Study Guide

MW00817315

Essentials of Business Law
and the Legal Environment
NINTH EDITION

Richard A. Mann

Professor of Business Law

The University of North Carolina at Chapel Hill

Member of the North Carolina Bar

Barry S. Roberts

Professor of Business Law

The University of North Carolina at Chapel Hill

Member of the North Carolina and Pennsylvania Bars

Prepared by

Ronald L. Taylor

Metropolitan State College of Denver

SOUTH-WESTERN
CENGAGE Learning™

Australia • Brazil • Japan • Korea • Mexico • Singapore • Spain • United Kingdom • United States

SOUTH-WESTERN
CENGAGE Learning™

Study Guide: Essentials of Business Law and the Legal Environment, Ninth Edition
Richard A. Mann, Barry S. Roberts

VP/Editorial Director: Jack W. Calhoun

Editor-in-Chief: Alex von Rosenberg

Publisher: Rob Dewey

Acquisitions Editor: Steve Silverstein Esq.

Senior Developmental Editor: Bob Sandman

Executive Marketing Manager: Lisa Lysne

Senior Media Technology Editor: Vicky True

Senior Production Project Manager: Deanna Quinn

Technology Project Editor: Pam Wallace

Website Coordinator: Scott Cook

Print Buyer: Charlene Taylor

Art Director: Michelle Kunkler

Cover Designer: Patti Hudepohl

Cover Image(s): © Corbis and JupiterImages

© 2007 South-Western Cengage Learning

ALL RIGHTS RESERVED. No part of this work covered by the copyright herein may be reproduced, transmitted, stored or used in any form or by any means graphic, electronic, or mechanical, including but not limited to photocopying, recording, scanning, digitizing, taping, Web distribution, information networks, or information storage and retrieval systems, except as permitted under Section 107 or 108 of the 1976 United States Copyright Act, without the prior written permission of the publisher.

For product information and technology assistance, contact us at
Cengage Learning Customer & Sales Support, 1-800-354-9706

For permission to use material from this text or product, submit all requests online at **cengage.com/permissions**
Further permissions questions can be emailed to
permissionrequest@cengage.com

ISBN-13: 978-0-324-37513-8

ISBN-10: 0-324-37513-1

South-Western
5191 Natorp Boulevard
Mason, OH 45040
USA

Cengage Learning is a leading provider of customized learning solutions with office locations around the globe, including Singapore, the United Kingdom, Australia, Mexico, Brazil, and Japan. Locate your local office at:
international.cengage.com/region

Cengage Learning products are represented in Canada by Nelson Education, Ltd.

For your course and learning solutions, visit **academic.cengage.com**

Purchase any of our products at your local college store or at our preferred online store **www.ichapters.com**

Printed in the United States of America
3 4 5 6 7   12 11 10 09 08

ED336

Table of Contents

Part I   Introduction to Law and Ethics
Chapter 1   Introduction to Law.. 1
Chapter 2   Business Ethics 10

Part II   The Legal Environment of Business
Chapter 3   Civil Dispute Resolution 18
Chapter 4   Constitutional Law.. 31
Chapter 5   Administrative Law 41
Chapter 6   Criminal Law 48
Chapter 7   Intentional Torts 58
Chapter 8   Negligence and Strict Liability 66
Parts I & II   Sample Examination 75

Part III   Contracts
Chapter 9   Introduction to Contracts.. 79
Chapter 10   Mutual Assent 87
Chapter 11   Conduct Invalidating Assent 96
Chapter 12   Consideration... 104
Chapter 13   Illegal Bargains 113
Chapter 14   Contractual Capacity 121
Chapter 15   Contracts in Writing 128
Chapter 16   Third Parties to Contracts 138
Chapter 17   Performance, Breach, and Discharge........................ 147
Chapter 18   Contract Remedies... 155
Part III   Sample Examination 164

Part IV   Sales
Chapter 19   Introduction to Sales and Leases 169
Chapter 20   Performance 178
Chapter 21   Transfer of Title and Risk of Loss 187
Chapter 22   Product Liability: Warranties and Strict Liability....... 196
Chapter 23   Sales Remedies 206
Part IV   Sample Examination 216

Part V   Negotiable Instruments
Chapter 24   Form and Content 221
Chapter 25   Transfer 230
Chapter 26   Holder in Due Course 238
Chapter 27   Liability of Parties 247
Chapter 28   Bank Deposits, Collections, and Funds Transfers 257
Part V   Sample Examination 268

Part VI   Agency
Chapter 29   Relationship of Principal and Agent 273
Chapter 30   Relationship with Third Parties 282
Part VI   Sample Examination 291

Part VII   Business Associations
Chapter 31   Formation and Internal Relations of General Partnerships 294
Chapter 32   Operation and Dissolution of General Partnerships 305
Chapter 33   Limited Partnerships and Limited Liability Companies 315
Chapter 34   Nature and Formation of Corporations 326
Chapter 35   Financial Structure of Corporations 337
Chapter 36   Management Structure of Corporations 348
Chapter 37   Fundamental Changes of Corporations 361
Part VII   Sample Examination 369

Part VIII   Debtor and Creditor Relations
Chapter 38   Secured Transactions and Suretyship 373
Chapter 39   Bankruptcy.. 388
Part VIII   Sample Examination 402

Part IX   Regulation of Business
Chapter 40   Securities Regulation... 407
Chapter 41   Intellectual Property.. 421
Chapter 42   Employment Law... 431
Chapter 43   Antitrust.. 442
Chapter 44   Accountants' Legal Liability 452
Chapter 45   Consumer Protection 461
Chapter 46   Environmental Law 471
Chapter 47   International Business Law 481
Part IX   Sample Examination 490
Chapter 48   CyberLaw... 494

Part X   Property
Chapter 49   Introduction to Property, Property Insurance, Bailments, and
               Documents of Title 505
Chapter 50   Interests in Real Property 523
Chapter 51   Transfer and Control of Real Property 534
Chapter 52   Trusts and Wills 544
Part X   Sample Examination 554

Answers   558

Chapter 1
Introduction to Law

PURPOSE

This chapter introduces the nature, classification, and sources of law in the American legal system. The chapter discusses the concept of law in a general sense, and then examines the classifications and sources of American law. Most of the chapter deals with the science of law, known as jurisprudence. The chapter introduces the student to important basic terminology, concepts, and principles that are essential to an understanding of later chapters.

CHAPTER CHECKPOINTS

After reading and studying this chapter, you should be able to:

1. Give a definition of law and distinguish between "law and morality" and "law and justice."

2. Define substantive law and procedural law and compare public law and private law.

3. Distinguish between civil law and criminal law and between law and equity.

4. Define the term "*stare decisis*" and discuss its importance to common law systems of law such as the one in the United States.

5. Identify and describe the sources of law in the American legal system.

6. Identify the four basic steps for analyzing a reported judicial decision.

CHAPTER OUTLINE

A. Nature of Law–Law is a pervasive instrument of social control whose function is to regulate, within certain limitations, human conduct and human relations. It has evolved slowly and will continue to change, because it is not a pure science that is based upon unchanging and universal truths, but rather, it results from a continuous striving to develop a workable set of rules that balance the individual and group rights of a society.

   1. Definition of Law–Numerous philosophers and jurists have attempted to define law. American jurists Oliver Wendell Holmes and Benjamin Cardozo defined law as predictions of the way that a court will decide specific legal questions. The English jurist Blackstone defined law as "a rule of civil conduct prescribed by the supreme power in a state, commanding what is right, and prohibiting what is wrong."

   2. Functions of Law–The primary function of law is to maintain stability in the social, political, and economic system while at the same time permitting change. A second function is to protect private ownership of property and to assist in the making of voluntary agreements. A third function is the preservation of the state.

   3. Law and Morals–The law is greatly affected by moral concepts; however, law and morality are not the same. There are ideas that are both moral and legal, yet many rules of law are completely unrelated to morals, and many moral precepts are not enforced by law.

   4. Law and Justice–These are separate and distinct concepts, although without law, there can be no justice in the sense of fair, equitable, and impartial treatment of competing interests and desires with due regard for the common good.

B. Classification of Law–There are a number of ways in which law can be classified. Basic to understanding these classifications are the terms *right* and *duty*. A *right* is the capacity of a person, with the aid of the law, to require another person or persons to perform, or refrain from performing, a certain act. A *duty* is the obligation imposed by law upon a person by which he or she is required to perform a certain act or to refrain from performing a certain act. There can be no right in one person without a corresponding duty resting upon some other person, or in some cases upon all other persons.

   1. Substantive and Procedural Law–Substantive law creates, defines, and regulates legal rights and duties. Procedural law states the rules for enforcing rights that exist because of substantive law.

   2. Public and Private Law–Public law is the branch of substantive law that deals with the government's rights and powers and its relationship to individuals or groups. It consists of constitutional, administrative, and criminal law. Private law is that part of substantive law governing individuals and legal entities in their relationships with one another. Business law is primarily private law.

   3. Civil and Criminal Law–Civil law is the law dealing with the rights and duties of individuals among themselves and is a part of private law. Criminal law is the law that involves offenses against the entire community and is a part of public law. In a civil action, the injured party (plaintiff) begins a lawsuit (sues) to recover compensation for the damages resulting from the defendant's wrongful conduct. The plaintiff has the burden of proof which must be sustained by a preponderance (greater weight) of the evidence. The principal forms of relief under civil law are money damages and decrees ordering the defendant to perform a specified act or to stop

specified conduct. In a criminal action, the government brings a criminal proceeding against (prosecutes) a person accused of committing a crime. A crime is any act prohibited or omission required by public law in the interest of protection of the public and made punishable by the government in a judicial proceeding brought by it. The government must prove criminal guilt beyond a reasonable doubt, a higher burden of proof than that required in a civil action. The principal sanctions under criminal law are capital punishment, imprisonment, and fines.

C. Sources of Law–The sources of law in the U.S. legal system are the federal and state constitutions, federal treaties, interstate compacts, federal and state statutes, the ordinances of countless local municipal governments, executive orders, the rules and regulations of federal and state administrative agencies, and an ever-increasing volume of reported federal and state court decisions. The supreme law of the land is the U. S. Constitution. The U. S. Constitution provides that federal statutes and treaties shall be paramount to state constitutions and statutes. Federal legislation and court decisions are significant sources of law. The paramount law of each state is contained in its constitution; state statutes and state case law are subordinate. A state constitution cannot deprive citizens of federal constitutional rights, but it can guarantee rights beyond those provided in the U. S. Constitution.

1. Constitutional Law–A constitution is the fundamental law of a government, establishing the governmental structure and allocating power among the levels of government, thereby defining political relationship. All other law in the United States is subordinate to the federal Constitution. Incorporated into our Constitution is the principle of separation of powers, meaning that there are three distinct and independent branches of government–the federal judiciary, the Congress, and the executive branch. Courts have the authority to determine the constitutionality of legislative and executive acts under the principle of judicial review. The Constitution of the United States also specifies the rights and liberties of the people.

2. Judicial Law–The common law is a body of law that originated in England and is derived from judicial decisions. The U.S. legal system is a common law system that relies heavily on the judiciary as a source of law and on the adversary system for settling disputes. The adversary system is one in which opposing parties initiate and present their cases. In contrast to common law systems are civil law systems, which are based on Roman law and depend upon comprehensive legislative enactments called codes and the inquisitorial system of determining disputes. In an inquisitorial system, the judiciary initiates, conducts, and decides cases.

    a. Common Law–The courts in common law systems have developed a body of law that serves as precedent for determination of later controversies. This law is called case law, judge-made law, or common law. In order to evolve in a stable and predictable manner, the common law has developed by application of *stare decisis*. *Stare decisis* literally means "to stand by the decisions" and is the principle that courts should apply rules decided by them or by courts superior to them in prior, substantially similar cases.

    b. Equity–Equity is a body of law based upon principles distinct from common law and providing remedies not available at law. Equity developed because the common law in England became overly rigid and beset with technicalities and law courts could provide only limited remedies, usually in the form of money damages. Individuals who could not obtain adequate relief from monetary awards began to petition the king directly for justice. He delegated these petitions to his chancellor who eventually developed a new second system of courts known as chancery or equity courts. An important difference between law and equity is that the chancellor could issue a decree ordering a party to perform a contractual duty (specific performance) or a decree ordering a party to do or refrain from doing a specified act (injunction). Reformation is an equitable remedy rewriting a contract to conform with the original intent of the contracting parties. Rescission is an equitable remedy invalidating a contract. Discretion was exercised by the courts of equity in providing remedies according to general legal principles, known as maxims, developed over the years.

   c. Restatements of Law–The American Law Institute is composed of a distinguished group of lawyers, judges, and law teachers who have set out to prepare "an orderly restatement of the general common law of the United States." The Restatements they have developed cover many of the important areas of common law and are regarded as the authoritative statement of the common law of the United States, though not actually binding law in themselves.

3. Legislative Law–Since the end of the nineteenth century, legislation has become the primary source of new law and ordered social change in the United States. This emphasis on legislative or statutory law has occurred because common law is not well suited to making drastic or comprehensive changes. Some business law topics, such as contracts, agency, property, and trusts, remain governed principally by the common law. However, most areas of commercial law have become largely statutory. In the second half of the twentieth century, there has been an increased need for uniformity and codification of business or commercial law. The National Conference of Commissioners on Uniform State Laws (NCCUSL) has drafted over 200 uniform laws, i.e., model acts, that states may enact in order to bring greater uniformity to states' laws. An example of is the Uniform Commercial Code (UCC) which has been adopted by all fifty states.

   a. Treaties–A treaty is an agreement between or among independent nations. The U. S. Constitution authorizes the president to enter into treaties with the advice and consent of the Senate "provided two thirds of the senators present concur."

   b. Executive Orders–An executive order is a law issued by the president of the United States or by the governor of a state.

4. Administrative Law–Administrative law is a branch of public law created by administrative agencies in the form of rules, regulations, orders, and decisions to carry out the regulatory powers and duties of those agencies. Because of the increasing complexity of the social, economic, and industrial life of the nation, the scope of administrative law has expanded enormously.

D. Legal Analysis–This refers to the method of analyzing and briefing federal and state judicial decisions. Decisions of many state supreme courts and courts of appeal can be found in a regional reporter published by West Publishing Company. A citation that says 86 P.3d 689 (2001) means that the case cited is found in volume 86 of the Pacific Reporter, Third Series, and beginning on page 689 and that it was decided in 2001. The appellant is the party who appeals a decision. In appellate court decisions, the name of the appellant will sometimes appear first in the citation even though the appellant was the defendant in the trial court. Four basic steps to analyze a reported decision are: (1) state the facts of the case; (2) determine the legal issue or question involved; (3) state the decision of the court; and (4) explain the legal reasons or basis for the court's decision.

Four important points to remember when reading legal opinions are: (1) a court must decide the specific legal dispute before it; (2) a court can decide only the specific legal dispute before it; (3) a court can decide the legal dispute before it only according to general rules that cover the whole class of similar disputes; and (4) everything stated in the opinion must be read regarding the legal dispute.

KEY TERMS

1. Substantive law
2. Procedural law
3. Public law
4. Private law
5. Civil law
6. Criminal law
7. Defendant
8. Plaintiff
9. Constitution
10. Common law system

11. Adversary system
12. Civil law system
13. Inquisitorial system
14. *Stare decisis*
15. Equity
16. Restatements
17. Legislative law
18. Treaty
19. Executive order
20. Administrative law

TRUE/FALSE

_____ 1. Although the law is greatly affected by moral concepts, morals and law are not the same.

_____ 2. In a civil trial, the plaintiff must show that the defendant is guilty beyond a reasonable doubt.

_____ 3. A state statute may be valid even though it violates the federal constitution.

_____ 4. The courts of equity arose to provide relief to those who had no adequate remedy at common law.

_____ 5. Over the past century, the emphasis in law making has shifted from legislatively enacted (statutory) law to judge-made (common) law.

_____ 6. A constitution is a fundamental law of a particular level of government.

_____ 7. Because of the many statutes enacted by the legislatures of the states and by the federal government, the American legal system is considered to be a civil law system.

_____ 8. Under the principle of judicial review, the courts have the authority to determine the constitutionality of legislative and executive acts.

_____ 9. Restatements of law are a source of law written by legal scholars, and Restatements are binding on the courts.

_____ 10. The law is constantly changing in an effort to meet the evolving needs of society.

_____ 11. In a civil action, the plaintiff must prove the case by a preponderance of the evidence.

_____ 12. The Supreme Court of the United States ultimately decides the constitutionality of any law.

_____ 13. Business law is primarily public law.

_____ 14. The Uniform Commercial Code is a federal statute that was adopted by Congress to make the law uniform among the states.

_____ 15. Forms of relief in civil law include judgments for money damages and equitable remedies.

MULTIPLE CHOICE

_____ 1. Which of the following is *not* a primary function of law?
   a. Maintain stability in the social, political, and economic system
   b. Protect ownership of private property
   c. Insure to all a minimum living
   d. Preservation of the state

_____ 2. Which of the following is not a category of private law?
   a. Tort law
   b. Contract law
   c. Criminal law
   d. Property law

_____ 3. Which of the following is not a category of public law?
   a. Constitutional law
   b. Criminal law
   c. Contract law
   d. Administrative law

_____ 4. While the principle of *stare decisis* provides that courts will follow their precedents in making subsequent decisions, nevertheless a court may decline to follow its precedents:
   a. to correct an erroneous decision.
   b. to choose among conflicting precedents.
   c. in recognition of the fact that the needs of society change over time.
   d. all of the above.

_____ 5. Which of the following is NOT a characteristic of a court of equity?
   a. It may provide injunctive relief.
   b. It may reform or rescind a contract.
   c. It presides over jury trials.
   d. It may command a person to perform a contract.

_____ 6. A person who is injured by the wrongful act of another may bring a civil suit to:
   a. recover money damages.
   b. have the wrongdoer thrown in jail.
   c. order the wrongdoer to engage in or desist from certain conduct.
   d. (a) and (c), but not (b).

_____ 7. The appeals court decision in the case of State v. Dawson, 282 S.E.2d 284, may be found at:
   a. page 282 of volume 284 of the Southeastern Reporter, second series.
   b. page 284 of volume 282 of the Southeastern Reporter, second series.
   c. pages 282–284 of volume 2 of the Southeastern Reporter.
   d. none of the above.

_____ 8. Which of the following is NOT true of an action brought under criminal law?
   a. It involves a wrongful act.
   b. Criminal guilt must be proven beyond a reasonable doubt.
   c. It must be brought by the government.
   d. The main purpose of the suit is to require payment of money damages to the victim.

_____ 9. Sources of state law include:
   a. state judicial decisions.
   b. state constitutions.
   c. state statutes.
   d. all of the above.

_____ 10. In the criminal trial of State of West Virginia v. Dawson, the defendant in the action was:
   a. Dawson.
   b. the State of West Virginia.
   c. the victim of the crime.
   d. the federal government.

_____ 11. The highest source of law in the United States is:
   a. an executive order of the president.
   b. an interstate compact.
   c. the federal Constitution.
   d. the state constitutions.

_____ 12. The most successful work by the National Conference of Commissioners on Uniform State Laws and the American Law Institute has been the:
   a. Uniform Commercial Code.
   b. Uniform Limited Partnership Act.
   c. Model Business Corporation Act.
   d. Uniform Probate Code.

_____ 13. A major difference between law and equity is that:
   a. today, in most states, courts of law decide law cases and courts of equity decide equity cases.
   b. law originated in America and equity was developed in England.
   c. the plaintiff could seek money damages under law, while the plaintiff could seek specific performance under equity.
   d. equity was overly rigid, while law provided various remedies.

_____ 14. Which of the following is/are equitable remedies?
   a. Injunction
   b. Reformation
   c. Rescission
   d. All of the above

_____ 15. Bill Businessman files a lawsuit against Carl Contractor for breach of contract. This case is a(n):
   a. equitable action.
   b. criminal proceeding.
   c. civil lawsuit.
   d. public law case.

SHORT ESSAY

1. What are the major differences between common law systems and civil law systems?

   _____

   _____

   _____

   _____

2. Explain the concepts of "right" and "duty" as they relate to law.

   _____

   _____

   _____

   _____

3. Define *stare decisis* and give a brief explanation.

_____

_____

_____

_____

4. How are the Restatements of Law and the Uniform Commercial Code similar? How are they different?

_____

_____

_____

_____

5. George, who is driving while intoxicated, crashed into Alice. Alice was injured, and her car sustained damage. State the two types of actions that could be brought and list the differences between them.

_____

_____

_____

_____

Chapter 2
Business Ethics

PURPOSE

Business ethics, as a branch of applied ethics, is the study and determination of right and good in business settings. Business ethics seeks to understand the moral issues that arise from business practices, institutions, and decision-making and their relationship to generalized human values. Unlike the law, analyses of ethics have no central authority, such as court or legislatures, upon which to rely, nor do they have well-defined universal standards. In this chapter, you study the most prominent ethical theories, examine ethical standards and responsibilities of business, and explore the ethical issues facing five businesses.

CHAPTER CHECKPOINTS

After reading and studying this chapter, you should be able to:

1. Define business ethics.

2. Distinguish between law and ethics.

3. Identify and compare significant ethical theories.

4. Explain Kohlberg's stages of moral development.

5. Discuss the ethical responsibilities of business.

CHAPTER OUTLINE

A. Law Versus Ethics—Law and morality are not the same. It is possible for acts that are legal to be immoral and equally possible for acts that are illegal to be considered morally preferable to following the law. Although legality is a guide to moral behavior, it cannot be relied upon as an infallible standard for action. The individual must engage in independent determinations of both the legal requirements and the moral requirements of a course of action.

10

B. Ethical Theories–Philosophers have provided various ethical theories that help analyze issues of business ethics.

1. Ethical Fundamentalism–Under ethical fundamentalism or absolutism, individuals look to a central authority or set of rules to guide them in ethical decision making.

2. Ethical Relativism–This is a doctrine asserting that actions must be judged by what individuals subjectively feel is right or wrong for themselves. It holds that when any two individuals or cultures differ regarding the morality of a particular issue or action, they are both correct because morality is relative. Situational ethics, another theory, holds that a person's actions must be judged by first putting oneself in the actor's situation.

3. Utilitarianism–This doctrine assesses good and evil in terms of the consequences of actions. It holds that moral actions are those that produce the greatest net pleasure compared to the net pain. Act utilitarianism assesses each separate act according to whether it maximizes pleasure over pain. Rule utilitarianism supports rules that on balance produce the greatest good. Utilitarian notions underlie cost-benefit analysis, an analytical tool used by many business and government managers.

4. Deontology–Deontology holds that actions must be judged by their motives and means as well as their results. Immanuel Kant proffered the best-known deontological theory. Under Kant's categorical imperative, for an action to be moral it must (1) be possible for it to be made a universal law to be applied consistently and (2) be respectful of the autonomy and rationality of all human beings and not treat them as an expedient.

5. Social Ethics Theories–Social ethics theories assert that special obligations arise from the social nature of human beings. These theories judge society in moral terms by its organization and by the way in which it distributes goods and services. Social egalitarians believe that society should provide all members with equal amounts of goods and services irrespective of their relative contributions. John Rawls proposed the theory of distributive justice which stresses equality of opportunity rather than results, while Robert Nozick proposed the libertarian theory which stresses market outcomes as the basis for distributing society's rewards.

6. Other Theories–Intuitionism holds that a rational person possesses inherent powers to assess the correctness of actions. The good person philosophy declares that if individuals wish to act morally, they should seek out and emulate the behavior of those individuals who always seem to know what the right choice is in any given situation and who always seem to do the right thing. The "Television Test" directs us to imagine that every ethical decision we make is being broadcast on nationwide television.

C. Ethical Standards in Business–Many ethical theories can be applied to the world of business.

1. Choosing an Ethical System–Lawrence Kohlberg observed that people progress through stages of moral development according to two major variables: age and reasoning. During the first level–the preconventional level–a child's conduct is a reaction to the fear of punishment and, later, to the pleasure of reward. During adolescence–Kohlberg's conventional level–people conform their behavior to meet the expectations of groups, such as family, peers, or society. Some people reach the third level–the postconventional level–where they accept and conform to moral principles because they understand why the principles are right and binding.

2. Corporations as Moral Agents–Some insist that only people can engage in behavior that can be judged in moral terms. Opponents of this view insist that a sufficient number of attributes of re-

sponsibility inhere in corporations to permit judging corporate behavior from a moral perspective.

D. Ethical Responsibilities of Business–Our system has always recognized the need for some form of regulation of business, whether it be by competition, self-regulation, or government regulation.

1. Regulation of Business–Increased government intervention has occurred not only to preserve the competitive process in our economic system but also to achieve social goals extrinsic to the efficient allocation of resources. Such intervention attempts (1) to regulate both "legal" monopolies and "natural" monopolies; (2) to correct imperfections in the market system to preserve competition; (3) to protect specific groups from failures of the marketplace; and (4) to promote other social goals.

2. Corporate Governance–The five thousand largest U.S. firms currently produce over half of the nation's gross national product. Many observers insist that companies playing such an important role in economic life should have a responsibility to undertake projects that benefit society in ways that go beyond mere financial efficiency in producing goods and services.

3. Arguments against Social Responsibility–A number of arguments oppose business involvement in socially responsible activities.

   a. Profitability–Some argue that businesses are not organized to engage in social activities; they are structured to produce goods and services for which they receive money, and their social obligation is to return as much of this money to their direct stakeholders as possible.

   b. Unfairness–Whenever companies stray from their designated role of profit maker, they take unfair advantage of company employees and shareholders.

   c. Accountability–Corporations are private institutions that are subject to a lower standard of accountability than are public bodies.

   d. Expertise–Even though a corporation has an expertise in producing and selling its product, it may not possess a talent for recognizing or managing socially useful activities.

4. Arguments in Favor of Social Responsibility–Some critics of business contend that business must help to resolve societal problems and offer a number of arguments in support of their position.

   a. The Social Contract–Supporters of social roles for corporations assert that limited liability and other rights granted to companies carry a responsibility. Companies owe a moral debt to society to contribute to its overall well-being. A derivative of this social contract theory is the stakeholder model which would impose on the corporation a fiduciary responsibility to all stakeholders (including employees, suppliers, and customers), not just its stockholders.

   b. Less Government Regulation–Not only does anticipatory corporate action lessen the likelihood of government regulation, but social involvement by companies creates a climate of trust and respect that reduces the inclination of government to interfere in company business.

   c. Long-Run Profits–In the long run, enhanced goodwill created by involvement in social causes means stronger profits. Corporate actions to improve the well-being of their communities make these communities more attractive to citizens and more profitable for business.

KEY TERMS

1. Ethics

2. Business ethics

3. Ethical fundamentalism

4. Ethical relativism

5. Situational ethics

6. Utilitarianism

7. Act utilitarianism

8. Rule utilitarianism

9. Cost-benefit analysis

10. Deontology

11. Social egalitarians

12. Distributive justice

13. Libertarians

14. Intuitionism

TRUE/FALSE

_____ 1. One definition of ethics is the study of what is right or good for human beings.

_____ 2. Under ethical relativism, individuals look to a central authority or set of rules to guide them in ethical decision making.

_____ 3. Rule utilitarianism supports rules that on balance produce the greatest good.

_____ 4. Lawrence Kohlberg felt that the two major variables in the stages of moral development were age and education.

_____ 5. The "Television Test" directs individuals to imagine that every ethical decision they make is being broadcast on nationwide television.

_____ 6. According to Kohlberg, most adults operate at the postconventional level where they accept and conform to moral principles because they understand why the principles are right and binding.

_____ 7. Enhanced goodwill due to corporate involvement in social causes often means stronger profits in the long run.

_____ 8. Intuitionism holds that rational persons possess inherent powers to assess the correctness of actions.

_____ 9. Libertarians stress market outcomes as the basis for distributing society's rewards.

_____ 10. Ethics, like law, relies upon the courts and legislatures for well-defined, universal standards.

_____ 11. Distributive justice stresses equality of opportunity rather than results.

_____ 12. The chief criticism of utilitarianism is that in some important instances it ignores justice.

_____ 13. Deontologists believe that society should provide all persons with equal amounts of goods and services irrespective of the contribution each makes to increase society's wealth.

_____ 14. Social egalitarianism holds that actions must be judged by their motives and means as well as by their results.

_____ 15. An argument in favor of corporate social responsibility is that the more responsibly companies act on their own, the less the government must regulate them.

MULTIPLE CHOICE

_____ 1. Which of the following is/are a major form of utilitarianism?
   a. Act utilitarianism
   b. Rule utilitarianism
   c. Distributive justice
   d. Both a and b

_____ 2. Dan religiously follows the teachings of the Bible. The approach Dan will take to ethical decision making is best described as:
   a. intuitionism.
   b. deontological.
   c. utilitarian.
   d. none of the above.

_____ 3. The relationship between a business and its owners results in ethical questions involving:
   a. corporate governance.
   b. shareholder voting.
   c. management's duties to shareholders.
   d. all of the above.

_____ 4. Which of the following statements is correct?
   a. Law and morality are the same.
   b. If something is legal, it is moral.
   c. The law is strongly affected by moral concepts.
   d. All of the above are correct.

_____ 5. The ethical theory which asserts that actions must be judged by what individuals feel is right or wrong for themselves is:
   a. ethical relativism.
   b. ethical fundamentalism.
   c. situational ethics.
   d. utilitarianism.

_____ 6. The approach to ethical decision making where the person judging actually puts herself in the other person's shoes to understand what motivated him to make a particular decision is known as:
   a. act utilitarianism.
   b. situational ethics.
   c. ethical relativism.
   d. none of the above.

_____ 7. Ethical fundamentalism is also known as:
   a. situational ethics.
   b. utilitarianism.
   c. absolutism.
   d. none of the above.

_____ 8. The deontologist who proposed the categorical imperative similar to the Golden Rule was:
   a. John Rawls.
   b. Jeremy Bentham.
   c. Robert Nozick.
   d. Immanuel Kant.

_____ 9. The ethical theory that underlies the cost-benefit analysis is:
   a. distributive justice.
   b. deontology.
   c. ethical fundamentalism.
   d. none of the above.

_____ 10. Aaron is a good student and citizen who conforms to the expectations of his family and peers as a result of loyalty, affection, and trust. Aaron is in what stage of moral development according to Kohlberg's observations?
a. Preconventional
b. Conventional
c. Postconventional
d. None of the above

_____ 11. Arguments that have been used to support business involvement in socially responsible activities include:
a. long-run profits.
b. less government regulation.
c. social contract.
d. all of the above.

_____ 12. Arguments that have been used against business involvement in socially responsible activities include:
a. profitability.
b. unfairness.
c. accountability.
d. all of the above.

_____ 13. Martin is employed by a company to design aircraft. He chooses to work to design the safest aircraft possible, because he wants to save lives and feels a duty to provide the public with the safest possible aircraft. Martin is best described as a(n):
a. utilitarian.
b. ethical fundamentalist.
c. deontologist.
d. libertarian.

_____ 14. Martin is employed by a company to design aircraft. He uses a cost-benefit analysis and designs an aircraft that will have the most favorable cost-benefit ratio, ignoring safety devices that could significantly affect the safety of the aircraft. This decision making approach is known as:
a. utilitarianism.
b. deontological.
c. ethical fundamentalism.
d. none of the above.

_____ 15. The ethical theory which asserts that society should provide all members with equal amounts of goods and services irrespective of their relative contributions is:
a. distributive justice.
b. ethical relativism.
c. utilitarianism.
d. social egalitarianism.

SHORT ESSAY

1. Compare the ethical theories of utilitarians and deontologists.

_____

_____

_____

_____

2. Explain the categorical imperative.

_____

_____

_____

_____

3. What are the arguments for and against corporate social responsibility?

_____

_____

_____

_____

4. List and describe three social ethics theories.

_____

_____

_____

_____

5. You would like to propose to the board of directors of Big Bucks, Inc. that the corporation distribute three percent of its annual income to help the homeless. Discuss the ethical considerations of your proposal.

_____

_____

_____

Chapter 3
Civil Dispute Resolution

PURPOSE

The purpose of this chapter is to introduce the student to procedural law and to the process of dispute resolution. The first part of the chapter discusses the structure and function of the federal and state court systems. The second part deals with jurisdiction, or the power of a court to hear and decide a case. The third part of the chapter discusses civil dispute resolution, including the procedure in civil lawsuits.

CHAPTER CHECKPOINTS

After reading and studying the chapter, you should be able to:

1. Outline the courts in a state court system and in the federal court system.

2. Identify and define the various types of jurisdiction and compare the subject matter jurisdiction of the state courts to that of the federal courts.

3. Distinguish between "jurisdiction" and "venue."

4. Outline, using correct terminology, the process by which a civil lawsuit is begun and proceeds through the court system.

5. Discuss and compare the relative advantages and disadvantages of court adjudication and the methods of alternative dispute resolution.

CHAPTER OUTLINE

I. The Court System–Courts are impartial tribunals established by government to settle disputes. A court may make a binding decision in a case only when it has jurisdiction over both the dispute and the parties to that dispute. The United States has a dual court system in which the federal government as well as each of the fifty states has its own independent system.

A. The Federal Courts–Article III of the U.S. Constitution says that judicial power of the United States shall be vested in one Supreme Court and such lower courts as Congress may establish. The federal court system consists of district courts, courts of appeals, a number of special courts, and the U.S. Supreme Court. Judges in the federal court system are appointed by the president for life, subject to confirmation by the Senate.

1. District Courts–The district courts are general trial courts in the federal system. Most federal cases begin in the district court where the issues of fact are decided. Appeals generally go to the Circuit Court of Appeals of the appropriate circuit. In most cases, that decision is final. Congress has established judicial districts. Each state has at least one district, while certain states have more.

2. Courts of Appeals–Congress has established eleven numbered circuits plus the D.C. circuit. Each circuit has a court of appeals, which hears appeals from the district courts located within the circuit. U.S. Courts of Appeals also review decisions of administrative agencies, the Tax Court, and the Bankruptcy Court. U.S. Courts of Appeals usually hear cases in panels of three judges, although they will sometimes hear cases *en banc* with all judges of the circuit. The function of appellate courts is to examine the record of a case on appeal and to determine whether the trial court committed prejudicial error. If so, the appellate court will reverse or modify the judgment of a lower court and if necessary remand or send the case back to the lower court for further proceeding. If there is no error, the appellate court will affirm the decision of the lower court.

3. The Supreme Court–The U.S. Supreme Court is the nation's highest tribunal. It consists of nine justices (Chief Justice and eight Associate Justices) who hear cases in Washington, D.C. A quorum consists of any six justices. The Court's principal function is to review decisions of the federal Courts of Appeals and, sometimes those of the highest state courts, but the Supreme Court does have original jurisdiction in certain types of cases. Appeal by right is mandatory review by a higher court. Very few cases that come before the U.S. Supreme Court are appeals by right, because this method of appeal was virtually eliminated by legislation enacted by Congress in 1988. Writ of certiorari refers to discretionary review by a higher court. Now almost all cases reaching the U.S. Supreme Court come to it by writ of certiorari. However, only a small percentage of the petitions for review are granted.

4. Special Courts–Special courts in the federal judicial system include the U.S. Court of Federal Claims, the U.S. Bankruptcy Courts, the U.S. Tax Court, and the U.S. Court of Appeals for the Federal Circuit. Each of these courts has jurisdiction over a particular subject matter.

B. State Courts–Each state and the District of Columbia has its own independent court system. The structure varies from state to state. In most states, judges are elected for a stated term.

1. Inferior Trial Courts–These courts decide the least serious criminal and civil matters and usually do not keep a complete written record of their proceedings. Minor criminal cases such as traffic offenses are heard by inferior trial courts, which are referred to as municipal courts, justice of the peace courts, or traffic courts. Small claims courts are also inferior trial courts, which hear civil cases involving a limited amount of money. Appeal from the decision of a small claims court is to a trial court of general jurisdiction where the appellant is entitled to a new trial (trial *de novo*).

2. Trial Courts–Each state has trial courts of general jurisdiction, which may be called county, district, superior, circuit, or common pleas courts. These courts do not have a dollar limitation on their jurisdiction in civil cases and hear all criminal cases except minor offenses. These courts maintain formal records of their proceedings. Many states also have special trial courts, such as probate courts and family courts. For example, a state may have a special court called a probate court with jurisdiction over wills and estates and a family court, which has jurisdiction over divorce and child custody cases. Appeal is to the general state appellate courts.

3. Appellate Courts–The state's court of last resort is a reviewing court generally called the supreme court of the state. Except for those cases reviewed by the U.S. Supreme Court, the decision of this highest reviewing court is final. In addition, most states have intermediate appellate courts to handle the large volume of cases which are appealed.

II. Jurisdiction–Jurisdiction means the power or authority of a court to hear and decide a case. To resolve a lawsuit, a court must have both jurisdiction over the subject matter of the lawsuit and jurisdiction over the parties to a lawsuit.

A. Subject Matter Jurisdiction–Subject matter jurisdiction refers to the authority of a court to judge a controversy of a particular kind. Federal courts have limited subject matter jurisdiction, whereas state courts have jurisdiction over all matters that have not been given exclusively to the federal courts or expressly taken from the state courts by Congress or the Constitution.

1. Federal Jurisdiction-The federal courts have exclusive jurisdiction over some areas if Congress so provides, either explicitly or implicitly. Federal courts also have concurrent jurisdiction which is the authority of either federal or state courts to hear the same case.

    a. Exclusive Federal Jurisdiction–The federal courts have exclusive jurisdiction over federal criminal prosecutions, admiralty, bankruptcy, antitrust, patent, trademark and copyright cases, suits against the United States, and cases arising under certain federal statutes.

    b. Concurrent Federal Jurisdiction–There are two types of concurrent federal jurisdiction: federal question jurisdiction and diversity jurisdiction. Federal question jurisdiction allows a court to hear any case arising under the Constitution, statutes, or treaties of the United States, over which the federal courts do not have exclusive jurisdiction. Diversity of citizenship jurisdiction allows the federal courts to hear a case involving state law where there is diversity of citizenship and the amount in controversy exceeds $75,000. Diversity exists (1) when the plaintiffs are citizens of a state or states different from the state or states of which the defendants are citizens; (2) when a foreign country brings an action against citizens of the United States; or (3) when the controversy is between citizens of a state and citizens of a foreign country. In any case involving concurrent jurisdiction, the plaintiff has the choice of bringing the action in either federal or state court. If a state court hears a concurrent federal question case, it applies federal substantive law but its own procedural law.

2. Exclusive State Jurisdiction–State courts have exclusive jurisdiction over all other matters. All matters not granted to the federal courts in the Constitution or by Congress are solely within the jurisdiction of the states. These areas include but are not limited to property, torts, contracts, agency, commercial transactions, and most crimes. Also included would be cases involving diversity of citizenship where the amount in controversy is $75,000 or less. Even though some or all of the relevant events occur in state *X*, a court in state *Y* may be a proper forum. Conflict of laws rules vary from state to state.

3. *Stare Decisis* in the Dual Court System–The doctrine of *stare decisis* presents certain problems when there are two parallel court systems, but there are rules which determine which decisions are binding and which are persuasive.

B. Jurisdiction over the Parties–Jurisdiction over the parties is the power of a court to bind the parties involved in the dispute. Its requirements may be met by (1) *in personam* jurisdiction; (2) *in rem* jurisdiction; or (3) attachment jurisdiction. The court's exercise of jurisdiction is valid under the due process clause of the Constitution if it satisfies the requirements of reasonable notification and reasonable opportunity to be heard and if the defendant has sufficient minimum contacts with the state.

1. *In Personam* Jurisdiction–*In personam* jurisdiction is personal jurisdiction of a court over the parties to a lawsuit in contrast to jurisdiction over their property. The plaintiff automatically grants the court personal jurisdiction when he or she files a complaint. Personal jurisdiction over the defendant may be obtained (1) by serving process on the party within the state in which the court is located, or (2) by reasonable notification to a party outside the state in those instances where a "long-arm statute" applies. To serve process means to deliver a summons, which is an order to respond to a complaint lodged against a party. Most states have adopted long-arm statutes to expand their jurisdictional reach. These statutes allow courts to obtain jurisdiction over nonresident defendants under conditions that do not offend traditional notions of fair play and substantial justice. Personal jurisdiction may also arise from a party's consent, such as when parties agree in a contract that any dispute will be subject to the jurisdiction of a specific court.

2. *In Rem* Jurisdiction–*In rem* jurisdiction is jurisdiction based on claims against property. Courts in a state have jurisdiction to adjudicate claims to property situated within the state if the plaintiff gives reasonable notice and an opportunity to be heard to those persons who have an interest in the property.

3. Attachment Jurisdiction–Attachment jurisdiction, or *quasi in rem* jurisdiction, is jurisdiction over property not based on claims against it. Like *in rem* jurisdiction, it is jurisdiction over property rather than over a person, but it is invoked by seizing the defendant's property located within the state to obtain payment of a claim against the defendant that is unrelated to the property seized. The basis of jurisdiction is the state's connection with the property; it does not depend on any connection between the state and the defendant.

4. Venue–Venue is the particular geographical place where a court with jurisdiction may hear a case. It is often confused with jurisdiction. Its purpose is to regulate the distribution of cases within a specific court system and to identify a convenient forum. Federal rules of venue determine the district or districts in a state in which the suit may be brought, while state rules of venue typically require that the suit be brought in a county where one of the defendants lives.

III. Civil Dispute Resolution–Our legal system has established an elaborate set of governmental mechanisms to settle disputes. The most prominent of these is judicial dispute resolution—called litigation—which is governed by the rules of civil procedure. In addition, there are several nongovernmental methods of dispute resolution, referred to as alternative dispute resolution.

A. Civil Procedure–Civil disputes must follow the rules of civil procedure that are designed to resolve the dispute in a just, prompt, and inexpensive way.

1. The Pleadings–Pleadings are a series of responsive, formal, written statements in which each side to a lawsuit states its claims and defenses. The purpose of pleadings is to give notice and to establish the disputed issues of fact and law. An "issue of fact" is a dispute between the parties regarding the events that gave rise to the lawsuit. An "issue of law" is a dispute between the parties as to what legal rule applies to these facts. The jury decides issues of fact, and the judge decides issues of law.

a. Complaint and Summons–The lawsuit begins when the plaintiff files the complaint with the clerk of the trial court. The complaint is the initial pleading by the plaintiff stating his case. The county sheriff or deputy serves a summons and a copy of the complaint on the defendant commanding him to file an answer within a specific time. The summons is a written document that gives notice to the defendant that a suit has been brought against him. Proper service of the summons establishes the court's jurisdiction over the defendant.

b. Responses to Complaint–If the defendant fails to respond at all to the summons and complaint, a default judgment will be entered against the defendant for the relief requested in the complaint. The defendant may make pretrial motions contesting the court's jurisdiction over him or asserting that the action is barred by the statute of limitations. A demurrer is a motion to dismiss for failure to state a claim. An answer is the defendant's pleading in response to the plaintiff's complaint. If the defendant does not make any pretrial motions, or if they are denied, the defendant must respond by filing an answer, which may contain denials, admissions, affirmative defenses, and counterclaims. A reply is a pleading by the plaintiff in response to the defendant's answer. It may also contain admissions, denials, or affirmative defenses.

2. Pretrial Procedure

a. Judgment on the Pleadings–A judgment on the pleadings is a final, binding determination on the merits of the case made by the judge after the pleadings. Either party may move for judgment on the pleadings which requests the judge to rule as a matter of law whether the facts as alleged in the pleadings of the nonmoving party are sufficient to grant the requested relief.

b. Discovery–Discovery is the pretrial exchange of information between opposing parties to a lawsuit. In preparation for trial, each party has the right to obtain relevant evidence, or facts that may lead to evidence, from the other party. Pretrial discovery includes (1) pretrial depositions consisting of sworn, out-of-court testimony of the opposing party or other witnesses; (2) sworn answers by the opposing party to written interrogatories or questions; (3) production of documents and physical objects in the possession of the opposing party or by a court-ordered subpoena from a third party; (4) court-ordered examination by a physician of the physical and/or mental condition of the opposing party; and (5) admissions of facts set forth in a request for admissions submitted to the opposing party.

c. Pretrial Conference–A pretrial conference between the judge and the attorneys representing the parties may also be held (1) to simplify the issues in dispute; and (2) to encourage settlement of the dispute without a trial.

d. Summary Judgment–If the evidence disclosed by discovery becomes so clear that a trial to determine the facts becomes unnecessary, one party may move for a summary judgment. A summary judgment is a final, binding determination on the merits made by the judge before a trial.

3. Trial–In all federal civil cases at common law involving more than $20, the U.S. Constitution guarantees the right to a jury trial. State constitutions often provide a similar right. Statutes also may grant the right to a jury trial in other situations. Jury trials are not available in equity cases.

a. Jury Selection–Assuming a timely demand for a jury has been made, the trial begins by selection of a jury. *Voir dire* is the preliminary examination of potential jurors. Each party has an unlimited number of challenges for cause, which allow a party to prevent a prospective juror from serving if the juror is biased or cannot be fair and impartial. Each party also has a limited number of peremptory challenges for which no cause is required to disqualify a prospective juror. By Supreme Court decision, the U.S. Constitution prohibits discrimination in jury selection based on race or gender.

b. Conduct of Trial–After the jury has been selected, both attorneys make an opening statement about the facts that they expect to prove in the trial. The plaintiff and her witnesses then testify on direct examination by the plaintiff's attorney. Each is subject to cross-examination by the defendant's attorney. If the judge does not allow certain evidence to be introduced or certain testimony to be given, the attorney must make an offer of proof to preserve for review on appeal the question of its admissibility. After cross-examination, followed by redirect examination of witnesses, the plaintiff rests her case. At this time, the defendant may move for a directed verdict in his favor. A directed verdict is a final, binding determination on the merits made by the judge after a trial has begun but before the jury renders a verdict. The judge may deny the motion for a directed verdict if there is any evidence on which the jury might possibly render a verdict for the plaintiff. If the judge denies the motion for a directed verdict, the defendant then has the opportunity to present evidence. After the defendant has presented his evidence and both parties have rested, then each party may move for a directed verdict. A directed verdict takes the case away from the jury and enters judgment for the party making the motion, because the evidence is so clear that reasonable persons could not differ about the outcome of the case. If these motions are denied, then the attorneys make closing arguments to the jury.

c. Jury Instructions–The attorneys have previously given written jury instructions on the applicable law to the trial judge, who gives those which he approves to the jury. These instructions are called charges in some states and advise the jury of the particular rules of law. The judge may give the jury instructions of his own.

d. Verdict–The jury then retires to the jury room to deliberate and to reach its verdict. A verdict is a formal decision by the jury on the questions submitted to it. In some jurisdictions, a special verdict is used, by which the jury makes specific written findings on each factual issue. The judge then applies the law to these findings and renders a judgment.

e. Motions Challenging Verdict–The unsuccessful party may then file a written motion for a new trial or for judgment notwithstanding the verdict. A motion for a new trial may be granted if (1) the judge committed prejudicial error; (2) the verdict is against the weight of the evidence; (3) the damages are excessive; or (4) the trial was not fair. A motion for judgment notwithstanding the verdict is similar to a motion for a directed verdict, except that it is made after the jury's verdict. A judgment notwithstanding the verdict is a final, binding determination on the merits. The judge makes it after and contrary to the jury's verdict. If a judgment n.o.v. is reversed on appeal, the jury's verdict is reinstated.

4. Appeal–To appeal a verdict, an attorney files a notice of appeal with the clerk of the trial court within the prescribed time. Where there is an intermediate court of appeals, it will usually be the reviewing court. In other states, the party appealing may appeal directly from the trial court to the state supreme court. The purpose of an appeal is to determine whether the trial court committed prejudicial error. An appeal typically can only be made from a final judgment. Generally, an appellate court reviews solely errors of law. The appellate court does not hear any evidence. It decides the case on the records, abstracts, briefs, and sometimes oral argument by the attorneys. The court prepares a written opinion containing the reasons for its decision, the rules of law that apply, and its judgment.

5. Enforcement–If the judgment favors the plaintiff and the defendant does not appeal, or the reviewing court affirms the judgment upon an appeal, the prevailing party may collect the judgment damages through execution or garnishment.

B. Alternative Dispute Resolution (ADR)–Because litigation is complex, time-consuming, and expensive, several nonjudicial methods of dealing with disputes have developed. The most important alternative to litigation is arbitration. Others include conciliation, mediation, and mini-trials. Advantages of ADR include privacy, speed, and preservation of continuing relations.

1. Arbitration–Arbitration is a nonjudicial proceeding where a neutral third party selected by the disputants renders a binding decision. The parties in many cases are able to select an arbitrator with special expertise concerning the subject of the dispute. There are two basic types of arbitration–consensual and compulsory. Consensual arbitration occurs whenever parties to a dispute agree to submit the controversy to arbitration. They may do this in advance by agreeing in their contract that disputes will be resolved by arbitration or after a dispute arises by then agreeing to submit the dispute to arbitration. Consensual arbitration is the most common. Compulsory arbitration is required by statute for certain disputes such as those involving public employees like police officers. The arbitrator's decision is called an award and is binding on the parties. Under the Federal Arbitration Act and the Revised Uniform Arbitration Act, which has been adopted by a few states, grounds for appealing an award are narrow and include (1) the award was procured by corruption, fraud, or other undue means; (2) the arbitrators were partial or corrupt; (3) the arbitrators were guilty of misconduct prejudicing the rights of a party to the arbitration proceeding; and (4) the arbitrators exceeded their powers.

2. Conciliation–Conciliation is a nonbinding process in which a third party (the conciliator) selected by the parties attempts to help them reach a mutually acceptable agreement.

3. Mediation–Mediation is a process in which a third party (the mediator) selected by the disputants helps them to reach a resolution of their disagreement. The mediator, unlike the conciliator, proposes possible solutions for the parties to consider, but like the conciliator the mediator does not have the power to render a binding decision.

4. Mini-Trial–A mini-trial is a nonbinding process in which attorneys for the disputing parties present evidence to managers of the disputing parties and a neutral third party, and then the managers attempt to negotiate a settlement in consultation with the third party. A mini-trial typically occurs when both disputants are corporations.
5. Summary Jury Trial–A mock trial presented to a jury. The jury will return a nonbinding verdict which should, however, influence the parties in their negotiations.
6. Negotiation–Negotiation is a consensual bargaining process between the parties without involvement of third parties.

KEY TERMS

1. Appeal by right
2. Writ of *certiorari*
3. Subject matter jurisdiction
4. Exclusive jurisdiction
5. Concurrent jurisdiction
6. Federal question
7. Diversity of citizenship
8. *In personam* jurisdiction
9. Long-arm statute
10. *In rem* jurisdiction
11. Attachment jurisdiction
12. Venue
13. Pleadings
14. Complaint
15. Summons
16. Default judgment
17. Demurrer

18. Answer
19. Reply
20. Judgment on the pleadings
21. Discovery
22. Summary judgment
23. *Voir dire*
24. Directed verdict
25. Motion for new trial
26. Judgment notwithstanding the verdict
27. Execution
28. Garnishment
29. Arbitration
30. Conciliation
31. Mediation
32. Mini-trial
33. Summary jury trial
34. Negotiation

TRUE/FALSE

_____ 1. A court may render a binding decision whether or not it has jurisdiction over the dispute and the parties to that dispute.

_____ 2. A quorum of the U.S. Supreme Court consists of any six justices.

_____ 3. The U.S. district courts are the trial courts in the federal court system.

_____ 4. State court judges in most states receive lifetime appointments from the governor.

_____ 5. U.S. Supreme Court Justices are appointed for life by the president.

_____ 6. A corporation may be a citizen of more than one state for diversity of citizenship purposes.

_____ 7. A state court may have exclusive jurisdiction to hear a case involving diversity of citizenship.

_____ 8. There is no right to trial by jury in civil cases.

_____ 9. The decision of an arbitrator is binding on the parties.

_____ 10. Venue is the power of a court to hear and decide a case.

_____ 11. The U.S. Supreme Court normally exercises appellate jurisdiction, although in certain instances it does exercise original jurisdiction.

_____ 12. A motion for a directed verdict is similar to a motion for judgment notwithstanding the verdict in that they are both made after the jury returns a verdict..

_____ 13. A deposition is a method of discovery consisting of sworn testimony of the opposing party or witness taken out of court.

_____ 14. The federal courts have exclusive jurisdiction of cases involving federal questions.

_____ 15. The Supreme Court has held that the U.S. Constitution prohibits discrimination in jury selection on the basis of race or gender.

MULTIPLE CHOICE

_____ 1. To render a binding decision, a court must have:
   a. subject matter jurisdiction.
   b. jurisdiction over the parties to the dispute.
   c. *quasi in rem* jurisdiction.
   d. a and b above

_____ 2. The main function of the appellate courts is to:
   a. keep criminals out of jail.
   b. review the decisions of the trial courts for prejudicial error.
   c. hear the testimony of witnesses.
   d. determine questions of fact.

_____ 3. Helena was born in Florida. While she was in school, she and her family moved to Texas, where she stayed to attend college. After graduation from college, Helena accepted an exciting job with an advertising agency in New York, and she moved to an apartment in New Jersey. She is now named a defendant in a diversity of citizenship lawsuit. Helena would be considered a citizen of:
   a. Florida.
   b. New York.
   c. New Jersey.
   d. Florida, Texas, New York, and New Jersey.

_____ 4. Diversity of citizenship exists when:
   a. the plaintiff and defendant are citizens of different states.
   b. a foreign country brings an action against U.S. citizens.
   c. U.S. citizens bring an action against citizens of a foreign country.
   d. all of the above.

_____ 5. In a case where the appropriate state and federal courts have concurrent jurisdiction to hear the matter, the plaintiff may bring the action:
   a. in the state court only.
   b. in the federal court only.
   c. in the state court or the federal court.
   d. none of the above.

_____ 6. A party to a civil action who feels that there are no issues of fact to be determined by trial would most likely move for:
   a. a new trial.
   b. a summary judgment.
   c. a directed verdict.
   d. a judgment notwithstanding the verdict.

_____ 7. Which of the following is/are a part of the pleadings stage in civil procedure?
   a. answer
   b. discovery
   c. interrogatory
   d. all of the above

_____ 8. Paul Plaintiff, a resident of Texas, and David Defendant, a resident of Colorado, are involved in a contractual dispute amounting to $80,000. The contract was executed in Texas. Paul may sue in:
   a. Colorado state court.
   b. Texas state court.
   c. Texas federal court.
   d. either Texas state court or Texas federal court.

_____ 9. In a civil action, the plaintiff is the party more likely to file:
   a. an answer.
   b. a reply.
   c. a counterclaim.
   d. a demurrer.

_____ 10. In a civil action, proper service of the summons establishes:
   a. the court's venue.
   b. the court's subject matter jurisdiction over the controversy.
   c. the court's jurisdiction over the defendant.
   d. all of the above.

_____ 11. Jurisdiction of a court over a party to a lawsuit is:
   a. *in personam.*
   b. *in rem.*
   c. attachment.
   d. venue.

_____ 12. Which of the following is a special court in the federal judicial system?
   a. U.S. Court of Federal Claims
   b. U.S. Tax Court
   c. U.S. Court of Appeals for the Federal Circuit
   d. all of the above

_____ 13. Most states have adopted long-arm statutes to expand their jurisdiction. Under such statutes nonresident defendants may be served if they:
    a. have committed a tort (civil wrong) within the state.
    b. own property within the state and that property is the subject of the lawsuit.
    c. have entered into a contract within the state.
    d. all of the above.

_____ 14. A binding process in which a third party acts as an intermediary between the disputing parties is a(n):
    a. arbitration.
    b. conciliation.
    c. mediation.
    d. mini-trial.

_____ 15. Paul Plaintiff wants to be certain that a prospective juror is not selected. He may accomplish this through the use of:
    a. a writ of *certiorari*.
    b. a peremptory challenge.
    c. *voir dire* examination.
    d. a demurrer.

SHORT ESSAY

1. Distinguish between "jurisdiction" and "venue."

_____

_____

_____

_____

2. In a civil trial, what procedure does the judge use in deciding whether to grant or deny a motion for a directed verdict?

_____

_____

_____

_____

3. Compare the relative advantages and disadvantages of court adjudication, arbitration, and mediation.

_____

_____

_____

_____

4. Distinguish between *in personam* and *in rem* jurisdiction.

_____

_____

_____

_____

5. Outline, using correct terminology, the process by which a civil lawsuit is begun and proceeds through the court system.

_____

_____

_____

_____

Chapter 4
Constitutional Law

PURPOSE

The purpose of this chapter is to introduce you to constitutional law as it relates to business and commerce. The first part of the chapter surveys some of the basic principles of constitutional law. The second part examines the allocation of power between the federal and state governments with respect to the regulation of business, with particular emphasis on the commerce clause. Finally, the third part discusses the constitutional restrictions imposed on the power of government to regulate business, with particular emphasis on the Bill of Rights.

CHAPTER CHECKPOINTS

After reading and studying this chapter, you should be able to:

1. Compare the principles of judicial review and preemption.

2. List the powers possessed by the federal government to regulate business and the Constitutional source of each power, as well as the powers possessed by the states.

3. List the limitations on government action to regulate business and identify the Constitutional source of each limitation.

4. Discuss the difference between substantive and procedural due process.

5. Identify the three tests used by courts in applying the Equal Protection Clause when deciding whether to uphold or to set aside a statute or administrative rule.

CHAPTER OUTLINE

A. Basic Principles–A number of concepts are basic to constitutional law in the United States.
1. Federalism–Federalism means that governing power is divided between the federal government and the states. The U.S. Constitution states the powers of the federal government and reserves to the states or the people the powers not expressly delegated to the federal government.
2. Federal Supremacy and Preemption–The supremacy clause of the U.S. Constitution provides that the federal constitution and federal laws are the supreme law of the land. Accordingly, any state constitutional provision or law that conflicts with the U.S. Constitution or valid federal laws or treaties is unconstitutional and may not be given effect. Federal preemption refers to the right of the federal government to regulate matters within its powers to the possible exclusion of state regulation. Federal regulation overrides conflicting state regulation.
3. Judicial Review–Judicial review describes the process by which the courts examine governmental actions to determine whether they conform to the U.S. Constitution. If governmental action violates the U.S. Constitution, under judicial review the courts will invalidate that action. Judicial review extends to legislation, acts of the executive branch, and the decisions of inferior courts. It includes the actions of both the federal and state governments, and it applies the same standards of constitutionality to both governments. The U.S. Supreme Court is the final authority as to the constitutionality of any federal or state law.
4. Separation of Powers–Separation of powers is the allocation of powers among the legislative, executive, and judicial branches of government. The purpose of this doctrine is to prevent any branch of government from gaining too much power. It also permits each branch to function without interference from any other branch.
5. State Action–State action refers to actions taken by governments as opposed to actions taken by private individuals. The Thirteenth Amendment, abolishing slavery or involuntary servitude, applies to the actions of private individuals, but other Constitutional protections apply only to state action. "State action" includes any actions of the federal and state governments and their subdivisions, such as city or county governments and agencies. It also may include action taken by private citizens if the state exercises coercive power over the challenged private action or has significantly encouraged the action.

B. Powers of Government–The U.S. Constitution created a federal government of enumerated powers. The Tenth Amendment declares "the powers not delegated to the United States by the Constitution, nor prohibited by it to the States, are reserved to the States respectively, or to the people." Legislation enacted by Congress must, therefore, be based on a specific power granted to the federal government by the Constitution, or be reasonably necessary for carrying out an enumerated power. Only the federal government may exercise some governmental powers, while others are concurrent powers of the federal and state governments.
1. Federal Commerce Power–The U.S. Constitution provides that Congress has the power to regulate commerce with foreign nations and among the states. This commerce clause has two important effects: (1) it is a broad source of commerce power for the federal government to regulate the economy, and (2) it operates as a restriction on state regulations that obstruct or unduly burden interstate commerce. The U.S. Supreme Court interprets the commerce clause as granting virtually complete power to Congress to regulate the economy and business. Legislation

enacted under the commerce clause may only be invalidated (1) if it is clear that the activity regulated by the legislation does not affect interstate commerce, or (2) if it is clear that there is no reasonable connection between the regulatory means selected and the stated ends.

2. State Regulation of Commerce–In addition to acting as a broad source of federal power, the commerce clause also implicitly restricts the states' power to regulate activities if the result obstructs or unduly burdens interstate commerce.

   a. Regulations–In determining the extent of permissible state regulation affecting interstate commerce, the Court weighs and balances (1) the necessity and importance of the state regulation, (2) the burden it imposes on interstate commerce, and (3) the extent to which it discriminates against interstate commerce in favor of local concerns.

   b. Taxation–The commerce clause in conjunction with the import-export clause limits the power of the states to tax. The import-export clause provides: "No State shall, without the Consent of the Congress, lay any Imposts or Duties on Imports or Exports." Once goods enter the stream of interstate or foreign commerce, the power of the state to tax ceases and does not resume until the goods are delivered to the purchaser or the owner terminates the movement of the goods through commerce. The due process clause of the Fourteenth Amendment also restricts the power of states to tax by requiring a sufficient connection between the state and the person, thing, or activity to be taxed.

3. Federal Fiscal Powers–The federal government exerts a dominating influence over the national economy through its control of financial matters. In addition to the powers granted in the commerce clause, the sources of federal fiscal regulatory power include (1) the power to tax, (2) the power to spend, (3) the power to borrow and coin money, and (4) the power of eminent domain.

   a. Taxation–The federal government has broad power to tax, limited by the following: (1) direct taxes other than income taxes must be apportioned among the states, (2) all custom duties and excise taxes must be uniform throughout the United States, and (3) no duties may be levied on exports from any state.

   b. Spending Power–The Constitution authorizes the federal government to pay debts and spend for the common defense and general welfare of the U.S. The spending power of Congress is extremely broad.

   c. Borrowing and Coining Money–The U.S. Constitution also grants Congress the power to borrow money on the credit of the United States and to coin money. These two powers have enabled the federal government to establish a national banking system, the Federal Reserve System, and specialized federal lending programs such as the Federal Land Bank.

   d. Eminent Domain–Eminent domain is the power of government to take private property for public use upon payment of fair compensation. The power is one of the inherent powers of government in the federal Constitution and in the constitutions of the states. However, the Fifth Amendment limits the power by stating: "nor shall private property be taken for public use without just compensation" and through the Fourteenth Amendment limit also applies to the states. The Takings Clause requires just compensation only if a governmental taking actually occurs or a regulation deprives an owner of all economic use of the property. Compensation is not required if governmental regulation only reduces the value of property.

C. Limitations on Government–The U.S. Constitution specifies certain powers that are granted to the federal government. Other, unspecified powers have been reserved to the states. The limitations most applicable to business are: (1) the contract clause, (2) the First Amendment, (3) due process, and (4) equal protection. The first of these–the contract clause–applies only to the actions of state government, whereas the other three apply to both the federal government and the states. None of these restrictions operates as an absolute limitation but instead triggers review to determine whether the governmental power exercised encroaches impermissibly upon the interest protected by the Constitution. Three levels of scrutiny are used. The least rigorous test is the rational relationship test, which requires that the regulation conceivably bear a rational relationship to a legitimate governmental interest. The most exacting test is the strict scrutiny test, which requires that legislation be necessary to promote a compelling governmental interest. The intermediate test requires that legislation have a substantial relationship to an important governmental objective.

1. Contract Clause–Article 1, Section 10 of the Constitution provides: "No State shall . . . pass any Law impairing the Obligation of Contracts . . . ." The Supreme Court has used the contract clause to restrict states from retroactively modifying public charters and private contracts. Although the contract clause does not apply to the federal government, due process limits the federal government's power to impair contracts.

2. First Amendment–The First Amendment contains a guarantee of free speech, but that protection is not absolute. Some forms of speech, such as obscenity, receive no protection.
    a. Corporate Political Speech–The First Amendment's guarantee of free speech applies not only to individuals but also to corporations, which may not be prohibited from speaking out on political issues. However, the U.S. Supreme Court has upheld a narrowly tailored state statute prohibiting corporations from using general treasury funds to make independent expenditures in elections for public office but permitting such expenditures from segregated funds used solely for political purposes.
    b. Commercial Speech–Commercial speech is expression related to the economic interests of the speaker and his audience, such as advertisements. Commercial speech that does no more than propose a commercial transaction is entitled to a "lesser degree" of constitutional protection, but it is not wholly outside the protection of the First Amendment.
    c. Defamation–Defamation is a civil wrong or tort consisting of a false communication that injures a person's reputation. Because defamation involves a communication, the protection extended to speech by the First Amendment applies. Public figures who pursue a cause of action for the tort of defamation or injury to their reputation by publication of false statements must prove actual malice or prove the defendant had knowledge of the falsity of the communication or acted in reckless disregard of its truth or falsity. In a defamation suit brought by a private person (not a public official or public figure), the plaintiff must prove that the defendant published the defamatory comment with malice or negligence.

3. Due Process–The Fifth and Fourteenth Amendments respectively prohibit the federal and state governments from depriving any person of life, liberty, or property without due process of law. Due process has two different aspects: substantive due process and procedural due process.
    a. Substantive Due Process–Substantive due process requires that governmental action be compatible with individual liberties. Where fundamental rights of individuals under the Constitution are affected, the Court will carefully scrutinize the legislation to determine if the legislation is necessary to promote a compelling state interest. Substantive due process addresses the constitutionality of the substance of a legal rule, not the fairness of the process by which the rule is applied.

b. Procedural Due Process–Procedural due process requires that governmental action depriving a person of life, liberty, or property be done through a fair procedure. Liberty for purposes of procedural due process generally includes the ability of individuals to engage in freedom of action and choice regarding their personal lives. Property, for the purpose of procedural due process, includes not only all forms of real and personal property but also certain benefits (entitlements) conferred by government, such as Social Security payments and food stamps.

4. Equal Protection–Equal protection requires that similarly situated persons be treated similarly by governmental action. The Fourteenth Amendment provides that "nor shall any State . . . deny to any person within its jurisdiction the equal protection of the laws." Although this amendment applies only to the actions of state governments, the Supreme Court has interpreted the due process clause of the Fifth Amendment to subject federal actions to the same standards of review. When governmental action involves classification of people, the equal protection guarantee applies. In equal protection cases, the Supreme Court will use one of three standards of review: (1) the rational relationship test, (2) the strict scrutiny test, or (3) the intermediate test.

a. Rational Relationship Test–This test applies to economic regulation and only requires that it is conceivable that a classification bears some rational relationship to a legitimate governmental interest furthered by the classification. Courts will overturn a governmental action only if clear and convincing evidence shows there is no reasonable basis justifying it.

b. Strict Scrutiny Test–The strict scrutiny test is more exacting and requires courts to determine whether a classification is constitutionally permissible because it is necessary to promote a compelling governmental interest. This test is applied when the governmental action affects fundamental rights or involves suspect classifications. Fundamental rights include most of the provisions of the Bill of Rights and some other rights, such as a right to vote. Suspect classifications include those based on race or national origin.

c. Intermediate Test–The intermediate test requires the governmental action to have a substantial relationship to an important governmental objective. This test has been applied to governmental action based on gender and legitimacy.

KEY TERMS

1. Supremacy clause

2. Federal preemption

3. Judicial review

4. Separation of powers

5. State action

6. Commerce clause

7. Federal fiscal powers

8. Eminent domain

9. Contract clause

10. Commercial speech

11. Substantive due process

12. Procedural due process

13. Equal protection

14. Rational relationship test

15. Strict scrutiny test

16. Intermediate test

TRUE/FALSE

_____ 1. Judicial review is the process by which courts review the constitutionality of government actions.

_____ 2. The doctrine of federal preemption requires a conflicting state law give way to the federal legislation.

_____ 3. The Contract Clause invalidates state laws that burden interstate commerce.

_____ 4. Federal supremacy means that federal law takes precedence over conflicting state laws.

_____ 5. The right of eminent domain permits the taking of private property for any purpose by government with fair compensation.

_____ 6. Under the process of judicial review, the U.S. Supreme Court is the final authority as to the constitutionality of federal and state laws.

_____ 7. Substantive due process refers to the decision-making process that results in depriving a person of life, liberty, or property.

_____ 8. Under the First Amendment, a governmental ban is appropriate and lawful on forms of communication more likely to deceive the public than to inform it.

_____ 9. The contract clause of the U.S. Constitution applies only to the actions of state governments.

_____ 10. Commercial speech receives the highest degree of protection under the First Amendment.

_____ 11. While goods are in the stream of interstate commerce, they may be taxed by individual states.

_____ 12. An activity conducted solely in one state is not subject to regulation by federal government.

_____ 13. The strict scrutiny test requires that the legislature's classification be necessary to promote a compelling or overriding governmental interest.

_____ 14. The Fourteenth Amendment provides that states shall not deny equal protection to persons.

_____ 15. The Supreme Court recently held that governmental restrictions of commercial speech must be absolutely the least severe necessary to achieve the governmental objective.

MULTIPLE CHOICE

_____ 1. Which of the following are considered to be fundamental principles, which apply to both the powers of and the limitations on government?
   a. Federal supremacy
   b. Judicial review
   c. Separation of powers
   d. All of the above

_____ 2. Exclusive federal powers include which of the following?
   a. To establish post offices
   b. To coin currency
   c. To grant patents
   d. All of the above are exclusive federal powers.

_____ 3. The equal protection clause is contained in the:
   a. Fifth Amendment.
   b. Fourteenth Amendment.
   c. First Amendment.
   d. Fourth Amendment.

_____ 4. Substantive due process rights would include all of the following except:
   a. right of privacy.
   b. right to interstate travel.
   c. right to have certain evidence excluded from a trial.
   d. right to vote.

_____ 5. For the purposes of procedural due process, the term "property" includes:
   a. real property and personal property only.
   b. real property and entitlements only.
   c. personal property and entitlements only.
   d. real property, personal property, and entitlements.

_____ 6. In equal protection cases involving fundamental rights or suspect classifications, which test would be used for review by the Supreme Court?
   a.   Rational relationship test
   b.   Procedural due process test
   c.   Strict scrutiny test
   d.   Substantive relationship test

_____ 7. Which of the following would require application of the intermediate equal protection test?
   a.   Legitimacy
   b.   Nonprotected speech
   c.   Protected noncommercial speech
   d.   None of the above

_____ 8. The main purpose of the Bill of Rights is to:
   a.   provide restrictions on the powers of the states.
   b.   provide the authority for federal government to regulate business.
   c.   provide restrictions on the powers of the federal government.
   d.   None of the above.

_____ 9. The Contract Clause restricts:
   a.   the federal government from retroactively modifying contracts.
   b.   the states from retroactively modifying contracts.
   c.   the states from exercising the power of eminent domain.
   d.   None of the above.

_____ 10. Which of the following federal "powers" stem from the Commerce Clause?
   a.   The power to coin money
   b.   The power to tax
   c.   The power of eminent domain
   d.   Environmental protection

_____ 11. The protection of the _____ Amendment applies to cases involving the tort of defamation.
   a. First
   b. Fourth
   c. Fifth
   d. Ninth

_____ 12. Which of the following would be considered property for purposes of procedural due process?
   a. Social Security payments
   b. Food stamps
   c. Both Social Security and food stamps
   d. Neither Social Security nor food stamps

_____ 13. The _____ operates as a restriction on state regulations that obstruct or unduly burden interstate commerce.
   a. First Amendment
   b. Commerce Clause
   c. Contract Clause
   d. Due Process Clause

_____ 14. Which of the following is a true statement with regard to the Commerce Clause of the U.S. Constitution?
   a. It expressly excludes state regulation of interstate commerce.
   b. It expressly permits federal regulation of interstate commerce.
   c. It expressly excludes state regulation and expressly permits federal regulation.
   d. The U.S. Constitution makes no statement regarding regulation of commerce.

_____ 15. Which of the following constitutional limitations of power, most applicable to business, applies only to actions of state governments?
   a. The Contract Clause
   b. The First Amendment
   c. Due Process
   d. Equal protection

SHORT ESSAY

1. Briefly explain the difference between procedural and substantive due process.

   _____

   _____

   _____

   _____

2. In equal protection cases, how does the rational relationship test compare with the strict scrutiny test?

   _____

   _____

   _____

   _____

3. Describe the factors used by the Supreme Court when deciding the extent to which state regulation may affect interstate commerce.

   _____

   _____

   _____

   _____

4. How does the Commerce Clause restrict the ability of states to regulate interstate commerce?

   _____

   _____

   _____

   _____

5. Explain the First Amendment's protection of free speech with respect to corporate political speech, commercial speech, and defamation.

   _____

   _____

   _____

   _____

Chapter 5
Administrative Law

PURPOSE

The purpose of this chapter is to introduce you to administrative agencies and examine the significant and necessary role of federal administrative agencies in our society. Administrative agencies are governmental entities (other than courts and legislatures) having authority to affect the rights of private parties. The chapter discusses the operation of administrative agencies and limits on administrative agencies.

CHAPTER CHECKPOINTS

After reading and studying this chapter, you should be able to:

1. List the three basic functions of administrative agencies.

2. Discuss pertinent provisions of the Administrative Procedure Act.

3. Compare the three types of rules promulgated by administrative agencies.

4. Explain formal and informal methods of adjudication.

5. Identify the limits placed upon administrative agencies.

CHAPTER OUTLINE

    A. Operation of Administrative Agencies–Most administrative agencies perform three basic functions: (1) to make rules, (2) to enforce the law, and (3) to adjudicate controversies. The term *administrative process* refers to the entire set of activities in which administrative agencies engage while carrying out their rulemaking, enforcement, and adjudicative functions. To address the issues raised by the concentration of these three functions in the same agency and to address questions raised regarding the propriety of having the same bodies which establish the rules also act as prosecutor and judge in determining whether the rules have been violated, Congress passed the Administrative Procedure Act (APA) in 1946. The APA also established procedural reforms.

1. Rulemaking–Rulemaking is the process by which an administrative agency enacts or promulgates rules of law. Under the APA, a rule is "the whole or a part of an agency statement of general or particular applicability and future effect designed to implement, interpret, or process law or policy." Three types of rules are promulgated by administrative agencies: legislative rules, interpretative rules, and procedural rules.

    a. Legislative Rules–Legislative rules, often called regulations, are substantive rules issued by an administrative agency under the authority delegated to it by the legislature. Legislative rules must be promulgated in accordance with the procedural requirements of the APA. In 1990, Congress enacted the Negotiated Rulemaking Act which authorizes agencies to use negotiated rulemaking but does not require it. Legislative rules, in contrast to interpretative and procedural rules, have the binding force and effect of law.

    b. Interpretative Rules–Interpretative rules are statements issued by an administrative agency indicating its construction of its governing statute. Interpretative rules are exempt from the notice and comment requirement of the APA. They are not binding, although they are persuasive and are given substantial weight by the courts.

    c. Procedural Rules–Procedural rules are non-binding rules issued by an administrative agency establishing its organization, method of operation, and rules of conduct for practicing before it. Procedural rules are also exempt from the notice and comment requirements of the APA.

2. Enforcement–Agencies also investigate conduct to determine whether the statute creating the agency or the agency's legislative rules have been violated. Agencies have traditionally been given great discretion to compel disclosure of information, subject to constitutional limitations.

3. Adjudication–After concluding an investigation, the agency may use formal or informal methods to resolve the matter. Most matters are informally adjudicated by procedures including advising, negotiating, and settling. While not required to be used, the Administrative Dispute Resolution Act authorizes and encourages federal agencies to use alternative dispute resolution. The formal procedure by which an agency resolves a matter (called adjudication) involves finding facts, applying legal rules to the facts, and formulating orders. An order is the final disposition made by an agency. Adjudication is in essence an administrative trial governed by certain standards set forth in the APA. The APA requires that notice be given of the hearing; that the agency give all interested parties the opportunity to submit "facts, arguments, offers of settlement, or proposals of adjustment"; and that a hearing be held if no settlement is reached. The hearing is presided over by an administrative law judge (ALJ) and is prosecuted by the agency. Juries are never used. Either party may introduce oral and documentary evidence. All decisions must include a statement of findings of fact and conclusions of law and the reasons or basis for them as well as a statement of the appropriate rule, order, sanction, or relief. In most instances orders are final unless appealed, and failure to comply with an order is subject to statutory penalty.

B. Limits on Administrative Agencies–An important and fundamental part of administrative law is the limits imposed by judicial review upon the activities of administrative agencies. Courts are not supposed to substitute their judgment on matters of policy for the agency's judgment, but the legislature and the executive branch may address the wisdom and correctness of an agency's action. Legally required public disclosure of agency actions provides further protection for the public.

1. Judicial Review–In exercising judicial review, the court may either compel agency action unlawfully withheld or set aside impermissible agency action if the error is prejudicial. This process acts as a check on the conduct of an agency.

   a. General Requirements–It is necessary for parties seeking to challenge agency action to (a) have standing and (b) have exhausted their administrative remedies. Judicial review is ordinarily available only for final agency action. In conducting a review, the court decides all relevant questions of law, interprets constitutional and statutory provisions, and determines the meaning or applicability of the terms of agency action.

   b. Questions of Law–A review of questions of law includes determining whether the agency has: (1) exceeded its authority, (2) properly interpreted the applicable law, (3) violated any constitutional provision, or (4) acted contrary to the procedural requirements of the law.

   c. Questions of Fact–One of three different standards will be used when reviewing factual determinations. The tests applied are: (a) the arbitrary and capricious test, (b) the substantial evidence test, or (c) the unwarranted by the facts standard.

2. Legislative Control–Congress may exercise control through its budgetary power; by amending the agency's enabling statute; by establishing general guidelines such as the APA; by reversing or changing an agency rule through legislation; through review of agencies by Congressional oversight committees; and through Congressional power to confirm high-level administrative appointments. Congress must approve new, major rules before they take effect.

3. Control by Executive Branch–The president has the power to appoint and remove the chief administrators of executive agencies. He has less control of independent agencies, because commissioners serve for a fixed term that is staggered with the president's term of office. The president also controls agencies through the budgeting process. In extreme cases, the president can impound moneys or restructure agencies unless disapproved by Congress.

4. Disclosure of Information–Congress has enacted disclosure statutes to enhance public and political oversight of agency activities. These statutes include:

   a. Freedom of Information Act–The FOIA gives the public access to most records in the files of federal administrative agencies.

   b. Privacy Act–Among other things, this Act generally forbids the unauthorized disclosure of individuals' personal records that are kept by a federal agency and allows an individual the right to review and copy these records and to find out if they have been disclosed to others.

   c. Government in the Sunshine Act–The Government in the Sunshine Act applies to multi-member bodies whose members are appointed by the president with the advice and consent of the Senate. This act requires such bodies to hold their meetings open to the public.

KEY TERMS

1. Administrative law
2. Administrative agency
3. Administrative process
4. Legislative rules

5. Interpretative rules
6. Procedural rules
7. Adjudication
8. Order

TRUE/FALSE

_____ 1. Interpretative rules establish an administrative agency's organization and method of operation.

_____ 2. Administrative law is a branch of private law.

_____ 3. Administrative agencies create more legal rules and adjudicate more controversies than all the legislatures and courts combined.

_____ 4. To be valid legislative rules must not exceed the actual authority granted to the agency by the enabling statute.

_____ 5. Enabling statutes require that all administrative rules be made only after the opportunity for an agency hearing.

_____ 6. A person who is involved in a hearing with an administrative agency has a right to a trial by jury.

_____ 7. Administrative agencies promulgate three types of rules: legislative, interpretative, and procedural.

_____ 8. Most legislative rules are issued in accordance with the informal rulemaking procedures of the Administrative Procedure Act.

_____ 9. Courts, by adjudicating, formulate more policy than do administrative agencies.

_____ 10. The order of an administrative law judge may be appealed to the governing body of the agency.

_____ 11. Judicial review acts as a check by a court on an order of an administrative agency.

_____ 12. Unless there is good cause, an agency must provide notice of a proposed rule and give the public an opportunity to comment.

_____ 13. Most matters that come before administrative agencies are resolved by informal adjudication.

_____ 14. The Administrative Dispute Resolution Act requires agencies to use alternative dispute resolution.

_____ 15. The Negotiated Rulemaking Act requires agencies to use negotiated rulemaking.

MULTIPLE CHOICE

_____ 1. Federal administrative agencies are charged with which of the following?
   a. Citizenship and naturalization
   b. Environmental protection
   c. Telecommunications
   d. All of the above

_____ 2. A decision by an administrative agency may be overturned if the agency:
   a. exceeded its authority.
   b. acted arbitrarily or capriciously.
   c. reached conclusions not supported by substantial evidence.
   d. all of the above.

_____ 3. Limits placed on administrative agencies include:
   a. judicial review of agency actions.
   b. appointment of administrators by the president.
   c. control of the budget by Congress.
   d. all of the above.

_____ 4. Rules issued by an administrative agency which are in effect "administrative statutes" are:
   a. interpretative rules.
   b. procedural rules.
   c. legislative rules.
   d. judicial rules.

_____ 5. In exercising judicial review, the court may:
   a. compel agency action unlawfully withheld.
   b. set aside impermissible agency action.
   c. both a and b.
   d. none of the above.

_____ 6. Which of the following are considered to be basic functions of most administrative agencies?
   a. To make rules
   b. To enforce the law
   c. Adjudication
   d. All of the above

_____ 7. In conducting an investigation, the Securities and Exchange Commission could:
   a. issue subpoenas requiring production of documents.
   b. conduct searches without a warrant.
   c. compel disclosure of privileged information.
   d. none of the above.

_____ 8. In exercising its adjudicative power, an agency may:
   a. impose a fine.
   b. seize property.
   c. revoke a license.
   d. all of the above.

_____ 9. Which of the following is not an administrative agency?
   a. Food and Drug Administration
   b. Equal Employment Opportunity Commission
   c. Consumer Product Safety Commission
   d. All of the above are administrative agencies.

_____ 10. The decision of the administrative law judge:
   a. is not subject to review by the courts.
   b. can be set aside by the courts if the ALJ made a prejudicial error.
   c. will automatically be reviewed by the agency.
   d. none of the above.

_____ 11. The legislature can exercise control over administrative agencies by:
   a. its budgetary power.
   b. by amending the enabling statute.
   c. changing an agency rule by specific legislation.
   d. all of the above.

_____ 12. Before OSHA can issue a regulation regarding safety in the workplace, it must:
   a. provide an opportunity for interested parties to participate in the rulemaking.
   b. determine that Congress supports the regulation.
   c. publish the regulation in the Code of Federal Regulations.
   d. all of the above.

_____ 13. In _____ rulemaking, the agency must base its rules upon consideration of the record of the agency hearing and include a statement of findings and conclusions on all material issues.
   a. informal
   b formal
   c. hybrid
   d. none of the above

_____ 14. In exercising judicial review the court will inquire into whether the agency has:
   a. exceeded its authority.
   b. properly interpreted the applicable law.
   c. acted contrary to the procedural requirements of the law.
   d. all of the above.

_____ 15. Which of the following would not have to be disclosed under the Freedom of Information Act?
   a. National defense secrets
   b. Records of an agency's internal practices
   c. Trade secrets
   d. None of the above would have to be disclosed.

SHORT ESSAY

1. Discuss the three basic functions of administrative agencies.

_____

_____

_____

2. Compare the formal, informal, and hybrid rulemaking processes.

_____

_____

_____

3. Explain the process of judicial review upon the activities of administrative agencies.

_____

_____

_____

4. Briefly discuss some limitations on administrative agencies.

_____

_____

_____

5. Define the three types of rules promulgated by administrative agencies.

_____

_____

_____

Chapter 6
Criminal Law

PURPOSE

Whereas civil law defines duties, the violation of which constitutes a wrong against the injured party, the criminal law establishes duties, the violation of which is a wrong against the whole community. Civil law is a part of private law; criminal law is a part of public law. In a civil case, the injured party sues to recover compensation for the injury sustained. In a criminal case, the government brings a case against a person for a wrong against society. If the person accused is convicted, the wrongdoer will be punished by a fine or imprisonment or both. Some conduct may be both a crime and a civil wrong, or tort. The purpose of this chapter is to introduce the general principles of criminal law and criminal procedure as well as specific crimes and defenses relevant to business. Because of the increasing use of criminal sanctions to enforce governmental regulation of business, criminal law is an essential part of business law.

CHAPTER CHECKPOINTS

After reading and studying the chapter, you should be able to:

1. Distinguish between a tort and a crime and identify the essential elements of a crime.

2. Compare the procedure used in initiating and pursuing a civil case to the procedure used in initiating and pursuing a criminal case.

3. Identify and define the common crimes against property and the common defenses.

4. Identify the constitutional protections for criminal defendants and the source of each of these constitutional rights.

5. Using appropriate legal terminology, outline the steps in a criminal prosecution.

CHAPTER OUTLINE

A. Nature of Crimes–A crime is any act or omission forbidden by public law in the interest of protecting society and made punishable by the government in a judicial proceeding brought by it. Crimes are prohibited and punished on grounds of public policy, which may include the protection of government, human life, or property. Other purposes of the criminal law include deterrence, rehabilitation, and retribution. Historically, criminal law was primarily common law, but today it is almost exclusively statutory.

1. Essential Elements–*Actus reus* is a wrongful or overt act. *Mens rea* is a criminal intent or mental fault. In general, both of these elements must be present to have a crime. *Actus reus* refers to all the nonmental elements of a crime, including the physical act that must be performed, the circumstances under which it must be performed, and the consequences of that act. *Mens rea,* or mental fault, refers to the mental element of a crime. Most common law and some statutory crimes require subjective fault, which includes purposeful, knowing, or reckless conduct. Other crimes require a lesser degree of mental fault, called objective fault. Objective fault involves gross deviation from the standard of care that a reasonable person would observe under the circumstances. Statutes usually refer to objective fault by such terms as "carelessness" or "negligence." Many regulatory statutes have totally dispensed with the mental element of a crime and impose liability without fault. Criminal liability without fault makes it a crime to do a specific act or to bring about a certain result without regard to the care exercised by that person.

2. Classification–Historically, crimes have been classified as *mala in se,* which are crimes such as murder that are morally wrong in themselves, or *mala prohibita,* which are crimes such as minor traffic offenses that are not morally wrong in themselves but that have been declared wrong by law. Today crimes are usually classified by their seriousness. A felony is a serious crime punishable by imprisonment in a penitentiary or by death. A misdemeanor is a less serious crime punishable by a fine or imprisonment in a local jail.

3. Vicarious Liability–Vicarious liability is liability imposed on one person for the acts of another person. Employers are vicariously liable for authorized criminal acts of their employees if the employer directed, participated in, or approved of the acts. Employers are ordinarily not liable for the unauthorized criminal acts of their employees. However, employers may be subject to a criminal penalty for the unauthorized act of an advisory or managerial person acting in the scope of employment. Moreover, employers may be criminally liable under liability without fault statutes for certain unauthorized acts of its employees, whether the employees are managerial or not.

4. Liability of a Corporation–Historically, corporations were not held criminally liable, because they did not possess the requisite criminal intent and, therefore, were incapable of committing a crime. Under the modern approach, a corporation may be liable for violation of statutes imposing liability without fault. In addition, a corporation may be liable where a high corporate officer or the board of directors perpetrates the offense. Punishment of a corporation is necessarily by fine and not imprisonment. Nonetheless, the individuals bearing responsibility for the criminal act face either/or both fines and imprisonment. The Federal Organizational Corporate Sentencing Guidelines became effective in 1991, with an overall purpose of imposing sanctions which will provide just punishment and adequate deterrence. In the most extreme case, a corporation's charter can be revoked.

B. White-Collar Crime–The Justice Department defines white-collar crime as nonviolent crime involving deceit, corruption, or breach of trust. It includes crimes committed by individuals–such as embezzlement and forgery–as well as crimes committed on behalf of a corporation–such as commercial bribery, product safety and health crimes, false advertising, and antitrust violations.

In 2002, Congress passed the Sarbanes-Oxley Act (see Chapter 40 for further discussion). This Act seeks to prevent various forms of corporate wrongdoing by increasing corporate responsibility; mandating greater corporate financial disclosure, creating new criminal offenses and strengthening existing ones, and creating an Accounting Oversight Board that has the power to review and discipline auditors. This Act, for instance, makes it a federal crime to defraud any person or to obtain any money or property fraudulently in connection with any security of a public company, or to knowingly alter, destroy, mutilate, or falsify any document in order to impede a federal investigation.

1. Computer Crime–Computer crime is a special type of white-collar crime. Computer crime includes the use of a computer to steal money or services, to remove personal or business information, and to tamper with information. These crimes can be broken down into five general categories: (1) theft of computer hardware, software, or secrets; (2) unauthorized use of computer services; (3) theft of money by computer; (4) vandalism of computer hardware or software; and (5) theft of computer data.

2. Racketeer Influenced and Corrupt Organizations Act–RICO was enacted in 1970 with the stated purpose of terminating the infiltration by organized crime into legitimate business. The act subjects enterprises that engage in a pattern of racketeering to severe civil and criminal penalties. A pattern of racketeering is defined as the commission of two or more predicate acts within a period of ten years. A predicate act is any of several criminal offenses listed in RICO. RICO is controversial, because businesses that are not involved in organized crime but that meet the "pattern of racketeering" test may be subjected to fines, forfeiture of property obtained due to a RICO violation, prison terms, and treble damages in civil suits.

C. Crimes Against Business–Criminal offenses against property greatly affect businesses.
1. Larceny–Larceny is the trespassory taking and carrying away of personal property of another with the intent to deprive the victim permanently of the goods.
2. Embezzlement–Embezzlement is the fraudulent conversion of another's property by one who was in lawful possession of it. A conversion is any act that seriously interferes with the owner's rights in the property. In both larceny and embezzlement there is a misuse of the property of another, but in larceny the thief unlawfully possesses the property, whereas in embezzlement the thief lawfully possesses it.
3. False Pretenses–False pretenses is the crime of obtaining title to property of another by means of materially false representations of an existing fact, with knowledge of its falsity, and made with the intent to defraud. Larceny does not cover this situation, because the victim of the crime of false pretenses voluntarily transfers the property to the thief. Other specialized crimes that are similar to false pretenses include mail fraud and securities fraud.
4. Robbery–Robbery is larceny with the additional elements that the property is taken directly from the victim or in the immediate presence of the victim, and the taking is accomplished through either force or threat of force. Many statutes distinguish between simple robbery and aggravated robbery.

5. Burglary–At common law, burglary was defined as the breaking and entering of the dwelling of another at night with the intent to commit a felony. Modern statutes vary, but many simply require that there be an entry into a building with the intent to commit a felony in the building.

6. Extortion and Bribery–Extortion, or blackmail, is generally held to be the making of threats for the purpose of obtaining money or property. Bribery is the offer of money or property to a public official to influence the official's decision. Some jurisdictions make commercial bribery illegal. Commercial bribery is the use of bribery to acquire new business, obtain secret information or processes, or obtain kickbacks.

7. Forgery–Forgery is the intentional falsification or false making of a document with the intent to defraud.

8. Bad Checks–All jurisdictions have now enacted laws making it a crime to issue bad checks; that is, writing a check when there is not enough money in the account to cover the check.

D. Defenses to Crimes–The defenses most relevant to white-collar crimes and crimes against business include defense of property, duress, mistake of fact, and entrapment.

1. Defense of Person or Property–Individuals may use reasonable force to protect themselves, other individuals, and property. This defense enables a person to commit, without any criminal liability, what would otherwise be considered the crime of assault, battery, manslaughter, or murder. Under the majority rule, deadly force is never reasonable to protect property.

2. Duress–A person who is threatened with immediate, serious bodily harm to himself or another unless he engages in criminal conduct other than murder may raise the defense of duress.

3. Mistake of Fact–Persons who reasonably believe the facts to be such that their conduct would not constitute crimes may use this defense to justify their conduct.

4. Entrapment–This defense arises when a law enforcement official induces a person to commit a crime when that person would not have done so without the persuasion of the police officer.

E. Criminal Procedure–Each of the states and the federal government have procedures for initiating and coordinating criminal prosecutions. In addition, the first ten amendments to the U.S. Constitution (called the Bill of Rights) guarantee many defenses and rights of an accused. Most state constitutions have similar provisions. In addition, the Fourteenth Amendment prohibits state governments from depriving any person of life, liberty, or property without due process of law.

1. Steps in Criminal Prosecution–Particulars of criminal procedure vary from state to state. In general, after arrest, the accused is booked and appears before a magistrate, commissioner, or justice of the peace, where the accused is given formal notice of the charges, the accused is advised of his rights, and bail is set. Then a preliminary hearing is held to determine whether there is probable cause to believe the defendant is the one who committed the crime. The defendant is usually entitled to be represented by counsel. If there is probable cause, the case will be brought before a grand jury which issues an indictment or true bill if it finds sufficient evidence to justify a trial. The indictment is a grand jury charge that the defendant should stand trial. An information is used rather than an indictment in misdemeanor cases and in some felony cases in states not requiring indictments. An information is a formal accusation of a crime brought by a prosecuting officer and not a grand jury. The next step is an arraignment where the defendant is informed of the charge against him and he enters a plea. If his plea is "not guilty," he must stand trial and is entitled to a jury in most cases. In a criminal trial, (1) the defendant is presumed

innocent, (2) the burden of proof on the prosecution is to prove guilt beyond a reasonable doubt, and (3) the defendant is not required to testify. If the jury's verdict is not guilty, the matter ends there. If the verdict is guilty, the judge will enter a judgment of conviction and set the case for the sentencing. The defendant may make a motion for a new trial or appeal to a reviewing court.

2. Fourth Amendment–The Fourth Amendment protects individuals against unreasonable searches and seizures. The amendment is designed to protect the privacy and security of individuals against arbitrary invasions by government officials. Although the Fourth Amendment by its terms applies only to the federal government, the Fourteenth Amendment makes it applicable to the states. When there is a violation of the Fourth Amendment, the exclusionary rule prohibits the introduction of the illegally seized evidence. The purpose of this rule is to discourage illegal police conduct and to protect individual liberty. To obtain a search warrant of a particular person, place, or thing, the law enforcement official must demonstrate to a magistrate that there is probable cause to believe that the search will reveal evidence of criminal activity. Probable cause means "[t]he task of the issuing magistrate is simply to make a practical, common sense decision whether, given all the circumstances set forth . . . before him, . . ., there is a fair probability that contraband or evidence of a crime will be found in a particular place." A search without a warrant is permissible where: (1) there is hot pursuit of a fugitive, (2) voluntary consent is given, (3) an emergency requires such action, (4) there has been a lawful arrest, (5) evidence of a crime is in plain view of the law enforcement officer, or (6) delay would present a significant obstacle to the investigation.

3. Fifth Amendment–The Fifth Amendment protects persons against self-incrimination, double jeopardy, and being charged with a capital or infamous crime except by grand jury indictment. The prohibitions against self-incrimination and double jeopardy, but not the grand jury clause, also apply to the states through the due process clause of the Fourteenth Amendment. The privilege against self-incrimination extends only to testimonial evidence and not to physical evidence. Due process is basically the guarantee of a fair trial. In criminal cases, the defendant has the right to counsel, to confront and cross-examine adverse witnesses, to testify in his own behalf, to produce witnesses and offer other evidence, and to be free of any and all prejudicial conduct and statements.

4. Sixth Amendment–The Sixth Amendment provides that the federal government shall provide the accused with a speedy and public trial by an impartial jury, inform him of the nature and cause of the accusation, confront him with the witnesses against him, have compulsory process for obtaining witnesses in his favor, and have the assistance of counsel for his defense. The Fourteenth Amendment extends these guarantees to the states.

KEY TERMS

1. Crime

2. *Actus reus*

3. *Mens rea*

4. Subjective fault

5. Objective fault

6. Liability without fault

7. Felony

8. Misdemeanor

9. Vicarious liability

10. White-collar crime

11. Computer crime

12. RICO

13. Larceny

14. Embezzlement

15. False pretenses

16. Robbery

17. Burglary

18. Extortion

19. Bribery

20. Forgery

21. Bad checks

22. Defense of person or property

23. Duress

24. Mistake of fact

25. Entrapment

26. Preliminary hearing

27. Grand jury

28. Indictment

29. Information

30. Arraignment

31. Exclusionary rule

32. Probable cause

33. Sarbaness-Oxley Act

TRUE/FALSE

_____ 1. Criminal law establishes duties, the violation of which constitutes wrongs against other individuals.

_____ 2. *Mala prohibita* means that the conduct is wrong in itself or morally wrong.

_____ 3. A corporation cannot be held criminally liable because a corporation cannot possess the requisite criminal intent.

_____ 4. The most severe punishment against a corporation would be removal of its corporate charter.

_____ 5. A grand jury issues a decision called an indictment.

_____ 6. To establish the crime of larceny, it is not necessary to prove that there was an intent to deprive the victim permanently of her goods.

_____ 7. The Fifth Amendment protects individuals against unreasonable searches and seizures.

_____ 8. The exclusionary rule prohibits illegally seized evidence from being introduced into court.

_____ 9. The Sixth Amendment provides the right to a jury trial.

_____ 10. In a criminal trial, the prosecution must establish guilt beyond a reasonable doubt.

_____ 11. The right to counsel is found in the Fifth Amendment.

_____ 12. Duress can never be raised as a defense to the commission of a crime.

_____ 13. A woman may use deadly force to protect herself against an attack that threatens death or serious bodily harm.

_____ 14. A pattern of racketeering under RICO is defined as the commission of two or more predicate acts within a period of ten years.

_____ 15. The privilege against self-incrimination extends to both physical evidence and testimonial evidence.

MULTIPLE CHOICE

_____ 1. Which of the following would not be a defense available to a criminal defendant?
  a. Mistake of fact
  b. Entrapment
  c. Duress
  d. Contributory negligence

_____ 2. Generally, a crime consists of which of the following?
  a. A wrongful or overt act
  b. The requisite criminal intent
  c. Both a and b
  d. None of the above

_____ 3. A crime punishable by a fine or imprisonment in local jail is called a:
  a. misdemeanor.
  b. felony.
  c. white collar crime.
  d. *mala in se.*

_____ 4. Which of the following crimes involves an intentional misrepresentation of fact in order to defraud another?
  a. Extortion
  b. Robbery
  c. Burglary
  d. False pretenses

_____ 5. The stage of a criminal trial when the defendant is brought before the court, informed of the charge, and allowed to enter a plea, is the:
   a. preliminary hearing.
   b. arraignment.
   c. sentencing.
   d. indictment.

_____ 6. A trespassory taking of the goods of another with intent to permanently deprive is:
   a. extortion.
   b. robbery.
   c. embezzlement.
   d. larceny.

_____ 7. Which of the following is not an essential element of robbery?
   a. Non-trespassory taking
   b. Carrying away of another's personal property
   c. Directly from the victim or in the victim's presence
   d. With the intent to deprive the victim permanently of the goods

_____ 8. Individuals are protected against unreasonable searches and seizures by the:
   a. Fourth Amendment.
   b. Fifth Amendment.
   c. Sixth Amendment.
   d. Fourteenth Amendment.

_____ 9. The right to be represented by legal counsel is provided by:
   a. the Sixth Amendment.
   b. the Fourth Amendment.
   c. the Fourteenth Amendment.
   d. custom.

_____ 10. Computer crime involves the use of a computer:
   a. to steal money or services.
   b. to remove personal or business information.
   c. to tamper with information.
   d. all of the above.

_____ 11. A warrant is not required for a search by the police when:
   a. they have just witnessed a crime.
   b. a homeowner agrees to allow the police to enter and search her garage.
   c. they would like to wiretap the phone of a suspected drug dealer.
   d. two of the above (a and b).

_____ 12. Violations of RICO could be considered:
   a. a civil wrong.
   b. a criminal wrong.
   c. a and b above.
   d. none of the above.

_____ 13. The rule which prohibits the introduction of illegally seized evidence is the:
   a. *mala in se* rule.
   b. exclusionary rule.
   c. due process rule.
   d. predicate act rule.

_____ 14. How are crimes distinguished from other forms of unlawful conduct?
   a. They are prosecuted by the victims.
   b. They result in payment of damages to the victim.
   c. They are offenses against all of society and are punishable by a fine and/or imprisonment.
   d. All of the above

_____ 15. If an employee of Risky Corporation dies because of unsafe conditions at the company plant and company officers were aware of and did nothing to alleviate those conditions, then:
   a. the officers only would be liable.
   b. the company only would be liable.
   c. both the officers and the company would be liable.
   d. neither the officers nor the company would be liable.

SHORT ESSAY

1. Distinguish between a tort and a crime and identify the essential elements of a crime.

    _____

    _____

    _____

    _____

2. Discuss the four defenses most relevant to white-collar crimes and crimes against business.

    _____

    _____

    _____

    _____

3. State the purpose of the Racketeer Influenced and Corrupt Organizations Act (RICO).

    _____

    _____

    _____

    _____

4. Under the Fourth Amendment, a search warrant is not required in what situations?

    _____

    _____

    _____

    _____

5. Identify and discuss the major constitutional protections for the accused in our criminal justice system.

    _____

    _____

    _____

    _____

Chapter 7
Intentional Torts

PURPOSE

The purpose of this chapter is to introduce you to the law of intentional torts. The law of torts reallocates losses caused by human misconduct. A tort is defined as a civil wrong causing injury to persons, their property, or their economic interests. In general, a tort is committed when a person owing a duty to another, breaches that duty and that breach proximately causes injury or damage to the owner of a legally protected interest. Torts may be inflicted intentionally, negligently, or without fault (strict liability). This chapter summarizes the general common law of intentional torts. All of the torts studied in this chapter require the element of intent. In tort law, "intent" is not necessarily the desire to harm, but rather the desire to cause the consequences of an act or knowledge that the consequences are substantially certain to result from the act.

CHAPTER CHECKPOINTS

After reading and studying this chapter, you should be able to:

1. Define "intent" as used in the law of intentional torts and recognize fact situations where intent to commit a tort exists.

2. Identify and define the intentional torts that cause harm to the person and to the right of dignity.

3. Discuss the various privileges that protect a defendant from liability for defamation.

4. Identify and define the torts that involve interference with property.

5. Identify and define the business torts that cause harm to economic interests.

CHAPTER OUTLINE

A. Intent–In tort law, intent does not require a hostile or evil motive. It is enough that the actor desires to cause the consequences of his act or even that he believes those consequences are substantially certain to result.

B. Harm to the Person–The law provides protection against harm to the person.
   1. Battery–The intentional infliction of harmful or offensive bodily contact constitutes a battery.
   2. Assault–The intentional infliction of apprehension of immediate bodily harm or offensive contact is an assault.
   3. False Imprisonment–Intentional interference with a person's freedom of movement by unlawful confinement is false imprisonment.
   4. Infliction of Emotional Distress–Extreme and outrageous conduct intentionally or recklessly causing severe emotional distress is known as the intentional infliction of emotional distress. Recklessness is conduct that evidences a person's conscious disregard of or an indifference to the consequences of the his or her act.

C. Harm to the Right of Dignity–The law also protects a person against interference with, or harm to, his right of dignity.
   1. Defamation–This tort consists of injury to a person's reputation by means of the unprivileged publication of a false statement.
      a. Elements of Defamation–The burden of proof is on the plaintiff to prove the falsity of the defamatory statement. Slander is oral defamation. Libel is defamation that is communicated by writing, television, radio or the like. In either case, there must be a publication, which is communication to a person or persons other than the one who is defamed.
      b. Defenses to Defamation–Privilege is immunity from tort liability. There are three kinds of privileges that apply to defamation: absolute, conditional, and constitutional. Absolute privilege protects the defendant regardless of his motive or intent and applies to statements made during a judicial proceeding, statements made by members of Congress on the floor of Congress, statements made by certain executive officers performing governmental duty, and statements made between spouses when they are alone. Qualified or conditional privilege depends on proper use of the privilege, such as when a person publishes defamatory matter to protect his own legitimate interests or interests of others. It would also apply to letters of reference. Constitutional privilege applies to comments about public officials or public figures so long as the comments are made without malice. Malice is knowledge of the falsity or reckless disregard of the truth.

      Congress recently enacted legislation that grants Internet service providers immunity from liability for defamation when they merely publish information originating from a third party.
   2. Invasion of Privacy–Four distinct torts are included within invasion of privacy.
      a. Appropriation–The unauthorized use of another person's name or likeness for one's own benefit constitutes the tort of appropriation.
      b. Intrusion–Unreasonable and highly offensive interference with the seclusion of another is the tort of intrusion.

    c. Public Disclosure of Private Facts–Offensive communication to the public at large of private information about another person is the public disclosure of private facts.

    d. False Light–Offensive publicity placing another in a false light is the tort of false light.

    e. Defenses–Absolute, conditional, and constitutional privilege are the allowable defenses.

  3. Misuse of Legal Procedure–Three torts comprise the misuse of legal procedure: malicious prosecution, wrongful civil proceedings, and abuse of process. Each protects individuals from unjustifiable litigation. Malicious prosecution and wrongful civil proceedings impose liability for damages caused by improperly brought proceedings. Abuse of process consists of the use of a legal proceeding in order to accomplish a purpose for which the proceeding is not designed.

D. Harm to Property–The law also provides protection against invasions of a person's interests in property.

  1. Real Property–Land and anything attached to it, such as buildings, trees, and minerals.

    a. Trespass–Wrongful entry onto another's land is trespass to real property.

    b. Nuisance–Nontrespassory invasion of another's interest in the private use and enjoyment of his land constitutes the tort of nuisance.

  2. Personal Property–Any property other than an interest in land is considered personal property.

    a. Trespass–An intentional dispossession or unauthorized use of the personal property of another is considered a trespass to personal property.

    b. Conversion–The intentional exercise of dominion or control over another's personal property is considered to be conversion.

E. Harm to Economic Interests–Economic or pecuniary interests include a person's existing and prospective contractual relations, a person's business reputation, a person's name and likeness, and a person's freedom from deception.

  1. Interference with Contractual Relations–Intentionally, improperly causing one of the parties to a contract not to perform the contract is the tort of interference with contractual relations.

  2. Disparagement–Publication of false statements resulting in harm to another's monetary interests constitutes disparagement.

  3. Fraudulent Misrepresentation–A false statement made with knowledge of its falsity and with the intent to deceive constitutes the tort of fraudulent misrepresentation, which is also known as fraud in the inducement when associated with a contract.

KEY TERMS

1. Tort

2. Exemplary or punitive damages

3. Intent

4. Battery

5. Assault

6. Recklessness

7. False imprisonment

8. Infliction of emotional distress

9. Defamation

10. Libel

11. Slander

12. Misuse of legal procedure

13. Absolute privilege

14. Conditional privilege

15. Constitutional privilege

16. Appropriation

17. Intrusion

18. Public disclosure of private facts

19. False light

20. Trespass to real property

21. Nuisance

22. Trespass to personal property

23. Conversion

24. Interference with contractual relations

25. Disparagement

26. Fraudulent misrepresentation

TRUE/FALSE

_____ 1. The purpose of tort law, unlike criminal law, is to compensate the injured party, not to punish the wrongdoer.

_____ 2. A person may be assaulted even though he is not afraid for his safety.

_____ 3. A person may be falsely imprisoned only if he is aware of the confinement.

_____ 4. Appropriation of a person's name or likeness must be unreasonable to be an invasion of privacy.

_____ 5. Intent, as used in tort law, does not require a hostile or evil motive.

_____ 6. A person may be liable for trespass to real property even though he causes no actual damage to the property itself.

_____ 7. A person may be liable for trespass to personal property even though he causes no actual damage to the property itself.

_____ 8. Truth is a complete defense to the tort of disparagement.

_____ 9. The same conduct may constitute both a crime and a tort.

_____ 10. Sexual harassment on the job is an example of intentional infliction of emotional distress.

_____ 11. Abuse of process consists of using a legal proceeding to accomplish a purpose for which the proceeding is not designed.

_____ 12. Arthur has a grudge against Bill. When Bill asks him to write a letter of reference to a prospective employer, Arthur readily agrees. He makes untrue statements in the letter, which prevent Bill from getting the job. Arthur is guilty of defamation.

_____ 13.   Harold Homeowner signs a consent form to allow Dr. Bright to perform surgery on his left knee. Through a mix-up, Dr. Bright operates on Harold's right elbow. Dr. Bright has committed the tort of battery.

_____ 14.   The key elements of false imprisonment are the plaintiff's being detained against her will and the plaintiff's knowing of no reasonable means of escape.

_____ 15.   Sarah is detained by a salesclerk and store manager at Marlin's Department Store and accused of shoplifting. The clerk is mistaken, having confused Sarah with someone else. Sarah is locked in a room for an hour and prevented from leaving. Marlin's is guilty of false imprisonment.

MULTIPLE CHOICE

_____ 1.   Which of the following are principal objectives of the law of torts?
   a.   To compensate persons who sustain loss or harm resulting from another's conduct
   b.   To place the cost of that compensation on society as a whole through a common fund
   c.   To prevent future harms and losses
   d.   (a) and (c), but not (b)

_____ 2.   *A* has committed an assault if he:
   a.   aims an unloaded gun at *B*, tells her that he is going to shoot her, and she reasonably believes it.
   b.   tells *B* that he is going to shoot her the next time he sees her with *C*.
   c.   kisses *B* while she is sleeping.
   d.   all of the above

_____ 3.   *A* is liable for defamation if she:
   a.   tells *B* that *C* is an adulteress when *C* is an adulteress.
   b.   tells *D*, her husband, that *C* is an adulteress when *C* actually is not an adulteress.
   c.   tells *E* that *C* is an adulteress when *C* actually is not an adulteress.
   d.   none of the above

_____ 4.   The unreasonable and highly offensive interference with the solitude or seclusion of another is an element of:
   a.   defamation.
   b.   intrusion.
   c.   public disclosure of private facts.
   d.   false light.

_____ 5. *A* is liable for trespass to real property if he:
   a.   unknowingly crosses *B*'s land while jogging.
   b.   plays his stereo so loudly that *C*, his neighbor, can't sleep at night.
   c.   tosses a gum wrapper and a cigarette butt onto *D*'s front yard.
   d.   (a) and (c), but not (b)

_____ 6. *A* is liable for interference with contractual relations if she:
   a.   intends to interfere with the performance of another's contract.
   b.   knows that her actions are substantially certain to interfere with the performance of another's contract.
   c.   intends to interfere with another's prospective contractual relation.
   d.   all of the above

_____ 7. *A* is liable for fraudulent misrepresentation if she:
   a.   induces *B* to rely justifiably on her false statements of fact.
   b.   induces *B* to rely justifiably on her false statements of opinion.
   c.   induces *B* to rely unjustifiably on her false statements of fact.
   d.   induces *B* to rely unjustifiably on her true statements of fact.

_____ 8. Which of the following is not required in the commission of an intentional tort?
   a.   A duty owed
   b.   A breach of the duty
   c.   Injury or damage to another
   d.   All of the above are required.

_____ 9. If Calvin offers Becky, an employee of Fran under a contract that has two years left, a yearly salary of $5,000 per year more than the contract between Becky and Fran, and Calvin is aware of the existing contract, he may be liable for:
   a.   conversion.
   b.   interference with contractual relations.
   c.   disparagement.
   d.   fraud.

_____ 10. The tort of conversion:
   a. includes the intentional destruction of personal property.
   b. includes the use of personal property in an unauthorized manner.
   c. is also always a trespass.
   d. all of the above.

_____ 11. As used in tort law, _____ denotes that the actor desires to cause the consequences of his act.
   a. assault
   b. retaliation
   c. intent
   d. privilege

_____ 12. Arthur throws his garbage over the fence into Brian's yard. Arthur has committed the tort of:
   a. nuisance.
   b. trespass to real property.
   c. outrageous conduct.
   d. conversion.

_____ 13. In a defamation case, the defendant raises an issue involving the First Amendment to the U.S. Constitution. This is the defense of:
   a. consent.
   b. privilege.
   c. self-defense.
   d. defense of public property.

_____ 14. Which of the following are torts against the person?
   a. Battery and assault
   b. False imprisonment and trespass
   c. Defamation and conversion
   d. All of the above are torts against the person.

_____ 15. The unauthorized use of a person's name or likeness is:
   a. appropriation.
   b. intrusion.
   c. public disclosure of private facts.
   d. false light.

SHORT ESSAYS

1. What is the difference between trespass and nuisance?

_____

_____

_____

_____

2. Explain the meaning of "intent" as used in the law of torts.

_____

_____

_____

_____

3. Discuss business torts that cause harm to economic interests.

_____

_____

_____

_____

4. Arnold needs money to buy drugs, so he beats up Benjamin and steals his wallet. (a) What, if any, torts has Arnold committed? Explain. (b) What, if any, crimes has Arnold committed? Explain. (c) Discuss the differences between the civil tort action and the criminal action.

_____

_____

_____

_____

5. Discuss the types of torts that cause harm to the right of dignity.

_____

_____

_____

_____

Chapter 8
Negligence and Strict Liability

PURPOSE

This chapter introduces you to the law of negligence and strict liability. Negligence involves conduct that creates an unreasonable risk of harm. Liability based upon negligence results from the failure to exercise reasonable care under the circumstances which failure proximately causes injury to another person and/or damage to his property. Negligence liability is not based upon the intent to do something like the intentional torts. Strict liability is liability without fault and without intent to commit an act which causes harm. Instead it is based upon the nature of the activity in which a person is engaging.

CHAPTER CHECKPOINTS

After reading and studying this chapter, you should be able to:

1. List and discuss the basic elements of negligence.

2. Define the reasonable person standard and how it is applied to various groups of people.

3. Compare the duty of care which a possessor of land has to trespassers, licensees, and invitees.

4. Identify the defenses that are available in a tort action in negligence and those that are available in a tort action in strict liability.

5. List and discuss the activities which give rise to strict liability.

CHAPTER OUTLINE

I. Negligence–A person is negligent if he fails to exercise reasonable care under the circumstances. According to the Restatement, negligence is "conduct which falls below the standard established by law for the protection of others against unreasonable risk of harm." An action for negligence consists of three elements: (1) breach of duty of care, (2) proximate cause, and (3) injury.

A. Breach of Duty of Care–A breach of duty of care occurs when the defendant fails to conform to the required standard of conduct established for the protection of others.

   1. Reasonable Person Standard–This is an objective and external standard which is the duty of care required to avoid being negligent. It is imposed by law and measured by the degree of carefulness that a reasonable person would exercise in a given situation. The reasonable person is a fictitious individual who is always careful and prudent and never negligent.

      a. Children–To avoid negligence, children must conform to the standard of a reasonable person of like age, intelligence, and experience under like circumstances.

      b. Physical Disability–A person who is ill or physically disabled must conform to the standard of a reasonable person under like disability.

      c. Mental Deficiency–No allowance is made for insanity or other mental deficiency.

      d. Superior Skill or Knowledge–A person who is qualified to practice a profession or trade that requires special skill and expertise is required to use the same care and skill normally possessed by members of that profession or trade.

      e. Emergencies–In sudden, unexpected events that call for immediate action, the standard is that of a reasonable person under the circumstances—the emergency is considered part of the circumstances.

      f. Violation of Statute–If a statute sets a reasonable person standard of conduct, the unexcused violation of it is negligence per se; that is, it is conclusive on the issue of negligent conduct.

   2. Duty to Act–Except in special circumstances, no one is required to aid another in peril. Exceptions include situations where special relations between the parties exist and where a person's conduct has injured another and left him helpless and in danger of further harm. For example, special relations that give rise to a duty to aid or protect another include common carrier-passenger, innkeeper-guest, employer-employee, and parent-child.

   3. Duties of Possessors of Land –The right of possessors of land to use that land for their own benefit and enjoyment is limited by their duty to do so in a reasonable manner. The possessor of land is required to exercise reasonable care in carrying on activities on the land in order to protect others who are not on the property. The duty to persons who come on the land depends on whether that person is a trespasser, a licensee, or an invitee.

      a. Duty to Trespassers–A trespasser is a person who enters or remains on the land of another without permission or privilege to do so. Except to children, there is no duty to maintain land in a reasonably safe condition for the benefit of trespassers. But an owner cannot intentionally hurt a trespasser, and most courts hold that upon discovering the presence of trespassers, the lawful occupier of land must use reasonable care in carrying on his or her activities and warn trespassers of dangerous conditions that they are unlikely to discover.

      b. Duty to Licensees–A licensee is a person privileged to enter or remain on land by the consent of the lawful possessor. Licensees include members of the household, social guests, and salespersons calling at homes. The possessor must warn a licensee of dangerous activities and conditions that the possessor know of and which the licensee does not and is not likely to discover. Some states have extended to licensees the same protection traditionally accorded invitees. A number of states have included social guests in the invitee category.

    c. Duty to Invitees–An invitee is a person invited upon land as a member of the public or for a business purpose. The duty of the possessor is to exercise reasonable care to protect them against dangerous conditions they are unlikely to discover.

4. Res Ipsa Loquitur–This term means "the thing speaks for itself." It permits the jury to infer both negligent conduct and causation from the mere occurrence of certain types of events. It applies when the event is of a kind that ordinarily does not occur in the absence of negligence.

B. Proximate Cause–Proximate cause is judicially imposed limitations on a person's liability for the consequences of his negligence. In strict liability cases the courts impose a narrower rule of proximate cause than they do for negligence cases.

1. Causation in Fact–The defendant's negligence must be the actual cause of the plaintiff's injury. Under the "but for rule," the conduct is a cause of an event if the event would not have occurred in the absence of the person's negligent conduct. The "substantial factor test" states that the conduct is a cause of the event if the conduct is a substantial factor in bringing about the harm.

2. Limitations on Causation in Fact–Unforeseeable consequences and superseding causes are taken into account in determining limitations on the causal connection between the defendant's negligence and the plaintiff's injury.

    a. Unforeseeable Consequences–The Restatement and a majority of the courts have adopted the position that even if the defendant's negligence is a cause in fact of the harm to the plaintiff, the conduct is not a proximate cause unless the defendant could have reasonably anticipated injuring the plaintiff or a class of persons of which the plaintiff is a member.

    b. Superseding Cause–A superseding cause is an intervening event or act that occurs after the defendant's negligent conduct. It relieves the defendant of liability for harm to the plaintiff caused in fact by both the defendant's negligence and the intervening event or act.

C. Injury–The plaintiff must prove that the defendant's negligence proximately caused harm to a legally protected interest.

D. Defenses to Negligence–As a general rule, any defense to an intentional tort is also available in an action in negligence, but there are additional defenses available in negligence cases.

1. Contributory Negligence–Contributory negligence is conduct on the part of the plaintiff that falls below the standard to which he should conform for his own protection and that is a legal cause of the plaintiff's harm. In the few states where contributory negligence is still recognized, a negligent plaintiff cannot recover any damages from the defendant. However, if the plaintiff was contributorily negligent, but the defendant had the last clear chance to avoid injury and did not do so, the contributory negligence of the plaintiff does not bar his recovery of damages.

2. Comparative Negligence–Most states have rejected the contributory negligence doctrine in favor of the comparative negligence doctrine. Under comparative negligence, damages are divided between parties in proportion to their relative fault. About 12 states have a "pure" comparative negligence system under which a plaintiff recovers the percentage of total damages that is attributable to the defendant's fault. Other states have adopted the "modified" comparative

negligence doctrine which operates the same as "pure" comparative negligence, except a plaintiff recovers nothing if his or her negligence is 50% or more the legal cause of the harm.

3. Assumption of Risk–Traditionally, a plaintiff who voluntarily and knowingly assumes the risk of harm arising from a defendant's negligence cannot recover for such harm. Assumption of the risk may be express, such as an exculpatory contract. Courts strictly interpret this type of agreement and hold that a plaintiff assumes a risk only if the terms are clear and do not violate a statute or public policy. Assumption of the risk also may be implied if a plaintiff voluntarily proceeds to encounter a known danger, e.g., spectator attends a hockey game. Some states and the Third Restatement of Torts have abolished the implied assumption of risk defense. A plaintiff's unreasonable willing confrontation of a known risk instead may give rise to the defense of contributory or comparative negligence.

II. Strict Liability–In some instances, persons may be held liable for injuries even though they have not acted intentionally or negligently. Such liability is called strict liability, absolute liability, or liability without fault. The doctrine of strict liability is not based on any particular fault of the defendant, but rather on the nature of the activity in which the defendant is engaging.

A. Activities Giving Rise to Strict Liability–These activities are: (1) performing abnormally dangerous activities, (2) keeping animals, and (3) selling defective, unreasonably dangerous products.

1. Abnormally Dangerous Activities–Strict liability is imposed for extraordinary, unusual, abnormal, or exceptional activities, as determined in light of the place, time, and manner in which the activity is conducted. An abnormally dangerous activity is one which (1) necessarily involves a high degree of risk of serious harm to the person and/or property of others, which risk cannot be eliminated by the exercise of reasonable care, and (2) is not a matter of common usage. Activities to which the rule has been applied include storing explosives or flammable liquids in large quantities, blasting, crop dusting, drilling for or refining oil in populated areas, and emitting noxious gases or fumes into a settled community.

2. Keeping of Animals–Strict liability for harm caused by animals existed at common law and continues today. As a general rule, those who possess animals for their own purposes do so at their peril and must protect against harm those animals cause to people and property.

   a. Trespassing Animals–Keepers of animals are generally held liable for any damages done if their animals trespass on the property of another. There are three exceptions to this rule: (1) keepers of cats and dogs are liable only for negligence; (2) keepers of animals are not strictly liable for animals straying from a highway on which they are being lawfully driven; and (3) in some western states, keepers of farm animals are not strictly liable for harm caused by their trespassing animals that are allowed to graze freely.

   b. Nontrespassing Animals–Keepers of wild animals are strictly liable for harm caused by such animals, whether or not they are trespassing. Wild animals are defined as those that cannot be considered safe no matter how domesticated. This category includes bears, lions, elephants, monkeys, tigers, deer, and raccoons. Domestic animals are, as a class, considered safe and include dogs, cats, horses, cattle, and sheep.

3. Products Liability–A recent and important trend in the law is the imposition of a limited form of strict liability on the manufacturers and merchants who sell goods in a defective condition unreasonably dangerous to the user or consumer. Liability is imposed regardless of the seller's due care and applies to all merchant sellers.

B. Defenses to Strict Liability–Since the strict liability of one who carries on an abnormally dangerous activity, keeps animals, or sells defective, unreasonably dangerous goods is not based on negligence, a plaintiff's ordinary contributory negligence is not a defense.   In strict liability cases, the responsibility for preventing harm is on the defendant.   Despite the rationale that disallows contributory negligence as a defense to strict liability, some states apply the doctrine of comparative negligence to products liability. Voluntary assumption of risk is a defense based on strict liability. In most states comparative negligence is allowed as a defense in strict products liability cases.

KEY TERMS

1. Negligence

2. Reasonable person standard

3. Duty of care

4. Negligence *per se*

5. Trespasser

6. Licensee

7. Invitee

8. *Res ipsa loquitur*

9.   Proximate cause

10. Causation in fact

11. But for rule

12. Substantial factor test

13. Superseding cause

14. Contributory negligence

15. Last clear chance

16. Comparative negligence

17. Assumption of risk

18. Strict liability

19. Abnormally dangerous activities

20. Products liability

TRUE/FALSE

_____   1. It is possible to be liable for injuries caused to another even though you have used reasonable care to prevent those injuries.

_____   2. Negligence is defined as conduct which falls below the standard established by law for the protection of others against unreasonable risk of harm.

_____   3. A possessor of land may inflict intentional injury upon a trespasser to eject him upon discovery of his presence on the land.

_____   4. The standard of conduct to which a child must conform is that of a reasonable person of like age, intelligence, and experience under like circumstances.

_____   5. The standard of conduct which is the basis for the law of negligence is usually determined by a cost-benefit analysis.

_____ 6. Although persons may not have a duty to help another, they nevertheless do have a duty not to hinder others who are trying to help.

_____ 7. A plaintiff who has proved all the required elements of a negligence action may nevertheless be denied recovery.

_____ 8. Whether an activity is considered abnormally dangerous or not usually depends on the circumstances under which the activity is conducted.

_____ 9. A defendant whose own negligence created an emergency situation is liable for the consequences of this conduct even though the defendant acted reasonably in the resulting situation.

_____ 10. A person living on property adjoining land later designated a blasting zone for a new highway has assumed the risk of harm and may not recover for damages if he fails to move away.

_____ 11. The "but for" rule is a test for determining strict liability.

_____ 12. A person with a mental deficiency will be held to the same reasonable person standard as a person of normal intelligence.

_____ 13. The possessor of land owes a higher duty of care to a licensee than to an invitee.

_____ 14. A violation of a statute constitutes negligence *per se* if the injured party is a member of the class protected by the statute.

_____ 15. The doctrine of strict liability is *not* based on any particular fault of the defendant, but rather on the nature of the activity in which the defendant is engaging.

MULTIPLE CHOICE

_____ 1. *P* was injured when *D* drove his golf ball into the back of *P*'s head. If *P* wants to recover against *D* in negligence, he must show which of the following?
   a. Breach of duty of care
   b. Proximate cause
   c. Injury
   d. All of the above

_____ 2. The standard of care applicable to a child is that of:
   a. the reasonable person.
   b. a reasonable person who is incapable of exercising the judgment of an adult.
   c. a reasonable person of like age, intelligence, and experience.
   d. a reasonable person who is mentally deficient.

_____ 3. Assume *F* violates a statute which is intended to protect restaurant patrons from food poisoning by requiring restaurant owners to install special refrigeration equipment. *F* may be sued under a standard of care based upon this statute if:
  a. *A*, a patron, falls down a poorly lit staircase on his way to the salad bar.
  b. *B*, a patron, becomes violently ill after eating tainted chicken salad.
  c. *C*, a patron, chokes on a chicken bone which was in his fruit salad.
  d. *D*, a waitress, dies after eating tainted chicken salad.

_____ 4. *A* is under an affirmative duty to come to the aid of *B* who is in danger if:
  a. *A* is *B*'s best friend.
  b. *A* is responsible for *B*'s predicament.
  c. *A* is a doctor.
  d. none of the above.

_____ 5. A possessor of land is liable for the injuries to his licensee if he fails to:
  a. warn her of a known defect which she is unlikely to discover.
  b. repair a known defect.
  c. warn her of a known defect which she is likely to discover.
  d. discover a defect.

_____ 6. A plaintiff who sues under *res ipsa loquitur* must show that:
  a. an event occurred which would not normally occur in the absence of negligence.
  b. the event which occurred would not normally occur in the absence of negligence.
  c. other possible causes have been eliminated by the evidence.
  d. none of the above.

_____ 7. *A* may be relieved of liability for negligent harm to *B* if an intervening act:
  a. occurs after *A*'s negligent conduct.
  b. is a cause in fact of *B*'s injury.
  c. is a normal consequence of the situation created by *A*'s negligent conduct.
  d. (a) and (b), but not (c).

_____ 8. In a state which does NOT recognize the doctrine of comparative negligence, *A* may recover from *B* for injuries proximately caused by *B*'s negligence and *A*'s contributory negligence if:
  a. *B*'s fault was greater than *A*'s fault.
  b. *B*'s fault was less than *A*'s fault.
  c. *B* had the last clear chance to avoid the injury.
  d. none of the above.

_____ 9. *A*, the owner of a dog, is strictly liable to *B* for harm caused by the dog if it:
  a. digs out from under its fenced yard and digs up *B*'s flowerbed.
  b. bites *B* when it has never attacked or bitten anyone before.
  c. bites *B* when it has bitten someone before.
  d. bites *B* when *A* knows that it frequently chases bicycle riders.

_____ 10. If *A*'s abnormally dangerous activity injures *B*, *B* may not recover for her injuries if she:
   a. assumed the risk of harm.
   b. was more at fault than *A*.
   c. had the last clear chance to avoid the danger.
   d. was contributorily negligent.

_____ 11. Which of the following would not give rise to an action in strict liability?
   a. Storing explosives in large quantity
   b. Crop dusting
   c. Blasting or pile driving
   d. All of the above would give rise to an action.

_____ 12. The standard of care of a person who practices a profession is that of:
   a. the reasonable person.
   b. a reasonable person of like education and training.
   c. a reasonable person of the same age.
   d. none of the above.

_____ 13. Matthew negligently drives his automobile into Nancy who is crossing against the light. Nancy sustains damages in the amount of $10,000 and sues Matthew. The jury determines that Matthew's negligence contributed 75 percent to Nancy's injury and that Nancy's negligence contributed 25 percent to her injury. Under the doctrine of comparative negligence, Nancy can recover:
   a. $0.
   b. $2,500.
   c. $7,500.
   d. $10,000.

_____ 14. Zane Zookeeper is fleeing from an escaped tiger. You see his plight and wave for him to come into your house. He leaps up your front steps and slips on your skateboard which was left there from the night before. Your duty to Zane is:
   a. not to intentionally injure him.
   b. to warn him the skateboard is there.
   c. to exercise reasonable care to protect him from falling on the skateboard.
   d. you have no duty to Zane.

_____ 15. Sarah Student goes to Glamour Department Store to buy a dress. Sarah is a:
   a. trespasser.
   b. licensee.
   c. public invitee.
   d. business invitee.

SHORT ESSAY

1. Explain the reasonable person standard of care. When may the courts apply a statutory standard of care in determining negligence?

   _____

   _____

   _____

   _____

2. Explain the concept of *res ipsa loquitur*.

   _____

   _____

   _____

   _____

3. Discuss strict liability and indicate activities which give rise to the application thereof.

   _____

   _____

   _____

   _____

4. Distinguish between the duty of care a possessor of property has to trespassers, licensees, and invitees.

   _____

   _____

   _____

   _____

5. Compare the doctrine of contributory negligence and the doctrine of comparative negligence.

   _____

   _____

   _____

   _____

Parts I & II
Sample Examination

MULTIPLE CHOICE

_____ 1. That law which deals with the relationship between government and individuals is commonly known as:
   a. substantive law.
   b. public law.
   c. private law.
   d. civil law.

_____ 2. The civil law system is:
   a. a system in which the judiciary initiates, conducts, and decides cases.
   b. a legal system in which the body of law is derived from Roman law and based upon comprehensive legislative enactments.
   c. a system in which opposing parties initiate and present their cases.
   d. none of the above.

_____ 3. The federal courts have exclusive jurisdiction over _____ cases.
   a. bankruptcy
   b. federal question
   c. diversity of citizenship
   d. bankruptcy, federal question, and diversity of citizenship

_____ 4. The ethical theory that holds moral actions must be judged by their motives and means as well as their results is:
   a. utilitarianism.
   b. ethical fundamentalism.
   c. deontology.
   d. ethical relativism.

_____ 5. An equitable remedy rewriting a contract to conform to the original intent of the contracting parties is known as:
   a. rescission.
   b. specific performance.
   c. reformation.
   d. none of the above.

_____ 6. The U.S. Supreme Court interprets the _____ as granting virtually complete power to Congress to regulate the economy and business.
   a. contract clause
   b. equal protection clause
   c. federal power to tax and spend
   d. commerce clause

_____ 7. Which of the following elements need not be proven in a negligence action?
   a. Breach of duty of care
   b. An unreasonably dangerous activity
   c. Proximate cause
   d. Injury

_____ 8. The nonbinding process in which a third party is selected to help reach a mutually acceptable agreement is known as:
   a. negotiation.
   b. arbitration.
   c. conciliation.
   d. consensual arbitration.

_____ 9. Authority of a particular court to adjudicate a controversy of a particular kind is known as:
   a. *in personam* jurisdiction.
   b. *in rem* jurisdiction.
   c. venue.
   d. subject matter jurisdiction.

_____ 10. The _____ protects all individuals against unreasonable searches and seizures and is intended to protect the privacy and security of individuals against arbitrary invasions by government officials.
   a. First Amendment
   b. Fourth Amendment
   c. Fifth Amendment
   d. Sixth Amendment

_____ 11. Which of the following activities will *not* give rise to a strict liability claim?
   a. Performing abnormally dangerous activities
   b. Keeping of wild animals
   c. Selling defective, unreasonably dangerous goods
   d. All of the above will give rise to a strict liability claim.

_____ 12. Albert, a citizen of California, is injured in an auto accident which occurs in Colorado and involves another car which is driven by Barbara, a citizen of Nebraska. Albert's medical expenses and property damage amount to $85,000. Albert sues in federal court based upon diversity jurisdiction.
   a. No diversity of citizenship exists, because both Albert and Barbara are U.S. citizens.
   b. Diversity exists because Albert is a citizen of California and the accident occurred in Colorado.
   c. Diversity exists because Albert is a citizen of California and Barbara is a citizen of Nebraska.
   d. The federal court will dismiss the suit, because the amount in controversy is less than the minimum jurisdiction amount.

_____ 13. For purposes of procedural due process, "property" includes:
   a. Social Security payments.
   b. food stamps.
   c. land.
   d. all of the above

_____ 14. The intentional exercise of dominion or control over another's personal property that so seriously interferes with the other's right of control and which justly requires the payment of full value for the property is known as:
   a. theft.
   b. trespass to personal property.
   c. conversion.
   d. two of the above, (a) and (b).

_____ 15. Pablo Plaintiff has a case which can be brought in either the state or the federal court. Jurisdiction in the case is:
   a. *in rem.*
   b. concurrent.
   c. exclusive.
   d. *quasi in rem.*

_____ 16. The constitutional protection which guarantees the right to a speedy, public trial by jury is found in the:
   a. First Amendment.
   b. Fourth Amendment.
   c. Fifth Amendment.
   d. Sixth Amendment.

_____ 17. At the _____, the accused is informed of the charge against him and he enters his plea.
   a. arraignment
   b. preliminary hearing
   c. information
   d. trial

_____ 18. At common law, _____ was defined as a breaking and entering of a dwelling house at night with the intent to commit a felony.
   a. theft
   b. robbery
   c. burglary
   d. stealing

_____ 19. The first right of the federal government to regulate matters within its powers to the possible exclusion of state regulation is known as:
   a. federal supremacy.
   b. federal preemption.
   c. judicial review.
   d. state action.

_____ 20. The Elmville City Council passed an ordinance stating that no person of Iranian extraction shall be allowed to purchase property within the city limits. Mohammed Abou came to the United States as a student ten years ago from Iran. He has now graduated, works as an engineer in Elmville, and would like to buy a house there. His attorney tells him the ordinance is unconstitutional and should be challenged. If Mohammed sues to challenge the ordinance, the court will apply the _____ standard.
   a. rational relationship
   b. strict scrutiny
   c. intermediate
   d. beyond a reasonable doubt

Try the Web

When and where was Ruth Bader Ginsburg born?

   Solution: Log onto the Internet
      Go to: http://www.law.cornell.edu/
      Select - court opinions - U.S. Supreme Court
      Select - ... the justices: present and past
      Select - Ginsburg

Chapter 9
Introduction to Contracts

PURPOSE

Knowledge of contract law is important to anyone involved in business, but it is especially important for anyone in management. Virtually every business transaction and many of the everyday personal transactions into which we enter involve one or more contracts. Ordering something from a catalog, buying an item at a store, agreeing to work as an employee or hiring someone to work as an employee, opening a bank account, and signing a purchase agreement to buy real estate all involve contracts. This chapter summarizes the basic requisites of a binding contract, discusses the sources of contract law, and introduces the basic terminology involved in contract law.

CHAPTER CHECKPOINTS

After reading and studying this chapter, you should be able to:

1. Define the term "contract."

2. Discuss the development of contract law and identify what type of law governs certain contracts.

3. List the essential elements of a contract.

4. Identify and define the various classifications of contracts.

5. Define the terms "promissory estoppel" and "quasi contract" and explain why certain promises are enforceable even though they do not meet all the requirements of a contract.

CHAPTER OUTLINE

A. Development of the Law of Contracts–In the nineteenth century, contract liability was imposed only when the parties complied strictly with the required formalities. Today contractual obligations are usually recognized whenever the parties clearly intend to be bound. In addition, promises are now enforced in certain circumstances even though they do not comply strictly with the basic requirements of a contract.

1. Common Law–Contracts are primarily governed by state common law. An orderly presentation of this law is found in the Restatements of the law of contracts.

2. The Uniform Commercial Code (UCC)–Article 2 of the UCC governs sales of goods. A sale is a contract involving the transfer of title to goods from seller to buyer for a price. Goods are tangible personal property. Personal property is any property other than an interest in real property (land or anything attached to the land).

3. Types of Contracts Outside the Code–The UCC does not apply to employment contracts, service contracts, insurance contracts, contracts involving real property, and contracts for the sale of intangibles, such as patents and copyrights. All of these contracts are governed by general contract law or common law.

B. Definition of Contract–A contract is a binding agreement that the courts will enforce. The Restatement defines a contract as "a promise or a set of promises for the breach of which the law gives a remedy, or the performance of which the law in some way recognizes a duty." A breach is the failure to properly perform a contractual obligation.

C. Requirements of a Contract–The four basic requirements of a contract as follows:

1. Manifestation of mutual assent–the parties must manifest by words or conduct that they have agreed to enter into a contract

2. Consideration–each party must intentionally exchange a legal benefit or incur a legal detriment as an inducement to the other party to make a return exchange.

3. Legality of object–contract must be for a lawful purpose and not otherwise against public policy

4. Capacity–parties must have contractual capacity.

D. Classification of Contracts–Contracts can be classified by their method of formation, their content, and their legal effect.

1. Express and Implied Contracts–An express contract is an agreement of parties that is stated in words either in writing or orally; an implied in fact contract is one where agreement of the parties is inferred from their conduct.

2. Bilateral and Unilateral Contracts–A bilateral contract is one in which both parties exchange promises; a unilateral contract is one in which only one party makes a promise.

3. Valid, Void, Voidable, and Unenforceable Contracts–A valid contract is one that meets all of the requirements of a binding contract and is, therefore, an enforceable agreement. A void agreement is no contract at all and is without legal effect. A voidable contract is not wholly lacking in legal effect; it is a contract, but because of the manner in which it was formed or a lack of capacity of a party to it, the law permits one or more of the parties to avoid the legal

duties created by the contract. An unenforceable contract is one for the breach of which the law provides no remedy.

4. Executed and Executory–An executed contract is one that has been fully performed by all of the parties. An executory contract has not been fully performed by one or more of the parties.

E. Promissory Estoppel–Promissory estoppel is a doctrine enforcing noncontractual promises where there has been justifiable reliance on the promise and justice requires the enforcement of the promise. A noncontractual promise is enforceable when it is made under circumstances that should lead the promisor reasonably to expect that the promisee will be induced by the promise to take definite and substantial action or forbearance in reliance on the promise, and the promisee does take such action or forbearance.

F. Quasi Contracts–This is an obligation not based upon contract that is imposed by law to avoid injustice; also called a contract implied in law. The elements of recovery in quasi contract are: (1) a benefit conferred on the defendant by the plaintiff; (2) an appreciation or knowledge by the defendant of the benefit; and (3) acceptance or retention by the defendant of the benefit under circumstances making it inequitable for the defendant to retain the benefit without paying the plaintiff for its value.

KEY TERMS

1. Sale
2. Goods
3. Contract
4. Breach
5. Mutual assent
6. Consideration
7. Capacity
8. Implied in fact contract
9. Express contract
10. Bilateral contract
11. Unilateral contract
12. Promisor
13. Promisee
14. Valid contract
15. Void contract
16. Voidable contract
17. Unenforceable contract
18. Executed contract
19. Executory contract
20. Promissory estoppel
21. Quasi contract

TRUE/FALSE

_____ 1. Most contracts are primarily governed by state common law.

_____ 2. As defined by the UCC, a sale is the transfer of title to goods from seller to buyer for a price.

_____ 3. A contract to provide legal services for a fee is governed by Article 2 of the UCC.

_____ 4. As defined by the UCC, goods are movable, tangible and intangible personal property.

_____ 5. Where general contract law has not been specifically modified by the UCC, the common law of contracts continues to apply.

_____ 6. Nearly every business transaction is based on contract, and even the most common transactions may involve multiple contracts.

_____ 7. A contract may be formed orally or by a writing, but it may not be inferred merely from the conduct of the parties.

_____ 8. The courts will presume that the parties intended to form a bilateral contract when it is unclear whether a unilateral or a bilateral contract has been formed.

_____ 9. A bilateral contract results from the exchange of a promise for an act, whereas a unilateral contract results from the exchange of a promise for a return promise.

_____ 10. An executory contract is one in which there are one or more unperformed promises by any party to the contract.

_____ 11. A quasi contract is not a contract, but rather is an obligation imposed regardless of the intention of the parties in order to assure a just and equitable result.

_____ 12. A voidable contract is an agreement that does not meet all of the requirements of a binding contract; thus, it is no contract at all and has no legal effect.

_____ 13. In certain circumstances, noncontractual promises are enforced under the doctrine of promissory estoppel in order to avoid injustice.

_____ 14. Thomas says to Steve, "If you will paint my garage, I will pay you $75." Steve replies, "Would you make it $85?" Under these facts, Thomas and Steve are both promisors and promisees.

_____ 15. In a "quasi-contract" situation, the remedy granted will be similar to a breach of contract remedy.

MULTIPLE CHOICE

_____ 1. All of the following are relevant to defining the principles of contract law EXCEPT:
   a. federal common law.
   b. state common law.
   c. Restatements of the Law of Contracts.
   d. Uniform Commercial Code.

_____ 2. The Uniform Commercial Code defines goods as:
   a. tangible and intangible personal property.
   b. tangible personal property.
   c. land and anything attached to it.
   d. none of the above.

_____ 3. *CPA:* Kay, an art collector, promised Hammer, an art student, that if Hammer could obtain certain rare artifacts within two weeks, Kay would pay for Hammer's post-graduate education. At considerable effort and expense, Hammer obtained the specified artifacts within the two-week period. When Hammer requested payment, Kay refused. Kay claimed that there was no consideration for the promise. Hammer would prevail against Kay based on:
   a. unilateral contract.
   b. unjust enrichment.
   c. public policy.
   d. quasi contract.

_____ 4. The remedies provided for breach of contract include:
   a. compensatory damages.
   b. punitive damages.
   c. reliance damages.
   d. (a) and (c), but not (b).

_____ 5. An executed contract is one in which:
   a. all duties under it have been performed by all parties to the contract.
   b. at least one party has performed all of its duties under the contract.
   c. there are one or more unperformed promises by any party to the contract.
   d. the contract is wholly unperformed by one or more of the parties.

_____ 6. Each of the following is an essential element of a binding promise EXCEPT:
   a. mutual assent.
   b. consideration.
   c. capacity.
   d. a writing signed by the parties.

_____ 7. A promise or a set of promises for the breach of which the law gives a remedy, or the performance of which the law in some way recognizes a duty, is best described as:
   a. a promise.
   b. an agreement.
   c. a contract.
   d. none of the above.

_____ 8. A manifestation of the intention to act or refrain from acting in a specified way is best described as:
   a. a promise.
   b. an agreement.
   c. a contract.
   d. none of the above.

_____ 9. A contract in which the parties indicate their assent in words is a(n):
   a. quasi-contract.
   b. implied contract.
   c. express contract.
   d. unlawful contract.

_____ 10. UCC Article 2 applies to contracts involving which of the following?
   a. The services of an accountant
   b. An employment relationship
   c. The sale of a television set
   d. The sale of a private residence

_____ 11. A contract in which both parties exchange promises is a(n):
   a. formal contract.
   b. quasi contract.
   c. implied in fact contract.
   d. bilateral contract.

_____ 12. A contract in which one party seeks an act in exchange for a promise is a(n):
   a. quasi contract.
   b. unilateral contract.
   c. implied in fact contract.
   d. bilateral contract.

_____ 13. A contract which fails to satisfy the requirements of the statute of frauds is:
   a. valid.
   b. void.
   c. voidable.
   d. unenforceable.

_____ 14. Bill Businessman places an ad in the local newspaper saying, "Reward: $50 for return of my golden retriever named Fido." The ad lists his address and telephone number. If Tim Teenager finds Fido and returns him to Bill, there will be:
   a. an executed contract requiring that Bill pay Tim $50.
   b. a bilateral contract, because two people are involved.
   c. an implied in fact contract requiring that Bill pay Tim $50.
   d. a unilateral contract, because Bill has promised to pay $50 but Tim hasn't promised anything.

_____ 15. Contract law:
   a. has more relaxed requirements today than in the nineteenth century.
   b. has more rigid requirements today than in the nineteenth century.
   c. has remained static throughout the nineteenth and twentieth centuries.
   d. is governed primarily by the Uniform Commercial Code.

SHORT ESSAY

1. Discuss how state common law, the Restatements of the Law of Contracts, and Article 2 of the UCC combine to form the law of contracts.

_____

_____

_____

_____

2. Arthur Accountant orally agrees to serve as an accountant for Clem Client in exchange for Clem's promise to pay Arthur an annual salary of $15,000. Describe this contract in terms of the following classifications: (a) express and implied; (b) unilateral and bilateral; (c) valid, void, voidable, and unenforceable; and (d) executory and executed.

_____

_____

_____

_____

3. Explain why and how certain promises are enforceable even though they do not meet all the requirements of a contract.

_____

_____

_____

_____

4. Distinguish between a contract and a gift and explain why one is enforceable and the other is not.

_____

_____

_____

5. What is promissory estoppel? Explain your answer.

_____

_____

_____

_____

Chapter 10
Mutual Assent

PURPOSE

For a contract to exist, the parties must have an agreement. This agreement can be either oral or written. In a bilateral contract, the agreement involves a promise for a promise; in a unilateral contract, the agreement involves a promise for either an act or a forbearance to act. In determining whether there is an agreement, it is necessary to analyze whether there has been an offer and whether there has been an acceptance of that offer by someone to whom it was made. The test for making this determination is an objective standard based upon intent as determined from the words and actions of the parties. This chapter examines the essentials of an offer, the duration of offers, and acceptance of offers. In this chapter, you must learn both the common law contract rules and the rules that are found in Article 2 of the UCC, because both rules are essential to a complete understanding of contract law.

CHAPTER CHECKPOINTS

After reading and studying the chapter, you should be able to:

1. List the elements of an offer, define offeror and offeree, and recognize when an offer comes to an end.

2. Compare the traditional common law approach to the requirement of definiteness to that found in Article 2 of the UCC and the Restatement.

3. Define the common law "mirror image rule" and explain how this rule has been modified by the Code's battle-of-the-forms provision.

4. Recognize the when an acceptance is made and discuss the effect of the means of acceptance.

5. Identify a firm offer and explain how the Code's firm offer provision differs from the rule at common law.

CHAPTER OUTLINE

I. Offer–An offer is defined as an indication of willingness to enter into a contract. An offeror is the person making the offer. An offeree is the person to whom the offer is made.

A. Essentials of an Offer–An offer must be communicated to the offeree, must manifest an intent to enter into a contract, and must be sufficiently definite and certain.

    1. Communication–To have the mutual assent required to form a contract, the offeree must know about the offer. The offeror must communicate the offer in an intended manner. The communication must be made or authorized by the offeror. An offer need not be stated or communicated by words. Conduct from which a reasonable person may infer a proposal in return for either an act or a promise amounts to an offer. An offer may be made to the general public, but no person can accept such an offer unless he knows that the offer exists.

    2. Intent–To have legal effect, an offer must manifest an intent to enter into a contract.

        a. Preliminary Negotiations–Initial communications between the potential parties to a contract in many cases take the form of preliminary negotiations rather than an offer. A statement that may indicate a willingness to make an offer is not itself an offer.

        b. Advertisements–Advertisements are generally considered to be invitations to make offers, because they are not sufficiently definite and certain. However, if the advertisement or announcement contains a definite promise of something in exchange for something else and confers a power of acceptance, it may constitute an offer.

        c. Auction Sales–The auctioneer at an auction sale does not make offers to sell the property being auctioned but invites offers to buy. The bid is an offer, and if it is accepted, a contract results. A bidder is free to withdraw his bid at any time prior to its acceptance, and the auctioneer is free to withdraw the goods unless the sale is advertised to be without reserve.

    3. Definiteness–The terms must be clear enough to provide a court with a basis for determining the existence of a breach and for giving an appropriate remedy.

        a. Open Terms–Under the UCC, an offer for the purchase or sale of goods may leave open particulars of performance. The Code provides standards to determine open terms and requires such specification be made in good faith and within limits set by commercial reasonableness. Good faith is defined as honesty in fact in the conduct or transaction concerned. Commercial reasonableness is a standard measured by the judgment of reasonable persons familiar with the customary practices in the type of transaction involved and with regard to the facts and circumstances of the case.

        b. Output and Requirements Contracts–Output and requirements contracts are valid under the Code so long as there is an objective standard for their application and the parties act in good faith. An output contract is an agreement of a buyer to purchase the entire output of a seller's factory for a stated period. A requirements contract is an agreement of a seller to supply a buyer with all his requirements for certain goods.

B. Duration of Offers–An offeree's power to accept an offer continues until the offer terminates.

    1. Lapse of Time–An offer remains open for the specified time period. If no time is stated, the offer will terminate after a reasonable period of time.

2. Revocation–Cancellation of an offer by an offeror brings an offer to an end. The offeror may revoke the offer by giving notice to the offeree. The notice effectively terminates the offer when the notice is received by the offeree. An offer made to the general public is revoked only by giving equivalent publicity to the revocation as was given to the offer. Certain limitations have been imposed on the offeror's power to revoke.

   a. Option Contracts–Contracts which provide that an offer will stay open for a specified period of time are enforceable if they comply with all of the requirements of a contract, including the payment of consideration by the offeree to the offeror, and such offers cannot be revoked during the specified time.

   b. Firm Offers under the Code–A merchant is bound to hold open an offer to buy or sell goods for a stated period not over three months, if the merchant gives assurance in a signed writing that it will be held open. The firm offer is enforceable even though no consideration is given.

   c. Statutory Irrevocability–Some offers, such as bids for the construction of a building or public work made to a governmental body, are made irrevocable by statute.

   d. Irrevocable Offers of Unilateral Contracts–The offeror is obligated not to revoke the offer for a reasonable time where the requested act necessarily requires time and effort on the part of the offeree. This obligation arises when the offeree begins the invited performance and the offeror's duty of performance is conditional on completion of the invited performance according to the terms of the offer.

   e. Promissory Estoppel–An offeror may be prevented from revoking an offer prior to its acceptance if the offer was made under circumstances that should lead the offeror reasonably to expect that the offeree will be induced by the offer to take action in reliance on the offer.

3. Rejection–The refusal of an offeree to accept an offer is effective when received by the offeror. Express or implied rejection terminates the power of acceptance.

4. Counteroffer–A counteroffer is a counterproposal from the offeree to the offeror that indicates a willingness to contract but on terms different from the original offer. It operates as a rejection and terminates the original offer upon receipt by the offeror. It also operates as a new offer. A conditional acceptance claims to accept an offer, but it is contingent upon the acceptance of an additional or different term. It is therefore a counteroffer that terminates the original offer.

5. Death or Incompetency–Death or incompetency of either the offeror or the offeree ordinarily terminates an offer, other than one contained in an option.

6. Destruction of Subject Matter–If the specific subject matter of the offer is destroyed, the offer is terminated.

7. Subsequent Illegality–If the purpose or subject matter of the offer becomes illegal, the offer is terminated.

II. Acceptance of Offer–Acceptance is a manifestation of a willingness to enter into a contract on the terms of the offer.

   A. Communication of Acceptance

   1. General Rule–In the case of a bilateral offer, acceptance must be communicated to the offeror. In the case of a unilateral offer, however, notice of acceptance is usually not required.

   2. Silence as Acceptance–Silence is usually not an acceptance unless it becomes one by custom, usage, or course of dealing. There is no legal duty to reply to an offer.

3. Effective Moment of Acceptance–An offer, revocation, rejection, and counteroffer are effective when received. An acceptance is generally effective upon dispatch unless the offer specifically provides otherwise, the offeree uses an unauthorized means of communication, or the acceptance follows a prior rejection.

   a. Stipulated Provisions in the Offer–If the offer specifically stipulates the means of communication to be used by the offeree, the acceptance must conform to that specification. Moreover, the rule that an acceptance is effective when dispatched or sent does not apply where the offer provides that the acceptance must be received by the offeror.

   b. Authorized Means–Historically, an authorized means of communication was the means expressly authorized by the offeror, or if none was authorized, it was the means used by the offeror. The Restatement and the Code both now provide that where the language in the offer or the circumstances do not otherwise indicate, an offer to make a contract shall be construed to authorize acceptance in any reasonable manner. Under this rule, an authorized means is any reasonable means of communication.

   c. Unauthorized Means–When the means used by the offeree is unauthorized, the traditional rule is that acceptance is effective when and if received by the offeror, provided it is received within the time the authorized means would have arrived. Under the Restatement, if these conditions are met, then the effective time for the acceptance is the moment of dispatch.

   d. Acceptance Following a Prior Rejection–When an acceptance follows a prior rejection, the first communication received by the offeror is the effective one.

4. Defective Acceptances–A late or defective acceptance does not create a contract. It is a new offer.

B. Variant Acceptances–A variant acceptance is one that contains terms different from or additional to those in the offer. It receives different treatment by the common law and the Code.

   1. Common Law–An acceptance must be positive and unequivocal. It must be a mirror image of the offer. The mirror image rule provides that an acceptance cannot deviate from the terms of the offer. Any communication by the offeree that attempts to modify the offer is not an acceptance but a counteroffer.

   2. Code–The mirror image rule is modified by the UCC. The Code focuses on the intent of the parties and attempts to alleviate the battle of the forms where the buyer uses a standardized form which favors the buyer and the seller uses a standardized form which favors the seller. If the offeree does not expressly make acceptance conditional upon the offeror's assent to the additional or different terms, a contract is formed.

KEY TERMS

1. Objective standard
2. Offer
3. Offeror
4. Offeree

5. Auction sale
6. Without reserve
7. Open terms
8. Good faith

9. Commercial reasonableness

10. Output contract

11. Requirements contract

12. Revocation

13. Option contract

14. Firm offer

15. Rejection

16. Counteroffer

17. Conditional acceptance

18. Acceptance

19. Authorized means

20. Mirror image rule

21. Battle of the forms

TRUE/FALSE

_____ 1. An offer is a proposal, expressed either in words or by conduct, by one person to another indicating a willingness to enter into a contract.

_____ 2. In order to have the mutual assent requisite to the formation of a contract, the offeror must have communicated the offer and the offeree must have knowledge of the offer.

_____ 3. A contract exists if either party's actions manifest recognition of a contract's existence.

_____ 4. An offeror's manifestation of intent to enter into a contract is judged by a subjective standard.

_____ 5. The UCC imposes an obligation of good faith in the performance or enforcement of every contract within its scope.

_____ 6. A contract for the sale of goods need not specify the price in order to have an effective contract.

_____ 7. If an offer does not state the time within which the offeree may accept, the offer will terminate upon the expiration of a reasonable time.

_____ 8. In order for an offeror's revocation of the offer to be effective, notice of the revocation must be directly communicated to the offeree before acceptance.

_____ 9. A rejection is effective at the moment of its dispatch by the offeree.

_____ 10. Under the common law mirror image rule, an offeree's acceptance will not be effective if it deviates from the exact terms of the offer.

_____ 11. Under the UCC, if both parties are merchants, additional terms contained in the offeree's unconditional acceptance will become part of the contract provided they do not materially alter the agreement and are not objected to either in the offer itself or within a reasonable period of time.

_____ 12. Under the Restatements of Contracts and the Code, unless language in the offer, or the circumstances under which it is made indicate otherwise, an offer shall be construed as inviting acceptance in any reasonable manner.

_____ 13. William, who just purchased a new computer which won't work properly, screams, "I'll sell this thing for $10," and thereby makes an offer.

_____ 14. Although an offeree is generally under no duty to reply to an offer, by custom, usage, or course of dealing, silence or inaction by the offeree may operate as an acceptance.

_____ 15. At an auction announced to be "without reserve," the auctioneer is free to withdraw the goods from sale at any time prior to a bid's acceptance.

MULTIPLE CHOICE

_____ 1. In order for an offer to have legal effect, it must:
   a. be communicated to the offeree.
   b. manifest an intent to enter into a contract.
   c. be sufficiently definite and certain in its terms.
   d. all of the above.

_____ 2. An offer can be effectively communicated to an offeree by:
   a. a writing only.
   b. spoken words only.
   c. a writing or by spoken words only.
   d. a writing, by spoken words, or by conduct from which a reasonable person could infer a promise.

_____ 3. Which of the following would be an offer?
   a. Will you buy my computer for $1000?
   b. I sure would like to sell this computer for $1000.
   c. I'll sell you this computer for $1000.
   d. None of the above are offers.

_____ 4. Advertisements, circulars, quotation sheets, and other similar business communications usually do not constitute offers because:
   a. they do not contain a promise.
   b. they leave unexpressed many terms which would be necessary to the making of a contract.
   c. both (a) and (b).
   d. none of the above.

_____ 5. Whether or not a person's words or conduct constitutes an offer is determined according to:
   a. the subjective intent of the offeror.
   b. the subjective intent of the offeree.
   c. the objective, reasonable person standard.
   d. none of the above.

_____ 6. With respect to agreements for the sale of goods, the Code provides standards by which omitted terms may be ascertained, provided:
   a. the parties actually agreed upon the open term but negligently failed to include it in the written contract.
   b. the parties actually discussed the open term but intentionally failed to include it in the written contract.
   c. the parties intended to enter into a binding contract regardless of whether they actually discussed the open term or not.
   d. the parties did not intend to enter into a binding contract regardless of whether they actually discussed the open term or not.

_____ 7. _CPA:_ On April 1, Fine Corp. faxed Moss an offer to purchase Moss' warehouse for $500,000. The offer stated that it would remain open only until April 4 and that acceptance must be received to be effective. Moss sent an acceptance on April 4 by overnight mail and Fine received it on April 5. Which of the following statements is correct?
   a. No contract was formed because Moss sent the acceptance by an unauthorized method.
   b. No contract was formed because Fine received Moss' acceptance after April 4.
   c. A contract was formed when Moss sent the acceptance.
   d. A contract was formed when Fine received Moss' acceptance.

_____ 8. An offeree generally may cancel or revoke an offer at any time prior to its acceptance unless the offer:
   a. is an option contract.
   b. is a merchant's firm offer under the Code.
   c. contemplates a unilateral contract and the offeree has begun the invited performance.
   d. all of the above.

_____ 9. A rejection of an offer by the offeree is effective:
   a. at the moment that the offeree signs the notice of rejection.
   b. at the moment that the offeree dispatches the notice of rejection.
   c. at the moment that the offeror receives the notice of rejection.
   d. none of the above

_____ 10. Under the Code, if two parties, at least one of whom is not a merchant, intend to enter into a binding contract but the offeree in her acceptance includes additional terms for the contract, those terms are construed as:
   a. mere surplus and are ignored.
   b. proposals for addition to the contract.
   c. terms of the contract provided they do not materially alter the agreement.
   d. terms of the contract provided they are not material and are not objected to by the offeror within a reasonable time.

_____ 11. Pat mails Trish an offer to buy Blackacre. Trish receives the offer on May 1. On May 2, Trish delivers a letter of acceptance to National Express, but due to their error the letter is not sent by the company until May 3. Pat receives the acceptance on May 4. A contract is formed on:
   a. May 1
   b. May 2
   c. May 3
   d. May 4

_____ 12. Which of the following would be subject to Article 2 of the UCC?
   a. An agreement to clean someone's yard for $25
   b. An option to buy a vacant lot
   c. An agreement to perform at a charity fundraiser
   d. None of the above is subject to the UCC.

_____ 13. A leading manufacturer of electronic equipment writes a letter to its wholesale distributors offering to sell its most popular VCR for $100 and stating that it will accept orders at that price for 30 days. This is a(n):
   a. option to sell.
   b. auction without reserve.
   c. firm offer.
   d. requirements contract.

_____ 14. *CPA:* Opal offered, in writing, to sell Larkin a parcel of land for $300,000. If Opal dies, the offer will:
   a. terminate prior to Larkin's acceptance only if Larkin received notice of Opal's death.
   b. remain open for a reasonable period of time after Opal's death.
   c. automatically terminate despite Larkin's prior acceptance.
   d. automatically terminate prior to Larkin's acceptance.

_____ 15. Carol Customer sees an ad in a newspaper for a clock radio for $8. She goes to the store and wants to buy the item advertised in the newspaper at the price quoted. Carol is:
   a. making a counteroffer.
   b. making an offer to buy.
   c. making an acceptance of the store's offer to sell.
   d. making an acceptance of the store's firm offer.

SHORT ESSAY

1. Distinguish between an offer and a preliminary negotiation by indicating the necessary elements of a valid offer.

    _____

    _____

    _____

    _____

2. An offer confers upon the offeree a power of acceptance that continues until the offer terminates. Identify and discuss briefly seven ways in which an offer may be terminated other than by acceptance.

    _____

    _____

    _____

    _____

3. Compare briefly the traditional and modern theories of variant acceptance of an offer as shown by the common law "mirror image rule" and by the rules of the UCC.

    _____

    _____

    _____

    _____

4. Distinguish between an option contract and a firm offer under the Code.

    _____

    _____

    _____

    _____

5. List two situations where the Code rule differs from the common law. Give both the Code rule and the common law rule.

    _____

    _____

    _____

    _____

Chapter 11
Conduct Invalidating Assent

PURPOSE

This chapter explains situations in which an apparent acceptance of an offer and consent to a contract will be legally ineffective. In general, the law says in certain situations the manifested consent by one of the parties is not effective, because it was not knowingly and voluntarily given. In some situations what seems to be a contract will be considered to be a void agreement, or one that is totally lacking in legal effect and cannot be enforced by either party. In other situations, a contract will be merely voidable. If a contract is voidable, it can either be enforced or avoided by one party, or in some cases, either party. Some of these situations include duress, undue influence, fraud, nonfraudulent misrepresentation, and mistake.

CHAPTER CHECKPOINTS

After reading and studying this chapter, you should be able to:

1. Distinguish between duress by threats of physical force and duress by improper threats and discuss the legal effect of each type of duress.

2. Distinguish between a fraudulent misrepresentation and a nonfraudulent misrepresentation.

3. List the elements of fraud in the inducement and distinguish between fraud in the inducement and fraud in the execution.

4. Distinguish between unilateral mistake of fact and mutual mistake of fact and discuss the legal effect of each type of mistake.

5. Identify fact situations involving duress, undue influence, fraud, nonfraudulent misrepresentation, and mistake.

CHAPTER OUTLINE

A. Duress–Duress is the wrongful or unlawful act or threat that overcomes the free will of a party. It leaves the victim with no reasonable alternative. There are two basic types of duress.
   1. Physical Compulsion–Physical duress or coercion occurs when a party compels another to manifest assent to a contract through actual physical force, and it renders the agreement void.
   2. Improper Threats–Duress by means of improper threats or acts, including economic and social coercion, makes the contract voidable at the option of the coerced party. This second type of duress is more common. The threat may be explicit or inferred The test for duress is subjective.

B. Undue Influence–The unfair persuasion of a person by a party in a dominant position based on a relationship of trust or confidence renders a contract voidable. The law very carefully scrutinizes contracts between those in a relationship of trust and confidence that is likely to permit one party to take unfair advantage of the other, such as a guardian and ward.

C. Fraud–There are two distinct types of fraud: fraud in the execution and fraud in the inducement.
   1. Fraud in the Execution–This type of fraud is extremely rare and renders a contract void. It consists of a misrepresentation that deceives the other party as to the nature of the document evidencing the contract.
   2. Fraud in the Inducement–Fraud in the inducement, generally referred to as fraud or deceit, is an intentional misrepresentation of a material fact by one party to the other, who consents to enter into a contract in justifiable reliance on the misrepresentation. When this type of fraud exists, there is a contract, but it is voidable at the option of the defrauded party. There are five requisite elements to fraud in the inducement.
      a. False Representation–A false representation or misrepresentation is a positive statement or conduct that misleads. Concealment, which is action taken to keep another from learning a fact, can form the basis for fraud. Silence ordinarily will not constitute a misrepresentation except in the case of a fiduciary who owes a duty of trust, loyalty, and confidence to another.
      b. Fact–For fraud there must be a misrepresentation of a material fact. Only on rare occasions will the misrepresentation of an opinion form a basis for fraud, such as an expression of opinion by someone holding himself out as an expert. Statements of value by a salesperson are generally considered to be puffing or sales talk. A statement of fact should also be distinguished from a prediction of the future. Representations of law are generally not considered to be representations of fact, but rather of opinion.
      c. Materiality–A misrepresentation is material if (1) it would be likely to induce a reasonable person to manifest his assent or (2) the maker knows that it would be likely to induce the recipient to do so.
      d. Knowledge of Falsity and Intention to Deceive–The misrepresentation must have been known by the one making it to be false and must have been made with intent to deceive, or scienter, which can consist of actual knowledge, lack of belief in the statement's truthfulness, or reckless indifference to its truthfulness.
      e. Justifiable Reliance–A person is not entitled to relief unless he has justifiably relied on the misrepresentation. There is no fraud if the complaining party's decision was in no way influenced by the misrepresentation.

D. Nonfraudulent Misrepresentation–Nonfraudulent misrepresentation is a material, false statement that induces another to rely justifiably but is made without scienter. Negligent misrepresentation is a false representation made without due care in ascertaining its truthfulness; innocent misrepresentation is a false representation made without knowledge of its falsity but with due care. To obtain relief for nonfraudulent misrepresentation, all other elements of fraud must be present and the misrepresentation must be material.

E. Mistake–A mistake is an understanding that is not in accord with existing fact.
1. Mutual Mistake–A mutual mistake is one where both parties have a common but erroneous belief forming the basis of a contract. If the mistake relates to a basic assumption on which the contract is made and has a material effect on the agreed exchange, then it is voidable by the adversely affected party unless he bears the risk of the mistake.
2. Unilateral Mistake–A unilateral mistake is an erroneous belief of only one of the parties to a contract. Relief will be granted only where the nonmistaken party knows, or reasonably should know, that such a mistake has been made or where the mistake was caused by the fault of the nonmistaken party.
3. Assumption of Risk of Mistake–A party who has undertaken to bear the risk of mistake will not be able to avoid the contract even though the mutual or unilateral mistake would have otherwise permitted the party to do so.
4. Effect of Fault upon Mistake–The Restatement provides that a mistaken party's fault in not knowing or discovering a fact before making a contract does not prevent him from avoiding the contract "unless his fault amounts to a failure to act in good faith and in accordance with reasonable standards of fair dealing." This rule does not, however, apply to failure to read a contract.
5. Mistake in Meaning of Terms–There is no manifestation of mutual assent where the parties attach materially different meanings to their manifestations and neither party knows or has reason to know the meaning attached by the other.

KEY TERMS

1. Duress

2. Undue influence

3. Fraud in the execution

4. Fraud in the inducement

5. Misrepresentation

6. Concealment

7. Fiduciary

8. Puffing

9. Scienter

10. Negligent misrepresentation

11. Innocent misrepresentation

12. Mutual mistake

13. Unilateral mistake

TRUE/FALSE

_____ 1. Duress in the form of physical force renders the resulting agreement voidable.

_____ 2. Duress in the form of improper threats must be explicit in order to render the resulting contract voidable.

_____ 3. In deciding whether a threat is sufficient to constitute duress, the fact that the act or threat would not affect a person of average strength and intelligence is determinative.

_____ 4. It has generally been held that contracts induced by threats of criminal prosecution are voidable, regardless of whether the coerced party had committed an unlawful act.

_____ 5. Before one can avoid a contractual obligation based upon undue influence, there must exist a confidential relationship between the parties involved.

_____ 6. Fraud in the execution consists of a misrepresentation that deceives the defrauded person as to the very nature of the contract being entered.

_____ 7. Fraud in the inducement will result in the contract being voidable.

_____ 8. Actionable fraud can usually be based on a statement of opinion as well as a statement of fact.

_____ 9. Active concealment, or action intended or known to be likely to keep another from learning a fact he otherwise would have learned, can form the basis for fraud.

_____ 10. When parties are dealing at arm's length, silence or nondisclosure usually constitutes fraud.

_____ 11. Justifiable reliance requires that the misrepresentation contribute substantially to the misled party's decision to enter into the contract.

_____ 12. A contract induced by an innocent misrepresentation is actionable provided all of the remaining elements of fraud are present and the misrepresentation is material.

_____ 13. In a legally challenged contract between a guardian and his ward, the law presumes that the guardian took advantage of the ward.

_____ 14. Harold Homeowner went to Al's Auto Dealership to look at cars. Harold found a 1980 Plymouth Horizon that he thought would be a good car for his teenagers to drive to school. Al said, "This is the best car in town." Harold buys it for $1,000. Two weeks later, the car breaks down. Al is guilty of fraud in the inducement.

_____ 15. Bill Businessman has decided to buy a copying machine on an installment contract from the Business Supply Store. After looking at machines, Bill is in a hurry, so he signs the agreement without reading it. Later, he discovers that the interest rate is 22% and that there are no guarantees on the machine. Bill can avoid the contract based on mistake.

MULTIPLE CHOICE

_____ 1. A contract assented to by a party acting under improper physical coercion is:
   a. void.
   b. voidable at the election of the coerced party.
   c. binding on both parties.
   d. none of the above.

_____ 2. In determining whether an improper threat constitutes duress, it must be shown that:
   a. the threat would have induced a reasonable person to assent to the contract.
   b. the threat was intended by the coercing party to coerce assent on the part of the person claiming to be the victim of duress.
   c. the threat actually coerced assent on the part of the person claiming to be the victim of duress.
   d. none of the above

_____ 3. In which of the following situations would silence constitute a misrepresentation?
   a. The parties are dealing at arm's length in a business transaction.
   b. A person fails to disclose a fact which she knows would correct a mistake upon which the other party is relying, and the nondisclosure is a failure to act in good faith.
   c. A buyer knows that a new highway is proposed through the seller's property, making it more valuable than the seller realizes.
   d. All of the above.

_____ 4. The requisite elements of fraud in the inducement include:
   a. a false representation of material fact.
   b. a representation made with knowledge of its falsity and the intention to deceive.
   c. a false representation justifiably relied upon.
   d. All of the elements above are required to be shown.

_____ 5. A misrepresentation is material in which of the following cases:
   a. Seller believes goods are of less value than buyer believes them to be, but seller remains silent.
   b. Seller represents a fact knowing it would be likely to induce a reasonable buyer to manifest his assent.
   c. Seller knows the misrepresentation would be likely to induce the buyer to act.
   d. (b) or (c), but not (a).

_____ 6. Knowledge of falsity and intention to deceive under fraud in the inducement may be shown by:
    a. actual knowledge.
    b. lack of belief of the statement's truthfulness.
    c. reckless indifference as to its truthfulness.
    d. all of the above.

_____ 7. A package is delivered to your door and the delivery person asks you to sign a receipt for the package. You actually sign a promissory note promising to pay the delivery person $5,000! The note is:
    a. void due to fraud in the execution.
    b. voidable due to fraud in the execution.
    c. void due to fraud in the inducement.
    d. voidable due to fraud in the inducement.

_____ 8. The law grants relief in a situation involving mistake only where there has been:
    a. a unilateral mistake by one party as to the nature of the subject matter of the contract.
    b. a mutual mistake of material fact.
    c. a unilateral mistake by one party to the contract occasioned by his failure to read the document before assenting to it.
    d. a unilateral mistake by one party to the contract as to its legal effect.

_____ 9. In order for an act or threat to constitute duress, it needs to be at least:
    a. contrary to public policy.
    b. tortious, but not necessarily criminal.
    c. a criminal act or threat.
    d. none of the above.

_____ 10. A contract entered into or induced by undue influence on the part of the dominant party is:
    a. valid.
    b. void.
    c. voidable.
    d. unenforceable.

_____ 11. Carl Contractor submits a bid that contains a substantial error in addition.
   a.   This is a unilateral mistake. Carl is bound by the error.
   b.   Carl is guilty of fraud in the inducement.
   c.   If the error is an obvious one that the other party knew of when it accepted the contract, Carl can avoid the contract.
   d.   Carl can avoid the contract based upon duress.

_____ 12. Which of the following would be a statement of fact?
   a.   For the price, this is the best typewriter available.
   b.   This is the one that I would recommend.
   c.   This furniture was refinished last year.
   d.   With a few more lessons, you should be able to compete in the regional dance competition.

_____ 13. A fiduciary owes which of the following duties?
   a.   Trust
   b.   Loyalty
   c.   Confidence
   d.   All of the above

_____ 14. The courts would not carefully scrutinize a contract between the parties in which of the following relationships?
   a.   Trustee and beneficiary.
   b.   Manufacturer and wholesaler.
   c.   Agent and principal.
   d.   Physician and patient.

_____ 15. *CPA:* In order for a purchaser of land to avoid a contract with the seller based on duress, it must be shown that the seller's improper threats:
   a.   constituted a crime or tort.
   b.   actually induced the purchaser to assent to the contract.
   c.   would have induced a reasonably prudent person to assent to the contract.
   d.   were made with the intent that the purchaser be influenced by them.

SHORT ESSAY

1. Identify the types of duress and discuss the legal effect of each.

_____

_____

_____

_____

2. a. List the elements necessary to establish *fraud in the inducement*.
   b. Can the statement of an opinion constitute fraud in the inducement? Explain.
   c. What is the difference between a false statement of fact and "puffing"? Explain.

   _____

   _____

   _____

   _____

3. The Main Street Gazette and Ned of Ned's Newsstand have entered into a contract under the terms of which the Gazette has agreed to ship its newspaper, the *Morning Disturber*, to Ned, a newspaper distributor in Elmville, U.S.A. In order to sell a morning newspaper, Ned must receive the papers and have them on the newsstand by 12 midnight. Accordingly, the parties agreed that the Gazette would ship the papers from its plant in Metro City to Elmville on the Silver Streak, a train that arrives in Elmville at 10:00 p.m. Unbeknownst to either party, however, the Silver Streak's schedule has been changed effective the first date of their contract so that the newspaper will not arrive in Elmville until 2:00 a.m., which is too late for distribution. No other trains pass through Elmville and the shipment of the newspapers by truck or airplane is impractical. Ned sues the Main Street Gazette for breach of contract when the first shipment arrives too late for him to sell. Discuss the enforceability of the contract.

   _____

   _____

   _____

   _____

4. Discuss materiality.

   _____

   _____

   _____

5. Define *undue influence* and describe the circumstances under which it generally occurs.

   _____

   _____

   _____

Chapter 12
Consideration

PURPOSE

For an agreement to be a binding contract, there must be legally sufficient consideration. Consideration is the "price" paid to make a promise enforceable; it is the bargained-for element of exchange that is necessary to make a contract binding on the parties. Generally, a promise made without consideration, which is known as a gratuitous promise, is not enforceable. This chapter discusses the two basic elements of consideration: (1) legal sufficiency (something of value) and (2) bargained-for exchange. It also discusses certain contracts that are enforceable without consideration.

CHAPTER CHECKPOINTS

After reading and studying this chapter, you should be able to:

1. Distinguish between legal sufficiency of consideration and adequacy of consideration and recognize when there is legally sufficient consideration to enter into a bilateral or a unilateral contract.

2. Distinguish between an illusory promise and a promise that constitutes legally sufficient consideration in fact situations involving output and requirements contracts, exclusive dealing contracts, and conditional promises.

3. Discuss why a contractual agreement to perform a preexisting obligation lacks consideration, why the settlement of a disputed debt for a lesser amount discharges the debt, and why the settlement of an undisputed debt for a lesser amount lacks consideration.

4. Explain the concept of bargained-for exchange and discuss whether it is present in fact situations involving past consideration and third parties.

5. Identify and discuss contracts that are enforceable even though they are not supported by consideration.

CHAPTER OUTLINE

A. Legal Sufficiency–As a general rule, a contract cannot be enforced without legally sufficient consideration. A gratuitous promise is one made without consideration, and therefore it is not legally enforceable. To be legally sufficient, the consideration for the promise must be either a legal detriment to the promisee or a legal benefit to the promisor. Legal detriment means (1) the doing (or promising to do) something that the promisee has no prior legal obligation to do, or (2) the refraining from doing (or promising to refrain from doing) something that he has no legal obligation to refrain from doing. Legal benefit means obtaining something that one had no prior legal right to obtain. Usually, where there is a legal detriment to the promisee, there is also a legal benefit to the promisor. The promisor is the person making the promise. The promisee is the person receiving a promise.

1. Adequacy–The requirement of legal sufficiency is not at all concerned with whether the bargain was good or bad. Adequacy is not required where the parties have freely agreed to the exchange.

2. Unilateral Contracts–In a unilateral contract the offeror makes a promise in exchange for a completed act or a forbearance to act by the offeree. Since only one promise exists, the promisor gives consideration in the form of the promise while the promisee gives consideration in the form of either an act or a forbearance to act.

3. Bilateral Contracts–In a bilateral contract there is an exchange of promises. Thus, each party is both a promisor and a promisee. The promises are binding provided there is either a legal benefit to the promisor or a legal detriment to the promisee. Each promise is the consideration for the other party's promise, which is referred to as mutuality of obligation.

4. Illusory Promises–A promise that imposes no obligation on the maker of the statement is illusory, and it cannot serve as consideration. An illusory promise can be distinguished from other promises that do impose obligations of performance upon the promisor and thus can be legally sufficient consideration.

   a. Output and Requirements Contracts–An output contract is an agreement to sell all of one's production to a particular buyer. A requirements contract is a purchaser's agreement to buy from a certain seller all of that purchaser's needs. These contracts are not illusory.

   b. Exclusive Dealing Contracts–An exclusive dealing contract is one where a manufacturer grants to a distributor the sole right to sell goods in a defined market. There is an implied obligation imposed on the manufacturer to use its best efforts to supply the goods and on the distributor to use her best efforts to promote their sale. With these implied obligations there is legally sufficient consideration.

   c. Conditional Promises–A conditional promise is one where obligations are contingent upon the occurrence or nonoccurrence of a stated, uncertain event. It is sufficient consideration unless the promisor knows at the time of making the promise that the condition cannot occur.

5. Preexisting Obligations–The law does not regard the performance of or promise to perform a preexisting legal duty, public or private, as either a legal detriment or a legal benefit. A public duty is one that does not arise out of contract but is imposed by common law or statute. Public officials are under a preexisting obligation to perform their duties by virtue of their public office. Performance of or promise to perform a preexisting contractual duty which is neither doubtful nor the subject of an honest dispute is also legally insufficient consideration, because the doing of what one is legally bound to do is neither a detriment to a promisee nor a benefit to a promisor.

a. Modification of a Preexisting Contract–Under common law, a modification of an existing contract must be supported by mutual consideration to be enforceable. The UCC modified this rule by providing that a contract for the sale of goods can be modified without new consideration, if the parties act in good faith and both parties intend to modify it.

b. Substituted Contracts–In a substituted contract the parties agree to rescind their original contract and to enter into a new one. Substituted contracts are perfectly valid and effective to discharge the original contract and to impose the obligations under the new contract.

c. Settlement of an Undisputed Debt–An undisputed debt is an obligation whose existence and amount is not contested. Under the common law, payment of a lesser sum of money than is owed in consideration of a promise to discharge such a liquidated debt is legally insufficient to support the promise of discharge. An early payment or a payment in a different manner than originally agreed can constitute legally sufficient consideration.

d. Settlement of a Disputed Debt–A disputed debt is an obligation whose existence or amount is contested. A promise to settle a validly disputed claim in exchange for an agreed payment or other performance is supported by consideration.

B. Bargained-For Exchange–A bargained-for exchange is a mutually agreed-upon exchange.
   1. Past Consideration–The element of exchange is absent where a promise is given for an act already done. Therefore, unbargained-for past events are not consideration, despite their designation as past consideration.
   2. Third Parties–Consideration to support a promise may be given to a person other than the promisor if the promisor bargains for that exchange. Also, consideration may be given by some person other than the promisee.

C. Contracts Without Consideration–Certain transactions are enforceable without consideration.
   1. Promises to Perform Prior Unenforceable Obligations–In certain circumstances the courts will enforce new promises to perform an obligation that originally was not enforceable or that has become unenforceable by operation of law.
      a. Promise to Pay Debt Barred by the Statute of Limitations–Every state has a statute of limitations which provides a time period in which a lawsuit to enforce a debt must be initiated. A new, written promise by the debtor to pay the debt is binding without consideration and renews the running of the statute for a second statutory period.
      b. Promise to Pay Debt Discharged in Bankruptcy–Such a promise is enforceable without consideration. However, the Bankruptcy Code imposes a number of requirements before the promise may be enforced.
      c. Voidable Promises–A new promise to perform a voidable obligation that has not previously been avoided is enforceable without new consideration.
      d. Moral Obligation–A promise made to satisfy a preexisting moral obligation is unenforceable for lack of consideration. The Restatement, however, provides that a promise made for "a benefit previously received by the promisor from the promisee is binding to the extent necessary to prevent injustice."
   2. Promissory Estoppel–This is a doctrine that makes gratuitous promises enforceable to avoid injustice and applies when a promise that the promisor should reasonably expect to induce detrimental reliance does induce such action or forbearance by the promisee. A common application of the doctrine is to charitable subscriptions. The Restatement has relaxed the

reliance requirement for charitable subscriptions so that actual reliance need not be shown; probability of reliance is sufficient.

3. Contracts Under Seal–Under the common law, no consideration for a promise under seal was necessary. Some states still follow this rule.

4. Promises Made Enforceable by Statute–Some gratuitous promises that would otherwise be unenforceable have been made binding by statute.

   a. Contract Modifications–The UCC states that a contract for the sale of goods can be effectively modified without new consideration if the modification is made in good faith.

   b. Renunciation–Under the Code, any claim or right arising out of an alleged breach of contract can be discharged without consideration by a written waiver or renunciation signed and delivered by the aggrieved party.

   c. Firm Offers–Under the Code, a written offer signed by a merchant offeror to buy or sell goods is not revocable for lack of consideration during the time stated (but not to exceed three months) or , if no time is stated, for a reasonable time.

KEY TERMS

1. Consideration
2. Gratuitous promise
3. Legal sufficiency
4. Legal detriment
5. Legal benefit
6. Adequacy of consideration
7. Promisor
8. Promisee
9. Mutuality of obligation
10. Illusory promise
11. Output contract

12. Requirements contract
13. Exclusive dealing contract
14. Conditional promise
15. Substituted contract
16. Undisputed debt
17. Disputed debt
18. Bargained-for-exchange
19. Past consideration
20. Statute of limitations
21. Promissory estoppel
22. Contract under seal

TRUE/FALSE

_____ 1. The doctrine of consideration requires only that the promise or performance of one party be legally sufficient.

_____ 2. To be legally sufficient, the consideration for the promise must be either a legal detriment to the promisee or a legal benefit to the promisor.

_____ 3. The adequacy of consideration is the same as the legal sufficiency of consideration.

_____ 4. A contract under which the parties' obligation to perform arises only on the happening of a stated event lacks the requisite mutuality of obligation if the specified event may never occur.

_____ 5. The performance of a preexisting contractual obligation that is neither doubtful nor the subject of honest dispute is not legally sufficient consideration, because the doing of what one is legally bound to do is neither a detriment to the promisee nor a benefit to the promisor.

_____ 6. At common law, a modification of an existing contract must be supported by new consideration in order for the reformed agreement to be enforceable.

_____ 7. In a unilateral contract, each promise is the consideration for the other, a relationship that has been referred to as mutuality of obligation.

_____ 8. Words of promise that make the performance of the purported promisor entirely optional result in an illusory contract.

_____ 9. The agreement of a seller to sell her entire production to a particular purchaser is an illusory agreement because the purchaser doesn't know the quantity being purchased.

_____ 10. In the absence of legal consideration, a promise may nevertheless be enforceable under the doctrine of promissory estoppel if the promisee has relied on the promise to his detriment.

_____ 11. Under the Code, a merchant's offer to buy or sell goods is not revocable for lack of consideration during the time stated that it is open or if no time is stated, for a reasonable time, but in either event for a period not to exceed three months.

_____ 12. Under the Code, the modification of a contract for the sale of goods requires the furnishing of additional consideration, just as required under the common law.

_____ 13. Bill Businessman agrees to buy 2,000 widgets from the Widget Corporation of America next year for $60 a widget if he wants to for his business. This is an illusory contract.

_____ 14. Bill purchased 500 pairs of shoes from Sam at a contract price of $1,000. Fifty pairs were defective and a dispute arose as to the amount owing under the contract. Finally, Bill sent a check for $800, marked it "paid in full," and sent a letter to Sam explaining his reasons for thinking $800 was fair. Sam didn't respond, but he cashed the check. The debt is discharged.

_____ 15. Bill Businessman has a bad day one Monday morning and signs a contract to buy a piece of real property for $250,000. Later he realizes he has been had, because the property is only worth $100,000. Bill can avoid the contract based on inadequacy of consideration.

MULTIPLE CHOICE

_____ 1. The requirement of consideration is satisfied by:
   a. a promise exchanged for a promise.
   b. a promise exchanged for an act.
   c. both (a) and (b).
   d. neither (a) nor (b).

_____ 2. To be legally sufficient, the consideration for a promise must be:
   a. a legal detriment to the promisee.
   b. a legal benefit to the promisor.
   c. either (a) or (b).
   d. neither (a) nor (b).

_____ 3. Debbie promises to pay Bill $2,000 if Bill paints Debbie's house. Bill doesn't say a word but paints Debbie's house. This is an example of:
   a. a unilateral contract.
   b. a bilateral contract.
   c. a gratuitous contract.
   d. none of the above.

_____ 4. Which of the following would be an illusory promise?
   a. Sara agrees to sell her total production to Bill.
   b. Bill agrees to buy his total widget requirement from Sara.
   c. Bill agrees to buy all the widgets he wants from Sara.
   d. Bill agrees to buy Sara's total production of widgets if he inherits enough money from Uncle John to do so.

_____ 5. Which of the following is legally sufficient consideration?
   a. The performance of a preexisting public obligation
   b. The performance of a preexisting contractual obligation
   c. The settlement of an undisputed matured debt of $10,000 arising out of the purchase of land for $8,500
   d. The settlement of a debt subject to honest dispute as to its amount

_____ 6. Which of the following is necessary in order to satisfy the consideration requirement?
   a. Legal sufficiency
   b. Bargained-for exchange
   c. Both (a) and (b)
   d. Neither (a) nor (b)

_____ 7. Which of the following promises must be supported by consideration to be enforceable?
   a. A promise to pay a debt barred by the statute of limitations
   b. A promise to pay a debt discharged in bankruptcy
   c. A promise that has been justifiably relied on by the promisee to his detriment
   d. A modification of an existing contract under common law

_____ 8. A promise by Andrew to pay Barry $1,000 if he refrains from suing Andrew, which is accepted by Barry not suing is:
   a. supported by consideration.
   b. enforceable because Barry has incurred a legal detriment by refraining from bringing suit.
   c. enforceable because Andrew has received a legal benefit.
   d. all of the above.

_____ 9. *CPA:* Which of the following will be legally binding on all the parties despite the lack of consideration?
   a. A promise to donate money to a charity which was relied upon by the charity in incurring large expenditures
   b. An employer's promise to pay an employee an additional $400 per month for the remainder of the employee's agreed-upon year of employment.
   c. An oral promise by a merchant to keep its offer open for 60 days.
   d. A material modification signed by the parties to a contract to purchase and sell a parcel of land.

_____ 10. *CPA:* In order to satisfy the consideration requirement to form a contract, the consideration exchanged by the parties must:
   a. have a monetary value.
   b. conform to the parties' subjective intent.
   c. be legally sufficient.
   d. have approximately the same value.

_____ 11. Widget Manufacturing Corporation of America contracts with the Poly Plastic Company of Wisconsin to buy from Poly all of the plastic it will need next year in its manufacturing process. This is an example of a(n):
   a. illusory contract.
   b. requirements contract.
   c. output contract.
   d. exclusive dealing contract.

_____ 12. Crime Stoppers offers a reward of $500 for information leading to the arrest and conviction of a criminal who has committed several recent burglaries. Paul Police Officer has been working on the case and applies for the reward based upon information he has gathered while on duty. Paul cannot collect the reward under the:
   a. legal detriment rule.
   b. inadequacy of consideration rule.
   c. preexisting duty rule.
   d. promissory estoppel rule.

_____ 13. Slick owes Gullible $50. Slick offers to let Gullible have Slick's pocket knife if he will accept $25 and forgive the rest of the debt. Later Gullible sues for the balance of the debt.
   a. Gullible will win because there was no consideration.
   b. Gullible will lose because he should have sued as soon as he got the knife.
   c. Slick will win because the knife constituted legally sufficient consideration.
   d. Slick will lose because he still owes $25.

_____ 14. Carl Contractor pledges to contribute $500 to the local United Fund for charity.
   a. This promise lacks consideration and will not be enforced.
   b. This promise is a firm offer under the Code and will be enforced.
   c. There is the probability of reliance by the United Fund and the promise will be enforced under the doctrine of promissory estoppel.
   d. This promise is a preexisting public obligation and will be enforced.

_____ 15. Colleen agrees to pay $10 for David's computer which is worth $300. Colleen's consideration:
   a. is not legally sufficient.
   b. appears to be inadequate but is probably legally sufficient.
   c. is a forbearance.
   d. is inadequate but the contract will be enforced based on moral obligation.

SHORT ESSAY

1. Discuss briefly what is meant by "mutuality of consideration." Define the terms "legal detriment" and "legal benefit."

_____

_____

_____

_____

2. What are the essential elements of consideration? Is the adequacy of consideration a concern in determining legal sufficiency? Explain.

_____

_____

_____

_____

3. Explain the concept of promissory estoppel.

_____

_____

_____

_____

4. Sam Student has just graduated from Ivory Towers University and has been offered a graduate assistantship if he wants to pursue an MBA. Big Bucks, Inc., offers him a $35,000 management position if he will move to California and begin work in three weeks. Based on this promise of a job, Sam turns down the graduate assistantship and moves to California. When he contacts Big Bucks, they say they decided that they no longer need him. What recourse does Sam have? Explain.

_____

_____

_____

_____

5. Give some examples of transactions which are enforceable even though they are not supported by consideration.

_____

_____

_____

_____

Chapter 13
Illegal Bargains

PURPOSE

This chapter discusses the requirement that a promise or agreement have a lawful objective in order to be binding. Such a promise or agreement is illegal and unenforceable if the formation or performance of it is criminal, tortious, or otherwise contrary to public policy. Such agreements are properly termed "illegal bargains" or "illegal agreements," because by definition the term "contract" denotes an agreement which is legally enforceable. The chapter divides the topic into agreements that are (1) violations of statutes and (2) violations of public policy. It then discusses the effect of illegality and some exceptions to the general rule that illegal agreements are not enforceable.

CHAPTER CHECKPOINTS

After reading and studying the chapter, you should be able to:

1. Identify the types of statutes that frequently raise issues regarding enforceability of an agreement.

2. Distinguish between a regulatory license and a revenue-raising license and explain the effect of an unlicensed person's agreement to perform services in situations involving both types of licenses.

3. Identify the two types of situations where restraints of trade typically arise and give an example of enforceable and unenforceable restraints in each type of situation.

4. Define the term "exculpatory clause" and give an example of an enforceable and an unenforceable exculpatory clause.

5. Explain why illegal bargains are generally unenforceable; then list five situations where such an agreement will be enforced despite its illegality.

CHAPTER OUTLINE

A. Violations of Statutes–Generally, agreements declared illegal by statute will not be enforced by the courts.

   1. Licensing Statutes–A license is a formal authorization to engage in certain practices. A regulatory license is a measure designed to protect the public against unqualified practitioners. Examples are licenses to practice law or medicine. A revenue license is a measure to raise money. If the license is regulatory, a person cannot ordinarily recover fees for professional services rendered unless he has the required license. However, if the law is for revenue purposes only, agreements for unlicensed services are enforceable.

   2. Gambling Statutes–A wager is an agreement that one party will win or lose depending upon the outcome of an event in which the parties' only interest is that gain or loss. Courts generally refuse to recognize the enforceability of a gambling agreement, although some states permit certain regulated gambling such as state-operated lotteries.

   3. Usury Statutes–Usury laws establish maximum permissible rates of interest. Rates and applications vary greatly from state to state. For a transaction to be usurious, courts require evidence of the following factors: (a) a loan (b) of money (c) that is repayable absolutely and in all events, and (d) for which an interest charge is exacted in excess of the interest rate allowed by law.

B. Violations of Public Policy–Certain agreements have a tendency to be injurious to the public or public good and, as such, are contrary to public policy.

   1. Common Law Restraint of Trade–A restraint of trade is any agreement that eliminates or tends to eliminate competition or otherwise obstructs trade or commerce. One type of restraint of trade is a covenant not to compete, which is an agreement to refrain from entering into a competing trade, profession, or business. Today, covenants not to compete are enforceable if: (1) the purpose of the restraint is to protect a property interest of the promisee, and (2) the restraint is no more extensive than is reasonably necessary to protect that interest. Restraints typically arise in two situations: (a) the sale of a business, and (b) employment contracts.

      a. Sale of a Business–As part of an agreement to sell a business, the seller frequently promises not to compete in a particular business in a defined area for a stated period of time. Courts will enforce these if they are reasonable as to time period, geographic area, and hardship imposed upon the promisor and the public.

      b. Employment Contracts–Employees are frequently required to sign employment contracts prohibiting them from competing with their employers during the time of employment and for a stated period after termination. Such agreements are readily enforced during employment. After termination, the employer must demonstrate the restriction is necessary to protect legitimate interests, such as trade secrets. Some courts have held that non-compete agreements for employees of Internet companies are valid for only short durations, with some courts considering a non-compete clause of one year to be unreasonably long.

   2. Exculpatory Clauses–An exculpatory clause excuses one party from liability for his own tortious conduct. Generally, exculpatory clauses relieving a person from tort liability for harm caused intentionally or recklessly are unenforceable as violating public policy. Ones that excuse a party

from liability for harm caused by negligent conduct are scrutinized carefully by the courts and have also been held unenforceable in certain cases.

3. Unconscionable Contracts–An unconscionable contract is unfair or unduly harsh. The Code and Restatement both limit the enforcement of unconscionable contracts. *Procedural unconscionability* refers to unfair or irregular bargaining, while *substantive unconscionability* refers to oppressive or grossly unfair contractual terms. These concepts are applied to determine the enforceability of certain contracts, such as adhesion contracts which are standard-form contracts where the preparer offers the other party the contract on a "take-it-or-leave-it" basis. Some courts hold that there must be both procedural and substantive unconscionability present to render a contract unenforceable.

4. Tortious Conduct–A promise to commit a tort is unenforceable as contrary to public policy.

5. Corrupting Public Officials–Agreements that may adversely affect the public interest through the corruption of public officials or the impairment of the legislative process are unenforceable.

C. Effect of Illegality–In most cases, neither party can recover under an illegal agreement, because both parties are *in pari delicto* (in equal fault). Exceptions are as follows:

1. Party Withdrawing Before Performance–A party to an illegal agreement may, before performance, withdraw from the transaction and recover whatever has been contributed, if the party has not engaged in serious misconduct.

2. Party Protected by Statute–If a statute makes an agreement illegal in order to protect one of the parties, the protected party usually has the right to withdraw from the illegal agreement and to recover the money paid. For example, an investor protected by a law prohibiting the sale of unregistered securities may have the right to recover the money paid.

3. Party Not Equally at Fault–A party who enters into an illegal agreement due to fraud, duress, or undue influence is not equally at fault and may recover payments made or property transferred.

4. Excusable Ignorance–An agreement that appears to be entirely permissible may be illegal by reason of facts and circumstances of which one of the parties is unaware. The courts permit the party who is ignorant of the illegality to maintain a lawsuit against the other party for damages.

5. Partial Illegality–A contract may be partly unlawful and partly lawful. If it is possible to separate the illegal from the legal part, some courts will enforce the legal part.

KEY TERMS

1. Licensing statute

2. Regulatory license

3. Revenue license

4. Wager

5. Usury statute

6. Restraint of trade

7. Covenant not to compete

8. Exculpatory clause

9. Unconscionable contracts

10. Procedural unconscionability

11. Substantive unconscionability

TRUE/FALSE

_____ 1. The courts will not enforce an agreement declared illegal by statute.

_____ 2. In the absence of a specific statutory provision, an unlicensed person engaged in a business or profession for which a license is required cannot recover for services rendered if the licensing statute was enacted in order to raise revenue.

_____ 3. A revenue licensing statute is one designed to protect the public against unqualified persons.

_____ 4. Sara bets Bill that Hilltop High will win the big game. This is an enforceable agreement.

_____ 5. Usury statutes establish the minimum rate of permissible interest that may be contracted for between a lender and a borrower of money.

_____ 6. An exculpatory clause is a contractual clause that exempts a party from liability for his own poor business judgment in entering into a contract.

_____ 7. If a court finds that a part of a contract is unconscionable, it must deny enforcement of the entire contract.

_____ 8. When evaluating the enforceability of covenants not to compete in employment contracts, courts must carefully balance the public policy favoring the employer's right to protect his business interests against the public policy favoring full opportunity for individuals to gain employment.

_____ 9. Subject to a few exceptions, neither party to an illegal contract can sue the other for breach nor recover for any performance rendered.

_____ 10. First Bank issues a consumer loan to Happy Homemaker at an annual rate of interest of 16%. In most states, this would be an illegal contract, because First Bank is in violation of a usury law.

_____ 11. Big Bucks, Inc. pays Andrew Attorney to lobby for a law that would increase its annual income. This is an illegal contract.

_____ 12. Donna is in her last semester of dental school. On weekends she cleans her friends' teeth and then sends them a bill for $25. These are illegal contracts, because Donna is not yet licensed.

_____ 13. Procedural unconscionability involves scrutiny for the presence of "bargaining naughtiness."

_____ 14. The president of Big Bucks, Inc. pays a state official $500 to give the corporation's application for a government contract special consideration. This is an illegal contract.

_____ 15. Carol Customer signs a consumer purchase agreement for a VCR in which she agrees to make monthly payments. In fine print on the back, the contract also provides that if she misses a payment, she will confess judgment and pay all costs necessary in enforcing the contract without raising any defenses against the lender. This is an unconscionable contract.

MULTIPLE CHOICE

_____ 1. An agreement is illegal and unenforceable if its formation or performance is:
   a. criminal.
   b. tortious.
   c. contrary to public policy.
   d. all of the above.

_____ 2. A regulatory licensing statute is one intended to:
   a. raise revenue.
   b. protect the public against unqualified persons.
   c. prevent gambling.
   d. prevent excessive rates of interest.

_____ 3. Which of the following is not required in order to have a usurious transaction?
   a. Evidence of a loan
   b. Evidence of money
   c. Evidence of repayability in all events
   d. Interest within allowable legal limits

_____ 4. In general, an agreement not to compete with an employer while employed is enforceable if:
   a. the purpose of the restraint is to protect the employer's business.
   b. the restraint is no greater than is reasonably needed to protect the employer's business.
   c. both (a) and (b).
   d. neither (a) nor (b).

_____ 5. An agreement in a contract that attempts to excuse one party from liability for her own negligence is called:
   a. a clause obstructing the administration of justice.
   b. an exculpatory clause.
   c. a restraint of trade.
   d. an illusory promise.

_____ 6. An agreement to refrain from a particular trade, profession, or business is enforceable if:
   a. the purpose of the restraint is to protect a property interest of the promisee.
   b. the restraint is no more extensive than is reasonably necessary to protect the interest.
   c. the secretary of state has approved the agreement.
   d. (a) and (b), but not (c).

_____ 7. In considering whether a covenant not to compete included in the sale of a business is reasonable, courts will consider all of the following factors except:
a. the geographic area covered.
b. the time period for which the restraint is to be in effect.
c. the hardship imposed on the promisor.
d. the price that the promisee paid for the business.

_____ 8. In general, if a promise is illegal:
a. only the promisor can sue the promisee for breach and recover any performance rendered.
b. only the promisee can sue the promisor for breach and recover any performance rendered.
c. neither the promisor nor the promisee can sue the other for breach and recover any performance rendered.
d. both the promisor and the promisee can sue the other for breach and recover any performance rendered.

_____ 9. All of the following situations represent exceptions to the strict rule of unenforceability of illegal agreements except:
a. where a party to the illegal agreement withdraws from the transaction prior to the performance.
b. where one of the parties to the agreement is a party protected by the statute violated.
c. where the parties are not equally at fault.
d. where the parties are _in pari delicto._

_____ 10. Where one party to an illegal contract is less at fault than the other, she may:
a. enforce the entire contract.
b. receive no assistance from the court at all.
c. recover out-of-pocket expenses only.
d. recover payments made or property transferred.

_____ 11. Which of the following would most likely be considered a regulatory licensing law?
a. A state statute requiring a license to practice medicine
b. A state statute requiring that beauticians pass an examination and pay a yearly licensing fee
c. A state statute requiring that public school teachers complete a required course of study and pay a yearly licensing fee
d. All of the above

_____ 12. Lucky Larson runs an illegal gambling business. Every month he pays a local judge $500 for protection. If Lucky is arrested and convicted in a trial before the same judge, and then sues the judge for breach of contract, what will be the likely result?
a. The contract will be unenforceable because it is a violation of public policy.
b. The contract will be enforced, because both parties are _in pari delicto._
c. Lucky will be able to have the contract rescinded and get back the payments he made to the judge.
d. The judge will be ordered to pay the money to the government as a fine.

_____ 13. A man and a woman make mutual promises to marry. Unknown to the woman, the man is already married.
   a. This is an agreement to commit a crime, which renders the agreement void.
   b. Both parties are *in pari delicto*.
   c. If the woman is unaware of the man's other marriage, she could pursue an action for money damages against him.
   d. Two of the above are correct, (a) and (c).

_____ 14. *CPA:* Todd is a licensed real estate broker in Ohio. One of Todd's largest clients, Sun Corp., contracted in writing with Todd to find a purchaser for its plant in New York and agreed to pay him a 6% commission if he were successful. Todd located a buyer who purchased the plant. Unknown to Todd, New York has a real estate broker's licensing statute which is regulatory in nature, intended to protect the public against unqualified persons. Todd violated the licensing statute by failing to obtain a New York license. If Sun refuses to pay Todd any commission and Todd brings an action against Sun, he will be entitled to recover:
   a. nothing.
   b. a fee based on the actual hours spent.
   c. the commission agreed upon.
   d. out of pocket expenses only.

_____ 15. *CPA:*   Wert, an employee of Salam Corp., signed an agreement not to compete with Salam during and after being employed with Salam. Wert is the director of research and has knowledge of many of Salam's trade secrets. If Wert's employment with Salam is terminated and Wert wishes to compete with Salam, which of the following statements is **not** correct?
   a. The agreement is only enforceable if Wert voluntarily terminates his employment with Salam.
   b. The agreement must be necessary to protect Salam's legitimate interests in order to be enforceable.
   c. The geographic area covered by the agreement must be reasonable in order to be enforceable.
   d. The court will consider Wert's ability to obtain other employment against Salam's right to protect its business.

SHORT ESSAY

1. Explain the "Restatement" approach to unconscionable contracts.

_____

_____

_____

_____

2. What are the two types of licensing statutes? How do they differ in their legal effect if violated?

_____

_____

_____

_____

3. Distinguish between "unconscionable contracts" and "contracts of adhesion."

_____

_____

_____

_____

4. Briefly discuss the effect of illegality and the exceptions to the general rule.

_____

_____

_____

_____

5. Explain when a covenant not to compete will be upheld.

_____

_____

_____

_____

Chapter 14
Contractual Capacity

PURPOSE

Everyone is regarded as having the capacity to enter into a binding promise or agreement unless the law, for public policy reasons, holds that an individual lacks such capacity. In this chapter, you learn the classes of persons who lack contractual capacity and the effect on the agreement when one of the parties to it is a member of a protected class. The classes lacking contractual capacity include minors, incompetent persons, and intoxicated persons. Most of this chapter focuses on how a protected party can successfully avoid a contract and the situations in which a protected party will be held responsible for a contractual obligation despite having membership in a protected class.

CHAPTER CHECKPOINTS

After reading and studying this chapter, you should be able to:

1. List the classes of persons who lack contractual capacity and discuss the effect of lack of capacity on the contracts of each class.

2. Recognize "necessaries" for a minor and discuss a minor's liability for necessary items.

3. Recognize when a minor has disaffirmed a contract in contrast to when a minor has ratified a contract, and discuss the effect of a minor's misrepresentation of age on the power to disaffirm.

4. Discuss the liability of minors for torts connected with a contract.

5. Compare the liability of minors to that of incompetent persons and to that of intoxicated persons.

CHAPTER OUTLINE

A. Minors–A minor is a person who is under the age of legal majority, which is 18 in most jurisdictions today.

   1. Liability on Contracts–A minor's contracts are voidable at the minor's option. In other words, a minor has the power to disaffirm (avoid) a contract or to enforce it against the other party.

      a. Disaffirmance–The exercise of a minor's power to avoid a contract is known as disaffirmance. A minor may disaffirm a contract at any time before reaching the age of majority and within a reasonable time after coming of age, as long as the minor has not already ratified the contract. Disaffirmance may be either express or implied; no particular form is necessary so long as it shows an intention not to be bound. Some contracts, such as those for student loans or medical care may not be avoided. The majority of courts hold that the minor's duty upon disaffirmance is to return any property received from the other party, provided the minor has it in his possession at the time of disaffirmance. Under the UCC, a person who buys goods from a minor and therefore has voidable title has the power to transfer valid title to a good faith purchaser for value.

      b. Ratification–A minor has the option of ratifying a contract after reaching majority; it makes the contract binding from the beginning. Ratification must validate the whole contract, both as to burdens and benefits. Ratification can occur in three ways: (1) through express language, (2) as implied from conduct, and (3) by failure to make a timely disaffirmance.

   2. Liability for Necessaries–Necessaries are items that suitably and reasonably supply a person's needs. Minors are liable for the reasonable value of necessary items, which may be different from the contract or selling price. Necessaries include those things that the minors need to maintain themselves in a particular station in life.

   3. Liability for Misrepresentation of Age–The states do not agree whether a minor who fraudulently misrepresents her age when entering into a contract has the power to disaffirm. The prevailing view is that a minor may nevertheless disaffirm. Other states either require the minor to restore the other party to the position she had before the contract or allow the defrauded party to recover damages against the minor in tort.

   4. Liability for Tort Connected with Contract–Generally minors are liable for their torts. However, if a tort and a contract are so connected that to enforce the tort action the court must enforce the contract, the minor is not liable in tort.

B. Incompetent Persons

   1. Person Under Guardianship–A guardianship is the relationship under which a person (the guardian) is appointed to preserve and control the property of another (the ward). Contracts made by a person under guardianship by court order are void. However, the person dealing with the ward may be able to recover the fair value of any necessaries provided to the incompetent. The contracts of the ward may be ratified by the guardian during the period of guardianship or by the ward if the guardianship is terminated.

   2. Mental Illness or Defect–Mentally incompetent persons are ones who are unable to understand the nature and effect of their acts. Agreements of persons who are mentally incompetent are voidable. Under the traditional test, persons are mentally incompetent if they are unable to comprehend the subject of the contract, its nature, and its probable consequences. Such persons

are liable for the reasonable value of necessaries on the principle of quasi contract. Incompetent persons may ratify or disaffirm contracts when they become competent or during lucid periods.

C. Intoxicated Persons–The defense of intoxication is similar to the defense of incompetency. A person may avoid a contract that he enters into if the other party has reason to know that, because of intoxication, he is unable to understand the nature and consequences of his actions. The options of ratification or disaffirmance remain, although most courts are more strict with the requirement of restitution on disaffirmance than they are with the agreements of an incompetent person, and require an intoxicated person to act promptly and to restore what has been received. Intoxicated persons are liable in quasi contract for necessaries furnished during their incapacity.

KEY TERMS

1. Contractual capacity

2. Minor

3. Disaffirmance

4. Ratification

5. Necessaries

6. Guardianship

7. Mentally incompetent

TRUE/FALSE

_____ 1. As a general rule, a contract entered into by a minor is voidable at the minor's option.

_____ 2. Recovery for necessaries furnished to a minor is based upon the reasonable value of the item furnished and not the contract price.

_____ 3. A minor has the option of ratifying a contract after reaching majority, which makes the contract binding *ab initio*.

_____ 4. Except in the case of a contract to transfer land, a minor can disaffirm a contract before attaining majority or within a reasonable time thereafter.

_____ 5. Disaffirmance may be either express or implied.

_____ 6. Under the Code, a person buying goods from a minor has the power to transfer valid title to the goods to a good faith purchaser for value.

_____ 7. In most states, minors who fraudulently misrepresented their age at the time a contract was entered into may nevertheless disaffirm the contract.

_____ 8. If a tort and a contract are so connected that to enforce the tort action the court must enforce the minor's contract, the court will enforce the contract and the minor will be liable in tort.

_____ 9. In order to prove that a person with a mental defect lacks the necessary capacity to enter into a contract, it must be shown that the person is permanently insane.

_____ 10. A person may be able to avoid a contractual agreement even though she understands what she is doing but cannot control her behavior, thereby failing to act in a reasonable or rational way.

_____ 11. To avoid a contract, an intoxicated person must act promptly, upon regaining capacity, to disaffirm.

_____ 12. A minor who contracts for a necessary will be liable for the full contract price.

_____ 13. Seventeen-year-old Tim Teenager has just completed a course in business law. He now wants to disaffirm his student loan agreements. Most states allow a minor to avoid contracts for student loans.

_____ 14. Under the traditional cognitive ability test, a person is mentally incompetent if unable to comprehend the subject of the contract, its nature, and its probable consequences.

_____ 15. In determining contractual capacity under the cognitive ability test, individuals who are taking prescribed medication are treated the same as those who are incompetent.

MULTIPLE CHOICE

_____ 1. Which of the following would lack contractual capacity?
   a. Bill, who is 16, wants to buy a speedboat.
   b. Sara, who has been adjudicated mentally incompetent, buys a fur coat.
   c. Richard, who is seriously intoxicated, agrees to sell his car.
   d. All of the above.

_____ 2. Which of the following would be required of a minor who disaffirms her contract?
   a. She must return any property she has received from the other party, provided it is in her possession.
   b. She must pay a reasonable amount for the use of the property.
   c. She must make restitution.
   d. All of the above are possible depending on the jurisdiction.

_____ 3. A contract entered into by a minor is:
   a. voidable at the election of the minor only.
   b. voidable at the election of the other party only.
   c. voidable at the election of either.
   d. voidable only if it is executory.

_____ 4. In a contract for necessaries, a minor is liable for:
   a. the list price of the items furnished.
   b. the agreed price of the items furnished.
   c. the reasonable value of the items furnished.
   d. the wholesale cost of the items furnished.

_____ 5. If a minor purchases a car and then continues to use it for one year after obtaining majority, this action constitutes:
   a. a disaffirmance of the contract.
   b. a ratification of the contract.
   c. a breach of the contract.
   d. none of the above.

_____ 6. A minor may disaffirm a contract for personal property:
   a. before attaining majority.
   b. on the day of attaining majority.
   c. within a reasonable time after reaching majority.
   d. all of the above.

_____ 7. A person who lacks sufficient mental capacity to enter into a contract is one who is:
   a. adjudicated incompetent by a court decree.
   b. incompetent, although not adjudicated as such by a court decree.
   c. unable to understand the nature and effect of her acts.
   d. all of the above.

_____ 8. One does not possess sufficient contractual capacity to enter into a contract if it is shown that he is:
   a. slightly intoxicated.
   b. intoxicated and unable to understand the nature and consequences of his acts.
   c. both of the above.
   d. none of the above.

_____ 9. Which of the following is/are liable in quasi-contract for necessaries furnished to them during their incapacity?
   a. Emancipated minors
   b. Persons incompetent but not so adjudicated
   c. Intoxicated persons
   d. All of the above

_____ 10. Which of the following would constitute an effective ratification?
   a. Ratification through express language
   b. Ratification through conduct
   c. Ratification through failure to make a timely disaffirmance
   d. Any of the above

_____ 11. Which of the following is NOT true with regard to necessary items?
  a. A car can be a necessary item.
  b. A contract for medical care can be avoided.
  c. What is necessary will vary from person to person.
  d. The liability for necessary items will be the reasonable value of the items, which may differ from the contract amount.

_____ 12. When can a minor disaffirm a contract?
  a. Only before reaching the age of majority
  b. At any time after reaching the age of majority
  c. At any time either prior to or immediately after reaching the age of majority
  d. None of the above

_____ 13. Martha, who is a minor, contracts with Alice, who is an adult.
  a. Alice may disaffirm the contract at any time.
  b. Alice may disaffirm the contract when Martha becomes an adult.
  c. Alice may ratify the contract when Martha reaches the age of 18.
  d. Alice may not disaffirm the contract.

_____ 14. *CPA:* Meed entered into a written agreement to sell a parcel of land to Beel for $80,000. At the time the agreement was executed, Meed had consumed a large amount of alcohol which significantly impaired Meed's ability to understand the nature and terms of the contract. Beel knew Meed was very intoxicated and that the land had been appraised at $125,000. Meed wishes to avoid the contract. The contract is:
  a. void.
  b. legally binding on both parties in the absence of fraud or undue influence.
  c. voidable at Meed's option.
  d. voidable at Meed's option only if the intoxication was involuntary.

_____ 15. *CPA:* On May 1, 1999, Mint, a 16-year-old, purchased a sailboat from Sly Boats. Mint used the boat for six months, at which time he advertised it for sale. Which of the following statements is correct?
  a. The sale of the boat to Mint was void, thereby requiring Mint to return the boat and Sly to return the money received.
  b. The sale of the boat to Mint may be avoided by Sly at its option.
  c. Mint's use of the boat for six months after the sale on May 1 constituted a ratification of that contract.
  d. Mint may disaffirm the May 1 contract at any time prior to reaching majority.

SHORT ESSAY

1. Indicate the classes of persons lacking contractual capacity and the effect of that incapacity.

2. Explain a minor's liability for necessaries.

3. Discuss ratification and how it may be accomplished.

4. Tyrone, who is 17 years old, shows a false ID to the loan officer at First Bank. Believing that Tyrone is of legal age, the bank officer gives him a $10,000 loan to buy a used sports car. Tyrone defaults on the loan two months later, after the car has been destroyed in a collision. Tyrone, who is still 17, informs the bank that he has decided to avoid the contract. What are Tyrone's rights? What are the bank's rights?

5. Don, who is mentally incompetent, enters into a contract with Lucy Landowner to purchase some land. Discuss the enforceability of the contract. If Don has been adjudicated incompetent by a court and enters such a contract, what would the result be?

Chapter 15
Contracts in Writing

PURPOSE

In general, oral contracts are just as enforceable as written contracts. However, there are some exceptions to this general rule. In this chapter, you will study (1) the types of contracts that must be evidenced by a writing to be enforceable, (2) the parol evidence rule, and (3) the rules of contractual interpretation. The statute of frauds specifies those contracts that must be in writing to be enforceable. If a given contract is within the statute of frauds, it must comply with the requirements of the statute to be enforceable.

In this chapter, you also study the parol evidence rule. When the parties have reduced their agreement to a complete and final written expression, the parol evidence rule honors this written document by not allowing the parties to introduce any evidence in a lawsuit that would vary or contradict the terms of the written document. There are some situations or exceptions when this rule does not apply and parol evidence is admissible. Further, the Restatement and the Code permit supplemental consistent evidence to be introduced into a court proceeding.

The chapter ends with the rules for interpretation of contracts that are found in the Restatement. These rules are a useful aid in determining the meaning of a contract by applying a legal standard to the words contained in the agreement.

CHAPTER CHECKPOINTS

After reading and studying the chapter, you should be able to:

1. List and discuss the situations that fall within the general statute of frauds.

2. Summarize and discuss the provisions of the UCC Article 2 statute of frauds.

3. Define the parol evidence rule, and identify at least six general types of situations in which the rule does not apply and parol evidence can be used even though there is a written contract.

4. Define the terms "course of performance," "course of dealing" and "usage of trade," and discuss their relevance to contractual interpretation and the UCC parol evidence rule.

5. Summarize the rules for interpretation of contracts that are found in the Restatement.

CHAPTER OUTLINE

I. Statute of Frauds–The statute of frauds requires that in order to be enforceable, certain contracts must be evidenced by a written memorandum signed by the party to be charged (the one you want to sue). The statute of frauds does not relate to any kind of fraud practiced in the making of a contract but rather is aimed at preventing fraud in the proof or evidence of oral contracts by perjured testimony in court.

The Uniform Electronic Transactions Act (UETA), adopted by more than 40 states, generally provides that electronic contracts should not be denied enforceability due to the statute of frauds. Similarly, the federal Electronic Signatures in Global and National Commerce Act (E-Sign) generally validates electronic records (including electronic contracts) and signatures for many transactions in interstate and foreign commerce.

  A. Contracts within the Statute of Frauds–If a contract is "within" the statute, it must comply with the requirements of the statute, i.e., a writing is necessary.

  1. Suretyship Provision–A suretyship is a promise to pay a debt or perform duties of a third person if the principal debtor fails to do so. The surety is the person who promises to perform. The principal debtor is the person whose debt is being supported. The suretyship provision applies to a contractual promise by a surety (the promisor) to a creditor (the promisee) to perform the duties or obligations of a third person (the principal debtor) if the principal debtor does not perform.

  a. Original Promise–If the promisor makes an original promise by undertaking to become primarily liable, then the statute of frauds does not apply. The statute only applies to a collateral promise. A collateral promise is an undertaking to be secondarily liable, that is, liable if the principal debtor does not perform. "If X doesn't pay, I will," is collateral, because the promisor is not the one who is primarily liable, X is. An original promise (one to become primarily liable) is not collateral.

  b. Main Purpose Doctrine–This is an exception that the courts have developed to the suretyship provision. It is also known as the leading object rule. If the main purpose of the promisor/surety is to provide an economic benefit to herself, then the promise comes within the exception and is outside the statute, i.e., no writing is necessary to enforce the promise.

  c. Promise Made to Debtor–Courts have interpreted the suretyship provision NOT to include promises made to the debtor. A promise made to a debtor is enforceable without writing.

  2. Executor–Administrator Provision–An executor or administrator is a person appointed to settle a decedent's estate. If an executor or administrator promises to answer personally for a duty of the decedent, the promise is unenforceable unless in writing. This provision is a specific application of the suretyship provision.

3. Marriage Provision–The marriage provision does NOT apply to mutual promises to marry. A writing is required only if a promise to marry is made in consideration of some other promise, such as if a man's parents promise a woman to convey title to property if she marries their son.

4. Land Contract Provision–An interest in land is any right, privilege, power, or immunity in real property. It includes ownership interests in land, long-term leases, mortgages, options, and easements. Under this provision, a promise to transfer an interest in land must be in writing. However, under the part performance exception, if the transferee has paid a portion or all of the purchase price and either taken possession of the property or started to make valuable improvements on the land in reasonable reliance on the contract, an oral contract is enforceable.

5. One-Year Provision–The statute of frauds requires that all contracts that cannot be fully performed within one year of the making of the contract must be in writing.

   a. The Possibility Test–The test for whether a contract is within the one-year provision is whether it is possible, under the terms of the contract, for the contract to be performed within one year; the test is not whether it is likely to be performed within one year.

   b. Computation of Time–The year runs from the time the agreement is made, not from when the performance is to begin.

   c. Full Performance by One Party–When one party has fully performed, most courts hold that the promise of the other party is enforceable even if performance was not possible within one year.

6. Sales of Goods–The UCC provides that a contract for the sale of goods for the price of $500 or more is not enforceable without a writing.

   a. Admission–The Code permits an oral contract for the sale of goods to be enforced against a party who in a pleading, testimony, or otherwise in court admits that a contract was made, but the Code limits enforcement to the quantity of goods the party admits.

   b. Specially Manufactured Goods–The Code permits enforcement of an oral contract for goods specially manufactured for a buyer which cannot be readily resold in the ordinary course of the seller's business.

   c. Delivery or Payment and Acceptance–Under the Code, delivery and acceptance of part of the goods or payment and acceptance of part of the price validates part of the oral contract.

7. Modification or Rescission of Contracts within the Statute of Frauds–Oral contracts modifying existing contracts are unenforceable if the resulting contract is within the statute of frauds.

B. Compliance with the Statute of Frauds–If a contract is within the statute of frauds, it will be enforced if there is a sufficient writing, memorandum or record that meets the requirements of the statute.

1. General Contract Provisions–The general statutes require that the writing (1) specify the parties to the contract; (2) specify the subject matter and essential terms of the unperformed promises; and (3) be signed by the party to be charged or by her agent. The note or memorandum may be formal or informal. The signature may be by initials, printed, or typewritten, and need not be at the bottom of the page. A personal letter or handwritten note would suffice. It may consist of several papers, none of which would be sufficient by itself.

2. Sale of Goods–The Article 2 statute of frauds provision is more liberal. It requires merely a writing (a) sufficient to indicate that a contract has been made between the parties; (b) signed by the party against whom enforcement is sought or by her authorized agent or broker; and (c) specifying the quantity of goods to be sold.

C. Effect of Noncompliance–The oral contract that should fall within the statute is unenforceable.
1. Full Performance–After all the promises of an oral contract have been performed by all parties, the statute of frauds no longer applies.
2. Restitution–If a party to a contract that is unenforceable because of the statute of frauds has acted in reliance upon the contract, the party may recover in restitution the benefits conferred upon the other.
3. Promissory Estoppel–Oral contracts within the statute of frauds have been enforced where the party seeking enforcement has reasonably and foreseeably relied upon a promise, and injustice can only be avoided by enforcement of the promise.

II. Parol Evidence Rule–Neither party to a final, complete written contract is later permitted to show that the contract they made is different from the terms and provisions that appear in the written agreement.

A. The Rule–When a contract is expressed in a writing that is intended to be the complete and final expression of the rights and duties of the parties, the parol evidence rule, which also applies to wills and deeds, excludes evidence of prior oral or written negotiations or agreements of the parties or their contemporaneous oral agreements that vary or change the integrated written contract.

B. Situations to Which the Rule Does Not Apply–The rule is considered to be a substantive rule of law that defines the limits of a contract. It does not apply to the following situations: (1) a contract that is partly written and partly oral; (2) a clerical or typographical error that obviously does not represent the agreement of the parties; (3) the lack of contractual capacity of one of the parties, such as proof of minority, intoxication, or mental incompetency; (4) a defense of fraud, misrepresentation, duress, undue influence, mistake, illegality, lack of consideration, or other invalidating cause; (5) a condition precedent that was orally agreed upon at the time of the contract's execution and to which the entire agreement was made subject; (6) a subsequent mutual rescission or modification of the contract; (7) *ambiguous* terms are found in the contract; and (8) there was a separate, distinct contract between the same parties.

C. Supplemental Evidence–Under the Restatement and the Code, a written contract may be explained or supplemented by course of dealing, usage of trade, course of performance, or evidence of consistent, additional terms. A course of dealing is a sequence of previous conduct between the parties that establishes a common basis for understanding. A usage of trade is a practice or method of dealing regularly observed and followed in a place, vocation, or trade. Course of performance is the manner and extent to which the respective parties have accepted successive tenders of performance by the other party without objection. Supplemental consistent evidence is admissible if it does not contradict the terms of the original agreement and would probably not have been included in the original contract.

III. Interpretation of Contracts–The Restatement defines interpretation as the ascertainment of the meaning of a promise or agreement or a term of the promise or agreement. Rules for interpretation include: (1) all the circumstances are considered and the principal purpose of the parties is given great weight; (2) a writing is interpreted as a whole; (3) commonly accepted meanings are used unless a different intention is manifested; (4) technical terms are given their technical meaning; (5) wherever possible, the intentions of the parties are interpreted as consistent with each other and with course of performance, course of dealing, or usage of trade; (6) an interpretation that gives a reasonable, lawful, and effective meaning to all terms is preferred; (7) specific terms are given greater weight than general language; (8) separately negotiated terms are given greater weight than standardized terms or those not separately negotiated; (9) express terms, course of performance, course of dealing, and usage of trade are weighted in that order; and (10) where a term has several possible meanings, the term will be interpreted against the party who supplied the contract or term; (11) written provisions prevail over inconsistent typed or printed provisions, and typed provisions prevail over printed; and (12) if an amount payable is set forth in conflicting words and figures, the words control the figures.

KEY TERMS

1. Statute of frauds

2. Suretyship

3. Surety

4. Collateral promise

5. Main purpose doctrine

6. Parol evidence rule

7. Integrated contract

8. Course of dealing

9. Usage of trade

10. Course of performance

TRUE/FALSE

_____ 1. It is optional with the parties, under the statute of frauds, whether to reduce their agreement to writing.

_____ 2. The statute of frauds does not relate to the circumstances surrounding the making of a contract or to the validity of a contract.

_____ 3. A collateral promise is an undertaking to be secondarily liable.

_____ 4. Where the "main purpose" of the promisor is to obtain an economic benefit for herself that she did not previously have, the promise is outside the statute, and need not be in writing to be enforceable.

_____ 5. The suretyship provision has been interpreted not to include promises made to a debtor.

_____ 6. The UCC provides that a contract for the sale of goods for the price of $500 or more must satisfy the requirements of the statute of frauds.

_____ 7. In order to comply with the requirements of most statutes of frauds, the writing or memorandum must be signed by both parties to the agreement.

_____ 8. The parol evidence rule applies to all integrated, written contracts and deals with what terms are part of the contract.

_____ 9. The parol evidence rule is a rule of evidence that prohibits the parties from subsequently orally modifying their written contract.

_____ 10. The "marriage provision" of the statute of frauds applies only if a promise to marry is made in consideration for some promise other than a mutual promise to marry.

_____ 11. A writing required under the UCC, Article 2 statute of frauds must be signed at the end of the writing with the intent to authenticate the writing.

_____ 12. A course of dealing is a practice or method of dealing regularly observed and followed in a place, vocation, or trade.

_____ 13. Under the parol evidence rule, words can be introduced in court which vary or contradict the terms of an integrated contract.

_____ 14. Under the "main purpose rule," an oral contract which would ordinarily require a writing can be enforced.

_____ 15. The parol evidence rule does not apply to parol evidence which is used to show a subsequent mutual rescission of a contract.

MULTIPLE CHOICE

_____ 1. The following promises or contracts are within the statute of frauds EXCEPT:
   a. the promise of an executor or administrator that he personally will pay all of the decedent's creditors in full.
   b. a promise to marry made in consideration for some promise other than a reciprocal promise to marry.
   c. a promise made by a father to his son by which the father will pay the son's debt in the event of his son's default.
   d. a promise made by a father to his son's creditor to pay the son's debt in the event of his son's default.

_____ 2. Which of the following contracts are within the statute of frauds and therefore must meet its requirements in order to be enforceable?
   a. A contract to sell half-acre lots of land in a 60-acre subdivision
   b. A six-month lease of an apartment
   c. A deed granting an easement
   d. (a) and (c) above

_____ 3. In a contract for the sale of goods costing more than $500, the statute of frauds provisions apply except:
   a. where an admission has been made.
   b. where the goods have been specially manufactured.
   c. where there has been a delivery of and payment for the goods.
   d. all the above are exceptions to statute of frauds provisions.

_____ 4. All of the following are required of a writing to satisfy the requirements of the general statute of frauds EXCEPT:
   a. it must be signed by the party to be charged or his agent.
   b. it must be signed by the party seeking to enforce the contract or his agent.
   c. it must specify the parties to the contract.
   d. it must specify with reasonable certainty the subject matter of the unperformed promises as well as their essential terms.

_____ 5. Under the statute of frauds provision of the UCC, if a writing that is otherwise sufficient incorrectly states the quantity term agreed upon by the parties, the contract is:
   a. unenforceable.
   b. enforceable, but only to the extent of the quantity of goods stated in the writing.
   c. enforceable to the extent of the quantity term orally agreed upon by the parties.
   d. enforceable to the extent determined by the court to be fair and reasonable at the time of enforcement of the contract.

_____ 6. By an oral agreement entered into on January 1, 2000, A hires B to work for eleven months starting on February 1, 2000. This contract is:
   a. enforceable because this contract is outside the statute of frauds.
   b. enforceable because it can be performed within a year of the start of performance.
   c. unenforceable because it cannot be performed within one year of when it was made.
   d. (a) and (b) above.

_____ 7. If a contract is expressed in a writing that is intended by the parties to be the complete and final expression of their rights and duties under the contract, the parol evidence rule precludes the admission into evidence of all of the following EXCEPT:
   a. prior oral negotiations or agreements of the parties.
   b. prior written negotiations of the parties.
   c. a subsequent oral agreement between the parties to modify the terms of the contract.
   d. a contemporaneous oral agreement between the parties that varies or changes the written contract.

_____ 8. The parol evidence rule will bar the introduction of:
   a. evidence that one of the parties to the contract was a minor.
   b. evidence of fraud in the formation of the contract.
   c. evidence of usage and custom that is not inconsistent with the terms of the written agreement.
   d. evidence of a letter written prior to the execution of the final contract stating that the price to be charged for the goods was $2.00 each rather than $2.10 as provided in the final contract.

_____ 9. A party seeks to introduce evidence of a subsequent oral agreement modifying a written employment contract from 2 to 3 years. The oral agreement is
   a. admissible under the parol evidence rule and valid under the statute of frauds.
   b. admissible under the parol evidence rule, but invalid because of the statute of frauds.
   c. inadmissible under the parol evidence rule, but valid under the statute of frauds.
   d. inadmissible under the parol evidence rule and invalid under the statute of frauds.

_____ 10. Which of the following is not a rule of contract interpretation?
   a. Words and other conduct are interpreted in light of all the circumstances, and if the principal purpose is ascertainable, it is given greater weight.
   b. Unless a different intention is manifested, technical terms and words of art are given their technical meaning.
   c. Express terms, usage of trade, course of dealing, and course of performance are weighed in that order.
   d. Separately negotiated or added terms are given greater weight than standardized terms or other terms not separately negotiated.

_____ 11. Arthur writes a letter to Bob in which he promises to pay Clark's debts if Clark doesn't pay.
   a. Arthur's promise is a primary promise.
   b. Arthur's promise is an original promise.
   c. Arthur's promise is a collateral promise.
   d. Arthur's promise falls within the main purpose doctrine.

_____ 12. Which of the following contracts need not be in writing to be enforced?
   a. Arthur agrees to buy Bob's house for $60,000.
   b. Clara's Aunt Amanda promises Clara $1,000 if she will marry Brad.
   c. Bill Buyer agrees to buy $450 in goods from Sam Seller.
   d. Oscar agrees to work for Big Bucks, Inc., for two years beginning June 1.

_____ 13. In which of the following situations would an oral contract that should have been within the statute of frauds no longer have to be written to be enforceable?
   a.   The contract has been fully performed.
   b.   The contract has been partially performed.
   c.   The parties had a previous course of dealing.
   d.   Oral contracts are a common practice in that trade.

_____ 14. *CPA:* The statute of frauds:
   a.   prevents the use of oral evidence to contradict the terms of a written contract.
   b.   applies to all contracts having consideration valued at $500 or more.
   c.   requires the independent promise to pay the debt of another to be in writing.
   d.   applies to all real estate leases.

_____ 15. *CPA:* Sand orally promised Frost a $10,000 bonus, in addition to a monthly salary, if Frost would work for two years for Sand. If Frost works for the two years, will the statute of frauds prevent Frost from collecting the bonus?
   a.   No, because Frost fully performed in reliance on the oral promise.
   b.   No, because the contract did **not** involve an interest in real estate.
   c.   Yes, because the contract could **not** be performed within one year.
   d.   Yes, because the monthly salary was the consideration of the contract.

SHORT ESSAY

1.   Identify five situations which fall within the statute of frauds.

   _____

   _____

   _____

   _____

2.   Identify two instances in which a contract to transfer an interest in land need not be in writing, and give an example of each.

   _____

   _____

   _____

   _____

3. Compare the requirements for a writing to comply with the general statute of frauds and the UCC version. Which is easier to satisfy? Why? List three alternative methods of compliance with the UCC version.

_____

_____

_____

_____

4. Briefly explain the "parol evidence" rule.

_____

_____

_____

_____

5. Interlock, Inc. hires Betty as human resources director under a two-year employment contract. After six months, the president of Interlock and Betty orally agree to modify her existing contract including a change in salary and job description. Discuss the enforceability of the oral contract modifying the existing contract.

_____

_____

_____

_____

Chapter 16
Third Parties to Contracts

PURPOSE

In prior chapters, you studied contracts that involved only two parties. In this chapter, you study the rights and duties of third parties who are not parties to the contract, but who have rights or duties under the contract. These rights or duties arise by (1) an assignment of the rights of a party to the contract, (2) a delegation of the duties of a party to the contract, or (3) the express terms of a contract entered into for the benefit of a third person.

The early common law placed a great deal of emphasis on privity of contract. Because of this principle, under ordinary circumstances, only the original parties to a contract may bring an action to enforce it in the event of a breach. However, today third party beneficiaries and assignees are frequently allowed to enforce a contract against the original parties. With some exceptions, a party to a contract today can assign rights or delegate duties to a third party.

CHAPTER CHECKPOINTS

After reading and studying the chapter, you should be able to:

1. Distinguish between an assignment of rights and a delegation of duties, and identify situations in which assignments and delegations are not permitted by the law.

2. Recognize the assignor, the assignee, the delegator, the delegatee, the obligor, and the obligee in various fact situations.

3. Discuss the majority rule, the minority rule, and the Restatement rule for situations involving successive assignments of the same right and the priorities of assignee claimants.

4. Distinguish third-party beneficiary contracts and novations from assignments and delegations.

5. Identify intended donee beneficiaries, intended creditor beneficiaries, and incidental beneficiaries, and discuss the relative rights of each in enforcing a contract.

CHAPTER OUTLINE

A. Assignment of Rights–Every contract creates both rights and duties. An assignment is the voluntary transfer to a third party of the rights arising from a contract. The assignor is the party making an assignment. The assignee is the party to whom the contract rights are assigned. An obligor is a party who owes a duty under a contract, while an obligee is a party to whom a duty is owed under a contract. The delegation of a duty is the transfer to a third party of a contractual obligation. The delegator is the party who delegates a duty to a third party. The delegatee is a third party to whom the delegator's duty is delegated.

1. Requirements of an Assignment–The Restatement defines an assignment as a manifestation of the assignor's intention to transfer a contract right so that the assignor's right to performance is extinguished and the assignee acquires a right to such performance. Although no special form or words are needed to create an assignment, the UCC imposes a writing requirement on all assignments beyond $5,000. No consideration is necessary to make an assignment effective.

    a. Revocability of Assignments–If the assignee gives consideration in exchange for the assignment, then there is a contract and the assignor may not revoke the assignment without the assent of the assignee. If the assignment is gratuitous, it is revocable by the assignor and is terminated by the assignor's death, incapacity, or subsequent assignment, unless effective delivery has been made.

    b. Partial Assignments–A partial assignment is a transfer of a portion of the contractual rights to one or more assignees.

2. Rights that are Assignable–Most contract rights are assignable. The right to the payment of money is the most common contractual right that may be assigned.

3. Rights that are Not Assignable–Some contract rights, including the following, are not assignable.

    a. Assignments that Materially Increase the Duty, Risk, or Burden–An assignment is ineffective where performance by the obligor to the assignee would be materially different from performance to the assignor, such as an automobile liability insurance policy.

    b. Assignments of Personal Rights–Where the rights under a contract are of a highly personal nature, they cannot be assigned. An example would be an agreement of two persons to marry one another.

    c. Express Prohibition Against Assignment–The Restatement and Article 2 of the Code say that unless circumstances indicate the contrary, a prohibition of assignment of the contract will be construed as barring only the delegation to the assignee of the assignor's duty of performance and not the assignment of rights.

    d. Assignments Prohibited by Law–Federal and state statutes prohibit or regulate certain assignments, such as those of the right to future wages.

4. Rights of the Assignee
   a. Obtains Rights of Assignor–The assignee stands in the shoes of the assignor, but acquires no new rights. The assignee takes the assigned right with all of the defenses, defects, and infirmities that the obligor would have against the assignor. The obligor may assert rights of setoff or counterclaim. Waivers of claims or defenses against assignees are valid under the Code, but the FTC has invalidated waivers of defenses in consumer credit transactions.
   b. Notice–A valid assignment does not require that notice be given to the obligor; however, such notice is advisable because an assignee will lose his rights against the obligor if the obligor pays the assignor without notice of the assignment.
5. Implied Warranties of Assignor–Four implied warranties are imposed by law upon the transferor of contract rights for value. The four warranties are (1) that he will do nothing to defeat or impair the assignment; (2) that the assigned right actually exists and is subject to no limitations or defenses other than those apparent or stated; (3) that any writing evidencing the right is genuine; and (4) that he has no knowledge of any fact that would impair the value of the assignment.
6. Express Warranties of Assignor–The assignor is bound by any explicitly made contractual promises regarding the contract rights transferred.
7. Successive Assignments of the Same Right–The majority rule in the United States is that the first assignee in point of time prevails over later assignees. In England and a minority of states, the first assignee to notify the obligor prevails. The Restatement adopts a third view.

B. Delegation of Duties–Duties are not assignable, but their performance generally may be delegated to a third person. A delegation of duties is a transfer to a third party of a contractual obligation. It does not extinguish the delegator's obligation to perform. When the delegatee accepts the delegated duty, both the delegator and the delegatee are liable for performance of the contractual duty to the obligee.
1. Delegable Duties–Contractual duties are generally delegable, however, a delegation will not be permitted if (1) the nature of the duties are personal; (2) the performance is expressly made nondelegable; or (3) the delegation is prohibited by statute or public policy.
2. Duties of the Parties–When there has been a delegation of duties and an assumption of the delegated duties, both the delegator and the delegatee are liable to the obligee for proper performance of the original contractual duty. A delegator who desires to be discharged of the duty may enter into a novation, which is an agreement obtaining the consent of the obligee to substitute a third person in the delegator's place. The delegator is then discharged and the third party is bound to the obligee.

C. Third-Party Beneficiary Contracts–Third-party beneficiary contracts are contracts in which one party promises to render performance to a third person.
1. Intended Beneficiary–An intended beneficiary is a third party intended by the two contracting parties to receive a benefit from their contract.
   a. Donee Beneficiary–A third party is an intended donee beneficiary if the promisee's purpose in bargaining for the agreement is to make a gift of the promised performance to the beneficiary. An example is the beneficiary of a life insurance policy.

    b. Creditor Beneficiary–A third person is an intended creditor beneficiary if the promisee intends the performance of the promise to satisfy a legal duty owed to the beneficiary, who is a creditor of the promisee.

    c. Rights of Intended Beneficiary–An intended donee beneficiary may enforce the contract against the promisor only. An intended creditor beneficiary may sue either or both parties. In an action by an intended beneficiary to enforce a promise, the promisor may raise any defense that would be available if the action had been brought by the promisee.

    d. Vesting of Rights–A contract for the benefit of an intended beneficiary confers rights that the beneficiary may enforce. Until the rights vest, however, the promisor and promisee may vary or completely discharge these rights. There is considerable variation among the states as to when vesting takes place. These views include: (1) immediately upon making the contract, (2) when the third party learns of the contract and assents to it, and (3) when the third party changes his position in reliance upon the promise made for his benefit.

    e. Defenses Against Beneficiary- An intended beneficiary is subject to any defense that the promisor could assert against the promisee.

  2. Incidental Beneficiaries–An incidental beneficiary is one whom the parties to a contract did not intend to benefit, but who nevertheless would derive some benefit from its performance. Incidental beneficiaries have no rights under a contract.

KEY TERMS

1. Obligor

2. Obligee

3. Assignment of rights

4. Assignor

5. Assignee

6. Delegation of duties

7. Delegator

8. Delegatee

9. Partial assignment

10. Implied warranty

11. Express warranty

12. Novation

13. Third-party beneficiary contract

14. Intended beneficiary

15. Incidental beneficiary

16. Donee beneficiary

17. Creditor beneficiary

18. Vesting of rights

TRUE/FALSE

_____ 1. An assignment of rights is the voluntary transfer to a third party of the rights arising from the contract..

_____ 2. After an effective assignment of rights, both the assignor and the assignee have a right to the obligor's performance.

_____ 3. After an effective delegation of duties, both the delegator and the delegatee are liable to the obligee for performance of the contractual duty.

_____ 4. Although no special words or particular form are necessary to create an assignment, an assignment must be supported by consideration to be effective.

_____ 5. Where the assignee gives consideration in exchange for an assignment, a contract exists between the assignor and the assignee and the assignor may not revoke the assignment.

_____ 6. In a novation, the delegator will be discharged and the third party will become directly bound on her promise to the obligee.

_____ 7. Under the Restatement and the Code, unless the language or circumstances indicate otherwise, an assignment of "all my rights under the contract" is both an assignment of rights and a delegation of the assignor's duties under the contract.

_____ 8. If successive assignments have taken place, the majority rule is that the first assignee to notify the obligor will prevail in a dispute among the successive assignees.

_____ 9. A third party is an intended beneficiary if the promisee's purpose in bargaining for and obtaining the promisor's promise was to make a gift to the beneficiary.

_____ 10. The rights of an intended beneficiary vest at the time of the making of the contract or at the time he learns of its making, whichever is later.

_____ 11. In an action by the intended beneficiary of a third-party beneficiary contract, the promisor may assert any defense that would have been available to him had the action been brought by the promisee.

_____ 12. Most contract rights, including rights under an option contract, are assignable.

_____ 13. Harold sells his used car to Tina and assigns his rights in his auto liability insurance policy to her. This is a valid assignment.

_____ 14. Sarah orders a microwave oven from Myriad's Department Store and requests that it be delivered to her sister Theresa. Theresa is a third-party intended beneficiary.

_____ 15. An implied warranty is an explicitly made contractual promise regarding contract rights transferred.

MULTIPLE CHOICE

_____ 1. A gratuitous assignment is:
   a. valid even though not supported by consideration.
   b. not revocable by the assignor.
   c. not terminated by the assignor's death.
   d. all of the above.

_____ 2. In the case of a gratuitous assignment, which of the following would not be revocable?
   a. The donee-assignee receives payment of the claim from the obligor.
   b. The donee-assignee obtains a judgment against the obligor.
   c. The donee-assignee obtains a new contract with the obligor.
   d. None of the above would be revocable.

_____ 3. Which of the following assignments of contract rights are not assignable?
   a. Assignments that would materially increase the risk or burden on the obligor
   b. Assignments which would transfer a personal contract right
   c. Assignments which are prohibited by law
   d. All of the above

_____ 4. An assignee of a contract right:
   a. acquires all of the rights of the assignor.
   b. acquires new, additional rights by virtue of the assignment.
   c. takes the assigned rights free of all of the defenses to which the rights would be subject in an action by the assignor against the obligor.
   d. all of the above

_____ 5. Which of the following would not be assignable?
   a. _A_ owes _B_ $50. _B_ assigns to _C_ the right to collect the money.
   b. Pedro assigns a contract right to land to Chung.
   c. Teacher assigns to her best friend her contract right to teach.
   d. All of the above

_____ 6. In the absence of an expressed intention to the contrary, an assignor who receives value makes all of the following implied warranties to the assignee with respect to the assigned right EXCEPT:
a. that he will do nothing to defeat or impair the assignment.
b. that the obligor will pay the assigned debt.
c. that the assigned right actually exists.
d. that he has no knowledge of any fact that would impair the value of the assignment.

_____ 7. A delegation of contractual duties will not be permitted if:
a. the duties are of a personal nature.
b. the contract is silent with respect to the assignment.
c. the delegation is for payment of money.
d. None of the above will be permitted.

_____ 8. The delegator remains bound to perform her contractual duties even after a delegation unless the delegation is:
a. a gratuitous delegation.
b. a delegation for value.
c. a novation.
d. none of the above.

_____ 9. A contract in which the promisor agrees to render a certain performance to a third person is called:
a. a third-party beneficiary contract.
b. an assignment of rights.
c. a delegation of duties.
d. a novation.

_____ 10. An intended creditor beneficiary of a third-party beneficiary contract has rights against:
a. the promisee/debtor only.
b. the promisor only.
c. both the promisee and the promisor.
d. neither the promisee nor the promisor.

_____ 11. A life insurance policy naming a spouse as a beneficiary is a common example of a(n):
a. assignment.
b. delegation of duties.
c. third-party donee beneficiary contract.
d. third-party incidental beneficiary contract.

_____ 12. Clara sells her house to Donald. The house has a mortgage which is held by First Bank. As part of the transaction, First Bank agrees to discharge Clara from the mortgage and to allow Donald to assume the obligation. This is a(n):
a. assignment of rights.
b. novation.
c. delegation of duties.
d. third-party creditor beneficiary contract.

_____ 13. Arthur and Bob enter into a contract. Bob later delegates his duty of performance to Clark. Which of the following is true?
a. If Clark fails to perform, Bob has a duty to perform.
b. Arthur will always have to accept Clark's performance.
c. The delegation is valid only if all three parties agree.
d. Bob must compensate Clark for accepting the delegation.

_____ 14. *CPA:* Graham contracted with the city of Harris to train and employ high school dropouts residing in Harris. Graham breached the contract. Long, a resident of Harris and a high school dropout, sued Graham for damages. Under the circumstances, Long will:
a. win, because Long is a third-party beneficiary entitled to enforce the contract.
b. win, because the intent of the contract was to confer a benefit on all high school dropouts residing in Harris.
c. lose, because Long is merely an incidental beneficiary of the contract.
d. lose, because Harris did **not** assign its contract rights to Long.

_____ 15. *CPA:* Krieg was the owner of an office building encumbered by a mortgage securing Krieg's promissory note to Muni Bank. Park purchased the building that was subject to Muni's mortgage. As a result of the sale to Park:
a. Muni is **not** a third party creditor beneficiary.
b. Krieg is a third party creditor beneficiary.
c. Park is liable for any deficiency resulting from a default note.
d. Krieg was automatically released from any liability on the note.

SHORT ESSAY

1. Identify the parties involved in an assignment/delegation.

_____

_____

_____

_____

2. Distinguish between an assignment of rights and a delegation of duties. How does an assignor's rights after an assignment differ from a delegator's duties after a delegation?

_____

_____

_____

_____

3. Briefly explain the majority rule with regard to successive assignments of the same right.

_____

_____

_____

_____

4. The Student Center at ABC University contracts with Rocky Nelson, a famous rock singer, to perform at the university. Can Rocky assign his rights and delegate his duties under this contract? Explain.

_____

_____

_____

_____

5. Identify the classes of third party beneficiaries and discuss the relative enforcement rights of each.

_____

_____

_____

_____

Chapter 17
Performance, Breach and Discharge

PURPOSE

In this chapter, you study the termination of contractual duties and the methods by which a party who has been bound by contractual duties is discharged from those duties. Most contracts are discharged by performance when the parties do what they have promised to do. However, performance may be defective, in which case there is a breach. In such a case, the defaulting party is not discharged. The consequences to the breaching party depend upon the seriousness of the breach. The contract may also be discharged by the agreement of the parties to a rescission, substituted agreement, novation, or an accord and satisfaction. In some situations, the contract may be discharged by operation of law. Such is the case when a party is discharged by impossibility, bankruptcy, or the statute of limitations. Also, many contractual promises are not absolute promises to perform but rather are conditional promises that depend on the happening or nonhappening of a specific event.

CHAPTER CHECKPOINTS

After reading and studying the chapter, you should be able to:

1. Recognize express conditions, implied-in-fact conditions, implied-in-law conditions, concurrent conditions, conditions precedent, and conditions subsequent, and discuss the effect of each type of condition upon a contract.

2. Identify fact situations in which discharge by agreement of the parties occurs and distinguish a mutual rescission, a substituted contract, an accord and satisfaction, and a novation.

3. Identify and discuss the ways in which discharge may be brought about by operation of law.

4. Compare the common law concept of material breach to the perfect tender rule of the UCC.

5. Distinguish between full performance, tender of performance, and substantial performance.

CHAPTER OUTLINE

A. Conditions–A condition is an event whose happening or nonhappening affects a duty of performance.
   1. Express Conditions–An express condition is explicitly set forth in language. It exists where performance is explicitly made contingent on the happening or nonhappening of a stated event.
       a. Satisfaction of a Contracting Party–The parties to a contract may agree that performance by one of them shall be to the satisfaction of the other, who will not be obligated to perform unless he is satisfied. This is an express condition to the duty to perform. If the contract does not clearly indicate that satisfaction is subjective, the law assumes an objective satisfaction standard.
       b. Satisfaction of a Third Party–A contract may condition the performance of a party on the approval of a third party.
   2. Implied-in-Fact Conditions–These are conditions that are understood but not expressed. They may be inferred from terms of the contract, nature of the transaction, or conduct of the parties.
   3. Implied-in-Law Conditions–These are not contained in the language of the contract or inferred from it but are imposed by law in order to accomplish a just and fair result.
   4. Concurrent Conditions–These occur when the mutual duties of performance are to take place at the same time.
   5. Condition Precedent–This is an event which must occur or not occur before performance is due.
   6. Condition Subsequent–This is an event which terminates an existing duty of performance.

B. Discharge by Performance–A discharge is a termination of a contractual duty. Performance is the fulfillment of a contractual obligation. Discharge by performance is the most frequent method of discharging a contractual duty. A tender is an offer of performance. In a bilateral contract, the refusal of a tender is a repudiation that discharges the tendering party from further duty to perform the contract.

C. Discharge by Breach–A breach is a wrongful failure to perform the terms of a contract. A breach is always a basis for an action for damages by the injured party.
   1. Material Breach–An unjustified failure to substantially perform the promised obligations in a contract is a material breach. An uncured material breach by one party discharges the aggrieved party from any further duty under the contract.
       a. Prevention of Performance–One party's substantial interference with or prevention of performance by the other generally constitutes a material breach and discharges the other party to the contract.
       b. Perfect Tender Rule–The Code alters the common law doctrine of material breach by adopting what is known as the perfect tender rule. This rule says that performance must strictly comply with contractual duties and any deviation discharges the aggrieved party.

2. Substantial Performance–This is performance that is incomplete but basically fulfills the purpose of the contract. If a party substantially performs, the common law will generally allow that party to obtain the other party's performance less any damages caused by the partial performance.

3. Anticipatory Repudiation–This is a breach of contract before performance is due by announcing that one will not perform or by committing an act which makes it impossible to perform. Anticipatory repudiation is treated as a breach, discharging the nonrepudiating party and permitting her to bring suit immediately as if it were a breach.

4. Material Alteration of Written Contract–A material, fraudulent alteration of a written contract by a party to the contract or an agent of a party discharges the entire contract.

D. Discharge by Agreement of the Parties–The parties may by agreement discharge each other from performance. This may be by rescission, substituted contract, accord and satisfaction, or novation.

1. Mutual Rescission–A rescission is an agreement between the parties to terminate their duties under a contract. It is a contract to end a contract.

2. Substituted Contracts–A substituted contract is a new contract accepted by both parties in satisfaction of their duties under their old contract. It immediately discharges the old contract.

3. Accord and Satisfaction–An accord is a contract by which the obligee promises to accept a stated performance in satisfaction of the obligor's existing contractual duty. The performance of the accord is the satisfaction.

4. Novation–A novation is a substituted contract involving a new third-party promisor or promisee.

E. Discharge by Operation of Law–Discharge can be brought about by operation of law.

1. Impossibility–Impossibility means that the performance cannot be done. There are two types of impossibility–subjective and objective. Subjective impossibility refers to the situation where it is impossible for the promisor to perform due to financial inability or because he personally lacks the capability to do so. Subjective impossibility does not excuse the promisor from liability for breach of contract. Objective impossibility means that no one would be able to perform. It will generally be held to excuse the promisor or to discharge the duty of performance. Destruction of the subject matter without the fault of the promisor is an excusable impossibility.

a. Subsequent Illegality–If performance becomes illegal or impractical as a result of a change in the law, the duty of performance is discharged.

b. Frustration of Purpose–Where the purpose of a contract has been frustrated by unexpected circumstances that deprive the performance of the value attached to it by the parties, the courts generally regard the frustration as a discharge.

c. Commercial Impracticability–Commercial impracticability means that performance can only be accomplished under unforeseen and unjust hardship. The Restatement and the Code take the view that commercial impracticability will excuse performance, even though the performance is not literally impossible.

2. Bankruptcy–This is a method of discharge which is available to a debtor who obtains an order of discharge by the bankruptcy court.

3. Statute of Limitations–All states have statutes providing time limitations within which to bring an action. When the statute of limitations has run, the debt is not discharged, but the creditor cannot maintain an action against the debtor.

KEY TERMS

1. Condition
2. Express condition
3. Implied-in-fact condition
4. Implied-in-law condition
5. Concurrent conditions
6. Condition precedent
7. Condition subsequent
8. Discharge
9. Performance
10. Tender
11. Breach

12. Material breach
13. Perfect tender rule
14. Substantial performance
15. Anticipatory repudiation
16. Material alteration
17. Mutual rescission
18. Substituted contract
19. Accord and satisfaction
20. Novation
21. Frustration of purpose
22. Commercial impracticability

TRUE/FALSE

_____ 1. Once contractual promises have been made, there is no way for the parties to escape from liability for nonperformance.

_____ 2. Even if a contract for interior decorating is expressly made subject to a subjective condition of satisfaction, courts will apply an objective, reasonable person standard to evaluate performance.

_____ 3. In the absence of an agreement to the contrary, the law assumes that the respective performances under a contract are concurrent conditions.

_____ 4. A condition is an event whose happening or nonhappening affects a duty of performance under a contract.

_____ 5. Under the Code, any deviation from the promised performance in a sales contract will be considered a material breach.

_____ 6. Under the perfect performance rule, the Code provides that a deviation in performance by a party in any contract constitutes a material breach.

_____ 7. A contract may condition the performance of a party upon the approval of a third party.

_____ 8. A promisor's good faith, personal belief that she lacks the necessary capability or competence to perform her contractual duties will excuse her from liability for nonperformance.

_____ 9. Under the Restatement and Code view of impossibility, commercial impracticability will excuse nonperformance.

_____ 10. A constructive condition is one imposed by law in order to accomplish a just and fair result.

_____ 11. Scott has a household insurance policy which requires that he notify the company within two weeks of any loss before he is eligible to receive payment for his loss. The notification requirement is a condition precedent.

_____ 12. Kevin builds a house for Paul and Virginia Demmit. The contract calls for extra grade, stain-resistant carpet. The pattern selected by the Demmits is not available when the carpeting is supposed to be installed, so Kevin substitutes a comparable grade similar carpet. Kevin has substantially performed the contract. Substantial performance plus a small amount of damages will discharge Kevin's contractual obligations, even if the Demmits think the substituted carpet ruins the house.

_____ 13. An unauthorized change in the terms of a written contract by a person who is not a party to the contract will discharge the contract.

_____ 14. CMC Contracting has a contract with Leonize, Inc., to build a new office complex. The contract provides that CMC must furnish a certificate of occupancy and conformity with the fire code before Leonize has an obligation to pay. The furnishing of the certificate is an implied-in-fact condition subsequent to the construction of the building.

_____ 15. Brian owes Albert $500. Brian, Albert, and Clarence agree that Brian will be discharged from the obligation and that Clarence will pay the debt. This is a novation.

MULTIPLE CHOICE

_____ 1. A condition that is understood by the parties to be part of their agreement, but is not included in their express contract, is called:
   a. an implied-in-law condition.
   b. an implied-in-fact condition.
   c. a concurrent condition.
   d. a condition precedent.

_____ 2. Which of the following would constitute a discharge of the contract?
   a. Full performance by all of the parties
   b. Breach of the contract by either or both parties
   c. Agreement of the parties to rescind
   d. All of the above

_____ 3. An uncured material breach of contract:
   a. gives rise to a cause of action for damages by the aggrieved party.
   b. operates as an excuse for nonperformance by the aggrieved party.
   c. discharges the aggrieved party from any further duty under the contract.
   d. all of the above.

_____ 4. The happening or nonhappening of a condition:
   a. prevents a party from acquiring a right.
   b. deprives a party of a right.
   c. subjects both parties to liability.
   d. (a) or (b), but not (c).

_____ 5. Which one of the following statements is NOT a correct principle to be applied in determining what constitutes a material breach?
   a. A failure to timely perform a promise is a material breach even if time is not of the essence.
   b. Partial performance is a material breach if an essential part of the contract is not performed.
   c. If quantitatively significant, a breach will be considered material.
   d. An intentional breach of a contract is generally held to be material.

_____ 6. Which of the following has occurred if, prior to the date that performance is due, a party announces that he will not perform or commits an act that renders him unable to perform?
   a. An anticipatory novation
   b. An anticipatory repudiation
   c. A prevention of performance
   d. A material alteration of a written contract

_____ 7. An agreement between three parties to substitute a new promisee or promisor in place of an existing promisee or promisor is called:
   a. a condition subsequent.
   b. a mutual rescission.
   c. an accord and satisfaction.
   d. a novation.

_____ 8. Which of the following would not be considered a discharge by agreement?
   a. A novation
   b. A mutual rescission
   c. An accord and satisfaction
   d. An anticipatory repudiation

_____ 9. A promisor may be excused for failure to perform a contract on grounds of impossibility when:
   a. she is financially unable to perform.
   b. she personally lacks the capability or competency to perform.
   c. no one, including the promisor, is able to perform.
   d. all of the above.

_____ 10. The effect of a party's failure to sue before the statute of limitations expires is:
   a. to discharge the promisor from liability.
   b. to act as a mutual rescission.
   c. to bar the right to bring an action.
   d. to act as an accord and satisfaction.

_____ 11. A contract in which the promisee agrees to accept and the promisor agrees to render a substituted performance in satisfaction of an existing contractual duty is called:
   a. a material alteration of a written contract.
   b. an accord.
   c. a substantial performance.
   d. a novation.

_____ 12. Edward has agreed to buy Donna's CD player. Edward agrees to pay Donna when the CD player is delivered. This transaction involves:
   a. implied-in-fact conditions subsequent.
   b. implied-in-law conditions subsequent.
   c. express concurrent conditions.
   d. express conditions precedent.

_____ 13. David and Sharon entered into a written contract involving the performance of some marketing services. A week later, they both changed their minds and agreed in writing to cancel the contract. This is an example of:
   a. accord and satisfaction.
   b. novation.
   c. substituted contract.
   d. mutual rescission.

_____ 14. *CPA:* To cancel a contract and to restore the parties to their original positions before the contract, the parties should execute a:
   a. novation.
   b. release.
   c. rescission.
   d. revocation.

_____ 15. *CPA:* In September 1999, Cobb Company contracted with Thrifty Oil Company for delivery of 100,000 gallons of heating oil at the price of $1.20 per gallon at regular specified intervals during the upcoming winter. Due to an unseasonably warm winter, Cobb took delivery on only 70,000 gallons. In a suit against Cobb for breach of contract, Thrifty will:
   a. lose, because Cobb acted in good faith.
   b. lose, because both parties are merchants and the UCC recognizes commercial impracticability.
   c. win, because this is a requirements contract.
   d. win, because the change of circumstances could have been contemplated by the parties.

SHORT ESSAY

1. Discuss "satisfaction" and the role it plays in conditional contracts.

    _____

    _____

    _____

    _____

2. At common law, when is a party excused from liability for nonperformance of a contractual duty on grounds of impossibility? How have the Restatement and the Code altered this rule?

    _____

    _____

    _____

    _____

3. Explain the "perfect tender rule" and how it differs from the common law approach.

    _____

    _____

    _____

    _____

4. Identify and briefly discuss the ways a contract might be discharged by agreement of the parties.

    _____

    _____

    _____

    _____

5. Give an example of a condition precedent, condition subsequent, and concurrent conditions.

    _____

    _____

    _____

    _____

Chapter 18
Contract Remedies

PURPOSE

This chapter discusses the remedies that are available to the injured party when the other party breaches the contract by failing to perform contractual duties. The primary objective of contract remedies is to compensate the injured party for the loss resulting from the breach. The relief the court can give an injured party is what it regards as an equivalent of the promised performance. In this chapter, you study the most common remedies available for breach of contract. These include the legal remedy of money damages and the equitable remedies of specific performance, injunction, and reformation. You also study the remedy of restitution, which is available as an alternative remedy for a party injured by breach and to a party who has avoided a contract for reasons such as lack of capacity, duress, undue influence, or fraud. Sometimes more than one remedy is available, and the injured party must elect a remedy and then cannot pursue another inconsistent remedy. Remedies under Article 2 of the Code differ from those available at common law. UCC remedies for breaches of sales contracts are discussed in Chapter 23.

CHAPTER CHECKPOINTS

After reading and studying the chapter, you should be able to:

1. List and discuss the various types of monetary damages.

2. Identify and discuss the two ways to measure damages for misrepresentation.

3. Identify the equitable remedies that are available for breach of contract and discuss the circumstances under which these remedies are available.

4. Define restitution and list the situations when restitution is available to the injured party.

5. List and discuss situations where the remedies of the injured party will be limited.

CHAPTER OUTLINE

A. Interests Protected by Contract Remedies–One or more of the following interests are protected:
  1. Expectation Interest–Interest in having the benefit of their bargain.
  2. Reliance Interest–Interest in being reimbursed for loss caused by reliance on the contract.
  3. Restitution Interest–Interest in having restored to them any benefit they conferred on other party.

B. Monetary Damages–A judgment awarding monetary damages is the most frequently granted judicial remedy for breach of contract.
  1. Compensatory Damages–These are contract damages placing the injured party in as good a position as if the other party had performed. The amount of damages is generally the loss of value to the injured party caused by the other party's failure to perform or by his deficient performance minus the loss or cost avoided by the injured party plus incidental damages plus consequential damages. The right to recover compensatory damages is always available.
     a. Loss of Value–In general, this is the difference between the value of the promised performance of the breaching party and the value of the actual performance rendered by the breaching party.
     b. Cost Avoided–The recovery by the injured party is reduced by any cost or loss she has avoided by not having to perform.
     c. Incidental Damages–These are damages arising directly out of a breach of contract, such as costs incurred to acquire the nondelivered performance from another source. Incidental damages are added to the loss of value.
     d. Consequential Damages–These are damages not arising directly out of a breach but that are a foreseeable result of the breach, such as lost profits and injury to persons or property resulting from defective performance.
  2. Reliance Damages–Instead of seeking compensatory damages, the injured party may seek reimbursement for foreseeable loss caused by reliance on the contract. This results in placing the injured party in as good a position as he would have been in had the contract not been made. These might be preferred when an injured party is unable to establish lost profits with reasonable certainty or when the contract itself is unprofitable.
  3. Nominal Damages–These are a small sum of money awarded where a contract has been breached but the loss is either negligible or unproved.
  4. Damages for Misrepresentation–The basic remedy for misrepresentation is rescission of the contract, but an alternative remedy under common law and an additional remedy under the Code is a suit for damages. The measure of damages generally depends upon whether the misrepresentation is fraudulent or nonfraudulent.
     a. Fraud–A minority of states allow the injured party to recover out-of-pocket damages, which is the difference between the value received and the value given. The majority of states permit the defrauded party to recover damages based upon the benefit-of-the-bargain rule, which is the difference between the value received and the value of the fraudulent party's performance as represented.
     b. Nonfraudulent Misrepresentation–The Restatement permits out-of-pocket damages but not benefit-of-the-bargain damages where the misrepresentation is not fraudulent or negligent.

5. Punitive Damages–Punitive damages are monetary damages in addition to compensatory damages awarded to a plaintiff in certain situations involving willful, wanton, or malicious conduct. Their purpose is to punish the defendant and thus to discourage him and others from similar wrongful conduct. The Restatement provides that punitive damages are not recoverable for a breach of contract unless the conduct constituting the breach is also a tort for which punitive damages are recoverable.

6. Liquidated Damages–These are reasonable damages agreed to in advance by the parties to a contract. If the liquidated damages clause is a reasonable forecast of the loss that may result from the breach, the provision will be enforced. If the sum bears no reasonable relationship to the amount of probable loss, it is unenforceable as a penalty. If the clause is invalid, a party is entitled to ordinary breach of contract remedies.

7. Limitations on Damages–Certain limits apply to monetary damages to ensure that damages can be taken foreseen at the time of contracting, that damages are compensatory and not speculative, and that damages do not include loss that could have been avoided by reasonable efforts.

   a. Foreseeability of Damages–Compensatory or reliance damages are recoverable only for loss that the party in breach had reason to foresee as a probable result of the breach when the contract was made. The test of foreseeable damages is objective, based on what the breaching party had reason to foresee.

   b. Certainty of Damages–Damages are not recoverable for loss beyond an amount that the injured party can establish with reasonable certainty.

   c. Mitigation of Damages–When a breach of contract occurs, the injured party may not recover damages for loss that he could have avoided by reasonable effort and without undue risk, burden, or humiliation.

C. Remedies in Equity–If damages will not adequately compensate an injured party, the court may, in its discretion, grant a remedy in equity.

   1. Specific Performance–This is a court decree ordering the breaching party to render the promised performance. It is not ordinarily available for breach of contract, because the usual remedy for breach is an action at law for money damages. It is available only in the case of breach of contract for the sale of personal property where the goods are rare or unique, such as for a famous painting or statue, an original manuscript, a patent or copyright, shares of stock in a closely held corporation, or an heirloom. Courts will always grant specific performance in case of breach of contract for the sale of real property. Specific performance is not available in contracts for personal services.

   2. Injunctions–An injunction is a court order prohibiting a party from doing a specific act. Where damages for breach would be inadequate, a court may grant an injunction against breach of a contractual duty. An employee's promise of exclusive personal services may be enforced by an injunction against serving another employer as long as the employee would have other reasonable means of making a living and the services are unusual in character.

D. Restitution–This is the restoration of the injured party to the position he was in before the contract was made. It is available (1) as an alternative remedy for a party injured by breach, (2) for a party in default, (3) for a party who may not enforce the contract because of the statute of frauds, and (4) on rescission of a voidable contract.

1. Party Injured by Breach–Restitution is available if the other party totally breaches the contract by nonperformance or repudiation.
2. Party in Default–The party who has partly performed but is in default such that the other party's duty to perform is discharged is entitled to restitution for any benefit she has conferred in excess of the loss she has caused by her breach.
3. Statute of Frauds–Where a contract is unenforceable because of the statute of frauds, but the party has nevertheless acted in reliance on the contract, the party may recover in restitution the benefits conferred on the other in reliance on the contract.
4. Voidable Contracts–A party who has avoided a contract for lack of capacity, duress, undue influence, fraud in the inducement, nonfraudulent misrepresentation, or mistake is entitled to restitution for any benefit he has conferred on the other party.

E. Limitations on Remedies
1. Election of Remedies–If a party is injured by a breach of contract and has more than one remedy available, he may pursue more than one remedy unless the remedies are inconsistent or the other party materially changes his position in reliance on the choice of one of them.
2. Loss of Power of Avoidance–A party may lose the power of avoidance in the following cases:
   a. Affirmance–A party who has the power to avoid a contract for lack of capacity, duress, undue influence, fraud in the inducement, nonfraudulent misrepresentation, or mistake will lose that power by affirming the contract.
   b. Delay–If a party has the power to rescind a contract but does not do so within a reasonable time, then the power of avoidance may be lost.
   c. Rights of Third Parties–The power of avoidance is limited by the intervening rights of third parties. For example, the right to rescind may be lost where a third party good faith purchaser acquires an interest in the subject matter of the contract before the right to rescind has been exercised.

KEY TERMS

1. Compensatory damages

2. Incidental damages

3. Consequential damages

4. Benefit-of-the-bargain damages

5. Punitive damages

6. Liquidated damages

7. Foreseeable damages

8. Mitigation of damages

9. Reliance damages

10. Nominal damages

11. Out-of-pocket damages

12. Reformation

13. Specific performance

14. Injunction

15. Restitution

16. Election of remedies

TRUE/FALSE

_____ 1. The primary purpose of contract remedies is to compensate the injured party for the loss resulting from the contract breach by attempting to provide an equivalent of the promised performance.

_____ 2. Loss of value is the difference between the value of the promised performance of the breaching party and the value of the expected performance to the non-breaching party.

_____ 3. Generally the breaching party will not be liable in damages for a loss that was not foreseeable at the time of entering into the contract.

_____ 4. Consequential damages include lost profits and property damage resulting from defective performance.

_____ 5. Even if an unforeseeable, extraordinary loss results from a breach of contract, the injured party may still recover for any ordinary loss resulting from the breach.

_____ 6. In most states, the measure of damages for misrepresentation depends upon whether the misrepresentation was fraudulent or nonfraudulent.

_____ 7. The Restatement provides that punitive damages are not recoverable for a breach of contract unless the breach also gives rise to a tort for which punitive damages are recoverable.

_____ 8. A contract term that sets the amount of damages to be paid in event of a breach of contract is enforceable even if it is not a reasonable forecast of the loss that would result from the breach.

_____ 9. When a breach of contract occurs, the injured party has a duty to take steps to minimize the damages that may be sustained.

_____ 10. Specific performance may be ordered in a contract situation calling for personal services.

_____ 11. A court may grant an equitable remedy, even though the terms of the agreement prohibit such relief, if the court feels an injustice would otherwise occur.

_____ 12. Under the doctrine of election of remedies, the injured party's choice of one available remedy will bar the choice of an additional, consistent remedy.

_____ 13. The power of avoidance may be lost if the party having the power does not rescind within a reasonable time.

_____ 14. Compensatory damages are only recoverable for damages that the party in breach had reason to foresee as a probable result of a breach when the contract was made.

_____ 15. An action to recover damages for breach of contract may be maintained even though the plaintiff has not sustained any loss from the breach.

MULTIPLE CHOICE

_____ 1. Contract remedies are available to protect which of the following interests of the injured party?
   a. Expectation interest
   b. Reliance interest
   c. Restitution interest
   d. All of the above

_____ 2. Which of the following would not be an appropriate measure of monetary damages?
   a. Compensatory damages
   b. Consequential damages
   c. Unforeseeable damages
   d. Incidental damages

_____ 3. Monetary damages are only recoverable for losses that the party in breach had reason to foresee as a probable result of such breach at the time that:
   a. the parties began negotiations.
   b. the parties entered into the contract.
   c. the breach occurred.
   d. none of the above

_____ 4. Acting in reliance on X's intentional misrepresentation as to a drill press's capabilities, Y purchases the press from X for $17,000. Although the value of the press, if it had performed as promised, would be $10,000, its actual delivered value is $4,000. Under the benefit-of-the-bargain rule, Y could recover:
   a. nothing.
   b. $3,000.
   c. $6,000.
   d. $7,000.

_____ 5. Through a clerical error, an annuity policy that should be paying $500 per month is actually paying $50 per month. Upon proper proof of the error, a court of equity might elect which of the following remedies?
   a. Specific performance
   b. An injunction
   c. Reformation
   d. Restitution

_____ 6. An equitable remedy would be granted in which of the following?
   a. Where the remedy at law is inadequate
   b. Where the contract is without consideration
   c. Where relief would cause the defendant unreasonable hardship
   d. Where the contract involves undue influence

_____ 7. In which of the following instances is restitution available as a remedy for breach of contract?
   a. When one party totally fails to perform its obligations
   b. When a party may not enforce the contract because of the statute of frauds
   c. Upon the avoidance of a voidable contract
   d. All of the above

_____ 8. A party with a power of avoidance may lose that power if:
   a. he affirms the contract.
   b. he delays unreasonably in exercising the power of disaffirmance.
   c. the rights of third parties intervene.
   d. all of the above.

_____ 9. *CPA:* Kaye contracted to sell Hodges a building for $310,000. The contract required Hodges to pay the entire amount at closing. Kaye refused to close the sale of the building. Hodges sued Kaye. To what relief is Hodges entitled?
   a. Punitive damages and compensatory damages
   b. Specific performance and compensatory damages
   c. Consequential damages or punitive damages
   d. Specific performance

_____ 10. *CPA:* In general, a clause in a real estate contract entitling the seller to retain the purchaser's down payment as liquidated damages if the purchaser fails to close the transaction is enforceable:
   a. in all cases, when the parties have signed a contract.
   b. if the amount of the down payment bears a reasonable relationship to the probable loss.
   c. as a penalty, if the purchaser intentionally defaults.
   d. only when the seller cannot compel specific performance.

_____ 11. Sam Seller contracts to sell 200 tables to Bill Buyer at a price of $50 a table. Bill repudiates the contract, whereupon Sam sells the tables to Paula Purchaser at a price of $45 a table. Sam's action in selling the chairs to another buyer is known as:
   a. liquidated damages.
   b. specific performance.
   c. mitigation of damages.
   d. restitution.

_____ 12. Central Contracting has a contract to build an office complex for Woodmenn, Inc. A clause in the contract calls for Central to pay $2,000 a day for each day's delay after the date the contract is scheduled for completion.
   a. This is a compensatory damages clause.
   b. This is a liquidated damages clause that may be an unenforceable penalty clause.
   c. Woodmenn will be given the benefit-of-the-bargain in calculating damages.
   d. Woodmenn will only be allowed to recover nominal damages in the case of a breach.

_____ 13. Arthur, a world-famous rock star, has a contract to perform at the Superdome on New Year's Eve. However, he decides he would rather spend the night with his family and friends so he informs the owners of the Superdome.
   a. The owners of the Superdome are entitled to specific performance, because Arthur's services are unique.
   b. The owners of the Superdome will have to wait until after January 1 to sue for breach of contract.
   c. The owners of the Superdome are entitled to damages, but they are not entitled to specific performance.
   d. Because an adequate remedy at law is available here, a court would be unable to issue an injunction prohibiting Arthur from performing at Madison Square Garden on New Year's Eve if they gave him a better offer.

_____ 14. Sam Seller has a contract to provide 100 widgets to Bill Buyer at a price of $10 a widget. Delivery is to be on October 1. Due to unanticipated delays, Sam is unable to get the widgets to Bill until October 2. Bill is not harmed by the delay but sues anyway, because he is angry with Sam.
   a. Sam's failure to deliver the goods on October 1 is a violation of the Code's perfect tender rule, even if it is not a material breach.
   b. Bill cannot sue, because this is not a material breach.
   c. If Bill cannot establish any incidental or consequential damages as a result of the breach, he will only be able to recover nominal damages.
   d. Two of the above are correct, (a) and (c).

_____ 15. Michael pays $500 down on a new computer to be used in the office. The salesperson told him the computer has a 100,000 megabyte memory. Michael learns from other sources that this is blatantly untrue and realizes now that the salesperson induced him to enter into the contract based upon fraud in the inducement. The company refuses to return the down payment. If Michael sues, an appropriate remedy would be:
   a. injunction.
   b. punitive damages.
   c. nominal damages.
   d. rescission and restitution.

SHORT ESSAY

1. Briefly explain "election of remedies."

_____

_____

_____

_____

2. What is the doctrine of mitigation of damages? What will the effect be of the injured party's failure to take the appropriate steps?

_____

_____

_____

_____

3. What are the two major types of equitable remedies? Discuss each type, including an explanation of when each is available.

_____

_____

_____

_____

4. What is restitution? Explain when it might be appropriate.

_____

_____

_____

_____

5. American Link, Inc. hires Jill for one year for $20,000 as an administrative assistant. American fires Jill without cause after one month, and she incurs $300 in fees to find comparable employment which will pay her $18,000 annually. How much and what types of damages, if any, may Jill recover from American?

_____

_____

_____

_____

Part III
Sample Examination

MULTIPLE CHOICE

_____ 1. Damages that are calculated by taking the difference between the value received and the value given are _____ damages.
  a. reliance
  b. nominal
  c. out-of-pocket
  d. benefit-of-the-bargain

_____ 2. A contract involving the exchange of a promise for an act is a(n) _____ contract.
  a. unilateral
  b. bilateral
  c. formal
  d. informal

_____ 3. Article 2 of the UCC applies to sales of:
  a. real property.
  b. secured transactions.
  c. goods.
  d. services.

_____ 4. A minor's oral promise to mow a lawn in exchange for the landowner's promise to pay $25 upon completion is an example of a(n) _____ contract.
  a. unilateral
  b. express
  c. implied
  d. void

5. In consideration of $500 being paid to Amanda by Barbara, Amanda gives Barbara the right to purchase her house for a price of $85,000 any time within 30 days. This is an example of a(n):
   a. firm offer.
   b. option.
   c. implied condition subsequent.
   d. revocation.

6. David owes Charles an undisputed debt of $500. David writes a check for $400, and then puts "paid in full" in the notation section of the check. Charles cashes the check.
   a. This is a valid accord and satisfaction.
   b. This is a valid novation.
   c. Charles can still collect the $100, because there was no consideration given for accepting less than the full amount of the debt.
   d. None of the above

7. Which of the following will invalidate a contract?
   a. Unilateral mistake
   b. A material misstatement of opinion
   c. Undue influence
   d. Failure to read a document

8. Which of the following will terminate an offer?
   a. Rejection
   b. Counteroffer
   c. Death of the offeree
   d. All of the above

9. Words such as "provided that," "on condition that," and "as soon as" usually precede a(n):
   a. express condition.
   b. implied-in-fact condition.
   c. implied-in-law condition.
   d. condition subsequent.

_____ 10. Which of the following is untrue regarding an enforceable restraint on trade?
   a. The purpose must be to protect a property interest of the promisee.
   b. The restraint can be no more extensive than is reasonably necessary to protect the interest.
   c. The restraints frequently involve the sale of a business.
   d. The reasonableness of the restraint has no relationship to the geographic area covered.

_____ 11. Barbara owes Anita $1,000. On June 1, Anita for value assigns the debt to Carly. Thereafter, on June 15, Anita assigns the same right to Darla.
   a. Under the majority rule in the United States, Carly will prevail over Darla.
   b. Under the English rule which is followed in a minority of states, the first assignee to notify Barbara will prevail.
   c. Under the Restatement, the first assignee to notify Barbara will prevail.
   d. Two of the above are correct, (a) and (b).

_____ 12. A(n) _____ does have a right to enforce a contract.
   a. creditor beneficiary
   b. donee beneficiary
   c. incidental beneficiary
   d. (a) and (b), but not (c)

_____ 13. Ron Roadbuilder has a contract to build a highway for the state of Wisconsin. The contract requires that the highway be completed by September 15. If the highway is not completed by that date, the contract requires that Ron be assessed $200 per day in damages. The $200 per day is:
   a. punitive damages.
   b. liquidated damages.
   c. nominal damages.
   d. an illegal penalty.

_____ 14. Daley Builders has a contract to build a house. Daley delegates the plumbing to Paul's Plumbing Company. Paul's Plumbing improperly performs the job.
   a. Daley remains responsible, even though it delegated the duty.
   b. Paul alone has responsibility for the improperly performed plumbing.
   c. Daley can assign its rights under the contract, but cannot delegate its duties.
   d. Two of the above are correct, (a) and (c).

_____ 15. Damages that arise directly out of the breach, such as the costs incurred to acquire the nondelivered performance from another source are known as _____ damages.
   a. consequential
   b. incidental
   c. nominal
   d. reliance

_____ 16. Sarah agrees to go to work for Pro-Com, Inc. upon her graduation from Eastern University on June 12. The contract is for one year, beginning on September 1. She agrees to the contract in a telephone conversation on May 1.
   a. Sarah needs a writing signed by Pro-Com in order to enforce the contract, because the contract cannot by its terms be performed within one year from her graduation on June 12.
   b. Sarah needs a writing signed by Pro-Com in order to enforce the contract, because the contract cannot by its terms be performed within one year from its making on May 1.
   c. Sarah does not need a writing to enforce this contract, because it can be performed within one year of September 1.
   d. This is a contract between merchants, which requires no writing under the UCC statute of frauds.

_____ 17. *CPA:* The president of Deal Corp. wrote to Boyd offering to sell the Deal factory for $300,000. The offer was sent by Deal on June 5 and was received on June 9. The offer stated that it would remain open until December 20. The offer:
   a. constitutes an enforceable option.
   b. may be revoked by Deal any time prior to Boyd's acceptance.
   c. is a firm offer under the UCC but will be irrevocable for only three months.
   d. is a firm offer under the UCC because it is in writing.

_____ 18. *CPA:* Which of the following requires consideration to be binding on the parties?
   a. Material modification of a contract involving the sale of real estate
   b. Ratification of a contract by a person after reaching the age of majority
   c. A written promise signed by a merchant to keep an offer of goods open for 10 days
   d. Material modification of a sale of goods contract under the UCC

_____ 19. *CPA:* Which of the following would be unenforceable because the subject matter is illegal?

    a. A contingent fee charged by an attorney to represent a plaintiff in a negligence action

    b. An arbitration clause in a supply contract

    c. A restrictive covenant in an employment contract prohibiting a former employee from using the employer's trade secrets

    d. An employer's promise not to press embezzlement charges against an employee who agrees to make restitution

_____ 20. *CPA:* If a buyer accepts an offer containing an immaterial unilateral mistake, the resulting contract will be:

    a. void as a matter of law.

    b. void at the election of the buyer.

    c. valid as to both parties.

    d. voidable at the election of the seller.

Try the Web

1. Locate a form contract for:

    a. contract assignment.

    b. sale of motor vehicle.

    Solution:

        Go to http://www.lectlaw.com/

        Select: Legal Forms

        Select: Business & General Forms

        Select: assignment of contracts, or

        Select: contract, sale of motor vehicle

Chapter 19
Introduction to Sales and Lease

PURPOSE

The sale of goods is the most common and important of all commercial transactions. The law of sales was originally part of the law merchant. It was eventually absorbed into the common law and then codified in Article 2 of the Uniform Commercial Code. Article 2 has been adopted in all states, except Louisiana, as well as in the District of Columbia and the Virgin Islands. The critical role of the law of sales is to establish a framework in which present and future exchanges may take place in a predictable, certain, and orderly fashion with a minimum of transaction costs. In this chapter, you begin your study of Article 2 of the UCC, which governs contracts involving the sale of goods and is a specialized branch of both the law of contracts and the law of personal property. Chapter 19 covers the basic definitions and the fundamental principles of UCC Articles 2 and 2A, governing leases of goods.

CHAPTER CHECKPOINTS

After reading and studying the chapter, you should be able to:

1. Define the terms "sale" and "goods" and distinguish a sale of goods from a lease of goods.

2. List and discuss the fundamental principles of Articles 2 and 2A.

3. Identify the topics found in Article 2 that have separate rules that apply to merchants.

4. Summarize the UCC battle of the forms provision and discuss how it varies from the common law mirror image rule.

5. Compare the UCC parol evidence rule and statute of frauds provisions to the common law parol evidence rule and the general statute of frauds provisions discussed earlier in this text.

CHAPTER OUTLINE

I.   Nature of Sales and Leases–The law of sales, governed by UCC Article 2, is a specialized branch of the law of both contracts and personal property. Article 2A of the UCC governs leases of personal property.

    A. Definitions
       1. Goods–Goods are movable, tangible, personal property and include the unborn young of animals, growing crops, and other items attached to real property but removed by the seller. Under Article 2A, minerals cannot be leased prior to their extraction.
       2. Sale–The Code defines a sale as the transfer of title to goods from seller to buyer for a price. The price can be money, services, other goods, or real property.
       3. Lease–Article 2A defines a lease of goods as a "transfer of the right to possession and use of goods for a term in return for consideration, but . . . retention or creation of a security interest is not a lease." The distinction between a lease and a security interest is important to the parties as well as to third persons. If the transaction is determined to be a lease, the residual interest in the goods belongs to the lessor, who need not file publicly to protect this interest. UCC Article 9 governs security interests.
          a. Consumer Leases–If a lease falls within the definition of a consumer lease under UCC Article 2A, the provisions of Article 2A that apply may not be changed by the agreement of the parties to the lease. Consumer leases within Article 2A are those between a lessor who is regularly engaged in the business of leasing or selling goods and lessee who is an individual taking the lease primarily for a personal, family, or household purpose. Total payments under the lease cannot exceed $25,000 to be an Article 2A consumer lease.
          b. Finance Leases–A finance lease generally involves three parties—the lessor and the supplier are separate parties, unlike in the typical lease situation. The lessor in a finance lease provides financing to the lessee for a lease of goods provided by the supplier. As primarily a source of credit, the finance lessor typically has no special expertise as to the goods.
       4. Governing Law–Sales transactions are governed by Article 2 of the Code, but where general contract law has not been specifically modified by the Code, general contract law continues to apply. Transactions not within the scope of Article 2 include employment contracts, service contracts, insurance contracts, contracts involving real property, and contracts for the sale of intangibles such as stocks, bonds, patents, and copyrights. Leases of personal property are governed by Article 2A, but general contract law applies where Article 2A has not modified it.

    B. Fundamental Principles of Article 2 and Article 2A–The purpose of Article 2 is to modernize, clarify, simplify, and make uniform the law of sales. The Code's open-ended drafting, intended to provide flexibility, includes the following fundamental concepts.
       1. Good Faith–All parties to contracts under the Code must perform their obligations in good faith. The Code defines good faith as honesty in fact in the conduct or transaction concerned. In the case of a merchant, it also includes the observance of reasonable commercial standards of fair dealing in the trade.
       2. Unconscionability–Every contract of sale or lease of personal property may be scrutinized by the courts to determine whether in its commercial setting, purpose, and effect, it is unconscionable. The court may refuse to enforce an unconscionable contract or any part of it found to be

unconscionable or may limit its application to prevent an unconscionable result. Procedural unconscionability involves scrutiny for the presence of "bargaining naughtiness." In other words, it involves an analysis of the fairness of the bargaining process or the presence of procedural irregularities, such as burying important terms in the fine print of a contract. Substantive unconscionability deals with the actual terms of the contract and looks for oppressive or grossly unfair provisions, such as an exorbitant price or an unfair exclusion or limitation of contractual remedies. A court finding unconscionability in a consumer lease may award attorney's fees.

3. Expansion of Commercial Practices–The Code places great emphasis on course of dealing and usage of trade in interpreting agreements. A course of dealing is a sequence of previous conduct between the parties that may fairly be regarded as establishing a common basis of understanding for interpreting their expressions and agreement. A usage of trade is a practice or method of dealing regularly observed and followed in a place, vocation, or trade.

4. Sales By and Between Merchants–The Code establishes separate rules that apply to transactions between merchants or involving a merchant as a party. A merchant is a dealer in goods or a person who by his occupation holds himself out as having knowledge or skill peculiar to the goods or practices involved, or who employs an agent or broker whom he holds out as having such knowledge or skill. These rules exact a higher standard of conduct from merchants because of their knowledge of trade and commerce and because merchants as a class generally set these standards for themselves.

5. Liberal Administration of Remedies–The Code provides that its remedies shall be liberally administered in order to place the aggrieved party in as good a position as if the defaulting party had fully performed. It also provides that where no specific remedy is expressly provided, the courts should provide an appropriate remedy.

6. Freedom of Contract–Most Code provisions are not mandatory, but instead permit the parties by agreement to vary or displace them altogether, except that the obligations of good faith, diligence, reasonableness, and care may not be disclaimed by agreement.

7. Validation and Preservation of Sales Contracts–The Code reduces formal requisites to the bare minimum and attempts to preserve agreements whenever the parties manifest an intention to enter into a contract

II. Formation of Sales and Lease Contracts–The Code's approach to validation is to recognize contracts whenever the parties manifest an intent to contract.

A. Manifestation of Mutual Assent–In order for a contract to exist there must be an objective manifestation of mutual assent: an offer and an acceptance.

1. Definiteness of an Offer–At common law, the terms of a contract were required to be definite and complete. The Code, however, provides that a contract does not fail for indefiniteness even though one or more terms may have been omitted. The Code provides standards by which omitted essential terms may be ascertained and supplied, provided the parties intended to enter into a binding agreement.

a. Open Price–The parties may enter into a contract for the sale of goods even though they have no agreement on price. The Code provides that the price be a reasonable one at the time for delivery where the agreement (1) says nothing as to price, (2) provides that the parties shall agree later as to the price and they fail to do so, or (3) fixes the price in terms of some agreed market or other standard or as set by a third person or agency and the price is not so set.

   b. Open Quantity: Output and Requirements Contracts–Output contracts, which are agreements for the buyer to purchase the entire output of a seller for a stated period, and requirements contracts, which are agreements for the seller to supply the buyer with all her requirements of certain goods, are enforceable by the application of an objective standard based on the good faith of both parties. The quantities may not be disproportionate to any stated estimate or to prior output or requirements.

2. Irrevocable Offer–A firm offer is a signed writing by a merchant to hold open an offer for the sale or purchase of goods. Such an offer is irrevocable for the stated period up to a maximum of three months, even if no consideration is given to the merchant offeror for the promise. An option is a contract to hold open an offer; it is binding on the offeror.

3. Variant Acceptances–The Code modifies the common law mirror image rule under which an acceptance cannot vary from the terms of the offer. Under the common law rule, where two businesses exchange preprinted forms with varying terms, no contract exists, even if the parties intend that there be a contract. The Code addresses this battle of the forms problem by focusing on the intent of the parties. The issue then becomes whether the offeree's different or additional terms become part of the contract. If both parties are merchants, the additional terms will be part of the contract if they do not materially alter the agreement and no objection is raised. If either of the parties is not a merchant or if the additional terms do materially alter the offer, they are merely construed as proposals for addition to the contract. Different terms proposed by the offeree will not become part of the contract unless specifically accepted by the offeror. If the offeree expressly makes the acceptance conditioned upon assent to the additional or different terms, no contract is formed.

4. Manner of Acceptance–An offer to make a sales contract invites acceptance in any manner and by any medium reasonable under the circumstances unless indicated otherwise. An offer to buy goods for prompt shipment may be accepted by a prompt promise to ship or by prompt shipment.

5. Auctions–If an auction sale is explicitly advertised or announced to be without reserve, the auctioneer may not withdraw the articles put up for sale unless no bid is made within a reasonable time. Unless the sale is advertised as being without reserve, it is with reserve.

B. Consideration–The Code has relaxed the common law rule in several respects. A contract for the sale of goods can be modified without new consideration. In addition, a written waiver or renunciation signed and delivered by the aggrieved party discharges a claim of right arising out of a breach, even if there is no consideration. A firm offer is not revocable for lack of consideration.

C. Form of the Contract

1. Statute of Frauds–The Code provides that a contract for the sale of goods costing $500 or more is not enforceable unless there is some writing (or electronic record) sufficient to evidence the existence of a contract between the parties. For leases, the figure is $1,000 or more. (See Chapter 48 for rules regarding electronic contracts, records and signatures).

   a. Modification of Contracts–Under Article 2 but not 2A, an agreement modifying a contract must be in writing if the resulting contract is within the statute of frauds. Conversely, a modification that takes a contract outside of the statute of frauds may be oral.

  b. Written Compliance–The statute of frauds compliance provisions under the Code are more liberal than the rules under general contract law.   The Code requires some writing (1) sufficient to indicate that a contract has been made between the parties, (2) signed by the party against whom enforcement is sought or by her authorized agent or broker, and (3) including a term specifying the quantity of goods.   Under the Code a writing may be sufficient even if it omits or incorrectly states an agreed-upon term.

  c. Exceptions–An oral contract for the sale of goods is enforceable against a party who admits in his pleading, testimony, or otherwise in court that a contract was made.   Enforcement is limited to the quantity of goods admitted.   An oral contract for specially manufactured goods is also enforceable against the buyer.   Finally, delivery and acceptance of part of the goods or payment of part of the price and acceptance of the payment validates the contract but only for the goods that have been delivered and accepted or for which payment has been accepted.

 2. Parol Evidence–Contractual terms that are set forth in a writing intended by the parties as a final expression of their agreement may not be contradicted by evidence of any prior agreement or of a contemporaneous oral agreement, but under the Code they may be explained or supplemented by: (a) course of dealing, usage of trade, or course of performance, and (b) evidence of consistent, additional terms, unless the writing was intended to be complete and exclusive.

KEY TERMS

1. Goods
2. Sale
3. Consumer lease
4. Finance lease
5. Good faith
6. Procedural unconscionability
7. Substantive unconscionability
8. Course of dealing
9. Usage of trade
10. Merchant
11. Freedom of contract
12. Option
13. Firm offer
14. Auction

TRUE/FALSE

_____ 1. A sale is defined as the transfer of title of goods from seller to buyer for a price.

_____ 2. Principles of general contract law govern where not been specifically modified by UCC Article 2.

_____ 3. "Goods" include unborn young of animals and growing crops.

_____ 4. The doctrine of unconscionability permits the courts to resolve issues of unfairness explicitly on that basis without recourse to formalistic rules or legal fictions.

_____ 5. Good faith means honesty in fact in the conduct or transaction concerned.

_____ 6. A merchant's firm offer is irrevocable for the stated period, not to exceed 3 months, even though no consideration is given to the merchant-offeror for that promise.

_____ 7. The Code has adopted the common law mirror image rule stating that an acceptance cannot deviate from the terms of the offer.

_____ 8. Under the Code, a unilateral offer must be accepted by a prompt shipment of the goods accompanied by notice to the buyer within a reasonable time.

_____ 9. Under the Code, a modification of an existing contract must be supported by consideration to be binding.

_____ 10. Under the Code, if a contract that was previously within the statute of frauds is modified so as to no longer fall within it, the modified contract must be in writing.

_____ 11. A farmer who grows corn is a merchant with respect to corn.

_____ 12. If an auction is not announced as being "without reserve" it is, under the Code, "with reserve."

_____ 13. Firm offers are not revocable for lack of consideration.

_____ 14. When Article 2 applies, parol evidence may be used to establish a course of dealing.

_____ 15. For a sale of goods contract to be enforceable under the Code, it must specify the price.

MULTIPLE CHOICE

_____ 1. Which of the following transactions would be governed by Article 2 of the UCC?
   a.   The sale of a house
   b.   The sale of a typewriter
   c.   The lease of a typewriter
   d.   A contract of employment

_____ 2. Which of the following would be governed by Article 2A of the UCC?
   a.   Employment contract
   b.   Service contract
   c.   Lease transaction involving a lessor, a lessee, and a supplier of goods
   d.   Lease of a building for two years

_____ 3. For a merchant, "good faith" requires:
   a.   "honesty in fact in the conduct or transaction concerned."
   b.   "reasonable commercial standards of fair dealing in the trade."
   c.   neither (a) nor (b).
   d.   both (a) and (b).

_____ 4. A "merchant" is defined by the Code as a person:
    a. who is a dealer in the goods involved.
    b. who by his occupation holds himself out as having knowledge or skill peculiar to the goods or practices involved.
    c. who employs an agent or broker whom he holds out as having knowledge or skill peculiar to the goods or practices involved.
    d. all of the above

_____ 5. Which of the following is not a requirement for a consumer lease?
    a. The lessor be regularly engaged in the business of leasing or selling goods
    b. The lessee be an individual, not an organization
    c. The lessee take the lease interest primarily for a personal, family, or household purpose
    d. The total payments under the lease not exceed $15,000

_____ 6. Under the Code, if a nonmerchant seller's acceptance contains a term in addition to those contained in the nonmerchant buyer's offer, the additional term is:
    a. construed as a proposal for an addition to the contract.
    b. ignored.
    c. construed as part of the contract even if it materially alters the agreement.
    d. construed as part of the contract unless the buyer expressly objects to its inclusion.

_____ 7. Under the Code, which of the following requires consideration to be binding?
    a. A modification of an existing contract
    b. A merchant's firm offer
    c. A contract to sell goods
    d. A written discharge of a claim after a breach of contract

_____ 8. In order to comply with the Code's version of the statute of frauds, the party seeking to enforce the contract must have a writing that:
    a. is sufficient to indicate a contract has been made.
    b. is signed by the party sought to be charged.
    c. indicates the quantity of goods to be exchanged.
    d. all of the above

_____ 9. Under the Code, an auction sale:
    a. operates under the assumption that the seller will be involved in the bidding process.
    b. is with reserve unless advertised as being without reserve.
    c. forbids a bidder from retracting a bid once properly made.
    d. allows retraction of a bid at any time prior to the auctioneer's acceptance, and a retraction revives the previous bid.

_____ 10. A practice or method of dealing regularly observed and followed in a place, vocation, or trade describes:
   a. a "usage of trade."
   b. a "course of performance."
   c. a "course of dealing."
   d. an express term in a contract.

_____ 11. A signed writing by a merchant to hold open an offer is:
   a. an option.
   b. a firm offer.
   c. parol evidence of an agreement.
   d. none of the above.

_____ 12. Under the UCC statute of frauds, which of the following must be included in the required memoranda?
   a. The signatures of both parties
   b. The shipment terms
   c. The quantity of goods sold
   d. The time for delivery

_____ 13. The UCC statute of frauds applies to contracts for the sale of goods of a price of _____ or more.
   a. $100
   b. $300
   c. $500
   d. $5,000

_____ 14. *CPA:* Under the UCC Sales Article, which of the following statements is correct concerning a contract involving a merchant seller and a nonmerchant buyer?
   a. Only the seller is obligated to perform the contract in good faith.
   b. The contract will be either a sale or return or sale on approval contract.
   c. The contract may **not** involve the sale of personal property with a price of more than $500.
   d. Whether the UCC Sales Article is applicable does **not** depend on the price of the goods involved.

_____ 15. *CPA:* To satisfy the UCC statute of frauds regarding the sale of goods, which of the following must generally be in writing?
   a. Designation of the parties as buyer and seller
   b. Delivery terms
   c. Quantity of the goods
   d. Warranties to be made

SHORT ESSAY

1. When is Article 2 of the UCC applicable? When is it inapplicable?

_____

_____

_____

_____

2. Define the terms "sale" and "goods."

_____

_____

_____

_____

3. Define and briefly explain "unconscionability."

_____

_____

_____

_____

4. What is a "firm offer?" What are its characteristics?

_____

_____

_____

_____

5. If the parties have an oral contract for the sale of 100 bushels of wheat at a price of $4.50 per bushel and later orally agree to increase the quantity to 150 bushels at the same price per bushel, is the agreement, as modified, enforceable? Why or why not?

_____

_____

_____

_____

Chapter 20
Performance

PURPOSE

In a sales contract, as in other contracts, the obligations of the parties are determined by their contractual agreement. The contract may expressly state whether the seller must deliver the goods prior to the buyer's payment of the price, or whether the buyer must pay the price before the seller must deliver the goods. However, if there is no specific agreement of the parties, the particulars will be supplied by the Code, common law, course of dealing, usage of trade, and course of performance. Performance is the carrying out of contractual obligations according to the terms of the contract so that the obligations are discharged. The basic obligation of the seller in a contract for the sale of goods is to transfer and deliver goods that conform to the contract terms. The basic obligation of the buyer is to accept and pay for the goods in accordance with the contract. In a lease, the basic obligation of the lessor is to transfer possession of the goods for the lease term. The basic obligation of the lessee is to pay the agreed rent. In this chapter, you study the Code provisions that apply to the performance by the buyer and seller in a sales contract. These provisions vary depending upon the contract terms and whether there has been a breach by one of the parties. You also study the circumstances under which the buyer or the seller may be excused from contractual obligations.

CHAPTER CHECKPOINTS

After reading and studying the chapter, you should be able to:

1. Distinguish a shipment contract from a destination contract and discuss the Code provisions regarding tender in each type of contract.

2. Explain the perfect tender rule and three limitations on it.

3. Distinguish between rejection and revocation of acceptance by the buyer and discuss the circumstances under which the buyer may exercise each of these rights.

4. Identify and discuss the excuses for nonperformance.

5. Discuss how a breach by one of the parties affects the obligations of performance by the other in various fact situations.

CHAPTER OUTLINE

A. Performance by the Seller–Unless the parties have agreed otherwise, tender of performance by one party is a condition to performance by the other party. Tender of delivery requires that the seller put and hold goods that conform to the contract at the buyer's disposition and that he give the buyer reasonable notification to enable him to take delivery. Tender must be made at a reasonable time and be kept open for a reasonable period of time.

   1. Time of Tender–Tender must be made at a reasonable time, and the goods tendered must be kept available for the period reasonably necessary to enable the buyer to take possession of them. If no definite time for delivery is fixed by the terms of the contract, the seller is allowed a reasonable time after entering into the contract within which to tender the goods to the buyer. The buyer has a reasonable time within which to accept delivery. A contract may not be performed piecemeal or in installments unless the parties so agree.

   2. Place of Tender–If no place is specified in the contract, the place for delivery is the seller's place of business or, if he has none, his residence. If the contract is for the sale of identified goods that the parties know at the time of making the contract are located elsewhere than the seller's place of business or residence, the location of the goods is the place for delivery. Any agreements by the parties using delivery terms, such as F.O.B. place of shipment, determine the place where the seller must tender delivery of the goods.

      a. Shipment Contracts–The delivery terms "F.O.B. place of shipment," "F.A.S. seller's port," "C.I.F.," and "C. & F." indicate shipment contracts. In these cases, the seller's tender of performance occurs at the point of shipment, provided the seller meets certain specified conditions designed to protect the interests of the absent buyer. The seller is required to: (1) deliver the goods to a carrier; (2) make a contract for their transportation that is reasonable according to the nature of the goods and the other circumstances; (3) obtain and promptly deliver or tender to the buyer any document necessary to enable the buyer to obtain possession of the goods from the carrier; and (4) promptly notify the buyer of the shipment.

      b. Destination Contracts–The terms "F.O.B. city of buyer," "ex-ship," and "no arrival, no sale" indicate a destination contract. A destination contract requires the seller to tender delivery of conforming goods at a specified destination. The seller must place the goods at the buyer's disposition and give the buyer reasonable notice to enable him to take delivery. The seller must also tender any necessary documents of title.

      c. Goods Held by Bailee–The seller may either tender a document of title or obtain an acknowledgment by the bailee of the buyer's right to possess the goods where they are in the possession of a bailee and they are to be delivered without being moved.

3. Perfect Tender Rule–Under this UCC rule, the seller's tender of performance must conform exactly to the contract. If the goods or the tender fail in any respect to conform to the contract, the buyer may (1) reject the whole lot, (2) accept the whole lot, or (3) accept any commercial unit or units and reject the rest. There are three qualifications of the buyer's right to reject the goods upon the seller's failure to comply with the perfect tender rule.
    a. Agreement Between the Parties–The parties may agree to limit operation of the perfect tender rule.
    b. Cure by the Seller–When the time for performance under the contract has not expired or when the seller has shipped nonconforming goods in the belief that the nonconforming tender would be acceptable, the Code recognizes that a seller may cure or correct the nonconforming tender.
    c. Installment Contracts–The buyer generally does not have to pay any part of the price of the goods until the entire quantity specified in the contract has been delivered or tendered to her. However, an installment contract expressly provides for delivery of the goods in separate lots or installments and usually for payment of the price in installments. If the contract is silent as to payment, the seller may demand payment for each lot if the price can be apportioned. The buyer may reject a nonconforming installment if it substantially impairs the value of that installment and cannot be cured. When the nonconformity or default of one or more of the installments substantially impairs the value of the whole contract, the buyer can treat the breach as a breach of the whole contract.

B. Performance by the Buyer–A buyer is obligated to accept conforming goods and to pay for them according to the contract terms. Unless otherwise agreed, payment or tender of payment by the buyer is a condition to the seller's duty to tender and to complete any delivery.
    1. Inspection–Unless otherwise agreed, the buyer has a right to inspect the goods before payment or acceptance to determine whether they conform to the contract. In a C.O.D. contract, payment must be made prior to inspection, but payment in such cases is not acceptance of the goods. The buyer is allowed a reasonable time to inspect the goods and may lose the right to reject them or to revoke acceptance by failing to inspect the goods within a reasonable time.
    2. Rejection–This is a manifestation by the buyer of unwillingness to become the owner of the goods. It must be made within a reasonable time after the goods have been tendered or delivered. It is not effective unless the buyer reasonably notifies the seller. A merchant buyer who has rightfully rejected goods is obligated to follow reasonable instructions from the seller about disposing of the goods, when the seller has no business or agent at the place of rejection. If the rejected goods are perishable or threaten to decline in value speedily, the buyer is obligated to make reasonable efforts to sell them for the seller's account.
    3. Acceptance–Acceptance means the buyer is willing to become the owner of the goods tendered or delivered by the seller. Acceptance precludes any later rejection of the goods accepted. Acceptance may be express or implied. It occurs when the buyer, after reasonable opportunity to inspect: (1) signifies to the seller that the goods conform to the contract, (2) signifies to the seller the goods will be taken in spite of their nonconformity, or (3) fails to make an effective rejection of the goods. Acceptance of any part of a commercial unit is acceptance of the entire unit.

4. Revocation of Acceptance—The buyer may rescind acceptance of the goods based upon their nonconformity if the nonconformity substantially impairs their value and acceptance had been based on a reasonable but false assumption that the seller would cure the nonconformity or acceptance was made without discovering a hard-to-find nonconformity. Revocation is not effective until notice is given to the seller, within a reasonable time. Revocation of acceptance gives the buyer the same rights and duties with respect to the goods as if they had been rejected.

5. Obligation of Payment—In the absence of an agreement, payment is due at the time and place the buyer is to receive the goods, even though the place of shipment is the place of delivery. Unless the seller demands cash, tender of payment may be by any means current in the ordinary course of business.

C. Obligations of Both Parties—If parties to a sales or lease of goods contract fail to allocate risks that future events may or may not occur, the Code contains provisions which allocate these risks and relieve the parties from the obligation of full performance under the contract.

1. Casualty to Identified Goods—If the contract is for goods that are identified when the contract was made, and those goods are totally lost or damaged without fault of either party and before the risk of loss has passed to the buyer, the contract is avoided. Each party is excused from its performance obligation under the contract. Where the goods are partially destroyed, the buyer has the option to avoid the contract or to accept the goods with due allowance for the deterioration or deficiency in quantity.

2. Nonhappening of Presupposed Condition—The seller is excused from the duty of performance on the nonoccurrence of presupposed conditions that were a basic assumption of the contract, unless the seller has expressly assumed the risk. The Code excuses performance when performance may not be literally impossible, but where it is commercially impracticable. This requires more than mere hardship or increased cost. The impracticability must be a result of an unforeseen supervening event not within the contemplation of the parties at the time of contracting.

3. Substituted Performance—Where neither party is at fault and the agreed manner of delivery of goods becomes commercially impracticable, a substituted manner of performance, if commercially reasonable, must be tendered and accepted.

4. Right to Adequate Assurance of Performance—When reasonable grounds for insecurity arise regarding either party's performance, the other party may demand a written assurance and suspend his own performance until he receives that assurance. If the assurance is not received within a reasonable time not exceeding thirty days, the contract is repudiated.

5. Right to Cooperation—Where performance is dependent upon one party's cooperation which is not forthcoming, the other party is excused regarding delay in performance and may either proceed to perform in any reasonable manner or may treat the failure to cooperate as a breach.

6. Anticipatory Repudiation—This is a clear indication by either contracting party that he is unwilling or unable to perform his duties under the contract before performance is due. If the anticipatory repudiation substantially impairs the value of the contract, the aggrieved party may (1) await performance for a commercially reasonable time or (2) resort to any remedy for breach.

KEY TERMS

1. Performance	11. Perfect tender rule
2. Tender of delivery	12. Cure
3. Shipment contract	13. Installment contract
4. F.O.B.	14. Inspection
5. F.A.S.	15. Rejection
6. C.I.F.	16. Acceptance
7. C. & F.	17. Revocation of acceptance
8. Destination contract	18. Identified goods
9. Ex-ship	19. Commercial impracticability
10. No arrival, no sale	20. Anticipatory repudiation

TRUE/FALSE

_____ 1. Tender of performance by one party is a condition to performance by the other party.

_____ 2. In a tender of delivery, the seller makes available to the buyer goods that conform to the contract.

_____ 3. Under the Code, the seller must tender all of the goods purchased under the contract in a single delivery, and payment by the buyer is due on such tender, unless the parties specify otherwise in the contract.

_____ 4. Unless the parties agree otherwise, the buyer has a right to inspect the goods before payment or acceptance.

_____ 5. Under a shipment contract, the seller need only deliver the goods to a carrier and make a reasonable contract for their shipment.

_____ 6. Under the Code, the operation of the perfect tender rule may not be limited by agreement of the parties to the contract.

_____ 7. If a buyer refuses a tender of nonconforming goods without informing the seller of the nature of the defect, he cannot then assert that defect as a breach of contract by the seller if the defect was curable.

_____ 8. If a nonconforming installment of goods substantially impairs the value of the whole contract, then the buyer can treat the breach of the installment as a breach of the whole contract.

_____ 9. The buyer may lose the right to revoke acceptance in a C.O.D. shipment by failing to inspect the goods within a reasonable time.

_____ 10. If goods that were identified when the contract was made are totally lost or damaged without fault of either party and before risk of loss passes to the buyer, the contract is avoided.

_____ 11. A party is not excused from the duty of performance under a contract upon the nonoccurrence of a presupposed condition unless that condition was a basic assumption underlying the contract.

_____ 12. A seller may "cure" a nonconforming tender anytime before the time for performance.

_____ 13. Under a shipment contract, a seller is required to tender delivery of the goods to a carrier for delivery to the buyer.

_____ 14. The delivery terms "F.O.B. city of buyer," "ex-ship," and "no arrival, no sale" indicate that the contract is a shipment contract.

_____ 15. Where a practical alternative exists, neither seller nor buyer is excused from a sales contract on the grounds that delivery in the express manner provided in the contract is impossible.

MULTIPLE CHOICE

_____ 1. A party may fulfill her contractual duty of performance and place the other party in default by all of the following except by:
   a. performing according to the contract.
   b. tendering her performance according to the contract.
   c. assuming that the other party will not perform according to the contract.
   d. being excused from tender of performance under the contract.

_____ 2. Tender of conforming goods by the seller entitles him to:
   a. acceptance of the goods by the buyer.
   b. payment of the contract price by the buyer.
   c. both acceptance of the goods and payment of the contract price by the buyer.
   d. neither acceptance of the goods nor payment of the contract price by the buyer.

_____ 3. Which of the following is not correct?
   a. The seller has a duty to keep goods tendered for a period reasonably necessary for the buyer to take possession of them.
   b. A destination contract requires a seller to tender conforming goods at a specified destination.
   c. Unless otherwise agreed, a contract is performable in installments.
   d. None of the above is correct.

_____ 4. If either the tender of delivery or the goods fail in any respect to conform to the contract, the buyer may:
   a.   reject the whole lot.
   b.   accept the whole lot.
   c.   accept any commercial unit(s) and reject the rest.
   d.   all of the above.

_____ 5. Under a destination contract, the seller must do all of the following except:
   a.   place the goods at the buyer's disposition at the specified destination.
   b.   give the buyer reasonable notice to enable the buyer to take delivery.
   c.   tender the necessary documents of title if such documents are involved in the transaction.
   d.   inspect the goods upon arrival at the specified destination to ensure that they are conforming.

_____ 6. Under a shipment contract, the seller is required to do which of the following?
   a.   Deliver the goods to a carrier
   b.   Promptly notify the buyer of the shipment
   c.   Provide the buyer with any necessary documents to obtain possession of the goods
   d.   All of the above

_____ 7. The buyer must reject nonconforming goods under the perfect tender rule except where:
   a.   the parties agree to limit the buyer's right to reject nonconforming goods.
   b.   the seller refuses to cure a nonconforming tender of delivery.
   c.   the nonconformity of an installment does not substantially impair the value of the whole contract.
   d.   all of the above

_____ 8. Which of the following is an incorrect statement concerning a buyer's right to inspect goods upon delivery?
   a.   Unless the parties agree otherwise, the buyer has the right to inspect the goods before payment or acceptance.
   b.   If the contract requires payment for the goods before acceptance, payment is required before inspection and operates as an acceptance of the goods.
   c.   The buyer may lose the right to reject or revoke acceptance of nonconforming goods by failing to inspect them within a reasonable time.
   d.   The buyer must bear the expenses of inspection, but may recover those costs from the seller if the goods prove to be nonconforming and are rejected.

_____ 9. After rejection of nonperishable goods, a merchant buyer who has received no instructions from the seller within a reasonable time after notice of rejection may:
   a.   store the goods for the seller's account.
   b.   reship the goods to the seller.
   c.   resell the goods for the seller's account.
   d.   all of the above.

_____ 10. An effective acceptance occurs when the buyer:
   a. signifies to the seller that the goods conform to the contract.
   b. signifies to the seller the intention to keep the goods.
   c. fails to make an effective rejection of the goods.
   d. all of the above.

_____ 11. Acceptance of the goods precludes a buyer from:
   a. rejecting the goods.
   b. revoking his acceptance.
   c. suing the seller for breach for any nonconformity that could not be reasonably discovered by inspection.
   d. all of the above.

_____ 12. If the goods contracted for are partially destroyed before risk of loss has passed to the buyer:
   a. the contract is avoided.
   b. the contract is voidable at the buyer's option.
   c. the contract is voidable at the seller's option.
   d. the contract is neither void nor voidable at either party's election.

_____ 13. Which of the following would indicate a shipment contract?
   a. Ex-ship
   b. No arrival, no sale
   c. C.I.F.
   d. All of the above

_____ 14. **CPA:** Jefferson Hardware ordered 300 Ram hammers from Ajax Hardware. Ajax accepted the order in writing. On the final date allowed for delivery, Ajax discovered it did not have enough Ram hammers to fill the order. Instead, Ajax sent 300 Strong hammers. Ajax stated on the invoice that the shipment was sent only as an accommodation. Which of the following statements is correct?
   a. Ajax's note of accommodation cancels the contract between Jefferson and Ajax.
   b. Jefferson's order can only be accepted by Ajax's shipment of the goods ordered.
   c. Ajax's shipment of Strong hammers is a breach of contract.
   d. Ajax's shipment of Strong hammers is a counteroffer and **no** contract exists between Jefferson and Ajax.

_____ 15. **CPA:** With regard to a contract governed by the UCC Sales Article, which of the following statements is correct?
   a. Merchants and nonmerchants are treated alike.
   b. The contract may involve the sale of any type of personal property.
   c. The obligations of the parties to the contract must be performed in good faith.
   d. The contract must involve the sale of goods for a price of more than $500.

SHORT ESSAY

1. What constitutes "tender"?

_____

_____

_____

_____

2. What must a seller do to discharge her obligation to tender delivery of goods under a shipment contract?

_____

_____

_____

_____

3. What is meant by the "perfect tender rule"?

_____

_____

_____

_____

4. Contrast rejection and revocation of acceptance. Explain a buyer's rights under each?

_____

_____

_____

_____

5. Under what circumstances may a buyer revoke acceptance?

_____

_____

_____

_____

Chapter 21
Transfer of Title and Risk of Loss

PURPOSE

The common law historically determined the rights and duties of the buyer and seller arising out of a sales contract based upon the principle of title. Under the Code, title has some significance, but the Code approaches each legal issue arising in a sales contract on its own merits. It provides separate and specific rules to control various transactional situations. In this chapter, you study the Code rules governing transfer of title and other property rights, the passage of risk of loss, and the transfer of goods sold in bulk.

CHAPTER CHECKPOINTS

After reading and studying this chapter, you should be able to:

1. Distinguish between a shipment contract and a destination contract and discuss the Code rules for risk of loss for each type of contract.

2. Explain the rules for passage of title and risk of loss in situations where there is no movement of the goods and (a) the seller is a merchant, (b) the seller is not a merchant, (c) there is a document of title, and (d) there is no document of title.

3. Distinguish between a void title and a voidable title and discuss the Code rule that applies when the owner of goods entrusts them to a merchant who then sells them to a good faith purchaser in the ordinary course of business.

4. Distinguish between a sale on approval and a sale or return and give the Code rule for risk of loss in each situation.

5. Define the term "bulk transfer" and summarize the Code provisions regarding such a transfer of assets.

CHAPTER OUTLINE

A. Transfer of Title–Transfer of title is fundamental to the existence of a sale of goods. Title cannot pass under a sales contract until existing goods have been identified to the contract. Future goods cannot be the subject of a present sale. If a buyer rejects the goods, title goes back to the seller. Title does not pass under a lease; the lessee obtains the right to possess and use the goods for a period of time in exchange for consideration..

   1. Identification–This is the designation of specific goods as goods to which the contract of sale refers. Identification may be made at any time and in any manner agreed upon by the parties. Identification may be made by either the buyer of seller. If the goods are fungible, identification of a share of undivided goods occurs when the contract is entered into.

      a. Security Interest–The Code defines "security interest" as an interest in personal property or fixtures that ensures payment or performance of an obligation. Security interests are governed by Article 9 of the Code.

      b. Insurable Interest–For a contract or policy of insurance to be valid, the insured must have an insurable interest in the subject matter. The Code extends an insurable interest to a buyer's interest in goods that have been identified to the contract, enabling the buyer to purchase insurance on the goods. The seller also has an insurable interest in the goods while he has title or a security interest in them. A lessor retains an insurable interest in goods if the lessee has an option to buy them.

   2. Passage of Title–Title passes when the parties intend it to pass, provided the goods are in existence and have been identified. If there is no explicit agreement of the parties, the Code controls.

      a. Physical Movement of the Goods–When delivery is to be made by moving the goods, title passes at the time and place where the seller completes performance with respect to delivery. When and where delivery occurs depends upon whether the contract is a shipment contract or a destination contract. In a shipment contract, the seller is required to tender delivery of the goods to a carrier for delivery to the buyer. Title passes to the buyer at the time and place that the seller delivers the goods to the carrier for shipment to the buyer. In a destination contract, the seller is required to tender delivery of the goods at a particular destination. Title passes to the buyer on tender of the goods at the destination. Tender means that the seller offers conforming goods to the buyer and gives the buyer notice that the goods are available.

      b. No Movement of the Goods–When delivery is to be made without moving the goods, title passes either (a) on delivery of a document of title where the contract calls for delivery of such a document; or (b) at the time and place of contracting where the goods at that time have been identified either by the seller or the buyer as the goods to which the contract refers and no documents are to be delivered. Where the goods are not identified at the time of contracting, title passes when the goods are identified.

   3. Power to Transfer Title–A seller who is the rightful owner or is authorized to sell the goods has the *right* to transfer title. In some situations unauthorized sellers may have the *power* to transfer good title to certain buyers. In general, the purchaser of goods obtains such title as the transferor either has or had the power to transfer. A purported sale by a thief or finder or ordinary bailee of goods does not transfer title to the purchaser. However, to encourage and make secure good faith acquisitions of goods, it is necessary that bona fide (good faith) purchasers for value be

protected under certain circumstances.   A good faith purchaser is defined as one who acts honestly, gives value, and takes the goods without notice or knowledge of any defect in the title of the transferor.

    a. Void and Voidable Title to Goods–A void title is no title. A thief or finder of goods has no title and can transfer none. A voidable title is one acquired under circumstances that permit the former owner to rescind the transfer and revest herself with title, as in the case of mistake, common duress, undue influence, fraud in the inducement, misrepresentation, or sale by a person without contractual capacity. If a buyer who has voidable title should resell the goods to a good faith purchaser for value, before the seller rescinds transfer of title, the good faith purchaser acquires good title, and the original seller's right of rescission is cut off.

    b. Entrusting of Goods to a Merchant–The Code protects buyers of goods in the ordinary course of business from merchants who deal in goods of that kind, where the owner has entrusted possession of the goods to the merchant. Buyers in the ordinary course of business are persons who buy in ordinary course, in good faith, and without knowledge that the sales to them are in violation of anyone's ownership rights. When merchants wrongfully sell items that have been entrusted to them, as between a good faith purchaser in the ordinary course of business and the owner who entrusted the goods to the merchant, the good faith purchaser from the merchant is preferred. The original owner's recourse is against the merchant for money damages; the original owner cannot get back the goods. However, the Code does not protect the bona fide purchaser from a merchant when the goods have been entrusted to the merchant by a thief or finder or by someone who is completely unauthorized to entrust the goods.

B. Risk of Loss–This term addresses the allocation of loss between seller and buyer where the goods have been damaged, destroyed, or lost without the fault of either the seller or the buyer.

    1. Risk of Loss Where There is a Breach–Where one party breaches the contract, the Code places the risk of loss on that party.

        a. Breach by the Seller–If the seller ships to the buyer goods that do not conform to the contract, the risk of loss remains on the seller until the buyer has accepted the goods or the seller has remedied the defect. Under Article 2A, leases of goods have a similar rule.

        b. Breach by the Buyer–Where conforming goods have been identified to the contract that the buyer repudiates or breaches before risk of loss has passed to the buyer, the seller may treat the risk of loss as resting on the buyer "for a commercially reasonable time" to the extent of any deficiency in the seller's effective insurance coverage.

    2. Risk of Loss in Absence of a Breach–Where there is no breach, risk of loss may be allocated by agreement of the parties.

        a. Agreement of the Parties–The parties may, by agreement, shift the allocation of risk of loss or divide the risk between them.

b. Trial Sales–Under the Code there are two types of trial sales: a sale on approval and a sale or return. Unless otherwise agreed, if trial-sale goods are delivered primarily for the buyer's use, the transaction is a sale on approval; if they are delivered primarily for resale, it is a sale or return. In a sale on approval, possession of, but not title to, the goods is transferred to the buyer for a stated period of time or, if none is stated, for a reasonable time. Both title and risk of loss remain with the seller until "approval" or acceptance of the goods by the buyer. In a sale or return, the goods are sold and delivered to the buyer with an option to return them to the seller. The risk of loss is on the buyer, who also has title until she revests it in the seller by a return of the goods. A consignment is a delivery of possession of personal property to an agent for sale by the agent. Under the Code, it is regarded as a sale or return.

c. Contracts Involving Carriers–If the contract does not require the seller to deliver the goods at a particular destination but merely to the carrier (a shipment contract), risk of loss passes to the buyer when the goods are delivered to the common carrier. If the seller is required to deliver the goods to a particular destination (a destination contract), risk of loss passes to the buyer at the destination when the goods are tendered to the buyer.

d. Goods in Possession of Bailee–When goods held by a bailee are to be delivered without being moved, the risk of loss passes to the buyer (1) if a negotiable document of title is involved, when the buyer receives the document; (2) if a nonnegotiable document of title is involved, when the document is tendered to the buyer; and (3) if no documents of title are used, either (a) when the seller tenders to the buyer written directions to the bailee to deliver the goods to the buyer or (b) when the bailee acknowledges the buyer's right to possession.

e. All Other Sales–If the seller is a merchant, risk of loss passes to the buyer on the buyer's receipt of the goods. If the seller is not a merchant, it passes on tender of the goods from the seller to the buyer.

C. Bulk Sales–Article 6 of the Code applies to such sales and defines a bulk transfer as a transfer not in the ordinary course of the transferor's business of a major part of its inventory. Bulk sales law is designed to prevent debtors from secretly liquidating all or a major part of their assets by bulk sale and concealing or diverting the proceeds of the sale without paying their creditors. In 1988, drafters of the Code recommended that Article 6 be repealed by the states because the changes in the business and legal contexts in which sales are conducted have made regulation of bulk sales unnecessary. More than two-thirds of the states have repealed UCC Article 6. A few states have enacted revised Article 6, which is designed to afford better protection to creditors and minimize obstacles to good faith transactions.

KEY TERMS

1. Identification

2. Fungible

3. Security interest

4. Insurable interest

5. Shipment contract

6. Destination contract

7. Good faith purchaser

8. Buyer in ordinary course of business

9. Entrustment

10. Risk of loss

11. Sale on approval

12. Sale or return

13. Consignment

14. Bulk transfer

TRUE/FALSE

_____ 1. If a buyer's rejection of conforming goods is not justified, title to the goods remains with the buyer.

_____ 2. A security interest in personal property ensures payment or performance of an obligation.

_____ 3. Under the Code, only those persons with title to or a lien on goods have an insurable interest in those goods.

_____ 4. When goods are to be moved to be delivered, title passes whenever the seller completes performance with reference to delivery of the goods.

_____ 5. A seller may have the power but not the right to sell goods in its possession to certain buyers.

_____ 6. If a minor sells goods to a good faith purchaser for value, the Code, as the common law, allows the minor to disaffirm and retake the goods.

_____ 7. A buyer in the ordinary course of business is defined by the Code as one who acts honestly, gives value, and takes without notice or knowledge of any defect in the title of the transferor.

_____ 8. If risk of loss is placed on the seller, then the seller has no right to recover the purchase price for lost or damaged goods from the buyer.

_____ 9. Under both the common law and the Code, risk of loss is determined by ownership of the goods and whether title has been transferred.

_____ 10. Under the Code, the parties to an agreement cannot allocate the risk of loss between themselves.

_____ 11. In a lease of goods under Article 2A, the lessee receives title to the goods for a period of time in return for consideration.

_____ 12. Under the Code, a sale on consignment is regarded as a sale or return.

_____ 13. If the seller is required to deliver the goods to a carrier for delivery to the buyer, there is a destination contract.

_____ 14. If a seller breaches a contract by shipping nonconforming goods to the buyer, risk of loss remains on the buyer until the buyer properly returns the goods to the seller.

_____ 15. In the case of a nonmerchant seller, risk of loss passes to the buyer upon tender of the goods.

MULTIPLE CHOICE

_____ 1. A destination contract requires the seller to deliver the goods to a particular destination, and title passes to the buyer:
   a. at the time and place that the seller delivers the goods to the carrier for shipment to the buyer's place of business.
   b. upon tender of the goods to the buyer at that destination.
   c. upon delivery of a document of title.
   d. at the time and place that the contract is entered.

_____ 2. A seller has an insurable interest in goods if:
   a. the goods have been identified as the goods to which the contract of sale refers.
   b. the seller has title to the goods.
   c. the seller has a security interest in the goods.
   d. all of the above.

_____ 3. Tender requires the seller to do all of the following except:
   a. put and hold conforming goods at the buyer's disposition.
   b. notify the buyer goods are available.
   c. supply the buyer with a bill of exchange.
   d. keep goods available for a reasonable time.

_____ 4. If goods are to be delivered without movement and are represented by a document of title, title passes:
   a. at time and place of contract.
   b. upon delivery of document of title.
   c. upon tender of delivery.
   d. none of the above

_____ 5. Under the Code, a merchant entrusted with the possession of goods has the power to transfer good title to a buyer in the ordinary course of business if the entruster is:
   a. a thief.
   b. the owner of the goods.
   c. one who found the goods.
   d. all of the above.

_____ 6. Unless otherwise agreed, if the goods are delivered primarily for the buyer's use, the transaction is a:
   a. bulk sale.
   b. sale on approval.
   c. sale or return.
   d. consignment.

_____ 7. In a sale on approval, risk of loss passes to the buyer when:
   a. the contract is entered into by the parties.
   b. the goods are sent by the seller.
   c. the goods are received by the buyer.
   d. the goods are accepted by the buyer.

_____ 8. In a shipment contract, risk of loss passes to the buyer when:
   a. the parties enter into the contract.
   b. the goods leave the seller's business.
   c. the goods are delivered to a carrier.
   d. the goods are received by the buyer.

_____ 9. Lisa operates a boutique in New York City. She orders ten gowns from Ferre, a designer in California. They are sent "F.O.B. New York City," but they do not arrive at the boutique. Which statement is true?
   a. Lisa bears the risk of loss because this is a shipment contract.
   b. Ferre bears the risk of loss because this is a destination contract.
   c. In this type of contract, risk of loss passes to the buyer when the goods are delivered to the common carrier.
   d. None of the above

_____ 10. In an ordinary contract in which the merchant-seller is required to tender or deliver the goods to a nonmerchant buyer, risk of loss passes to the buyer:
   a. when the parties enter into the contract.
   b. upon the seller's tender of the goods to the buyer.
   c. when the buyer receives the goods.
   d. none of the above

_____ 11. If the seller ships nonconforming goods to the buyer, the risk of loss remains on the seller until:
   a. the buyer accepts the goods.
   b. the seller remedies the defect in the goods.
   c. (a) or (b)
   d. both (a) and (b)

_____ 12. Margaret goes to Jack's furniture store, selects a dining table, and pays Jack $400 for it. Jack agrees to stain the table a darker color and deliver it. Jack stains the table and notifies Margaret that it is ready for delivery. Prior to delivery the table is accidentally destroyed by fire. Which statement is true?
   a. Margaret can recover the $400 payment from Jack.
   b. Margaret cannot recover the $400 payment from Jack.
   c. The risk of loss is on the buyer, Margaret.
   d. None of the above.

_____ 13. Goods that are not existing or identified are classified as:
   a. inventory goods.
   b. consumer goods.
   c. future goods.
   d. none of the above.

_____ 14. *CPA:* Under the UCC Sales Article, a seller will be entitled to recover the full contract price from the buyer when:
   a. goods are destroyed after title passed to the buyer.
   b. goods are destroyed while risk of loss is with the buyer.
   c. the buyer revokes its acceptance of the goods.
   d. the buyer rejects some of the goods.

_____ 15. *CPA:* Sutter purchased a computer from Harp. Harp is not in the business of selling computers. Harp tendered delivery of the computer after receiving payment in full from Sutter. Sutter informed Harp that Sutter was unable to take possession of the computer at that time, but would return later that day. Before Sutter returned, the computer was destroyed by fire. The risk of loss:
   a. remained with Harp, since title had **not** yet passed to Sutter.
   b. passed to Sutter upon Harp's tender of delivery.
   c. remained with Harp, since Sutter had **not** yet received the computer.
   d. passed to Sutter at the time the contract was formed and payment was made.

SHORT ESSAY

1. Compare the significance of the concept of title under the common law with its role under the Code in allocating risk of loss.

_____

_____

_____

_____

2. Identify and discuss the various types of trial sales.

_____

_____

_____

_____

3. Explain the significance of entrusting goods to a merchant and what effect that has on title to those goods.

_____

_____

_____

_____

4. Sterling Seller delivers nonconforming goods to Brenda Buyer, and she accepts. Later, Brenda discovers a hidden defect in the goods and revokes her acceptance. If the goods are subsequently destroyed by an accidental fire and Brenda has insured the goods for 80% of their fair market value of $10,000, who will bear the risk of loss?

_____

_____

_____

_____

5. Discuss briefly when one obtains an insurable interest.

_____

_____

_____

_____

Chapter 22
Product Liability:
Warranties and Strict Liability

PURPOSE

In this chapter you study the liability of manufacturers and sellers of goods to buyers, users, consumers, and bystanders for damages caused by defective products. A buyer of goods expects that a purchase will meet certain standards. If these standards are not met, then the manufacturer or seller may be liable for damages based on negligence, misrepresentation, statutory liability, breach of warranty, or strict liability in tort. Product liability is now considered to be a separate and distinct field of law that combines and enforces rules and principles of contracts, sales, negligence, strict liability, and statutory law. In this chapter, you study warranties and strict liability in tort.

CHAPTER CHECKPOINTS

After reading and studying this chapter, you should be able to:

1. Identify and describe the warranties found in Articles 2 and 2Aof the Code.

2. Compare the provisions of the Code's implied warranty of merchantability to the implied warranty of fitness for a particular purpose.

3. Discuss the defenses that may be raised by the seller in an action based on warranty and compare the defenses to an action based on warranty of merchantability to those in an action based on section 402A of the Restatement of Torts.

4. Discuss the concept of privity of contract and how the Code approaches the issue of horizontal privity.

5. List and discuss the elements of an action based upon strict liability in tort under Section 402A of the Restatement of Torts.

CHAPTER OUTLINE

I. Warranties–A warranty is an obligation of the seller to the buyer concerning title, quality, characteristics, or condition of goods. A seller is not required to warrant goods, but when the warranties are prescribed by the Code, the seller must act affirmatively in the manner prescribed by the Code to effectively disclaim liability for these implied warranties.

   A. Types of Warranties–A warranty may arise out of the mere existence of a sale (warranty of title), any affirmation of fact or promise made by the seller to the buyer (express warranty), or the circumstances under which the sale is made (implied warranty). Warranties under Article 2A are virtually identical to the warranties under Article 2 except for warranties of title and infringement, warranties for finance leases, and provisions for the exclusion and modification of warranties.

      1. Warranty of Title–Under the Code, the seller implicitly warrants that (1) the title conveyed is good and its transfer rightful and (2) the goods have no security interest or other lien of which the buyer had no knowledge at the time of contracting. Article 2A protects the lessee's right of use.

      2. Express Warranties–An express warranty is an affirmation of fact or promise about the goods, a description of the goods, or a sample or model of the goods, which becomes part of the basis of the bargain. The seller need not use formal words such as "warrant" or "guarantee" or have knowledge of the falsity of a statement in order to be liable for breach of an express warranty.

         a. Creation–An express warranty can be created by the seller either orally or in writing by an affirmation of fact or promise that relates to the goods, a description of the goods, or a sample or model of the goods, which becomes part of the basis of the bargain. The warranty can be in regard to quality, condition, capacity, performability, or safety of the goods. As a general rule, statements of value or opinion do not create a warranty.

         b. Basis of Bargain–Statements or models and samples made or used by the seller constitute a part of the basis of the bargain if they are part of the buyer's assumption underlying the sale.

      3. Implied Warranties–An implied warranty is a contractual obligation arising out of certain circumstances of the sale. It exists by operation of law, not in the language of the sales contract.

         a. Merchantability–Under the Code a merchant seller makes an implied warranty of the merchantability of goods that are of the kind in which he deals. This is a warranty of the merchant seller that the goods are reasonably fit for the ordinary purposes for which they are used, that they pass without objection in the trade under the contract description, and that they are of fair, average quality.

         b. Fitness for Particular Purpose–Any seller, whether a merchant or not, makes an implied warranty that the goods are fit for a particular purpose, provided the seller selects the product knowing the buyer's intended use and that the buyer is relying on the seller's judgment. This warranty pertains to the buyer's specific purpose, rather than the ordinary purpose, of the goods. A seller's conduct may involve both the implied warranty of merchantability and the implied warranty of fitness for a particular purpose.

   B. Obstacles to Warranty Actions–A number of obstacles can limit the effectiveness of warranty as a basis for recovery.

      1. Disclaimer of Warranties–A disclaimer is a negation of a warranty. The Code calls for a reasonable construction of words or conduct to disclaim or limit warranties.

    a. Express Exclusions–A warranty of title may be excluded only by specific language or by certain circumstances, including judicial sale or a sale by a sheriff, executor, or foreclosing lienor. In such cases the seller is clearly offering to sell only such title as he or a third person has in the goods. The language of a disclaimer or modification of an implied warranty of merchantability must mention "merchantability" and, in the case of a writing, it must be conspicuous. A disclaimer of an implied warranty of fitness for the particular purpose of the buyer must be in writing and conspicuous. Unless the circumstances indicate otherwise, all implied warranties are excluded by expressions like "as is," "with all faults," or other language calling the buyer's attention to the exclusion of warranties. Implied warranties may also be excluded by course of dealing, course of performance, or usage of trade.

    b. Buyer's Examination or Refusal to Examine–If the buyer inspects goods before making the contract, implied warranties do not apply to defects that are apparent on examination. There are no implied warranties as to defects that an examination ought to have revealed where the buyer has examined as fully as she desires or when the buyer refuses to examine the goods.

    c. Federal Legislation Relating to Warranties of Consumer Goods–The Federal Trade Commission administers and enforces the Magnuson–Moss Warranty Act. The act is designed to protect purchasers of consumer goods by providing that warranty information be clear and useful. The act defines consumer goods as those that are normally used for personal, family, or household purposes. It provides that a seller who makes a written warranty cannot disclaim any implied warranty. Some courts have applied the act to leases.

2. Limitation or Modification of Warranties–The Code permits a seller to limit or modify a buyer's remedies for breach of warranty. A seller may not, however, use unconscionable limitations or exclude consequential damages. Article 2A has a similar provision for leases of goods.

3. Privity of Contract–During the nineteenth century, the law became established that a plaintiff could not recover for breach of warranty unless he was in a contractual relationship with the defendant. This relationship is known as privity of contract. Horizontal privity determines who benefits from a warranty and therefore may sue for breach. It pertains to noncontracting parties who are injured by the defective goods, including users, consumers, and bystanders who are not the contracting purchaser. The Code provides three alternatives, which state different limits for horizontal privity. The least comprehensive and most widely adopted alternative provides that a seller's warranty, whether express or implied, extends to any natural person who is in the family or household of the buyer or who is a guest in his home if it is reasonable to expect that such a person may use, consume, or be affected by the goods and who is injured in person by breach of the warranty. A seller may not exclude or limit the operation of this section for injury to a person. Alternative B extends Alternative A to "any natural person who may reasonably be expected to use, consume or be affected by the goods." Alternative C further expands the coverage of the section to any person, not just natural persons, and to property damage as well as personal injury. Vertical privity, in determining who is liable for breach of warranty, pertains to remote sellers within the chain of distribution, such as manufacturers and wholesalers, with whom the consumer purchaser has not entered into a contract. Courts in most states have eliminated the requirement of vertical privity in warranty actions.

4. Notice of Breach of Warranty–A buyer who fails to notify the seller of any breach within a reasonable time is barred from any remedy against the seller.

5. Plaintiff's Conduct–Contributory negligence of the buyer is no defense to an action against the seller for breach of warranty. However, a buyer who discovers a defect in the goods that may cause an injury and nevertheless proceeds to make use of them, will not be permitted to recover damages from the seller. This is the voluntary assumption of a known risk.

II. Strict Liability in Tort–Section 402A of the Restatement, Second, of Torts, imposes strict liability in tort on merchant sellers for both personal injuries and property damage resulting from selling a product in a defective condition, unreasonably dangerous to the user or consumer. The essential distinction between strict liability in tort and negligence is that actions in strict liability do not require the plaintiff to prove that the injury-producing defect resulted from any specific act of negligence of the seller. It applies even though the seller has exercised all possible care in the preparation and sale of the product.

A. Requirements of Strict Liability in Tort–Section 402A imposes strict liability in tort if: (1) the defendant was engaged in the business of selling such a product; (2) the defendant sold the product in a defective condition; (3) the defective condition made the product unreasonably dangerous to the user or consumer or to his property; (4) the defect in the product existed at the time it left the hands of the defendant; (5) the plaintiff sustained physical harm or property damage by use or consumption of the product; and (6) the defective condition was the proximate cause of the injury or the damage. Liability based on Section 402A is tort liability and arises out of the common law, not out of the UCC. The liability is imposed by law as a matter of public policy and does not depend on contract.

1. Merchant Sellers–Section 402A imposes liability only upon a person who is in the business of selling the product involved.

2. Defective Condition–In an action to recover damages under the rule of strict liability in tort, the plaintiff must prove a defective condition in the product, but need not prove how or why the product became defective. Defects may arise through faulty manufacture, faulty product design, or inadequate warning, labeling, packaging, or instructions.

   a. Manufacturing Defect–A defect of this kind occurs when the product is not properly made. Thus, it fails to meet its own manufacturing specifications. A chair that was missing screws would constitute a manufacturing defect.

   b. Design Defect–A defect of this kind occurs when a product is made as specified but is dangerous or hazardous because the design is inadequate. Design defects result from poor engineering, poor choice of materials, or poor packaging. (Restatement (Third) of Torts does not impose strict liability for design defect or failure to give proper warnings or instructions.)

   c. Failure to Warn–A seller has a duty to provide adequate warning of possible danger, to provide appropriate directions for safe use, and to package the product in a safe manner.

3. Unreasonably Dangerous–Section 402A liability applies only if the defective product is unreasonably dangerous. An unreasonably dangerous product is one that poses a danger beyond that which would be contemplated by an ordinary consumer who buys it with common knowledge of its characteristics. Most courts let the jury decide what a consumer would expect.

B. Obstacles to Recovery–Obstacles to recovery in warranty cases generally do not present problems in strict liability actions under Section 402A. The section was drafted to avoid most of these obstacles.

1. Disclaimers and Notice–Strict liability is based on tort law and is not subject to contractual defenses. It is not governed by the Code, not affected by contract limitations or disclaimers, and

not subject to any requirement that notice be given to the seller within a reasonable time. In commercial transactions, however, most courts have allowed enforcement of clear and specific disclaimers of Section 402A liability between merchants of relatively equal economic power.

2. Privity–With respect to horizontal privity, strict liability in tort of manufacturers and other sellers extends not only to buyers, users, and consumers, but also to injured bystanders. In terms of vertical privity, strict liability extends to any seller who is in the business of selling the product, including a wholesaler or distributor as well as the manufacturer and the retailer. The rule of strict liability in tort also applies to the manufacturer of a defective component part.

3. Plaintiff's Conduct–The element common to all products liability defenses based on the plaintiff's conduct is that the plaintiff's improper conduct played such a contributing role in the injury that it would be unfair to blame the product or its seller.

   a. Contributory Negligence–Contributory negligence is conduct on the part of a plaintiff that falls below the standard to which he should conform and that is the legal cause of the plaintiff's harm. Section 402A rejects contributory negligence as a defense.

   b. Comparative Negligence–Under comparative negligence, damages are apportioned between the parties in proportion to the degree of fault or negligence found against the parties. Most courts apply comparative negligence to strict liability cases.

   c. Voluntary Assumption of the Risk–Assumption of risk is the plaintiff's express or implied consent to encounter a known danger. This is a defense in an action based on strict liability in tort. The burden of proof of this defense is on the defendant.

   d. Misuse or Abuse of the Product–Misuse or abuse occurs when the injured party knows, or should know, that he is using the product in a manner not contemplated by the seller. This is a defense to a strict liability case. A manufacturer will not avoid liability using this defense if the misuse of the product was foreseeable.

   e. Subsequent Alteration–Section 402A provides that liability only exists if the product reaches "the user or consumer without substantial change in the condition in which it is sold."

4. Statute of Repose–Lawsuits often are brought against manufacturers years after products are sold. In response, many states have adopted statutes of repose, which limit the time period for which a manufacturer is liable for injury caused by its product. After the statutory time period elapses, a manufacturer ceases to be liable for harm caused by its defective products.

5. Limitations on Damages–More than 50% of the states limit punitive damages in product liability lawsuits. Such limits include (a) limiting the amount of punitive damages that may be awarded, (b) giving to the state all or a portion of punitive damages awarded, (c) mandating separate hearings to determine liability and punitive damages, (d) requiring clear and convincing evidence in order to recover punitive damages, and (e) limiting punitive damages to an amount that is no greater than a certain percentage of compensatory damages awarded.

III. Restatement (Third) Of Torts: Products Liability–This Restatement changes product liability and expands Section 402A. Liability applies to anyone in the business of selling or distributing a products if a defective product harms persons or property. This Restatement does not use the term strict liability. It instead defines different liability standards for manufacturing defects, design defects, and failure to warn. It imposes strict liability only for manufacturing defects. Liability for inadequate design or warning is imposed only for foreseeable risks of harm that were avoidable by using an alternative reasonable design, warning, or instruction.

A. Manufacturing Defect–A product has a manufacturing defect when it departs from its intended design even though reasonable care is exercised in making and marketing the product. Sellers and distributors of products therefore remain strictly liable for manufacturing defects.

B. Design Defect–Section 2(b) states: "A product ... is defective in design when the foreseeable risks of harm posed by the product could have been reduced or avoided by the adoption of a reasonable alternative design ... and the omission of the reasonable alternative design renders the product not reasonably safe." This rule thus creates a quasi-negligence standard for design defects. A plaintiff must prove the existence of a reasonable, safer alternative design that would reduce the foreseeable risk of harm, and consumer expectations are not the standard for determining design defectiveness.

C. Failure to Warn–Section 2(c) states: "A product ... is defective because of inadequate instructions or warnings when the foreseeable risks of harm posed by the product could have been reduced or avoided by the provision of reasonable instructions or warnings...." A seller therefore must warn about a risk only if he or she knew or should have known about the risk. Warnings are not adequate, however, if a reasonable, safer alternative design for the product is available.

KEY TERMS

1. Warranty
2. Warranty of title
3. Express warranty
4. Basis of the bargain
5. Implied warranty
6. Implied warranty of merchantability
7. Implied warranty of fitness for particular purpose
8. Disclaimer of warranties
9. Consumer goods
10. Privity
11. Horizontal privity
12. Vertical privity
13. Strict liability in tort
14. Manufacturing defect
15. Design defect
16. State of the art
17. Statute of repose

TRUE/FALSE

_____ 1. A warranty creates a duty on the part of the seller to ensure that the goods it sells will conform to certain qualities, characteristics, or conditions.

_____ 2. The Code requires that a seller make certain warranties, which cannot be disclaimed.

_____ 3. The Code's implied warranty of merchantability is a warranty by a merchant seller that the goods are reasonably fit for the ordinary purposes for which they are manufactured and sold.

_____ 4. Application of the implied warranty of fitness for a particular purpose does not depend on whether the seller is a merchant.

_____ 5. The expression "as is" will only disclaim the implied warranty of merchantability if it is in writing and conspicuous.

_____ 6. Most states have eliminated the requirements of horizontal privity but have retained vertical privity requirements in warranty actions.

_____ 7. Strict liability in tort generally is not subject to disclaimer, exclusion, or modifications by contractual agreement.

_____ 8. Strict liability in tort may arise from a manufacturing defect but not from a defective design.

_____ 9. The strict liability in tort of manufacturers extends only to buyers and their families.

_____ 10. The doctrine of strict liability in tort may be held to be applicable to merchant sellers for personal injuries but not property damage.

_____ 11. There is no implied warranty on defects that an examination ought to have revealed.

_____ 12. Under the Magnuson-Moss Act, no seller providing a written warranty can effectively disclaim any implied warranty.

_____ 13. Contributory negligence by the user of a defective product that is unreasonably dangerous will prevent the user from pursuing a claim based on Section 402A.

_____ 14. Any seller can make an implied warranty of fitness for a particular purpose, but only a merchant can make an implied warranty of merchantability.

_____ 15. Heidi Homeowner buys a defective toaster at a neighborhood garage sale and is injured when it explodes. Heidi can sue her neighbor for breach of the implied warranty of merchantability.

MULTIPLE CHOICE

_____ 1. Under the Code, a promise made by the seller constitutes an express warranty provided:
   a. the buyer relied upon the promise.
   b. the promise constitutes a part of the basis of the bargain.
   c. either (a) or (b).
   d. both (a) and (b).

_____ 2. A warranty is an obligation of the seller to the buyer concerning which of the following?
   a. Title
   b. Quality
   c. Condition of the goods
   d. Any of the above

_____ 3. In order for the implied warranty of fitness for a particular purpose to apply:
   a. the seller must, at the time of contracting, have reason to know of the particular purpose.
   b. the buyer must actually rely on the seller's skill and judgment to furnish suitable goods.
   c. (a) or (b).
   d. both (a) and (b).

_____ 4. Which of the following will NOT bar an injured buyer from recovering in an action against the seller for breach of warranty?

    a. The buyer's failure to notify the seller of any breach of warranty within a reasonable time after discovering it.

    b. The buyer's contributory negligence.

    c. The buyer's voluntary assumption of the known risk.

    d. An explicit, conspicuous disclaimer.

_____ 5. The doctrine of strict liability in tort applies only if:

    a. the seller is engaged in the business of selling the product that caused the harm.

    b. the product was sold in a defective condition unreasonably dangerous to the user or consumer.

    c. the plaintiff sustained physical harm or property damage by use or consumption of the product.

    d. all of the above.

_____ 6. A party injured by a defective product can establish that it was defective by showing that the product had which of the following?

    a. A manufacturing defect

    b. A design defect

    c. Inadequate instructions enclosed

    d. All of the above

_____ 7. Strict liability in tort is applicable only if the product is:

    a. defective.

    b. somewhat dangerous to the user or consumer.

    c. (a) and (b).

    d. either (a) or (b).

_____ 8. An injured party's recovery under the doctrine of strict liability in tort will be barred by:

    a. a valid disclaimer of liability included in the contract of sale.

    b. the failure of the injured party to give notice to the seller within a reasonable time.

    c. subsequent alteration of the product.

    d. the lack of privity between the injured party and the seller.

_____ 9. A party injured by a product that is defective because of a defective component can bring an action under the doctrine of strict liability in tort against all of the following EXCEPT:

    a. the seller of the finished product.

    b. the assembler of the finished product.

    c. the manufacturer of a nondefective chassis to which the assembler attached the defective component.

    d. the manufacturer of the defective component used without essential change in the final product.

_____ 10. Which of the following, even if properly shown, is NOT a complete defense to a claim of strict liability in tort?
   a. Comparative negligence
   b. Voluntary assumption of the risk
   c. Product misuse
   d. Subsequent alteration

_____ 11. Mel Merchant sells lawnmowers at his retail store. Mel impliedly warrants:
   a. that the mowers are the best available.
   b. that the mowers are fit for lawn mowing and are of fair, average quality.
   c. that all possible safety devices have been incorporated into the design.
   d. that the mowers will last at least two years.

_____ 12. In order to establish the defense of voluntary assumption of the risk, the defendant must show which of the following?
   a. That the plaintiff was aware of the particular risk involved
   b. That the plaintiff voluntarily and unreasonably decided to encounter the known risk
   c. (a) or (b)
   d. Both (a) and (b)

_____ 13. Which of the following would constitute an express warranty?
   a. Sam Seller shows a sample to Bill Buyer and says the product in the box is just like it.
   b. Sam Seller says the VCR Bill Buyer wants to buy is "the best around."
   c. Sam Seller says the VCR Bill Buyer wants to buy will give him many hours of enjoyment.
   d. Sam Seller tells Bill Buyer that he really likes the RCA VCR better than the Sharpe one.

_____ 14. *CPA:* Which of the following conditions must be met for an implied warranty of fitness for a particular purpose to arise in connection with a sale of goods?
   I. The warranty must be in writing.
   II. The seller must know that the buyer was relying on the seller in selecting the goods.
   a. I only
   b. II only
   c. Both I and II
   d. Neither I nor II

_____ 15. *CPA:* To establish a cause of action based on strict liability in tort for personal injuries resulting from using a defective product, one of the elements the plaintiff must prove is that the seller (defendant):
   a. defectively designed the product.
   b. was engaged in the business of selling the product.
   c. was in privity of contract with the plaintiff.
   d. failed to exercise due care.

SHORT ESSAY

1. List and describe several types of warranties found in Article 2 of the Code.

_____

_____

_____

_____

2. Compare and contrast the implied warranties of merchantability and fitness for a particular purpose. Can either be disclaimed? How?

_____

_____

_____

3. Under the Restatement Second, what must an injured party show to recover under a theory of strict liability in tort? What obstacles, if any, will bar recovery and what traditional defenses will not?

_____

_____

_____

_____

4. List and discuss the kinds of defects which can give rise to a defective condition in a product.

_____

_____

_____

_____

5. Briefly describe the Magnuson-Moss Warranty Act.

_____

_____

_____

_____

Chapter 23
Sales Remedies

PURPOSE

Breach is the failure of a party to perform the obligations under the contract. In a sales contract, breach may consist of the seller's delivery of defective goods, too few goods, the wrong goods, or no goods. The buyer may breach by failing to accept conforming goods or by failing to pay for conforming goods, which have been accepted. In this chapter, you study the remedies that are available to the buyer and the seller in the case of a breach by the other party. The Code provides separate and distinct remedies for the seller and for the buyer. Each of the remedies available is specifically keyed to the type of breach and the situation of the goods. The purpose of the remedies provided by the Code is to put the aggrieved party in as good a position as if the other party had fully performed. The Code provides that its remedies should be liberally administered to accomplish this purpose. In providing its various remedies, the Code has rejected the doctrine of election of remedies by providing that the remedies for breach are cumulative. Whether one remedy bars another depends entirely on the facts of the individual case.

CHAPTER CHECKPOINTS

After reading and studying this chapter, you should be able to:

1. List and describe the remedies available to the seller under the Code.

2. List and describe the remedies available to the buyer under the Code.

3. Identify and discuss the various kinds of money damages available to the seller and the buyer.

4. Distinguish between specific performance and replevin and discuss under what circumstances each is available.

5. Identify and describe the basic types of contractual provisions that affect the remedies available in the event of a breach and the limitations that the Code imposes upon these provisions.

CHAPTER OUTLINE

A. Remedies of the Seller–When the buyer defaults, the seller has been deprived of the rights for which it bargained. The buyer's default may consist of (1) wrongfully rejecting the goods; (2) wrongfully revoking acceptance; (3) failing to make a payment due on or before delivery; or (4) repudiating the contract in whole or in part. The seller's goods-oriented remedies for these defaults are withholding delivery of the goods, stopping delivery of the goods by a carrier, identifying conforming goods to the contract not already identified, and reclaiming the goods on the buyer's insolvency. The seller's money-oriented remedies include reselling the goods and recovering damages, recovering damages for nonacceptance of the goods or repudiation of the contract, recovering the price, and recovering incidental damages. The seller can also cancel the contract, which is an obligation-oriented remedy. The Code's remedies are cumulative; more than one may be used by an aggrieved seller.

1. To Withhold Delivery of the Goods–A seller may withhold delivery of the goods to a buyer who has wrongfully rejected or revoked acceptance of the goods, who has failed to make a payment due on or before delivery, or who has repudiated the contract. Where the contract calls for installments, any breach of an installment that impairs the value of the whole contract will permit the seller to withhold the entire undelivered balance of the goods. If the seller discovers that the buyer is insolvent, the seller may refuse to deliver the goods except for cash.

2. To Stop Delivery of the Goods–If the buyer is insolvent, the seller may stop any delivery. If the buyer repudiates or otherwise breaches, the seller may stop carload, truckload, planeload, or larger shipments. The seller must timely notify the carrier or other bailee to stop delivery of the goods. After this notification, the carrier or bailee who holds the goods must deliver them in accordance with the directions of the seller. The seller must pay any charges or damages incurred by the carrier or bailee.

3. To Identify Goods to the Contract–On breach by the buyer, the seller may identify to the contract conforming goods in its possession or control that were not so identified at the time it learned of the breach. The seller may either complete the manufacture of unfinished goods and identify them to the contract or cease the manufacture and resell the unfinished goods for scrap or salvage value. The seller must exercise reasonable judgment to minimize its loss.

4. To Resell the Goods and Recover Damages–In the case of wrongful rejection or revocation, repudiation, or failure to make timely payment, the seller may resell the goods concerned or the undelivered balance of the goods. If the resale is made in good faith and in a commercially reasonable manner, the seller may recover the difference between the contract price and the resale price, together with any incidental damages, less expenses saved because of the buyer's breach. The seller is not accountable to the buyer for any profit made on any resale of the goods. A good faith purchaser at a resale takes the goods free of any rights of the original buyer.

5. To Recover Damages for Nonacceptance or Repudiation–In the event of the buyer's wrongful rejection or revocation, repudiation, or failure to make timely payment, the seller may recover damages from the buyer measured by the difference between the unpaid contract price and the

market price at the time and place of tender of the goods, plus incidental damages, less expenses saved in consequence of the buyer's breach. This remedy is an alternative to reselling the goods.

6. To Recover the Price–The Code permits the seller to recover the price in three situations: (1) where the buyer has accepted the goods; (2) where the goods have been lost or damaged after the risk of loss has passed to the buyer; and (3) where the goods have been identified to the contract and there is no ready market available for their resale at a reasonable price.

7. To Recover Incidental Damages–In the same action in which the seller seeks damages for the difference between the contract price and the resale price or in cases to recover the price or damages, the seller may recover incidental damages. Incidental damages include any commercially reasonable charges, expenses, or commissions resulting from the breach.

8. To Cancel the Contract–Where the buyer wrongfully rejects or revokes acceptance of the goods, or fails to make a payment due on or before delivery, or repudiates the contract in whole or in part, the seller may cancel the part of the contract that concerns the goods directly affected. If the breach is of an installment contract and it substantially impairs the whole contract, the seller may cancel the entire contract. The Code defines cancellation as one party's putting an end to the contract by reason of a breach by the other.

9. To Reclaim the Goods upon the Buyer's Insolvency–The unpaid seller may reclaim goods from an insolvent buyer by demand made to the buyer within ten days after the buyer has received the goods. If the buyer has committed fraud by a misrepresentation of solvency made to the seller in writing within three months prior to delivery of the goods, the ten-day limitation does not apply. This right is subject to the rights of a buyer in the ordinary course of business or other good faith purchaser. Use of this remedy precludes the use of other remedies.

B. Remedies of the Buyer–The seller's default may consist of repudiating the contract, failing to deliver the goods without repudiation, or delivering goods that do not conform to the contract. The buyer's obligation-oriented remedy for these defaults is cancellation of the contract. The money-oriented remedies include recovery of payments made, cover and recovery of damages, recovery of damages for nondelivery, recovery of damages for breach of warranty, recovery of incidental damages, and recovery of consequential damages. The goods-oriented remedies of the buyer are to recover identified goods if the seller is insolvent, replevy the goods, obtain specific performance, or obtain a security interest in the goods. The buyer, upon proper notice to the seller, may deduct from the price due damages for any breach by the seller.

1. To Cancel the Contract–Where the seller fails to make delivery or repudiates the contract, or where the buyer rightfully rejects or justifiably revokes acceptance of goods tendered or delivered, the buyer may cancel the contract with respect to any goods involved. If the breach concerns the whole contract, the buyer may cancel the entire contract. The buyer must give notice of cancellation and is excused from further performance or tender.

2. To Recover Payments Made–On the seller's breach, the buyer may recover as much of the price as the buyer has paid.

3. To Cover–On the seller's breach, the buyer may obtain "cover." This means that the buyer may in good faith and without unreasonable delay proceed to purchase goods or make a contract to purchase goods in substitution for those due under the contract of the seller. The buyer may also recover the difference between the cost of cover and the contract price, plus any incidental and consequential damages, less expenses saved in consequence of the seller's breach. The buyer is

not required to obtain cover. Failure to do so does not bar any other remedy provided in the Code, but the buyer may not recover consequential damages that could have been prevented by cover. In a lease, recovery is the difference between the present values of the new and old rents.

4. To Recover Damages for Nondelivery or Repudiation—If the seller repudiates the contract or fails to deliver the goods, or if the buyer rightfully rejects or justifiably revokes acceptance, the buyer is entitled to recover damages measured by the difference between the market price at the time the buyer learned of the breach and the contract price, together with incidental and consequential damages, less expenses saved in consequence of the seller's breach. This remedy is an alternative to cover and is available only to the extent the buyer has not covered. A buyer electing this remedy may not recover consequential damages that could have been avoided by cover. In a lease, recovery is the difference between the present values of the market rent and old rent.

5. To Recover Identified Goods on the Seller's Insolvency—Where existing goods are identified to the contract of sale, the buyer acquires a special property interest in the goods. This interest exists even though the goods are nonconforming, and the buyer has the right to return or reject them. Identification may be made by either the buyer or the seller. Under the Code the buyer has the right to recover from an insolvent seller goods in which the buyer has a special property interest. This right exists where the seller, who is in possession or control of the goods, becomes insolvent within ten days after receipt of the first installment of the price. To exercise the right, the buyer must tender to the seller any unpaid portion of the price. If the buyer has identified the goods, the buyer may recover the goods only if they conform to the contract.

6. To Sue for Replevin—Replevin is an action at law to recover specific goods in the possession of a defendant that are being unlawfully withheld from the plaintiff. The buyer may replevy goods where the seller has repudiated or breached the contract if (1) the buyer is unable to obtain cover or (2) the goods have been shipped under reservation of a security interest in the seller and satisfaction of this security interest has been made or tendered.

7. To Sue for Specific Performance—This is an equitable remedy compelling the party in breach to perform the contract according to its terms. At common law, specific performance is available only if the legal remedies are inadequate. The Code continues the availability of specific performance and has sought to further a more liberal attitude towards its use.

8. To Enforce a Security Interest in the Goods—A buyer who has rightfully rejected or justifiably revoked acceptance of goods that remain in its possession or control has a security interest in these goods to the extent of any payment of the price that the buyer has made and for any expenses reasonably incurred in their inspection, receipt, transportation, care, and custody. The buyer may hold such goods and resell them in the same manner as an aggrieved seller may resell goods. The buyer must account to the seller for any excess of net proceeds of the resale over the amount of the security interest.

9. To Recover Damages for Breach in Regard to Accepted Goods—Where the buyer has accepted nonconforming goods and has given timely notification to the seller of the breach of contract, the buyer is entitled to recover from the seller the damages resulting in the ordinary course of events from the seller's breach. In the event of breach of warranty, the measure of damages is the difference between the value of the goods that have been accepted and the value that the goods would have had if they had been as warranted. Incidental and consequential damages may also be recovered.

10. To Recover Incidental Damages–The buyer may recover incidental damages in addition to covering, damages for nondelivery or repudiation, and breach of warranty. Incidental damages include expenses reasonably incurred in inspection, receipt, transportation, care and custody of goods rightfully rejected and any commercially reasonable expense connected to obtaining cover or to the delay or other breach.

11. To Recover Consequential Damages–In many cases the above remedies will not fully compensate the aggrieved buyer for losses. Under the Code, the buyer has the opportunity to recover consequential damages resulting from the seller's breach, including (1) any loss resulting from the buyer's requirements and needs of which the seller at the time of contracting had reason to know and which could not reasonably be prevented by cover or otherwise, and (2) injury to person or property proximately resulting from any breach of warranty.

C. Contractual Provisions Affecting Remedies–The parties to a sales contract may modify, exclude, or limit by agreement the remedies or damages available for breach of that contract.

1. Liquidation or Limitation of Damages–The parties may specify the amount or measure of damages that either party may recover in the event of a breach by the other party. The amount of such damages must be reasonable in light of the anticipated or actual loss resulting from a breach, the difficulties of proof of loss, and the inconvenience or lack of feasibility of otherwise obtaining an adequate remedy. A provision fixing unreasonably large liquidated damages is void as a penalty, while an unreasonably small amount might be stricken on the grounds of unconscionability.

2. Modification or Limitation of Remedy by Agreement–The contract between the parties may expressly provide for remedies in addition to those in the Code. It may also limit or change the measure of damages recoverable for breach. A remedy in a contract is optional unless it is expressly agreed to be exclusive of other remedies. Where an exclusive remedy fails in its essential purpose, resort may be had to the remedies provided by the Code. The contract may limit or exclude consequential damages unless such limitation or exclusion would be unconscionable. Limitation of consequential damages for personal injury from breach of warranty in the sale of consumer goods is *prima facie* unconscionable, whereas limitation of such damages where the loss is commercial is not.

KEY TERMS

1. Insolvency

2. Incidental damages

3. Cancellation

4. Cover

5. Replevin

6. Specific performance

7. Consequential damages

8. Liquidated damages

TRUE/FALSE

_____ 1. The purpose of the Code's remedial provisions is to place the aggrieved party in as good a position as if the other party had fully performed.

_____ 2. An obligation-oriented remedy is one that provides the aggrieved party with the opportunity to recover monetary damages.

_____ 3. The Code has rejected the doctrine of election of remedies, providing that remedies for breach are cumulative in nature.

_____ 4. The aggrieved seller's right to stop delivery of goods by a carrier or other bailee upon learning of the buyer's insolvency ceases when a negotiable document of title covering the goods is negotiated to the buyer.

_____ 5. If a seller in good faith and in a commercially reasonable manner resells goods that were wrongfully rejected by the buyer, the seller may recover from the buyer the difference between the contract price and the resale price, plus any incidental damages incurred.

_____ 6. A seller who discovers that the buyer is insolvent may stop any delivery.

_____ 7. The Code permits an aggrieved seller to bring an action to recover the price where the goods have been identified to the contract and there is no ready market available for their resale.

_____ 8. If a buyer breaches an installment contract in a manner that substantially impairs the whole contract, the seller may cancel the entire contract.

_____ 9. An aggrieved buyer may make a reasonable contract of cover and then seek to recover from the seller the difference between the cost of cover and the market price, plus any incidental and consequential damages.

_____ 10. In the event of a breach of warranty, the measure of damages is the difference at the time and place of the acceptance between the value of the accepted goods and the value of the goods as warranted.

_____ 11. Under the Code the parties may, by agreement, limit, modify, or exclude remedies or damages available for breach.

_____ 12. The Code allows parties to a contract to specify the extent of damages in the event of a breach.

_____ 13. The Code has rejected the common law remedy of cover.

_____ 14. A buyer cannot recover consequential damages that could have been prevented by cover.

_____ 15. Upon discovering that the seller is insolvent, a buyer may recover goods from the seller in which she has as special property interest and for which she had paid part or all of the price.

MULTIPLE CHOICE

_____ 1. Which of the following is not a money-oriented remedy?
   a. Cover and obtain damages
   b. An action to recover market price damages
   c. Cancellation
   d. An action to recover damages for nonconformity

_____ 2. Under the Code, the equity meaning of insolvency is:
   a. that a person has no assets.
   b. that a person is unable to pay debts as they become due.
   c. that a person's total liabilities exceed the value of all her assets.
   d. none of the above.

_____ 3. Which of the following is not a seller's remedy?
   a. Withhold delivery
   b. Cover
   c. Resell the goods
   d. Cancel the contract

_____ 4. Spence Seller in Seattle agrees to sell goods to Beth Buyer in Buffalo for $20,000 F.O.B. Buffalo, delivery on June 15. Beth wrongfully rejects the goods. The market price of the goods on June 15 in Buffalo is $15,000. Spence incurred $1,000 in incidental expenses while saving $500 in expenses. How much would Spence be allowed to recover from Beth?
   a. $20,000
   b. $15,000
   c. $5,500
   d. $5,000

_____ 5. A seller's right to stop delivery ceases when:
   a. the buyer receives the goods.
   b. the bailee of goods notifies the buyer that he holds them for the buyer..
   c. a negotiable document of title is negotiated to the buyer.
   d. any of the above.

_____ 6. The Code permits the seller to bring an action to recover the price in all of the following cases except:
   a. where the buyer has accepted the goods but has failed to make a payment.
   b. where the goods have been identified to the contract and a ready market is available for their resale at a reasonable price.
   c. where conforming goods have been lost or damaged after risk of loss has passed to the buyer.
   d. all of the above.

7. If an aggrieved party rightfully cancels a contract:
    a. he discharges any obligation of future performance that he might have under the contract.
    b. he retains any remedy for breach of the whole contract or of any unperformed balance.
    c. neither (a) nor (b)
    d. both (a) and (b)

8. Which of the following is not a correct statement concerning an unpaid seller's attempt to reclaim goods from an insolvent buyer?
    a. The seller must demand that the goods be returned within twenty days after the buyer has received them unless the buyer has fraudulently misrepresented his solvency to the seller.
    b. The seller, if successful in reclaiming the goods from an insolvent buyer, may not seek other remedies with respect to the goods.
    c. The seller's right to reclaim the goods is subject to the rights of a buyer in the ordinary course of business or other good faith purchaser.
    d. All of the above

9. Of the following remedies, which is not available to the buyer?
    a. To sue for replevin
    b. To resell the goods
    c. To cover
    d. To cancel the contract

10. Where a seller fails to make delivery, or repudiates, the buyer may:
    a. cover and recover damages.
    b. recover payments made.
    c. recover market price damages.
    d. all of the above.

11. If the seller repudiates the contract, the buyer is entitled to recover damages from the seller in an amount equal to the difference between the contract price and the market price of goods when:
    a. the parties entered into the contract.
    b. the breach occurred.
    c. the buyer learned of the breach.
    d. none of the above.

12. Brian Buyer contracted to buy 1000 widgets from Sal Seller for $5,000. Sal shipped defective widgets, but Brian accepted them and properly notified Sal of the breach. As warranted, the widgets were valued at $7,000, but as received they were worth $4,000. If Brian is successful in his suit for breach of warranty against Sal, he will be allowed to recover:
    a. $1,000.
    b. $2,000.
    c. $3,000.
    d. $7,000.

_____ 13. Susan Seller has shipped 100 widgets to Bob Buyer pursuant to a contract. The next day Susan discovers that Bob is insolvent. On learning this:
   a. Susan may stop delivery.
   b. Susan must cancel the contract.
   c. Susan has no recourse available under the Code.
   d. Susan may cover and sue for damages.

_____ 14. *CPA:* On February 15, Mazur Corp. contracted to sell 1,000 bushels of wheat to Good Bread, Inc. at $6.00 per bushel, with delivery to be made on June 23. On June 1, Good advised Mazur that it would not accept or pay for the wheat. On June 2, Mazur sold the wheat to another customer at the market price of $5.00 per bushel. Mazur had advised Good that it intended to resell the wheat. Which of the following statements is true?
   a. Mazur can successfully sue Good for the difference between the resale price and the contract price.
   b. Mazur can resell the wheat only after June 23.
   c. Good can retract its anticipatory breach at any time before June 23.
   d. Good can successfully sue Mazur for specific performance.

_____ 15. *CPA:* Under the UCC Sales Article, a plaintiff who proves fraud in the formation of a contract may:
   a. elect to rescind the contract and need **not** return the consideration received from the other party.
   b. be entitled to rescind the contract and sue for damages resulting from the fraud.
   c. be entitled to punitive damages provided physical injuries resulted from the fraud.
   d. rescind the contract even if there was **no** reliance on the fraudulent statement.

SHORT ESSAY

1. What remedies are available to a buyer who rightfully rejects a seller's tender of nonconforming goods?

_____

_____

_____

_____

2. What remedies are available to a buyer after the seller repudiates their contract?

_____

_____

_____

_____

3. What remedies are available to the seller after the buyer has wrongfully rejected a conforming tender of goods?

_____

_____

_____

_____

4. Explain the remedy of cover.

_____

_____

_____

_____

5. What is liquidation of damages?

_____

_____

_____

_____

Part IV
Sample Examination

MULTIPLE CHOICE

_____ 1. A contract involving the rendition of a service is governed primarily by the:
   a. federal law.
   b. state common law.
   c. UCC.
   d. none of the above

_____ 2. Mike Mechanic has a used car that he would like to sell. He puts an ad in the local newspaper. Boris Buyer comes to his house to look at the car and asks what kind of condition it is in. Mike says, "As a mechanic, I think the car is in good running order and should give you no problems for at least 60 days." Based on that statement, Boris purchases the car.
   a. Mike's statement is an express warranty.
   b. The sale by Mike gives rise to a warranty of merchantability.
   c. Mike's statement does not constitute an express warranty.
   d. None of the above

_____ 3. Sarah Seller agrees to sell 100 widgets to Bart Buyer at a price of $600. No mention is made of the time for delivery.
   a. The goods must be delivered within two weeks.
   b. The goods must be delivered within a reasonable time.
   c. The goods must be delivered within 30 days.
   d. There is no contract, because an essential term has been omitted.

_____ 4. Catherine telephoned Al's Office Supply and ordered ten boxes of pens at $30 a box. Later that day, she decided that since the pens were on sale she would order 20 boxes. She called the store back to modify her order. What result?
   a. There is no consideration, so the contract is unenforceable.
   b. The modified contract is unenforceable because a writing was required.
   c. The modified contract is enforceable.
   d. None of the above.

_____ 5. Which of the following doctrines would a court apply where the seller's price was exorbitant?
   a. Validation
   b. Substantive unconscionability
   c. Procedural unconscionability
   d. None of the above.

_____ 6. Silvia Seller learns of Ben Buyer's insolvency while the goods are in transit.
   a. Silvia is out of luck and can't do much.
   b. Silvia can stop delivery.
   c. If Silvia stops delivery, she will be in breach of contract.
   d. Silvia will have to deliver the goods and then file a claim with the bankruptcy court.

_____ 7. A form of action at law that a party may use to recover specific goods that are in possession of the defendant is known as:
   a. specific performance.
   b. replevin.
   c. stopping goods in transit.
   d. reclaiming of the goods.

_____ 8. Hazel Homemaker brings her VCR to Al's Quick Fix Repair Shop to have the head cleaned. While the VCR is in the shop, Carmen Customer comes to the store and asks Al its price. Al says $50, so Carmen pays him $50 cash and takes the VCR home. When Hazel comes to the shop to pick up her VCR, it isn't there.
   a. Hazel has entrusted the VCR to Al's Repair Shop.
   b. Al can transfer good title to the VCR to Carmen.
   c. If Hazel brings a replevin action against Carmen, she will recover the goods.
   d. Two of the above are correct, (a) and (b).

_____ 9. If a buyer in good faith purchases replacement goods for those that were not delivered as required by a sales contract, then the buyer is utilizing the remedy of:
   a. replevin.
   b. cover.
   c. tender of delivery.
   d. specific performance.

_____ 10. To protect purchasers of consumer goods, Congress enacted the:
   a. Statute of frauds.
   b. Magnuson-Moss Warranty Act.
   c. UCC.
   d. All of the above.

_____ 11. In an action based upon Section 402A of the Restatement, the defendant manufacturer can raise the defense(s) of:
   a. misuse or abuse of the product.
   b. voluntary assumption of the risk.
   c. comparative negligence.
   d. all of the above.

_____ 12. Bernice Buyer accepts 1,000 widgets from Sergio Seller, and then discovers a latent defect in them that could not have been found earlier by a reasonable inspection.
   a. Bernice must keep the goods, because she has already accepted them.
   b. Bernice may revoke her acceptance.
   c. Bernice is entitled to the difference between the value of the goods which have been accepted and the value that the goods would have had if they had been as warranted.
   d. Two of the above are correct, (b) and (c).

_____ 13. Henry Homeowner used his lawn mower to trim his hedges. In the process he severely injured his hand. In a lawsuit against the manufacturer, the manufacturer is likely to raise the defense of:
   a. comparative negligence.
   b. assumption of the risk.
   c. misuse of the product.
   d. subsequent alteration.

_____ 14. Unless otherwise agreed by the parties, transfer of title in a shipment contract occurs when:
   a. the documents of title are delivered.
   b. payment is received.
   c. the seller delivers the goods to the carrier for shipment to the buyer.
   d. the goods are delivered to the buyer.

_____ 15. Steve Seller, who is located in New York, has a contract to sell 1,000 widgets to Brent Buyer, who is located in San Francisco. The contract is a shipment contract. Steve delivers the goods to Downs Transport for delivery. En route to San Francisco, the goods are destroyed.
   a. Brent bears the risk of loss.
   b. Steve bears the risk of loss.
   c. Brent and Steve will each share half of the loss.
   d. Brent has no interest in the goods, because he has not yet accepted them.

16. Sheila Seller ships nonconforming goods to Bev Buyer. The risk of loss remains on Sheila until:
    a. the goods are delivered to the carrier.
    b. Bev has had an opportunity to inspect the goods.
    c. Sheila corrects the defect in the goods.
    d. Bev pays for the goods.

17. *CPA:* Dunne and Cook signed a contract requiring Cook to rebind 500 of Dunne's books at 80 cents per book. Later, Dunne requested, in good faith, that the price be reduced to 70 cents per book. Cook agreed orally to reduce the price to 70 cents. Under the circumstances, the oral agreement is:
    a. enforceable, but proof of it is inadmissible into evidence.
    b. enforceable, and proof of it is admissible into evidence.
    c. unenforceable, because Dunne failed to give consideration, but proof of it is otherwise admissible into evidence.
    d. unenforceable, due to the statute of frauds, and proof of it is inadmissible into evidence.

18. *CPA:* Which of the following factors results in an express warranty with respect to a sale of goods?
    I. The seller's description of the goods as part of the basis of the bargain.
    II. The seller's selection of goods, knowing the buyer's intended use.
    a. I only
    b. II only
    c. Both I and II
    d. Neither I nor II

19. *CPA:* In a contract governed by the UCC Sales Article, which of the following statements is correct?
    a. Unless both the seller and the buyer are merchants, neither party is obligated to perform the contract in good faith.
    b. The contract will **not** be enforceable if it fails to expressly specify a time and a place for delivery of the goods.
    c. The seller may be excused from performance if the goods are accidentally destroyed before the risk of loss passes to the buyer.
    d. If the price of the goods is less than $500, the goods need **not** be identified to the contract for title to pass to the buyer.

_____ 20. *CPA:* On April 5, Anker, Inc., furnished Bold Corp. with Anker's financial statements dated March 31, of the same year. The financial statements contained misrepresentations which indicated that Anker was solvent when in fact it was insolvent. Based on Anker's financial statements, Bold agreed to sell Anker 90 computers "F.O.B.-Bold's loading dock." On April 14, Anker received 60 of the computers. The remaining 30 computers are in the possession of the common carrier and in transit to Anker. With respect to the remaining 30 computers in transit, which of the following statements is correct if Anker refuses to pay Bold in cash and Anker is **not** in possession of a negotiable document of title covering the computers?

    a. Bold may stop delivery of the computers to Anker since their contract is void due to Anker's furnishing of the false financial statements.

    b. Bold may stop delivery of the computers to Anker despite the fact that title had passed to Anker.

    c. Bold must deliver the computers to Anker on credit since Anker has **not** breached the contract.

    d. Bold must deliver the computers to Anker since the risk of loss has passed to Anker.

Try the Web

1. Locate Article 2-513 (buyer's right to inspect goods) of the UCC.

    Solution:

        Go to http://www.law.cornell.edu

        Select - Law about – commerce

        Select - Sales

        Select - Article Two of the Uniform Commercial Code (UCC)

        Drag down to 2-513 and click on it.

2. Is the "Wool Products Labeling Act" administered by the Federal Trade Commission?

    Solution:

        Go to: http://www.ftc.gov/

        Drag to and click on – For Business

        Drag to and click on - Textile, Wool, Fur & Apparel Matters

        Select - Wool Products Labeling Act of 1939

        Select - § 68d - Enforcement of subchapter

Chapter 24
Form And Content

PURPOSE

Modern business could not be conducted without the use of checks, drafts, promissory notes, and certificates of deposit, all of which are negotiable instruments. The way rights and obligations are acquired in negotiable instruments is important because of the huge volume of daily transactions in these instruments. In this chapter, you study the concept of negotiability and the form necessary for an instrument to qualify as a "negotiable instrument" (previously called "commercial paper" under Article 3 of the UCC). Negotiability invests negotiable instruments with a high degree of marketability and commercial utility. It allows negotiable instruments to be freely transferable and enforceable by a person with the rights of a holder in due course against any person obligated on the instrument, subject only to a limited number of defenses.

CHAPTER CHECKPOINTS

After reading and studying this chapter, you should be able to:

1. Discuss the concept and importance of negotiability.

2. Identify the parties on a check, draft, note, and certificate of deposit.

3. Identify and discuss the types of negotiable instruments that are promises to pay and those that are orders to pay.

4. List and discuss the formal requirements that an instrument must meet in order to qualify as a negotiable instrument.

5. Discuss the effect of the following on negotiability: (1) postdating, antedating, or not dating an instrument; (2) an incomplete instrument; and (3) an ambiguity within an instrument.

CHAPTER OUTLINE

A. Negotiability–This is a legal concept that makes written instruments freely transferable and therefore a readily accepted form of payment in substitution for money.

1. Development of Law of Negotiable Instruments–Originally, a contract right to the payment of money could not be assigned because a contractual promise ran to the specific promisee. This rule prevented the owner of the right from selling or disposing of it. Eventually, the law permitted an assignment of contractual rights and allowed the assignee to recover against the obligor. However, an innocent assignee bringing an action against the obligor was subject to all defenses available to the obligor, and the obligor has the same liability to the assignee as to the assignor. Since the promise to pay was subject to all of the defenses available against the assignor, transferees were reluctant to acquire the promise and to pay for it. Accordingly, the law of negotiable instruments developed the concept of the holder in due course, whereby certain good faith transferees who gave value acquired the right to be paid, free of most of the defenses to which an assignee would be subject. Under the holder in due course doctrine, a transferee of a negotiable instrument can acquire greater rights than the transferor, whereas an assignee acquires only the rights of the assignor. In July 1990, the American Law Institute and the National Conference of Commissioners on Uniform Laws approved a Revised Article 3. The new Article, which has been adopted by nearly all of the states, maintains the basic scope and content of the prior Article 3.

2. Assignment Compared with Negotiation–The concept of negotiability applies to negotiable instruments, governed by Article 3 of the Uniform Commercial Code, to documents of title, governed by Article 7, and to investment securities, governed by Article 8. Negotiability invests negotiable instruments with a high degree of marketability and commercial utility. It allows negotiable instruments to be freely transferable and enforceable by a person with the rights of a holder in due course against any person obligated on the instrument, subject only to a limited number of defenses. To have the full benefit of negotiability, a negotiable instrument must not only meet the requirements of negotiability, but it must also be acquired by a "holder in due course."

B. Types of Negotiable Instruments–There are four types of negotiable instruments. Drafts and checks are orders or directions to pay money. Notes and certificates of deposit are promises to pay money.

1. Drafts–A draft involves three parties. The drawer orders the drawee to pay a fixed amount in money to the payee. The same party may appear in more than one capacity; for instance, the drawer may also be the payee. A time draft is one payable at a specified future date. A sight draft is payable on presentation to the drawee.

2. Checks–A check is a specialized form of draft, namely an order to pay money drawn on a bank and payable on demand. There are three parties also involved in a check: the drawer, who orders the drawee, a bank, to pay the payee on demand. Checks are by far the most widely used form of negotiable instrument. A cashier's check is a check drawn by a bank on itself to the order of a named payee. The Check Clearing for the 21st Century Act (called "Check 21" or "Check Truncation Act") creates a new instrument called a substitute check or image replacement document (IRD). (See Chapter 30).

3. Notes–A promissory note involves two parties. One party, the maker, promises to pay to the order of a second party, the payee, a stated sum of money, either on demand or at a stated future date.

4. Certificates of Deposit–A certificate of deposit is a specialized form of promise to pay money that is given by a bank or thrift association. The bank is the maker and promises to pay the payee, who is named in the CD.

C. Formal Requirements of Negotiable Instruments–Negotiability is wholly a matter of form. All of the information required to determine whether an instrument is negotiable must be found within the four corners of the instrument. No reference to any other source is required or permitted. To be negotiable, an instrument must (1) be in writing, (2) be signed, (3) contain a promise or order to pay, (4) be unconditional, (5) be for a fixed amount ("sum certain" under prior Article 3) in money, (6) contain no other promise or order, (7) be payable on demand or at a definite time, and (8) be payable to order or to bearer.

1. Writing–The writing requirement is broadly construed. Any tangible expression is sufficient. Most negotiable instruments are written on paper, but this is not required.

2. Signed–A note or certificate of deposit must be signed by the maker; a draft or check must be signed by the drawer. A signature is any symbol executed or adopted by a party with the intention to validate a writing. An "X," a thumbprint, initials, trade name, or assumed name will suffice. Normally, a maker or drawer signs in the lower right-hand corner of the instrument, but this is not required.

3. Promise or Order to Pay–A negotiable instrument must contain a promise to pay money in the case of a note or certificate of deposit, or an order to pay in the case of a draft or check. A promise must be more than a mere acknowledgment of indebtedness. An "I.O.U." is not a promise to pay. An order is a direction or command to pay. It must be more than an authorization or request, and it must identify with reasonable certainty the person to be paid. The usual way to express an order is by the use of the word "pay" or the phrases "Pay to the order of," or "Pay bearer."

4. Unconditional–This requirement is to prevent the inclusion of any term that could reduce the promised obligation. A promise or order to pay is unconditional if it is absolute and not subject to any contingencies or qualifications. A promise or order is unconditional unless it states (a) there is an express condition to payment, (b) that it is subject to or governed by another writing, or (c) that rights or obligations concerning the order or promise are stated in another writing.

   a. Reference to Other Agreements–The restriction against reference to another agreement is to enable any person to determine the right to payment provided by the instrument without having to look beyond its four corners. If such right is made subject to the terms of another agreement, the instrument is nonnegotiable.

   b. The Particular Fund Doctrine–Revised Article 3 eliminates the particular fund doctrine by providing that a promise or order is not made conditional because payment is to be made only out of a particular fund. Under prior Article 3, an order or promise to pay only out of a particular fund was conditional and destroyed negotiability, because payment depended on the existence and sufficiency of the particular fund. However, a promise or order to pay, coupled with a mere indication of a particular fund out of which reimbursement was to be made or a particular account to be debited with the amount, did not impair negotiability, because the drawer's or the maker's general credit is relied on and charging a particular account is merely a bookkeeping entry to be followed after payment.

5. Fixed Amount–This requirement must be considered from the point of view of the holder, not the maker or drawer. The holder must be assured of a determinable minimum payment. Revised Article 3 applies the fixed amount requirement only to the principal, not interest, costs of collection, and attorney's fees on default in payment. Negotiability is not affected by the inclusion or omission of a stated rate of interest. Interest may be expressed as a fixed or variable rate or amount. A sum payable is a fixed amount even though it is payable in installments, or with a fixed discount if paid before maturity, or a fixed addition if paid after maturity.

6. Money–This term means a legal tender authorized or adopted by a sovereign government as part of its currency. An instrument payable in a fixed amount in French francs, German marks, Italian lira, Japanese yen, or other foreign currency is negotiable.

7. No Other Undertaking or Instruction–An instrument that contains an undertaking or instruction, promise or order to do an act in addition to the payment of money, is not negotiable. However, the Code sets out a list of terms that may be included without adversely affecting negotiability.

8. Payable on Demand or at a Definite Time–This requirement is intended to promote certainty in determining the present value of a negotiable instrument.

   a. Demand–Demand paper has always been considered sufficiently certain as to time of payment, because it is the holder who makes the demand and thus sets the time for payment. An instrument is considered payable on demand if it is payable "at sight" or on presentment.

   b. Definite Time–Instruments payable at a definite time are called time paper. A promise or order is payable at a definite time if it is payable: (1) at a fixed date or dates, (2) at a definite period of time after sight or acceptance, or (3) at a time readily ascertainable at the time the promise or order is issued. An instrument that by its terms is payable only on an act or event whose time of occurrence is uncertain is not payable at a definite time. A time that is readily ascertainable at the time the promise or order is issued is a definite time.

   c. At a Definite Time and on Demand–If an instrument is payable at a fixed date and also states it is payable on demand made before the fixed date, the instrument is negotiable.

9. Payable to Order or to Bearer–A negotiable instrument must contain words indicating that the maker or drawer intends that it pass into the hands of someone other than the payee. The magic words of negotiability are "payable to order or to bearer."

   a. Payable to Order–The following are correct forms for order instruments: "Pay to the order of Jane Jones" or "Pay to Jane Jones or her order." The person to whose order the instrument is payable must be designated with reasonable certainty. If an instrument is ambiguous as to whether it is payable to order or bearer, it is payable to bearer. A writing, other than a check, that names a person without indicating it is payable to order is not a negotiable instrument.

   b. Payable to Bearer–An instrument is payable to bearer if it (1) states it is payable to bearer or the order of bearer, (2) does not state a payee, or (3) states it is payable to "cash" or to the order of "cash."

10. Terms and Omissions and Their Effect on Negotiability

   a. Dating of the Instrument–In general, the negotiability of an instrument is not affected by the fact that it is undated, antedated, or postdated. If an instrument is undated, its date is the date of issuance. If unissued, its date is the date it first comes into the possession of a holder.

    b. Incomplete Instruments–If an essential term such as a promise or order, the designation of the payee, the amount payable, or the time for payment is omitted, the instrument is not negotiable until it is completed.

    c. Ambiguous Instruments–The Code establishes rules to resolve common ambiguities. This promotes negotiability by providing a degree of certainty to the holder. If it is unclear whether an instrument is a draft or a note, the holder may treat it as either and present it for payment to the drawee or the person signing it. Handwritten words control typewritten words, and typewritten words control printed words. If the amount payable is set forth on the face of instrument in both figures and words and the amounts differ, the words control the figures.

KEY TERMS

1. Negotiable instruments
2. Instrument
3. Negotiability
4. Draft
5. Drawer
6. Drawee
7. Payee
8. Check
9. Demand
10. Promissory note
11. Maker
12. Certificate of deposit
13. Writing
14. Signature
15. Promise to pay
16. Order to pay
17. Unconditional promise or order
18. Money
19. Demand paper
20. Time paper
21. Order paper
22. Bearer paper

TRUE/FALSE

_____ 1. Negotiability is a legal concept that makes written instruments an accepted form of payment in substitution for money.

_____ 2. A draft involves only two parties, the drawer and the drawee.

_____ 3. A note is a written promise by a maker to pay a payee and is thus a two-party instrument.

_____ 4. An instrument is nonnegotiable if the obligor may extend the maturity of the instrument for a definite period of time.

_____ 5. An instrument is nonnegotiable if the holder may extend the maturity of the instrument for an indefinite period of time.

_____ 6. The concept of holder in due course was developed to make transferees subject to defenses.

_____ 7. An instrument, otherwise negotiable, is negotiable bearer paper if by its terms it is payable to "cash."

_____ 8. An instrument is negotiable even though it is incomplete as to the amount payable.

_____ 9. Under Revised Article 3, an order to pay only out of a particular fund makes the instrument conditional and thus destroys negotiability.

_____ 10. In resolving ambiguities, printed words control typewritten and handwritten words, and typewritten words control handwritten words.

_____ 11. A cashier's check is a check drawn by a bank on itself to the order of a named payee.

_____ 12. A note must be signed by the drawer, while a draft must be signed by the maker.

_____ 13. Greater rights are given to the transferee under assignment than under negotiation.

_____ 14. An instrument payable with a stated, variable rate of interest is an obligation for a fixed amount.

_____ 15. The treasurer of Image, Inc. uses a stamp to sign checks drawn on the corporate account. This meets the signature requirement of negotiability.

MULTIPLE CHOICE

_____ 1. Which of the following are negotiable instruments?
   a. A draft
   b. A check
   c. A promissory note
   d. All of the above

_____ 2. A check drawn by a bank upon itself to the order of a named payee is a:
   a. promissory note.
   b. certificate of deposit.
   c. cashier's check.
   d. none of the above.

_____ 3. The legal concept of negotiability makes written instruments:
   a. acceptable as a substitute for money.
   b. acceptable as a credit device.
   c. both (a) and (b).
   d. none of the above.

_____ 4. A signature on an instrument may:
   a. appear in the upper right-hand corner.
   b. be a thumbprint.
   c. be an assumed name.
   d. be all of the above.

_____ 5. An instrument is nonnegotiable if it:
   a. refers to the existence of a separate agreement.
   b. states that it is subject to the terms of a separate agreement.
   c. is attached to a separate agreement.
   d. is made payable to the order of an office rather than a specified individual.

_____ 6. An instrument is nonnegotiable if it:
   a. relies upon the general credit of the drawer or maker.
   b. directs that a particular account be debited after payment.
   c. has no name but contains an accidental thumbprint of the maker.
   d. states that it is given in consideration for the purchase of a blue suit.

_____ 7. An instrument is nonnegotiable if:
   a. it is payable at a stated rate of interest which will increase by 2% upon default.
   b. it provides for the recovery of costs and attorney's fees upon default.
   c. it is payable with a fixed addition if paid after maturity.
   d. none of the above.

_____ 8. An instrument is nonnegotiable if it:
   a. contains a promise or order to pay 800 French francs.
   b. provides that the payee, by cashing it, acknowledges full satisfaction of an obligation of the drawer.
   c. contains a promise to deliver goods.
   d. is payable on or before a specified date.

_____ 9. An instrument is nonnegotiable if:
   a. it is payable upon an event uncertain as to time of occurrence.
   b. it is postdated.
   c. the obligor may extend the maturity of the instrument for a definite period of time.
   d. all of the above.

_____ 10. A certificate of deposit is a written acknowledgment by a bank of the receipt of money wherein the bank promises which of the following? To repay:
   a. at a stated future date.
   b. with a stated rate of interest.
   c. both of the above.
   d. none of the above.

_____ 11. Which of the following is negotiable and subject to Article 3 of the UCC?
   a. A check that states "Pay to Jose Martinez."
   b. A draft that states "Pay to Jose Martinez."
   c. A draft that states "I wish you would pay Jose Martinez."
   d. A note that states, "Due Jose Martinez $200."

_____ 12. First Bank is the holder of a note which states that it is secured by a mortgage.
   a. The note is nonnegotiable, because it refers to another agreement.
   b. The note is nonnegotiable, because it is subject to another agreement.
   c. The note is nonnegotiable, because it violates the particular fund doctrine.
   d. The note is negotiable.

_____ 13. Christina Customer deposits $5,000 at First Bank and gets a certificate of deposit from the bank.
   a. Christina is the maker of the certificate.
   b. First Bank is the maker of the certificate.
   c. Christina is the drawer of the certificate.
   d. First Bank is the drawer of the certificate.

_____ 14. *CPA:* A bank issues a negotiable instrument that acknowledges receipt of $40,000. The instrument also provides that the bank will repay the $40,000 plus 6% interest per annum to the bearer 90 days from the date of the instrument. The instrument is a:
   a. certificate of deposit.
   b. time draft.
   c. trade or banker's acceptance.
   d. cashier's check.

_____ 15. *CPA:* Assuming each of the following is negotiable, which qualifies as a draft under the UCC Negotiable Instruments Article?
   a. A warehouse receipt
   b. A demand promissory note
   c. A document of title
   d. A cashier's check.

SHORT ESSAY

1. Explain the concept of negotiability and discuss its importance.

_____

_____

_____

_____

2. Is the following instrument, "I.O.U., Adam Brown $100, /s/ Joe Green," negotiable? Explain.

_____

_____

_____

_____

3. Distinguish between "order" paper and "bearer" paper.

_____

_____

_____

_____

4. Carol Contractor is the holder of an otherwise negotiable draft that contains the following notation: "Charge this against Construction Account 7890." What effect does this notation have upon the negotiability of the instrument? Explain.

_____

_____

_____

_____

5. Explain briefly the effect on negotiability of referring to another agreement within the instrument.

_____

_____

_____

_____

Chapter 25
Transfer

PURPOSE

The primary advantage of negotiable instruments is the ease with which they can be transferred. Negotiation is the transfer of a negotiable instrument in such a manner that the transferee becomes a holder. This concept is important, because only a holder of an instrument can become a holder in due course and thus be entitled to greater rights than the transferor may have possessed. The rights of a holder in due course are the reason why negotiable instruments move easily in the marketplace. In this chapter you study the methods by which negotiable instruments may be transferred. In particular, you study the requirements of negotiation and the methods by which bearer paper and order paper may be negotiated.

CHAPTER CHECKPOINTS

After reading and studying this chapter, you should be able to:

1. Distinguish a transfer by negotiation from a transfer by assignment and discuss the ramifications of the distinction.

2. Define the term "holder" and discuss how a person becomes a holder of bearer paper in contrast to how a person becomes the holder of order paper.

3. Distinguish between a blank indorsement and a special indorsement and give an example of each.

4. Distinguish between a qualified indorsement and an unqualified indorsement and give an example of each.

5. List the various types of restrictive indorsements and give an example of each.

CHAPTER OUTLINE

A. Negotiation–Negotiation is the transfer of a negotiable instrument in such a manner that the transferee becomes a holder. A holder is defined as "a person who is in possession of an instrument drawn, issued, or indorsed to him or his order or to bearer or in blank." The transfer of a nonnegotiable instrument operates as an assignment. An assignment is the voluntary transfer to a third party of the rights arising from a contract. Whether a transfer is by "assignment" or "negotiation," the transferee acquires the rights that the transferor had. If a transfer is by negotiation and the person to whom it is negotiated is a holder in due course, then the transferee may acquire more rights than the transferor had. The requirements for negotiation depend upon whether the instrument is bearer paper or order paper.

   1. Negotiation of Bearer Paper–A bearer instrument is transferred by mere possession and is therefore comparable to cash. Because bearer paper (an instrument payable to bearer) runs to whoever is in possession of it, a finder or a thief of bearer paper would be a holder even though possession was not gained by voluntary transfer.

   2. Negotiation of Order Paper–If the instrument is order paper (an instrument payable to order), both possession and indorsement (signatures) by the appropriate parties are necessary for the transferee to become a holder. Any transfer for value of an instrument not payable to bearer gives the transferee the specifically enforceable right to have the unqualified indorsement of the transferor, unless the parties otherwise agreed. Negotiation takes effect only when a proper indorsement is made, at which time the transferee of order paper becomes a holder of the instrument. Otherwise, the transferee has nothing more than the contract rights of an assignee.

      a. The Impostor Rule–This rule is an exception to the general rule that negotiation of an order instrument requires a valid indorsement by the person to whose order the instrument is payable. It involves a situation where a confidence man impersonates someone and deceives a third party into delivering a negotiable instrument to the impostor in the name of the other person. The Code provides that the indorsement of the impostor or of any other person in the name of the named payee is effective if the impostor has induced the maker or drawer to issue the instrument to him using the name of the payee.

      b. The Fictitious Payee Rule–Under this rule an indorsement by any person in the name of a named payee is effective if an agent or employee of the maker or drawer has supplied her with the name of the payee for fraudulent purposes. The rule also applies where a person signs as or on behalf of a maker or drawer and does not intend the payee to have an interest in the instrument.

   3. Negotiations Subject to Rescission–If a negotiation conforms to the appropriate requirements, it is effective to transfer the instrument though the transaction in which it occurs is voidable or even void.

B. Indorsements–An indorsement is a signature other than that of a maker, drawer, or acceptor that alone or accompanied by other words is made on an instrument for the purpose of (i) negotiating the instrument, (ii) restricting payment of the instrument, or (iii) incurring liability on the instrument. The type of indorsement used affects its subsequent negotiation. Every indorsement is either (1) blank or special, (2) restrictive or nonrestrictive, and (3) qualified or unqualified, but these indorsements are not mutually exclusive. An indorser who merely signs her name on the back of an instrument makes a blank, nonrestrictive, unqualified indorsement.

1. Blank Indorsements–A blank indorsement specifies no indorsee and may consist of merely the signature of the indorser or her authorized agent. A blank indorsement converts order paper into bearer paper and thereafter may be negotiated by delivery alone without further indorsement.

2. Special Indorsements–A special indorsement specifically designates the person to whom or to whose order the instrument is to be payable (order paper). An indorsement reading "Pay Edward" is interpreted as meaning "Pay to the order of Edward." Any further negotiation would require Edward's indorsement. A holder of an instrument with a blank indorsement may protect himself by converting the blank indorsement to a special indorsement by writing over the signature of the indorser any contract consistent with the character of the indorsement.

3. Restrictive Indorsements–A restrictive indorsement attempts to restrict the rights of the indorsee in some fashion. The UCC defines four kinds of restrictive indorsements: conditional indorsements, indorsements prohibiting further transfer, indorsements for deposit or collection, and indorsements in trust. Only the last two are effective.

   a. Indorsements for Deposit or Collection–These are the most frequently used restrictive indorsements. They are designed to place the instrument in the banking system for deposit or collection. Examples include: "for collection," "for deposit," and "pay any bank." Such indorsements effectively limit further negotiations to those consistent with the limitation and put all nonbanking persons on notice as to who has a valid interest in the paper.

   b. Indorsements in Trust–In this type of indorsement the indorser creates a trust for the benefit of himself or others. Examples are: "Pay Trish in trust for Boris," "Pay Trish for Boris," "Pay Trish for the account of Boris," and "Pay Trish as agent for Boris." In these indorsements, Trish is a fiduciary subject to liability for any breach of her obligation.

   c. Indorsements with Ineffective Restrictions–In a conditional indorsement, the indorser makes the rights of the indorsee subject to the happening or nonhappening of a specified event. Example: "Pay Adam, but only if the good ship Jolly Jack arrives in Chicago harbor by September 15, 2006." In the instrument itself this language would make it nonnegotiable. Revised Article 3 nullifies the effect of conditional indorsements by providing that an indorsement that states a condition to the right of a holder to receive payment is ineffective to condition payment.

   An indorsement may by its express terms attempt to prohibit further transfer, such as an indorsement stating "Pay only Tom Thomas." The Code provides that no restrictive indorsement prevents further transfer or negotiation of the instrument. In effect, an indorsement that purports to prohibit further transfer of the instrument operates the same as an unrestricted indorsement.

4. Qualified and Unqualified Indorsements–Unqualified indorsers guarantee payment of the instrument if certain conditions are met. An indorser may disclaim liability on the contract of indorsement, but only if the indorsement so declares and the disclaimer is written on the instrument. The customary manner of disclaiming an indorser's liability is to add the words "without recourse," either before or after his signature. A "without recourse" indorsement is called a qualified indorsement. A qualified indorsement does not eliminate all liability of an indorser. It disclaims contract liability, but it does not entirely remove the warranty liability of the indorser.

5. Formal Requirements of Indorsements
   a. Place of Indorsement–An indorsement must be written on the instrument or on a paper, called an allonge, affixed to the instrument. An allonge may be used even if the instrument contains sufficient space for the indorsement. Customarily, indorsements are made on the back or reverse side of the instrument, starting at the top and continuing down. Failure to follow Federal Reserve Board guidelines for indorsements does not destroy negotiability.
   b. Incorrect or Misspelled Indorsement–If the name of the payee or indorsee is misspelled, or is a name different from that of the holder, the holder may require the indorsement in the name stated or in the holder's correct name or both. The person paying or taking the instrument for value may require the indorser to sign both names.

KEY TERMS

1. Holder

2. Negotiation

3. Assignment

4. Shelter rule

5. Indorsement

6. Blank indorsement

7. Special indorsement

8. Restrictive indorsement

9. Qualified indorsement

10. Allonge

TRUE/FALSE

_____ 1. A nonnegotiable instrument is not transferable.

_____ 2. An indorsement written on a piece of paper clipped to the instrument is not valid.

_____ 3. The indorsement of an impostor or of any other person in the name of the named payee is effective if the impostor has induced the maker or drawer to issue the instrument to him.

_____ 4. The transfer of a nonnegotiable promise or order operates as an assignment.

_____ 5. Negotiation of a bearer instrument requires a valid indorsement.

_____ 6. Assignment is the transfer of a negotiable instrument in such a manner that the transferee becomes a holder.

_____ 7. Requirements for negotiation depend on whether the instrument is bearer paper or order paper.

_____ 8. A qualified indorsement destroys the instrument's negotiability.

_____ 9. A person can be a holder only if the instrument has been transferred to that person by negotiation.

_____ 10. A restrictive indorsement attempts to limit the rights of the indorsee.

_____ 11. A check which is "payable to cash" requires an appropriate indorsement for further negotiation.

_____ 12. A thief or finder of order paper which has been indorsed in blank can transfer good title to a subsequent holder who may qualify as a holder in due course.

_____ 13. An indorser who has indorsed a negotiable instrument with a qualified indorsement stating that it is "without recourse" has no liability of any kind to subsequent holders.

_____ 14. A blank indorsement can be converted into a special indorsement.

_____ 15. An allonge may be used only if the instrument does not contain sufficient space for an indorsement.

MULTIPLE CHOICE

_____ 1. Indorsement by the appropriate parties is necessary to:
   a. transfer an instrument by assignment.
   b. negotiate a bearer instrument.
   c. negotiate an order instrument.
   d. (a) and (c), but not (b).

_____ 2. Which of the following is needed to be a holder of a bearer instrument?
   a. A transfer for value
   b. Possession of the instrument
   c. The indorsement of the transferor
   d. An allonge

_____ 3. The Code provision which holds that a transferee acquires the rights of a holder in due course if the transferor has such right is known as:
   a. an allonge.
   b. the shelter rule.
   c. the impostor rule.
   d. none of the above.

_____ 4. Negotiability is destroyed if an instrument is indorsed with the words:
   a. "pay to A only."
   b. "pay to the order of A."
   c. "pay to A or his order."
   d. none of the above.

_____   5. An indorsement is ineffective as a negotiation if it:
   a.   is not dated.
   b.   conveys only the unpaid balance on the instrument.
   c.   is forged.
   d.   (b) and (c) but not (a).

_____   6. Bearer paper may be converted into order paper by:
   a.   a blank indorsement.
   b.   a special indorsement.
   c.   a restrictive indorsement.
   d.   a qualified indorsement.

_____   7. If H, the holder of a note, indorses it, "Pay A, but only if P is elected president in November," the indorsement is:
   a.   blank, restrictive, qualified.
   b.   special, nonrestrictive, qualified.
   c.   blank, nonrestrictive, unqualified.
   d.   special, restrictive, unqualified.

_____   8. An indorsement which reads "Pay only if the goods are delivered by December 1, without recourse, Jane Jones" is:
   a.   blank, nonrestrictive, qualified.
   b.   blank, restrictive, unqualified.
   c.   blank, restrictive, qualified.
   d.   special, restrictive, unqualified.

_____   9. Which of the following statements, written on the back of a check, is an example of an effective restrictive indorsement?
   a.   "Pay A only."
   b.   "Pay any bank."
   c.   "Pay A, without recourse."
   d.   All of the above.

_____   10. With respect to negotiation, which of the following is true?
   a.   The transferee becomes a holder.
   b.   An impostor may never transfer a negotiable instrument.
   c.   The transferor has no liability with respect to the transferred instrument.
   d.   None of the above are true.

_____ 11. First Bank issued a certificate of deposit to Howard Homeowner. At Howard's request, the instrument was made payable to bearer.
   a. A thief could never redeem the certificate.
   b. The instrument needs a blank indorsement to be redeemed.
   c. If Howard places a special, unqualified indorsement on the instrument, he will avoid making a guarantee of its payment.
   d. None of the above.

_____ 12. Robyn indorsed her paycheck with her signature and the words "for deposit only." This indorsement is a:
   a. blank indorsement.
   b. special indorsement.
   c. restrictive indorsement.
   d. blank, restrictive indorsement.

_____ 13. A negotiation conforming to Code requirements is effective to transfer the instrument even if it is:
   a. made by a person without capacity.
   b. made as part of an illegal transaction.
   c. both of the above.
   d. neither of the above.

_____ 14. *CPA:* The following indorsements appear on the back of a negotiable promissory note made payable "to bearer." Clark has possession of the note.

Pay to Sam North
Alice Fox

Sam North
(Without recourse)

Which of the following statements is correct?
   a. Clark's unqualified indorsement is required to further negotiate the note.
   b. To negotiate the note, Clark must have given value for it.
   c. Clark is **not** a holder because North's qualified indorsement makes the note nonnegotiable.
   d. Clark can negotiate the note by delivery alone.

_____ 15. *CPA:* Hand executed and delivered to Rex a $1,000 negotiable note payable to Rex or bearer. Rex then transferred it to Ford after indorsing it on the back by merely signing his name. Which of the following is a correct statement?
   a. Rex's indorsement was a special indorsement.
   b. Rex's indorsement was necessary to Ford's qualification as a holder.
   c. The instrument initially being bearer paper **cannot** be converted to order paper.
   d. The instrument is bearer paper, but Ford can convert it to order paper by writing "pay to the order of Ford" above Rex's signature.

SHORT ESSAY

1. Distinguish between order paper and bearer paper. Explain how each is negotiated.

_____

_____

_____

_____

2. Explain the difference between a transfer by negotiation and a transfer by assignment.

_____

_____

_____

_____

3. Identify and discuss restrictive indorsements.

_____

_____

_____

_____

4. Can a negotiation be set aside if the underlying transaction is void or voidable? Explain.

_____

_____

_____

_____

5. Explain an indorsement "without recourse."

_____

_____

_____

_____

Chapter 26
Holder in Due Course

PURPOSE

The concept of holder in due course is the most significant aspect of negotiability; it is a concept that is unique to negotiable instruments. A mere holder of an instrument acquires it subject to all claims and defenses against it. However, a holder in due course in a nonconsumer credit transaction takes the instrument free of all claims of other parties and free of all defenses to the instrument except for a very limited number of claims that are specifically set forth in the Code. The holder in due course has a preferred position in the law, because such a position encourages the free transferability of negotiable instruments by minimizing the risks that are assumed by an innocent purchaser of the instrument. A holder is a person in possession of an instrument that contains all necessary indorsements. However, not every holder is a holder in due course. In addition to being a holder, a holder in due course must have taken the instrument for value, in good faith, without notice that it is overdue or dishonored, and without notice of any defense or claim to it on the part of any person. In this chapter, you study how a transferee becomes a holder in due course and the advantages of being a holder in due course.

CHAPTER CHECKPOINTS

After reading and studying this chapter, you should be able to:

1. List and discuss the requirements for becoming a holder in due course.

2. Discuss the preferred position of a holder in due course and determine whether a holder is a holder in due course.

3. Explain the shelter rule and the limitations of the rule.

4. Distinguish between real and personal defenses and identify the most common examples of each.

5. Discuss the effect of the Federal Trade Commission rule upon the status of a holder in due course.

CHAPTER OUTLINE

A. Requirements of a Holder in Due Course–To acquire the preferential rights of a holder in due course, a person must meet the requirements of the Code or must "inherit" these rights under the shelter rule.

1. Holder–A holder is a person who has both possession of an instrument and all necessary indorsements. A holder is a person who is in possession of a negotiable instrument that is payable to bearer or to an identified person if the identified person is in possession.

2. Value–A holder in due course must have given value. A holder who was given an instrument as a gift cannot be a holder in due course, because she has not given value. Value in the law of negotiable instruments differs from consideration under the law of contracts. Value, for purposes of negotiable instruments, is defined as: (1) the actual performing of the agreed promise; (2) the acquiring of a security interest or other lien on the instrument; (3) the taking of the instrument in payment of or as security for an antecedent debt; (4) the giving of a negotiable instrument; or (5) the giving of an irrevocable obligation to a third party.

   a. Executory Promise–An executory promise, an unperformed obligation, is not the giving of value to support holder-in-due-course status because it has not been performed. A holder takes an instrument for value to the extent that the agreed consideration has been given. The Code provides two exceptions to the executory promise rule: (1) the giving of a negotiable instrument, and (2) the making of an irrevocable commitment to a third party.

   b. Security Interest–Where an instrument is given as security for an obligation, the lender is regarded as having given value to the extent of the security interest.

   c. Antecedent Debt–Under the Code, a holder gives value when taking an instrument in payment of or as security for an antecedent debt.

3. Good Faith–The Code defines good faith as "honesty in fact and the observance of reasonable commercial standards of fair dealing." The observance of reasonable commercial standards of fair dealing is comparable to the definition of good faith applicable to merchants under the Code.

4. Lack of Notice–To become a holder in due course, a holder must take the instrument without notice that it is: (1) overdue, (2) dishonored, (3) forged or altered, or (4) subject to any claim or defense. A person has notice of a fact when (a) he has actual knowledge of it; or (b) he has received a notice or notification of it; or (c) from all the facts and circumstances known to him at the time in question he has reason to know that it exists. Since the applicable standard is "actual notice," "notice received," or "reason to know," constructive notice through public filing or recording is not of itself sufficient notice to prevent a person from becoming a holder in due course. To be effective, notice must be received at such a time and way that will give the recipient a reasonable opportunity to act on it.

   a. Notice an Instrument is Overdue–To be a holder in due course, the purchaser must take the instrument without notice that it is overdue. Time paper is due on its stated due date if the stated day is a business day or, if not, on the next business day. Demand paper is not overdue for purposes of holder in due course status unless the purchaser has notice that she is taking it after demand has been made, or until it has been outstanding for a reasonable length of time. In the case of a check, a reasonable time is ninety days after its date. For other demand instruments, the reasonable period of time varies depending on the facts of each case.

b. Notice an Instrument Has Been Dishonored–Dishonor is the refusal to pay or accept an instrument when it becomes due. A transferee who has notice that an instrument has been dishonored, cannot become a holder in due course.

c. Notice of a Claim or Defense–A purchaser of an instrument cannot become a holder in due course if purchasing it with notice of a defense or claim to it. A defense to the instrument is a justification or shield protecting a person from liability on it, whereas a claim to the instrument is an assertion of ownership to it.

5. Without Reason to Question its Authenticity–A party may be a holder in due course only if the instrument "does not bear such apparent evidence of forgery or alteration or is not otherwise so irregular or incomplete as to call into question its authenticity." It does not matter if the holder does not have notice of such irregularity or incompleteness; it depends only on whether the instrument's defect is apparent and whether the taker should have reason to know of the problem.

B. Holder in Due Course Status–A payee may become a holder in due course. Also, a transferee of a holder in due course acquires this status.

1. A Payee May Be a Holder in Due Course–The Code provides that a payee who satisfies the holder-in-due-course requirements may be a holder in due course. A payee who is not an immediate party to the transaction will not be subject to any claims and most defenses if the payee meets the requirements of a holder in due course.

2. The Shelter Rule–The transferee of an instrument acquires the same rights in the instrument that the transferor had. Therefore, a holder who does not qualify to be a holder in due course acquires all the rights of one if some previous holder of the instrument has been a holder in due course. However, a transferee (1) who has been a party to any fraud or illegality affecting the instrument, or (2) who as a prior holder had notice of a claim or defense, may not obtain the rights of a holder in due course by reacquiring the instrument from a subsequent holder who is either a holder in due course or who has the rights of one. In other words, a transferee cannot improve his position by reacquiring the instrument.

C. The Preferred Position of a Holder in Due Course–In a nonconsumer transaction, a holder in due course takes the instrument (1) free from all claims on the part of any person and (2) free from all defenses of any party with whom he has not dealt, except for a limited number of defenses that are available against anyone, including a holder in due course.

1. Real Defenses–Real defenses are available against all holders, including holders in due course. The real defenses are as follows:

a. Infancy–The Code does not state when infancy is available as a defense or the conditions under which it may be asserted. Rather, it provides that infancy is a defense available against a holder in due course to the extent that it is a defense to a simple contract under the laws of the state involved.

b. Void Obligations–When the obligation on an instrument originates in such a way that under the law of the state involved it is void, the Code authorizes the use of this defense against a holder in due course. Incapacity, duress, and illegality of the transaction are defenses that may render the obligation of a party voidable or void. To the extent that the underlying transaction is voidable only, the defense (other than minority) is ineffective against a holder in due course.

c. Fraud in the Execution–Fraud in the execution of an instrument renders the instrument void and therefore is a valid defense against a holder in due course. The Code describes fraud in the execution as misrepresentation that induced the party to sign the instrument with neither knowledge nor a reasonable opportunity to learn of its character or its essential terms.

d. Discharge in Insolvency Proceedings–A party whose obligation on an instrument is discharged in a bankruptcy or any other insolvency proceeding has a valid defense in an action on the instrument, including one by a holder in due course.

e. Discharge of Which the Holder Has Notice–Any holder, including a holder in due course, takes the instrument subject to any discharge of which he has notice at the time of taking. If a holder acquires an instrument with notice that all prior parties have been discharged, he cannot become a holder in due course.

f. Unauthorized Signature–A person's signature on an instrument is unauthorized when it is made without authority. A person whose signature is unauthorized or forged cannot be held liable on the instrument in the absence of estoppel or ratification, even if the instrument is negotiated to a holder in due course. Any unauthorized signature is totally invalid as that of the person whose name is signed unless he ratifies it or is precluded from denying it. The signature operates only as the signature of the unauthorized signer. A person may, however, be estopped from asserting this defense because her conduct caused reliance by a third party.

g. Fraudulent Alteration–An alteration is any unauthorized change that modifies the obligation of any party to the instrument or an unauthorized addition or change to an incomplete instrument concerning the obligation of a party. An alteration that is fraudulently made discharges a party whose obligation is affected, except where that party assents or is precluded by his own negligence from raising the defense.

2. Personal Defenses–These are contractual defenses that are good against assignees and holders but not holders in due course. Personal defenses include (1) lack of consideration; (2) failure of consideration; (3) breach of contract; (4) fraud in the inducement; (5) illegality that does not render the transaction void; (6) duress, undue influence, mistake, misrepresentation, or incapacity that does not render the transaction void; (7) setoff or counterclaim; (8) discharge of which a holder in due course has no notice; (9) nondelivery of an instrument; (10) unauthorized completion of an incomplete instrument; (11) payment without obtaining surrender of the instrument; (12) theft of a bearer instrument or an instrument payable to him; and (13) lack of authority of a corporate officer or an agent or partner as to the particular instrument.

D. Limitations Upon Holder in Due Course Rights–The preferential position of a holder in due course is limited by a Federal Trade Commission rule that applies to consumer credit contracts. This rule applies to sellers and lessors of consumer goods, i.e., goods for personal, family, or household use. It also applies to lenders that advance money to finance a consumer's purchase of consumer goods or services. Under the UCC, if a buyer executes and delivers to the seller a negotiable instrument that the seller then negotiates to a holder in due course, then the consumer must continue to make payments to the holder in due course even if products or services purchased are defective or the transaction involves fraud in the inducement. These defenses cannot ordinarily be asserted against a holder in due course of the instrument. The FTC rule, however, requires a conspicuous notice in a consumer credit contract that preserves these defenses for consumer purchasers against subsequent holders in due course, in effect placing holders in due course in the position of assignees.

KEY TERMS

1. Holder
2. Holder in due course
3. Value
4. Executory promise
5. Antecedent debt
6. Good faith

7. Dishonor
8. Shelter rule
9. Real defense
10. Personal defense
11. Alteration

TRUE/FALSE

_____ 1. In order to become a holder in due course, the transferee must first be a holder.

_____ 2. A person may acquire the rights of a holder in due course even though he does not take the instrument for value.

_____ 3. The concept of value in the law of negotiable instruments is the same as that of consideration under the law of contracts.

_____ 4. A check is presumed overdue if it has been outstanding more than 30 days.

_____ 5. Revised Article 3 of the Code defines "good faith" as honesty in fact and the observance of reasonable commercial standards of fair dealing.

_____ 6. Personal defenses may not be asserted against a holder in due course.

_____ 7. A person may be a holder in due course even if taking the instrument after all of the parties to the instrument have been discharged, regardless of whether or not he has notice of the discharge.

_____ 8. The Federal Trade Commission rule treats a holder in due course of an instrument in the same manner as an assignee if the instrument concerns a debt arising out of a consumer credit contract.

_____ 9. When an incomplete instrument has been completed in an authorized manner, a subsequent holder in due course may enforce the instrument as completed.

_____ 10. Under the Code, a person has notice of a fact if he has reason to know that it exists from all of the facts and circumstances known to him at the time in question.

_____ 11. An executory promise is not ordinarily considered the giving of value to support holder in due course status.

_____ 12. Buford Buyer issued a note to Sarita Seller in return for goods to be used as inventory. Buford's customers later complained that the goods were defective, so Buford dishonored the note. Sarita can assert holder in due course status to enforce the note against Buford.

_____ 13. Under the shelter rule a transferee will acquire the rights of a holder in due course regardless of the rights held by the transferor.

_____ 14. Haley issues a $25 check to her niece for graduation from high school. The niece is a holder in due course.

_____ 15. Leo holds a gun to John's head and forces him to sign a note for $5,000. Leo then transfers the note to First Bank who now wants to collect $5,000 from John. John can assert the defense of duress against First Bank in order to avoid payment.

MULTIPLE CHOICE

_____ 1. Persons are holders if they possess instruments:
   a.   issued to their order or to bearer.
   b.   indorsed to them.
   c.   (a) or (b).
   d.   (a) and (b).

_____ 2. Persons may acquire the rights of a holder in due course if they take the instrument:
   a.   for value.
   b.   in bad faith.
   c.   with notice that it has been dishonored.
   d.   all of the above.

_____ 3. Holders take instruments for value when they:
   a.   make irrevocable commitments to their transferors.
   b.   promise to pay the agreed consideration.
   c.   take the instruments as security for antecedent debts.
   d.   (a) and (c), but not (b).

_____ 4. A purchaser takes an instrument in good faith if:
   a.   he believes there is nothing wrong with it.
   b.   he knows there is something wrong with it.
   c.   a prudent man under the circumstances would not have known that something was wrong with it, but the purchaser in fact knows something is wrong with it.
   d.   (a) and (c), but not (b).

_____ 5. The shelter rule does not apply in which of the following situations?
   a. Where the holder has been party to a fraud affecting the instrument.
   b. Where the holder has been party to an illegal act affecting the instrument.
   c. The shelter rule applies in both situation (a) and situation (b).
   d. The shelter rule does not apply in either situation (a) or situation (b).

_____ 6. *M* issues a note to *P* which is successively negotiated to *A*, *B*, *C*, and *H*. If *H* is a holder in due course with respect to all parties, then *H* is subject to the personal defenses of:
   a. *A* only.
   b. *B* only.
   c. *C* only.
   d. none of the above.

_____ 7. Assume *M* issues a note to *P* which is successively negotiated to *A*, *B*, *C*, and *H*. If *H* is a holder in due course with respect to all the parties to the instrument, then *H* is subject to the real defenses of:
   a. *A* only.
   b. *B* only.
   c. *C* only.
   d. all of the above.

_____ 8. A party to an instrument has a real defense if his obligation on the instrument:
   a. is void.
   b. is the result of duress.
   c. has been discharged without notice to the him.
   d. is the result of fraud in the inducement.

_____ 9. A forged signature operates as the signature of:
   a. the person whose name is forged.
   b. the forger.
   c. any person who takes the instrument with notice that the signature has been forged.
   d. none of the above.

_____ 10. Under the FTC's holder in due course rule, the consumer may successfully assert:
   a. real defenses.
   b. personal defenses.
   c. real and personal defenses.
   d. none of the above.

_____ 11. Which of the following constitutes value for purposes of holder in due course status?
   a. The taking of an instrument in payment of an antecedent debt
   b. An executory promise to pay money
   c. The acquiring of a security interest in the instrument
   d. (a) and (c) only

_____ 12. *CPA:* To the extent that a holder of a negotiable promissory note is a holder in due course, the holder takes the note free of which of the following defenses?
   a. Minority of the maker where it is a defense to enforcement or a contract
   b. Forgery of the maker's signature
   c. Discharge of the maker in bankruptcy
   d. Nonperformance of a condition precedent

_____ 13. *CPA:* A subsequent holder of a negotiable instrument may cause the discharge of a prior holder of the instrument by any of the following actions **except**:
   a. unexcused delay in presentment of a time draft.
   b. procuring certification of a check.
   c. giving notice of dishonor the day after dishonor.
   d. material alteration of a note.

_____ 14. Paula Payee by means of fraud in the inducement induces Michael Maker to sign an instrument payable to her. Paula subsequently negotiates the instrument to Hannah Holder, a holder in due course. Paula later reacquires the note from Hannah.
   a. Paula can invoke the shelter rule.
   b. Paula is a holder in due course if she gave value to Hannah.
   c. Paula remains subject to the defense of fraud and cannot invoke the shelter rule.
   d. Paula can invoke the shelter rule and may be a holder in due course if she gave value to Hannah.

_____ 15. Tonya has a checking account with First Bank. She deposits a $300 check in her account and then writes a check to Independent Department Store in the amount of $100 which First Bank then pays from her account.
   a. First Bank is a holder in due course in the amount of $300.
   b. First Bank is a holder in due course in the amount of $100.
   c. First Bank is not a holder in due course, because it has not given value.
   d. First Bank is not a holder in due course, because it has a customer relationship with Tonya.

SHORT ESSAY

1. What are the requirements for becoming a holder in due course?

_____

_____

_____

_____

2. Explain the difference between a holder and a holder in due course.

_____

_____

_____

_____

3. Explain the shelter rule and limitations thereon.

_____

_____

_____

_____

4. *P* induces *M*, by fraud in the inducement, to make a note payable to her order and then negotiates it to *H*, a holder in due course. After the note is overdue, *H* gives it to *B*, who has notice of the fraud. What are the rights of *B*?

_____

_____

_____

_____

5. Gary makes a note payable to the order of Estill for $2,000. Estill negotiates it to Jason, who changes the amount to $20,000 and negotiates it to Melissa, who qualifies as a holder in due course. What rights does Melissa have in the instrument? Explain.

_____

_____

_____

_____

Chapter 27
Liability of Parties

PURPOSE

In this chapter, you study the liability of parties arising out of negotiable instruments and the ways in which liability may be terminated. There are two types of liability associated with negotiable instruments: (1) contractual liability, which may be either primary liability on the instrument or secondary liability on the instrument; and (2) warranty liability, which applies to persons who transfer an instrument and to persons who receive payment or acceptance of an instrument. Contractual liability on the instrument is only imposed upon persons who have signed the instrument. However, warranty liability is not based upon having signed the instrument; it may be imposed upon both signers and nonsigners of an instrument.

CHAPTER CHECKPOINTS

After reading and studying this chapter, you should be able to:

1. Distinguish between and discuss contractual liability and warranty liability.

2. Discuss the liability for authorized signatures and for unauthorized signatures.

3. Summarize the liability of makers, acceptors, drawees, drawers, indorsers, and accommodation parties.

4. Compare the warranties on transfer with those on presentment.

5. Discuss the ways that liability of the parties to an instrument may be terminated.

CHAPTER OUTLINE

I. Contractual Liability–All parties whose signatures appear on a negotiable instrument incur certain contractual liabilities, unless they disclaim liability. The maker of a promissory note and the acceptor of a draft assume primary or unconditional liability. Primary liability is an absolute obligation to pay a negotiable instrument. Drawers of drafts and checks and indorsers of all instruments incur secondary or conditional liability if the instrument is not paid. Secondary liability is an obligation to pay a negotiable instrument subject to conditions of presentment, dishonor, notice of dishonor, and sometimes protest. Accommodation parties sign a negotiable instrument for the purpose of lending their credit to another party. Accommodation parties have liability based upon the manner in which they sign. If they sign as makers, they have primary liability; if they sign as indorsers, they have secondary liability.

   A. Signature–Signature is broadly defined to include any name, word, or mark, whether handwritten, typed, or printed so long as it is made with the intention of authenticating the instrument. It may be made by the individual or the individual's agent.

   1. Authorized Signatures–An agent who executes a negotiable instrument on behalf of a principal is not liable on the instrument if it is executed properly and the agent is authorized. The correct form for an agent to sign and avoid liability is "P, principal, by A, agent." An authorized agent may improperly sign an instrument by (a) only signing his own name to the instrument, (b) signing his own name and stating that he is signing in a representative capacity without stating the principal's name, or (c) signing his own name and the name of the principal but failing to state that he is signing in a representative capacity. In all of these situations, the following rules apply:
      - The agent is liable on the instrument only to a holder in due course who takes the instrument without notice that the agent was not intended to be liable.
      - The principal is liable to all holders (based on contract and agency law principles).
      - Under Revised Article 3, an authorized agent is not liable on the instrument if the agent only signs his name as the drawer of a *check* without indicating his representative status and the check is payable from the principal's account.

   2. Unauthorized Signatures–This includes both forgeries and signatures made by an agent without proper authority to do so. An unauthorized signature is generally not binding on the person whose name appears on the instrument, but it is binding on the unauthorized signer whether or not her own name appears on the instrument. However, an unauthorized signature does bind the person whose name is signed if that person by his negligence substantially contributes to the making of the unauthorized signature. A subsequent holder in due course will not be subject to the defense of unauthorized signature. Also, an unauthorized signature may be ratified by the person whose name appears on the instrument.

      a. Ratification of Unauthorized Signature–The person whose name appears on the instrument may ratify an unauthorized signature, relieving the actual signer from liability on the instrument. This does not of itself affect any rights the person ratifying the signature may have against the actual signer.

      b. Negligence Contributing to Forged Signature–Any person who, by negligence, substantially contributes to the making of an unauthorized signature will be estopped from asserting the lack of authority as a defense against a holder in due course or one who has paid the instrument in good faith or who took it for value or for collection.

B. Liability of Primary Parties–The makers and acceptors are primarily liable.
1. Makers–The maker of a note is obligated to pay the instrument according to its terms at the time of issuance, or in the case of an incomplete instrument, according to its terms when completed. Primary liability also applies to issuers of cashier's checks and to issuers of drafts drawn on the drawer.
2. Acceptors–A drawee has no liability on the instrument until she accepts it, at which time she becomes an acceptor and primarily liable. Certification is a special type of acceptance consisting of the drawee bank's promise to pay the check when presented for payment.

C. Liability of Secondary Parties–The drawers and indorsers (including a payee who indorses) are secondarily liable.
1. Drawers–If the instrument is not paid by a primary party and the conditions precedent to the liability of secondary parties are satisfied, then a secondary party is liable unless the secondary party has disclaimed liability or has a valid defense.
2. Indorsers–Indorsers promise that upon dishonor of the instrument *and* notice of dishonor, they will pay the instrument according to its terms at the time it was indorsed.
3. Effect of Acceptance–When a draft is accepted by a bank, the drawer and all prior indorsers are discharged.
4. Disclaimer of Liability by Secondary Parties–Both drawers and indorsers may disclaim their secondary liability by drawing or indorsing instruments "without recourse." Drawers of checks may not disclaim contractual liability. A person drawing or indorsing an instrument "without recourse" does not incur normal contractual liability, but may be liable for breach of warranty.
5. Conditions Precedent to Liability–A condition precedent is an event, or events, that must occur before liability arises. The condition precedent to the liability of the drawer of an unaccepted draft is dishonor. Conditions precedent to the liability of any indorser or the drawer of an accepted draft by a nonbank are dishonor and notice of dishonor. If these conditions are not met, a party's conditional obligation on the instrument is discharged unless the conditions are excused.
   a. Dishonor–Dishonor generally involves the refusal to pay an instrument when demand is made by or on behalf of a person entitled to enforce the instrument. What constitutes dishonor varies depending upon the type of instrument and whether presentment is required.
      (1) Note–A demand note is dishonored if the maker does not pay it on the day of presentment. A note payable at a definite time is dishonored if it is not paid on the date it is presented or its due date, whichever is later if (i) the terms of the note require presentment or (ii) the note is payable at or through a bank. All other time notes need not be presented and are dishonored if they are not paid on their due dates.
      (2) Drafts–An unaccepted draft payable on demand is dishonored if not paid upon presentment. An accepted demand draft is dishonored if the acceptor does not pay it on the day presented.
      (3) Checks–A check is dishonored where it is presented for payment directly to the payor/drawee bank for immediate payment and there is a refusal to pay. More

commonly, a check being presented through the normal collection process is dishonored if the payor bank makes timely return of the check, sends timely notice of dishonor or nonpayment, or becomes accountable for the amount of the check.

b. Notice of Dishonor–The obligation of an indorser of any instrument and of a drawer of a draft accepted by a nonbank is not enforceable unless the indorser or drawer are given notice of dishonor or the notice is otherwise excused.

c. Presentment and Notice of Dishonor Excused–Presentment will be excused if (i) the person entitled to enforce the instrument cannot reasonably present the instrument, (ii) the maker or acceptor has repudiated the obligation to pay, is dead, or is in insolvency proceedings, (iii) the terms of the instrument do not require presentment in order to hold the indorser or drawer liable, (iv) the drawer or indorser has waived the right of presentment, (v) the drawer instructed the drawee not to pay or accept the draft, or (vi) the drawee was not obligated to the drawer to pay the draft.

6. Liability for Conversion–Conversion is a tort whereby a person becomes liable in damages because of the wrongful control over the personal property of another. The law applicable to conversion of personal property applies to instruments.

D. Termination of Liability–The Code specifies the methods by and extent to which the liability of any party, primary or secondary, is discharged. It also specifies when the liability of *all* parties is discharged.

1. Payment–Payment to a party entitled to enforce the instrument will discharge liability.

2. Tender of Payment–Any party liable on an instrument who makes tender of full payment to a person entitled to enforce the instrument when or after payment is due is discharged from all subsequent proper liability for interest. The party is still liable for the face amount of the instrument or any interest accrued until the time of tender, should tender be refused.

3. Cancellation and Renunciation–Intentional cancellation of the instrument by the person entitled to enforce the instrument results in a discharge of all parties. Accidental destruction or cancellation does not have such an effect. A party entitled to enforce an instrument may renounce the rights to the instrument by a writing, signed and delivered to the party to be discharged. Cancellation or renunciation needs no consideration to be effective.

II. Liability Based on Warranty–There are two types of Article 3 implied warranties: transferor's warranties and presenter's warranties. The warranties may be disclaimed by agreement between the immediate parties, but they are effective otherwise whether or not the transferor or presenter signs the instrument.

A. Warranties on Transfer–These warranties are given by any person who transfers, by negotiation or assignment, an instrument and receives consideration. If the transfer is by delivery alone, the warranties run only to the immediate transferee. If the transfer is by indorsement, whether qualified or unqualified, the transfer warranties run to "any subsequent transferee." Transfer means that the delivery of possession is voluntary. The warranties of the transferor are as follows:

1. Entitlement to Enforce–The transferor warrants that he has the entitlement to enforce the instrument to obtain payment or acceptance on behalf of one who has good title and that the transfer is otherwise rightful.

2. Authentic and Authorized Signatures–The transferor warrants that all signatures are authentic and authorized.
3. No Alteration–The transferor warrants that the instrument has not been materially altered.
4. No Defenses–The transferor warrants that the instrument is not subject to defense or claim in recoupment of any party.
5. No Knowledge of Insolvency–The transferor warrants that he has no knowledge of any insolvency proceedings instituted by the maker, acceptor, or drawer of an unaccepted instrument.

B. Warranties on Presentment–Any party who pays or accepts an instrument must do so in strict compliance with the orders contained in that instrument. In the case of a note, a maker who pays the wrong person will not be discharged from the obligation to pay the correct person. A drawee who pays the wrong person generally cannot charge the drawer's account. What warranties are given by presenters depend on who is the payor or acceptor. The greatest protection is given to drawees of unaccepted drafts. All other payors receive significantly less protection..
1. Drawees of Unaccepted Drafts–A drawee of an unaccepted draft who pays or accepts in good faith, receives a presentment warranty from the person obtaining payment or acceptance and from all prior transferors of the draft. These parties warrant that the warrantor is entitled to enforce the draft, the draft has not been altered, and the warrantor has no knowledge the drawer's signature is unauthorized.
    a. Entitled to Enforce–Presenters of unaccepted checks give the same warranty of entitlement to enforce to persons who pay or accept as is granted to transferees under the transferor's warranty.
    b. No Alteration–Presenters warrant that there has been no alteration.
    c. Genuineness of Drawer's Signature–Presenters warrant that they have no knowledge that the signature of drawer is unauthorized.
2. All other Payors–The only warranty given is that the warrantor is a person entitled to enforce the instrument or is authorized to obtain payment on behalf of the person entitled to enforce it.

KEY TERMS

1. Contractual liability
2. Warranty liability
3. Primary liability
4. Secondary liability
5. Accommodation party
6. Acceptance
7. Acceptor

8. Certification
9. Dishonor
10. Presentment
11. Discharge
12. Cancellation
13. Transferor's warranties
14. Presenter's warranties

TRUE/FALSE

_____ 1. A person may be liable on a negotiable instrument even without signing it.

_____ 2. A forger will be liable on an instrument even though he signs someone else's name and not his own.

_____ 3. The liability of an accommodation party is determined by the capacity in which she signs.

_____ 4. The acceptor of a draft or check assumes secondary liability on the instrument.

_____ 5. An unauthorized signature may not be ratified even by the person whose name appears on the instrument.

_____ 6. A bank that pays an instrument on a forged indorsement will be liable for conversion even though it acted in good faith.

_____ 7. If an authorized agent signs his name as drawer on a check that bears the name of the principal on whose account the check is drawn but the agent fails to state that he is signing only as an agent of the principal, then both the agent and the principal are liable on the instrument.

_____ 8. An indorser may disclaim contractual liability by using the notation "without recourse."

_____ 9. If an instrument is transferred by delivery alone (without indorsement) warranties in transfer run to the immediate transferee only.

_____ 10. An indorser is completely discharged from liability on an instrument if due presentment for payment has not been made.

_____ 11. Noncompliance with conditions precedent has a different effect on the liability of an indorser than on the liability of a drawer.

_____ 12. Andrew is the indorser of a note for $1,000 on which Michael is the maker. Andrew becomes immediately liable for the face amount when the note becomes due.

_____ 13. The discharge of a party is not effective against a subsequent holder in due course unless she has notice of the discharge when she takes the instrument.

_____ 14. David Drawer wrote a check for $1,000 payable to Paul Payee. Paul altered the check to read $11,000 and negotiated the check to Heather, a holder in due course. Paul is liable to Heather under the transferor's warranties.

_____ 15. Any necessary notice of dishonor must be given by a bank before midnight on the first banking day after the banking day when it receives notice of dishonor.

MULTIPLE CHOICE

_____ 1. A signature may be:
   a. printed.
   b. made by an authorized agent.
   c. typed.
   d. all of the above.

_____ 2. A drawee bank becomes liable on a check when:
   a. the check is written.
   b. the drawer issues the check.
   c. the payee indorses the check.
   d. the bank accepts the check.

_____ 3. An indorser may disclaim contractual liability on an instrument if his indorsement contains the words:
   a. "time is of the essence."
   b. "Caveat Emptor."
   c. "without recourse."
   d. "notice of dishonor."

_____ 4. Presentment may be made by which of the following?
   a. Mail.
   b. At a place specified in the instrument.
   c. Through a clearinghouse.
   d. All of the above.

_____ 5. Warranty liability:
   a. is based on signature on negotiable instruments.
   b. is imposed on both signers and nonsigners of negotiable instruments.
   c. is based on contract.
   d. may not be disclaimed by agreement between immediate parties.

_____ 6. Jackie, without authority, signs Kenneth's name to an instrument. Which of the following is true?
   a. Kenneth is liable for the instrument.
   b. Jackie is liable on the instrument.
   c. Neither Kenneth nor Jackie is liable on the instrument.
   d. Both Kenneth and Jackie are liable, but Jackie has primary liability.

_____ 7. Which of the following is not a warranty of transfer?
   a. No material alteration.
   b. Maker is solvent.
   c. Entitlement to enforce.
   d. Signatures genuine.

_____ 8. The parties that are secondarily liable for payment of an instrument include:
   a. makers and acceptors.
   b. makers and drawers.
   c. drawers and indorsers.
   d. drawers and acceptors.

_____ 9. Which of the following is not an example of conversion?
   a. A drawee to whom a draft is delivered for acceptance refuses to return it on demand.
   b. An instrument is paid on a forged indorsement.
   c. A holder unjustifiably impairs any collateral given on an instrument by a party to that instrument.
   d. A drawee to whom an instrument is delivered for payment refuses on demand either to pay or to return it.

_____ 10. A holder who intentionally strikes out an indorser's signature:
   a. has discharged that indorser.
   b. is liable for conversion.
   c. has broken the chain of title.
   d. is not entitled to payment.

_____ 11. An indorser who is required to pay an instrument has no right of recourse against:
   a. subsequent indorsers.
   b. prior indorsers.
   c. makers and acceptors.
   d. any party.

_____ 12. Susan Kalinowsky owns a business and is known for business purposes as Susan Monroe. She signs her business checks and notes as Susan Monroe.
   a. Susan is liable on these checks and notes, because her signature is valid.
   b. Susan has no liability, because her signature is under an assumed name.
   c. Susan is a fictitious payee.
   d. Susan has secondary liability because the business has primary liability.

_____ 13. A person obtaining payment warrants to a drawee of an unaccepted draft who pays in good faith:
   a. that all signatures are genuine and authorized.
   b. that there are no defenses against the instrument.
   c. that he has entitlement to enforce.
   d. that no defenses are good against him.

_____ 14. _CPA:_ Which of the following actions does **not** discharge a prior party to a negotiable instrument?
   a. Good faith payment or satisfaction of the instrument
   b. Cancellation of that prior party's indorsement
   c. The holder's oral renunciation of that prior party's liability
   d. The holder's intentional destruction of the instrument

_____ 15. _CPA:_ Blare bought a house and provided the required funds in the form of a certified check from a bank. Which of the following statements correctly describes the legal liability of Blare and the Bank?
   a. The bank has accepted; therefore, Blare is without liability.
   b. The bank has **not** accepted; therefore, Blare has primary liability.
   c. The bank has accepted, but Blare has secondary liability.
   d. The bank has **not** accepted, but Blare has secondary liability.

SHORT ESSAY

1. Explain the difference between contractual liability and warranty liability.

_____

_____

_____

_____

2. Your roommate writes a check to you and you indorse it "Pay to Cathy" and your signature, and give it to Cathy to pay a debt you owe her. Cathy writes "Without recourse, Cathy" and gives it to Ben. Ben quickly presents it to the bank for payment, but payment is refused. What can Ben do?

_____

_____

_____

_____

3. What are the differences between primary and secondary liability?

_____

_____

_____

_____

4. Discuss briefly the difference between authorized and unauthorized signatures.

_____

_____

_____

_____

5. You are the president of XYZ, Inc. and are authorized to sign instruments on behalf of XYZ, Inc. You execute a promissory note on behalf of the XYZ, Inc. payable to the order of Jim Farrow. You sign the note with your name and indicate that you are president, but the name of XYZ, Inc. does not appear on the note. Jim Farrow, however, understands that you are signing the note only as a representative of XYZ, Inc. Under these facts, who is liable on the note?

_____

_____

_____

_____

Chapter 28
Bank Deposits, Collections, and Funds Transfers

PURPOSE

Today most goods and services are bought and sold without a physical transfer of cash. Credit cards, charge accounts, and various deferred payment plans have made cash sales increasingly rare. The credit sales are usually settled by check rather than cash. Generally, the buyer's check must journey from the seller-payee's bank (depositary bank), where the check is deposited by the seller for credit to its account, to the buyer-drawer's bank (payor bank) for payment. In the collection process, checks can also pass through one or more banks (intermediary banks) so that it may be collected and the appropriate entries recorded. In recent years, the amount of payment made by electronic funds transfers has also increased. The dollar volume of commercial payments made by wire transfer far exceeds the dollar amount made by checks and credit cards. In this chapter you study the bank deposit-collection system and electronic funds transfers.

CHAPTER CHECKPOINTS

After reading and studying this chapter, you should be able to:

1. Define and distinguish among the depositary, payor, intermediary, and collecting banks.

2. Define provisional credit, and discuss how and when credit becomes final.

3. Discuss the obligations imposed on the customer and on the payor bank as part of their relationship.

4. Define electronic fund transfer, compare it to the check collection process of Article 4, and outline the major provisions of the Electronic Fund Transfers Act.

5. Discuss the scope of Article 4A of the UCC which covers wholesale funds transfers.

CHAPTER OUTLINE

I. Bank Deposits and Collections–Article 4 of the UCC provides the principal rules governing the bank collection process.

   A. Collection of Items–The depositary bank is the bank in which the payee or holder deposits a check for credit. Provisional credit is tentative credit for the deposit of an instrument until final credit is given. If the bank permits a customer to draw funds against provisional credit, the bank has given value and, provided it meets the other requirements, is a holder in due course. When the amount of the check has been collected from the payor bank, which is also the drawee bank, the credit becomes final. The Competitive Equality Banking Act of 1987 expedited the availability of funds by establishing maximum time periods for a bank to hold various types of instruments. A bank may be both the depositary bank and the payor bank; however, in most cases they are different banks. When the two are different banks, a check must pass from one bank to the other, either directly through a clearinghouse or through one or more intermediary banks. An intermediary bank is a bank involved in the collection process other than the depositary or payor bank. A clearinghouse is an association of banks or other payors for the purpose of settling accounts on a daily basis.

   1. Collecting Banks–A collecting bank is any bank, except the payor bank, handling the item for payment. In the usual situation where the depositary and payor banks are different, the depositary bank gives a provisional credit to its customer, transfers the item to the next bank in the chain, receiving a provisional credit or "settlement" from it, and so on to the payor bank, which then debits the drawer's account. When the check is paid, the provisional settlements become final. If the payor bank does not pay the item, the process must be reversed so that ultimately the depositary bank charges the account of the customer who deposited the check. He must then seek recovery from the drawer or indorsers. A collecting bank is an agent of the owner of the check until settlement becomes final. Any credit given is provisional until settlement becomes final at which time the depositary collecting bank changes from an agent of the depositor to a debtor of the depositor. The effect of this agency rule is that the risk of loss remains with the owner and any chargebacks go to her, not to the collecting bank.

       a. Duty of Care–A collecting bank must use ordinary care in handling an item transferred to it for collection. It must act within a reasonable time after receipt of the item and must choose a reasonable method of forwarding the item for presentment.

       b. Duty to Act Timely–A collecting bank acts timely if it acts within the midnight deadline. The midnight deadline means midnight of the banking day following the banking day on which the bank receives the item or notice of its dishonor. If a bank receives a check on Monday, it must take proper action by midnight on Tuesday. The Code allows banks to fix an afternoon hour of 2:00 p.m. or later as a cutoff hour for bookkeeping purposes in order to meet the midnight deadline.

       c. Indorsements–When an item is restrictively indorsed with words such as "pay any bank," it is locked into the bank collection system. When a bank forwards an item for collection, it normally indorses it "pay any bank." This protects the bank by making it impossible for the item to stray from regular collection channels. If there was no indorsement, the bank still becomes a holder when it takes possession, if the customer was a holder at the time of delivery to the bank. If the bank meets the other requirements, it will become a holder in due course.

    d. Warranties–Customers and collecting banks give basically the same warranties as those given by parties under Article 3 of the Code upon presentment and transfer.

    e. Final Payment–Under the Code, final payment occurs when the payor bank first does any of the following: (1) pays an item in cash; (2) settles and does not have the right to revoke the settlement through agreement, statute, or clearinghouse rule; or (3) makes a provisional settlement and does not revoke it in the time and manner permitted by statute, clearinghouse rule, or agreement.

2. Payor Banks–Under its contract with the drawer, the payor or drawee bank agrees to pay to the payee or his order checks that are issued by the drawer, provided the order is not countermanded by a stop payment order and provided there are sufficient funds in the drawer's account. When a payor bank that is not also a depositary bank receives a demand item other than for immediate payment over the counter, it must either return the item or give its transferor a provisional settlement before midnight of the banking day on which the item is received.

B. Relationship Between Payor Bank and Its Customer–The relationship between a payor bank and its checking account customer is primarily the product of their contractual arrangement. A bank may not (1) disclaim responsibility for its lack of good faith; (2) disclaim responsibility for its failure to exercise ordinary care; or (3) limit its damages for breach of such lack or failure.

1. Payment of an Item–A payor bank owes a duty to its customer, the drawer, to pay checks properly drawn by her on an account that has sufficient funds to cover the items. The drawee is not liable on a check until it accepts the item. However, if a bank improperly refuses payment, it will incur liability to its customer from whose account the item should have been paid. If the customer had enough money on deposit and there is no other valid reason for refusing to pay, the bank is liable to the customer for wrongful dishonor. If a wrongful dishonor occurs through mistake, the bank's liability is limited to actual damages proved, including damages for arrest or other consequential damages. A payor bank is under no obligation to pay an uncertified check that is over six months old. However, a bank is not obligated to dishonor such a check. When a payor receives an item for which there are insufficient funds in the account, but which is otherwise properly payable, the bank may either (1) dishonor the item and return it; or (2) pay the item and charge the customer's account even though an overdraft is created as a result. The customer may be liable to pay a service charge and interest on the overdraft.

2. Substitute Check–The Check Clearing for the 21st Century Act (called Check 21 or Check Truncation Act) allows banks to replace checks with either (1) a substitute check or (2) by agreement, information relating to the original check. Under the Act a substitute check in the correct form is the legal equivalent of an original check for all purposes, and parties cannot refuse to accept a substitute check that satisfies requirements of the Act.

3. Stop Payment Orders–The drawer of a check may issue a stop payment order. To be effective, a stop payment order must be received by the bank in time to give it a reasonable opportunity to act on it. An oral stop payment order is binding on the bank for fourteen calendar days. The normal practice is for a customer to confirm an oral stop payment order in writing. The written order is effective for six months and may be renewed in writing. It is possible that when the

check is dishonored by the bank, the drawer may incur liability to the holder, particularly if the holder is a holder in due course against whom personal defenses are not effective.

4. Bank's Right to Subrogation on Improper Payment–If a payor bank pays an item over a stop payment order or otherwise in violation of its contract with the drawer or maker, the payor bank is subrogated to the rights of (a) any holder in due course on the item against the drawer or maker; (b) the payee or any other holder against the drawer or maker; and (c) the drawer or maker against the payee or any other holder. This allows a bank to pay a holder in due course when the drawer's defense is a personal one notwithstanding the fact that the drawer has issued a valid stop payment order.

5. Disclosure Requirements–In 1992, Congress enacted the Truth in Savings Act, which provides that disclosures must be made in clear and conspicuous writing and must be given to consumers when an account is opened or service is provided. The disclosure must include the following: (a) the annual percentage yield and the percentage rate; (b) how variable rates are calculated and when the rates may be changed; (c) balance information; (d) when and how interest is calculated and credited; (e) the amount of fees that may be charged and how they are calculated; and (f) any limitation on the number or amount of withdrawals or deposits.

6. Customer's Death or Incompetence–If either a payor or collecting bank does not know that a customer has been adjudicated incompetent, the bank's authority to accept, pay, or collect the item is not impaired. Neither death nor adjudication of incompetence of a customer revokes a payor or collecting bank's authority to accept, pay, or collect an item until the bank knows of the condition and has a reasonable opportunity to act on this knowledge. Even though the bank knows of the death of its customer, it may for ten days after the date of death act on the instrument unless a person claiming an interest in the account orders the bank to stop making payments.

7. Customer's Duties–The Code imposes affirmative duties on bank customers and fixes time limits within which they must assert their rights. The customer is required to exercise reasonable care and promptness in examining the bank statement and items to discover an unauthorized signature or an alteration and must notify the bank promptly. The customer must examine the statement and items within a reasonable time, which in no event may exceed thirty calendar days and must notify the bank of unauthorized signatures and alterations. Any alterations or unauthorized signatures on instruments by the same wrongdoer and paid by the bank during that period will still be the responsibility of the bank, but any paid thereafter but before the customer notifies the bank may not be asserted against it. The customer must always report an alteration or unauthorized signature within one year from the time the statement or items were made available or be barred from asserting them against the bank. Any unauthorized indorsement must be asserted within three years from the time the bank statements and items containing such indorsements are made available to the customer.

II. Electronic Funds Transfer–Financial institutions seek to substitute EFTs for checks to eliminate the paperwork involved in processing checks and to eliminate the "float" that a drawer of a check enjoys as a result of having the use of funds during the check-processing period between issuing the check and final payment. An electronic funds transfer has been defined as "any transfer of funds, other than a transaction originated by check, draft, or similar paper instrument, which is initiated through an electronic terminal, telephonic instrument, or computer or magnetic tape so as to order, instruct, or authorize a financial institution to debit or credit an account." EFTs have brought about considerable confusion concerning the legal rights of customers and financial institutions. A partial solution has been the enactment of the Electronic Fund Transfers Act, but important legal problems remain.

A. Types of Electronic Funds Transfers–Currently there are several EFTs in use.
1. Automated Teller Machines–ATMs permit customers to conduct various transactions with their bank through the use of electronic terminals. After activating an ATM with a plastic identification card and a secret number, customers can deposit and withdraw funds from their accounts, transfer funds between accounts, obtain cash advances from bank credit card accounts, and make payments on loans.
2. Point-of-Sale Systems–Point-of-sale (POS) systems permit consumers to transfer funds from their bank accounts to merchants automatically. The POS machines are located within the merchant's store and are activated by the consumer's identification card and code.
3. Direct Deposits and Withdrawals–Direct deposits of payroll, Social Security, and other payments can be made through an electronic terminal when the deposit has been authorized in advance by the consumer. Automatic withdrawals to pay insurance premiums, utility bills, or automobile loan payments are common examples of this type of EFT.
4. Pay-by-Phone Systems–These permit customers to pay bills by telephoning the bank's computer system and directing a transfer of funds to a designated third party or between accounts.
5. Wholesale Electronic Funds Transfers–These are commonly called wholesale wire transfers and involve the movement of funds between financial institutions, between financial institutions and businesses, and between businesses.

B. Consumer Funds Transfers–Because of the unique characteristics of electronic systems and inadequate legislation, Congress enacted the Electronic Fund Transfers Act (EFTA). This act "provides a basic framework establishing the rights, liabilities, and responsibilities of participants in electronic fund transfers" with primary emphasis on "the provision of individual consumer rights." The act does not govern electronic transfers between financial institutions, between financial institutions and businesses, or between businesses. The act is administered by the Board of Governors of the Federal Reserve System.
1. Disclosure–The terms of an electronic funds transfer involving a consumer must be disclosed in readily understandable language at the time the consumer contracts for such services.
2. Documentation and Periodic Statements–The financial institution must provide the consumer with written documentation of each transfer made from an electronic terminal at the time of the transfer–a receipt. The receipt must clearly state the amount involved, the date, the type of transfer, the identity of the consumer's accounts involved, the identity of any third party involved, and the location of the terminal involved. The institution must also provide periodic statements for each consumer account that may be accessed by means of an EFT.
3. Preauthorized Transfers–A preauthorized transfer from a consumer's account must be authorized in advance by the consumer in writing, and a copy of the authorization must be provided to the consumer when the transfer is made. A consumer may stop payment of any preauthorized EFT

by notifying the financial institution orally or in writing at any time up to three business days before the scheduled transfer.

4. Error Resolution–The consumer has sixty days after the financial institution sends a periodic statement in which to notify the financial institution of any errors that appear on the statement. The financial institution is required to investigate and report the results within ten business days. If it determines that an error did occur, it must properly correct it. Failure to investigate in good faith makes the financial institution liable for treble damages.

5. Consumer Liability–A consumer's liability for an unauthorized electronic funds transfer is limited to a maximum of $50 if the consumer notifies the financial institution within two days after learning of the loss or theft. A consumer who does not report the unauthorized use within two days is liable for losses up to $500. A consumer who fails to report the unauthorized use within sixty days is liable for losses resulting from any unauthorized EFT that would not have occurred but for the failure of the consumer to report the loss within sixty days.

6. Liability of Financial Institution–A financial institution is liable to a consumer for all damages proximately caused by its failure to make an EFT according to the terms and conditions of an account. However, it will not be liable if (1) the consumer's account has insufficient funds through no fault of the financial institution, (2) the funds are subject to legal process, (3) the transfer would exceed an established credit limit, (4) an electronic terminal has insufficient cash, or (5) circumstances beyond the institution's control prevent the transfer. The institution is also liable for failure to stop payment of a preauthorized transfer when instructed to do so in accordance with the terms and conditions of the account.

C. Wholesale Funds Transfers–Article 4A, Funds Transfers, is designed to provide a statutory framework for a payment system that is not covered by existing Articles of the UCC or by the EFTA. It provides that the rights and obligations of the parties to a funds transfer covered by the article are subject to contrary agreement of the parties.

1. Scope of Article–Article 4A covers wholesale funds transfers and defines a funds transfer as a "series of transactions, beginning with the originator's payment order, made for the purpose of making payment to the beneficiary of the order. The term includes any payment order issued by the originator's bank or an intermediary bank intended to carry out the originator's payment order. A funds transfer is completed by acceptance by the beneficiary's bank of a payment order for the benefit of the beneficiary of the originator's payment order."

   a. Payment Order–This is an oral or written instruction of a sender to a receiving bank to pay, or to cause another bank to pay, a fixed or determinable amount of money to a beneficiary.

   b. Parties–The originator sends the payment order or, in a series of payment orders, it sends the first payment order. A sender is the party who gives an instruction to the receiving bank. The bank to which the sender's instruction is addressed is the receiving bank. The originator's bank is either the bank that receives the original payment order or the originator if the originator is a bank. The beneficiary's bank is the bank identified in a payment order to credit the beneficiary's account and is the last bank in the chain of transfer. A beneficiary is the person to be paid by the beneficiary bank. An intermediary bank is any receiving bank, other than an originator's bank or a beneficiary's bank, that receives a payment order.

    c. Excluded Transactions–If any part of a funds transfer is governed by the EFTA, such coverage is excluded from Article 4A coverage. Article 4A also excludes debit transactions.

2. Acceptance–If a receiving bank is not the beneficiary's bank, it does not subject itself to any liability until it accepts the instrument. Acceptance by a receiving bank other than the beneficiary's bank occurs when the receiving bank executes the payment order. If a beneficiary's bank accepts a payment order, the bank is obliged to pay the beneficiary.

3. Erroneous Execution of Payment Orders–If a receiving bank mistakenly executes a payment order for an amount greater than the authorized amount, the bank is only entitled to payment of the amount of the sender's correct order. The receiving bank is entitled to recover from the beneficiary of the erroneous order the amount in excess of the authorized amount.

4. Unauthorized Payment Orders–If a bank establishes commercially reasonable security measures agreed to by the customer for preventing unauthorized transmissions and properly follows its process, the customer must pay an order even if it was unauthorized.

KEY TERMS

1. Depositary bank
2. Provisional credit
3. Final Credit
4. Intermediary bank
5. Clearinghouse
6. Collecting bank
7. Midnight deadline
8. Payor bank
9. Stop payment order
10. Electronic funds transfer

TRUE/FALSE

_____ 1. When Travis deposits a check in his bank, the bank credits his account and at that time receives a final credit in the amount of the check.

_____ 2. Under the Competitive Equality Banking Act, local checks must clear within one intervening business day.

_____ 3. Once a check is restrictively indorsed with words such as "pay any bank," only a bank may acquire the rights of a holder.

_____ 4. A payor bank which dishonors an item must either return the item or send written notice of dishonor before midnight of the banking day on which the item is received.

_____ 5. A collecting bank is the payor bank.

_____ 6. Where there are insufficient funds in a customer's account, the bank may pay a check properly payable from the account and charge the account, even if it creates an overdraft.

_____ 7. A bank is required to dishonor its customer's check if the check is over six months old.

_____ 8. An oral stop payment order is binding on the bank for fourteen days.

_____ 9. A consumer's liability for an unauthorized electronic funds transfer is limited to $100 if the consumer notifies the financial institution within two days after learning of the loss.

_____ 10. Point-of-sale systems enable a consumer automatically to transfer funds from his bank account to a merchant seller.

_____ 11. The payor bank and the drawee bank are the same bank.

_____ 12. The first bank to receive a check for payment is the payee bank.

_____ 13. Under Article 4A of the UCC, a funds transfer is completed by acceptance by the beneficiary's bank of a payment order for the benefit of the beneficiary of the originator's payment order.

_____ 14. A collecting bank has a debtor-creditor relationship with a check's owner until final settlement.

_____ 15. Check 21 is a federal Act that allows banks to replace original checks with substitute checks in connection with processing checks.

MULTIPLE CHOICE

_____ 1. If a check is not paid for any reason, the payor bank should:
   a. return it to the drawer.
   b. return it to the drawee.
   c. return it to its transferor.
   d. throw it away.

_____ 2. A depositary bank may treat a check as having been received on Monday if the check was actually received late in the afternoon on:
   a. Tuesday.
   b. Wednesday.
   c. Thursday.
   d. Friday.

_____ 3. In presenting an item for payment, a collecting bank may delay presentment for up to:
   a. one calendar day.
   b. one banking day.
   c. three banking days.
   d. one week.

_____ 4. Which of the following is responsible for examining a check for prior restrictive indorsements?
  a. The depositary bank
  b. The intermediary bank
  c. The payor bank
  d. All of the above must examine it for restrictive indorsements.

_____ 5. Final payment of an item occurs during the processing of the item by:
  a. the depositary bank.
  b. the intermediary bank.
  c. the payor bank.
  d. none of the above.

_____ 6. Which is not true under the Competitive Equality Banking Act?
  a. Wire transfers must clear by the next business day.
  b. Local checks must clear within one business day.
  c. Nonlocal checks must clear in seven intervening business days.
  d. Government checks must clear by the next business day.

_____ 7. A collecting bank that transfers an item and receives settlement gives what warranty:
  a. It is entitled to enforce the instrument.
  b. All signatures are authentic and authorized.
  c. Both (a) and (b)
  d. Neither (a) nor (b)

_____ 8. Banks may not do which of the following?
  a. Disclaim responsibility for lack of good faith
  b. Disclaim responsibility for failure to exercise ordinary care
  c. Limit their damages for breach
  d. They may not do any of the above.

_____ 9. A written stop payment order:
  a. is valid for 60 days.
  b. is valid for 90 days.
  c. may be renewed in writing.
  d. (a) and (c), but not (b).

_____ 10. If a consumer does not report the loss or theft of his electronic funds transfer card within two days he is liable for losses up to:
  a. $500.
  b. $250.
  c. $50.
  d. any unauthorized use.

_____ 11. The Electronic Fund Transfers Act imposes liability on a customer for unauthorized transfers in the maximum amount of:
   a. $50 if the consumer notifies the financial institution within two days after learning of a loss.
   b. $100 in most circumstances.
   c. $500 if a consumer fails to notify a financial institution within 2 days after learning of a loss.
   d.   (a) and (c) only.

_____ 12. Any bank to which an item is transferred in the course of collection, other than the depositary or payor banks, is a(n) _____ bank.
   a.   drawee
   b.   intermediary
   c.   clearinghouse
   d.   federal

_____ 13. First Bank pays a check over a stop payment order of its customer.
   a.   First Bank is subrogated to the rights of any holder in due course on the item against the drawer or maker.
   b.   First Bank is subrogated to the rights of the payee or any other holder against the drawer or maker.
   c.   First Bank is subrogated to the rights of the drawer or maker against the payee or any other holder.
   d.   All of the above are correct.

_____ 14. Financial institutions seek to substitute electronic funds transfers for checks for which of the following reasons?
   a.   To eliminate the float a drawer of a check enjoys and to eliminate the paperwork involved in processing checks
   b.   To have a clearer basis of determining legal rights of customers
   c.   To eliminate the need for providing customers with statements of account
   d.   To eliminate bank fraud

_____ 15. *CPA:* For which of the following negotiable instruments is a bank **not** an acceptor?
   a.   Cashier's check
   b.   Certified check
   c.   Certificate of deposit
   d.   None of the above

SHORT ESSAY

1. Explain the effect of a restrictive indorsement with words such as "pay any bank."

_____

_____

_____

_____

2. Explain the effect of a "stop payment order."

_____

_____

_____

_____

3. Arthur issued a check to Brad. Carl stole the check, forged Brad's indorsement, and cashed the check at Arthur's bank. What are the rights of Arthur and of the bank?

_____

_____

_____

_____

4. David had a bank card that he used for EFT transactions with First Bank. On Tuesday, a thief stole David's wallet, including the bank card. David immediately notified the bank. Nevertheless, the thief withdrew $1,000 from David's account on Wednesday using the card. Discuss David's liability.

_____

_____

_____

_____

5. East Company instructs its bank, First National Bank, to pay $1,000,000 to West Company, also a customer of First National Bank. First National executes the payment order by crediting West's account with $1,000,000 and notifying West that the credit has been made and is available. Identify the parties to this funds transfer under Article 4A of the UCC.

_____

_____

_____

_____

Part V
Sample Examination

MULTIPLE CHOICE

_____ 1. Carl Criminal breaks into Brenda's apartment, steals her checkbook, then makes a check for $100 payable to "cash" and signs Brenda's name in the lower right-hand corner of the check. Which of the following is correct regarding this instrument?
   a. Carl is the drawer of the check.
   b. Brenda is the drawer of the check.
   c. The instrument is nonnegotiable.
   d. Carl is a fictitious payee.

_____ 2. Bob has a bearer instrument for $200. He transfers it to Acme Corporation, but does not indorse it. Which of the following is correct regarding this transaction?
   a. Bob incurs contract liability, but not warranty liability by transferring this bearer instrument.
   b. Bob incurs warranty liability, but not contract liability by transferring this bearer instrument.
   c. Bob incurs both contract and warranty liability by transferring this bearer instrument.
   d. Bob incurs neither contract nor warranty liability by transferring this bearer instrument.

_____ 3. First Bank pays an instrument with a forged indorsement which is drawn on the account of Shiloh, Inc.
   a. First Bank may charge the account of Shiloh.
   b. First Bank has no recourse against the person from whom it received the check.
   c. First Bank is liable to the named payee for conversion.
   d. None of the above is correct.

_____ 4. Midtown Bank receives a check drawn on one of its accounts from American Bank, an intermediary collecting bank, at 10:00 a.m. Monday during banking hours. When must Midtown Bank either pay or dishonor the item?
   a. Immediately
   b. By midnight on Monday
   c. By midnight on Tuesday
   d. By 3:00 p.m. on Tuesday

_____ 5. Michael calls First Bank to issue a stop payment order on a check he has issued to a door-to-door salesperson selling magazines.
a. The stop payment order is binding on the bank for ten days.
b. The stop payment order is binding on the bank for 14 days.
c. The stop payment order is binding on the bank for six months.
d. Oral stop payment orders have no validity under the Code.

_____ 6. Which of the following is a type of commercial paper?
a. Check
b. Note
c. Certificate of deposit
d. All the above

_____ 7. Which of the following is not a valid purpose of an indorsement?
a. To negotiate the instrument
b. To restrict payment of the instrument
c. To validate the instrument
d. To incur liability on the instrument

_____ 8. After a busy day of running errands, Janet stops at the grocery store, writes a check for groceries, but fails to insert the date. The instrument as issued by Janet is:
a. a negotiable demand instrument.
b. a negotiable time instrument.
c. nonnegotiable.
d. an assignment of funds to the grocery store.

_____ 9. Tyler indorses a check "For deposit only." This is a _____ indorsement.
a. qualified
b. restrictive
c. special
d. blank

_____ 10. Evelyn has a check that is payable to her order. She indorses it in blank. The instrument is now:
a. nonnegotiable.
b. bearer paper.
c. an incomplete instrument.
d. order paper.

_____ 11. Roger signs a blank check and then leaves it on his desk. His son Junior picks it up, and then uses it to buy a $500 VCR from the local electronics store by completing the instrument and making it payable to the store. As the drawer of the check, Roger:
   a. has no liability on the instrument because it was an incomplete instrument when he signed it.
   b. has no liability, because it was not completed according to his authorization.
   c. will be liable since his negligence in leaving the blank check on his desk contributed to the unauthorized completion of the check.
   d. can sue the bank if they pay the check from his account.

_____ 12. Which is required to become a holder in due course?
   a. Take the instrument for value
   b. Take the instrument in good faith
   c. Take the instrument without notice it is overdue or has been dishonored
   d. All of the above are required

_____ 13. Chung is a holder in due course of a negotiable instrument. He takes it:
   a. free from all defenses.
   b. subject to real defenses.
   c. subject to personal defenses.
   d. subject to all defenses.

_____ 14. Yvonne issues a check for $500 payable to the order of Martin and drawn on Security Bank.
   a. Security Bank is the drawer; Martin is the drawee; and Yvonne is the payee.
   b. Yvonne is the drawer; Martin is the payee; and Security Bank is the drawee.
   c. Yvonne is the drawer; Martin is the drawee; and Security Bank is the payee.
   d. Security Bank is the holder; Martin is the payor; and Yvonne is the drawee.

_____ 15. Aaron accepted a $400 negotiable demand note from Gary for goods he sold to him. Aaron then negotiated the note to Carl who qualified as a holder in due course. Carl later indorsed the note to his son Junior as a gift. Unfortunately, Aaron had misrepresented the goods to Gary and Gary now wants to dishonor the note based upon fraud in the inducement. Junior, of course, knew nothing about the dealings between Aaron and Gary when he accepted the $400 note as a gift from his father.
   a. Junior is a holder in due course.
   b. The defense of fraud in the inducement can be asserted against Junior, because he is not a holder in due course.
   c. Junior is not a holder in due course, but under the shelter rule he has the rights of one. The defense of fraud in the inducement cannot be asserted against him.
   d. Junior is a mere assignee and has no right to collect the note.

_____ 16. In order for a transferee of a negotiable instrument to become a holder, the transfer must be made by:
   a. negotiation.
   b. indorsement.
   c. assignment.
   d. delivery.

_____ 17. *CPA:* Which of the following negotiable instruments is subject to the provisions of the UCC Negotiable Instruments Article?
   a. Installment note payable on the first day of each month
   b. Warehouse receipt
   c. Bill of lading payable to order
   d. Corporate bearer bond with a maturity date of January 1, 2004

_____ 18. *CPA:* For a person to be a holder in due course of a promissory note:
   a. the note must be payable in U.S. currency to the holder.
   b. the holder must be the payee of the note.
   c. the note must be negotiable.
   d. all prior holders must have been holders in due course.

_____ 19. *CPA:* A $5,000 promissory note payable to the order of Neptune is discounted to Bane by blank indorsement for $4,000. King steals the note from Bane and sells it to Ott, who promises to pay King $4,500. After paying King $3,000, Ott learns that King stole the note. Ott makes no further payment to King. Ott is:
   a. a holder in due course to the extent of $5,000.
   b. an ordinary holder to the extent of $4,500.
   c. a holder in due course to the extent of $3,000.
   d. an ordinary holder to the extent of $0.

_____ 20. *CPA:* Bond fraudulently induced Teal to make a note payable to Wilk, to whom Bond was indebted. Bond delivered the note to Wilk. Wilk negotiated the instrument to Monk, who purchased it with knowledge of the fraud after it was overdue. If Wilk qualifies as a holder in due course, which of the following statements is correct?
   a. Monk has the standing of a holder in due course through Wilk.
   b. Teal can successfully assert the defense of fraud in the inducement against Monk.
   c. Monk personally qualifies as a holder in due course.
   d. Teal can successfully assert the defense of fraud in the inducement against Wilk.

Try The Web

1. Locate an article on investing.

   One solution:
         Go to: http://www.lectlaw.com/
         Select: The Library's Rotunda
         Select: laypeople's law lounge
         Review: information for investors

2. Review current U.S. economic conditions.

   One solution:
         Go to: net search on Yahoo
         Select: business and economy
         Select: finance and investment
         Select: statistics and indicators
         Select: economic
         Select: United States
         Select: Federal Reserve System Beige Book

Chapter 29
Relationship of Principal and Agent

PURPOSE

The law of agency is essential to business, because almost every type of contract or business transaction can be conducted through an agent. Agency is especially important in the case of partnerships and corporations. Partnership is founded on the agency of the partners; each partner is an agent of the partnership. Each partner has the authority to bind the partnership in transactions pertaining to partnership business. Sole proprietors may, and often do, employ agents to work for them. Because a corporation is an artificial entity, it can only act through the agency of its officers and employees. There are two main parts of agency law: (1) the internal part or the relationship between the principal and the agent, and (2) the external part or the relationship between the agent and the principal with third parties. In this chapter, you study the nature and function of agency and other topics involving the internal part of agency law. Agency is primarily governed by state common law, which is presented in the Restatement (Second) of the Law of Agency.

CHAPTER CHECKPOINTS

After reading and studying this chapter, you should be able to:

1. Distinguish among (a) an agency relationship, (b) an employment relationship, and (c) an independent contractor relationship.

2. Discuss how an agency relationship comes into existence.

3. List and discuss the duties owed by an agent to the principal.

4. List and discuss the duties owed by a principal to the agent.

5. Identify the ways in which an agency relationship is terminated.

CHAPTER OUTLINE

A. Nature of Agency–Agency is the relationship existing between two persons known as principal and agent through which the agent is authorized to act for and on behalf of the principal. An agent is one who represents a principal in business dealings with third persons. Agents may negotiate and bind the principal to contracts with third persons. The parties to the contract are the principal and third person; the agent is simply an intermediary if the principal's existence and identity are disclosed.

1. Scope of Agency Purposes–As a general rule, whatever business activity a person may accomplish personally, may be done through an agent.

2. Other Legal Relationships–Two other legal relationships overlap with agency: employer-employee and principal-independent contractor. The employment relationship is one in which the employer has the right to control the physical conduct of the employee. An independent contractor is a person who contracts with another to do a particular job and is not subject to the control of the other. Although all employees are agents, not all agents are employees. Agents who are not employees are independent contractors.

B. Creation of Agency–Agency is a consensual relationship that may be formed by contract or agreement between the principal and agent. Whether an agency relationship is created is determined by an objective test. An agency created without consideration is a gratuitous agency. Sometimes a person is held liable as a principal even though no actual agency was created.

1. Formalities–No formality is required in a contract of agency. The contract may be express or inferred from the conduct of the principal. Some states have an "equal dignity" rule, which requires an agent's appointment to be evidenced by a writing if the agency is for more than one year or involves a sale of land. A power of attorney is a written, formal appointment of an agent.

2. Capacity–The capacity to be a principal and act through an agent depends on the capacity of the principal to do the act herself. The appointment of an agent by a minor or an incompetent not under a guardianship and any resulting contracts are voidable. However, minors and incompetents not under guardianship can act as agents. The contract of agency may be voidable, but an authorized contract between the principal and the third party is valid. Most states have adopted the Uniform Durable Power of Attorney Statute. This law permits an agent's power to survive or be triggered by the principal's loss of mental competence. An "electronic agent" is a computer program or other automated instrumentality that independently initiates an action or response to electronic input in whole or in part without review or action by a natural person.

C. Duties of Agent to Principal–Because the relationship of principal and agent is ordinarily created by contract, the duties of the agent to the principal are primarily determined by the provisions of the contract. In addition, the agent is subject to various other duties imposed by law. An agent is liable for any loss caused to the principal for breach of any of these duties.

1. Duty of Obedience–This duty requires an agent to act in the principal's affairs only as authorized by the principal and to obey all reasonable instructions and directions of the principal. The principal has the right to control the agent's conduct regarding the subject matter of the agency. An agent however does not have a duty to follow illegal orders or to perform unethical acts. An agent is liable to the principal for unauthorized acts that result from the agent's misinterpretation of the principal's directions unless the instructions are ambiguous.

2. Duty of Diligence–An agent must act with reasonable care and skill in performing agency work.
3. Duty to Inform–An agent must use reasonable efforts to give the principal information that is relevant to the affairs entrusted to her and that, as the agent knows or should know, the principal would desire to have. Notice to an agent is notice to her principal.
4. Duty to Account–The agent is under a duty to maintain and provide the principal with a true and complete account of money or other property that the agent has received or expended on behalf of the principal. An agent must also keep the principal's property separate from his own.
5. Fiduciary Duty–A fiduciary duty is the duty to act with utmost loyalty and good faith.
   a. Conflicts of Interest–An agent must act solely in the interest of the principal and not in his own interest or in the interest of another. An agent may not represent his principal in any transaction in which he has a personal interest, nor act on behalf of adverse parties to a transaction, unless the principal consents.
   b. Self-Dealing–An agent must not be involved in a transaction with the principal without first fully disclosing the agent's interest in the matter and assuring that it is fair.
   c. Duty Not to Compete–An agent cannot compete with a principal or represent a competitor. An agent may compete against a former principal once an agency terminates without breach by the agent.
   d. Confidential Information–An agent may not use or disclose confidential information obtained in the course of the agency for her own benefit or contrary to the interest of her principal. Confidential information includes unique business methods, trade secrets, business plans, and customer lists. However, an agent may reveal confidential information that the principal is committing or is about to commit a crime.
   e. Duty to Account for Financial Benefits–An agent is under a duty to account to the principal for any financial benefit received by her as a direct result of transactions conducted on behalf of the principal, including bribes, kickbacks, and gifts. Also, an agent is not permitted to make a secret profit out of any transaction subject to the agency.

D. Duties of Principal to Agent–The agent has certain rights against the principal which result in certain duties that the principal owes to the agent.
   1. Contractual Duties–The contractual duties owed by a principal to an agent are the duties of compensation, reimbursement, and indemnification.
      a. Compensation–A principal has a duty to compensate her agent unless the agent has agreed to serve gratuitously. If the agreement does not specify a definite compensation, a principal is under a duty to pay the reasonable value of authorized services performed by her agent. An agent loses the right to compensation by (1) breaching the duty of obedience, (2) breaching the duty of loyalty, or (3) willfully breaching the agency contract.
      b. Reimbursement–A principal is under a duty to pay back authorized payments the agent has made on principal's behalf.
      c. Indemnification–A principal is under a duty to pay the agent for losses incurred while acting as directed by principal.
   2. Tort Duties–A principal is under a duty to disclose to an agent those risks involved in the agency, of which the principal knows or should know. If the agent is an employee, the principal also owes the duty to provide an employee with reasonably safe conditions of employment and to warn the employee of any unreasonable risk involved in the employment.

E. Termination of Agency–The agency is terminated when the consent of the principal is withdrawn or otherwise ceases to exist. On termination of the agency, the agent's actual authority ends, and she is not entitled to compensation for services subsequently rendered. Termination may take place by the acts of the parties or by operation of law.

1. Acts of the Parties–Termination by the acts of the parties may occur by the provisions of the original agreement, by the subsequent acts of both principal and agent, or by the subsequent act of either one of them.

   a. Lapse of Time–Authority conferred upon an agent for a specified time terminates at the expiration of that period. If no time is specified, authority terminates at the end of a reasonable period.

   b. Fulfillment of Purpose–The authority of an agent to perform a specific act or accomplish a particular result terminates when the act is done or the agent accomplishes the result.

   c. Mutual Agreement of the Parties–The agency relationship is created by agreement and may be terminated at any time by mutual agreement of the principal and the agent.

   d. Revocation of Authority–A principal may revoke an agent's authority at any time by giving the agent notification of revocation. But if such revocation constitutes a breach of contract by the principal, the agent may recover damages from the principal.

   e. Renunciation by the Agent–The agent has the power to put an end to the agency by notice to the principal that she renounces the authority given her by the principal. If the parties have contracted that the agency continues for a specified time, an unjustified renunciation prior to the expiration of the time is a breach of contract.

2. Operation of Law–As a matter of law, an agency relationship is terminated by the following:

   a. Bankruptcy–Bankruptcy is a proceeding in a federal court affording relief to financially troubled debtors. The filing of the petition in bankruptcy usually terminates all the debtor's existing agency relationships.

   b. Death–The death of the agent or principal terminates an agency.

   c. Incapacity–Incapacity of the principal that occurs after the formation of the agency terminates the agent's authority, unless the authority was granted through a durable power of attorney. Also, subsequent incapacity of an agent to perform the acts authorized by the principal terminates the agent's authority.

   d. Change in Circumstances–The authority of an agent is terminated by notice or knowledge of a change in the value of the subject matter or a change in business conditions from which the agent should reasonably infer that the principal would not consent to use of the authority.

   e. Loss or Destruction of Subject Matter–Where the authority of the agent relates to a specific subject matter that becomes lost or destroyed, agency authority is thereby terminated.

   f. Disloyalty of Agent–If an agent, without the knowledge of the principal, acquires interests adverse to those of the principal or otherwise breaches the duty of loyalty to the principal, authority to act on behalf of the principal is terminated.

   g. Change in Law–A change in the law that takes effect after the employment of the agent may cause the performance of the authorized act to be illegal or criminal. Such a change in the law terminates the agency relationship.

   h. Outbreak of War–When the outbreak of war places the principal and agent in the position of alien enemies, the authority of the agent is terminated because its exercise is illegal.

3. Irrevocable Agencies–When the agency is coupled with an interest of the agent (also known as a "power given as security"), it is an irrevocable agency. This occurs where the agent has a security interest in the subject matter of the agency. The authority of the agent may not be revoked by the principal. In addition, incapacity or bankruptcy of the principal will not terminate the authority of the agent. The death of the principal also will not terminate the agency unless the duty for which the security was given terminates with the death of the principal. This power is terminated, however, when the secured obligation is discharged.

KEY TERMS

1. Agency
2. Principal
3. Agent
4. Employment relationship
5. Independent contractor
6. Power of attorney
7. Fiduciary duty
8. Reimbursement
9. Indemnification
10. Agency coupled with an interest

TRUE/FALSE

_____ 1. Most contracts or business transactions can be created or conducted through an agent.

_____ 2. The relationship of principal and agent exists only when one party exercises the right of control over the actions of another.

_____ 3. An agent is under a duty to keep her principal's property separate from her own.

_____ 4. A principal is under no duty to reimburse his agent for unauthorized expenses the agent incurs.

_____ 5. Generally, any person has the capacity to be an agent.

_____ 6. A person who engages an independent contractor to do a specific job has a right to control the conduct and activities of the independent contractor in the performance of the contract.

_____ 7. The principal's right to control the conduct of the agent is the most significant factor in determining whether an employment relationship exists.

_____ 8. A power of attorney is a formal appointment of an agent.

_____ 9. An agent has no duty to account for property or gifts received.

_____ 10. An agency contract must be in writing.

_____ 11. The principal-agent relationship is a fiduciary relationship.

_____ 12. A principal may revoke an agent's authority at any time, but if he does, he may be in breach of his contract with the agent.

_____ 13. Brian is appointed an agent for Independent Investors, Inc. Two months later, Brian files for bankruptcy because of personal debts arising prior to beginning work for Independent. Brian's agency is terminated by the bankruptcy.

_____ 14. An agency coupled with an interest can be revoked at any time.

_____ 15. While an agent may not ordinarily use or disclose confidential information, she may reveal confidential information that the principal is about to commit a crime.

MULTIPLE CHOICE

_____ 1. An agent may be appointed to perform which of the following?
   a. Perform a contract for personal services
   b. Commit an illegal act
   c. Buy or sell goods
   d. More than one of the above

_____ 2. Any contracts resulting from the appointment of an agent by a minor are:
   a. void.
   b. voidable.
   c. unenforceable.
   d. none of the above.

_____ 3. An agent who violates a fiduciary duty is liable to the principal:
   a. for breach of contract.
   b. in tort for losses caused.
   c. in restitution for profits made.
   d. all of the above.

_____ 4. Assume that S wants to sell his house and B is interested in buying it. If A is an agent who normally handles such transactions, A may represent:
   a. S or B, but not both.
   b. S and B, but only with the informed consent of S.
   c. S and B, but only with the informed consent of B.
   d. S and B, but only with the informed consent of S and B.

_____ 5. If an agent has an interest in the agency subject matter, the agent's authority terminates upon:
   a. the death of the principal.
   b. the bankruptcy of the principal.
   c. a revocation of authority.
   d. the mutual agreement of the parties.

_____ 6. Mel owns a retail store. Elizabeth is a salesclerk for Mel in the store. The relationship between Elizabeth and Mel is an example of:
   a. employer and independent contractor only.
   b. employer and employee only.
   c. principal and agent only.
   d. both employer and employee, as well as principal and agent.

_____ 7. Charles hires Andrew, an attorney, to represent him in a lawsuit. The relationship between Charles and Andrew is an example of:
   a. employer and independent contractor only.
   b. employer and employee only.
   c. principal and agent only.
   d. both employer and independent contractor, as well as principal and agent.

_____ 8. Which of the following is not a duty owed by an agent to her principal?
   a. Obedience
   b. Accounting
   c. Information
   d. All of the above are duties of the agent.

_____ 9. Peter listed a real estate with Ron, a realtor, pursuant to a listing agreement, which was good for 90 days. Two months later, Peter decides not to sell the property and revokes Ron's authority.
   a. Peter cannot revoke Ron's authority.
   b. Peter has the power to revoke Ron's authority, but does not have the right to revoke it.
   c. Peter may be liable to Ron for damages for breach of contract.
   d. Two of the above are correct, (b) and (c).

_____ 10. A principal owes an agent a duty of:
   a. reimbursement.
   b. indemnification.
   c. compensation.
   d. all of the above.

_____ 11. An agency terminates by operation of law upon the occurrence of any of the following except:
   a. Bankruptcy
   b. Fulfillment of purpose
   c. Death of the principal
   d. Disloyalty of agent

_____ 12. Ann is authorized to sell her principal's property for $10,000. If Ann sells it for $11,000, then:
   a. she may pocket the additional $1,000.
   b. she has a duty to account to the principal for the additional $1,000.
   c. she must give the $1,000 back to the third party.
   d. none of the above.

_____ 13. Which of the following will not terminate an agency?
   a. Lapse of time
   b. Revocation of authority
   c. Renunciation by the agent
   d. All of the above will terminate the agency.

_____ 14. *CPA:* Simpson, Ogden Corp.'s agent, needs a written agency agreement to:
   a. enter into a series of sales contracts on Ogden's behalf.
   b. hire an attorney to collect a business debt owed by Ogden.
   c. purchase an interest in undeveloped land for Ogden.
   d. retain an independent general contractor to renovate Ogden's office building.

_____ 15. *CPA:* A principal and agent relationship requires a:
   a. written agreement.
   b. power of attorney.
   c. meeting of minds and consent to act.
   d. specified consideration.

SHORT ESSAY

1. How may an agency relationship be created?

_____

_____

_____

_____

2. What are the practical consequences of an agent's fiduciary duty?

_____

_____

_____

_____

3. What are the remedies available to the principal for violation of duties by an agent?

_____

_____

_____

_____

_____

4. What is an irrevocable agency? Explain.

_____

_____

_____

_____

5. *P* appoints *A* as her agent to sell goods in markets where the highest price can be obtained. *A* sells the goods in a market that is glutted and obtains a low price, although a higher price could have been obtained in another market. If *P* sues *A*, what would be the result?

_____

_____

_____

_____

Chapter 30
Relationship With Third Parties

PURPOSE

In this chapter, you study the external part of agency involving the relationship between the agent and third parties with reference to the liability of the agent and of the principal to those third parties. In general with regard to contracts, the principal and the third party are bound to those contracts the principal actually authorizes plus those the principal has apparently authorized. In addition to studying the contractual liability of the principal and agent, you also study the liability of the principal and agent for torts and crimes committed by the agent.

CHAPTER CHECKPOINTS

After reading and studying this chapter, you should be able to:

1. Distinguish between and identify actual authority and apparent authority.

2. Discuss the liability of principal and the agent to third parties upon termination of the agency relationship.

3. Distinguish between a disclosed principal, an undisclosed principal, and a partially disclosed principal and discuss the contract liability of each with respect to third parties.

4. Define the doctrine of *respondeat superior* and discuss when principals will be liable for the torts of their agents under the doctrine.

5. Discuss the contract liability and the tort liability of an agent to third parties.

CHAPTER OUTLINE

I. Relationship of Principal and Third Persons–The purpose of an agency relationship is to allow the principal to extend business activities by authorizing agents to enter into contracts with third persons on the principal's behalf. Pursuant to the agency relationship, the principal has contract liability and potential tort and criminal liability.

A. Contract Liability of the Principal–The power of an agent is the ability to change the legal status of the principal. An agent has the power to bind his principal whenever he has actual or apparent authority. This power of an agent to act for his principal in business transactions is the basis of agency. The contract liability of a principal also depends upon whether the principal is disclosed, partially disclosed, or undisclosed. A disclosed principal is one whose existence and identity are known. A partially disclosed principal (also known as an "unidentified principal") is one whose existence is known but whose identity is not known. An undisclosed principal is one whose existence and identity are not known.

1. Types of Authority–There are two basic types of authority: actual and apparent. Actual authority is the power conferred upon agent by actual consent given by principal. Apparent authority is power conferred upon an agent by acts or conduct of the principal that reasonably lead a third party to believe that the agent has such power.

a. Actual Express Authority–The express authority of an agent is found in the words of the principal, spoken or written, and communicated to the agent.

b. Actual Implied Authority–Implied authority is inferred from words or conduct manifested to the agent by the principal. It may arise from custom and usages of the principal's business. Also, general authority to manage a business for a principal confers certain implied authority on the agent.

c. Apparent Authority–Apparent authority is power that arises out of words or conduct of a disclosed or partially disclosed principal that, when manifested to third persons, reasonably induce them to rely upon the assumption that actual authority exists. When there is apparent authority but not actual authority the principal is still bound by the act of the agent. However, the agent has violated the duty of obedience and is liable to the principal. Apparent authority may arise: (i) when a principal appoints an agent to a position that third parties reasonably believe gives the agent authority to do certain acts; (ii) a principal gives an agent general authority regarding a certain transaction and later restricts the agent's authority without informing the third parties involved; (iii) a principal agrees to similar prior deals between the agent and a third party; (iv) the agent shows the third party a document from the principal that appears to authorize the agent; and (v) a principal terminates an agent without informing third parties with whom the agent has previously done business.

2. Delegation of Authority–If an agent is authorized to appoint or select other persons, called subagents, to perform or assist in the performance of the agent's duties, the acts of the subagent are binding on the principal to the same extent as if the agent had done them.

3. Effect of Termination of Agency Upon Authority–On the termination of an agency, the agent's actual authority ceases. Notice of such termination to third persons is not required if termination is by death, incapacity, or impossibility of performance. Bankruptcy of the principal terminates,

without notice, the power of an agent to affect the principal's property that passes to the trustee in bankruptcy. In other cases, apparent authority continues until the third party has knowledge or receives actual notice of the agent's termination if the third party is one (1) with whom the agent previously dealt on credit, (2) to whom the agent has been specially accredited, or (3) with whom the agent has begun to deal and the principal knows of such dealing. Actual notice is knowledge actually and expressly communicated. All other third parties must have actual knowledge or constructive notice. Constructive notice is knowledge imputed by law. It includes publication in a newspaper of general circulation in the area where the agency is regularly carried on.

4. Ratification–Ratification is the affirmance by one person of a prior unauthorized act that another has done as his agent. The ratification of such act or contract binds the principal and the third party as if the agent had been initially authorized.

    a. Requirements of Ratification–A principal must show intent to ratify an entire act or contract with knowledge of all material facts concerning a transaction. This may be manifested by express language or implied from the principal's conduct. If formalities are required to authorize an act, then these formalities must be met in order to ratify that act. Also, the principal must have existed at the time that the agent entered into the transaction and the principal must ratify before the third party gives notice that it is withdrawing.

    b. Effect of Ratification–Ratification is equivalent to prior authority. Therefore, the respective rights, duties, and remedies of the principal and the third party are the same as if the agent had originally possessed due authority.

5. Fundamental Rules of Contractual Liability–The following rules summarize the contractual relation between a principal and third party: (1) a disclosed principal and the third party are contractually bound if the agent acts within her actual or apparent authority in making the contract; (2) a partially disclosed principal and the third party are contractually bound if the agent acts within her actual or apparent authority in making the contract; (3) an undisclosed principal and the third party are contractually bound if the agent acts within her actual authority in making the contract unless the principal is excluded by the terms of the contract or his existence is fraudulently concealed; and (4) no principal is contractually bound to a third party if the agent acts without any authority, unless a disclosed or partially disclosed principal ratifies the contract.

B. Tort Liability of the Principal–Tort liability may arise directly or indirectly (vicariously) from authorized or unauthorized acts of the agent.

1. Direct Liability of Principal–A principal is directly liable in damages resulting from (1) directing an agent to commit a tort and (2) failing to exercise care in employing competent agents.

    a. Authorized Acts of Agent–A principal who authorizes his agent to commit a tort concerning the property or person of another is liable for the injury or loss sustained by that person.

    b. Unauthorized Acts of Agent–A principal who conducts activities through an employee or other agent is liable for harm resulting from the principal's negligent or reckless conduct in hiring, instructing, supervising, or controlling the employee or other agent, or where the principal either knew or should have known that the agent was violent or aggressive.

2. Vicarious Liability of Principal for Unauthorized Acts of Agent–Vicarious liability is indirect legal responsibility for the act of another. The liability of a principal for unauthorized torts by an agent depends primarily on whether the agent is an employee or not. An employee is an agent employed to perform services for a principal-employer and whose physical conduct in the

performance of the service is controlled or subject to the right to control by the principal. A principal is liable for an unauthorized tort committed by an employee in the course of employment. If the principal does not control the agent's physical conduct, then the agent is an independent contractor and the principal is not liable for tortious conduct.

    a. *Respondeat Superior*–This means "let the superior respond." This is a form of liability without fault and is based on the rationale that a person who carries out business activities through the use of employees should be liable for their tortious conduct in carrying out those business purposes.

    b. Torts of Independent Contractor–The doctrine of *respondeat superior* does not generally apply to torts committed by an independent contractor because he is not an employee.

C. Criminal Liability of the Principal–A principal is liable for the authorized criminal acts of his agents only if the principal directed, participated in, or approved of the acts.

II. Relationship of Agent and Third Persons–The function of an agent is to assist in the conduct of the principal's business by carrying out his orders. Generally, the agent acquires no rights against third parties and incurs no liabilities to them. However, there are several exceptions.

A. Contract Liability of Agent–The agent is not normally a party to the contract he makes with a third person on behalf of a disclosed principal.

    1. Disclosed Principal–When the agent is acting on behalf of a disclosed principal, the agent ordinarily incurs no liability on the contract to either party.

        a. Unauthorized Contracts–If an agent exceeds his actual and apparent authority, a principal is not bound. If the agent does not have authority to bind the principal, the agent is liable to the third party for damages if the agent expressly or impliedly warrants that he has authority unless the principal ratifies the contract or the third party knew the agent was unauthorized.

        b. Agent Assumes Liability–An agent may agree to become liable on a contract between the principal and the third party by making the contract in her own name, by co-making the contract with the principal, or by a guarantee of the contract.

    2. Partially Disclosed Principal–Whether the particular transaction is authorized or not, an agent for a partially disclosed principal is liable on the contract to the third party. If the agent is authorized to make the contract, then both the agent and the partially disclosed principal are liable.

    3. Undisclosed Principal–The agent is personally liable upon a contract she enters into with a third person on behalf of an undisclosed principal, unless the third person, after discovering the existence and identity of the principal, elects to hold the principal to the contract.

    4. Nonexistent or Incompetent Principal–A person who purports to act as agent for a principal, whom both the agent and the third party know to be nonexistent or incompetent, is personally liable on a contract entered into with a third person on behalf of such a principal.

B. Tort Liability of Agent–An agent is personally liable for his torts that injure third persons, whether or not the principal authorizes such acts and whether or not the principal may also be liable.

C. Rights of Agent Against Third Person–An agent who makes a contract with a third person on behalf of a disclosed principal usually has no right of action against the third person for breach of contract, because the agent is not a party to the contract.

KEY TERMS

1. Disclosed principal

2. Partially disclosed principal

3. Undisclosed principal

4. Actual authority

5. Apparent authority

6. Express authority

7. Implied authority

8. Subagent

9. Actual notice

10. Constructive notice

11. Ratification

12. Vicarious liability

13. *Respondeat superior*

TRUE/FALSE

_____ 1. For an agent to bind a principal, she must have either actual or apparent authority coming from the conduct or words of the principal.

_____ 2. Unless the principal is disclosed, an agent has no apparent authority.

_____ 3. An agent may not ordinarily appoint a subagent to perform the agent's duties.

_____ 4. An agent's actual authority is terminated by a revocation of authority.

_____ 5. An agent's apparent authority is terminated by a renunciation of authority.

_____ 6. A principal may not be held liable for the wrongful acts of his agent if the agent acted in flagrant disobedience of the principal's instructions.

_____ 7. Under the doctrine of *respondeat superior*, a principal may be held liable for the torts of her agent even though the agent is sufficiently solvent to pay for the damage himself.

_____ 8. Revocation of an agent's authority does **not** bind third parties until they receive notice of it.

_____ 9. The bankruptcy of the principal does not affect the agent's power with respect to property passing to a bankruptcy trustee.

_____ 10. An agent who is personally liable on a contract has no right of action against the third person for breach of the contract.

_____ 11. An undisclosed principal is one whose existence is known but whose identity is not known.

_____ 12. An agent who enters into a contract on behalf of an incompetent principal may be personally liable on that contract.

_____ 13 A principal-employer is vicariously liable for the unauthorized acts of an agent-employee.

_____ 14. Implied authority is actual authority derived from the written or spoken words of the principal.

_____ 15. A principal may be liable to a third party based upon an agent's apparent authority even though the agent had no actual authority.

MULTIPLE CHOICE

_____ 1. Dianna tells Ray that he may sell her stereo for her. Ray's authority is:
   a. express authority.
   b. actual authority.
   c. implied authority.
   d. (a) and (b), but not (c).

_____ 2. An agent may be liable to the principal for exceeding his actual authority even though his acts are within the scope of his:
   a. express authority.
   b. implied authority.
   c. apparent authority.
   d. none of the above.

_____ 3. An agent has apparent authority to bind the principal in any transaction in which:
   a. third persons have no knowledge of the agency relationship.
   b. the existence and identity of the principal are undisclosed.
   c. third persons reasonably rely upon the existence of actual authority as indicated by the principal's conduct.
   d. none of the above.

_____ 4. When an agency is terminated by revocation of authority, the agent's apparent authority continues with respect to third parties with whom the agent had previously dealt until they:
   a. receive actual notice of the termination.
   b. receive constructive notice of the termination.
   c. read of the termination in a newspaper of general circulation.
   d. none of the above.

_____ 5. Apparent authority continues until the third party has actual knowledge or notice of termination in which of the following situations?
   a. The agent has previously dealt with the third party on credit.
   b. The agent has been specially accredited.
   c. The principal should know that the agent has begun to deal with the third party.
   d. All of the above.

_____ 6. Ratification of an unauthorized contract is effective to bind the principal and a third person to the contract even though:
   a.   the principal does not ratify the entire contract.
   b.   the principal does not notify the third person of his intent to ratify the contract.
   c.   the third person has already notified the principal of his withdrawal from the contract.
   d.   the agent failed to indicate to the third person that his acts were on behalf of the principal.

_____ 7. Assume that *P* and *P*'s agent *A*, conspire to and actually injure *C* so that she can't run in the big race. Which of the following is true?
   a.   *P* has committed both a crime and a tort.
   b.   *P* has committed a tort but not a crime.
   c.   *A* has committed a tort and a crime.
   d.   Two of the above.

_____ 8. *CPA:* A principal will **not** be responsible to a third party for a tort committed by an agent:
   a.   unless the principal instructed the agent to commit the tort.
   b.   unless the tort was committed within the scope of the agency relationship.
   c.   if the agency agreement limits the principal's liability for the agent's tort.
   d.   if the tort is also regarded as a criminal act.

_____ 9. *CPA:* When an agent acts for an undisclosed principal, the principal will **not** be liable to a third party if the:
   a.   principal ratifies a contract entered into by the agent.
   b.   agent acts within an implied grant of authority.
   c.   agent acts outside the grant of actual authority.
   d.   principal seeks to conceal the agency relationship.

_____ 10. Assume that *A* enters into a contract with *T* on behalf of *A*'s undisclosed principal, *P*. If *T* discovers the existence and identity of *P*, whom may *T* hold to performance of the contract?
   a.   *A* only
   b.   *P* only
   c.   *A* or *P* but not both
   d.   Neither *A* nor *P*

_____ 11. General authority to manage or operate a business for a principal confers implied authority on the agent to do all except which one of the following:
   a.   hire employees.
   b.   purchase equipment and supplies.
   c.   make repairs.
   d.   the agent may do all of the above.

_____ 12. *P* writes a letter to *A* authorizing her to sell his car. *A* tries to sell the car to *C*, telling him that although it isn't her car, she has authority to sell it. In this case *P* would be a(n):
   a. disclosed principal.
   b. partially disclosed principal.
   c. undisclosed principal.
   d. none of the above.

_____ 13. *P* writes a letter to *A* authorizing her to sell his car and sends a copy of the letter to *T*, a prospective buyer. The next day *P* writes a letter to *A* revoking the authority to sell the car but does not send a copy of this letter to *T*. If *A* contracts to sell the car to *T*:
   a. *P* will be liable on the contract based upon *A*'s implied authority.
   b. *P* will be liable on the contract based upon *A*'s apparent authority.
   c. *P* will not be liable because *A* did not have actual authority.
   d. none of the above.

_____ 14. Page and Company hires Ed to deliver merchandise to Page's customers. While driving the company's truck on his way to make a delivery, Ed negligently causes the truck to hit Tim's car and injure Tim.
   a. Page is liable to Tim because Ed was acting within the scope of employment.
   b. Page is not liable to Tim because Ed was not acting within the scope of employment.
   c. Page is not liable to Tim because Ed is an independent contractor.
   d. None of the above.

_____ 15. Page and Company hires Ed to deliver merchandise to Page's customers. After making the scheduled deliveries, Ed drives the company's truck to a nearby city to visit his girlfriend. While in the city, Ed negligently causes the truck to hit Tony's car and injure Tony.
   a. Page is not liable to Tony because Ed is an independent contractor.
   b. Page is liable to Tony because Ed was acting within the scope of employment.
   c. Page is not liable to Tony because Ed was not acting within the scope of employment.
   d. None of the above.

SHORT ESSAY

1. What is the difference between actual authority and apparent authority?

_____

_____

_____

_____

2. What is the difference between having the power to bind one's principal and having the right to bind the principal?

_____

_____

_____

_____

3. Discuss the negligent hiring doctrine.

_____

_____

_____

_____

4. Explain vicarious liability of the principal for unauthorized acts of an agent.

_____

_____

_____

_____

5. Dan entered into a contract to remodel the Majestic Restaurant owned by Riverside Restaurant, Inc. Rob, part owner and president of Riverside, signed the contract, "Rob Swanton." When a dispute arose over the contract, Dan brought suit against Rob for breach of contract. Rob contends that he has no personal liability for the contract and that only Riverside is liable. What is the result?

_____

_____

_____

_____

Part VI
Sample Examination

TRUE/FALSE

_____ 1. If an agent is acting on behalf of a disclosed principal and is acting with authority, then the principal and the third party will be bound by a contract that the agent negotiates with the third party on behalf of the principal.

_____ 2. Under *respondent superior*, an employer may be liable for torts committed by an employee who, after conducting personal business, resumes his duties.

_____ 3. The principal generally retains the power to revoke the agent's authority, even though the principal may then be liable for resulting damage to the agent.

_____ 4. An employer has a duty to provide an employee with reasonably safe conditions of employment and to warn the employee of any unreasonable risk involved in the employment.

_____ 5. Should a principal file a petition in bankruptcy, the agent's authority terminates without notice.

_____ 6. To avoid personal liability on a contract, an agent must disclose both that she is acting as an agent and the identity of her principal.

_____ 7. Ken hires Andrew Attorney to negotiate a contract on his behalf. Andrew is both an independent contractor and an agent acting on behalf of Ken.

_____ 8. An employer is never liable for intentional torts committed by his employees.

_____ 9. Although the agent has duties to the principal, the principal has no duties to the agent.

_____ 10. Ron, a realtor, is hired by Lyle to find a purchaser for a 10-acre hobby farm he owns in the country. Two days later, Paula comes to Ron and asks him whether he would be willing to be her agent in finding a small amount of acreage in the country for her to buy. Ron agrees. Ron can serve as agent to both Lyle and Paula in arranging a deal between them without violating any of his duties as an agent.

MULTIPLE CHOICE

_____ 11. The Individual Indemnity Insurance company hires Audrey to sell insurance for it. Audrey makes her own hours and drives her own automobile to see prospects. While hurrying to see a customer, Audrey drives a little too fast for the weather conditions and negligently injures a pedestrian. The pedestrian sues Individual Indemnity for his injuries.
   a. The pedestrian can recover from Individual Indemnity.
   b. Audrey was an independent contractor for whose physical acts Individual Indemnity was not liable.
   c. Audrey's authority to sell insurance policies means that Individual Indemnity will be liable for policies which Audrey sells on its behalf.
   d. Two of the above are correct, (b) and (c).

_____ 12. Ratification by a principal of an unauthorized act may occur by:
   a. silence that indicates consent.
   b. express statements.
   c. acceptance of the benefits of the contract.
   d. all of the above.

_____ 13. When a principal terminates an agent who has dealt with third parties and has collected accounts on the principal's behalf, the principal must give the third parties _____ notice of the termination of the agent's authority.
   a. constructive
   b. actual
   c. no
   d. written

_____ 14. Power conferred upon an agent by acts or conduct of the principal that reasonably lead a third party to believe that the agent has such power is known as:
   a. actual authority.
   b. apparent authority.
   c. implied authority.
   d. constructive authority.

_____ 15. Sam is a salesperson at the Paymart Discount Store. He inadvertently misrepresents the capabilities of a computer which he sells to Thomas. Thomas is upset and sues the Paymart Store.
   a. Paymart has no liability, because it did not authorize the misrepresentation.
   b. Paymart has no liability, because Sam's misrepresentation was not a tort.
   c. Paymart is responsible for Sam's unauthorized misrepresentations.
   d. None of the above.

_____ 16. One who contracts with another to do a job but who is not subject to the control of the other is known as a(n):
   a. agent.
   b. principal.
   c. independent contractor.
   d. employee.

_____ 17. Apparent authority continues beyond termination, requiring actual notice if a third party is one:
   a. with whom the agent had previously dealt.
   b. to whom the agent has been specially accredited.
   c. both (a) and (b).
   d. neither (a) nor (b). Apparent authority never continues beyond termination.

_____ 18. *CPA:* Kent, without authority, contracted to buy equipment from Fox Corp. for Ace Corp. Kent told Fox that Kent was acting on Ace's behalf. For Ace to ratify the contract with Fox:
   a. Kent must be a general agent of Ace.
   b. Ace must know all material facts relating to the contract at the time it is ratified.
   c. Ace must notify Fox that Ace intends to ratify the contract.
   d. Kent must have acted reasonably and in Ace's best interest.

_____ 19. *CPA:* Ace engages Butler to manage Ace's retail business. Butler has the implied authority to do all of the following **except**:.
   a. purchase inventory for Ace's business.
   b. sell Ace's business fixtures.
   c. pay Ace's business debts.
   d. hire or discharge Ace's business employees.

_____ 20. *CPA:* Orr gives North a power of attorney. In general, the power of attorney:
   a. will be valid only if North is a licensed attorney at law.
   b. may continue in existence after Orr's death.
   c. may limit North's authority to specific transactions.
   d. must be signed by both Orr and North.

Try the Web

1. Try your hand at writing an employment contract between yourself (principal) and another (agent).

   Possible solution:
   Go to http://www.lectlaw.com
   Select: Legal Forms
   Select: Forms Room
   Select: Business & General Forms
   Select: Power of Attorney, Special

Chapter 31
Formation and Internal Relations of General Partnerships

PURPOSE

A business enterprise may do business as a sole proprietorship, joint venture, general partnership, limited partnership, limited liability company, corporation, or as some other form of business organization. You begin this chapter by studying various types of organizations and important factors that you should consider when choosing the most appropriate form. The remainder of the chapter and the next examine general partnerships. Partnerships allow individuals with different expertise, resources, and interests to bring their various skills together to form a competitive enterprise. The law of partnerships is fairly uniform throughout the United States because at least thirty states have adopted the Revised Uniform Partnership Act (RUPA) and many of the other states have adopted its predecessor, the Uniform Partnership Act (UPA). This material reflects the law as stated in the RUPA.

CHAPTER CHECKPOINTS

After reading and studying this chapter, you should be able to:

1. Identify the various types of business associations and discuss relevant factors in choosing the most appropriate form.

2. Identify and discuss the situations in which a partnership is treated as a legal entity and those situations for which it is treated as a legal aggregate.

3. Discuss the rights that a partner has in partnership property in contrast to the rights that a partner has in the partnership itself.

4. List and discuss the three principal duties owed by a partner to her copartners.

5. List and discuss the principal rights of a partner.

CHAPTER OUTLINE

I. Choosing a Business Association–Business owners determine the form of organization based on their specific circumstances.

    A. Factors Affecting the Choice–The relative importance of the factors will vary with each business.
       1. Ease of Formation–Some types can be created with no formality; others require state filings.
       2. Taxation–Some associations are separate taxable entities. In others, the owners are taxed.
       3. External Liability–In some business forms, owners have unlimited liability, which places their entire estate at risk for the obligations of the business. In other business forms, the owners have limited liability, which means their liability is limited to the extent of their capital contribution.
       4. Management and Control–The extent to which owners can share in operation and control of the business varies with the type of association.
       5. Transferability–In some types of business associations, the entire ownership interest is freely transferable. In others, transferability is limited to either the financial or the management interest.
       6. Continuity–Some business associations must dissolve upon the death, bankruptcy, or withdrawal of an owner. Others may continue operation.

    B. Forms of Business Associations
       1. Sole Proprietorship–This is an unincorporated business consisting of one person who owns and controls the business and has unlimited liability. A sole proprietorship is formed without any formality and is not a taxable entity. The proprietor's interest is freely transferable. Death of the sole proprietor dissolves the business.
       2. General Partnership–This is an unincorporated business consisting of two or more persons who co-own the business for profit. It can be formed without formality and may elect not to be taxed as a separate entity. Partners have equal rights to control the business and have unlimited liability. Death, bankruptcy, or withdrawal of a partner dissolves the partnership.
       3. Joint Venture–This is an unincorporated business association, usually of short duration, composed of persons who combine their property, money, efforts, skill, and knowledge to carry out a particular business enterprise for profit. Partnership law generally governs a joint venture.
       4. Limited Partnership–This is an unincorporated business association consisting of at least one general partner, who has unlimited liability and shares an equal right of control with any other general partners, and at least one limited partner, who has limited liability and no right to control. A certificate must be filed with the state to form a limited partnership.
       5. Limited Liability Company–This is an unincorporated business association in which all members have limited liability and share the right to participate in management. It may elect not to be a taxable entity. Death, bankruptcy, or withdrawal of a member dissolves an LLC.
       6. Limited Liability Partnership–This is a general partnership that files an application with the state to limit liability of the partners for some or all of the partnership's obligations.
       7. Limited Liability Limited Partnership–This is a limited partnership in which the liability of the general partners has been limited by registering as an LLLP.
       8. Corporation–This is a legal entity separate from its owners and it is formed by filing articles of incorporation with the state. A corporation is taxed as an entity and owners are taxed on

earnings distributed to them. Shareholders have limited liability, and shares are freely transferable. Death, bankruptcy, or withdrawal of an owner does not dissolve the corporation.

9. Business Trusts–These can be created by voluntary agreement of the parties without authorization of the state. A business trust is devoted to the conduct of a business. By the terms of the agreement, each beneficiary is entitled to a certificate evidencing an ownership interest. Trustees have the exclusive right to manage and control the business. Unless otherwise agreed, trustees are personally liable for the debts of the business.

II. Formation of General Partnerships–Partnerships allow individuals with different expertise, backgrounds, resources, and interests to bring their various skills together to form a more competitive enterprise.

A. Nature of Partnership–Today the law governing partnerships in a majority of states is the RUPA. Matters not provided for by the act are governed by the rules of law and equity.

1. Definition of Partnership–A partnership is "an association of two or more persons to carry on as co-owners, a business for profit." Comments to the RUPA indicate that other business entities, such as a limited liability company, may be a partner.

2. Entity Theory–A legal entity is an organization having a separate legal existence from its members. It is a unit with the capacity of possessing legal rights and being subject to legal duties. A legal entity may acquire, own, and dispose of property. It may also enter into contracts, commit wrongs, sue, and be sued. At common law, a partnership was regarded as a legal aggregate, a group of individuals not having a legal existence separate from its members. The RUPA treats a partnership as a legal entity for some purposes and as a legal aggregate for others.

a. Partnership as a Legal Entity–The RUPA has increased the extent to which a partnership is treated as a legal entity distinct from its owners. For instance: (1) partnership assets are considered separate from the individual assets of its members; (2) title to real estate may be acquired in the partnership name; (3) a partner is accountable as a fiduciary to the partnership; (4) every partner is considered an agent of the partnership; and (5) a partnership can sue or be sued in the firm name

b. Partnership as a Legal Aggregate–Under the legal aggregate theory of partnership law, partners have unlimited personal liability for the debts of the partnership. In addition, disassociation of a partner sometimes causes dissolution of a partnership.

B. Formation of a Partnership–Partnership formation is simple and a partnership may result from an oral or written agreement, an informal arrangement, or from the conduct of the parties. If two or more parties share control and profits of a business, the law may deem them partners regardless of how they characterize their relationship. A "term partnership" is one that is created for a specific term or until a specific task is completed. A "partnership at will" is one in which the partners have not agreed to remain partners until the expiration of a definite term or completion of a task.

1. Partnership Agreement–It is preferable but not usually required that the partners put their agreement in writing. A written agreement creating a partnership is referred to as the partnership agreement or the articles of partnership. Unless the agreement provides otherwise, the partners may amend it only by unanimous consent. Except as otherwise stated in the RUPA, a partnership agreement determines the rights and obligations between partners.

2. Statute of Frauds: While a writing ordinarily is not required to format a partnership, it is required by the statute of frauds if the partnership is to continue for a period longer than one year.

3. Firm name: The name of a partnership cannot be the same or deceptively similar to the name of another business. The name may include one or more names of the individual partners.

4. Tests of Partnership Existence–Partnerships can be formed without any formality. There are three components to the UPA definition, all of which have to be met to have a partnership: (1) an association of two or more persons, (2) conducting a business for profit, (3) which they co-own.

   a. Association–A partnership must have two or more persons who agree to become partners. Any natural person having full capacity may enter into a partnership. A minor may become a partner, but has the right to disaffirm the partnership agreement at any time in order to avoid personal liability. A nonadjudicated incompetent may become a partner, although incompetency affords the copartners a ground for seeking dissolution by court decree. A partnership agreement entered into by an adjudicated incompetent is void. A corporation is a "person" within the meaning of the UPA and may enter into a partnership; a partnership may also be a member of another partnership.

   b. Business for Profit–Co-ownership does not of itself establish a partnership, even though the co-owners share the profits derived from use of the property. There must be a business in addition to the co-ownership of property. Social clubs, fraternal orders, civic societies, and charitable organizations cannot be partnerships. Co-ownership of the means or instrumentality of accomplishing a single business transaction or a limited series of transactions may result in a joint venture but not a general partnership.

   c. Co-ownership–Although co-ownership of property used in business is not sufficient for the existence of a partnership, the co-ownership of a business is essential. In determining whether co-ownership of a business exists, the two most important factors are sharing of profits and the right to manage and control the business. The receipt of profits of a business is prima facie evidence a person is a partner in a business unless the profits are received in payment (1) of a debt; (2) of wages of an employee or rent to a landlord; (3) of an annuity to a widow or representative of a deceased partner; (4) of interest on a loan; or (5) as consideration for the sale of the goodwill of a business. The sharing of gross returns, in contrast to profits, does not of itself establish a partnership. Nor does participation in the management or control of a business furnish conclusive proof of a partnership relation. However, an agreement to share losses furnishes strong evidence of an ownership interest.

5. Partnership Capital and Property–The total money and property contributed by the partners and dedicated to the permanent use in the enterprise is the partnership capital. Partnership property is the sum of all of the partnership assets.

   Property is held to be partnership property if it is acquired (a) in the name of the partnership, (b) in the name of one or more partners in their capacity as partners, or in the name of one or more of the partners if the document transferring title acknowledges the existence of a partnership even if the its name is not stated.

   Absent any of the foregoing indications of partnership ownership, an item still may be partnership property. The RUPA provides two rebuttable presumptions that apply when the partners' intent is not stated. First, property bought with partnership funds or credit is presumed to be partnership property without regard to the name in which title is held. Second, property taken in the name of a partner without an indication of their capacity as partners and without use of partnership funds or credit is presumed to be the partner's separate property.

III. Relationships Among Partners

A. Duties Among Partners–The law imposes certain obligations on the parties to a partnership and also gives them specific rights. The parties may, by agreement, vary these rights and obligations so long as standards of fairness are met and so long as the rights of third parties are not affected.

B. Duties Among Partners–The principal legal duties imposed upon partners in their relationship are (1) the fiduciary duty (duty of loyalty), (2) the duty of obedience, and (3) the duty of care.
1. Fiduciary Duty–Each partner owes a duty (a) to account to the partnership and hold for it any property, profit, or benefit derived by the partner in conducting partnership business or derived from the use of partnership property, including the appropriation of a partnership opportunity; (b) to refrain from dealing with the partnership in the conduct or winding up of partnership business with an interest adverse to the partnership's interest; and (c) not to compete with the partnership before dissolution of the partnership. The RUPA provides, however, that a partner does not violate a duty of loyalty merely because the partner's conduct advances his or her own interest, and the fiduciary duty does not extend to formation of the partnership or events after a partner's dissociation. The RUPA requires that a partner act in good faith and fair dealing in connection with partnership affairs.
2. Duty of Obedience–A partner must act in obedience to the partnership agreement and to any business decisions properly made by the partnership. A partner who violates this duty is individually liable to the partners for any resulting loss.
3. Duty of Care–A partner must refrain from conduct that is grossly negligent or reckless, intentional misconduct, or a knowing violation of law. Honest errors of judgment or failure to use ordinary skill in transacting business do not breach the duty of care.

C. Rights Among Partners–Partners have certain rights including: (1) their right to use and possess partnership property for partnership purposes, (2) their transferable interests in a partnership, (3) their right to share in distributions, (4) their right to manage the partnership business, (5) their right to choose copartners, and (6) their enforcement rights.
1. Rights in Specific Partnership Property–The RUPA rejects the UPA's theory of tenancy in partnership (thus partners are not co-owners of partnership property) and instead holds that the partnership owns partnership property. Therefore a partner cannot voluntarily or involuntarily transfer a separate interest in partnership property and can use partnership property only for partnership purposes.
2. Partner's Interest in the Partnership–Each partner has an interest in the partnership defined as all of the partner's interest in the partnership including the his or her transferable interest and all management and other rights.
a. Assignability-A transferable interest only includes the partner's share of the partnership profits, losses, and distributions upon liquidation. A partner may transfer all or a portion of his or her transferable interest in a partnership. The transfer does not by itself cause the

partner's dissociation or a dissolution of the partnership. The new owner does not become a partner and does not enjoy any of the other rights of partners. The assignee is merely entitled to receive the partner's share of profits and rights and distribution on liquidation. However, the assignee may request a court-ordered dissolution. By unanimous vote, the remaining partners can expel the assigning partner unless the assignment was made as security for an obligation.

   b. Creditors' Rights–A partner's transferable interest is subject to the claims of that partner's creditors, who may obtain a charging order (a type of judicial lien) against the partner's transferable interest which empowers the court to order that payments due to the partner be paid to the creditor. A court also may order a foreclosure of the interest subject to the charging order at any time. The purchaser at the foreclosure sale has the rights of a transferee. Prior to foreclosure, an interest that is subject to a charging order may be redeemed by (a) the partner who is the debtor; (b) other partners with nonpartnership property; or (c) other partners with partnership property if all remaining partners consent.

3. Right to Share in Distributions–A distribution is a transfer of partnership property from the partnership to a partner. Distributions include a division of profits, a return of capital contributions, a repayment of a loan or advance made by a partner to the partnership, and a payment made to compensate a partner for services rendered to the partnership.

   a. Right to Share in Profits–Unless otherwise agreed, each partner is entitled to a share of the partnership profits and each partner is charged with a share of any partnership losses. If there is no agreement about dividing profits, the partners share profits equally regardless of the ratio of their financial contributions. Unless otherwise agreed, the partners bear losses in the same proportion in which they share profits.

   b. Right to Return of Capital– Unless otherwise agreed, a partner has no right to receive a distribution of the capital contributions in his account before his withdrawal or the liquidation of the partnership. Unless otherwise agreed, partners are not entitled to interest on their capital contributions absent unless there is a delay in the return of them.

   c. Right to Return of Advances–A partner who makes advances (loans) over and above a capital contribution is entitled to repayment of the advances plus interest. Under the RUPA, the partner's priority to repayment is the same as nonpartner creditors.

   d. Right to Compensation–Unless otherwise unanimously agreed, a partner is not entitled to remuneration for working in the partnership business. Partners are entitled to reasonable compensation for services rendered in winding up the partnership affairs.

4. Right to Participate in Management–Unless otherwise agreed, each partner has an equal vote in management of the business. A majority vote is required to authorize ordinary matters of partnership business. Unanimous authorization is required for extraordinary matters and to amend the partnership agreement.

5. Right to Choose Associates–*Delectus personae* refers to a partner's right to choose who may become a member of the partnership. It literally means "choice of the person." The RUPA provides that a person cannot become a partner without the consent of all the partners.

6. Enforcement Rights–Partnership law provides the partners with the means to enforce rights and duties created by the partnership relationship.

   a. Right to Information and Inspection of the Books–Every partner and the partnership must disclose to a partner, without demand, any information concerning the partnership that is needed for the proper exercise of the partner's partnership rights and duties. On demand, every partner and the partnership must furnish to a partner any other information concerning the partnership that is reasonable to request.

b. Legal Action–A formal account is a complete review of all financial transactions of the partnership. Under the RUPA, a partner may directly sue the partnership or other partners, with or without requesting an accounting of the partnership business, in order to enforce the partner's rights. The RUPA does not authorize partners to file derivative lawsuits on behalf of a partnership.

KEY TERMS

1. Sole proprietorship
2. General partnership
3. Joint venture
4. Limited partnership
5. Limited liability company
6. Limited liability partnership
7. Limited liability limited partnership
8. Corporation
9. Business trust
10. Partnership
11. Legal entity
12. Legal aggregate
13. Tenancy in partnership
14. Charging order
15. Distribution
16. *Delectus personae*
17. Formal account
18. Accounting
19. Transferability interest

TRUE/FALSE

_____ 1. The corporate form of business organization has an advantage over both the sole proprietorship and the general partnership in ease of formation.

_____ 2. The corporate form of business organization has an advantage over both the sole proprietorship and the general partnership in external liability for business debts.

_____ 3. A partnership is an association of two or more persons to carry on as co-owners a business for profit.

_____ 4. Any one partner may be held liable for the entire indebtedness of the partnership.

_____ 5. A limited partner is liable for the partnership debt only to the extent of her capital contribution.

_____ 6. A person may be a partner even though he has no authority to conduct the ordinary activities of the business.

_____ 7. A partner may withdraw his capital contribution without the consent of all the partners.

_____ 8. When a partner sells his interest in the partnership, the buyer becomes a new partner.

_____ 9. Every partner owes a duty of good faith, fairness, and loyalty to the other partners.

_____ 10. A partner who fails to use ordinary care and skill in discharging assigned duties will be personally liable to the partners for any resulting loss.

_____ 11. Unless otherwise agreed, partners bear losses equally even if profits are shared unequally.

_____ 12. The RUPA provides that amounts owing to partners for capital contributions are to be paid first upon dissolution of a partnership.

_____ 13. A partner who wrongfully withdraws from the partnership is liable to the remaining partners for damages resulting from the breach of the partnership agreement.

_____ 14. A partner's transferable interest does not include his or her entire partnership interest. It only includes the partner's share of the partnership profits, losses, and distributions upon liquidation.

_____ 15. A partner may engage in one or more competing businesses.

_____ 16. A partner who performs a disproportionate share of the partnership duties is entitled to a salary in addition to a share of the profits.

_____ 17. A partner may not ordinarily inspect the books of the partnership unless a majority of partners permit such inspection.

_____ 18. A partner's right to participate in the management of the partnership depends upon the size of that partner's capital contribution.

_____ 19. Unless otherwise agreed, a partner is entitled to interest on a capital contribution.

_____ 20. Partners may agree that losses will be shared differently than profits are shared.

MULTIPLE CHOICE

_____ 1. Which of the following forms of business organization is unaffected by the death, bankruptcy, or withdrawal of an owner?
   a. Corporation
   b. General partnership at will
   c. Limited partnership
   d. Sole proprietorship

_____ 2. Under the RUPA, a partnership may be formed by two or more:
   a. Individuals.
   b. Partnerships.
   c. Corporations.
   d. All of the above.

_____ 3. No person may become the member of a partnership without the consent of:
   a. At least one partner.
   b. Two or more partners.
   c. A majority of the partners.
   d. All of the partners.

_____ 4. Which of the following is not characteristic of the legal entity theory of partnerships?
   a. Assets of the firm are treated as those of the business.
   b. Title to real estate must be acquired by individual partners.
   c. Every partner is considered an agent of the partnership.
   d. Partnership creditors have the prior right to partnership assets.

_____ 5. Able and Baker are engaged in continuous transactions of buying and selling real estate over a period of time and are carrying on a business of trading in real estate. What are they?
   a. Partnership
   b. Corporation
   c. Joint venture
   d. None of the above

_____ 6. A person who is entitled to receive a share of the profits of a partnership is prima facie a partner unless the payment is of:
   a. A debt to a creditor.
   b. Rent to a landlord.
   c. Wages to an employee.
   d. All of the above.

_____ 7. _CPA:_ A partnership agreement must be in writing if:
   a. Any partner contributes more than $500 in capital.
   b. The partners reside in different states.
   c. The partnership's purpose cannot be completed within one year of formation.
   d. The partnership intends to own real estate.

_____ 8. _CPA:_ Which of the following is **not** necessary to create an express partnership?
   a. Execution of a written partnership agreement
   b. Agreement to share ownership of the partnership
   c. Intention to conduct a business for profit
   d. Intention to create a relationship recognized as a partnership

_____ 9. Which of the following is a legal duty imposed upon partners in their relationship with one another?
   a. Fiduciary duty
   b. Duty of obedience
   c. Duty of care
   d. All of the above

_____ 10. A partner has which of the following rights?
   a. Right to share in profits
   b. Right to return of capital upon demand
   c. Under the RUPA, a right to return of advances before nonpartner creditors are paid
   d. (a) and (b), but not (c)

_____ 11. A person who is entitled to participate in the management of a partnership is generally:
   a. An individual partner's assignee.
   b. An individual partner's judgment creditor.
   c. A receiver for an individual partner's interest.
   d. None of the above.

_____ 12. The fiduciary duty imposed upon partners requires which of the following?
   a. That a partner not engage in any activity except for partnership business
   b. That a partner not make a secret profit in connection with partnership business
   c. That a partner not own an interest in any other business other than the partnership
   d. All of the above

_____ 13. *CPA:* In a general partnership, the authorization of all partners is required for an individual partner to bind the partnership in a business transaction to:
   a. Purchase inventory.
   b. Hire employees.
   c. Sell goodwill.
   d. Sign advertising contracts.

_____ 14. Arthur breaches his fiduciary duty to the Main Street Partnership by usurping a partnership opportunity. As a result of his breach of this duty, the partnership suffered a loss of $10,000 and Arthur made a secret profit of $20,000.
   a. Arthur must pay the firm triple damages.
   b. Arthur must pay the firm $10,000.
   c. Arthur must pay the firm the $20,000 secret profit and the $10,000 loss.
   d. Arthur need not pay the firm anything.

_____ 15. *CPA:* Blake, a partner in QVM, a general partnership, wishes to withdraw from the partnership and sell her interest to Nolan. All of the other partners in QVM have agreed to admit Nolan as a partner and to hold him harmless for the past, present, and future liabilities of QVM. As a result of Blake's withdrawal and Nolan's admission to the partnership, Nolan:
   a. Must contribute cash or property to QVM to be admitted with the same rights as the other partners.
   b. Is personally liable for partnership liabilities arising before and after being admitted as a partner.
   c. Has the right to participate in QVM's management.
   d. Acquired only the right to receive Blake's share of QVM's profits.

SHORT ESSAY

1. What are the factors considered by a court in determining whether a partnership exists?

_____

_____

_____

_____

2. What are the main provisions that should be included in a partnership agreement?

_____

_____

_____

_____

3. Distinguish between the legal entity theory and the legal aggregate theory.

_____

_____

_____

_____

4. What are the principal rights of a partner?

_____

_____

_____

_____

5. What are the principal duties of a partner?

_____

_____

_____

_____

Chapter 32
Operation and Dissolution of
General Partnerships

PURPOSE

In this chapter, you study the interactions among the partners as well as with third persons in the operation and management of a partnership. The first part of the chapter focuses on the rights and duties of the partners among themselves. These rights and duties are determined by the partnership agreement, the common law, and the Revised Uniform Partnership Act (RUPA) in a majority of states. The second part of the chapter focuses on the relations of partners to third persons dealing with the partnership. These relations are governed by the laws of agency, contracts, and torts as well as by the RUPA. The material below relates to the RUPA. Some rules under the UPA are different.

CHAPTER CHECKPOINTS

After reading and studying this chapter, you should be able to:

1. Discuss the contract liability of a partner and of the partnership.

2. Explain under what circumstances the partnership and the partners will have tort liability.

3. Discuss the effect of notice to or knowledge of a partner.

4. Identify causes of dissolution of a partnership and the conditions under which partners have the right to continue the partnership after dissolution.

5. Explain the effect of dissolution on partners' authority and liability and the order of distribution of assets upon dissolution.

CHAPTER OUTLINE

I. Relationship of Partnership and Partners with Third Parties–Under agency law a principal is liable on contracts made on his behalf by his duly authorized agents and is liable in tort for the wrongful acts his employees commit in the course of their employment. Most problems between partners and third persons require the application of principles of agency law.

A. Contracts of Partnership–The act of every partner binds the partnership on transactions within the scope of partnership business unless the partner does not have actual or apparent authority to so act. If the partnership is bound, each general partner has unlimited personal liability. The RUPA provides that partners are jointly and severally liable on all partnership obligations. Joint and several liability means all partners may be sued jointly in one lawsuit or separate lawsuits may be filed against a partner individually.

   1. Authority to Bind Partnership–A partner may bind the partnership if (a) she has actual authority, express or implied, to perform the act, or (b) she has apparent authority to perform the act. Where there is no actual or apparent authority, the partnership is bound only if it ratifies the act.

      a. Actual Express Authority–Actual express authority of partners may be stated in the partnership agreement or in other agreements between the partners. A partner who does not have actual authority from all other partners cannot legally bind the partnership to any transaction that is not in the ordinary course the partnership business, such as: (i) execution of contracts of guaranty or suretyship, (ii) selling of partnership property that is not held for sale in the usual course of business, and (iii) payment of the partner's individual with partnership assets. The RUPA also authorizes the central filing of a statement of partnership authority, which may state the partners who are authorized to execute instruments transferring partnership real property, may limit a partner's authority of to transfer real property, or may grant extraordinary authority to some or all the partners or limit their ordinary authority. A filed statement is effective for up to five years.

      b. Actual Implied Authority–This is authority that is neither expressly granted nor expressly denied but is reasonably deduced from the nature of the partnership, the terms of the partnership agreement, or the relations of the partners. Examples include hiring and firing employees and purchasing property necessary for the business.

      c. Apparent Authority–It is authority that in view of the circumstances and the conduct of the parties, may be reasonably considered to exist by a third person who has no knowledge or notice of the lack of actual authority. A partner has apparent authority to indorse checks and notes, make warranties in selling goods, and enter into contracts for advertising.

   2. Partnership by Estoppel–Partnership by estoppel imposes partnership duties and liabilities on nonpartners who have either represented themselves or consented to be represented as partners.

B. Torts and Crimes of Partnership–The RUPA provides that a partnership is liable for loss or injury caused by any wrongful act or omission of any partner while acting within the ordinary course of the business of the partnership or with the authority of his copartners. If the partnership is liable, then each partner has unlimited personal liability for the partnership obligation. Partners are jointly and severally liable for a tort or breach of trust committed by any partner or by an employee of the firm in the course of partnership business. The partner committing the tort is directly liable to the third party and must also indemnify the partnership for damages it pays to the third party. A partner is not criminally liable for crimes committed by copartners unless the partner authorized or participated in them. A partnership is not criminally liable for the crimes committed by partners or employees unless a statute imposes vicarious liability.

C. Notice to a Partner–A partnership is bound by (1) notice to any partner of any matter relating to partnership affairs, (2) the knowledge of the partner acting in a particular matter if the knowledge was acquired while he was a partner, and (3) the knowledge of any other partner who reasonably could and should have communicated it to the acting partner. A demand on one partner as a representative of the firm is a demand on the partnership.

D. Liability of Incoming Partner–A person admitted as a partner into an existing partnership is liable for all of the obligations of the partnership arising before her admission as though she had been a partner when such obligations were incurred, although this liability may be satisfied only out of partnership property. Liability of incoming partners for preexisting debts and obligations of the firm is limited to their capital contributions. Liability for obligations that arise after their admission into the partnership is unlimited.

II. Dissociation and Dissolution of General Partnerships–"Dissociation" occurs when a partner is no longer associated in carrying on partnership business. "Dissolution" is a state that often triggers winding up and terminating a partnership. A partner's dissociation results in dissolution only in limited cases. When dissolution occurs, a partnership is not terminated but continues until the winding up of its affairs is complete. During winding up, unfinished business is completed, assets are collected, creditors are paid, and remaining assets are distributed to partners. Termination occurs when the foregoing is completed.

A. Dissociation–A partner has the *power* to dissociate at any time by expressing an intent to withdraw. A partner sometimes, however, does not have the *legal right* to dissociate. A partner who wrongfully dissociates is liable to the partnership for damages caused by his or her dissociation and the wrongfully dissociated partner does not have the right to participate in winding up the business.
   1. Wrongful Dissociations–Dissociation is wrongful if (a) it breaches the partnership agreement; or (b) in a term partnership if (i) dissociation occurs prior to expiration of the partnership term by the partner voluntarily withdrawing unless it occurs within 90 days after another partner's dissociation by death, bankruptcy, or wrongful dissociation, (ii) a partner is expelled for misconduct by judicial decree, (iii) the partner becomes a bankruptcy debtor; or (iv) the partner is an entity (other than a trust or estate) and is expelled or otherwise dissociated because its dissolution or termination was willful. A term partnership is one for a specific term or particular undertaking.
   2. Rightful Dissociations–Except as stated above, a partner's dissociation in any other situation is lawful, including death of a partner in any partnership, withdrawal of a partner in a partnership at will, and judicial decree that a partner is incapable of performing the partner's duties.
   3. Effect of Dissociation–After dissociation, a partner no longer participates in the management and conduct of the partnership business. If dissociation causes a dissolution and winding up, however, all partners who did not wrongfully dissociate may participate in winding up the

business. The duty not to compete terminates upon dissociation and a dissociated partner may immediately compete with the partnership.

B. Dissolution–In addition to the foregoing handful of dissociations that may cause a dissolution, the events below also may trigger dissolution.
   1. Causes of Dissolution–The RUPA provides that a partnership dissolves and its business must be wound up only if one of the following events occurs: (a) an act of the partners (see discussion regarding dissociations above), (b) operation of law, or (c) court order. The partners cannot vary the grounds for dissolution based on operation of law or court order.
      a. Dissolution by Act of the Partners–In a partnership at will, a partner may give notice of intent to withdraw at any time and this causes a dissolution. Death or bankruptcy of a partner does not dissolve a partnership at will. A term partnership may be dissolved in one of three ways.
         ▪ The partnership term expires. (Note: if the partners continue the partnership business, then the partnership is treated as a partnership at will.)
         ▪ All partners expressly agree to dissolve.
         ▪ A partner's dissociation results from the partner's death or incapacity, bankruptcy or similar financial impairment, or wrongful dissociation *and* within 90 days 50% or more of the remaining partners vote to wind up the partnership business.
      b. Dissolution by Operation of Law–A partnership dissolves by operation of law if it becomes unlawful to continue all or substantially all of the partnership's business.
      c. Dissolution by Court Order–On application by a partner, a court may order dissolution on based on any of the following grounds: (i) another partner's serious misconduct, (ii) the partnership's economic purpose is likely to be unreasonably frustrated; (iii) another partner has engaged in conduct relating to the partnership business that makes it unreasonable to carry on the partnership business with that partner, or (iv) it is not reasonably practicable to carry on the partnership business in conformity with the partnership agreement. The partners may not by agreement vary or eliminate the court's power to wind up a partnership.
      d. Effects of Dissolution–A partnership terminates when its affairs are wound up. The remaining partners may, however, continue the business after dissolution if all partners, including any dissociating partner other than a wrongfully dissociating partner, waive the right to have the partnership's business wound up and the partnership terminated.
         1. Authority Upon Dissolution–A partner's actual authority to act for the partnership terminates upon dissolution except as necessary to wind up partnership business. As an exception, a partner continues to have apparent authority following dissolution and can bind the partnership to a transaction if the partner's act would have bound the partnership before dissolution and the other party to the transaction did not have notice of the dissolution. A party has notice of dissolution if he or she (a) knows of it, (b) has received notification of it, (c) has reason to know it exists from all of the surrounding facts, or (d) more than 90 days have elapsed since a partner (who did not wrongfully dissociate) filed a statement of dissolution on the partnership's behalf.
         2. Liability–Partners are liable for their share of partnership liabilities incurred after dissolution.
         3. Winding Up–The process of liquidating a partnership is called winding up and involves many tasks needed to complete unfinished business, collect debts, reduce assets to cash,

pay creditors, and distribute the remaining assets to the partners. During this period, the fiduciary duties of the partners continue in effect except for the duty not to compete.

    a. Participation in Winding Up–After dissolution, partners who did not wrongfully dissociate may participate in winding up the partnership's business. Partners are entitled to reasonable compensation for services rendered in the winding up.

    b. Distribution of Assets–Under the RUPA, partnership assets are paid in the following order: (i) amounts owing to creditors, both partners and nonpartners, and (ii) any surplus is used to pay a liquidating distribution equal to the net amount distributable to partners in accordance with their right to distributions, which includes both return of capital and profits. Partners are entitled to a settlement of partnership accounts upon winding up. Any partner with a negative account balance must contribute to the partnership an amount equal to the negative balance in the partner's account. Partners share proportionately in the shortfall caused by partners who fail to contribute their proportionate share and a partner may recover from other partners any contributions paid in excess of that partner's share of the partnership's liabilities.

    c. Marshaling of Assets–The RUPA eliminates the marshalling of assets doctrine. It provides that partnership creditors are to be satisfied first out of partnership assets and unsatisfied partnership creditors may recover any deficiency out of the partners' individual assets on an equal footing with the partners' personal creditors.

C. Dissociation Without Dissolution–A dissociation of a partner frequently does not cause a dissolution and only requires the parties to provide for paying off a dissociated partner.

    1. Dissociations Not Causing Dissolution–See discussion above. Partners may by agreement change or eliminate the grounds for dissolution unless it is caused by the partnership carrying on an illegal business or a court-ordered dissolution on application of a partner or transferee of a partner's interest.

    2. Continuation after Dissociation–If a partner dissociates from a partnership without causing a dissolution, then the remaining partners have the right to continue the business. Creditors of the partnership remain creditors of the continued partnership. The partnership must purchase the dissociated partner's interest in the partnership. A partner in a term partnership who wrongfully dissociates is not entitled to any portion of the buyout price until the expiration of the term or completion of the undertaking unless the partner can prove that earlier payment will not cause undue hardship to the partnership. A partnership must indemnify a dissociated partner whose interest is being purchased against most partnership liabilities.

    3. Dissociated Partner's Power to Bind the Partnership–If a partner dissociates without causing a dissolution, then the partner for two years has apparent authority to bind the partnership if the dissociated partner would have bound the partnership before dissociation and at the time of entering into the transaction the third party (a) reasonably believed that the dissociated partner was a partner, (b) did not have notice of the partner's dissociation, and (c) did not have constructive notice of dissociation from a filed statement of dissociation. A dissociated partner is liable for any damage caused to the partnership arising from an obligation improperly incurred.

D. Dissociated Partner's Liability to Third Persons–A partner's dissociation does not itself discharge the partner's liability for partnership obligations incurred before dissociation. A dissociated partner is not liable for partnership obligations incurred more than two years after dissociation. For partnership obligations incurred within two years after a partner dissociates without resulting in a dissolution of the partnership business, a dissociated partner is liable for a partnership obligation if at the time of entering into the transaction the other party (a) reasonably believed that the dissociated partner was then a partner; (b) did not have notice of the partner's dissociation, and (c) did not have constructive notice of dissociation from a filed statement.

KEY TERMS

1. Partnership by estoppel

2. Joint liability

3. Dissolution

4. Winding up

5. Term partnership

6. Partnership at will

7. Disassociation

8. Joint and several liability

TRUE/FALSE

_____   1. Partnership by estoppel imposes partnership duties and liabilities on a nonpartner who has represented himself as a partner.

_____   2. A partner who, in violation of an agreement not to extend credit, sells goods on credit to an insolvent party is personally liable to the partnership for the unpaid debt.

_____   3. Unless otherwise agreed, partners bear losses in the same proportion in which they share profits.

_____   4. It is permissible, in a partnership agreement, to provide for admission of a new partner by a less-than-unanimous vote.

_____   5. A partner who commits a tort in the ordinary course of the business of the partnership must indemnify the partnership for any damages it pays to the third party.

_____   6. Under the RUPA, partners only have joint liability for partnership contractual or tort obligations.

_____   7. A majority vote of the partners is sufficient to admit a new partner into the partnership.

_____   8. An incoming partner has unlimited personal liability for antecedent debts of the partnership.

_____   9. On dissolution, a partnership is not terminated but continues until winding up of its affairs is completed.

_____ 10. During the winding up stage of dissolution, the partners no longer are bound by fiduciary duties one to another.

_____ 11. A partner's dissociation from a partnership does not discharge the partner's liability for partnership obligations incurred before his or her dissociation.

_____ 12. With certain limits, a partner who dissociates without causing a dissolution may have apparent authority to bind the partnership for two years following his or her dissociation.

_____ 13. The RUPA retains the marshalling of assets doctrine stated by the UPA.

_____ 14. In connection with distribution of assets, partner creditors stand on an even footing with other general creditors of the partnership.

_____ 15. Under the RUPA, death of a partner automatically dissolves a partnership at will.

MULTIPLE CHOICE

_____ 1. The rights and duties of the partners with respect to the third persons with whom the partnership deals are determined by:
   a. delectus personae.
   b. the Uniform Third Persons Act.
   c. the RUPA.
   d. none of the above.

_____ 2. A partner may bind the partnership by an act which is not apparently within the scope of the partnership business if he has:
   a. express authority to perform the act.
   b. implied authority to perform the act.
   c. either (a) or (b).
   d. neither (a) nor (b).

_____ 3. A partner who has actual authority from a majority of his copartners may bind the partnership to:
   a. an assignment of partnership property for the benefit of its creditors.
   b. a sale of partnership property held for sale in the usual course of business.
   c. a sale of partnership property not held for sale in the usual course of business.
   d. a contract of suretyship in the firm name.

_____ 4. The liability of an incoming partner for antecedent debts and obligations of the firm is:
   a. unlimited.
   b. limited to his capital contribution.
   c. limited to his accrued and unpaid share of the profits.
   d. none of the above.

_____ 5. Ann and Betty were partners in a business. They represented to First Bank that Carl was a partner with them. When contacted by First Bank, Carl did not deny the representation, because he was seriously considering the possibility of joining the business. First Bank loaned the money, but Ann and Betty defaulted. First Bank is entitled to collect from:
   a. Carl only.
   b. Ann, Betty, and Carl jointly.
   c. Ann, Betty, or Carl severally.
   d. Ann and Betty jointly, but not from Carl.

_____ 6. When a partner commits a crime in the course of partnership business:
   a. the partner is not criminally liable for his or her conduct.
   b. the partner is criminally liable for his or her conduct.
   c. the partnership cannot be held criminally liable for partner's conduct.
   d. a and c.

_____ 7. Dissolution is brought about by:
   a. The assignment of a partner's interest.
   b. a creditor's charging order on a partner's interest.
   c. unanimous vote of the partners even if prior to expiration of time for a term partnership.
   d. All of the above.

_____ 8. A court may order a dissolution if it finds that:
   a. a partner engages in serious misconduct.
   b. the partnership's economic purpose is likely to be unreasonably frustrated.
   c. the partnership's business is not as profitable as it was in the past.
   d. a and b.

_____ 9. When is a partner in a partnership at will legally entitled to dissociate from the partnership?
   a. Never.
   b. Only when a majority of the remaining partners consent to such dissociation.
   c. Only when all of the remaining partners consent to such dissociation.
   d. At any time the partner chooses.

_____ 10. Ashley, Barbara, and Clarence form a partnership with Ashley contributing $1,000 capital, Barbara contributing $5,000 capital, and Clarence contributing $10,000 capital. Each partner also loaned the partnership $2,000 which has not been repaid. When the partnership is liquidated, its assets are $50,000 and its liabilities to creditors are $25,000. Under the RUPA, how much will Ashley receive?
   a. $1,000.
   b. $2,000.
   c. $4,000.
   d. $10,000.

_____ 11. David, Elvis, and Fred are partners in the DEF Company. David wrongfully disassociates from the partnership in breach of the partnership agreement. Under these facts:
   a. David can compel the liquidation of the partnership.
   b. David is liable to Elvis and Fred for damages caused by the wrongful disassociation.
   c. Elvis and Fred can continue in business, but they must pay David for his interest in the firm less damages sustained as the result of his breach.
   d. b and c.

_____ 12. Select the correct answer.
   a. A partner is personally liable for a tort that the partner committed while carrying on the partnership business.
   b. A partner is not personally liable for a tort that the partner committed while carrying on the partnership business.
   c. A partnership is liable for a tort that one of its partners committed while carrying on the partnership business.
   d. a and c.

_____ 13. Select the correct answer(s):
   a. A partner cannot act as an agent of the partnership.
   b. A partner can act as an agent of the partnership.
   c. The liability of a partnership for actions of a partner are largely determined by ordinary rules of contract law, tort law, and agency law.
   d. b and c.

SHORT ESSAY

1. Explain the liability of an incoming partner into an existing partnership.

_____

_____

_____

_____

2. Arthur, Bob, and Clark have a partnership, but their agreement is silent as to the sharing of profits and losses. Arthur's capital contribution is $12,000; Bob's capital contribution is $6,000; Clark's contribution is a computer and other equipment valued at $3,400. How would the partners divide a $36,000 profit?

_____

_____

_____

_____

3. Fred, a partner in Fastime, an express mail delivery partnership, negligently drove the delivery truck and caused a wreck with Sue. Sue was injured, so she files a lawsuit. Discuss who is liable to Sue for her damages.

_____

_____

_____

_____

4. In what ways may a partnership be dissolved?

_____

_____

_____

_____

5. What is the order of distribution of assets in the winding up process under the RUPA?

_____

_____

_____

_____

Chapter 33
Limited Partnerships and
Limited Liability Companies

PURPOSE

In this chapter, you study limited partnerships, limited liability companies, limited liability partnerships, and limited liability limited partnerships. Although these forms of business associations are not as common as general partnerships, sole proprietorships, and corporations, they do meet special business and investment purposes that make each appropriate in certain circumstances. In recent years, limited partnerships have become more common as investment vehicles. The limited partnership has limited liability for limited partners and has certain tax advantages that make it an attractive vehicle for a variety of investments.

CHAPTER CHECKPOINTS

After reading and studying this chapter, you should be able to:

1. Compare a limited partnership to a general partnership with respect to formation, liability of the partners, management, and dissolution.

2. List and discuss the activities in which a limited partner may engage without forfeiting limited liability under the RULPA.

3. List the order in which the assets of a limited partnership are distributed to creditors, limited partners, and general partners.

4. Discuss the formation and dissolution of a limited liability company and the rights and duties of the members.

5. List the main characteristics of and distinguish among limited liability partnerships and limited liability limited partnerships.

CHAPTER OUTLINE

A. Limited Partnerships–Limited partnerships are statutory creations. All states except Louisiana have adopted either the 1976 Revised Uniform Limited Partnership Act (1976 RULPA) or the 1985 RULPA. These Acts generally govern limited partnerships although the Uniform Partnership Act applies to limited partnerships in any case not provided for in the RULPA.

   1. Definition–A limited partnership is a partnership formed by two or more persons under the laws of a state and that has one or more general and one or more limited partners. A person includes a natural person, partnership, limited partnership, trust, estate, association, or corporation. It differs from a general partnership in that (1) there must be a statute in effect providing for the formation of limited partnerships; (2) the limited partnership must substantially comply with the requirements of that statute; and (3) the liability of a limited partner for partnership debts or obligations is limited to the extent of the capital he has contributed or agreed to contribute.

   2. Formation–Although a general partnership may be formed without special procedures, a limited partnership requires substantial compliance with the limited partnership statute. Failure to do so may result in the limited partners not obtaining limited liability.

      a. Filing of Certificate–To form a limited partnership under the RULPA, two or more persons must file a signed certificate in the office of the secretary of state of the state in which the limited partnership has its principal office. The certificate must include the following information: (1) the name of the limited partnership; (2) the address of the office and the name and address of the agent for service of process; (3) the name and the business address of each general partner; (4) the latest date upon which the limited partnership is to dissolve; and (5) any other matters the general partners decide to include. The certificate of limited partnership must be amended if a new general partner is admitted, a partner withdraws, or a general partner becomes aware that any statement in the certificate was or has become false.

      b. Name–The surname of a limited partner may not be included in the partnership name unless it is also the surname of a general partner or unless the business had been carried on under that name before the admission of that limited partner. A limited partner who knowingly permits his name to be used in violation of this provision is liable to any creditor who did not know that he was a limited partner. The name may not be the same as or deceptively similar to that of any corporation or other limited partnership. The name must also contain without abbreviation the words "limited partnership."

      c. Contributions–The contribution of a partner may be cash, property, services rendered, a promissory note, or an obligation to contribute cash, property, or to perform services. A promise by a limited partner to contribute to the limited partnership is not enforceable unless it is in a signed writing. Should a partner fail to make a required capital contribution described in a signed writing, she may be held liable to contribute the cash value of the stated contribution.

      d. Defective Formation–The limited partnership is formed when the certificate is filed if it substantially complies with the requirements of the statute. If there is no certificate filed or if one is filed but it does not substantially meet the statutory requirements, the formation is defective. Where formation is defective, the limited liability of the limited partners is jeopardized. The 1985 RULPA greatly reduces the risk that a limited partner will be exposed to liability because of an inadvertent omission from the certificate.

   e. Foreign Limited Partnerships–A limited partnership is considered "foreign" in any state in which it has not been formed. The laws of the state under which a foreign limited partnership is organized govern its organization, internal affairs, and the liability of its limited partners. Under RULPA, all foreign limited partnerships must register with the secretary of state before transacting any business in the state. A partnership that fails to register may not bring enforcement actions in the state's courts, although it may defend itself there.

3. Rights–The rights of the parties are usually set forth in the articles of limited partnership and the limited partnership agreement. Unless otherwise agreed or provided in the act, a general partner in a limited partnership has all the rights and powers of a partner in a general partnership. A general partner may also be a limited partner.

   a. Control–The general partners have almost exclusive control and management of the limited partnership. A limited partner who shares in the management or control of the association may forfeit limited liability. Under the RULPA, a limited partner who participates in the control of the business is liable only to those persons who transact business with the limited partnership reasonably believing, based upon the limited partner's conduct, that the limited partner is a general partner. The RULPA enumerates certain activities in which a limited partner may engage without being deemed to have taken part in control of the business. They include but are not limited to: (1) being a contractor for, or an agent or employee of, the limited partnership or of a general partner; (2) consulting with and advising a general partner with respect to the business of the limited partnership; (3) acting as surety for the limited partnership; (4) approving or disapproving an amendment to the partnership agreement; and (5) voting on various fundamental changes in the limited partnership.

   b. Voting Rights–The partnership agreement may grant to all or a specified group of general or limited partners the right to vote on any matter. If, however, the agreement grants limited partners voting powers beyond the act's safe harbor provisions, a court may hold that the limited partners have participated in control of the business. The RULPA does not require that limited partners have the right to vote on matters as a class separate from the general partners, although the partnership agreement may provide for such a right.

   c. Choice of Associates–After the formation of a limited partnership, the admission of additional limited partners requires the written consent of all partners unless the partnership agreement provides otherwise, and new general partners may be admitted only with the specific written consent of all partners. Under the 1985 act, the written partnership agreement determines the procedure for authorizing the admission of additional general partners. The written consent of all partners is required only if the partnership agreement fails to deal with this issue.

   d. Withdrawal–A general partner may withdraw from a limited partnership at any time by giving written notice to the other partners. If the withdrawal violates the partnership agreement, the limited partnership may recover damages from the withdrawing general partner. A limited partner may withdraw as provided in the limited partnership certificate or, under the 1985 act, the written partnership agreement. Upon withdrawal, a withdrawing partner is entitled to receive any distribution to which she is entitled under the partnership agreement, subject to the amount restrictions discussed below. If the partnership agreement makes no provision, the partner is entitled to receive the fair value of her interest in the limited partnership as of the date of withdrawal based upon her right to share in distributions from the limited partnership.

e. Assignment of Partnership Interest–A partnership interest is a partner's share of the profits and losses of a limited partnership and the right to receive distributions of partnership assets. It is considered to be personal property. Unless otherwise provided in the partnership agreement, a partner may assign his partnership interest without dissolving the limited partnership, although the assignee does not become a partner and may not exercise the rights of a partner. An assignee may become a limited partner if all other partners consent.

f. Profit and Loss Sharing–The profits and losses are allocated among the partners as provided in the partnership agreement. If the partnership agreement has no such written provision, then the profits and losses are allocated on the basis of the value of contributions actually made by each partner. Limited partners are not liable for losses beyond their capital contribution. Under the 1985 act, the agreement for sharing profits and losses must be in writing.

g. Distributions–The partners share distributions of cash or other assets of a limited partnership as provided in writing in the partnership agreement. The 1985 Act requires such an agreement to be written. The RULPA allows partners to share in distributions in a different proportion than they share in profits. In the absence of an agreement in writing, the distributions are made on the basis of the value of contributions actually made by each partner. A partner who is entitled to a distribution has the status of a creditor, but a partner may not receive a distribution unless there are sufficient assets after the distribution to pay all liabilities other than those owing to partners on account of their partnership interests.

h. Loans–Both general and limited partners may be secured or unsecured creditors of the partnership, subject to applicable state and federal bankruptcy and fraudulent conveyance statutes.

i. Information–The partnership must maintain within the state an office at which basic organizational and financial records are kept. Each partner has the right to inspect and copy any of the partnership records.

j. Derivative Actions–A limited partner has the right to bring an action on behalf of a limited partnership to recover a judgment in its favor if the general partners have refused to bring the action.

4. Duties and Liabilities–The duties and liabilities of general partners are quite different from those of limited partners.

a. Duties–A general partner has a fiduciary relationship to the general and limited partners. It remains unclear whether a limited partner is a fiduciary to the general partners or to the partnership. The RULPA does not distinguish between the duty of care owed by a general partner to a general partnership and that owed by a general partner to a limited partnership. A limited partner owes no duty of care to a limited partnership as long as he remains a limited partner.

b. Liabilities–The limited personal liability offered to limited partners is one of the most appealing features of a limited partnership. Limited liability means that once a limited partner has paid her contribution she has no further liability to the limited partnership or its creditors. The general partners have unlimited external liability unless the limited partnership is a limited liability limited partnership (LLLP). Any general partner who knew or should have known that the limited partnership certificate contained a false statement is liable to anyone who suffers loss by reliance on that false statement.

5. Dissolution–As with a general partnership, the three steps are (1) dissolution, (2) winding up or liquidation, and (3) termination. The causes of dissolution and the priorities in the distribution of assets are different from those in a general partnership.

   a. Causes–The limited partners do not have the right or the power to dissolve the partnership, except by decree of the court. Under the RULPA the following events trigger a dissolution, after which the partnership must be liquidated: (1) the expiration of the time period specified in the certificate; (2) the happening of events specified in writing in the partnership agreement; (3) the unanimous written consent of all the partners; (4) the withdrawal of a general partner, unless either (a) the written provisions of the partnership agreement permit the remaining general partners to continue the business or (b) within 90 days all partners agree in writing to continue the business; or (5) a decree of judicial dissolution, which may be granted whenever it is not reasonably practicable to carry on the business in conformity with the partnership agreement.

   b. Winding Up–Unless otherwise provided in the partnership agreement, the general partners who have not wrongfully dissolved the partnership may wind up its affairs. Under certain circumstances, the limited partner may wind up the affairs.

   c. Distribution of Assets–The priorities for distribution are as follows: (1) creditors, including partners who are creditors except with respect to liabilities for distributions; (2) partners and ex-partners in satisfaction of liabilities for unpaid distributions; (3) partners for the return of contributions except as otherwise agreed; and (4) partners for their partnership interests in the proportions in which they share in distributions, except as otherwise agreed.

B. Limited Liability Companies

All states have enacted LLC statutes. A limited liability company is a noncorporate business organization that provides limited liability to all owners, permits all of its members to participate in management of the business, and, if properly structured, may be taxed as a partnership. (Note: publicly traded LLCs are subject to corporate income taxation.)

1. Formation–Formation requires substantial compliance with a state's limited liability company statute. All states allow an LLC to have only one member. Individual members then are not liable for the debts and obligations of the LLC. The LLC can contract in its own name and carry on any lawful business activity. Some states restrict the permissible activities of LLCs.

   a. Filing–LLC statutes generally require the central public filing of articles of organization in a designated state office. Most states provide for perpetual existence unless otherwise stated.

   b. Name–The words "limited liability company" or the abbreviation "LLC" are generally required to be a part of the name although some states allow "limited company."

   c. Contribution–Contributions by a member to an LLC may be cash, property, services rendered, a promissory note, or other obligation to contribute cash, property, or perform services.

    d. Operating Agreement–A required operating agreement is the basic contract governing the affairs of the company and the source of rights and duties of its members and managers.

    e. Foreign Limited Liability Companies–An LLC is "foreign" in any state other than that in which it was formed and must register with the secretary of state before transacting any business in the state. Failure to register deprives the company of filing enforcement actions until it does register, although it may defend itself in the state's courts.

2. Rights of Members–A member's interest in the LLC includes two components: (a) the financial interest, which is the right to distributions and (b) the management interest, which typically includes the right to manage, vote, obtain information, and bring enforcement actions.

    a. Profit and Loss Sharing–The operating agreement determines how the partners allocate the profits and losses which, in the absence of agreement, are typically allocated on the basis of the value of the member's contribution.

    b. Distribution–Distribution of cash or other assets is provided for in the operating agreement but, in the absence of agreement, is typically made on the basis of the contributions each member has made. Members have no right to distributions before withdrawal from the LLC.

    c. Withdrawal–Some statutes allow a member to withdraw upon giving notice as specified in the operating agreement and demand payment of her interest. Some states permit the operating agreement to deny members the right to withdraw.

    d. Management–In the absence of a contrary agreement, each member typically has equal rights in the management of an LLC. A manager may, but does not have to, be a member of the LLC.

    e. Voting–Voting rights are often expressed by statute, subject to a contrary provision in an LLC's operating agreement. Typically members have the right to vote to (i) adopt or amend the operating agreement, (ii) admit any person as a member, (iii) sell all or substantially all of the LLC's assets prior to dissolution, and (iv) merge the LLC with another LLC. In some states, members have equal voting rights. In other states, members' voting is based on their respective financial contributions to the LLC.

    f. Information–An LLC must keep organizational and financial records which members can inspect.

    g. Derivative Actions–A member has the right to bring an action on behalf of a limited liability company to recover a judgment in its favor if the managers or members with authority to bring the action have refused to do so.

    h. Assignment of LLC Interest–A member's financial interest may be assigned without affecting the LLC. The assignee does not become a member and may not exercise any rights of a member. A judgment creditor of a member may obtain a charging order against the member's financial interest in the LLC, which gives the creditor the rights of an assignee.

3. Duties–As with general and limited partnerships, the duties of care and loyalty apply to LLCs. Who has these duties depends upon whether the LLC is a manager-managed or member-managed LLC. Some state laws impose the duties of good faith and fair dealing.

    a. Manager-Managed LLCs–Managers generally have by statute a duty of care to refrain from grossly negligent, reckless, or intentional conduct; however, in some states, this duty is to act as a prudent person would in similar circumstances.

    b. Member-Managed LLCs–Members of member-managed LLCs have the same duties of care and loyalty that managers have in manager-managed LLCs.

4. Liabilities–A member or manager generally is not personally liable for an LLC's obligations, provided, that a member or manager is personally liable for a wrongful act that he or she commits or an LLC debt that he or she personally guarantees. A member who fails to make an agreed contribution is liable to the LLC for the deficiency. A member receiving a return of her contribution in violation of the LLC's operating agreement is liable to the LLC for the amount of the contribution wrongfully returned.

5. Dissolution–Dissolution occurs upon (a) the expiration of the LLC's agreed duration or the happening of any of the events specified in the articles, (b) the unanimous written consent of all members, or (c) a decree of judicial dissolution, typically issued because it is not reasonably practicable to carry on the LLC's business or in some states because the members or managers have acted illegally, fraudulently, or oppressively.

    a. Dissociation–Voluntary withdrawal, death, incompetence, expulsion, or bankruptcy all would constitute a member's dissociation with the LLC. Most statutes permit the non-dissociating members to continue the LLC by unanimous consent or by majority vote.

    b. Winding Up–An LLC continues after dissolution solely to wind up its business. The fiduciary duties of members and managers continue during this period.

    c. Authority Upon dissolution–The actual authority of a member or manager to act for the LLC terminates except as necessary to wind up the LLC's business.

    d. Distribution of Assets–Most statutes provide default rules for distributing the assets of a limited liability company.

    e. Protection of Creditors–Many states establish procedures to help protect creditors' interests.

6. Mergers and Conversions–Most states expressly provide for the merger of an LLC (the merged entity) into another LLC (the surviving entity), which then has all of the assets and obligations of the merged LLCs. Many states also allow an LLC to merge into other forms of entities, such as corporations, partnerships, and limited partnerships, or visa versa. LLC statutes vary with respect to the voting rights of the members of the merged entities.

C. Other Unincorporated Business Associations

    1. Limited Liability Partnerships (LLP or RLLP)–Nearly all the states have enacted limited liability partnership statutes authorizing a general partnership that limits the liability of its partners. Filing with the secretary of state is required and all LLPs must designate themselves as such. Earlier statutes only provided protection from liability for negligence of partners (partial shield statutes), whereas recent statutes often provide limited liability for all debts and obligations (full-shield statutes) except where (a) a partner committed the wrongful act or where (b) a partner supervised the partner, employee, or agent who committed the wrongful act.

    2. Limited Liability Limited Partnerships–An LLLP is a limited partnership in which the liability of the general partners has been limited to the same extent as in an LLP. Where authorized, the general partners in a LLLP obtain the same degree of liability limitation that general partners can achieve in LLPs.

KEY TERMS

1. Limited partnership
2. Limited liability
3. Limited liability company
4. Limited liability partnership
5. Limited liability limited partnership

TRUE/FALSE

_____ 1. The liability of a limited partner for partnership debts or obligations is usually limited to her capital contribution.

_____ 2. As in general partnerships, limited partnerships are governed primarily by state common law.

_____ 3. A limited partner is liable to the partnership for the difference between what he has actually contributed and that stated on the certificate.

_____ 4. False statements in a certificate or amendment that cause loss to third parties who rely on those statements may result in liability for general partners.

_____ 5. It is possible for a general partner to also be a limited partner.

_____ 6. A limited partner may not assign her interest without the consent of all of the partners.

_____ 7. Unless otherwise agreed, under the RULPA the profits of a limited partnership are allocated on the basis of the value of contributions actually made by each partner.

_____ 8. A limited liability partnership is a general partnership that, by making the statutorily required filing, limits the liability of its partners for some or all of the partnership's obligations.

_____ 9. The RULPA draws a distinction between the duty of care owed by a general partner to a general partnership and that owed to a limited partnership.

_____ 10. The liability of a general partner in a limited partnership for partnership debts or obligations is limited to his capital contribution.

_____ 11. If a member of an LLC assigns her financial interests, the LLC is dissolved.

_____ 12. Statutory compliance is required in the formation of a limited liability company.

_____ 13. A limited liability company permits all members to participate in management of the business.

_____ 14. A limited liability company is a noncorporate business organization that provides limited liability to all of its members.

_____ 15. In a limited liability company, all members may participate in management of the business without losing liability protection.

MULTIPLE CHOICE

_____ 1. A limited partnership may be composed of:
   a. one general partner and one limited partner.
   b. two limited partners.
   c. one general partner and two limited partners.
   d. (a) and (c), but not (b).

_____ 2. The names of all limited partners should be included in:
   a. the certificate of limited partnership.
   b. the name of the partnership.
   c. each partner's income tax return.
   d. all of the above.

_____ 3. The capital contribution of a limited partner may be made in:
   a. cash.
   b. services.
   c. property.
   d. all of the above.

_____ 4. Under the RULPA, if a limited partnership transacts business in a foreign state without first registering to transact business in that state:
   a. its limited partners will be liable as general partners in the foreign state's courts.
   b. it may not defend itself in the foreign state's courts.
   c. it may not bring enforcement actions in the foreign state's courts.
   d. (b) and (c), but not (a).

_____ 5. Under the RULPA, a limited partner forfeits limited liability by:
   a. becoming an agent of the limited partnership.
   b. advising a general partner with respect to the business of the limited partnership.
   c. voting on a change in the nature of the business.
   d. participating in the daily management of the business.

_____ 6. A limited partner who makes a loan to the partnership is entitled to repayment of the loan:
   a. before general creditors of the partnership are repaid.
   b. on a pro rata basis with general creditors of the partnership.
   c. after general creditors of the partnership are repaid.
   d. none of the above.

_____ 7. A limited partnership is dissolved upon:
   a. the death of a limited partner.
   b. the bankruptcy of a limited partner.
   c. the withdrawal of the only general partner.
   d. all of the above.

_____ 8. Under the RULPA, a limited partner is entitled to repayment of her capital contribution:
   a. before general partners are repaid their capital contributions.
   b. on a pro rata basis with general partners.
   c. after general partners are repaid their capital contributions.
   d. none of the above.

_____ 9. The first priority in distributing the assets of a limited partnership is:
   a. partners for their partnership interests.
   b. partners for the return of their contributions.
   c. partners in satisfaction of liabilities for unpaid distributions.
   d. creditors, including partners who are creditors.

_____ 10. Which of the following is not a condition necessary to protect the limited liability status of limited partners?
   a. A certificate of limited partnership must be filed.
   b. The surname of a limited partner must be used in the partnership name.
   c. A limited partner must not take part in control of the business.
   d. The certificate of limited partnership contains no false statements.

_____ 11. Under the 1985 act, which of the following need not be included in the certificate of limited partnership?
   a. The name of the limited partnership
   b. The address of its office
   c. The name and business address of each general partner
   d. The name and business address of each limited partner

_____ 12. Which of the following is a characteristic of a limited liability partnership under most statutes?
   a. A filing must be made with the secretary of state
   b. The firm's name must contain the full words "limited liability partnership"
   c. Under recent statutes liability is typically limited only for negligent acts of partners.
   d. All of the above.

_____ 13. In a limited liability company, each member has:
   a. unlimited liability.
   b. limited liability for all debts and obligations of the company.
   c. liability to $500.
   d. liability to $5,000.

_____ 14. *CPA:* Which of the following statements regarding a limited partner are generally correct?

	The limited partner is subject to personal liability for partnership debts	*The limited partner has the right to has the right to take part in management*
a.	Yes	Yes
b.	Yes	No
c.	No	Yes
d.	No	No

_____ 15. *CPA:* Which of the following statements is correct with respect to a limited partnership?
   a. A limited partner may **not** be an unsecured creditor of the limited partnership.
   b. A general partner may **not** also be a limited partner at the same time.
   c. A general partner may be a secured creditor of the limited partnership.
   d. A limited partnership can be formed with limited liability for all partners.

SHORT ESSAY

1. When may a limited partner rightfully withdraw from a limited partnership?

_____

_____

_____

_____

2. When may a limited partner be subject to unlimited personal liability for partnership obligations?

_____

_____

_____

_____

3. Explain what activities a limited partner may participate in without losing liability protection.

_____

_____

_____

4. Describe a limited liability company and indicate its advantages.

_____

_____

_____

5. Describe a limited liability partnership.

_____

_____

_____

Chapter 34
Nature And Formation
of Corporations

PURPOSE

A corporation is an entity separate from its shareholders. It is created by law and is distinct from the individuals who create it. The corporation is the dominant form of business organization in the United States, accounting for 90 percent of the gross revenues of all business entities. Corporations have achieved this dominance because their attributes of limited liability, free transferability of shares, and continuity enable them to attract great numbers of widespread investors. The use of the corporation as a means of doing business has allowed vast concentrations of wealth and capital that have transformed this country from an agrarian to an industrial economy. Corporate law differs slightly from state to state, because each state has its own business corporation statute. However, most statutes contain many of the provisions found in the Model Business Corporation Act or its revised form, the RMBCA (Revised Act). The MBCA or the RMBCA sets a standard for the statutory law of business corporations.

CHAPTER CHECKPOINTS

After reading and studying this chapter, you should be able to:

1. List the principal attributes of a corporation and compare the corporate form of organization to the partnership and limited partnership.

2. Discuss the liability of the promoter of a corporation and the fiduciary duty of a promoter.

3. Define a corporation *de jure* and a corporation *de facto* and compare the approach of the MBCA with regard to defective incorporation to that of the common law.

4. Define "piercing the corporate veil" and discuss the circumstances under which courts are likely to pierce a corporate veil.

5. Define the term *ultra vires* and discuss the common law and modern approaches to acts of a corporation that are *ultra vires*.

CHAPTER OUTLINE

I. Nature of Corporations–A corporation may be formed only by substantial compliance with a state incorporation statute.

    A. Corporate Attributes–The principal attributes of a corporation are that (1) it is a legal entity; (2) it provides limited liability to its shareholders; (3) its shares of stock are freely transferable; (4) it may have perpetual existence; (5) its management is centralized; and it is considered, for some purposes, (6) a person, and (7) a citizen.

        1. Legal Entity–A corporation is a legal entity separate and apart from its shareholders with rights and liabilities entirely distinct from theirs.

        2. Limited Liability–A corporation is a legal entity and is therefore liable out of its own assets for its debts. Generally, the shareholders have limited liability for the corporation's debts—that liability does not extend beyond the amount of their investment.

        3. Free Transferability of Corporate Shares–In the absence of contractual restrictions, shares in a corporation may be freely transferred by sale, gift, or pledge. Transfers of shares of stock are governed by Article 8 of the UCC.

        4. Perpetual Existence–Unless otherwise stated in its articles of incorporation, a corporation has perpetual existence and does not terminate upon the death, withdrawal, or addition of a shareholder, director, or officer.

        5. Centralized Management–The shareholders of a corporation elect the board of directors which manages the business affairs of the corporation. The board must then appoint officers to run the day-to-day operations of the business.

        6. As a Person–A corporation is considered a person within the meaning of the due process clause of the Fifth and Fourteenth Amendments to the U.S. Constitution and of the equal protection clause of the Fourteenth Amendment. A corporation also enjoys the right of a person to be secure against unreasonable searches and seizures, as provided for in the Fourth Amendment. However, a corporation is not a person within the meaning of the clause in the Fifth Amendment that protects a "person" against self-incrimination.

        7. As a Citizen–A corporation is regarded as a citizen of the state of its incorporation and of the state in which it has its principal office for the purpose of determining whether diversity of citizenship exists for jurisdiction in the federal courts. It is not a citizen as the term is used in the Fourteenth Amendment privileges and immunities of citizenship clause.

    B. Classification of Corporations–Corporations may be classified as public or private, profit or nonprofit, domestic or foreign, publicly held or closely held, Subchapter S, and professional. These classifications are not mutually exclusive.

        1. Public or Private–A public corporation is one that is created to administer a unit of local civil government or one created by the United States to conduct public business. A private

corporation is founded by and composed of private persons for private purposes and has no governmental duties.

2. Profit or Nonprofit–A profit corporation is one founded for the purpose of operating a business for profit. A nonprofit corporation is one whose profits must be used exclusively for the charitable, educational, or scientific purpose for which it was formed.

3. Domestic or Foreign–A corporation is a domestic corporation in the state in which it is incorporated. It is a foreign corporation in every other state or jurisdiction. In states other than the state of incorporation, a corporation must obtain a certificate of authority to do business. This involves filing certain information with the secretary of state, paying prescribed fees, and designating a resident agent. In most states, an unlicensed foreign corporation is not entitled to maintain a suit in the state courts until it has obtained a certificate of authority, but it may defend against an action brought against it. Many states impose fines on the corporation's officers and directors and hold them personally liable on contracts made within the state.

4. Publicly Held or Closely Held–A publicly held corporation is one whose shares are owned by a large number of people and are widely traded. A corporation is closely held when its outstanding shares of stock are held by a small number of persons, who frequently are relatives or friends. Shareholders are usually active in the management and control of the business. Generally, closely held corporations are subject to the general incorporation statute that governs all corporations. Some states have enacted special legislation to accommodate the needs of closely held corporations. A Statutory Close Corporation Supplement to the Model and Revised Acts has been promulgated.

5. Subchapter S Corporation–The Internal Revenue Code permits a corporation meeting specified requirements to elect to be taxed essentially as though it were a partnership. Requirements for a corporation qualifying for subchapter S treatment are (1) it must be a domestic corporation; (2) it must have no more than 100 shareholders; (3) each shareholder must be an individual, an estate or a certain type of trust; (4) no shareholder may be a nonresident alien; and (5) it may have only one class of stock although classes of common stock differing only in voting rights are permitted.

6. Professional Corporations–All states have statutes permitting duly licensed professionals to use the corporate form. There is a Model Professional Corporation Supplement to the MBCA.

II. Formation of a Corporation–Under a general incorporation statute, the formation of a corporation requires the performance of several acts by various groups, individuals, and state officials.

A. Organizing the Corporation–Promoters of a corporation procure offers by subscribers to buy stock. Promoters also prepare the incorporation papers. Incorporators then execute articles of incorporation and file them with the secretary of state who issues a charter or certificate of incorporation.

1. Promoters–A promoter is a person who takes the necessary steps to organize a corporation. This person arranges for the capital and financing of the corporation, assembles the necessary assets, equipment, licenses, personnel, leases, and services.

a. Promoters' Contracts–Promoters enter into contracts in anticipation of the creation of the corporation. If these contracts are executed by the promoter in her own name and there is no further action, the promoter is liable on such contracts and the corporation, when it is created, is not automatically liable. The corporation is liable only if it adopts the contract.

    b. Promoters' Fiduciary Duty–The promoters have a fiduciary relationship among themselves, and with the corporation, its subscribers, and its initial shareholders. This duty requires good faith, fair dealing, and full disclosure. Promoters must account for any secret profit; failure to do so may violate federal or state securities laws.

  2. Subscribers–A subscriber is a person who agrees to purchase initial stock in a corporation. A preincorporation subscription is an offer to purchase capital stock in a corporation yet to be formed. The majority of courts regards a subscription as a continuing offer to purchase stock from a nonexisting entity which is incapable of accepting the offer until created. Under this view, a subscription may be revoked at any time prior to its acceptance. A minority of jurisdictions treat a subscription as a contract among the various subscribers which is irrevocable except with the consent of all of them. The Revised Act provides that a subscription is irrevocable for a period of six months, unless otherwise provided in the subscription agreement or unless all of the subscribers consent to the revocation of the subscription. If the corporation accepts during the period of irrevocability, a binding contract exists.

B. Formalities of Incorporation–Typically, the incorporators execute and deliver to the secretary of state the articles of incorporation. Under the Revised Act, once the certificate of incorporation (charter) is issued, the board of directors holds an organizational meeting for the purpose of adopting bylaws, appointing officers, and carrying on any other business.

  1. Selection of Name–Most incorporation laws require that the name contain a word or words that clearly indicate it is a corporation. A name must be distinguishable from that of another domestic corporation or of a foreign corporation authorized to do business within the state.

  2. Incorporators–The incorporators are the persons who sign the articles of incorporation filed with the secretary of state of the state of incorporation.

  3. Articles of Incorporation–Under the Revised Act, the articles of incorporation (charter) must include the name of the corporation, the number of authorized shares, the street address of the registered office and the name of the registered agent, and the name and address of each incorporator.

  4. Organizational Meeting–The Revised Act requires that an organizational meeting be held to adopt bylaws, appoint officers, and carry on any other business brought before the meeting.

  5. Bylaws–The bylaws of a corporation are the rules and regulations that govern its internal management. The bylaws may contain any provision for managing the business and regulating the affairs of the corporation that is not inconsistent with law or the articles of incorporation. The bylaws do not have to be publicly filed. Under the Revised Act, the board of directors may amend or repeal the bylaws unless the articles of incorporation or other sections of the Revised Act reserve that power exclusively to the shareholders. Under the Statutory Close Corporation Supplement, a close corporation may elect not to adopt any bylaws if necessary information is included either in a shareholder agreement or in the articles of incorporation.

III. Recognition or Disregard of Corporateness–Because a corporation is a creature of the state, corporate attributes such as limited liability and perpetual existence are recognized when the enterprise complies with the state's requirements for incorporation. The consequences of noncompliance with the statutory incorporation procedure depend on the seriousness of the error.

A. Defective Incorporation–Simplified incorporation procedures have greatly reduced the frequency of defective incorporation. Possible consequences of defective incorporation include: (1) the state brings an action for involuntary dissolution; (2) associates are held personally liable to a third party; (3) the association asserts that it is not liable on an obligation; or (4) a third party asserts that it is not liable to the association.

   1. Common Law Approach–Under the common law, a defectively formed corporation was sometimes accorded corporate attributes.

      a. Corporation *de Jure*–A corporation *de jure* is one that has been formed in substantial compliance with the incorporation statute and the organizational procedure. Such a corporation may not be challenged by anyone.

      b. Corporation *de Facto*–A corporation *de facto* is one that is not *de jure,* because of a failure to comply substantially with the incorporation statute. Nevertheless, it is recognized for most purposes as a corporation. There must be a *bona fide* attempt to comply with the law organizing a corporation under a general incorporation statute, and there must be the actual exercise of corporate power by conducting business in the belief that a corporation has been formed. The state can challenge the existence of a *de facto* corporation in a *quo warranto* ("by what right") action.

      c. Corporation by Estoppel–Estoppel does not create a corporation. It operates only to prevent a person from raising the question of a corporation's existence where the necessary elements of holding out and reliance are present.

      d. Defective Corporation–If the associates who purported to form a corporation have not formed either a *de jure* or a *de facto* corporation and the doctrine of estoppel does not apply, then some or all of the associates will be held to have unlimited liability for the obligations of the business.

   2. Statutory Approach–Corporate existence begins either upon the filing of the articles of incorporation or their acceptance by the secretary of state. Moreover, under the Revised Act and most state statutes, the filing or acceptance of the articles of incorporation by the secretary of state is conclusive proof that the incorporators have satisfied all conditions for incorporation. The Revised Act imposes liability only on persons who purport to act as or on behalf of a corporation, with knowledge that there was no incorporation.

B. Piercing the Corporate Veil–Courts will pierce the corporate veil of a properly formed corporation when the corporate entity is used to defeat public convenience, commit wrongdoing, protect fraud, or circumvent the law. Courts have pierced the corporate veil most frequently with closely held corporations and in parent-subsidiary relationships.

   1. Closely Held Corporations–Courts will pierce the corporate veil where shareholders have: (1) not conducted the business on a corporate basis, (2) not provided an adequate financial basis for the business, or (3) used the corporation to defraud. Under the Statutory Close Corporation Supplement, a court may pierce the corporate veil of a close corporation if the same circumstances would justify imposing personal liability on the shareholders of a general business corporation, but a court may not pierce the corporate veil just because the corporation is a statutory close corporation. The Revised Act validates unanimous shareholder agreements by which the shareholders may relax traditional corporate formalities.

2. Parent-Subsidiary–A subsidiary corporation is one in which another corporation, the parent, owns at least a majority of the subsidiary's shares and therefore has control over it. Courts will pierce the corporate veil and hold the parent liable for the debts of the subsidiary if (1) both corporations are not adequately capitalized, or (2) the formalities of separate corporate procedures are not observed, or (3) each corporation is not held out to the public as a separate enterprise, or (4) the funds of the two corporations are commingled, or (5) the parent corporation completely dominates the operation of the subsidiary to advance only the parent's own interests.

IV. Corporate Powers–A corporation has only those powers that the state has conferred on it. These powers are those expressly set forth in the statute and articles of incorporation and powers reasonably implied from those documents.

A. Sources of Corporate Powers
   1. Statutory Powers–The general powers of a corporation are typically set forth in the incorporation statute and include: (1) to have perpetual succession; (2) to sue and be sued; (3) to acquire and dispose of property; (4) to make contracts, borrow money, and secure any of its debts; (5) to lend money; (6) to be a promoter, partner, member, associate, or manager of any partnership or other entity; (7) to conduct business within or without the state of incorporation (8) to establish pension plans and other employee benefit plans; and (9) to make charitable donations.
   2. Purposes–A corporation may be formed for any lawful purposes. The Revised Act permits a corporation's articles of incorporation to state a more limited purpose. Many state statutes, but not the RMBCA, require that the purposes for which a corporation is formed be stated in its articles of incorporation.

B. *Ultra Vires* Acts–Any action taken or contract made by a corporation that goes beyond the express and implied powers is *ultra vires*. This term means that the act is not within the scope and type of acts that the corporation is legally empowered to perform.
   1. Effect of *Ultra Vires* Acts–Traditionally, *ultra vires* contracts were unenforceable as null and void. Under the modern approach, courts allow the *ultra vires* defense where the contract is wholly executory on both sides. Almost all statutes, including the Revised Act, have abolished the defense of *ultra vires* in an action by or against a corporation.
   2. Remedies for *Ultra Vires* Acts–Although under modern statutes *ultra vires* may no longer be used defensively against liability, the following ways to redress *ultra vires* acts are provided by the Revised Act: (1) a shareholder may bring an action against the corporation to enjoin the act; (2) the corporation, or a shareholder derivatively, may bring an action against the incumbent or former directors or officers for exceeding their authority; or (3) the attorney general of the state of incorporation may bring an action to dissolve the corporation or to enjoin it from transacting unauthorized business.

C. Liability for Torts and Crimes–A corporation is liable for the torts and crimes committed by its agents in the course of their employment. The doctrine of *respondeat superior* imposes full liability on a corporation for torts committed by its agents and employees during the course of their employment. A corporation may be liable for violation of statutes imposing liability without fault. A corporation may also be liable where the offense is perpetuated by a high corporate officer or the board of directors. Punishment of a corporation for crimes is by fine.

KEY TERMS

1. Corporation
2. Legal entity
3. Limited liability
4. Public corporation
5. Private corporation
6. Profit corporation
7. Nonprofit corporation
8. Domestic corporation
9. Foreign corporation
10. Publicly held corporation
11. Closely held corporation
12. Professional corporation
13. Subchapter S corporation
14. Promoter
15. Subscriber
16. Incorporators
17. Articles of incorporation
18. Bylaws
19. Corporation *de jure*
20. Corporation *de facto*
21. Corporation by estoppel
22. Piercing the corporate veil
23. Subsidiary corporation
24. Parent corporation
25. *Ultra vires*

TRUE/FALSE

_____ 1. A corporation is an entity apart from its shareholders, with entirely distinct rights and liabilities.

_____ 2. A corporation may sue or be sued by any other party, as well as contract with any other party, including its own shareholders.

_____ 3. A shareholder is neither a principal nor an agent of the corporation.

_____ 4. A promoter is one who agrees to purchase the initial stock in a corporation.

_____ 5. A promoter who enters into a preincorporation contract in the name of the corporation is ordinarily personally liable on that contract.

_____ 6. A closely held corporation is owned by a few shareholders whose shares are not actively traded.

_____ 7. Under the Internal Revenue Code, Subchapter S, a corporation's *income*, if qualifying, is taxed only at the shareholder level.

_____ 8. The bylaws of a corporation may not be changed without shareholder approval.

_____ 9. A corporation *de facto* is a corporation in fact because it has been formed in substantial compliance with the applicable statutes.

_____ 10. Under the MBCA, persons who act as a corporation without authority to do so are subject to unlimited personal liability for the debts of the enterprise.

_____ 11. A general statement of corporate purpose is sufficient to give rise to all of the powers necessary to accomplish that purpose.

_____ 12. A corporation is liable for crimes committed by its agents in the course of their employment.

_____ 13. A corporation may be liable for torts committed by its employees within the scope of their employment.

_____ 14. The Revised Model Business Corporation Act is the federal statute governing corporations in the United States.

_____ 15. A public corporation, such as General Motors Corporation, is one that is created to do business with the general public.

MULTIPLE CHOICE

_____ 1. A corporation:
   a. may sue or be sued by one of its shareholders.
   b. is dissolved by a transfer of its stock from one individual to another.
   c. may not own or deal in real property.
   d. all of the above.

_____ 2. A corporation is dissolved by:
   a. the death of a director.
   b. the withdrawal of an officer.
   c. the bankruptcy of a shareholder.
   d. none of the above.

_____ 3. The officers of a corporation:
   a. must be shareholders of the corporation.
   b. are elected by the shareholders of the corporation.
   c. are appointed by the board of directors of the corporation.
   d. (a) and (c), but not (b).

_____ 4. A corporation recognized for most purposes as a corporation but not formed in compliance with statutory requirements is a:
   a. corporation *de jure*.
   b. corporation *de facto*.
   c. corporation by estoppel.
   d. defective corporation.

_____ 5. A corporation becomes liable on a preincorporation contract made by promoters in the name of the corporation and in its behalf when:
   a. the contract is executed.
   b. the corporation is formed.
   c. the corporation adopts or ratifies the contract.
   d. none of the above.

_____ 6. The promoters of a corporation owe a fiduciary duty to:
   a. each other.
   b. subscribers.
   c. initial shareholders.
   d. all of the above.

_____ 7. The existence of a *de facto* corporation can be challenged by:
   a. the state.
   b. creditors of the corporation.
   c. debtors of the corporation.
   d. none of the above.

_____ 8. Piercing the corporate veil:
   a. invalidates the contracts of the corporation.
   b. imposes personal liability upon the shareholders for the obligations of the corporation.
   c. denies the corporation access to the state's courts.
   d. (b) and (c), but not (a).

_____ 9. Under the RMBCA, a corporation may:
   a. lend money.
   b. be a shareholder in other corporations.
   c. make charitable contributions.
   d. all of the above.

_____ 10. Under the RMBCA, the defense of *ultra vires* in an action for breach of contract by or against a corporation:
   a. is unavailable.
   b. is available where the contract is wholly executory on both sides.
   c. is available where the corporation has received full performance from the other party.
   d. is available where the other party has received full performance from the corporation.

_____ 11. Possible consequences of a defective incorporation would include:
   a.   state action for involuntary dissolution.
   b.   associates are personally liable to third parties.
   c.   third parties may assert that they are not liable to the association.
   d.   all of the above.

_____ 12. The city of San Francisco would best be described as which of the following?
   a.   A public corporation
   b.   A corporation formed pursuant to the Model Business Corporation Act
   c.   A close corporation
   d.   A domestic corporation

_____ 13. Albert invested $500 in the stock of the Ajax Corporation. Six months later, Ajax filed for bankruptcy with debts of $50,000. What is the amount of Albert's liability?
   a. $500
   b. $50,000
   c.   Albert is liable for a portion of the debt based upon the ratio of the number of shares he held to the total number of shares outstanding, and he can be liable for more than his initial investment.
   d.   Albert has no personal liability, although he may lose his $500 investment.

_____ 14. *CPA:* Assuming all other requirements are met, a corporation may elect to be treated as an S corporation under the Internal Revenue Code if it has:
   a.   both common and preferred stockholders.
   b.   a partnership as a stockholder.
   c.   100 or fewer stockholders.
   d.   the consent of a majority of stockholders.

_____ 15. *CPA:* In general, which of the following must be contained in articles of incorporation?
   a.   The names of states in which the corporation will be doing business
   b.   The name of the registered agent
   c.   The names of the initial officers and their terms of office
   d.   The powers of the corporation

SHORT ESSAY

1.   Identify the attributes of a corporation.

_____

_____

_____

_____

2.   Indicate ways in which a corporation may be classified.

_____

_____

_____

_____

3.   When is a court likely to pierce the corporate veil?

_____

_____

_____

_____

4.   Albert, a truck driver employed by the Carryall Corporation, while on a business errand, negligently runs over Brenda, a pedestrian. Brenda sues Albert and Carryall Corporation to recover damages for her injuries. What is the result?

_____

_____

_____

_____

5.   What are the sources of corporate power?

_____

_____

_____

_____

Chapter 35
Financial Structure of Corporations

PURPOSE

In this chapter, you study debt and equity investment securities, which are the two principal sources for financing corporations. Equity securities represent an ownership interest in the corporation and include both common and preferred stock. Bonds are debt securities and do not represent an ownership interest in the corporation. Instead, they create a debtor-creditor relationship between the corporation and the bondholder. Retained earnings are also essential to the financial structure of a corporation. This chapter discusses debt and equity securities as well as payment of dividends and other distributions to shareholders.

CHAPTER CHECKPOINTS

After reading and studying this chapter, you should be able to:

1. Define the characteristics of and distinguish between debt and equity securities.

2. Identify and describe the principal types of debt and equity securities.

3. Give the RMBCA definition of the term "distribution."

4. List and summarize the various types of distributions.

5. List and discuss the legal restrictions upon the payment of dividends and other distributions. Compare the various tests for the legality of distributions that are commonly found in state corporate statutes.

CHAPTER OUTLINE

I. Debt Securities–Debt securities (also called bonds) are a source of capital creating no ownership interest and involving the corporation's promise to repay funds loaned to it.

   A. Authority to Issue Debt Securities–The RULPA provides that every corporation has the power to borrow money and issue its notes, bonds, and other obligations. The board may issue bonds without the authorization or consent of the shareholders.

   B. Types of Debt Securities–Debt securities are usually issued under an indenture, which is a debt agreement that specifies the terms of the loan in great detail.

      1. Unsecured Bonds–These are usually called debentures; the holders of them are only unsecured creditors who rank equally with other general creditors. Debenture agreements frequently impose limitations on corporate borrowing, payment of dividends, and redemption and reacquisition of shares. They may also require the maintenance of specified minimum reserves.

      2. Secured Bonds–Secured bonds are enforceable as liens on specific corporate property. These bonds provide the security of specific corporate property in addition to the general obligation of the corporation. After resorting to the specified security, the holder of the bond becomes a general creditor for the unsatisfied amount of the debt.

      3. Income Bonds–Income bonds condition the payment of interest on corporate earnings. Participating bonds call for a stated percentage of return regardless of earnings, with additional payments dependent on earnings.

      4. Convertible Bonds–Convertible bonds may be exchanged, usually at the option of the holder, for other securities of the corporation at a specified ratio.

      5. Callable Bonds–Callable bonds are subject to a redemption provision that permits the corporation to redeem or call (pay off) all or part of the issue before maturity at a specified redemption price.

II. Equity Securities–An equity security is a source of capital creating an ownership interest in the corporation. The shareholders of a corporation are owners of it who occupy a position of greater financial risk than creditors. Shares confer on their owner a threefold interest in the corporation: (1) the right to participate in control, (2) the right to participate in the earnings of the corporation, and (3) the right to participate in the residual assets of the corporation on dissolution.

   A. Issuance of Shares–The state of incorporation, the federal government, and each state in which shares are issued or sold regulate the issuance of shares.

      1. Authority to Issue–The initial amount of shares to be issued is determined by the promoters or incorporators. A corporation may only sell the number of shares authorized in the articles of incorporation. Any unauthorized shares that are purportedly issued by the corporation are void. Article 8 of the UCC provides remedies for the holders of unauthorized shares. The number of shares authorized can be increased or decreased only by amending the corporate charter. Thus, it is common for the articles of incorporation to authorize more shares than the board intends to immediately issue.

      2. Preemptive Rights–A shareholder's proportionate interest in the corporation can be changed by either a nonproportionate issuance of additional shares or a nonproportionate reacquisition of

outstanding shares. When additional shares are issued, a shareholder may have the preemptive right to purchase a proportionate part of the new issue. Preemptive rights are frequently used in closely held corporations, because without them shareholders may be unable to prevent a dilution of their ownership interests in the corporation. At common law, shareholders have preemptive rights to the issuance of additionally authorized shares. Modern statutes allow the articles of incorporation to deny or limit preemptive rights.

3. Amount of Consideration for Shares–Shares are deemed fully paid and nonassessable when a corporation receives the consideration for which the board of directors, or the shareholders if the charter so directs, authorized the issuance of the shares.

   a. Par Value Stock–Par value shares may be issued for any amount, not less than par, set by the board of directors or shareholders. The par value must be stated in the articles of incorporation. The par value consideration constitutes the stated capital of the corporation; any consideration in excess of par value constitutes capital surplus. The Revised Act, the 1980 amendments to the MBCA, and about twenty states have eliminated the concepts of par value, stated capital, and capital surplus. Under these acts, all shares may be issued for such consideration as authorized by the board of directors or, if the charter so provides, the shareholders.

   b. No Par Value Stock–Shares without par value may be issued for any amount set by the board of directors or shareholders. The entire consideration received constitutes stated capital unless the board of directors allocates a portion of the consideration to capital surplus. If there is a liquidation preference, only consideration in excess of that preference may be allocated to capital surplus.

   c. Treasury Stock–Treasury stock is shares that a corporation buys back after it has issued them; they are issued but not outstanding in contrast to shares owned by shareholders, which are issued and outstanding. The corporation may resell treasury stock for any amount set by the board of directors, even if that amount is less than par value. Treasury shares have neither voting rights nor preemptive rights. No dividend is paid on treasury stock.

4. Payment for Shares–The two major issues regarding payment for shares are (1) what type of consideration may validly be accepted in payment, and (2) who determines the value placed upon consideration received in payment.

   a. Type of Consideration–In some states, cash, property, and services actually rendered are acceptable as valid consideration, but promissory notes and future services are not. The Revised Act has liberalized these rules by specifically validating for the issuance of shares consideration consisting of any tangible or intangible property or benefit to the corporation, including cash, services performed, contracts for future services, and promissory notes.

   b. Valuation of Consideration–The directors are responsible for determining the value to be placed upon consideration exchanged for shares. In the majority of jurisdictions, the judgment of the board of directors as to the value of the consideration is conclusive so long as it is made without fraud and in good faith.

5. Liability for Shares–A purchaser of shares has no liability to the corporation or to its creditors with respect to shares except to pay the corporation the consideration for which the shares were authorized.

B. Classes of Shares–Corporations are generally authorized to issue more than one class of stock. The usual classifications are common and preferred shares. The Revised Act has eliminated the terms common and preferred, but it permits the issuance of classes of shares with different preferences, limitations, and relative rights.

   1. Common Stock–Common stock does not have any special contract rights or preferences. It generally represents the greatest proportion of the corporation's capital structure and bears the greatest risk of loss in the event the enterprise fails.

   2. Preferred Stock–Preferred stock has contractual rights superior to common stock with regard to dividends, assets on liquidation, or both. The contractual rights and preferences of preferred stock must be stated in the articles of incorporation.

      a. Dividend Preferences–No dividend is payable on any class of stock unless it has been declared by the board of directors. Preferred stock with a dividend preference receives full dividends before any dividend may be paid to holders of common stock. Preferred stock may provide that dividends are cumulative, noncumulative, or cumulative to the extent earned. If the board does not declare regular dividends on preferred stock with cumulative dividends, the omitted dividends cumulate. No dividend may be declared on the common stock until all dividend arrearages are declared and paid. If noncumulative, dividends do not cumulate. Cumulative-to-the-extent earned shares cumulate unpaid dividends only to the extent funds were legally available to pay such dividends in that period. Preferred stock may be participating. Participating preferred shares are entitled to their original dividend and, after common shares receive a specified dividend, participating preferred share with common shares in any additional dividends.

      b. Liquidation Preferences–After a corporation is dissolved, its assets liquidated, and the claims of its creditors satisfied, the remaining assets are distributed *pro rata* among the shareholders according to their priority as provided in the articles of incorporation. When a liquidation preference is provided, preferred stock has priority over common to the extent stated in the articles of incorporation. In addition, if specified, preferred shares may participate beyond the liquidation preference in a stated ratio with other classes of shares.

   3. Stock Options–A corporation may issue stock rights or stock options entitling the holders of them to purchase from the corporation shares of a specified class. A stock warrant is a type of stock option that typically has a longer term and is freely transferable. A stock right is a short-term warrant. Stock options and warrants are used for incentive compensation plans and for raising capital by making one class of securities more attractive by including rights to purchase shares in another class.

III. Dividends and Other Distributions–In its discretion, the board of directors determines when to declare distributions and dividends and in what amount. In determining its distribution policy, the board will be influenced by the corporation's working capital requirements, the expectations of shareholders, and the tax consequences of such distributions.

A. Types of Dividends and Other Distributions–The Revised Act defines a distribution as "a direct or indirect transfer of money or other property (except its own shares) or incurrence of indebtedness by a corporation to or for the benefit of its shareholders with respect to any of its shares. A distribution may be in the form of a declaration or payment of a dividend; a purchase, redemption, or other acquisition of shares; a distribution of indebtedness; or otherwise."

1. Cash Dividends–The most customary dividend is the cash dividend, declared and paid at regular intervals from legally available funds.
2. Property Dividends–Distributions to shareholders may be made in the form of property.
3. Liquidating Dividends–A distribution of capital assets to shareholders is referred to as a liquidating dividend in some jurisdictions. Most incorporation statutes require that the shareholder be informed if a distribution is a liquidating dividend.
4. Redemption of Shares–Redemption is the repurchase by the corporation of its own shares, usually at its own option. The Model Act and the statutes of many states permit preferred shares to be redeemed but do not allow common stock to be redeemed. The power of redemption must be expressly mentioned in the articles of incorporation.
5. Acquisition of Shares–A corporation may acquire its own shares, which are then referred to as treasury shares. Under the Revised Act, such shares are authorized but unissued. As with redemptions, the acquisition of shares is a distribution to shareholders and has an effect similar to that of a dividend.

B. Legal Restrictions on Dividends and Other Distributions–All states have statutes restricting the funds that are legally available for dividends and other distributions of corporate assets in order to protect creditors. Lenders impose restrictions that are even more stringent than the statutory restrictions on the declaration of dividends and distributions. The equity insolvency test prohibits the payment of any dividend or other distribution when the corporation is insolvent or when payment of the dividend would make the corporation insolvent. Insolvency means that the corporation is unable to pay its debts as they become due in the usual course of business. Additional restrictions are based upon the corporation's assets, whereas the equity insolvency test is based upon the corporation's cash flow.

1. Definitions–Asset-based restrictions involve the concepts of earned surplus, surplus, net assets, stated capital, and capital surplus. Earned surplus consists of the undistributed net profits, income, gains, and losses from the date of incorporation. Surplus means the excess of the net assets of the corporation over its stated capital. Net assets are the amount by which the total assets of a corporation exceed the total debts of the corporation. Stated capital is the sum of the consideration received for issued stock, except that part of the consideration properly allocated to capital surplus, and including any amount transferred to stated capital when stock dividends are declared. For par value shares, the amount of stated capital is the total par value of all of the issued shares. For no par shares, the stated capital is the consideration received for all the no par shares, except for that amount allocated to an account designated as capital surplus or paid-in surplus. Capital surplus means the entire surplus of a corporation other than its earned surplus. Capital surplus may result from the allocation of part of the consideration received for no par shares, or from any consideration in excess of par value received for par shares, or from a higher reappraisal of certain corporate assets.

2. Legal Restrictions on Cash Dividends
   a. Earned Surplus Test–Many states permit dividends to be paid only from earned surplus. Dividends may not be paid if the corporation is or would be rendered insolvent in the equity sense by the payment. The MBCA used this test until 1980.

b.   Surplus Test–A number of states are less restrictive and permit dividends to be paid out of any surplus–earned or capital. Some states express this test by prohibiting dividends that impair stated capital. Dividends may not be paid if the corporation is or would be rendered insolvent in the equity sense by the payment.

c.   Net Assets Test–The MBCA as amended in 1980 and the Revised Act have adopted a net asset test. Under this test, dividends may be paid unless the corporation's total assets after payment of the dividend would be less than the sum of its total liabilities and the maximum amount that then would be payable for all outstanding shares having preferential rights in liquidation.

3.   Legal Restrictions on Liquidating Distributions–Even those states that do not permit cash dividends to be paid from capital surplus will usually permit distributions in partial liquidation from that source. Prior to 1980 the MBCA followed the earned surplus test for the payment of cash dividends, but it nevertheless allowed dividends in partial liquidation to be paid from capital surplus. No such distribution may be made when the corporation is insolvent or would become insolvent by the distribution.

4.   Legal Restrictions on Redemption and Acquisition of Shares–Most states have statutory restrictions on redemption in order to protect creditors and the holders of other classes of stock. A corporation may not redeem or purchase its redeemable shares when insolvent or when such redemption or purchase would render it insolvent or reduce its net assets below the aggregate amount payable on shares having prior or equal rights to the assets of the corporation on involuntary dissolution. A corporation may purchase its own shares only out of earned surplus or if the articles of incorporation permit or if the shareholders approve, out of capital surplus.

C.   Declaration and Payment of Distributions–The board declares dividends and other distributions; this power may not be delegated. If the charter provides for mandatory dividends, the board must comply with the provision. There can be no discrimination among shareholders of the same class in the declaration of dividends.

1.   Shareholders' Right to Compel a Dividend–Where the directors have failed to declare a dividend, a shareholder may bring a suit in equity to require the directors to declare a dividend. However, courts are reluctant to issue such an injunction, because it involves substituting the court's business judgment for that of the directors elected by the shareholders.

2.   Effect of Declaration–A debtor-creditor relationship exists between a corporation and its shareholders once a dividend has been declared but has not yet been paid.

D.   Liability for Improper Dividends and Distributions–The Revised Act imposes personal liability on the directors of a corporation who vote for or assent to the declaration of a dividend or other distribution contrary to the state statute or the articles of incorporation. The damages are the amount of the dividend or distribution that exceeds the amount that could lawfully have been paid. A director is not liable if she acted in good faith, with due care, and in a manner she reasonably believed to be in the best interests of the corporation. A director is entitled to rely in good faith on financial statements presented by the corporation's officers, public accountants, or finance committee. The existence of statutory liability on the part of the directors does not relieve shareholders from the duty to make repayment. A shareholder who receives an illegal dividend with knowledge of their unlawful character has a duty to refund it to the corporation.

KEY TERMS

1. Blue sky laws
2. Debt security
3. Bond
4. Indenture
5. Debenture
6. Secured bond
7. Income bond
8. Participating bond
9. Convertible bond
10. Callable bond
11. Equity security
12. Share
13. Preemptive right
14. Par value stock
15. Stated capital
16. Capital surplus
17. No par value stock
18. Treasury stock
19. Common stock
20. Preferred stock
21. Cumulative dividend
22. Noncumulative dividend
23. Stock option
24. Distribution
25. Insolvent
26. Earned surplus
27. Surplus
28. Net assets

TRUE/FALSE

_____ 1. Equity securities create a debtor-creditor relationship between the corporation and the shareholder.

_____ 2. It is legal for a board of directors to issue bonds or other obligations in the corporate name without shareholder approval.

_____ 3. It is not necessary to amend the corporate charter in order to change the amount of authorized shares.

_____ 4. Shares without par value may be issued for any amount set by the board of directors.

_____ 5. The rights of preferred shareholders are subordinate to the rights of all of the creditors of the corporation.

_____ 6. The declaration of distributions is a function of the shareholders to be determined at a called meeting for that purpose.

_____ 7. Shares of common stock are frequently redeemable by the corporation at a call price stated in the stock certificate.

_____ 8. A secured creditor is one whose claim is not only enforceable against the general assets of the corporation, but also against individual shareholders within the same class.

_____ 9. Under the MBCA, a corporation may purchase its own shares only out of earned surplus.

_____ 10. Once properly declared, a cash dividend is a debt owed by a corporation to the shareholders.

_____ 11. In most states, an unsuspecting shareholder who receives an illegal dividend from an insolvent corporation cannot be compelled to make a refund.

_____ 12. Any director who assents to an improper dividend would be liable for the amount of the dividend under the Revised Act.

_____ 13. Under the earned surplus test, capital surplus may be used for the payment of dividends.

_____ 14. In most states, a corporation may not redeem shares when it is insolvent.

_____ 15. Under the RMBCA, it is not necessary to set a par value for the stock of a corporation.

MULTIPLE CHOICE

_____ 1. Kelacti Corporation issued bonds that provided the bondholder could exchange the bond for twenty shares of common stock. This bond is referred to as a:
   a. callable bond.
   b. secured bond.
   c. convertible bond.
   d. none of the above.

_____ 2. Which of the following is not included in a shareholder's interest in a corporation?
   a. The right to participate in control
   b. The right to participate in earnings
   c. The right to participate in residual assets upon dissolution
   d. The right to participate in daily management

_____ 3. The par value of a share of stock must:
   a. be stated in the articles of incorporation.
   b. reflect the actual value of the share.
   c. reflect the actual price paid to the corporation.
   d. (b) and (c), but not (a).

_____ 4. Treasury shares may be:
   a. voted.
   b. paid dividends.
   c. sold at less than par value.
   d. none of the above.

_____ 5. Under the Revised Act, valid consideration for the issuance of capital stock includes:
   a. promissory notes.
   b. real property.
   c. contracts for future services.
   d. all of the above.

_____ 6. A corporation's repurchase of its own shares is known as:
   a. a liquidating dividend.
   b. exercise of a stock option.
   c. an acquisition of shares.
   d. none of the above.

_____ 7. Capital surplus may result from:
   a. an allocation of part of the consideration received for no par shares.
   b. any consideration in excess of par value received for par shares.
   c. a reappraisal upward of certain corporate assets.
   d. all of the above.

_____ 8. A shareholder may maintain an action at law against the corporation to recover a dividend whenever:
   a. unreserved and unrestricted earned surplus is available for payment of the dividend.
   b. the dividend may be paid out of capital surplus without impairing stated capital.
   c. the dividend has been formally declared by resolution of the board of directors.
   d. all of the above.

_____ 9. A declared and proper cash dividend:
   a. may be revoked unless actually distributed.
   b. cannot be rescinded as against nonassenting shareholders.
   c. is considered a debt owing by the corporation to the shareholders.
   d. (b) and (c), but not (a).

_____ 10. The corporate board of a distillery declared and paid a dividend in bonded whiskey. Such a dividend would be classified as a:
   a. cash dividend.
   b. property dividend.
   c. liquid dividend.
   d. none of the above.

_____ 11. If 1,000 shares of stock are issued at a price of $100 a share and the par value is $75 per share, how much of the consideration constitutes stated capital?
   a. $25,000
   b. $100,000
   c. $75,000
   d. None of the above

_____ 12. Which of the following tests for the payment of dividends is the most restrictive?
   a. The surplus test
   b. The earned surplus test
   c. The net assets test
   d. The insolvency test

_____ 13. Which of the following tests for the payment of dividends is the least restrictive?
   a. The surplus test
   b. The earned surplus test
   c. The net assets test
   d. The insolvency test

_____ 14. *CPA:* All of the following distributions to stockholders are considered asset or capital distributions **except**:
   a. liquidating dividends.
   b. stock splits.
   c. property distributions.
   d. cash dividends.

_____ 15. *CPA:* Opal Corp. declared a 9% stock dividend on its common stock. The dividend:
   a. requires a vote of Opal's stockholders.
   b. has **no** effect on Opal's earnings and profits for federal income tax purposes.
   c. is includable in the gross income of the recipient taxpayers in the year of receipt.
   d. must be registered with the SEC pursuant to the Securities Act of 1933.

SHORT ESSAY

1. Give the RMBCA definition of a distribution and provide some examples.

_____

_____

_____

_____

2. Discuss the difference between debt securities and equity securities.

   _____

   _____

   _____

   _____

3. Explain the difference between cumulative, noncumulative, and cumulative to the extent earned dividends on preferred stock.

   _____

   _____

   _____

   _____

4. Discuss the liability of directors and shareholders for improper dividends and distributions.

   _____

   _____

   _____

   _____

5. Julie owns 100 shares of Filtrain, Inc. The total number of shares outstanding is 1,000, and Filtrain plans to issue 500 new shares. If Julie has preemptive rights, explain what she is entitled to do in this situation.

   _____

   _____

   _____

   _____

Chapter 36
Management Structure of Corporations

PURPOSE

In this chapter, you study the pyramidal corporate structure that is required by state incorporation statutes. Shareholders are the base of the pyramid as the residual owners of the corporation. Their role is to elect the board of directors who manage the ordinary business matters of the corporation. Directors have broad authority to delegate power to the officers and agents of the corporation. The directors appoint the officers, who in turn hire and fire the personnel necessary to operate and run the day-to-day affairs of the corporation. In this chapter, you study the statutory provisions regarding the management structure of corporations.

CHAPTER CHECKPOINTS

After reading and studying this chapter, you should be able to:

1. Compare the statutory model of corporate governance to the actual governance of closely held corporations and publicly held corporations.

2. Compare straight and cumulative voting and discuss who benefits from cumulative voting.

3. Summarize the role of the board of directors in corporate governance and discuss the liability of directors under the business judgment rule.

4. Summarize the enforcement rights of shareholders.

5. List and discuss the duties of directors and officers.

CHAPTER OUTLINE

I. Corporate Governance–The statutory model of corporate management accurately describes the actual governance of only a few corporations. The great majority of corporations are closely held by a small number of shareholders who take an active part in the management of the business. In most states, closely held corporations must adhere to the general corporate statutory model. The rigid formalities imposed by general corporation statutes impose a burden on the closely held corporation where the owners are usually the managers. These formalities may be necessary and desirable in publicly held corporations where management and ownership are separated, but in a closely held corporation they are unnecessary and meaningless.

Approximately 20 states have enacted legislation to accommodate closely held corporations. These statutes vary but they are optional and must be elected by eligible corporations. Eligibility typically is based on a corporation having fewer than a specified number of shareholders. These statutes permit corporate operation without a board of directors and authorize broad use of shareholder agreements.

In response to recent business scandals, Congress passed the Sarbanes-Oxley Act in 2002. This Act increases corporate responsibility; adding new financial disclosure requirements; creating new criminal offenses; increasing the penalties of existing federal crimes; and creating a powerful new five person Accounting Oversight Board with authority to review and discipline auditors.

II. Role of Shareholders–The role of the shareholders is generally restricted to electing directors, approving certain extraordinary matters, approving corporate transactions that are void or voidable unless ratified, and bringing suits to enforce these rights.

A. Voting Rights of Shareholders–In most states, a shareholder is entitled to one vote for each share of stock that she owns, unless the articles of incorporation provide otherwise. Statutes generally permit the issuance of one or more classes of nonvoting stock so long as one class of shares has voting rights.

1. Shareholder Meetings–Shareholders may exercise their voting rights at both annual and special shareholder meetings. Annual meetings are required and must be held at a time fixed by the by-laws. If the annual meeting is not held within the earlier of six months after the end of the corporation's fiscal year or fifteen months after its last annual meeting, any shareholder may petition and obtain a court order requiring that a meeting be held. The Close Corporation Supplement states that no annual meeting need be held unless a written request is made by a shareholder at least 30 days in advance of the date specified for the meeting. Special meetings may be called by the board of directors, holders of at least 10% of the shares, or such other persons authorized in the articles of incorporation. Written notice must be given in advance, but may be waived in writing by any shareholder entitled to notice.

2. Quorum and Voting–A quorum of shares must be represented at a shareholder meeting, either in person or by proxy, and once a quorum is present, it is present for the rest of the meeting. A quorum is usually a majority of shares entitled to vote.

3. Election of Directors–Directors are elected each year at the annual meeting of the shareholders. Where a board consists of nine or more directors, the charter or bylaws may provide for a classification or division of directors into two or three classes. If directors are divided into two classes, they are elected once a year in alternate years for a two-year term; if into three classes,

for three-year terms in order to provide continuity in the membership of the board. Where there are two or more classes of stock, each class may elect a specified number of directors.

    a.   Straight Voting–Normally, each shareholder has one vote for each share owned, and directors are elected by a plurality of votes.

    b.   Cumulative Voting–In most states and under the Revised Act, cumulative voting is permitted. Cumulative voting entitles the shareholders to multiply the number of votes they are entitled to cast by the number of directors for whom they are entitled to vote and cast the product for a single candidate or distribute the product among two or more candidates. It permits a minority shareholder, or group of shareholders, to obtain representation on the board. The formula for determining how many shares a minority shareholder with cumulative voting rights must have in order to secure representation on the board is as follows:

$$X = \frac{ac}{b + 1} + 1$$

a = the number of shares voting
b = the number of directors to be elected
c = the number of directors desired to be elected
X = the number of shares necessary to elect the number of directors desired

4. Removal of Directors–Directors may be removed with or without cause by a majority vote of the shareholders. If a corporation has cumulative voting, removal of a director requires sufficient votes to prevent his election.

5. Approval of Fundamental Changes–The board manages the ordinary affairs of the corporation. Extraordinary matters involving fundamental changes require shareholder approval.

6. Concentrations of Voting Power–Devices are available to enable shareholders to combine their voting power to obtain or maintain control or maximize the impact of cumulative voting.

    a.   Proxies–A proxy is the authorization by a shareholder to an agent to vote the shareholder's shares at a particular meeting or on a particular question. Generally, proxies must be in writing to be effective, and the duration is limited by statute to no more than eleven months. A proxy is revocable unless conspicuously stated to be irrevocable and coupled with an interest, such as when shares are held as collateral. The solicitation of proxies by publicly held corporations is regulated by the Securities Exchange Act of 1934.

    b.   Voting Trusts–A voting trust is a device by which one or more shareholders separate the voting rights of their shares from the ownership of them. The shareholders confer on a trustee the right to vote or act for them by signing an agreement and transferring their shares to the trustee. Most states limit the duration of these to ten years.

    c.   Shareholder Voting Agreements–Shareholders may agree in writing to vote in a specified manner for the election or removal of directors or on any matter subject to shareholder approval. These are not limited in duration as are voting trusts. Such agreements are often used in closely held corporations in order to provide each shareholder with greater control over who becomes a shareholder, which is sometimes referred to as *delectus personae.*

7. Restrictions on Transfer of Shares–The common law validates share transfer restrictions if they are adopted for a lawful purpose and are reasonable. The RMBCA and some state statutes permit reasonable transfer restrictions if they are noted conspicuously on the stock certificate.

B. Enforcement Rights of Shareholders–The law provides shareholders with certain enforcement rights to protect their interests in the corporation.

   1.   Right to Inspect Books and Records–In most states shareholders have the right to inspect books and records for a proper purpose and to copy parts of them. The Revised Act provides that every shareholder is entitled to examine specified corporate records upon prior written request if the demand is made in good faith, for a proper purpose, and during regular business hours at the corporation's principal office. Many states limit this right to shareholders who own a minimum number of shares or have been shareholders for a minimum period of time. The MBCA requires that a shareholder either must own 5% of the outstanding shares or must have owned his shares for at least six months, but a court may order an inspection when neither condition is met. Proper purpose for inspection means a purpose that is reasonably relevant to that shareholder's interest in the corporation; it includes determining its financial condition, the value of its shares, the existence of mismanagement, or the names of other shareholders for communication on corporate affairs.

   2.   Shareholder Suits–The ultimate recourse of a shareholder is to bring suit against or on behalf of the corporation. Shareholder suits are either direct suits or derivative suits.

      a.   Direct Suits–A direct suit may be brought by a shareholder to enforce a claim that the shareholder has against the corporation based on her ownership of shares. Any recovery goes to the shareholder plaintiff. A class suit is a direct suit in which one or more shareholders purport to act as a representative of a class of shareholders to recover for injuries to the entire class.

      b.   Derivative Suits–A derivative suit is a cause of action brought by one or more shareholders on behalf of the corporation to enforce a right belonging to the corporation. Recovery usually goes to the corporation's treasury so that all of the shareholders can benefit proportionately. In most states, a shareholder must have owned shares at the time the complained-of transaction occurred, and the shareholder must have made a demand on the board of directors to enforce the corporate right before bringing suit.

   3.   Shareholder's Right to Dissent–A shareholder has the right to dissent from certain corporate actions that require shareholder approval. These actions include most mergers, consolidations, compulsory share exchanges, and a sale or exchange of all or substantially all of the assets of the corporation not in the usual and regular course of business.

III. Role of Directors and Officers–Management of a corporation is vested by statute in its board of directors, which determines general corporate policy and appoints officers to execute that policy and to administer the day-to-day operations of the corporation. Both the directors and the officers owe certain duties to the corporation as well as to the shareholders and are liable for breaching these duties. Shareholders who own a sufficient number of shares to have effective control over the corporation are called "controlling shareholders." Controlling shareholders are in some instances held to the same duties as directors and officers. All shareholders in a close corporation are sometimes held to a fiduciary duty similar to that imposed upon partners.

A. Function of the Board of Directors–The directors are neither trustees nor agents of the shareholders or of the corporation. However, they are fiduciaries who must perform their duties in good faith, in the best interests of the corporation, and with due care. The Revised Act states that "all corporate powers shall be exercised by or under authority of, and the business and affairs of the corporation managed under the direction of, its board of directors, subject to any limitation set forth in the articles of incorporation." In some corporations, corporate powers are exercised by the board of directors. On the other hand, in publicly held corporations, the corporate powers are exercised under the authority of the board, which formulates major management policy but does not involve itself in the day-to-day management. Under the Revised Act, a corporation having fifty or fewer shareholders may dispense with or limit the authority of a board by describing in its articles of incorporation who will perform some or all of the duties of a board.

The Sarbanes-Oxley Act confers on the audit committee of every publicly held corporation direct responsibility for the appointment, compensation, and oversight of the work of the public accounting firm employed by the company to perform audit services and the public accounting firm must report directly to the audit committee. The audit committee is responsible for resolving disagreements between management and the auditor regarding the company's financial reporting. Each member of the audit committee must be independent.

1. Selection and Removal of Officers–In most states, the board of directors has the responsibility to choose the corporate officers and may remove any officer at any time. Officers are agents of the corporation and are delegated their responsibilities by the board of directors.

2. Capital Structure–The board of directors determines the capital structure and financial policy of the corporation. The board has the power to (1) fix the selling price of newly issued shares unless the power to do so is reserved to the shareholders by the articles of incorporation; (2) determine the value of the consideration received by the corporation in payment for shares issued; (3) borrow money, issue notes, bonds, and other obligations, and secure any of the corporation's obligations; and (4) sell, lease, or exchange assets of the corporation in the usual and regular course of business.

3. Fundamental Changes–The board of directors has the power to amend or repeal the bylaws, unless this power is reserved to the shareholders by the articles of incorporation. The board also initiates actions, such as proceedings to amend the articles of incorporation or to effect a merger, which require shareholder approval.

4. Dividends–The board declares the amount and type of dividends, subject to restrictions in the state statute, the articles of incorporation, and any corporate loan and preferred stock agreements. It also may purchase, redeem, or acquire shares of the corporation's equity securities.

5. Management Compensation–The board usually determines the compensation of officers and in a number of states, fixes the compensation of board members.

B. Election and Tenure of Directors–The incorporation statute, articles of incorporation, and the bylaws determine the qualifications that individuals must possess in order to serve as directors; they also determine the election, number, tenure, and compensation of directors.

1. Election, Number, and Tenure of Directors–The initial board of directors is generally named in the articles of incorporation and serves until the first meeting of the shareholders, at which directors are elected. Thereafter, directors are elected at annual meetings and hold office for one year unless their terms are staggered. If the shares represented at a meeting do not constitute a quorum, or the shareholders are deadlocked and unable to elect a new board, the incumbent directors continue as "holdover" directors until their successors are duly elected and qualified. Some states require three or more directors, but the trend is to permit one or more directors. The

number of directors may be increased or decreased, within statutory limits, by amendment to the bylaws or charter.

2. Vacancies and Removal of Directors–The Revised Act provides that a vacancy on the board may be filled by the shareholders or by the affirmative vote of a majority of the remaining directors. The term of a director elected to fill a vacancy expires at the next shareholders' meeting when directors are elected. The common law rule permits removal of a director for cause by action of the shareholders. The Revised Act permits removal of one or more of the directors or of the entire board by the shareholders. Such a removal can be with or without cause and would be at a special meeting called for that purpose. The Revised Act permits the articles to provide for removal of directors only for cause.

3. Compensation of Directors–Traditionally directors were paid a fee or honorarium for attendance at meetings, but they did not receive salaries for their services. The Revised Act now specifically authorizes the board to fix the compensation of directors unless there is a contrary provision in the articles or bylaws. bylaws. Under the Sarbanes-Oxley Act, if a publicly held company is required to issue an accounting restatement due to a material violation of securities law, the chief executive and chief financial officers must forfeit certain bonuses and compensation received, as well as any profit realized from the sale of the company's securities during the 12-month period following the issuance of a noncomplying financial document.

C. Exercise of Directors' Functions–Directors only have the power to bind the corporation when acting as a board. The board may act only at a meeting or by the written consent signed by all of the directors, if written consent without a meeting is authorized and not contrary to the charter or bylaws.

1. Quorum and Voting–A majority constitutes a quorum. Although most states do not permit a quorum to be set at less than a majority, the Revised Act allows the articles or bylaws to authorize a quorum to consist of as few as one-third. The articles or bylaws may require a greater number than a simple majority. If a quorum is present, the act of the majority in attendance is the act of the board, unless the articles or bylaws state otherwise. Closely held corporations sometimes require either a supermajority or unanimous quorum for all meetings or for votes on some matters. The Revised Act requires a quorum when "a vote is taken." Thus, a board may act only when a quorum is present.

2. Action Taken Without a Meeting–The Revised Act and most states provide that any action required or permitted by the statute to be taken at a meeting of the board may be taken without a meeting if consent in writing is signed by all of the directors.

3. Delegation of Board Powers–If allowed by the articles of incorporation or bylaws, the board of directors may appoint one or more committees by majority vote of the full board. All committee members must be directors. Committees may exercise all of the authority of the board except for certain matters specified in the statute.

4. Directors' Inspection Rights–Directors have the right to inspect corporate books and records so they can competently perform their duties.

D. Officers–The officers are appointed by the board of directors to hold the offices provided for in the bylaws. Statutes generally require that the officers consist of a president, one or more vice presidents, a secretary, and a treasurer. A person may hold more than one office at one time, except for the offices of president and secretary. The Revised Act permits a corporation to designate whatever officers it wants. No number is specified, but one officer must be delegated the responsibility for preparing the minutes and authenticating the records of the corporation. Under the Revised Act, the same individual may hold all of the offices of a corporation.

1. Selection and Removal of Officers–Under most state statutes, officers are appointed by the board and serve at its pleasure. They may be removed by the board either with or without cause.

2. Role of Officers–Officers are fiduciaries of the corporation. Unlike directors, however, they are agents of the corporation. The roles of the various officers are set forth in the corporate bylaws.

3. Authority of Officers–Under the RMBCA, officers have such authority as may be provided in the bylaws or prescribed by the board to the extent consistent with the bylaws. The authority of an officer to bind the corporation may be (1) actual express, (2) actual implied, or (3) apparent.

   a. Actual Express Authority–Actual express authority results from the manifestation of assent by the corporation to the officer to act on behalf of the corporation. This authority arises from the incorporation statute, the articles of incorporation, the bylaws, and resolutions of the board of directors.

   b. Actual Implied Authority–As agents of the corporation, officers have implied authority to do what is reasonably necessary to perform their actual, delegated authority.

   c. Apparent Authority–Apparent authority arises from acts of the principal that lead third parties to reasonably and in good faith believe that an officer has the required authority. It might arise when a third party relies upon the fact that an officer has exercised the same authority in the past with board consent.

   d. Ratification–A corporation may ratify the unauthorized acts of its officers. Ratification relates back to the original transaction; it may be express or implied from the corporation's acceptance of the benefits of the contract with full knowledge of the facts.

E. Duties of Directors and Officers–Directors and officers are not insurers of business success. Thus, a corporation may not recover damages from directors and officers for losses resulting from poor business judgment or honest mistakes of judgment. Generally, directors and officers owe the duties of obedience, diligence, and loyalty to the corporation.

1. Duty of Obedience–Directors and officers must act within their respective authority. In some jurisdictions they are held absolutely liable for unauthorized acts; in others, they are liable only for intentionally or negligently exceeding their authority.

2. Duty of Diligence–Directors and officers must exercise ordinary care and prudence. The Revised Act and most states require that a director or officer discharge corporate duties (1) in good faith; (2) with the care an ordinarily prudent person in a like position would exercise under similar circumstances; and (3) in a manner the director or officer reasonably believes to be in the best interests of the corporation. So long as good faith and due care were present, courts under the "business judgment rule" will not substitute their judgment for the board's or its officers'. Directors and officers are liable for bad faith, negligent conduct, and sometimes for failing to act.

   a. Reliance on Others–Directors and officers are permitted to entrust work to others. If they have carefully selected employees, they are not personally liable for the negligent or willful wrongs of employees. An officer or director will be held liable for losses resulting from an employee's carelessness, theft, or embezzlement if the officer or director knew or ought to have known about the losses. Directors may rely upon information provided them by officers or employees, committees of the board, legal counsel, or public accountants.

   b. Business Judgment Rule–The business judgment rule protects directors from liability for honest mistakes of judgment. To benefit from the business judgment rule, a director or officer must make an informed decision, in good faith without any conflict of interest, have a rational basis for reasonably believing it is in the best interests of the corporation.

3. Duty of Loyalty–The officers and directors owe a fiduciary duty of loyalty to the corporation and to its shareholders. The essence of a fiduciary duty is the subordination of self-interest to the interest of the person or persons to whom the duty is owing. The remedy for breach of this duty is a suit by the corporation, or a derivative suit by a shareholder, to require the fiduciary to pay the profits obtained through the breach.

   a. Conflict of Interests–A contract between an officer or director and the corporation will be upheld if it is honest and fair. The Revised Act and most states provide that such transactions are neither void nor voidable if, after full disclosure, they are approved by either the disinterested directors or by the shareholders or if they are fair and reasonable to the corporation.

   b. Loans to Directors and Officers–The Model Act and some states forbid loans to directors except with shareholder authorization for each loan. Most states permit loans either on a general or limited basis. The Revised Act permits such loans if either the board of disinterested directors or the shareholders approve them or if they are fair and reasonable to the corporation. With certain limited exceptions, the Sarbanes-Oxley Act forbids publicly held corporations from making personal loans to their directors or executive officers.

   c. Corporate Opportunity–Directors and officers may not usurp any corporate opportunity that in fairness belongs to the corporation. A corporate opportunity is an opportunity in which the corporation has a right, property interest, or expectancy. The Sarbanes-Oxley Act generally prohibits publicly held corporations from making personal loans to their directors or executive officers.

   d. Transactions in Shares–The issuance of shares at a favorable price to management to the exclusion of other shareholders violates the fiduciary duty. The duty is also violated by issuing shares to a director at a fair price if the purpose of the issuance is to perpetuate corporate control rather than to raise capital or serve some other interest of the corporation. Officers and directors have access to inside advance information not available to the public that may affect the market value of shares of the corporation. Federal statutes prohibit officers and directors from trading their corporation's stock without adequately disclosing all material facts in their possession that may affect the value of stock.

   e. Duty Not to Compete–Directors and officers may not compete with the corporation. A director or officer who breaches the fiduciary duty by competing with the corporation is liable for damages caused to the corporation. Officers and directors may not use corporate personnel, facilities, or funds for their own benefit or disclose the trade secrets of the corporation to others.

4. Indemnification of Directors and Officers–Directors and officers incur personal liability for breaching any of the duties they owe to the corporation and shareholders. Many modern incorporation statutes allow the corporation to indemnify an officer or director for liability if he acted in good faith and in a manner reasonably believed to be in the best interests of the

corporation, so long as he has not been adjudged negligent or liable for misconduct. The Revised Act provides for mandatory indemnification of directors and officers for reasonable expenses incurred by them in the wholly successful defense of any proceeding brought against them as directors or officers.

5. Liability Limitation Statutes–At least forty states have enacted a statute limiting the liability of directors. Most of these states, including Delaware, authorize corporations–with shareholder approval–to limit or eliminate the liability of directors for some breaches of duty. A few states permit limiting the liability of officers.

KEY TERMS

1. Quorum

2. Cumulative voting

3. Proxy

4. Voting trust

5. Shareholder agreement

6. Direct suit

7. Class suit

8. Derivative suit

9. Business judgment rule

10. Corporate opportunity

TRUE/FALSE

_____ 1. Special meetings of a corporation may be called by any shareholder who holds at least 10 percent of the shares.

_____ 2. Cumulative voting means a shareholder normally has one vote for each share owned.

_____ 3. Shareholders may exercise their right to vote only at annual meetings and may not vote at special meetings.

_____ 4. Any recovery in a shareholder's direct suit usually goes to the corporate treasury so that all shareholders can benefit proportionately.

_____ 5. A shareholder may not bring a derivative suit without first making demand upon the board of directors to enforce the corporate right.

_____ 6. Shareholders may agree in writing to vote in a specified manner for the election or removal of directors.

_____ 7. Once established, the number of directors may not be increased or decreased.

_____ 8. Shareholders have the right to inspect corporate books and records for any purpose reasonably related to that shareholder's interest in the corporation.

_____ 9. A shareholder may dissent from certain corporate actions that require shareholder approval.

_____ 10. Generally, proxies need not be in writing to be effective.

_____ 11. Although officers are fiduciaries to the corporation, they are not agents of the corporation.

_____ 12. Officers who breach their fiduciary duty forfeit the right to compensation during the period they engaged in the breach.

_____ 13. Cumulative voting permits a minority shareholder to obtain minority representation on the board of directors.

_____ 14. In some states the liability of directors and officers may be limited by shareholder action.

_____ 15. A voting trust is the written authorization by a shareholder to an agent to vote the shareholder's shares at a particular meeting.

MULTIPLE CHOICE

_____ 1. Special shareholder meetings may be called by:
   a. any member of the board of directors.
   b. any shareholder.
   c. any person so authorized in the articles of incorporation.
   d. all of the above.

_____ 2. The board of directors may be classified into:
   a. three groups.
   b. six groups.
   c. nine groups.
   d. none of the above.

_____ 3. Sharpe, Inc. has two shareholders, Arthur and Brad, and 100 shares of voting stock. If Sharpe, Inc. uses cumulative voting, how many shares would Arthur need to elect 3 of the 5 directors?
   a. 50
   b. 51
   c. 60
   d. 61

_____ 4. In general, a proxy:
   a. must be in writing to be effective.
   b. is not revocable unless coupled with an interest.
   c. transfers legal title to the stock.
   d. (a) and (b), but not (c).

_____ 5. A suit brought by a shareholder to enforce a right belonging to the corporation is a:
   a. direct suit.
   b. derivative suit.
   c. suit to pierce the corporate veil.
   d. none of the above.

_____ 6. In classifying directors with regard to their relationship to the corporation, they would probably best be classified as:
   a. trustees.
   b. agents.
   c. fiduciaries.
   d. none of the above.

_____ 7. Assume that Tyway, Inc. has nine directors. What is the minimum number of directors that may bind the corporation?
   a. One
   b. Three
   c. Five
   d. Nine

_____ 8. Which of the following could an executive committee appointed by the board properly do?
   a. Amend the bylaws
   b. Set management compensation
   c. Declare dividends
   d. All of the above

_____ 9. Under the RMBCA, the same person may not simultaneously hold the office of:
   a. president and vice-president.
   b. president and secretary.
   c. president and treasurer.
   d. none of the above.

_____ 10. A contract between a director and the corporation is neither void nor voidable, if:
   a. it is approved by the board of disinterested directors after full disclosure.
   b. it is fair and reasonable to the corporation.
   c. either (a) or (b).
   d. neither (a) nor (b).

_____ 11. In order for a director to effectively dissent from a board action she must do which of the following in addition to dissenting?
   a. Have her dissent entered in the minutes of the meeting.
   b. File a written dissent with the presiding officer before adjournment.
   c. Deliver a written dissent to the corporation immediately after adjournment.
   d. Any of the above is effective.

_____ 12. Which of the following is correct regarding the role of the shareholders of a corporation?
   a. They have no voice in policy matters.
   b. They exercise control over policy by electing directors.
   c. They are consulted regularly by management when decisions must be made on broad policy matters.
   d. Contracts which they make on behalf of the corporation are binding on it.

_____ 13. *CPA:* Knox, president of Quick Corp., contracted with Tine Office Supplies Inc. to supply Quick's stationery on customary terms and at a cost less than that charged by any other supplier. Knox later informed Quick's board of directors that Knox was a majority stockholder in Tine. Quick's contract with Tine is:
   a. void because of Knox's self-dealing.
   b. void because the disclosure was made after execution of the contract.
   c. valid because of Knox's full disclosure.
   d. valid because the contract is fair to Quick.

_____ 14. The Ajax Corporation has two shareholders–Shirley with 75 shares and Thomas with 25 shares. The board of directors consists of four directors. Under cumulative voting, how many shares must Thomas own in order to be assured of electing one director if all four directors come up for election at the same time?
   a. 20
   b. 21
   c. 24
   d. 25

_____ 15. *CPA:* Under the Revised Model Business Corporation Act, which of the following statements is correct regarding corporate officers of a public corporation?
   a. An officer may **not** simultaneously serve as a director.
   b. A corporation may be authorized to indemnify its officers for liability incurred in a suit by stockholders.
   c. Stockholders always have the right to elect a corporation's officers.
   d. An officer of a corporation is required to own at least one share of the corporation's stock.

SHORT ESSAY

1. When may a shareholder be denied the right to inspect the books and records of the corporation?

_____

_____

_____

_____

2. List five actions that may be initiated by the board of directors but require shareholder approval.

    _____

    _____

    _____

    _____

3. List four actions that may be taken by the board of directors without shareholder approval.

    _____

    _____

    _____

    _____

4. What duties do officers and directors owe to a corporation?

    _____

    _____

    _____

    _____

5. Explain the "business judgment rule."

    _____

    _____

    _____

    _____

Chapter 37
Fundamental Changes of Corporations

PURPOSE

Certain fundamental changes in a corporation require shareholder approval because they are outside the authority of the board of directors of the corporation. These include charter amendments, the sale or lease of all or substantially all of the corporation's assets, compulsory share exchanges, dissolution, mergers, and consolidations. Each of these is a fundamental change, because it alters the basic structure of the corporation. The approval of the shareholders does not usually need to be unanimous. This means that a minority of shareholders may oppose the change. In such cases, the minority shareholders have the right to recover the fair value of their shares if they follow the appraisal remedy procedure found in the state statute. In this chapter, you study the legal aspects of the various fundamental changes in a corporation.

CHAPTER CHECKPOINTS

After reading and studying this chapter, you should be able to:

1. List and discuss the charter amendments which do not require shareholder approval and those which give dissenting shareholders an appraisal remedy.

2. List and discuss the corporate combinations which do not require shareholder approval and those which give dissenting shareholders an appraisal remedy.

3. Discuss the relative rights of the shareholders and the board of directors in tender offers, going private transactions, and compulsory share exchanges.

4. Define a cash-out combination and a management buyout and discuss the fairness of each to shareholders.

5. List and discuss the ways in which voluntary and involuntary dissolutions may occur.

CHAPTER OUTLINE

A. Charter Amendments–Shareholders do not have a vested property right resulting from any provision in the articles of incorporation; therefore corporate charters may be amended.
  1. Approval by Directors and Shareholders–The typical procedure for amending the articles of incorporation requires the board of directors to adopt a resolution setting forth the proposed amendment, which then must be approved by a majority vote of the shareholders. After approval, articles of amendment are filed with the secretary of state. Under the RMBCA, the required shareholder approval is a majority of all votes entitled to be cast on the amendment if the amendment would give rise to dissenters' rights. All other amendments must only be approved by a majority of the votes cast unless the act or the charter requires a greater vote. (1999 amendments to the Revised Act provide that fundamental changes only need approval by a majority of the shares present at a meeting at which a quorum is present.)
  2. Approval by Directors–The RMBCA permits the board to adopt certain amendments without shareholder action unless the articles of incorporation provide otherwise.

B. Combinations–It may be desirable and profitable for a corporation to acquire all or substantially all of the assets of another corporation or corporations. This may be accomplished by (1) purchase or lease of the assets, (2) purchase of a controlling stock interest in other corporations, (3) merger with other corporations, or (4) consolidation with other corporations.
  1. Purchase or Lease of All or Substantially All of the Assets–In this transaction, there is no change in the legal personality of either corporation. Each corporation continues its separate existence with only the form or extent of the assets altered. Generally, the purchaser does not assume the other's liabilities.
    a. Regular Course of Business–If the sale or lease of all or substantially all of its assets is in the usual and regular course of business of the selling or lessor corporation, approval by its board of directors is required, but shareholder authorization is not.
    b. Other Than in Regular Course of Business–Shareholder approval is necessary if such a sale or lease is not in the usual and regular course of business. In most states, dissenting shareholders of the selling corporation are given an appraisal remedy.
  2. Purchase of Shares–The purchase of a corporation's stock is an alternative to the purchase of its assets. When one corporation acquires all or a controlling interest of the stock of another corporation, there is no change in the legal existence of either corporation. The acquiring corporation acts through its board of directors. The capital structure of the subsidiary remains unchanged. No formal shareholder approval of either corporation is required.
    a. Sale of Control–A privately negotiated transaction is possible when one or a few shareholders own a controlling interest. The sale must be made with due care. The controlling shareholders must make a reasonable investigation to establish that the transfer is not being made to purchasers who plan to act contrary to the best interests of the corporation.
    b. Tender Offer–A tender offer is a general invitation to all of the shareholders of a target company to tender their shares for sale at a specified price. Tender offers for publicly held companies are frequently subject to federal securities regulation.
  3. Compulsory Share Exchange–A compulsory share exchange is a transaction by which a corporation becomes the owner of all the outstanding shares of one or more classes of another

corporation by an exchange that is compulsory on all owners of the acquired shares. The directors of each corporation and the shareholders of the corporation whose shares are being acquired must approve the compulsory share exchange. Dissenting shareholders have an appraisal remedy. Shareholders of the acquiring corporation need not approve the transaction.

4. Merger–A merger is the combination of the assets of two or more corporations into one of the corporations. One corporation, known as the surviving corporation, receives title to all of the assets. The other corporation, known as the merged corporation, ceases to exist as a separate entity. The surviving corporation assumes all debts and other liabilities of the merged corporation. The board of directors and the shareholders of each corporation generally must approve the merger by a majority vote of the shares entitled to vote. In a short-form merger, a corporation that owns at least 90% of the outstanding shares of a subsidiary may merge the subsidiary into itself without approval by the shareholders of either corporation. Dissenting shareholders of the subsidiary have the right to obtain payment from the parent for their shares, but the shareholders of the parent do not have an appraisal remedy.

    Many states now permit the vote of the shareholders of a surviving corporation to be eliminated if a merger increases the number of outstanding shares by no more than 20 percent.

5. Consolidation–A consolidation is the combination of two or more corporations into a new corporation which is known as the consolidated corporation. The original corporations cease to exist and all of their debts are assumed by the new corporation. Consolidation requires the approval of the boards of each corporation and the affirmative vote of the holders of a majority of the shares entitled to vote. Dissenting shareholders have an appraisal remedy.

6. Going Private Transactions–Corporate combinations are sometimes used to take a publicly held corporation private. One method of going private is for a majority shareholder to acquire the corporation's shares through purchases on the open market or through a tender offer. Cash-out combinations or management buyouts are also possible.

    a. Cash-out Combinations–These are used to eliminate minority shareholders by forcing them to accept cash or property for their shares. A cash-out combination is often used after a person or company has acquired a large interest in a target company through a tender offer. The tender offeror then seeks to eliminate all other shareholders, thereby achieving complete control of the target company. Some states require that such cash-out combinations have a valid business purpose and that they are fair to all concerned.

    b. Management Buyout–A management buyout is a transaction in which existing management increases its ownership of a corporation and eliminates its public shareholders. Because of the extensive use of borrowed funds, management buyouts are commonly called leveraged buyouts. A critical issue in this type of transaction is its fairness to the shareholders.

7. Dissenting Shareholders–A dissenting shareholder is one who opposes a fundamental change and has the right to receive the fair value of her shares.

    a. Transactions Giving Rise to Dissenters' Rights–Most states grant dissenters' rights to dissenting shareholders of (1) a corporation selling all or nearly all of its property or assets not in the usual course of business; (2) each corporation that is a party to a merger (except short-form merger); and (3) each corporation that is a party to a consolidation.

    b. Procedure–Dissenting shareholders who take certain steps may get payment for their shares.

    c. Appraisal Remedy–Dissenting shareholders are entitled to be paid the fair value of their shares plus interest. Fair value means the value immediately before the action objected to.

C. Dissolution–Dissolution of a corporation may occur in several ways. Dissolution does not terminate the corporation, but does require that the corporation wind up its affairs and liquidate its assets.
   1. Voluntary Dissolution–Voluntary dissolution is initiated by a resolution of the board of directors which is approved by the affirmative vote of holders of a majority of the corporation's shares that are entitled to vote at a shareholder meeting duly called for that purpose. In many states, the unanimous consent of the shareholders to a dissolution eliminates the need for directors' action.
   2. Involuntary Dissolution–A corporation may be involuntarily dissolved by administrative dissolution or by judicial dissolution.
      a. Administrative Dissolution–The secretary of state may commence a proceeding to dissolve a corporation if (1) it does not pay within sixty days after they are due any franchise taxes or penalties; (2) it does not deliver its annual report to the secretary of state within sixty days after it is due; (3) it is without a registered agent or registered office for sixty days or more; (4) it does not notify the secretary of state within sixty days that its registered agent or registered office has been changed, that its registered agent has resigned, or that its registered office has been discontinued; or (5) the duration stated in its articles of incorporation expires.
      b. Judicial Dissolution–Judicial dissolution may occur by court action brought by: (1) the attorney general of the state of incorporation; (2) shareholders when it is shown that directors are deadlocked, that the directors' acts are illegal or fraudulent, that assets are being wasted, or that shareholders are deadlocked; and (3) a creditor on showing that the corporation is unable to pay its debts and obligations as they mature in the regular course of its business.
   3. Liquidation–A corporation must cease carrying on its business except as is necessary to wind up once dissolution has occurred. When a corporation is dissolved, its assets are liquidated and used first to pay the expenses of liquidation and its creditors according to their respective contract or lien rights. Any remainder is distributed to shareholders proportionately according to their contract rights. Stock with liquidation preference has a priority over common stock.
   4. Protection of Creditors–Statutory dissolution procedures usually dictate procedures to safeguard the interests of creditors of the corporation. Typically, notice must be mailed to known creditors, general publication of notice, and preservation of claims against the corporation.

KEY TERMS

1. Fundamental change
2. Tender offer
3. Compulsory share exchange
4. Merger
5. Short-form merger
6. Consolidation
7. Cash-out combination
8. Management or leveraged buyout
9. Dissenting shareholder
10. Appraisal remedy
11. Fair value
12. Voluntary dissolution
13. Involuntary administrative dissolution
14. Involuntary judicial dissolution
15. Liquidation

TRUE/FALSE

_____ 1. Changes which alter the basic structure of the corporation require only board approval.

_____ 2. Shareholder approval for fundamental changes requires a majority of all votes entitled to be cast.

_____ 3. A sale of substantially all of a corporation's assets within the usual course of business requires shareholder authorization.

_____ 4. Charter amendments do not affect the existing rights of nonshareholders.

_____ 5. If a purchaser of all of a corporation's assets continues the seller's product line, strict tort liability may be imposed upon the purchaser for defects in previously manufactured products.

_____ 6. In a consolidation of two corporations, each of the constituent corporations ceases to exist.

_____ 7. Voluntary dissolution may be brought about by action on the part of the holders of a majority of the outstanding shares of stock.

_____ 8. The creditors of the corporation may start involuntary dissolution by judicial proceeding.

_____ 9. All states require that cash-out combinations have a valid business purpose and that they be fair.

_____ 10. When liquidation is involuntary, a court-appointed receiver carries it out.

_____ 11. When a corporation is dissolved, its assets are liquidated and used first to pay the expenses of liquidation and the shareholders according to their respective contract rights.

_____ 12. A compulsory share exchange requires approval of the shareholders of the acquiring corporation.

_____ 13. A shareholder who dissents from certain fundamental changes and strictly complies with the provisions of the incorporating statute is entitled to receive the fair value of her shares.

_____ 14. All amendments to the articles of incorporation require shareholder approval.

_____ 15. There are no statutory provisions to protect creditors upon the dissolution of a corporation.

MULTIPLE CHOICE

_____ 1. Under the RMBCA, a board of directors may adopt which of the following charter amendments without shareholder approval?
   a. Minor change in corporate name
   b. Extend the duration of the corporation when there were no previous restrictions on duration
   c. Alteration of preferential rights of shares
   d. All of the above.

_____ 2. Charter amendments become effective upon:
   a. adoption of a resolution by the board setting forth the proposed amendment.
   b. approval by a majority vote of the shareholders.
   c. execution and filing of articles of amendment with the secretary of state.
   d. receipt of an appraisal remedy by the dissenting shareholders.

_____ 3. A corporation ceases to exist as a separate entity when:
   a. all or substantially all of its assets are purchased by another corporation.
   b. a controlling interest in its stock is purchased by another corporation.
   c. it is merged into another corporation.
   d. all of the above.

_____ 4. The sale or lease of all or substantially all of a corporation's assets in the usual course of its business requires approval by its:
   a. board of directors.
   b. shareholders.
   c. board of directors and shareholders.
   d. none of the above.

_____ 5. Directors cannot make which of the following charter amendments without shareholder action?
   a. Extend the duration of a corporation that is incorporated with a limited duration.
   b. Making minor name changes
   c. Altering a preferential right of the shares
   d. Changing each issued and unissued authorized share of an outstanding class into a greater number of whole shares if the corporation has only one class of shares

_____ 6. A corporation that buys another corporation's assets does not assume the other's liability unless:
   a. the purchaser agrees to assume the seller's liability.
   b. the transaction amounts to a merger.
   c. the purchaser is a mere continuation of the seller.
   d. all of the above.

_____ 7. A merger requires the approval of:
   a. the board of directors of the merged corporation.
   b. the board of directors of the surviving corporation.
   c. the shareholders of the surviving corporation.
   d. all of the above.

_____ 8. The merger of a wholly owned subsidiary into its parent requires the approval of:
   a. the board of directors of the parent corporation.
   b. the board of directors and shareholders of the subsidiary corporation.
   c. the board of directors and shareholders of each corporation.
   d. the shareholders of the subsidiary corporation.

_____ 9. If a wholly owned subsidiary is merged into its parent, an appraisal remedy is available to the shareholders of:
    a. the parent corporation.
    b. the subsidiary corporation.
    c. both the parent and the subsidiary.
    d. none of the above.

_____ 10. A consolidation requires the approval of:
    a. the board of directors of each constituent corporation.
    b. the shareholders of each constituent corporation.
    c. the board of directors and shareholders of each constituent corporation.
    d. none of the above.

_____ 11. A general invitation to all of the shareholders of a target company to tender their shares for sale at a specified price is referred to as a:
    a. consolidation.
    b. merger.
    c. compulsory share exchange.
    d. tender offer.

_____ 12. A _____ is a transaction by which existing management increases its ownership of a corporation and eliminates its public shareholders.
    a. short-form merger
    b. consolidation
    c. leveraged buyout
    d. compulsory share exchange

_____ 13. Involuntary dissolution may occur by administrative action taken by:
    a. the attorney general.
    b. shareholders under certain circumstances.
    c. both (a) and (b).
    d. neither (a) nor (b).

_____ 14. *CPA:* A parent corporation owned more than 90% of each class of the outstanding stock issued by a subsidiary corporation and decided to merge that subsidiary into itself. Under the Revised Model Business Corporation Act, which of the following actions must be taken?
    a. The subsidiary corporation's board of directors must pass a merger resolution.
    b. The subsidiary corporation's dissenting stockholders must be given an appraisal remedy.
    c. The parent corporation's stockholders must approve the merger.
    d. The parent corporation's dissenting stockholders must be given an appraisal remedy.

_____ 15. *CPA:* Which of the following statements is a requirement for the merger of two corporations?
  a. The merger plan must be approved unanimously by the stockholders of both corporations.
  b. The merger plan must be approved unanimously by the boards of both corporations.
  c. The absorbed corporation must amend its articles of incorporation.
  d. The stockholders of both corporations must be given due notice of a special meeting, including a copy or summary of the merger plan.

SHORT ESSAY

1. List five examples of fundamental changes.

   _____

   _____

   _____

   _____

2. Outline the procedure for amending the articles of incorporation.

   _____

   _____

   _____

   _____

3. By what methods may a corporation acquire all or substantially all of the assets of another corporation?

   _____

   _____

   _____

   _____

4. What transactions give rise to dissenters' rights in most states?

   _____

   _____

   _____

   _____

5. How may dissolution occur?

   _____

   _____

   _____

Part VII
Sample Examination

MULTIPLE CHOICE

_____ 1. A general partner may do which of the following without the consent or ratification of the limited partners?
   a. Admit a limited partner
   b. Act as an agent for the partnership
   c. Wind up the business, as long as he did not wrongfully dissolve the partnership
   d. (b) and (c), but not (a)

_____ 2. A limited partner has limited liability provided which of the following conditions is met?
   a. There is substantial good faith compliance with the requirement that a certificate of limited partnership be filed.
   b. The surname of the limited partner does not appear in the partnership name.
   c. The limited partner does not take part in control of the business.
   d. All of the above.

_____ 3. Arthur and Byron agree to form a partnership. Arthur contributes $3,000 in assets and agrees to devote full time to the partnership. Byron contributes $1,000 and agrees to devote one-third of his time to the partnership. If they do not agree otherwise, how will Arthur and Byron share their profits and losses?
   a. Arthur will get 3/4 and Byron 1/4.
   b. Arthur will get 2/3 and Byron 1/3.
   c. Arthur and Byron will share profits and losses equally.
   d. Arthur will get 1/3 and Byron will get 2/3.

_____ 4. Anita and Melva form an organization to collect donations and establish a food shelf for needy people. They raise money through a series of activities and jointly manage the enterprise. Are they a partnership?
   a. No, because they have no written partnership agreement.
   b. No, because they are not running a business for profit.
   c. Yes, because each has a voice in management.
   d. Yes, because they both contribute to the project.

_____ 5. Which of the following is/are required to form a limited liability company?
   a. File articles of organization in a designated state office
   b. Must have at least three members
   c. Must have a minimum of $500,000 capital
   d. All of the above

_____ 6. In which of the following situations will the directors of a corporation be liable?
   a. The directors refuse to declare dividends even though the corporation has retained earnings.
   b. Two directors miss a meeting because they are ill and don't notify the others.
   c. The directors violate the business judgment rule in their corporate dealings.
   d. The directors make an honest mistake in judgment when they decide to move the corporate headquarters to a new location.

_____ 7. The test which the RMBCA now uses to determine whether a corporation can legally pay a dividend is known as the _____ test.
   a. surplus
   b. earned surplus
   c. net asset
   d. none of the above:

_____ 8. A lawsuit brought by a shareholder on behalf of the corporation to enforce a right belonging to the corporation is known as:
   a. a direct suit.
   b. a class suit.
   c. a derivative suit.
   d. none of the above.

_____ 9. Under the RMBCA, directors who vote for or assent to the payment of an illegal dividend have liability to the:
   a. shareholders.
   b. corporation.
   c. creditors of the corporation.
   d. all of the above.

_____ 10. Dri-Ko Corporation has two shareholders. Ann has 64 shares and Bob has 36 shares. The board of directors consists of three directors. How many shares does Bob need to elect one director under cumulative voting?
   a. 26
   b. 36
   c. 40
   d. 51

_____ 11. In which of the following is shareholder approval required?
   a. A corporation sells substantially all of its assets outside of the regular course of business.
   b. There are amendments to the articles of incorporation.
   c. The board of directors has approved a merger of a corporation with another.
   d. All of the above situations require shareholder approval.

_____ 12. Will sues the Tel-Vyn Corporation in a stockholder derivative suit and wins the case. The judgment will be paid to:
  a. Will personally.
  b. all of the shareholders as a dividend.
  c. the corporate treasury.
  d. the board of directors.

_____ 13. Which of the following is a shareholder right?
  a. The right to elect the corporate directors
  b. The right to elect the corporate officers
  c. The right to determine the capital structure of the corporation
  d. The right to declare the amount and type of dividends to be paid

_____ 14. A corporation is considered to be a "person" for purposes of:
  a. the Fifth Amendment due process clause.
  b. the Fourteenth Amendment due process clause.
  c. the Fifth Amendment right against self-incrimination.
  d. the Fifth and Fourteenth Amendments due process clauses.

_____ 15. A corporation that is owned by a few shareholders and whose shares are not actively traded is known as a _____ corporation.
  a. closely held
  b. Subchapter S
  c. public
  d. nonprofit

_____ 16. The rules and regulations that govern the internal management of a corporation are normally found in the:
  a. articles of incorporation.
  b. corporate charter.
  c. corporate bylaws.
  d. state statute.

_____ 17. **CPA:** Generally, a corporation's articles of incorporation must include all of the following except the:
  a. name of the corporation's registered agent.
  b. name of each incorporator.
  c. number of authorized shares.
  d. quorum requirements.

_____ 18. **CPA:** In a general partnership, a partner's interest in specific partnership property is:
    a. transferable to a partner's individual creditors.
    b. subject to a partner's liability for alimony.
    c. transferable to a partner's estate upon death.
    d. subject to a surviving partner's right of survivorship.

_____ 19. **CPA:** A corporate stockholder is entitled to which of the following rights?
    a. Elect officers
    b. Receive annual dividends
    c. Approve dissolution
    d. Prevent corporate borrowing

_____ 20. **CPA:** A consolidation of two corporations usually requires all of the following **except**:
    a. approval by the board of directors of each corporation.
    b. receipt of voting stock by all stockholders of the original corporations.
    c. provision for an appraisal buyout of dissenting stockholders.
    d. an affirmative vote by the holders of a majority of each corporation's voting shares.

Try the Web

Review a sample (Virginia) Limited Liability Company statute.

Solution: Log onto the Internet
    Go to: http://www.state.va.us/
    Select: Government
    Select: Code of Virginia
    Select: Select Table of Contents
    Select: Title 13.1
    Select: Chapter 13

Chapter 38
Secured Transactions and Suretyship

PURPOSE

Today our economy runs on borrowed funds. The public policy and social issues created by today's enormous use of debt center on certain tenets, among which are: (1) The means by which debt is created and transferred should be as simple and as inexpensive as possible. (2) The risks to lenders should be minimized. (3) Lenders should have a way to collect unpaid debts. A lender typically incurs two types of collection risks: the borrower may be unwilling to repay the loan or the borrower may prove to be unable to repay. The law has developed devices to maximize the likelihood of repayment. These devices include consensual security interests (also called secured transactions) and suretyships. In this chapter, you study secured transactions in personal property including the rules of attachment, perfection, and priorities of secured parties. You will also study the nature and formation of suretyships, as well as the rights and defenses of sureties.

CHAPTER CHECKPOINTS

After reading and studying this chapter, you should be able to:

1. Define the terms "attachment" and "perfection" and identify when a security interest attaches and when it becomes perfected.

2. List the three classifications of collateral according to the nature of the collateral and explain how a security interest in each is perfected.

3. Explain what rights the creditor in a secured transaction has in the event of a default by the debtor.

4. Discuss the priorities among parties with competing interests in collateral.

5. Explain the requirements for the formation of a suretyship and discuss the right of the parties.

373

CHAPTER OUTLINE

I.   Secured Transactions in Personal Property–Often businesses or individuals cannot obtain credit without giving adequate security or can negotiate better terms by giving security. UCC Article 9 governs transactions involving security in personal property.

A. Essentials of Secured Transactions– A secured transaction is an agreement by which one party obtains a security interest in the personal property of another to secure the payment of a debt. Article 9 governs secured transactions if the agreement is *consensual*. In every consensual secured transaction there is a debtor, a secured party, collateral, a security agreement, and a security interest. A debtor is a person who owes payment or performance of an obligation. A secured party is the creditor-lender, seller, or other person who possesses the security interest in the collateral. Collateral is the property subject to the security interest. A security agreement is the agreement that creates a security interest, which in its broadest sense is an interest in personal property or fixtures that secures payment or performance of an obligation. A purchase money security interest is a security interest in goods purchased, which interest is retained either by the seller of the goods or by a lender who advances the purchase price. A security interest cannot exist apart from the debt it secures; discharging the debt in any way terminates the security interest.

B. Classification of Collateral–Some provisions of Article 9 state special rules that apply only to particular kinds of collateral. Collateral is classified according to its nature and its use.
1. Goods–Goods are tangible personal property that can be moved when the security interest in them becomes enforceable. Goods are subdivided into (a) consumer goods, (b) farm products, (c) inventory, and (d) equipment. An item may fall into different classifications depending on its use or purpose.
    a. Consumer Goods–Goods are consumer goods if they are used or bought for use primarily for personal, family, or household purposes.
    b. Farm Products–Farm products include "goods, other than standing timber, which are part of a farming operation and which are crops grown, growing or to be grown, including crops produced on trees, vines, and bushes...." Farm products also include livestock, born or unborn, including aquatic goods such as fish raised on a fish farm as well as supplies used or produced in a farming operation.
    c. Inventory–Inventory includes goods held for sale or lease and raw materials, work in process, or materials used or consumed in a business.
    d. Equipment–Goods are classified as equipment if they are used or purchased for use primarily in business. If goods used in a business are not categorized as inventory, farm products, or consumer goods, they are classified as equipment.
    e. Fixtures–Fixtures are goods that are so firmly attached to real property that they are considered part of the real estate. State law other than the Code determines whether and when goods become fixtures. A security interest under Article 9 may be created in goods that become fixtures.
2. Indispensable Paper–Four kinds of collateral involve rights evidenced by indispensable paper. These are (a) chattel paper, (b) instruments, (c) documents and (d) investment property.

a. Chattel Paper–Chattel paper is a record or records that evidence both a monetary obligation and a security interest in or a lease of specific goods. A secured party may borrow against or sell the security agreement of his debtor along with his interest in the collateral. A "record" is information written or stored in an electronic or other medium, which is retrievable in a tangible format.

b. Instruments–Instruments include negotiable instruments, stocks, bonds, and other investment securities. An instrument is any writing that evidences a right to payment of money, that is transferable by delivery with any necessary indorsement or assignment, and that is not of itself a security agreement or lease.

c. Documents–Documents include documents of title, such as bills of lading and warehouse receipts that may be either negotiable or nonnegotiable.

d. Investment Property–Investment property are investment securities, such as stocks and bonds, and securities accounts, commodity contracts and commodity accounts. A certificated security is represented by a paper certificate. An uncertificated security is not represented by a paper certificate but is recognized on the records of the issuing company.

3. Intangibles–The Code recognizes two other kinds of collateral: accounts and general intangibles.

   a. Accounts–An account or account receivable is the right to payment for goods sold or leased or for services rendered. An account is not evidenced by an instrument or chattel paper.

   b. General Intangibles–General intangibles are any personal property other than goods, accounts, chattel paper, commercial tort claims, deposit accounts, documents, instruments, investment property, letter-of-credit rights, money, and oil, gas and minerals before extraction. It includes software, goodwill, literary rights, and interests in patents, trademarks, and copyrights to the extent they are not regulated by federal statute.

4. Other Kinds of Collateral–Proceeds include whatever is received upon the sale, lease, license exchange or other disposition of collateral; whatever is collected on, or distributed on account of, collateral; or other rights arising out of collateral. Unless otherwise agreed, a security agreement gives the secured party rights to proceeds. Additional types of collateral include timber to be cut, minerals, motor vehicles, mobile goods (goods used in more than one jurisdiction), and money. Revised Article 9 also adds the following kinds of collateral: commercial tort claim, letter-of-credit rights and deposit accounts (e.g., accounts with a bank). In consumer transactions, however, deposit accounts may not be taken as original collateral.

C. Attachment–Attachment describes the creation of a security interest that is enforceable against the debtor. It is a prerequisite to a security interest's enforceability against parties other than the debtor. Until a security interest "attaches," it is ineffective against the debtor. A security interest attaches to the described collateral when: (1) the secured party gives value; (2) the debtor acquires rights in the collateral; and (3) the security agreement is signed by the debtor.

1. Value–Value is broadly defined to include consideration under contract law, a binding commitment to extend credit, and an antecedent debt.

2. Debtor's Rights in Collateral–As a general rule, the debtor is deemed to have rights in collateral if he owns the collateral, possesses it, or if he is in the process of acquiring it from the seller.

3. Security Agreement–A security agreement cannot attach unless there is an agreement between the debtor and creditor granting the creditor a security interest in the debtor's collateral. With the exception of pledges, the agreement must (a) be in writing, (b) be signed by the debtor, and

(c) contain a reasonable description of the collateral. No written security agreement is required when the collateral is pledged or is in the possession of the secured party pursuant to an agreement. A pledge is the delivery of personal property to a creditor as security for the payment of a debt.

    a. Authenticating record–In most situations, there must be a record of the security agreement authenticated by the debtor. Authentication may occur when a debtor signs a written security agreement or when a debtor executes or encrypts or processes a record in whole or in part with the intent of adopting or accepting the record (i.e., an electronic authentication).

    b. Authenticating Record Not Required–A security agreement is not required when certain types of collateral are pledged or in the possession of the secured party pursuant to an agreement. This rule applies to negotiable documents, goods, instruments, money, and tangible chattel paper. A pledge is the delivery of personal property to a creditor as security for the payment of a debt. An authenticated record also is not required when: (a) the collateral is a certificated security in registered form that has been delivered to the secured party; and (b) the collateral is a deposit account, electronic chattel paper, investment property, or letter-of-credit rights and the secured party has control over the collateral. Some additional concepts relating to security agreements include the following:

    c. Consumer Goods–Federal regulation prohibits a credit seller or lender from obtaining a consumer's grant of a nonpossessory security interest in household goods. This rule does not apply to purchase money security interests or to pledges.

    d. After-Acquired Property–A security agreement may provide a secured party with a security interest in after-acquired property, which is property the debtor does not own or have rights to but may acquire at some time in the future. The Code limits the operation of an after-acquired property clause against consumers. No such interest can be claimed in consumer goods acquired more than ten days after the secured party gives value.

    e. Future Advances–The obligations covered by a security agreement may include future advances. A debtor may obtain a line of credit from a creditor for advances to be made at some later time.

D. Perfection–Perfection refers to the enforceability of a security agreement against third parties. It occurs when a security interest attaches and all steps required for perfection have been taken. If these steps are taken before the security agreement attaches, it is perfected at the time it attaches. Depending upon the type of collateral, a security interest may be perfected in the following ways.

    1. Filing a Financing Statement–A common method of perfecting a security interest under Article 9 is filing a financing statement.

        a. What to File-A financing statement is a document filed by the secured party to provide notice of the security interest. It must contain the names and addresses of the secured party and the debtor, and reasonably identify the type or items of collateral. (Most states have certificate of title statutes for automobiles, trailers, mobile homes, boats, and farm tractors. A certificate of title is a government-issued document representing ownership of a good. In these states, filing requirements do not apply to perfecting a security interest in such collateral unless the collateral is inventory held by a dealer for sale.)

        b. Duration of Filing–Where no maturity date is stated on a financing statement, the statement is effective for five years from the date of filing. This period may be extended for an additional five-year period by the filing of a continuation statement within six months prior to the expiration. In most states, a security interest in motor vehicles must be perfected by a notation on the certificate of title rather than by filing a financing statement unless a dealer-owner holds the collateral as inventory for sale.

    c. Place of Filing–Except for real property-related collateral, financing statements are filed in a central location designated by the state. Financing statements for real property-related collateral are filed in the government office designated for the filing or recording of mortgages on the related real property, which is usually local. If a secured party fails to properly file a financing statement, then, the filing generally is ineffective.

    d. Subsequent Change of Debtor's Location–If a debtor moves to another state after the initial filing, the security interest remains perfected until the earliest of (i) the time the security interest would have terminated in the state in which perfection occurred; (ii) four months after the debtor moved to the new state; or (iii) the expiration of one year after the debtor transfers the collateral to a person (who becomes the debtor) in another state.

2. Possession–Possession by the secured party perfects a security interest in goods, instruments, negotiable documents, or tangible chattel paper. A secured party may perfect a security interest in a certificated security by taking delivery of it. In a field warehouse pledge, a warehouser establishes a warehouse on the debtor's premises by enclosing a portion of the premises and posting appropriate signs. The secured party controls the goods but allows the debtor access to the inventory.

3. Automatic Perfection–In some situations there is automatic perfection upon attachment. The most important situation to which automatic perfection applies is a purchase money security interest in consumer goods. There also is automatic perfection of a partial or isolated assignment of accounts that does not transfer a significant part of the outstanding accounts of the assignor.

4. Temporary Perfection–A security interest in a certificated security, negotiable document, or instrument is perfected upon attachment for a period of twenty days if the security interest is given for new value given under an authenticated security agreement. A perfected security interest in a certificated security or an instrument remains perfected for twenty days if the secured party delivers the security certificate or instrument to the debtor for the purpose of (a) sale or exchange or (b) presentation, collection, enforcement, renewal, or registration of transfer. original collateral was perfected.

5. Perfection by Control–A security interest in investment property, deposit accounts (not including consumer deposit accounts), electronic chattel paper, and letter-of-credit rights may be perfected by control of the collateral. A security interest in deposit accounts and letter-of-credit rights may be perfected only by control. What constitutes control varies with the type of collateral involved.

E. Priorities Among Competing Interests–A security interest must be perfected to be effective against other creditors of the debtor, the debtor's trustee in bankruptcy, and transferees of the debtor. However, perfection does not mean that the secured party will have priority over all third parties with an interest in the collateral. Article 9 establishes a complex set of rules that determine relative priorities among parties.

1. Against Unsecured Creditors–When a security interest attaches, it has priority over claims of other creditors without a security interest or lien. This priority does not depend upon perfection. Without attachment, the creditor is an unsecured or general creditor.

2. **Against Other Secured Creditors**–The rights of a secured creditor against other secured creditors depends upon which security interests are perfected, when they are perfected, and the type of collateral.

   a. **Perfected versus Unperfected**–A creditor with a perfected security interest has greater rights in the collateral than a creditor with an unperfected security interest.

   b. **Perfected versus Perfected**–If two parties each have perfected security interests, they rank according to priority in time of filing or perfection. The first party to file or perfect has priority, provided that there is no subsequent period when there is neither filing nor perfection. This rule gives special treatment to filing, because it can occur prior to attachment and thus grants priority from a time that may precede perfection.

      If there is a purchase money security interest (PMSI) in collateral, then the following rules apply: (i) a PMSI in noninventory collateral takes priority over a conflicting security interest if the PMSI is perfected at the time the debtor receives possession of the collateral or within 20 days of receipt; and (ii) a PMSI in inventory has priority over conflicting security interests if (a) the PMSI is perfected at the time the debtor receives the inventory; (b) the secured party sends an authenticated notification to the holder of any conflicting security interest; (c) the holder of the conflicting security interest receives the notification within 5 years before the debtor receives possession of the inventory; and (d) the notification states that the person sending the notification has or will acquire a PMSI in inventory of the debtor and describes the inventory. the following requirements are met.

   c. **Security interest perfected by control**–This type of security interest in deposit accounts, letter-of-credit rights, or investment property has priority over a conflicting perfected security interest held by a secured party who does not have control. If both conflicting security interests are perfected by control, they rank according to priority in time of obtaining control.

   d. **Unperfected versus Unperfected**–If neither security interest is perfected, then the first to attach has priority. If neither attaches, both creditors are general, unsecured creditors.

3. **Against Buyers**–A security interest continues in collateral even though it is sold unless the secured party authorizes the sale. The security interest also continues in any identifiable proceeds from the sale of the collateral.

   a. **Buyer vs. unperfected security interest**–Buyers of collateral prevail over an unperfected security interests in the following situations: (i) buyers of goods, tangible chattel paper, documents, instruments, or certificated securities who give value and receive delivery of collateral without knowledge of the security interest before it is perfected; and (ii) buyers of accounts, electronic chattel paper, general intangibles, or investment property other than certificated securities if the buyers give value without knowledge of the security interest and before it is perfected.

   b. **Buyers in the Ordinary Course of Business**–A buyer in the ordinary course of business takes collateral free of any security interest created by the seller, even if the security interest is perfected and the buyer knows of its existence. A buyer in the ordinary course of business is a person who buys from a merchant in good faith, without knowledge that the sale violates a security interest. This rule applies primarily to purchasers of inventory.

   c. **Buyers of Farm Products**–Buyers in the ordinary course of business of farm products, although not protected by Article 9, are protected by the Federal Food Security Act. This act defines a buyer in the ordinary course of business as "a person who, in the ordinary course of business, buys farm products from a person engaged in farming operations who is in the business of selling farm products." The act provides that such a buyer shall take free of most security interests created by the seller, even if it is perfected and the buyer knows of the existence of the interest.

    d. Buyers of Consumer Goods–A buyer who buys consumer goods without knowledge of a security interest, for value, and for personal, family, or household use, takes the goods free of any purchase money security interest automatically perfected, but takes the goods subject to a security interest perfected by filing.

4. Against Lien Creditors–A lien creditor is a creditor who has acquired a lien on the property by judicial decree and includes a trustee in bankruptcy. A trustee in bankruptcy is a representative of the estate in bankruptcy who is responsible for collecting, liquidating, and distributing the debtor's assets. A perfected security interest has priority over lien creditors who acquire their lien after perfection. An unperfected security interest is subordinate to the rights of a person who becomes a lien creditor before the security interest is perfected.

5. Against Trustee in Bankruptcy–The Bankruptcy Code empowers a trustee in bankruptcy to (a) take priority over an unperfected security interest, and (b) avoid preferential transfers.

    a. Priority over Unperfected Security Interest–A trustee in bankruptcy may invalidate any security interest that is voidable by a creditor who obtained a judicial lien on the date of the filing of the bankruptcy petition. Under the UCC and the Bankruptcy Code, the trustee has priority over a creditor with a security interest that was not perfected when the bankruptcy petition was filed. A creditor with a purchase money security interest who files within the statutory grace period after the debtor receives the collateral will defeat the trustee, even if the petition is filed before the creditor perfects and after the creation of the security interest.

    b. Avoidance of Preferential Transfers–In general, a trustee in bankruptcy may invalidate any transfer of property–including the granting of a security interest–from the debtor, provided that the transfer (1) was to or for a benefit of a creditor; (2) was made on account of an antecedent debt; (3) was made at a time the debtor was insolvent; (4) was made on or within 90 days before the filing of the bankruptcy petition, or if made to an insider, was made within one year before the date of filing; and (5) enabled the transferee to receive more than he would have received in bankruptcy. An insider includes a relative or general partner of a debtor as well as some others. If a security interest is invalidated as a preferential transfer, the creditor may make a claim for the unpaid debt, but the claim is unsecured.

F. Default–After default, the secured party may ask for a judgment or foreclosure or otherwise enforce the security interest by available judicial procedure. A debtor who has not waived rights in the collateral has a right of redemption, which is the right to free the collateral of the security interest by paying off the loan before the secured party has collected the collateral, disposed of the collateral, has entered a contract to dispose of it, or has discharged the obligation by accepting the collateral.

1. Repossession–Unless the parties have agreed otherwise, the secured party may take possession of the collateral on default without judicial process if it can be done without a breach of the peace. After default, the secured party may render the collateral unusable and leave it on the debtor's premises until disposing of it.

2. Sale of Collateral–The secured party may sell, lease, or otherwise dispose of any collateral in its existing condition at the time of default or following any commercially reasonable preparation or

processing. The debtor is entitled to any surplus and is liable for any deficiency, except that in the case of a sale of accounts or chattel paper, she is not entitled to any surplus or liable for a deficiency unless the security agreement so provides. One who purchases the collateral for value obtains all the debtor's rights and also discharges the security interest under which the sale occurred and all subordinate security interests and liens. The collateral may be disposed of at public or private sale, so long as all aspects of its disposition, including its method, time, place, and terms, are "commercially reasonable."

3. Acceptance of Collateral (strict foreclosure)–After default and repossession, the secured party may send written notice to the debtor that he proposes to retain the collateral in satisfaction of the obligation. If no authenticated objection is received within 20 days, the secured party may retain the collateral. If there is objection within the period, the collateral must be disposed of as provided in the Code. In the case of consumer goods, if the debtor has paid 60 percent of the obligation and has not signed a statement after default renouncing her rights, the secured party must dispose of the property by sale within 90 days after repossession.

II. Suretyship–A surety is someone who promises to fulfill an obligation if the principal debtor fails to do so.

A. Nature and Formation–A suretyship involves three parties: the principal debtor, the creditor, and the surety. Three contractual obligations are also involved: one between the principal debtor and the creditor, one between the principal debtor and the surety, and one between the surety and the creditor. The creditor's rights against the principal debtor are determined by the contract between them. A creditor may hold an absolute surety liable as soon as the principal debtor defaults, but a conditional guarantor of collection is liable only when and if the creditor first obtains, but is unable to collect, a judgment against the principal debtor. The terms surety and guarantor are almost synonymous in common usage. A surety who is required to pay the creditor is entitled to reimbursement by the principal debtor.

1. Types of Sureties–A suretyship is frequently used by creditors seeking to reduce the risk of default by their debtors. Another common suretyship arises when an owner of property subject to a mortgage sells the property to a purchaser who assumes the mortgage. The purchaser becomes the principal debtor, but the seller remains liable to the lender as a surety. There are numerous specialized kinds of suretyship including fidelity, performance, official, and judicial.

2. Formation–Suretyship is contractual and must satisfy the usual elements of a contract. No particular words are required, although the surety's promise must be in writing to be enforceable.

B. Rights of Surety–A surety's rights include exoneration, reimbursement, subrogation, and contribution.

1. Exoneration–The surety has the right to require that her principal debtor pay the creditor when the obligation is due. If the principal debtor fails to do so, the surety may obtain a decree ordering the principal to pay the creditor. This remedy does not affect the creditor's right to proceed against the surety. A surety also has a right of exoneration against cosureties for their proportionate shares of the debt.

2. Reimbursement–When a surety pays a creditor upon default of the principal debtor, the surety has the right of reimbursement, or repayment, against the principal debtor.

3. Subrogation–Upon payment of the principal debtor's entire obligation, the surety "steps into the shoes" of the creditor and obtains all the rights the creditor has against the principal debtor. These include the creditor's rights against the principal debtor, rights in security of the principal debtor, rights against third parties such as comakers, and rights against cosureties.

4. Contribution–Up to the amount of each surety's undertaking, cosureties are jointly and severally liable for the principal debtor's default. A surety who pays the principal debtor's obligation may require the cosureties to pay their proportionate shares of the obligation. This right of contribution exists even if the cosureties originally were unaware of each other or were bound on separate instruments.

C. Defenses of Surety and Principal Debtor–Obligations the principal debtor and the surety owe to the creditor arise out of contracts, so usual contract defenses apply.

1. Personal Defenses of Principal Debtor–Some defenses, such as incapacity, are available only to a principal debtor and not to the surety. A principal debtor who disaffirms the contract due to incapacity and returns the consideration received, thereby discharges the surety from liability.

2. Personal Defenses of Surety–Defenses available only to the surety include incapacity of the surety, noncompliance with the statute of frauds, or absence of mutual assent or consideration to support the surety's obligation. If a principal debtor and a creditor enter a binding modification of their contract, a surety who does not assent to the modification may be discharged. If the creditor releases or impairs the value of the security, the surety is discharged to that extent.

3. Defenses of Both Surety and Principal Debtor–Forgery of the principal debtor's signature, fraud or duress exerted by the creditor on the principal debtor, fraudulent and material alteration, illegality of the principal debtor's contract, and absence of mutual assent or consideration to support the principal debtor's obligation are defenses of both the surety and principal debtor.

KEY TERMS

1. Secured transaction

2. Debtor

3. Secured party

4. Collateral

5. Security agreement

6. Security interest

7. Purchase money security interest

8. Instruments

9. Documents

10. Intangibles

11. Accounts

12. General intangibles

13. Attachment

14. Value

15. Consumer goods

16. Farm products

17. Inventory

18. Equipment

19. Fixtures

20. Indispensable paper

21. Chattel paper

22. Automatic perfection

23. Lien creditor

24. Trustee in bankruptcy

25. Record

26. Pledge

27. After-acquired property

28. Proceeds

29. Perfection

30. Financing statement

31. Certificate of title

32. Field warehouse

33. Redemption

34. Surety

35. Conditional guarantor of collection

36. Investment property

TRUE/FALSE

_____ 1. Article 9 of the UCC governs financing transactions involving security in real property.

_____ 2. A security interest in property may continue even after the underlying debt is discharged.

_____ 3. A security interest must be in writing unless the secured party has possession of the collateral.

_____ 4. A security interest is perfected if the interest has attached and the secured party files a financing statement that has not been signed by the debtor.

_____ 5. A buyer in the ordinary course of business takes collateral free of any security interest created by any previous seller of the collateral.

_____ 6. A financing statement is generally effective for five years from the date of filing.

_____   7. Unless the parties agree otherwise, a security agreement covering the debtor's inventory does not give the secured party rights to the proceeds from the sale of that inventory.

_____   8. Unless the parties have otherwise agreed, after default the secured party may take possession of the collateral without judicial process if it can be done without a breach of the peace.

_____   9. Unless the debtor waived her rights in the collateral after default, she has a right of redemption at any time before the secured party disposes of the collateral or enters a contract to dispose of it.

_____ 10. Two parties, each having a perfected security interest, rank according to priority in time of filing or perfection

_____ 11. A fidelity bond guarantees the performance of the terms and conditions of the contract.

_____ 12. A surety who is required to pay the creditor has fulfilled his contractual obligation and has no recourse against the principal debtor.

_____ 13. Belinda is a conditional guarantor of collection on a note to First Bank on which Donald is the principal debtor. Belinda will only be liable when First Bank obtains a judgment against Donald and is unable to collect that judgment.

_____ 14. An uncompensated surety is discharged from her obligation if the principal debtor and the creditor enter into a binding, material modification of their contract.

_____ 15. The promise of a surety is binding without consideration.

MULTIPLE CHOICE

_____   1. A secured transaction includes which of the following?
   a.   A debt or obligation to pay money
   b.   An interest of the creditor in property of the debtor
   c.   Both (a) and (b)
   d.   Neither (a) nor (b)

_____   2. Every consensual secured transaction involves which of the following?
   a.   A debtor
   b.   A security agreement
   c.   A security interest
   d.   All of the above

_____ 3. In order for a security interest to attach, an agreement between the debtor and creditor must:
    a. be authenticated by the debtor.
    b. be notarized.
    c. describe the collateral.
    d. (a) and (c), but not (b).

_____ 4. A tractor that is used by a farmer to plow his land would be what type of collateral?
    a. farm products.
    b. equipment.
    c. either (a) or (b).
    d. both (a) and (b).

_____ 5. Under the Code, collateral is classified according to its nature. Which of the following are proper classifications?
    a. Goods
    b. Indispensable paper
    c. Both (a) and (b)
    d. Neither (a) nor (b)

_____ 6. A creditor with an unperfected, but attached, security interest has greater rights in the collateral than:
    a. the debtor's trustee in bankruptcy.
    b. the debtor's perfected secured creditors.
    c. the debtor.
    d. none of the above.

_____ 7. On the debtor's default, the secured party may do all of the following except:
    a. foreclose on the claim.
    b. take possession of the collateral even if it requires a breach of the peace.
    c. reduce the claim to judgment.
    d. render the collateral unusable on the debtor's premises.

_____ 8. Glenn takes out a $2,000 loan from Credit Corporation on May 15 to buy a new video camcorder to use in his photography business. He buys the camcorder immediately and signs a financing agreement. On May 20, before Credit Corporation files the financing statement, Glenn files for bankruptcy. Credit Corporation files the financing statement on May 22. It is now July and the trustee in bankruptcy claims that she is entitled to the camcorder to sell and use the proceeds to pay the expenses of administration and the general creditors of the estate. As between the trustee in bankruptcy and Credit Corporation, who is entitled to the video camcorder?
    a. Credit Corporation because its security interest attached before Glenn filed for bankruptcy.
    b. Credit Corporation because it has a perfected security interest.
    c. The trustee because this was a preferential transfer.
    d. The trustee because the trustee always has the power to invalidate a perfected security interest.

9. *CPA:* Pix Co., which is engaged in the business of selling appliances, borrowed $18,000 from Lux Bank. Pix executed a promissory note for that amount and pledged all of its customer installment receivables as collateral for the loan. Pix executed a security agreement that described the collateral, but Lux did not file a financing statement. With respect to this transaction:
   a. attachment of the security interest did **not** occur because Pix failed to file a financing statement.
   b. perfection of the security interest occurred despite Lux's failure to file a financing statement.
   c. attachment of the security interest took place when the loan was made and Pix executed the security agreement.
   d. perfection of the security interest did **not** occur because accounts receivable are intangibles.

10. *CPA:* Wine purchased a computer using the proceeds of a loan from MJC Finance Co. Wine gave MJC a security interest in the computer. Wine executed a security agreement and financing statement, which was filed by MJC. Wine used the computer to monitor Wine's personal investments. Later, Wine sold the computer to Jacobs, for Jacobs' family use. Jacobs was unaware of MJC's security interest. Wine now is in default under the MJC loan. May MJC repossess the computer from Jacobs?
    a. Yes, because MJC's security interest was perfected before Jacobs' purchase.
    b. Yes, because Jacobs' purchase of the computer made Jacobs personally liable to MJC.
    c. No, because Jacobs was unaware of the MJC security interest.
    d. No, because Jacobs intended to use the computer for family or household purposes.

11. Caldwell Corporation applies to First Bank for a loan. The bank refuses to extend credit unless Samuels, the sole shareholder, promises to repay the loan if Caldwell does not. Samuels is a:
    a. surety.
    b. principal debtor.
    c. creditor.
    d. none of the above.

12. Dan agreed to loan Ike $5,000 for his business for which Ike signed a promissory note. One week later, Dan heard that Ike's business was in trouble and he might not repay the loan. Dan therefore asked Rod to guarantee the loan. Rod gave a glowing oral endorsement of Ike and Ike's business and then orally promised to pay the $5,000 if Ike did not. Rod added that he has done business with Ike for five years and that Ike buys all of his supplies from Rod's lumberyard. Is Rod's agreement to pay the $5,000 if Ike does not enforceable?
    a. Yes, because it was made freely and without coercion.
    b. No, because the statute of frauds requires that the suretyship agreement is in writing.
    c. Yes, because even though the statute of frauds applies, the main purpose rule exception will probably make the agreement enforceable.
    d. No, because there is no consideration for Rod's promise.

_____ 13. Al approached Brad to borrow $15,000. Brad demanded that Al obtain a surety, and Clarence agreed to act as one. If Al defaults, which of the following defenses could Clarence raise?
   a. Al's fraud in securing Clarence as a surety.
   b. Al's having tendered payment to Brad, which Brad refused to accept.
   c. Al's insolvency at the time the loan was made.
   d. The fact that Al furnished no consideration to Clarence for agreeing to act as surety.

_____ 14. *CPA:* Which of the following events will release a noncompensated surety from liability?
   a. Filing of an involuntary petition in bankruptcy against the principal debtor
   b. Insanity of the principal debtor at the time the contract was entered into with the creditor
   c. Release of the principal debtor's obligation by the creditor but with the reservation of the creditor's rights against the surety
   d. Modification by the principal debtor and the creditor of their contract that materially increases the surety's risk of loss

_____ 15. *CPA:* Edwards Corp. loaned Lark $200,000. At Edwards' request, Lark entered into an agreement with Owen and Ward for them to act as compensated cosureties on the loan in the amount of $200,000 each. If Edwards releases Ward without Owen's or Lark's consent, and Lark later defaults, which of the following statements is correct?
   a. Lark will be released for 50% of the loan balance.
   b. Owen will be liable for the entire loan balance.
   c. Owen will be liable for 50% of the loan balance.
   d. Edwards' release of Ward will have **no** effect on Lark's and Owen's liability to Edwards.

SHORT ESSAY

1. Define "secured transaction" and describe its purpose.

_____

_____

_____

_____

2. Outline briefly the steps that a lender must go through to attain a perfected security interest in a boat as collateral for a loan.

_____

_____

_____

_____

3. List the classifications of collateral according to the nature of the collateral and give examples of each.

_____

_____

_____

_____

4. Equity Credit loaned $30,000 to Gamble's Store to buy televisions for its inventory. Gamble signed a financing agreement that Equity Credit appropriately filed. Jeremy purchased a television that was subject to the security interest held by Equity Credit. Whose interest in the television has priority?

_____

_____

_____

_____

5. List and briefly describe the rights of a surety.

_____

_____

_____

_____

Chapter 39
Bankruptcy

PURPOSE

Various solutions to the conflict between creditor rights and relief for the overburdened debtor have developed. These include voluntary adjustments and compromises requiring payment in installments over time. Other voluntary methods include compositions and assignments of assets by a debtor to a trustee or assignee for the benefit of creditors. However, the most adaptable and frequently employed method of debtor relief and the one that also affords some protection to creditors is a proceeding in a federal court under the federal bankruptcy laws. In this chapter, you study the various chapters of the U.S. Bankruptcy Code, as well as several forms of nonbankruptcy compromises to resolve conflicts among debtors and creditors.

CHAPTER CHECKPOINTS

After reading and studying this chapter, you should be able to:

1. Distinguish between Chapters 7, 11, and 13 bankruptcy proceedings.

2. Discuss the administration of a bankruptcy case including the filing of a voluntary or involuntary petition, automatic stay, duties and powers of the trustee, and meetings of creditors.

3. Outline the steps involved in a Chapter 7 bankruptcy and identify property of the estate, assets which are exempt, the priority in which the debtor's debts will be paid from the estate, nondischargeable debts, and events that result in denial of the discharge.

4. Distinguish between a fraudulent transfer and a voidable preference.

5. List the various forms of nonbankruptcy compromises and distinguish them from the relief available under the Bankruptcy Code.

CHAPTER OUTLINE

I. Federal Bankruptcy Law–Bankruptcy legislation serves a dual purpose: (1) to bring about an equitable distribution of the debtor's property among creditors, and (2) to discharge the debtor from her debts and enable her to start afresh. The legislation also provides uniform treatment of similarly situated creditors, preserves existing business relations, and stabilizes commercial usages. The 1994 Amendments to the Bankruptcy Act require that every three years, beginning in 1998, adjustments be made for inflation to figures within the Act. The U.S. Bankruptcy Abuse Prevention and Consumer Protection Act of 2005 (2005 Act) made extensive amendments to federal bankruptcy law.

A. Case Administration–Chapter 3–Chapter 3 of the Bankruptcy Code contains provisions dealing with the commencement of the case, the officers who administer the case, the meetings of creditors, and the administrative powers of the various officers.

1. Commencement of the Case–The filing of a voluntary or involuntary petition starts a bankruptcy case and confers jurisdiction on the bankruptcy court and the operation of the bankruptcy laws.

a. Voluntary Petitions–Any person eligible to be a debtor under a given bankruptcy proceeding may file a voluntary petition under that chapter. The debtor need not be insolvent to file the petition. Commencement of a voluntary case constitutes an automatic order for relief. The petition must include a list of all creditors (secured and unsecured), a list of all the debtor's property, a list of property claimed to be exempt, and a statement of the debtor's affairs. The 2005 Act requires most individual debtors to receive credit counseling from an approved nonprofit budget and credit counseling agency within 180 days prior to filing a petition.

b. Involuntary Petitions–An involuntary petition in bankruptcy may be filed only under Chapter 7 for liquidation or Chapter 11 for reorganization. It may be filed: (1) by 3 or more creditors who have undisputed unsecured claims that total $12,300 or more, or (2) if there are fewer than 12 creditors of the debtor, by one or more creditors whose total undisputed unsecured claims equal $12,300 or more. If the debtor does not contest the petition, the court will enter an order for relief against the debtor. If the debtor opposes the petition, the court may enter an order of relief only if (1) the debtor is not paying debts as they become due, or (2) within 120 days before the filing of the petition a custodian, assignee, or general receiver took possession of substantially all of the debtor's property.

2. Dismissal–The court may dismiss bankruptcy cases for cause after notice and a hearing. When an individual debtor whose debts are primarily consumer debts files a case the court may dismiss the case, or with the debtor's consent, convert it to one under Chapter 11 or 13 if the court finds that granting relief would be an abuse of Chapter 7.

3. Automatic Stays–The filing of a voluntary or involuntary petition operates as a stay against (prevents) attempts by creditors to begin or continue to recover claims against the debtor, to enforce judgments against the debtor, or to create or enforce liens against the debtor's property. The stay applies to both secured and unsecured creditors.

4. Trustees–The trustee is the representative of the estate and has the capacity to sue and be sued. Under Chapter 7, trustees are selected by a vote of the creditors; in Chapter 11 proceedings the creditors may elect a trustee if the court orders appointment of a trustee for cause; in Chapters 12 and 13, the trustee is appointed. The trustee collects, liquidates, and distributes the debtor's estate under Chapter 7. The trustee may (1) collect the property of the estate; (2) challenge

transfers of property of the estate; (3)use, sell, or lease property of the estate; (4) deposit or invest money of the estate; (5) employ attorneys, accountants, appraisers, or auctioneers; (6) assume or reject any executory contract or unexpired lease of the debtor; (7) object to improper creditor claims; and (8) oppose the debtor's discharge. Trustees under Chapters 11, 12, and 13 perform some but not all of the duties of a Chapter 7 trustee.

5. Meetings of Creditors–Within a reasonable time after relief is ordered, a meeting of creditors must be held. The debtor must appear and submit to examination by creditors and the trustee regarding his financial situation.

B. Creditors, the Debtor, and the Estate–Chapter 5
1. Creditors–A creditor is any entity having a claim against the debtor that arose at the time of or before the order for relief. A claim is a right to payment.
   a. Proofs of Claim–If a creditor does not file a proof of claim in a timely manner, the debtor or trustee may file a proof of such claim. Filed claims are allowed unless an interested party objects. The court will not allow a claim that (1) is unenforceable against the debtor, (2) is unmatured, (3) may be offset against a debt, or (4) is for services of an insider or attorney in excess of the reasonable value of such services. An insider includes a relative or general partner of the debtor, a partnership in which the debtor is a partner, or a corporation in which the debtor is an officer, director, or person in control.
   b. Secured and Unsecured Claims–A secured claim is one with a lien on property of the estate of the debtor. It is unsecured to the extent that the value of the secured interest is less than the allowed amount of the claim.
   c. Priority of Claims–After secured claims have been satisfied, the remaining assets are distributed among creditors with unsecured claims. Certain classes of unsecured claims have priority, which means that they have the right to be paid in full before any distribution is made to claims of lesser rank. Each claimant within a priority class shares pro rata if the assets are not sufficient to satisfy all claims within that class. The following claims have priority in the following order: (1) domestic support obligations (debts owed to a spouse, former spouse, or child of the debtor in the nature of alimony, maintenance, or support) subject to certain amounts of trustee administration expenses; (2) expenses of administration of the debtor's estate; (3) unsecured claims of "gap" creditors in an involuntary case; (4) unsecured claims of up to $10,000 for wages, salaries, or commissions earned within 180 days before the filing of the petition; (5) unsecured claims for contributions to employee benefit plans (subject to limits); (6) unsecured claims up to $4,925 for grain or fish producers against a storage facility; (7) unsecured claims up to $2,225 for consumer deposits; (8) specified income, property, employment, or excise taxes owed to the government; and (9) allowed claims for death or personal injuries resulting from the debtor's operation of a motor vehicle or vessel while legally intoxicated from alcohol, drugs, or other substances.
   d. Subordination of Claims–In proper cases, the bankruptcy court can in its discretion apply equitable priorities. By applying the doctrine of subordination of claims, when the bankruptcy court has two claims of equal priority, it may pay one in full before paying anything on the other claim. Subordination is applied when allowing a claim in full would be unfair and inequitable to other creditors.

2. Debtors–The Bankruptcy Code explicitly subjects the debtor to specified duties while exempting some of his property and discharging most of his debts.

   a. Debtor's Duties–A debtor must file a list of creditors, schedule of assets and liabilities, schedule of current income and expenditures, and statement of financial affairs. The debtor must cooperate with the trustee and surrender to the trustee all property of the estate and all records relating to property of the estate.

   b. Debtor's Exemptions–The Code exempts certain property of the debtor from the bankruptcy proceedings, including: (1) up to $18,450 in equity in a residence or burial plot; (2) up to $2,950 in equity in one motor vehicle; (3) up to $475 for any particular item of household furnishings, goods, or apparel; (4) up to $1,225 in jewelry; (5) any property up to $975 plus up to $9,250 of any unused amount of the first exemption; (6) up to $1,850 in implements, professional books, or tools of the debtor's trade; (7) unmatured life insurance contracts owned by the debtor; (8) professionally prescribed health aids; (9) social security, veteran's, and disability benefits; (10) unemployment compensation; (11) alimony and support payments; (12) payments from pension, profit-sharing, and annuity plans; (13) tax-exempt retirement funds; and (14) payments from a crime victim's reparation law, a wrongful death award, and up to $18,450, not including pain and suffering, from a personal injury award.

      A debtor has the option of using either the above exemptions from the Bankruptcy Code or the exemptions available under state law, but states may limit them to the exemptions provided by state law. The 2005 Act states that a debtor's exemption is governed by the law of the state where the debtor was domiciled for 730 days immediately before filing.

      For individual debtors, the 2005 Act states that tax exempt retirement accounts are exempt. IRAs are subject to a $1 million cap adjusted for inflation. The 2005 Act, however, renders exempt property liable for nondischargeable domestic support obligations.

      The 2005 Act limits state homestead exemptions in the following manner:

      - The homestead exemption is reduced to the extent that the homestead was obtained through fraudulent conversion of nonexempt assets during the 10 years prior to filing.
      - Regardless of the state homestead exemption, a debtor may exempt only up to $125,000 that was acquired within 1,215 days prior to filing (subject to exception).
      - A debtor may not exempt more than $125,000 if the debtor has committed one of a number of wrongs specified in the 2005 Act.

   c. Discharge–Discharge relieves the debtor from liability for all dischargeable debts. However, certain debts are nondischargeable, such as: (1) certain taxes and debts incurred to pay such taxes; (2) liabilities for money or property fraudulently obtained; (3) liability for willful and malicious injuries to the person or property of another; (4) domestic support obligations and divorce-related property settlements; (5) debts not scheduled, unless the creditor knew of the bankruptcy; (6) debts created by fraud or embezzlement while acting as a fiduciary; (7) student loans unless the debt would impose an undue hardship; (8) debts that could have been listed in a previous bankruptcy in which no discharge was issued; (9) consumer debts for luxury goods or services in excess of $500 per creditor if incurred within 90 days of the order for relief; (10) cash advances aggregating more than $750 obtained under an open-ended credit plan within 70 days before the order for relief; (11) liability for death or personal injury based upon operation of a motor vehicle while legally intoxicated; (12) fines, penalties, or forfeitures owed to a governmental entity; and (13) certain debts incurred for violations of securities fraud law.   The foregoing list applies in Chapter 7 and 11, and in most Chapter 13 cases.

A reaffirmation agreement between a debtor and a creditor permits the creditor to enforce a discharged debt. It is enforceable to the extent state law if it complies with a number of Bankruptcy Code requirements including that it be made before a discharge is granted.

3. The Estate–The commencement of a bankruptcy case creates a separate legal estate consisting of all legal and equitable interests of the debtor in nonexempt property at that time. The estate also includes property acquired within 180 days after the filing of the petition, by inheritance, property settlement, divorce decree, or from insurance. It includes property that the trustee recovers under powers (1) as a lien creditor, (2) to avoid voidable preferences, (3) to avoid fraudulent transfers, and (4) to avoid statutory liens.

a. Trustee as Lien Creditor–When the case commences, the trustee gains the rights and powers of any creditor with an unsatisfied judicial lien against the debtor, whether or not such a creditor exists. The trustee is an ideal creditor possessing every right and power conferred by the law of the state on its most favored creditor who has acquired a lien by legal or equitable proceedings. Thus, the trustee, as a hypothetical lien creditor, has priority over a creditor with a security interest that was not perfected when the bankruptcy petition was filed. A creditor with a purchase money security interest who files within the allowed grace period of the debtor's receiving the collateral will defeat the trustee.

b. Voidable Preferences–The Bankruptcy Code invalidates certain preferential transfers. The trustee may recover any transfer of property of the debtor (1) to or for the benefit of a creditor; (2) for or on account of an antecedent debt owed by the debtor before the transfer was made; (3) made while the debtor was insolvent; (4) made on or within ninety days before the date of the filing of the petition; or, if the creditor was an "insider" within one year of the date of the filing of the petition; and (5) that enables such creditor to receive more than he would have received under Chapter 7. A transfer is any voluntary or involuntary transfer of property or interest in property, including the retention of title as a security interest. The Code presumes the debtor has been insolvent on and during the 90 days immediately preceding the date of the filing of the petition. Insolvency is a financial condition where the sum of debts exceed the fair value of assets. Not all transfers made within 90 days of bankruptcy are voidable. Exceptions for pre-bankruptcy transfers include: (1) exchanges for new value, (2) enabling security interests, (3) payments in ordinary course, (4) payment of consumer debts for less than $600, (5) domestic support obligations, and (6) payment of nonconsumer debts by a business for less than $5,000.

c. Fraudulent Transfers–The trustee may avoid fraudulent transfers made on or within one year before the date of the filing of the petition or that violate state fraudulent conveyance law. One type of fraudulent transfer consists of the debtor's transferring property with the actual intent to hinder, delay, or defraud creditors. Another type is the transfer by the debtor of property for less than a reasonably equivalent consideration while she is insolvent or when the transfer would make her so. A fraudulent transfer includes a payment to an insider under an employment contract that is not in the ordinary course of business.

d. Statutory Liens–A statutory lien is one that arises solely by statute and does not include a security interest or judicial lien. The trustee may avoid a statutory lien on property of the debtor if the lien (1) first becomes effective when the debtor becomes insolvent, (2) is not perfected or enforceable on the date of the filing of the petition against a *bona fide* purchaser, or (3) is for rent.

C. Liquidation–Chapter 7–The Bankruptcy Code has established two approaches to accomplishing its goals: liquidation and adjustment of debts. Chapter 7 uses liquidation, whereas Chapters 11, 12, and 13 use the adjustment of debts.

1. Proceedings–Chapter 7 proceedings apply to all debtors except railroads, insurance companies, banks, savings and loan associations, homestead associations, and credit unions. Once a voluntary or involuntary petition has been filed, the court enters an order for relief and appoints an interim trustee who serves until a permanent trustee is selected by the creditors. Under Chapter 7, the trustee collects and reduces to money the property of the estate; accounts for all property received; investigates the financial affairs of the debtor; examines, and if appropriate, challenges proofs of claim; may oppose the discharge of the debtor; and makes a final report of the administration.

2. Dismissal–The court may dismiss a Chapter 7 case for cause. For a case filed by an individual debtor whose debts are primarily consumer debts, if the court finds that relief would be an abuse of Chapter 7, then the court may dismiss the case, or with the debtor's consent, convert the case to Chapter 11 or 13A. Abuse may be based: (1) on general grounds or (2) an unrebutted presumption of abuse based on a new means test established by the 2005 Act.

   Abuse is presumed under the means test for an individual debtor (1) whose net current monthly income is greater than the state median income and (2) either (a) the debtor has available net income (income minus allowed expenses) for repayment to creditors over 5 years totaling at least $10,000 or (b) the available net income for repayment to creditors over five years is between $6,000 and $10,000 and such available net income is at least 25% of the debtor's nonpriority unsecured claims.

3. Distribution of the Estate–After the assets have been collected, the trustee distributes them to the creditors. If any remain, they are distributed to the debtor. The order of distribution is as follows: (1) secured creditors on their security interests; (2) creditors with priority in the order provided in the statute; (3) unsecured creditors who filed claims on time, or tardily if they did not have notice or actual knowledge of the bankruptcy; (4) unsecured creditors who filed claims late; (5) claims for fines, and multiple, exemplary, or punitive damages; (6) interest at the legal rate from the date of the filing of the petition to all of the above claimants; and (7) the remainder, if any, to the debtor.

4. Discharge–A discharge under Chapter 7 relieves the debtor of all debts that arose before the date of the order for relief, except for those debts that are not dischargeable. After distribution of the estate, the court will grant the debtor a discharge unless the debtor (1) is not an individual, (2) has destroyed, failed to keep, or falsified records and books of account, (3) has committed fraud, (4) has transferred property, defrauding creditors, (5) under Chapter 7 or 11 has been granted a discharge within eight years, (6) has refused to obey a court order, (7) has failed to explain any losses of assets, or (8) has executed a court-approved waiver of discharge. A debtor will also be denied a discharge under Chapter 7 if she received a Chapter 13 discharge within the past six years unless payments under that Chapter's plan totaled at least (1) 100 percent of the allowed unsecured claims or (2) 70 percent of such claims and the plan was the debtor's best

effort. Discharge also is denied for an individual debtor who fails to complete a personal financial management course.

D. Reorganization–Chapter 11–Reorganization is the means by which a distressed business enterprise and its value as a going concern are preserved through the correction or elimination of factors causing the distress. Chapter 11 governs reorganization of eligible debtors, including partnerships, corporations, and individuals.

1. Proceedings–Any person who may be a debtor under Chapter 7 (except stockbrokers and commodity brokers) and railroads may be debtors under Chapter 11. Petitions may be voluntary or involuntary. Under the 1994 amendments, qualifying small businesses may elect streamlined procedures designed to expedite the administration of Chapter 11. After the order for relief, a committee of unsecured creditors is appointed, consisting of persons who hold the seven largest unsecured claims against the debtor. The court may order the appointment of additional committees. The committee may with court approval employ attorneys, accountants, and other agents to perform services. The debtor remains in possession and management of the property of the estate unless the court orders the appointment of a trustee to operate the debtor's business. One important duty of a trustee is to file a plan or to file a report on why there will be no plan or to recommend dismissal of the case or its conversion to Chapter 7.

2. Plan of Reorganization–The debtor may file a plan at any time and has the exclusive right to file a plan during the 120 days after the order for relief, unless a trustee has been appointed. Then other interested parties, including the trustee, or a creditors' committee may file a plan. A plan of reorganization must divide creditors' claims and shareholders' interests into classes, specify how each class will be treated, deal with claims within each class equally, and provide adequate means for implementing the plan. Information on the plan must be sent to each claim holder before the plan is accepted or rejected.

3. Acceptance of Plan–Each class of claims has the opportunity to accept or reject the proposed plan. A class of claims has accepted a plan if it has been accepted by creditors that hold at least two-thirds in amount and more than one-half in number of the allowed claims of such class. Acceptance of a plan by a class of interests requires acceptance by holders of at least two-thirds in amount of the allowed interests of such class.

4. Confirmation of Plan–The court must confirm a plan before it is binding on any parties. The plan must meet the requirements of good faith, feasibility, cash payments in full to certain classes of creditors, and acceptance by at least one class of claims.

5. Effect of Confirmation–After confirmation, the plan binds the debtor and any creditor, equity security holder, or general partner of the debtor. After the entry of a final decree closing the proceedings, the debtor is discharged from all debts and liabilities that arose before the date of confirmation of the plan except as otherwise provided in the plan, order of confirmation, or the Bankruptcy Code. A corporate debtor does not receive a discharge of any debt owed to the government due to fraud or arising from a fraudulent tax return or willful evasion of taxes.

An individual debtor is not discharged until all plan payments have been made. If the debtor fails to make all payments, the court in some cases may nonetheless grant a "hardship discharge." A discharge under Chapter 11 does not discharge an individual debtor from debts that are not dischargeable.

E. Adjustment of Debts of Individuals–Chapter 13–This chapter permits an individual debtor to file a repayment plan that will discharge him from almost all of his debts when he completes payments under the plan.

1. Proceedings–Chapter 13 provides for the adjustment of debts of an individual with regular income who owes liquidated, unsecured debts of less than $307,675 and secured debts of less than $922,975. Sole proprietorships also are eligible. A Chapter 13 case may only be initiated by a voluntary petition. A trustee is appointed in every case.

2. The Plan–The debtor files the plan and may modify it at any time before confirmation. It must meet three requirements. It must (1) require the debtor to submit all or any portion of future earnings or income of the debtor, as is necessary for the execution of the plan, to the supervision and control of the trustee; (2) provide for full payment on a deferred basis of all claims entitled to a priority unless a holder of a claim agrees to a different treatment of such claim; and (3) if the plan classifies claims, it must provide the same treatment for each claim in the same class. If the debtor's net current monthly income is equal to or greater than the state median income, then the plan may not provide for payments over a period longer than 5 years. If the debtor's net current monthly income is less than the state median income, the plan may not provide for payments over a period longer than 3 years unless the court approves a longer not to exceed 5 years.

3. Confirmation–The plan will be confirmed by the court if the plan meets the following requirements: (1) the plan must comply with applicable law and be proposed and filed in good faith; (2) the present value of the property to be distributed to unsecured creditors must be not less than would be paid them under Chapter 7; (3) either the secured creditors must accept the plan, or the plan must provide that the debtor will surrender to the secured creditors the collateral, or the plan must permit the secured creditors to retain their security interest and the value of the property to be distributed to them is not less than the allowed amount of their claim; (4) the debtor must be able to make all payments and comply with the plan; (5) if the trustee or holder of an unsecured claim objects to the confirmation of the plan, then the plan must either provide for payment in full of that claim or provide that all the debtor's disposable income for 3 or 5 years apply to the payments under the plan; and (6) the debtor must pay all domestic support obligations that became payable after the filing.

4. Effect of Confirmation–The provisions of a confirmed plan, which vest in the debtor all property of the estate free and clear of any creditor's claim or interest for which the plan provides, bind the debtor and all creditors. A plan may be modified after confirmation at the request of the debtor, the trustee, or a holder of an unsecured claim.

5. Discharge– Chapter 13 discharges only a few types of debts that are not discharged under Chapter 7. Even if all payments have not been made, the court may grant a "hardship discharge" provided certain conditions are met. Discharge under Chapter 13 is denied to a debtor who has received a discharge (1) in a Chapter 7 or 11 case filed during the 4 years preceding the filing of the Chapter 13 case or (2) in a Chapter 13 case filed within two years preceding the date of filing the current Chapter 13 case. Discharge also is denied if the debtor fails to complete a personal financial management course.

II. Creditors' Rights and Debtors' Relief Outside of Bankruptcy–The rights and remedies of debtors and creditors outside of bankruptcy are principally governed by state law. Bankruptcy is often viewed as a last resort, and it is often in the best interests of both debtor and creditors to resolve their claims outside of bankruptcy.

A. Creditor's Rights–When a debtor fails to pay a debt, the creditor may file suit to collect the debt. The objective of a lawsuit is to obtain a judgment and to collect that judgment.
   1. Prejudgment Remedies–Because litigation takes time, the creditor may use certain prejudgment remedies such as attachment to protect against the debtor's disposing of his assets. Attachment is the seizure of property to bring it under the custody of the court. Similar in purpose is the remedy of prejudgment garnishment, which is a proceeding by a creditor against a third person who owes money to the debtor or who has property belonging to the debtor.
   2. Postjudgment Remedies–If the debtor still has not paid the claim, the creditor may proceed to trial and try to obtain a court judgment against the debtor. If the debtor does not voluntarily pay the judgment, the creditor can use postjudgment remedies to collect. A writ of execution is an order served by the sheriff upon the debtor demanding payment of a court judgment against the debtor. Nonexempt property seized by the sheriff may be advertised for sale and sold at a public sale under the writ of execution. If the proceeds of the sale do not produce sufficient funds to pay the judgment, the creditor may institute a supplementary proceeding to locate money or other property belonging to the defendant. The creditor may also proceed by garnishment against the debtor's employer or a bank in which the debtor has an account.

B. Debtors' Relief–There are inherent conflicts between creditors' rights and debtor relief, which include: (1) the right of diligent creditors to pursue their claims to judgment and to satisfy their judgments by sale of property of the debtor; (2) the right of unsecured creditors who have refrained from suing the debtor; and (3) the social policy of giving relief to a debtor who has contracted debts beyond his ability to pay and who may be confronted by a lifetime burden. Various forms of nonbankruptcy compromises have been developed to resolve these conflicts.
   1. Compositions–A common law or nonstatutory composition (a "workout") is an ordinary contract or agreement between the debtor and creditors under which the creditors receive a proportional part of their claims and the debtor is discharged from the balance of the claims. It requires the formalities of a contract. The debtor in a composition is discharged from liability only on the claims of those creditors who voluntarily consent to the composition.
   2. Assignments for Benefit of Creditors–A common law or nonstatutory assignment for the benefit of creditors is a voluntary transfer by the debtor of some or all of his property to a trustee, who applies the property to the payment of all of the debtor's debts. The advantage of the assignment over the composition is that it prevents the debtor's assets from being attached or executed and halts the race of diligent creditors to attach. It does not require the consent of the creditors, and payment by the trustee of part of the claims does not discharge the debtor from the balance.

   Because assignments benefit creditors by protecting the debtor's assets from attachment, there have been statutory attempts to combine the idea of the assignment with a corresponding benefit to the debtor by discharging him from the balance of his debts. Since the United States Constitution prohibits a state from impairing the obligation of a contract between private citizens, it is impossible for a state to force all creditors to discharge a debtor on a *pro rata* distribution of assets, although the federal government does have such power and exercises it in the Bankruptcy Code. States have generally enacted assignment statutes permitting the debtor to obtain voluntary releases of the balance of claims from creditors who accept partial payments.

3. Equity Receiverships–The receiver is a disinterested person appointed by the court who collects and preserves the debtor's assets and income and disposes of them at the direction of the court. The court may instruct the receiver to (1) liquidate the assets by public or private sale; (2) operate the business as a going concern temporarily; or (3) conserve the assets until final disposition of the matter before the court. Petitions for appointment of a receiver will be granted when made by (1) a secured creditor seeking foreclosure of her security; (2) a judgment creditor after exhausting legal remedies to satisfy the judgment; or (3) a shareholder of a corporate debtor where it appears that the assets of the corporation will be dissipated by fraud or mismanagement. Insolvency is one of the factors considered by the court in appointing a receiver.

KEY TERMS

1. Voluntary petition
2. Involuntary petition
3. Automatic stay
4. Trustee
5. Claim
6. Insider
7. Secured claim
8. Priority
9. Subordination of claims
10. Discharge
11. Receivership
12. Attachment
13. Voidable preference
14. Insolvency
15. Fraudulent transfer
16. Statutory lien
17. Liquidation
18. Reorganization
19. Garnishment
20. Means test
21. Judicial lien
22. Composition
23. Estate
24. Writ of execution
25. Domestic support obligations
26. Assignment for benefit of creditors
27. Homestead exemption
28. Adjustment of debts of individuals
29. U.S. Bankruptcy Abuse Prevention and Consumer Protection Act of 2005

TRUE/FALSE

_____ 1. Federal bankruptcy law is generally superseded by state insolvency laws.

_____ 2. Chapter 13 of the Bankruptcy Code applies to individuals with regular income who owe liquidated, unsecured debts of less than $200,000 and secured debts of less than $1 million.

_____ 3. The jurisdiction of the bankruptcy court and the operation of the bankruptcy laws are commenced by the filing of a voluntary or involuntary petition.

_____ 4. Filing of a voluntary or involuntary petition prevents immediate enforcement of judgments against a debtor.

_____ 5. As the representative of the estate, the trustee in bankruptcy has the capacity to sue or to be sued.

_____ 6. A secured creditor's claim is secured to the extent of the allowed amount of his claim, even if that amount exceeds the value of his interest in the debtor's property.

_____ 7. After creditors with secured claims and creditors with claims having a priority have been satisfied, creditors with allowed, unsecured claims share proportionately in any remaining assets.

_____ 8. The debtor's estate in bankruptcy includes any property received by the debtor by inheritance or as a beneficiary of a life insurance policy within one year after commencement of the case.

_____ 9. A discharge of a debt voids any judgment obtained at any time concerning that debt.

_____ 10. Any individual who may be a debtor under Chapter 13 may be a debtor under Chapter 7.

_____ 11. Under Chapter 11, the debtor will remain in possession of and management of the property of the estate unless the court appoints a trustee, who then may operate the debtor's business.

_____ 12. A plan of reorganization under Chapter 11 is binding with or without court confirmation.

_____ 13. An individual debtor generally may exempt only up to $125,000 as a homestead exemption if the homestead was acquired within 1,215 days prior to filing of his or her bankruptcy petition.

_____ 14. A plan under Chapter 13 will not be confirmed by the bankruptcy court if the value of the property to be distributed to unsecured creditors under the plan is less than they would receive under Chapter 7.

_____ 15. The trustee may avoid fraudulent transfers made within one year before the date of the filing of the petition.

MULTIPLE CHOICE

_____ 1. Which chapter of the Bankruptcy Code deals with case administration?
a. Chapter 1.
b. Chapter 3.
c. Chapter 4.
d. Chapter 5.

_____ 2. Chapter 7 of the Bankruptcy Code applies to which of the following debtors?
a. Railroads
b. Insurance companies
c. Credit unions
d. None of the above

_____ 3. Which of the following individual debts may be discharged in bankruptcy?
a. Customs duties
b. Alimony and child support
c. Unsecured consumer loans
d. None of the above

_____ 4. Which of the following is not a duty or power of a trustee under the Bankruptcy Code?
  a. To use, sell, or lease property of the estate
  b. To deposit or invest money of the estate
  c. To conduct the affairs of the debtor's estate for the trustee's own benefit
  d. To assume or reject any executory contract or unexpired lease of the debtor

_____ 5. Under Chapter 3 of the Bankruptcy Code the filing of an involuntary petition operates as a stay against which of the following?
  a. Attempts by creditors to begin to recover claims against the debtor
  b. Attempts by creditors to continue to recover claims against the debtor
  c. The enforcement of judgments against the debtor
  d. All of the above

_____ 6. A creditor's claim will be denied by the bankruptcy court as that of an insider if the creditor is any of the following except:
  a. a general partner of the debtor.
  b. a partnership in which the debtor is a limited partner.
  c. a relative of the debtor.
  d. a corporation of which the debtor is a director.

_____ 7. Which of the following items of an individual debtor's property is exempted from the bankruptcy estate by the Bankruptcy Code?
  a. IRAs up to $1 million.
  b. Child support.
  c. Retirement accounts.
  d. All of the above.

_____ 8. Under the Bankruptcy Code, a trustee may recover property of the debtor which has been transferred in which of the following situations?
  a. Debtor purchases an automobile for $9,000.
  b. Debtor makes a payment in the ordinary course of business.
  c. Debtor makes a payment on a past due $1,000 obligation.
  d. Debtor purchases a refrigerator and grants seller a security interest which the seller perfects within one week.

_____ 9. The estate in bankruptcy includes property that the trustee recovers under powers:
  a. as a lien creditor.
  b. to avoid a voidable preference.
  c. to avoid a fraudulent transfer.
  d. all of the above.

_____ 10. The trustee may avoid a fraudulent transfer made by the debtor on or within _____
before the date of the filing of the petition.
   a. 60 days.
   b. 90 days.
   c. 180 days.
   d. one year.

_____ 11. After distribution of the estate in a Chapter 7 proceeding, the court will grant the debtor a
discharge unless the debtor:
   a. is an individual.
   b. has within ten years before the bankruptcy been granted a discharge under a prior Chapter 7
       bankruptcy.
   c. has destroyed or falsified records.
   d. all of the above.

_____ 12. A court will confirm a plan of reorganization under Chapter 11 of the Bankruptcy Code only if it
meets the requirements of the Code, including all of the following except:
   a. the plan must be accepted by all of the creditors.
   b. certain classes of creditors must have their allowed claims paid in full in cash immediately,
       or in some instances, upon a deferred basis.
   c. the court must find that the plan is feasible.
   d. the plan must have been proposed in good faith.

_____ 13. Under the exemptions found in the Bankruptcy Code, which of the following items may be kept
by the debtor?
   a. $18,450 equity in property used as a residence
   b. Automobile with up to $5,000 equity.
   c. Any household good regardless of value.
   d. B and c, but not a.

_____ 14. *CPA:* Rolf, an individual, filed a voluntary petition in bankruptcy. A general discharge in
bankruptcy will be denied if Rolf:
   a. negligently made preferential transfers to certain creditors within 90 days of the filing
       petition.
   b. unjustifiably failed to preserve Rolf's books and records.
   c. filed a fraudulent federal income tax return two years prior to filing the petition.
   d. obtained a loan by using financial statements that Rolf knew were false.

_____ 15. *CPA:* Decal Corp. incurred substantial operating losses for the past three years. Unable to meet
its current obligations, Decal filed a petition for reorganization under Chapter 11 of the federal
Bankruptcy Code. Which of the following statements is correct?
   a. A creditors' committee, if appointed, will consist of unsecured creditors.
   b. The court must appoint a trustee to manage Decal's affairs.
   c. Decal may continue in business only with the approval of a trustee.
   d. The creditors' committee must select a trustee to manage Decal's affairs.

SHORT ESSAY

1. Discuss the difference between voluntary and involuntary petitions in bankruptcy.

_____

_____

_____

_____

2. What is the effect of filing a petition in bankruptcy?

_____

_____

_____

_____

3. Distinguish between Chapters 7, 11, and 13 bankruptcy.

_____

_____

_____

_____

4. Frankie owned a sole proprietorship and he personally filed for bankruptcy. He has the following outstanding debts:

Child support payments in arrears	$6,000
Fees earned by attorneys of the bankruptcy estate	$3,000
Unsecured claim for income tax	$25,000
Claim for $50,000 secured by inventory worth $10,000	$50,000
Employee's claim for wages earned within 180 days of filing	$1,500

    In what order will these claims be paid?

_____

_____

_____

_____

5. Discuss briefly the adjustment of debt provisions in Chapter 13.

_____

_____

_____

_____

Part VIII
Sample Examination

MULTIPLE CHOICE

_____ 1. Which of the following is NOT covered by Article 9 of the UCC?
   a. A mortgage on an office building
   b. A mechanic's lien on a house
   c. The cash purchase of a TV
   d. None of the above are covered

_____ 2. Rebecca, an attorney, buys a set of tax books to include in her office library. She gives First Bank a security interest in the books in return for a $1,500 loan which she uses to purchase the books. Under Article 9 of the Code, the books would be classified as:
   a. consumer goods.
   b. equipment.
   c. inventory.
   d. fixtures.

_____ 3. Daryl, an attorney, buys a set of encyclopedias to include in his home library. He gives First Bank a security interest in the books in return for a $1,500 loan which he uses to purchase the books. Under Article 9 of the Code, the books would be classified as:
   a. consumer goods.
   b. equipment.
   c. inventory.
   d. fixtures.

_____ 4. Which of the following must be done in order for a security interest in goods to attach?
   a. The secured party must give value.
   b. The debtor must sign a security agreement which describes the goods.
   c. The debtor must retain possession of the goods.
   d. The secured party must properly file a financing statement.

_____ 5. Which of the following is/are necessary in a security agreement to create a security interest?
   a. Agreement must be in writing
   b. Agreement must be signed by the debtor
   c. Agreement must contain a reasonable description of collateral
   d. All of the above

_____ 6. In which of the following situations is a security interest automatically perfected?
   a. First Bank loans $1,000 to Leonard so that he may purchase a gold necklace for his wife which Leonard then gives to her on their anniversary.
   b. First Bank loans $1,000 to Leonard so that he may purchase a computer for his office which Leonard then purchases and allows his secretary to use.
   c. First Bank files a financing statement covering the computer which Leonard purchased for his office.
   d. Leonard purchases a refrigerator and uses his bank credit card to finance it.

_____ 7. Bill grants a security interest in a Picasso painting to Southern Bank. In accordance with the loan agreement, the bank advances $5,000 to Bill. Southern Bank then files a financing statement. Six months later, Bill needs more money and goes to his friend David who owns an art gallery and deals in art. David advances $2,000 to Bill based on Bill's pledge of the painting.
   a. Both Southern Bank and David have a perfected security interest in the painting.
   b. Southern Bank has a perfected security interest, but David does not, because he has not filed a financing statement.
   c. The interest of Southern Bank has priority over that of David, because Southern Bank was the first to file or perfect its security interest.
   d. Two of the above are correct, (a) and (c).

_____ 8. First Bank loans Rob $1,500 so that Rob may purchase a personal computer and printer for his son Mark to use in writing term papers for school. Rob signs a financing statement which First Bank duly files. Mark never uses the computer, so Rob puts an ad in the paper and sells it to Cheryl. If Rob defaults on the loan, which of the following is correct?
   a. The bank has a perfected security interest, because it has filed a financing statement.
   b. The bank has a perfected security interest, because it gave Rob the money to purchase an item of consumer goods, as a result of which its security interest is automatically perfected.
   c. As between the bank and Cheryl, Cheryl will prevail, because she is a buyer in the ordinary course of business.
   d. Two of the above are correct, (a) and (c).

_____ 9. First Bank loans Shawn $1,500 so that he may purchase a personal computer for his office. First Bank never files a financing statement. Shawn's secretary never uses the computer, so Shawn puts an ad in the paper and sells the computer to Ramona. If Shawn defaults on the loan, which of the following is correct?
   a. The bank has a perfected security interest even though it never filed a financing statement.
   b. The bank does not have a perfected security interest because it never filed a financing statement.
   c. As between the bank and Cheryl, the bank will prevail and be able to repossess the computer.
   d. Two of the above are correct, (a) and (c).

_____ 10. Second Bank loans Kim $1,500 so that she may purchase a computer for her office. Kim signs a financing statement which Second Bank duly files within ten days. After Kim purchases the computer, she takes out a loan at Valley Bank, gives the computer as collateral, and signs a financing statement, which Valley Bank then duly files. Kim's secretary never uses the computer, so Kim puts an ad in the paper and sells it to Travis. If Kim defaults on the loans, which of the following is correct?

a. Both Second Bank and Valley Bank have perfected security interests in the computer, which is classified as noninventory collateral.

b. Second Bank has a perfected purchase money security interest, while Valley Bank has only a perfected security interest.

c. Both Second Bank and Valley Bank have rights in the computer that are superior to those of Travis, even if he had no knowledge of the two security interests.

d. All of the above are correct.

_____ 11. Enterprise Bank loans Miller, who is the owner of Miller's Department Store, $15,000 so that he may purchase personal computers for the store's inventory. Miller signs a financing statement which Enterprise Bank duly files before Miller takes possession. After Miller purchases the computers, he then goes to Winton Bank and takes out a loan for which he gives the computers as collateral. Miller signs a financing agreement which Winton Bank then duly files. Later a consumer comes into the store and purchases one of the computers. If Miller defaults on the loans, which of the following is correct?

a. Enterprise Bank and Winton Bank both have perfected security interests in the computers.

b. Enterprise Bank has a purchase money security interest in inventory, which has priority over conflicting security interests if certain requirements have been met.

c. The customer is a buyer in the ordinary course of business whose interest in the computer is superior to that of both Enterprise Bank and Winton Bank.

d. All of the above are correct.

_____ 12. The right of a surety who has paid the creditor to be repaid by the debtor is:

a. exoneration.

b. reimbursement.

c. subrogation.

d. contribution.

_____ 13. Which chapter of the Bankruptcy Code is available for adjustment of debts of a family farmer?

a. Chapter 7

b. Chapter 9

c. Chapter 11

d. Chapter 12

_____ 14. A trustee in bankruptcy may avoid a statutory lien on property of the debtor if which of the following is true with respect to the lien?
   a. It first becomes effective when the debtor becomes insolvent.
   b. It is for rent.
   c. Both (a) and (b).
   d. Neither (a) nor (b).

_____ 15. If the only nonexempt asset in a bankruptcy estate is a piece of equipment valued at $25,000, which of the following claims will be paid first by the trustee in bankruptcy?
   a. A claim of $15,000 by a bank and secured by the piece of equipment where the bank has duly filed a financing statement.
   b. The necessary expenses of the trustee in administering the estate.
   c. Unsecured claims in the amount of $15,000.
   d. The wages, salaries, and commissions earned by employees within 90 days before the filing of the petition and the cessation of a business.

_____ 16. If the only nonexempt asset in a bankruptcy estate is a piece of equipment valued at $25,000, which of the following claims will be paid second by the trustee in bankruptcy?
   a. A claim of $15,000 by a bank and secured by the piece of equipment where the bank has duly filed a financing statement.
   b. The necessary expenses of the trustee in the administration of the estate.
   c. Unsecured claims in the amount of $15,000.
   d. The wages, salaries, and commissions earned by employees within 180 days before the filing of the petition and the cessation of the business.

_____ 17. _CPA:_ Sun Inc. manufactures and sells household appliances on credit directly to wholesalers, retailers, and consumers. Sun can perfect its security interest in the appliances without having to file a financing statement or take possession of the appliances if the sale is made by Sun to:
   a. consumers.
   b. wholesalers that sell to buyers in the ordinary course of business.
   c. retailers.
   d. wholesalers that sell to distributors for resale.

_____ 18. _CPA:_ Under the UCC, which of the following is correct regarding the disposition of collateral by a secured creditor after the debtor's default?
   a. It is improper for the secured creditor to purchase the collateral at a public sale.
   b. The collateral must be disposed of at a public sale.
   c. A good faith purchaser for value and without knowledge of any defects in the sale takes free of any subordinate liens or security interests.
   d. Secured creditors with subordinate claims retain the right to redeem the collateral after the disposition of the collateral to a third party.

_____ 19. **CPA:** Sorus and Ace have agreed, in writing, to act as guarantors of collection on a debt owed by Pepper to Towns Inc. The debt is evidenced by a promissory note. If Pepper defaults, Towns will be entitled to recover from Sorus and Ace unless:

a. Sorus and Ace are in the process of exercising their rights against Pepper.
b. Sorus and Ace prove that Pepper was insolvent at the time the note was signed.
c. Pepper dies before the note is due.
d. Towns has **not** attempted to enforce the promissory note against Pepper.

_____ 20. **CPA:** To file for bankruptcy under Chapter 7 of the federal Bankruptcy Code, an individual must:

a. have debts of any amount.
b. be insolvent.
c. be indebted to more than three creditors.
d. have debts in excess of $5,000.

Try The Web

Go deeper into bankruptcy.

Solution:
Go to: http://www.abiworld.org/

Chapter 40
Securities Regulation

PURPOSE

The primary purpose of federal securities regulation is to prevent fraudulent practices in the sale of securities and thereby foster public confidence in the securities market. Federal securities law consists principally of two statutes: the Securities Act of 1933, which focuses on the issuance of securities, and the Securities Exchange Act of 1934, which deals mainly with trading in issued securities. Both statutes are administered by the Securities and Exchange Commission (SEC), an independent, quasi-judicial agency. In addition to the federal laws regulating the sale of securities, there are also state laws, commonly known as Blue Sky Laws, which prohibit fraud in the sale of securities and sometimes require state registration. In this chapter, you study the 1933 act and the 1934 act.

CHAPTER CHECKPOINTS

After reading and studying this chapter, you should be able to:

1. Identify the scope and purpose of the Securities Act of 1933 and Securities Exchange Act of 1934.

2. Define a security and recognize exempt securities and exempt transactions..

3. Summarize the requirements and applications of Rule 10b-5.

4. Summarize the federal securities provisions dealing with proxy solicitations and tender offers.

5. Discuss the sanctions for noncompliance with the disclosure and antifraud requirements of the 1934 act.

CHAPTER OUTLINE

I. The Securities Act of 1933–This act, also called the "Truth in Securities Act," requires that a registration statement be filed with the SEC and become effective before any securities may be offered for sale to the public unless either the securities or the transaction in which they are offered are exempt from registration. The purpose of registration is to disclose financial and other information to potential investors. They must be furnished with a prospectus containing the important data set forth in the registration statement. The antifraud provisions of the act apply regardless of whether registration is required. Civil and criminal liability may be imposed for violations of the act. The National Securities Markets Improvements Act of 1996 broadly authorizes the SEC to issue regulations exempting any person, security, or transaction from provisions of the 1933 act or SEC rules promulgated thereunder.

A. Definition of a Security–The 1933 act defines the term security to include any note, stock, bond, debenture, evidence of indebtedness, preorganization certificate or subscription, investment contract, voting-trust certificate, fractional undivided interest in oil, gas, or other mineral rights, or in general, any interest or instrument commonly known as a security. Under the *Howey* test, a financial instrument or transaction that involves (1) an investment in a common venture (2) premised on a reasonable expectation of profit (3) to be derived from the efforts of others, constitutes an investment contract. Courts have interpreted the definition to include limited partnership interests, citrus groves, whiskey warehouse receipts, real estate condominiums, cattle, franchises, and pyramid schemes.

B. Registration of Securities–The 1933 act prohibits the offer or sale through the use of the mails or any means of interstate commerce of any security unless a registration statement for that security is in effect or an exemption from registration is secured. The purpose of registration is to provide adequate and accurate disclosure of financial and other information on which investors may judge the merits of securities. The SEC, however, does not judge the financial merits of securities.

1. Disclosure Requirements–In general, registration requires disclosure of the following information: (1) a description of the registrant's properties, business, and competition, (2) a description of the significant provisions of the security and its relationship to the registrant's other capital securities, (3) information about the management of the registrant, and (4) financial statements certified by independent public accountants. In 1992 new disclosure requirements regarding compensation paid to senior executives and directors were added. The registration statement must be signed by the issuer, its chief executive, financial and accounting officers, and a majority of the board of directors. The information becomes public immediately upon filing. It is unlawful to sell the securities until the effective date, although after the filing of the registration statement, the securities may be offered (1) orally; (2) by certain summaries of the information in the registration statement; (3) by a "tombstone advertisement" that identifies the security and its price; or (4) by a preliminary prospectus, called a "red herring".

2. Integrated Disclosure–The disclosure system under the 1933 act developed independently of that required under the 1934 act. As a result, issuers were compelled to provide duplicative or overlapping disclosure. In 1982 the SEC adopted an integrated disclosure system to reduce or eliminate unnecessary duplication. Under this system, there are three levels of disclosure. All issuers may use the detailed form. Corporations that have continuously reported under the 1934 act for at least three years are permitted to disclose less detailed information in the 1933 act

registration statement and to incorporate by reference information in reports filed under the 1934 act. Those corporations that have filed under the 1934 act and also have a minimum market value of publicly held stock of $75 million are permitted to disclose even less detail in the 1933 act registration and to incorporate even more information by reference to 1934 act reports.

3. Shelf Registrations–Shelf registrations permit certain qualified issuers to register securities that are to be offered and sold "off the shelf" on a delayed or continuous basis. The information in the original registration must be kept accurate and current, and the issuer must reasonably expect that the securities will be sold within two years of the effective date of the registration. Only companies eligible to use the shortest form of registration qualify for shelf registration.

C. Exempt Securities–The 1933 act exempts specific securities from its registration requirements.
1. Short-Term Commercial Paper–Notes, drafts, bankers' acceptances (drafts accepted by banks) issued for working capital, that have a maturity of not more than nine months when issued are exempt under the act. The exemption is not available if the proceeds are to be used for permanent purposes, such as the acquisition of a plant, or if the paper is not ordinarily of the type purchased by the general public.
2. Other Exempt Securities–The following kinds of securities are also exempt from registration: (1) securities of domestic governments; (2) securities of domestic banks and savings and loan associations; (3) securities of nonprofit charitable organizations; (4) securities issued by federally regulated common carriers; and (5) insurance policies and annuity contracts issued by state-regulated insurance companies. The Bankruptcy Code exempts securities issued by a debtor if they are offered under a reorganization plan.

D. Exempt Transactions for Issuers–An exempt transaction is the issuance of securities not subject to the registration requirements of the 1933 act. Exempt transactions include: (1) private placements, (2) limited offers not exceeding $5 million, (3) limited offers not exceeding $1 million, and (4) limited offers solely to accredited investors. Except for Rule 504, these registration exemptions apply only to transactions in which the securities are issued; therefore, any resale must be made by registration unless the resale qualifies as an exempt transaction. The 1933 act also identifies other exemptions which are in effect transaction exemptions including intrastate issues, exchanges between an issuer and its security holders, reorganization securities issued with court or government approval, and Regulation A which permits an issuer to sell a limited amount of securities in an unregistered public offering under certain conditions.
1. Limited Offers–Regulation D contains three separate exemptions (Rules 504, 505, and 506) each involving limited offers. Section 4(6) also provides for small issues. Securities sold under these exemptions are restricted securities and may be resold only by registration or in another transaction exempt from registration. An issuer who uses these exemptions must take reasonable care to assure against nonexempt, unregistered resales of the restricted securities. Reasonable care includes the following: (a) making a reasonable inquiry to determine if the purchaser is acquiring the securities for herself or for other persons; (b) providing written disclosure to each purchaser prior to the sale stating that the securities have not been registered and therefore cannot be resold unless they are registered or an exemption is available; and (c) placing a legend on the certificate stating that the securities have not been registered and are restricted securities.

a. Private Placements–The private placement provision exempts "transactions by an issuer not involving any public offering." Rule 506 of the SEC establishes a nonexclusive safe harbor for limited offers and sales without regard to the dollar amount of the offering. General advertising or solicitation is not permitted. The issue may be purchased by an unlimited number of "accredited investors" and by no more than 35 other purchasers. Accredited investors include banks, insurance companies, investment companies, executive officers or directors of the issuer, savings and loan associations, registered broker-dealers, certain employee benefit plans with total assets in excess of $5 million, any person whose net worth exceeds $1 million, and any person with an annual income over $200,000. Nonaccredited investors must be given specified material information before the sale about the issuer, its business, and the securities being offered. The issuer must take precautions against nonexempt, unregistered resales and must notify the SEC of sales made under the exemption.

b. Limited Offers Not Exceeding $5 Million–Rule 505 exempts from registration offerings by noninvestment company issuers that do not exceed $5 million over 12 months. General advertising or solicitation is not permitted. The issue may be purchased by an unlimited number of accredited investors and by no more than 35 other purchasers. Nonaccredited investors must be given specified material information before the sale about the issuer, its business, and the securities being offered. Unlike Rule 506, the issuer is not required to reasonably believe that each nonaccredited investor, either alone or with a representative, has sufficient knowledge and experience in financial matters to be capable of evaluating the merits and risks of the investment. The issuer must take precautions against nonexempt, unregistered resales and must notify the SEC of sales made under the exemption.

c. Limited Offers Not Exceeding $1 Million–Rule 504 provides private, noninvestment company issuers with an unconditional exemption from registration for small issues not exceeding $1 million within twelve months. Issuers required to report under the 1934 act and investment companies may not use Rule 504. The SEC must be notified. The rule permits sales to an unlimited number of investors and does not require any information to be furnished to them.

d. Limited Offers Solely to Accredited Investors–Section 4(6) provides an exemption for offers and sales by an issuer made solely to accredited investors if not in excess of $5 million. General advertising or public solicitation is not permitted. As with Rules 505 and 506, an unlimited number of accredited investors may purchase the issue; however, no unaccredited investors may purchase. The issuer must take precautions against nonexempt, unregistered resales and must notify the SEC of sales made under the exemption.

2. Regulation A–This regulation permits an issuer to offer up to $5 million of securities in any twelve-month period without registering them provided that the issuer files an offering statement with the SEC's regional office prior to the sale of the securities. An offering circular must be provided to offerees and purchasers. Filings are less detailed and time-consuming than full registration statements. Issuers required to report under the 1934 act and investment companies may not use Regulation A. Because each purchaser must be supplied with an offering circular, securities sold under Regulation A may be freely resold after issuance.

3. Intrastate Issues–An issue offered and sold only to persons who live in a single state where the issuer is resident and doing business is also exempt under the 1933 act. The exemption is intended to apply to local issues that represent local financing by local persons to be carried out

through local investments. Rule 147 provides a "nonexclusive safe harbor" for securing the intrastate exemption. Rule 147 requires that: (1) the issuer be incorporated in the state in which the issuance occurs; (2) the issuer be principally doing business in that state; (3) all offerees and purchasers be residents of that state; (4) no resales be made to nonresidents during the period of sale and for nine months thereafter; and (5) precautions be taken against interstate distributions.

E. Exempt Transactions for Non-Issuers–The 1933 act requires registration of any sale by any person (including non-issuers) of any nonexempt security unless there is an exemption. The act provides a transaction exemption for any person other than an issuer, underwriter, or dealer, as well as most transactions by dealers and brokers. These exemptions do not extend to some situations involving resale by non-issuers that must be made pursuant to registration, Rule 144, or Regulation A.

1. Rule 144–Rule 144 of the SEC sets forth conditions that, if met by an affiliate or any person selling restricted securities, exempt her from registering them. There must be adequate current public information about the issuer, the person selling the securities must have owned them for at least one year, must sell them only in limited amounts in unsolicited brokers' transactions, and must give notice of the sale to the SEC. An affiliate is a person who controls, is controlled by, or is under common control with the issuer.

2. Regulation A–Regulation A, in addition to providing an exemption for issuers from registration for securities up to $5 million, also provides an exemption for non-issuers. A $1.5 million limit is placed on the total amount of securities sold in any 12-month period by all non-affiliates. All conditions imposed on issuers by Regulation A must be met.

F. Liability–Sanctions for noncompliance with the 1933 act include SEC administrative remedies, civil liability to injured investors, and criminal penalties. The Reform Act provides "forward looking" statements a "safe harbor" from civil liability under the 1933 act based on an untrue statement of material fact or an omission of a material fact needed to make a statement not misleading.

1. Unregistered Sales–Section 12(a)(1) of the act imposes civil liability for the sale of an unregistered security that is required to be registered, the sale of a registered security without delivery of a prospectus, the sale of a security by use of a prospectus that is not current, or the offer of a sale before filing of the registration statement. There are no defenses. The person who purchases a security in violation of the act has the right to tender it back to the seller and recover the purchase price, or if the seller no longer owns it, to recover monetary damages.

2. False Registration Statements–Section 11 of the act imposes liability for the inclusion in the registration statement of any untrue statement or omission of a material fact. A matter is material if a reasonable investor would attach importance to it in deciding whether to purchase a security. Liability is imposed on: (1) the issuer; (2) all persons who signed the registration statement, including the principal executive officer, the principal financial officer, and the principal accounting officer; (3) every person who was a director or partner; (4) every accountant, engineer, appraiser, or expert who prepared or certified any part of the registration statement; and (5) all underwriters. Liability is joint and several. It extends to any person who acquires the security without knowledge of the untruth or omission. Liability is for the amount paid for the security less either its value at the time of suit or the price for which it was sold. Experts are liable only for the portion of the registration that they prepared or certified. Defendants other

than the issuer may assert the defense of due diligence. This defense requires that the defendant had a reasonable belief that there were no untrue statements or material omissions.

3. Antifraud Provisions–The 1933 act contains two broad antifraud provisions: Section 12(a)(2) and 17(a). In addition, Rule 10b-5 of the 1934 act applies to all securities. Section 12(a)(2) imposes liability on any person who offers or sells a security by means of a prospectus or oral communication that contains an untrue statement of material fact or an omission of a material fact. Liability extends only to the immediate purchaser, provided she did not know of the untruth. The seller may avoid liability by proving that he did not know and could not have known of the untrue statement or omission. The seller is liable for the amount paid. Section 17(a) makes it unlawful to (a) employ any device, scheme, or artifice to defraud; (b) obtain money or property by means of any untrue statement of a material fact or omission of a material fact; and (c) engage in a trans-action, practice, or course of business that would constitute a fraud or deceit on the purchaser.

4. Criminal Sanctions–The 1933 act imposes criminal sanctions on any person who willfully violates any of the provisions of the act or the rules and regulations promulgated by the SEC. A fine of not more than $10,000 or imprisonment for not more than five years or both may be imposed for criminal violations.

II. The Securities Exchange Act of 1934–This act deals mainly with the secondary distribution (resale) of securities. It seeks to ensure fair and orderly securities markets by establishing rules for the operation of the markets and by prohibiting fraudulent and manipulative practices. The act provides protection for holders of securities listed on national exchanges and holders of equity securities of companies traded over the counter if their assets exceed $10 million and they have a class of equity securities with 500 or more shareholders. The National Securities Markets Improvements Act of 1996 broadly authorized SEC to issue regulations, rules, or orders exempting any person, security, or transaction from any of the provisions of the 1934 act or SEC rules promulgated thereunder.

A. Disclosure–The 1934 act imposes significant disclosure requirements upon reporting companies including filing registrations of securities, periodic reports, disclosure statements for proxy solicitations, and disclosure statements for tender offers, as well as compliance with the Foreign Corrupt Practices Act. In 1992, the SEC started requiring disclosure of compensation paid to senior executives and directors.

1. Registration Requirements for Securities–The 1934 act requires all regulated publicly held companies to register with the SEC. These registrations are one-time registrations that apply to the entire class of securities. Registration requires disclosure of the organization, financial structure, and nature of the business; the terms, positions, rights, and privileges of the different classes of outstanding securities; the names of the directors, officers, and underwriters and each holder who owns more than 10% of any class of nonexempt equity security; bonus and profit-sharing arrangements; and balance sheets and profit and loss statements for the three preceding fiscal years.

2. Periodic Reporting Requirements–Annual and periodic updates must be filed by the issuer. Directors, officers, and any person who owns more than 10% of a registered equity security must file reports if there has been any change in their ownership. A report must be filed with the SEC before the end of the second business day after the day in which a change occurs.

The SEC has adopted rules under the Sarbanes-Oxley Act that require an issuer's chief executive and chief financial officers to certify financial and other information stated in the issuer's annual and quarterly reports as well as requiring these officers to certify other matters. A CEO or CFO who certifies while a report knowing that it does not comply is subject to a fines and/or imprisonment. This Act also requires that issuers disclose in plain English to the public on a rapid and current basis such additional information concerning material changes in the financial condition or operations of the issuer as the SEC decides is needed to protect investors

3. Proxy Solicitations–A proxy is a writing signed by a shareholder of a corporation authorizing a named person to vote his shares of stock at a specified meeting of the shareholders. The 1934 act regulates the proxy solicitation process. It makes it unlawful for any person to solicit any proxy concerning any registered security "in contravention of such rules and regulations as the Commission may prescribe." Solicitation includes any request for a proxy, any request not to execute a proxy, or any request to revoke a proxy.

   a. Proxy Statements–Solicitation is prohibited unless each person has been furnished with a written proxy statement containing specified information. A soliciting issuer must furnish security holders with a proxy statement, a proxy form, and in the case of the election of directors an annual report along with the proxy statement.

   b. Shareholder Proposals–Where management makes a solicitation, the corporation must, on written request, mail at the security holder's expense the communication of any security holder entitled to vote or furnish to the security holder a current list of other holders. Management must include any security holder's timely proposals for action at a forthcoming meeting in its proxy statement and provide security holders with an opportunity to vote for or against them. Management may omit a proposal if (1) under state law it is not a proper subject for shareholder action, (2) it would require the company to violate any law, (3) it is beyond the issuer's power to accomplish, (4) it relates to the conduct of the issuer's ordinary business operations, or (5) it relates to an election to office.

4. Tender Offers–A tender offer is a general invitation to the shareholders of a company to purchase their shares at a specified price. The 1968 Williams Act amended the 1934 act to extend reporting and disclosure requirements to tender offers and other block acquisitions. The purpose of the act is to provide public shareholders with full disclosure.

   a. Disclosure Requirements–The 1934 act imposes disclosure requirements in three situations: (1) a person or group acquires more than 5% of a class of voting securities registered under the act, (2) a person makes a tender offer for more than 5% of a class of registered equity securities, or (3) the issuer makes an offer to repurchase its own shares. The disclosure requirements for each is substantially the same. A statement must be filed with the SEC containing (1) the person's background, (2) the source of the funds used to acquire the securities, (3) the purpose of the acquisition, (4) the number of shares owned, (5) terms of the transaction, and (6) any relevant contracts, arrangements, or understandings. Anyone soliciting shareholders to accept or reject a tender offer is also subject to disclosure. The target company has ten days in which to respond to the bidder's tender offer by (1) recommending acceptance or rejection, (2) expressing no opinion and remaining neutral, or (3) stating that it is unable to take a position.

   b. Required Practices–A tender offer must be kept open for at least 20 business days and for at least ten days after any change in terms. Shareholders who tender their shares may withdraw them at any time during the offering period. All shares tendered must be purchased for the same price. A tender offeror who offers to purchase less than all the outstanding securities of the target must accept, on a *pro rata* basis, securities tendered during the offer.

   c. Defensive Tactics–When confronted by an uninvited takeover bid, or by a potential, uninvited bid, management of the target company may decide either to oppose the bid or to seek to prevent it. The tactics continue to evolve.

   d. State Regulation–More than two-thirds of the states have enacted statutes regulating tender offers. Most tend to protect the target company from an unwanted tender offer. Some give the state the power to review the merits of the offer or the adequacy of disclosure or impose waiting periods before the tender offer is effective. State statutes generally have more detailed disclosure requirements than are found in the Williams Act.

5. Foreign Corrupt Practices Act–In 1977 Congress enacted the Foreign Corrupt Practices Act. The act imposes internal control requirements on companies with registered securities and prohibits all domestic concerns from bribing foreign governmental officials. The accounting requirements of the FCPA were enacted (1) to assure that an issuer's books accurately reflect financial transactions, (2) to protect the integrity of independent audits of financial statements, and (3) to promote the reliability of financial information required by the 1934 act.

B. Liability–The 1934 act imposes sanctions for noncompliance with its disclosure and antifraud requirements including civil liability to injured parties, civil penalties, and criminal penalties.

1. Misleading Statements in Reports–Section 18 imposes civil liability upon any person who makes or causes to be made any false or misleading statement with respect to any material fact in any application, report, document, or registration filed with the SEC under the 1934 act. A person is not liable if she proves that she acted in good faith and had no knowledge that such statement was false or misleading.

2. Short-Swing Profits–Section 16(b) of the 1934 act imposes liability upon insiders–directors, officers, and any person owning more than 10% of the stock of a corporation listed on a national stock exchange or registered with the SEC–for all profits resulting from their short-swing trading in such stock. The corporation is entitled to recover any and all profit realized by an insider who sells such stock within six months from the date of its purchase or who purchases such stock within six months from the date of a sale of the stock. "Profit" is calculated by matching the highest sale price against the lowest purchase price within six months of each other, and losses cannot be used to offset profits.

3. Antifraud Provision–Section 10(b) of the 1934 act and SEC Rule 10b-5 make it unlawful for any person to do any of the following when using the mails or any other facilities of interstate commerce in connection with the purchase or sale of any security: (1) employ any device, scheme, or artifice to defraud; (2) make any untrue statement of a material fact; (3) omit to state a material fact without which the information is misleading; or (4) engage in any act, practice, or course of business that operates or would operate as a fraud or deceit on any person. The rule applies to the purchase and sale of any security regardless of whether it is registered, how it is traded, or whether it is part of an initial issuance or a secondary distribution.

   a. Requisites of Rule 10b-5–Required elements to prove include: (1) a misstatement or omission, (2) that is material, (3) made with scienter, and (4) relied upon (5) in connection with the purchase or sale of a security. Scienter is intentional and knowing conduct.

b. Insider Trading–Rule l0b-5 applies to sales or purchases of securities made by an "insider" who is aware of material information that is not available to the public. Insiders include directors, officers, employees, and agents of the issuer as well as those with whom the issuer has entrusted information solely for corporate purposes, such as underwriters, accountants, lawyers, and consultants. In some instances tippees, who are persons who receive material, nonpublic information from insiders, are also precluded from trading on that information.

SEC Rule 10b5–2 adopts the misappropriation theory of liability, which occurs if a person buys or sells a security of an issuer on the basis of material nonpublic information about that security or issuer in breach of trust or confidence that is owed to the issuer, the shareholders of that issuer or any other person who is the source of the material nonpublic information.

Under SEC Regulation FD, regulated issuers who disclose material nonpublic information to specified persons, such as securities analysts and mutual fund managers, must make public disclosure of that information. Regulation FD generally does not apply to disclosures made in connection with securities offering registered under the 1933 Act.

4. Express Insider Trading Liability–Section 20A imposes civil liability upon any person who violates the act by purchasing or selling a security while in possession of material, nonpublic information. The total amount of damages may not exceed the profit gained or loss avoided by the violation less any amount disgorged to the SEC pursuant to a court order.

5. Civil Penalties for Insider Trading–The SEC is authorized to bring an action in a U.S. district court to have a civil penalty imposed upon any person who purchases or sells a security while in possession of material, nonpublic information. Any person who controlled the violator is also liable if the controlling person knew or recklessly disregarded the fact that the controlled person was likely to commit a violation. The transaction must be on or through a national securities exchange or through a broker or dealer. The penalty may not exceed the greater of $1.275 million or three times the profit gained or the loss avoided as a result of the unlawful purchase or sale. "Profit gained" or "loss avoided" is "the difference between the purchase or sale price of the security and the value of that security as measured by the trading price of the security a reasonable period after public dissemination of the nonpublic information."

6. Misleading Proxy Statements–Any person who distributes a materially false or misleading proxy statement may be liable to a shareholder who suffers a loss caused by purchasing or selling a security in reliance upon the statement. A misstatement or omission is material if there is a substantial likelihood that a reasonable shareholder would consider it important in deciding how to vote. Remedies include injunction, rescission, damages, and attorneys' fees.

7. Fraudulent Tender Offers–Section 14(e) makes it unlawful for any person to make any untrue statement of material fact or omit to state any material fact or to engage in any fraudulent, deceptive, or manipulative practices in connection with any tender offer. Some courts have implied civil liability for violations of Section 14(e).

8. Antibribery Provision of FCPA–The FCPA makes it unlawful for any domestic concern or any of its officers, directors, employees, or agents to offer or give anything of value directly or indirectly to any foreign official, political party, or political official for the purpose of (1) influencing any act or decision of that person or party in his or its official capacity, (2) inducing an act or omission in violation of his or its lawful duty, or (3) inducing such person or party to use his or its influence to affect a decision of a foreign government in order to assist the domestic concern in obtaining or retaining business.

9. Criminal Sanctions–Section 32 of the 1934 act imposes criminal sanctions on any person who willfully violates any of the provisions of the act or the rules and regulations promulgated by the SEC pursuant to the act. Conviction may carry a fine of not more than $5 million or imprisonment of not more than 20 years, or both, for individuals. Business entities may be fined up to $25 million.

KEY TERMS

1. Blue Sky Laws

2. Prospectus

3. Security

4. Investment contract

5. Shelf registration

6. Restricted securities

7. Private placement

8. Accredited investors

9. Affiliate

10. Control

11. Due diligence defense

12. Proxy

13. Proxy statement

14. Tender offer

15. Short-swing profits

16. Insider

17. Tippee

TRUE/FALSE

_____ 1. A primary purpose in requiring a registration statement to be filed with the SEC is to allow the SEC to verify the information contained therein and guarantee its accuracy.

_____ 2. Exempt securities may be resold without registration.

_____ 3. Under the Securities Enforcement Remedies and Penny Stock Reform Act, the SEC may impose administrative, civil penalties up to $600,000.

_____ 4. The National Securities Markets Improvements Act of 1996 preempts state regulation of the offerings of certain securities.

_____ 5. Securities sold under the private placement exemption may be purchased by an unlimited number of purchasers.

_____ 6. Computer bulletin boards are defined by the SEC as electronic media and must therefore meet SEC requirements.

_____ 7. Courts will examine the economic realities of a transaction in determining whether a financial transaction is a security.

_____ 8. The Securities Exchange Act of 1934 applies only to companies whose assets exceed $10 million and who have a class of equity securities with 500 or more shareholders.

_____ 9. Under the integrated reporting system with respect to registration of securities, the SEC defines a small business issuer as a non-investment company whose annual revenues total less than $25 million and whose voting and nonvoting common stock has a market value of less than $25 million.

_____ 10. Liability under Rule 10b-5 may be imposed upon buyers as well as sellers.

_____ 11. Fines imposed upon individuals for violations of the Foreign Corrupt Practices Act may not be paid by the corporation on whose behalf they acted.

_____ 12. Scienter is required for an individual to violate the provisions of Rule 10b-5.

_____ 13. The 1934 act imposes disclosure requirements for a person who makes a tender offer for more than 5 percent of a class of registered equity securities.

_____ 14. Limited partnership interests are not considered securities as defined by the 1933 act.

_____ 15. The Reform Act provides "forward-looking" statements a "safe harbor" from civil liability.

MULTIPLE CHOICE

_____ 1. The effective date of a registration statement is:
   a. the day it is filed with the SEC.
   b. the tenth day after it is filed with the SEC.
   c. the twentieth day after it is filed with the SEC.
   d. none of the above.

_____ 2. The "forward-looking" safe harbor provision eliminates civil liability if the statement is:
   a. immaterial.
   b. made without knowledge of its falsity.
   c. either (a) or (b).
   d. neither (a) nor (b).

_____ 3. "Forward-looking" statements include which of the following?
   a. Projections of revenues
   b. Projected earnings per share
   c. Projections of capital expenditures
   d. All of the above

_____ 4. Under the *Howey* test, an investment contract must:
   a. involve an investment in a common venture.
   b. be premised on a reasonable expectation of profit.
   c. be derived from the efforts of others.
   d. all of the above.

_____ 5. Under Rule 506 of the SEC, an issuer may make a private placement of unregistered securities of up to:
   a. $500,000.
   b. $1,500,000.
   c. $5,000,000.
   d. Unlimited amount.

_____ 6. Violators of the 1933 act are subject to:
   a. administrative remedies by the SEC.
   b. civil liability to injured investors.
   c. criminal penalties.
   d. all of the above.

_____ 7. There are no defenses to:
   a. selling an unregistered security which is required to be registered.
   b. including in a registration statement any untrue statement or omission of material fact.
   c. selling a security by means of a prospectus which includes an untrue statement of material fact or an omission of a material fact.
   d. (b) and (c), but not (a).

_____ 8. Corporate insiders who buy the stock of the corporation will be liable to the corporation for any profits made pursuant to a sale of that stock within:
   a. 20 days.
   b. 90 days.
   c. 6 months.
   d. 12 months.

_____ 9. Assume Alice, an officer of the DHI Computer Corporation, buys 700 shares of DHI stock on January 1 for $10 per share and 800 shares of DHI stock on March 15 for $8 per share. If Alice then sells 600 of these shares on June 30 for $12 per share and the remaining 900 shares on October 15 for $14 per share, Alice will be liable to DHI for:
   a. $12,000.
   b. $2,000.
   c. $2,400.
   d. $4,000.

_____ 10. Under the 1933 act, which of the following transactions would be exempt from registration?
   a. Private placements
   b. Limited offers solely to accredited investors
   c. Limited offers not exceeding $1 million
   d. All of the above

_____ 11. Sanctions under the 1934 act for noncompliance with the act include which of the following?
   a. Civil liability to injured investors
   b. Civil penalties
   c. Criminal penalties
   d. All of the above

_____ 12. Which of the following is correct with respect to Section 16(b)?
   a. It applies only to transactions involving registered securities.
   b. It uses the same definition of "insider" as does Rule 10b-5.
   c. It requires that an insider possess material nonpublic information.
   d. All of the above are correct with respect to 16(b).

_____ 13. Which of the following are included within the definition of insiders for the purposes of Rule 10b-5?
   a. Directors
   b. Officers
   c. Employees
   d. Directors, officers, and employees are all insiders under Rule 10b-5

_____ 14. *CPA:* Under the Securities Act of 1933, which of the following securities must be registered?
   a. Bonds of a railroad corporation
   b. Common stock of an insurance corporation
   c. Preferred stock of a domestic bank corporation
   d. Long-term notes of a charitable corporation

_____ 15. *CPA:* Data Inc. intends to make a $375,000 common stock offering under Rule 504 of Regulation D of the Securities Act of 1933. Data:
   a. may sell the stock to an unlimited number of investors.
   b. may make the offering through a general advertising.
   c. must offer the stock for a period of more than 12 months.
   d. must provide all investors with a prospectus.

SHORT ESSAY

1. What is the primary purpose of federal securities regulation?

_____

_____

_____

_____

2. What information must typically be disclosed in a registration statement?

_____

_____

_____

_____

3. Define a security.

_____

_____

_____

_____

4. What is Rule 10b-5?

_____

_____

_____

_____

5. The Breakers Corporation has assets of $3 million and 300 shareholders owning common stock. The board of directors plans to issue $500,000 of common stock to raise additional capital. If Breakers plans to trade the stock over the counter, does it need to register with the SEC?

_____

_____

_____

_____

Chapter 41
Intellectual Property

PURPOSE

In this chapter, you study the law that has been developed to prevent businesses from taking unfair advantage of their competitors. An important part of this area of law involves the protection of intellectual property. Intellectual property includes trade secrets, trade symbols, copyrights, and patents. Businesses would be less willing to invest their resources in research and development unless the resulting discoveries, inventions, and processes were protected by patents and trade secrets. Similarly, business would not be secure in devoting time and money to the marketing of its products and services if its trade symbols and trade names were not protected. Without copyright protection, the publishing, entertainment, and computer software industries would be vulnerable. In this chapter, you study the law protecting (1) trade secrets; (2) trade symbols, which include trademarks, service marks, certification marks, collective marks, and trade names; (3) copyrights; and (4) patents.

CHAPTER CHECKPOINTS

After reading and studying this chapter, you should be able to:

1. Explain what is protected by trade secrets and how they may be infringed.

2. Distinguish among trademarks, service marks, certification marks, collective marks, and trade names.

3. Discuss the extent to which trade names are protected.

4. Distinguish between a patent and a copyright and compare the protection given to each.

5. List and discuss the remedies for copyright infringement and those for patent infringement.

CHAPTER OUTLINE

A. Trade Secrets–Every business has secret information.   This commercially valuable, secret information is considered a trade secret. The Uniform Trade Secrets Act has been adopted by nearly all states.

   1. Definition–A trade secret is commercially valuable information that is guarded from disclosure. Trade secrets include customer lists, contracts with suppliers and customers, secret formulas, processes, and methods used in the production of goods. Trade secrets are disclosed in confidence to employees with the understanding that they will not disclose the information.

   2. Misappropriation–Misappropriation is the wrongful use of a trade secret. Trade secrets are misappropriated in two ways: (1) an employee wrongfully uses or discloses it; or (2) a competitor wrongfully obtains it. An employee is under a duty of loyalty to the employer which includes the nondisclosure of trade secrets to competitors. In the absence of a contract restriction, after termination of employment, the employee may compete with a former employer, but may not use trade secrets or disclose them to third persons. A former employee is entitled to use skill, knowledge and general information acquired during the employment relationship. Industrial espionage by means of electronic surveillance, spies, or discovery of trade secrets by means other than one's own independent research efforts or inspection of the finished product is improper unless the other party voluntarily discloses the secret or fails to take reasonable precautions to protect its secrecy. Other improper means of acquiring trades secrets are theft, bribery, fraud, unauthorized interception, and breach of confidence.

   3. Remedies–Remedies for misappropriation are damages and, where appropriate, injunctive relief.

   4. Criminal Penalties–In 1996 Congress enacted the Economic Espionage Act prohibiting the theft of trade secrets and providing criminal penalties for violations. Theft is broadly defined under the act.

B. Trade Symbols–One of the earliest forms of unfair competition was the fraudulent marketing of one person's goods as those of another, referred to as "passing off" or "palming off." The federal Trademark Act (the Lanham Act) provides protection against palming off, a practice which results in deception of the public and loss of trade by honest businesses by cashing in on the good name, goodwill, and reputation of a competitor. This section also prohibits the false description or representation of a person's own goods or services. In 1988, the section was amended to prohibit misrepresentations of another's goods, services, or commercial activities. It also forbids "reverse palming off" which occurs when a producer misrepresents someone else's goods as his or her own. The Lanham Act established a federal registration of trade symbols and protection against misuse or infringement by injunctive relief and the right of action for damages against an infringer. Remedies include injunctive relief, an accounting for profits, damages, destruction of infringing articles, costs, and sometimes attorneys' fees.

   1. Types of Trade Symbols–The Lanham Act recognizes four types of trade symbols or marks. A trademark is a distinctive symbol, word, name, device, letter, number, design, picture, or combination in any form or arrangement that is adopted or used by a person to identify goods he manufactures or sells. A service mark is used to identify and distinguish the services of one person from those of another. The titles, character names, and other distinctive features of radio

and television shows may be registered as service marks. A certification mark is a distinctive symbol, work, or design used with goods or services to certify specific characteristics. These characteristics include regional or other origin, material, mode of manufacture, quality, accuracy, or other characteristics. The owner of the certification mark need not be the producer or provider of the goods or services. A collective mark is a distinctive mark or symbol used to indicate either membership in a trade union, trade association, fraternal society, or other organization, or that the goods or services are produced by members of a collective group. The owner of a collective mark is the group to which the producer or provider belongs.

2. Registration–To be protected by the Lanham Act, a mark must be distinctive so that it identifies the origin of the goods or services. Marks that are fanciful or arbitrary satisfy the distinctiveness requirement. In contrast, a descriptive or geographic designation is not inherently distinctive. The word "Plow" cannot be a trademark for plows, but it may be one for shoes.

Federal registration is not required to establish rights in a mark, but doing so provides certain additional protections. To obtain federal protection, the mark must be registered with the Patent and Trademark Office. Registration gives nationwide constructive notice of the mark to all users, and it permits the registrant to use the federal courts to enforce it. Registration of the mark is *prima facie* evidence of the registrant's exclusive right to use it. To retain trademark protection an owner must not abandon the mark by failing to make bona fide use of it in the ordinary course of trade. U.S. registration accords protection only in the United States. However, under the Madrid Protocol, U.S. trademark owners may file for registration in over 65 member countries by filing a single application. Registration is good for 10 years with unlimited 10-year renewals.

Descriptive or geographic names may become protected by acquiring distinctiveness through "secondary meaning." A mark acquires a secondary meaning when a substantial number of prospective buyers associate it with the product or service it identifies. The trademark office may accept as prima facie evidence of secondary meaning proof of substantially exclusive and continuous use for five years.

Federal registration cannot be obtained for marks that are immoral, deceptive, or scandalous or if they disparage or falsely suggest connection with persons, institutions, beliefs, or national symbols.

3. Infringement–Infringement occurs when a person without authorization uses an identical or substantially identical mark that is likely to cause confusion or mistake or to deceive. Neither intent to cause confusion nor proof of actual confusion is required. If an appreciable number of ordinarily prudent purchasers are likely to be confused or misled, then infringement occurs. Courts consider these factors in deciding whether infringement has occurred: the strength of the mark, the intent of the unauthorized user, the degree of similarity between the two marks, the relation between the two marks, the relation between the two products or services identified by the marks, and the marketing channels through which the goods or services are purchased.

The Federal Trademark Dilution Act of 1995 amended the Lanham Act to protect marks from dilution. Dilution is the lessening of a mark's ability to identify and distinguish goods or services even where there is no competition between the marks and the other party's use of the mark does not result in the likelihood of confusion.

4. Remedies– Remedies under the Lanham Act include: (1) injunctive relief, (2) an accounting for profits, (3) damages, (4) destruction of infringing articles; (5) attorneys' fees in exceptional

cases, and (6) costs. In assessing profits, the plaintiff need only prove the gross sales made by the defendant; the defendant must prove any costs to be deducted. The court may award an amount it determines to be just, and it may award up to three times the actual damages. When an infringement is knowing and intentional, the court may award attorney's fees plus the greater of treble profits or treble damages, unless there are extenuating circumstances, or the innocent party may claim statutory damages. Where a counterfeit mark is intentionally and knowingly used, criminal sanctions for the first offense may be imposed which include a fine of up to $2 million and/or imprisonment up to 10 years.

C. Trade Names–A trade name is a name used to identify a business, vocation, or occupation. Descriptive and generic words, and personal and generic names may become protected as trade names upon acquiring a special significance in the trade by virtue of a "secondary meaning." Although trade names are not federally registered, they are protected, and a person who palms off his goods or services is liable in damages and may be enjoined from doing so.

D. Copyrights–A copyright is the exclusive right to original works of authorship. Under the Federal Copyright Act, original works which can be protected include software, computer mask works, literary works, musical works, dramatic works, pantomimes, choreographic works, pictorial, graphic and sculptural works, motion pictures and other audiovisual works, sound recordings, architectural works and any other "original works of authorship in any tangible medium of expression, now known or later developed." Copyright protection cannot be obtained for an idea, procedure, process, system, method of operation, concept, principle, or discovery.

1. Procedure–Registration of a copyright is not required because copyright protection begins as soon as a work is fixed in a tangible medium. Registration is advisable, though, because it is a required in order to obtain certain remedies for infringement. When a work is published, a notice of copyright should be placed on all publicly distributed copies to give reasonable notice.

2. Rights–In most instances, copyright protection continues for the period of the author's life plus an additional 70 years. The Copyright Act gives the owner of the copyright the exclusive right, and the right to authorize others, to reproduce the work, prepare derivative works, distribute copies or recordings, perform the work publicly, and display the work publicly. These broad rights are subject to "compulsory licenses" and "fair use." Compulsory licenses permit certain limited uses of copyrighted materials upon the payment of specified royalties and compliance with statutory conditions. Under the act, the fair use of a copyrighted work for purposes such as criticism, comment, news reporting, teaching, scholarship, or research is not an infringement of the copyright. The following factors are used in determining whether a particular case is a fair use: (1) the purpose and character of the use, including whether such use is of a commercial nature or is for nonprofit educational purposes; (2) the nature of the copyrighted work; (3) the amount and substantiality of the portion used in relation to the work as a whole; and (4) the effect of the use upon the potential market for or value of the work.

3. Ownership–The "author" of a work is the owner of a copyright. Ownership may be transferred in whole or in part by conveyance, will, or intestate succession. A transfer of copyright ownership is not valid unless there is a note or memorandum of the transfer in writing and signed by the owner of the rights or by the owner's authorized agent. An author may terminate any transfer of copyright ownership, other than a work for hire, if timely done. Ownership of a

copyright or of the exclusive rights under a copyright is distinct from ownership of a material object in which the work is embodied. The purchase of a textbook does not affect the publisher's copyright, nor does it authorize the purchaser to make and sell copies of the book.

The actual creator of a work is the author (and owner) of a work except in two situations. First, if an employee prepares a work within the scope of her employment, then the employer is the author (and owner) of the work. Second, if a work is specially ordered or commissioned for certain purposes and the parties expressly agree in writing that the work shall be considered a work for hire, the person commissioning the work is deemed to be the author (and owner). In a work for hire situation, a copyright lasts for 95 years from the year of its first publication or 120 years from the year of its creation, whichever expires first.

4. Infringement and Remedies–Infringement occurs when someone without authorization exercises the rights exclusively reserved for the copyright owner. To prove infringement, the plaintiff must establish ownership of the copyright and prove that the defendant violated one or more of the exclusive rights under the copyright. The copyright must be registered in order to sue for infringement unless the work is a Berne Convention work and the country of origin is not the United States. If an infringement occurs after registration, the following remedies are available: (1) injunction, (2) impoundment and possible destruction of the infringing articles, (3) actual damages plus profits made by the infringer in addition to the statutory damages of at least $750, but no more than $30,000 and up to $150,000 if the infringement is willful, (4) in the court's discretion costs including reasonable attorneys' fees to the prevailing party, or (5) criminal penalties of a fine and/or up to one year in prison for willful infringement for purposes of commercial advantage or private gain. Other recent federal laws include:
   - The No Electronic Theft Act: increases criminal penalties for certain copyright violations;
   - The Digital Millenium Copyright Act of 1998: creates limits on liability of online providers for copyright infringement;
   - The Family Entertainment and Copyright Act of 2005: imposes criminal penalties for willful copyright infringement by bootlegging copyrighted audio and video works or recording a cinema-released film on videotape from the audience; and
   - The Anti-counterfeiting Amendments Act of 2004: forbids knowingly trafficking in counterfeit copies of a computer program, motion picture and certain other types of works.

E. Patents–A patent is a federal government grant to the inventor of the exclusive right to make, use, or sell the invention for the period of the patent. The owner may license others to use the patent on a royalty basis. However, the patent may not be renewed. Upon its expiration, the invention enters the "public domain" and anyone may use it. A U.S. patent applies only to the United States. A party must apply for patent protection in other desired countries. The Patent Cooperation Treaty helps facilitate this process.
1. Patentability–Under the Patent Act, any new and useful process, machine, manufacture, or composition of matter, or any new and useful improvement thereof may be patented as a utility patent. Naturally occurring substances, laws of nature, principles, systems of bookkeeping, fundamental truths, methods of calculation, and ideas are not patentable. Isolated computer programs are not patentable, but may be copyrighted. To be patentable, the process, machine, manufacture, or composition of matter must have three criteria: (1) novelty, (2) utility, and (3) nonobviousness. In addition to utility patents, the Patent Act provides for plant patents and

design patents.   Utility patents and   plant patents have a 20-year term from the date of application. Design patents have a term of 14 years.

2. Procedure–A patent is issued by the United States Patent and Trademark Office based on a patent application that contains a "specification" describing how the invention works, and "claims" describing the features of the invention that make it patentable. The applicant must be the inventor. The Patent Office then makes an examination and determines whether the submitted invention has novelty (i.e., does not conflict with a prior pending application or issued patent), utility, and is nonobvious. A patent application ordinarily is confidential, but the confidentiality ends upon the granting of the patent. (As an exception, certain utility and plant patent applications must be published 18 months after filing if the applications are filed in other countries that require publication after 18 months or publication is required under the Patent Cooperation Treaty.)

An applicant may apply for reexamination if an application is rejected. If the application is rejected again, the applicant may appeal to the Patent and Trademark Office's Board of Appeals. From there, appeal is to the federal courts. Unlike rights under a copyright, no monopoly rights arise until the Patent Office actually issues a patent.

3. Infringement–A direct infringer is anyone who makes, uses, or sells a patented invention without permission. Good faith or ignorance is not a defense to direct infringement. An indirect infringer is a person who actively encourages another to make, use, or sell a patented invention without permission. A contributory infringer knowingly sells or supplies a part or component of a patented invention unless the item supplied is a commodity suitable for a noninfringing use. Good faith and ignorance are defenses to contributory infringement.

4. Remedies–Under the Patent Act, remedies include: (1) injunctive relief, (2) damages adequate to compensate the plaintiff but "in no event less than a reasonable royalty for the use made of the invention by the infringer", (3) treble damages when appropriate, (4) attorneys' fees in exceptional cases such as knowing infringement, and (5) costs.

KEY TERMS

1. Infringement

2. Trade secret

3. Misappropriation

4. Mark

5. Trademark

6. Service mark

7. Certification mark

8. Collective mark

9. Secondary meaning

10. Trade name

11. Copyright

12. Compulsory license

13. Fair use

14. Works for hire

15. Utility patent

16. Design patent

17. Direct infringer

18. Contributory infringer

TRUE/FALSE

_____ 1. The granting of a patent guarantees the patent holder the exclusive right to make, use, or sell the invention for the period of the patent.

_____ 2. The owner of a certification mark must be the producer or provider of the mark.

_____ 3. Copyright protection may be used to protect an original idea or concept.

_____ 4. Under the "fair use" doctrine, use of a copyrighted work for teaching is an infringement.

_____ 5. Kohl Computer Company has been having problems with competitors copying and selling its computer software. Computer software may be copyrighted.

_____ 6. Kohl Computer Company has invented a new and innovative personal computer. A computer may be copyrighted.

_____ 7. In order to recover statutory damages and attorneys' fees for copyright infringement, the work must be registered.

_____ 8. A design patent has a term of 20 years.

_____ 9. The Lanham Act provides protection against the palming off of another's goods as one's own.

_____ 10. Elaine has worked as an engineer in the product development department of Techno Computer Company. Elaine may quit the Techno job and then sell to Techno's competitors the secret information she has learned in her job.

_____ 11. Ownership of a copyright is the same as ownership of a physical object that embodies the work.

_____ 12. Infringement of a mark may occur even without an intent to cause confusion among purchasers.

_____ 13. If a person misappropriates a trade secret, the owner of the information may obtain damages.

_____ 14. A counterfeit mark means a spurious mark that is identical to a registered mark.

_____ 15. Compulsory licenses permit certain limited uses of copyrighted material upon payment of specified royalties and compliance with statutory conditions.

MULTIPLE CHOICE

_____ 1. A _____ is often used to identify a provider's services.
   a. trademark
   b. service mark
   c. collective mark
   d. certification mark

_____ 2. To obtain federal protection, a mark must be registered and the registrant must have:
   a.   actually used the mark.
   b.   showed a bona fide intent to use the mark in commerce and actually use it within 6 months.
   c.   either (a) or (b).
   d.   neither (a) nor (b).

_____ 3. "Kodak," "Chef Boyardee" and the rainbow apple logo on Apple computers are examples of:
   a.   certification marks.
   b.   service marks.
   c.   trademarks.
   d.   copyrights.

_____ 4. Which of the following items would not be patentable?
   a.   A computer
   b.   A genetically engineered bacterium
   c.   A process by which to manufacture a new product
   d.   All of the above are patentable

_____ 5. The Lanham Act provides criminal sanctions for intentionally and knowingly using a counterfeit mark . These penalties include up to five years in prison and up to:
   a. $25,000.
   b. $200,000.
   c. $250,000.
   d. $500,000.

_____ 6. Who grants a patent?
   a.   The United States Patent and Trademark Office
   b.   The Secretary of State of the state where the inventor resides
   c.   The Federal Trade Commission
   d.   The Library of Congress

_____ 7. The big "G" on a box of General Mills breakfast cereal is an example of a:
   a.   service mark.
   b.   copyright.
   c.   collective mark.
   d.   trademark.

_____ 8. Brenda photocopies ten copies of an article from the *Wall Street Journal* and distributes them at the weekly management meeting of the TKY Company management team. Select the correct answer regarding the copyright on the article that is held by the *Wall Street Journal*.
   a.   Brenda has probably infringed the copyright if she neglected to obtain the permission of the *Wall Street Journal*.
   b.   Copyright protection does not extend to newspaper articles.
   c.   This is probably the fair use of the copyrighted article which is not an infringement.
   d.   Brenda appears to have violated the Piracy and Counterfeiting Amendments Act of 1982.

_____ 9. The "REAL" symbol used to identify genuine dairy products is an example of a:
    a. trademark.
    b. service mark.
    c. collective mark.
    d. certification mark.

_____ 10. To register a mark with the Patent and Trademark Office an applicant must:
    a. have actually used the mark in commerce.
    b. demonstrate a bona fide intent to use the mark in commerce and actually use it within six months.
    c. both (a) and (b).
    d. either (a) or (b).

_____ 11. If Jons, a famous musician, wants to protect one of his original works, he should use a:
    a. patent.
    b. copyright.
    c. trade name.
    d. trademark.

_____ 12. Marriott has a distinctive mark which is used to identify its hotels. This is an example of a:
    a. copyright.
    b. collective mark.
    c. service mark.
    d. certification mark.

_____ 13. Trade secrets are misappropriated by:
    a. an employee wrongfully using or disclosing it.
    b. a competitor wrongfully obtaining it.
    c. a competitor obtaining it by independent research efforts.
    d. two of the above are correct, (a) and (b).

_____ 14. Which of the following remedies are provided by the Lanham Act for infringement of a mark?
    a. Destruction of infringing articles
    b. An accounting for profits
    c. Damages
    d. All of the above

_____ 15. If Bobby actively encourages Giant M Company to make a machine and he knows it is a patented item and they do not have permission, Bobby is:
    a. an indirect infringer.
    b. a direct infringer.
    c. a contributory infringer.
    d. none of the above.

SHORT ESSAY

1. If registration of a copyright is not necessary and copyright protection begins as soon as the work is fixed in a tangible medium, what is the advantage in registering it?

   _____

   _____

   _____

   _____

2. Define the four types of trade symbols recognized by the Lanham Act.

   _____

   _____

   _____

   _____

3. Identify two limitations on the broad rights of a copyright owner.

   _____

   _____

   _____

   _____

4. Mark, a salesman for Briarton Company, resigns from his job. He then accepts employment with CompCo, a competitor of Briarton. Mark provides to CompCo a list of Briarton's customers which he had obtained as an employee of Briarton. What is the result?

   _____

   _____

   _____

   _____

5. What remedies are available for infringement of trade symbols?

   _____

   _____

   _____

   _____

Chapter 42
Employment Law

PURPOSE

The common law governed the relationship between employer and employee in terms of tort and contract duties. This common law has been supplemented or replaced by federal and state legislation. In this chapter, you study (1) labor law–the general framework in which management and labor negotiate and bargain over the terms of employment; (2) employment discrimination law–federal legislation to prohibit discrimination in employment based upon race, sex, religion, age, disability, or national origin; and (3) employee protection law–legislation which mandates that employers provide a safe and healthy work environment for their employees and provide compensation to employees injured during the course of employment.

CHAPTER CHECKPOINTS

After reading and studying this chapter, you should be able to:

1. List and discuss the major federal statutes that govern the relationship between an employer and a union representing employees.

2. List the unfair labor practices of an employer and of a union and distinguish between a closed shop and a union shop.

3. List the major federal statutes that govern the area of employment discrimination and discuss the provisions of each.

4. Discuss how the workers' compensation laws changed the common law with respect to injuries sustained by employees on the job.

5. List the major provisions of the OSHA and Social Security statutes and discuss the purpose and effect of OSHA on employment conditions.

CHAPTER OUTLINE

A. Labor Law–The following statutes provide the general framework in which management and labor negotiate and bargain over the terms of employment. They are designed to promote both labor-management harmony and the welfare of society at large.

1. Norris-LaGuardia Act–This act was enacted in 1932 in response to the growing criticism of the use of injunctions in peaceful labor disputes. It withdrew from the federal courts the power to issue injunctions in nonviolent labor disputes. The term labor dispute includes any controversy concerning terms or conditions of employment or union representation. The act declared the policy of the United States to be that labor has full freedom to form labor unions and prohibited "yellow dog" contracts requiring employees to promise not to join a union.

2. National Labor Relations Act–The NLRA or Wagner Act was enacted in 1935 and marked an affirmative effort by the federal government to support collective bargaining and unionization. The act provides that "the right to self-organization, to form, join or assist labor organizations, to bargain collectively through representatives of their own choosing, and to engage in concerted activities for the purpose of collective bargaining or other mutual aid or protection" is a federally protected right. The act gave employees the right to be represented by a union and enforces this right by prohibiting certain conduct known as unfair labor practices by employers and unions. Unfair employer practices prohibited by the act include interference with the right to unionize, discriminating against union members, and refusing to bargain in good faith. The act establishes the National Labor Relations Board (NLRB) to remedy unfair labor practices and to supervise elections.

3. Labor-Management Relations Act–The LMRA or Taft-Hartley Act was passed by Congress in 1947 in response to an increase in union membership and labor unrest following passage of the NLRA. The LMRA prohibits certain unfair union practices such as coercing employees to join a union, causing employers to discharge nonunion employees, refusing to bargain in good faith, levying excessive union dues, featherbedding, and engaging in secondary activities, such as boycotts, strikes, or picketing an employer with whom there is no labor dispute. The act also fosters employer free speech by declaring that no employer unfair labor practices can be based on a statement of opinion. The LMRA also prohibits the closed shop, which is a contract that requires the employer to hire only union members. A union shop contract permits the employer to hire nonunion members but requires them to join the union within a specified period after being hired. A right-to-work law is a state statute that prohibits union shop contracts. Finally, the act reinstates the civil injunctions in labor disputes if requested by the NLRB to prevent an unfair labor practice and grants the president the power to obtain an injunction for an 80-day cooling-off period for a strike likely to endanger national health or safety.

4. Labor-Management Reporting and Disclosure Act–This act, also known as the Landrum-Griffin Act, was passed in 1959 to eliminate corruption in labor unions. It established a reporting system and enacted a union "bill of rights" designed to make unions more democratic.

B. Employment Discrimination Law–These federal statutes prohibit discrimination in employment on the basis of race, sex, religion, national origin, age, and disability. Title VII of the 1964 Civil Rights Act is the cornerstone employment discrimination law. Two recent discrimination laws are: the

Civil Rights Act of 1991 and the Americans with Disabilities Act of 1990. Most states have enacted similar laws.

1. Equal Pay Act–This act prohibits an employer from discriminating between employees on the basis of sex by paying unequal wages for the same work. An employer may pay unequal wages for equal work to members of the opposite sex if the pay differential is based on a seniority system, a merit system, a system that measures earnings by quantity or quality of production, or any factor except gender. Remedies include back pay, an award of liquidated damages, and injunctions to prohibit further unlawful conduct. Today, the act is enforced by the Equal Employment Opportunity Commission (EEOC).

2. Civil Rights Act of 1964–Title VII of the Civil Rights Act of 1964 prohibits employment discrimination on the basis of race, color, sex, religion, or national origin in hiring, firing, compensating, promoting, or training and other employment-related processes. In 1978 Title VII benefits were extended to pregnant women. The act applies to employers in any business affecting commerce and having 15 or more employees, labor unions with 15 or more members, and the federal, state, and local governments. The EEOC is the enforcement agency.

   a. Proving Discrimination–The following types of conduct are prohibited by the act: (1) disparate treatment–a *prima facie* case of discrimination is shown if the plaintiff (a) is within a protected class, (b) applied for an open position, (c) was qualified for the position, (d) was denied the job, and (e) the employer continued to try to fill the position; (2) present effects of past discrimination–conduct by an employer that is "neutral" and nondiscriminatory on its face is illegal if it perpetuates past discriminatory practices; and (3) disparate impact–"neutral" rules are illegal if they have an adverse impact on a protected class and are not necessary to the business. A "mixed motive" case (i.e., employer considers both permissible and impermissible factors) also may give rise to certain remedies.

   b. Defenses–Defenses in the act include: (1) a *bona fide* seniority or merit system, (2) a professionally developed ability test, and (3) a *bona fide* occupational qualification (BFOQ); (4) a compensation system based on performance; and (5) a "business necessity" in connection with disparate impact cases.

   c. Remedies–These include injunction, appropriate affirmative action, and reinstatement of employees and award of back pay. Affirmative action is the active recruitment of a designated group of applicants.

   d. Reverse Discrimination–Reverse discrimination refers to affirmative action that directs an employer to remedy the under representation of a given race or sex in a traditionally segregated job by considering an individual's race or gender when hiring or promoting. When a state or local government adopts an affirmative action plan that is challenged as illegal reverse discrimination, the plan is subject to strict scrutiny under the Equal Protection Clause of the 14th Amendment.

   e. Sexual Harassment–In 1980, the EEOC issued a definition of sexual harassment. Sexual harassment may constitute sexual discrimination in violation of Title VII. An employer is liable for sexual harassment committed by an employee if it knew or should have known of the harassment. If the employee is an agent of the employer or is in a supervisory position over the victim, the employer may be liable even without knowledge or reason to know.

   f. Comparable Worth–Because the Equal Pay Act only requires equal pay for equal work, it does not apply to different jobs even if they are comparable. It provides no remedy for women whose traditional jobs have been systematically undervalued and underpaid. The concept of comparable worth provides that the relative values to an employer of different jobs should be measured through a rating system or job evaluation that is free of sex bias. The concept of comparable worth is covered by Title VII but has met with limited success in the courts. Some states have adopted requirements that public and private employers pay equally for comparable work.

3. Executive Order–In 1965 President Johnson issued an executive order that prohibited discrimination by federal contractors on the basis of race, color, sex, religion, or national origin on any work performed by the contractor during the period of the federal contract. It also requires affirmative action by federal contractors. The Secretary of Labor, Office of Federal Contract Compliance Programs (OFCCP) administers enforcement of the program.

4. Age Discrimination in Employment Act of 1967–This act prohibits discrimination in hiring, firing, compensating, or otherwise on the basis of age. It applies to private employers having 20 or more employees and to all governmental units. It also prohibits the mandatory retirement of most employees unless retirement is justified by a suitable defense. Statutory defenses include a *bona fide* occupational qualification, a *bona fide* seniority system, and any other reasonable action. Remedies include back pay, injunction, affirmative action, and liquidated damages.

5. Disability Law–The Rehabilitation Act of 1973 requires federal contractors and agencies to take affirmative action to hire qualified handicapped persons. It prohibits discrimination on the basis of handicap in federal programs and programs that receive federal financial assistance. A handicapped person is one who (1) has a physical or mental impairment that substantially affects one or more major life activities, (2) has a history of major life activity impairment, or (3) is regarded as having such an impairment. Alcohol and drug abuses are not handicaps under this statute.

C. Employee Protection–Employees are accorded a number of protections relating to their jobs including a limited right not to be unfairly dismissed, a right to a safe and healthy workplace, compensation for injuries sustained in the workplace, and some financial security upon retirement or loss of employment.

1. Employee Termination at Will–Under the common law, a contract of employment for other than a definite term is terminable at will by either party. Under this rule an employer may dismiss an employee at will "for good cause, for no cause, or even for cause morally wrong, without being thereby guilty of legal wrong." In recent years, judicial exceptions have developed, federal and state statutes have been enacted, and contractual agreements have been used to limit the rule.

  a. Statutory Limitations–Federal legislation that limits an employer's right to discharge include (1) those that protect certain employees from discriminatory discharge, (2) those that protect certain employees in the exercise of statutory rights, and (3) those that protect certain employees from discharge without cause. There are also state statutes that protect workers from discriminatory discharge for filing workers' compensation claims, as well as many state statutes that parallel federal legislation.

  b. Judicial Limitations–Judicial limitations on the employment-at-will doctrine have been based on contract law, tort law, or a public policy. Cases founded in contract theory have relied on arguments that include the employer's promise of work for a reasonable period, the breaking of implied-in-fact promises of employment for a specific duration, the existence of express or implied provisions of continued employment conditioned upon satisfactory work performance, the assurance of nondismissal except for cause, and the giving of additional consideration beyond the performance of services to support job security. Tort obligations imposed on employers are frequently based upon the torts of intentional infliction of emotional distress and interference with employment relations. A majority of states consider a discharge wrongful if it violates a statutory or other established public policy, which often includes termination because an employee (1) refuses to violate a statute, (2) exercises a statutory right, (3) performs a statutory obligation, or (4) reports an alleged violation of a statute of public interest.

2. Occupational Safety and Health Act–In 1970 Congress enacted this act, which established the Occupational Safety and Health Administration (OSHA) to develop standards, conduct inspections, monitor compliance, and institute enforcement actions against those who are not in compliance. The act requires each employer to meet the general duty to provide a work environment "free from recognized hazards that are causing or likely to cause death or serious physical harm to his employees." Employers and employees must comply with OSHA rules and regulations. Employers may not discharge or discriminate against employees who exercise rights under the act. OSHA inspects workplaces and issues citations for which an employer may be both civilly and criminally liable. Most states have some form of state regulation of health and safety in the workplace.

3. Employee Privacy–The fundamental right to privacy, a product of common law, protects employees from unwanted searches, electronic monitoring and other forms of surveillance, and disclosure of confidential records by the tort of invasion of privacy. This actually consists of four different torts: (1) unreasonable intrusion into the seclusion of another; (2) unreasonable public disclosure of private facts; (3) unreasonable publicity that places another in a false light; and (4) appropriation of a person's name or likeness. Additionally, employees receive protection from federal and some state legislation.

   a. Drug and Alcohol Testing–By U.S. Supreme Court decision it would appear that a government employer may use (1) random or universal testing where public health or safety or national security is involved and (2) selective drug testing where there is a sufficient cause to believe an employee has a drug problem. In the absence of a state statute, private sector employees have little or no protection from drug or alcohol tests. In a union setting such tests are subject to collective bargaining.

   b. Lie Detector Tests–The Federal Employee Polygraph Protection Act of 1988 prohibits private employers from requiring employees or prospective employees to undergo a lie detector test, inquiring about the results of such a test, or using the results of such a test or the refusal to be tested as grounds for an adverse employment decision. The act provides for certain exemptions with regard to government employers, security firms, and manufacturers of controlled substances. An employer, as part of an ongoing investigation of economic loss or injury to its business may test; however, the use of the test must meet certain requirements: (1) it must be designed to investigate a specific incident or activity, not a chronic problem; (2) the employee must have had access to the property that is the subject of the investigation, and (3) the employer must have reason to suspect the particular employee.

4. Workers' Compensation–In order to provide speedier and more certain relief to injured employees, all states have adopted statutes, which provide workers' compensation. These statutes create boards to determine whether an injured employee is entitled to receive compensation and, if so, the amount. The common law defenses have been abolished. Employees are entitled to compensation if the employee is injured and if the injury arose out of and in the course of employment. Actions at law against the employer by the employee are not permitted, because the courts have no jurisdiction except to review decisions of the workers' compensation board or commission.

5. Social Security and Unemployment Insurance–Social Security was enacted in 1935 to provide limited retirement and death benefits to certain employees. The system now covers almost all employees and contains four major benefit programs: (1) Old-Age and Survivors Insurance (OASI), (2) Disability Insurance (DI), (3) Hospitalization Insurance (Medicare), and (4) Supplemental Security Income (SSI). The system is financed by contributions (taxes) paid by employers, employees, and self-employed individuals. Benefits vary depending on the particular program and whether the beneficiary is "fully" insured. Dependents (spouses and children) are also eligible for certain Social Security benefits. The federal unemployment insurance system was initially created by Title IX of the Social Security Act of 1935. It has been supplemented by the Federal Unemployment Tax Act and numerous other federal statutes. Employees do not pay the tax. The purpose of the tax is to provide unemployment compensation, the exact amount of which is based on each state's formula, to workers who have lost their jobs and cannot find other employment.

6. Fair Labor Standards Act–The Fair Labor Standards Act (FLSA) regulates the employment of child labor outside of agriculture. The act prohibits the employment of anyone under age 14 in nonfarm work, except for newspaper deliverers and child actors. Fourteen and fifteen-year-olds may work a limited number of hours in nonhazardous occupations. Sixteen and seventeen-year-olds may work in any nonhazardous job, while eighteen-year-olds may work in any job. The FLSA imposes wage and hour requirements upon covered employers and provides for a minimum wage and overtime pay of time-and-a-half for hours worked in excess of 40 hours per week.

7. Worker Adjustment and Retraining Notification Act–WARN requires an employer to provide 60 days' advance notice of a plant closing or mass layoff. A "plant closing" is a permanent or temporary shutting down of a single site or units within a site if the shutdown results in 50 or more employees losing employment during any 30-day period. A "mass layoff" is a loss of employment during a 30-day period either for 500 employees or for at least one-third of the employees at a given site, if that one-third equals or exceeds 50 employees.

8. Family and Medical Leave Act of 1993–Employees must be given up to 12 weeks of leave during any 12-month period for the birth of a child; adopting or gaining foster care of a child; or the care of a spouse, child, or parent who suffers from a serious health condition. Eligibility is based upon an employee's having worked for the employer at least 12 months and having worked at least 1,250 hours during the 12 months preceding the leave request. The act applies to employers with 50 or more employees as well as governments at the federal, state, and local levels. The requested leave may be paid, unpaid, or a combination of both.

KEY TERMS

1. Labor dispute
2. Unfair labor practice
3. Unfair employer practice
4. Unfair union practice
5. Closed shop
6. Union shop
7. Right-to-work law
8. Equal pay
9. Employment discrimination
10. Affirmative action
11. Reverse discrimination
12. Sexual harassment
13. Comparable worth
14. Fellow servant rule
15. Workers' compensation
16. Social Security
17. Unemployment compensation

TRUE/FALSE

_____ 1. The National Labor Relations Act guarantees the right of employees to bargain collectively.

_____ 2. The Fair Labor Standards Act regulates the employment of child labor.

_____ 3. The Equal Pay Act prohibits an employer from discriminating between employees on the basis of race, color, sex, religion, or national origin by paying unequal wages for equal work.

_____ 4. The Civil Rights Act of 1964 applies to employers engaged in an industry affecting commerce and having 15 or more employees.

_____ 5. By presidential executive order, federal contractors are exempt from affirmative action in recruiting.

_____ 6. Title VII does not prohibit discrimination based on age.

_____ 7. The customers at Chez Chic Restaurant prefer to be served by male waiters. The restaurant owner can refuse to hire women based upon gender being a *bona fide* occupational qualification.

_____ 8. Sexual harassment is not covered by the federal discrimination laws.

_____ 9. If a state government's affirmative action plan is challenged, it is subject to strict scrutiny under the Equal Protection Clause.

_____ 10. The National Labor Relations Act prohibits union shops but allows closed shops.

_____ 11. The Social Security system is financed by taxes paid by employers, employees, and self-employed individuals.

_____ 12. Common law employer defenses such as the fellow-servant rule, contributory negligence, and voluntary assumption of the risk are eliminated by workers' compensation statutes.

_____ 13. The Family and Medical Leave Act of 1993 applies where there are 50 or more employees.

_____ 14. The Equal Pay Act applies to different jobs that are comparable as well as to jobs that are equal jobs.

_____ 15. The Pregnancy Discrimination Act extends the benefits of the Civil Rights Act to pregnant women.

MULTIPLE CHOICE

_____ 1. An employer who refuses to bargain in good faith with the duly established representatives of the employees has violated the:
   a. Norris-LaGuardia Act.
   b. National Labor Relations Act.
   c. Labor-Management Relations Act.
   d. Labor-Management Reporting and Disclosure Act.

_____ 2. A union which goes on strike to force an employer to fire a nonunion employee has violated the:
   a. Norris-LaGuardia Act.
   b. National Labor Relations Act.
   c. Labor-Management Relations Act.
   d. Labor-Management Reporting and Disclosure Act.

_____ 3. Under the NLRA, which of the following is/are unfair labor practices?
   a. To dominate a union
   b. To discriminate against union members
   c. To refuse to bargain in good faith
   d. All of the above

_____ 4. The federal statute that prohibits the mandatory retirement of most employees:
   a. Rehabilitation Act of 1973.
   b. Civil Rights Act of 1964.
   c. Age Discrimination in Employment Act of 1967.
   d. Executive Order of 1965.

_____ 5. An employee who sues an employer under a workers' compensation statute for injuries arising out of and in the course of employment is subject to the defense of:
   a. contributory negligence.
   b. assumption of the risk.
   c. the fellow servant rule.
   d. none of the above.

_____ 6. The _____ is responsible for enforcing federal antidiscrimination laws.
   a. NLRB
   b. OSHA
   c. EEOC
   d. Social Security Administration

_____ 7. Which of the following is a protection accorded an employee relating to the job?
   a. Right to a safe and healthy workplace
   b. Compensation for injuries sustained in the workplace
   c. Some financial security upon retirement
   d. All of the above

_____ 8. Under the common law, employers may dismiss their employees at will:
   a. for good cause.
   b. for no cause.
   c. both of the above.
   d. none of the above.

_____ 9. Which of the following employees would not be covered by the Rehabilitation Act of 1973?
   a. An alcoholic
   b. A victim of AIDS
   c. A victim of tuberculosis
   d. A polio victim in a wheelchair

_____ 10. The Americans with Disabilities Act provides assistance to the handicapped in which of the following?
   a. Rehabilitation training
   b. Access to public facilities
   c. Employment
   d. All of the above

_____ 11. Which of the following is a valid discrimination defense under the Civil Rights Act of 1964?
   a. A *bona fide* seniority or merit system
   b. A professionally developed ability test
   c. A bona fide occupational qualification
   d. All of the above

_____ 12. Which one of the following defenses may be used by an employer to avoid responsibility for paying an employee's claim for workers' compensation?
   a. The employee assumed the risk of the injury.
   b. The employee was contributorily negligent.
   c. A co-worker actually caused the injury.
   d. The injury did not occur on the job.

_____ 13. Under the Labor-Management Relations Act which of the following union activities would be considered an unfair labor practice?
   a. Causing an employer to discriminate against a nonunion employee
   b. Coercing an employee to join a union
   c. Levying excessive dues
   d. All of the above are unfair labor practices.

_____ 14. *CPA:* Under which of the following conditions is an onsite inspection of a workplace by an investigator from the Occupational Safety and Health Administration (OSHA) permissible?
   a. Only if OSHA obtains a search warrant after showing probable cause
   b. Only if the inspection is conducted after working hours
   c. At the request of the employees
   d. After OSHA provides the employer with at least 24-hours' notice of the inspection

_____ 15. *CPA:* Under the provisions of the Americans With Disabilities Act of 1990, in which of the following areas is a disabled person protected from discrimination?

	Public transportation	Privately operated public accommodations
a.	Yes	Yes
b.	Yes	No
c.	No	Yes
d.	No	No

SHORT ESSAY

1. Briefly describe the Civil Rights Act of 1964.

    _____
    _____
    _____
    _____

2. What are the remedies available to an employee who brings a successful employment discrimination action?

    _____
    _____
    _____
    _____

3. What is the doctrine of comparable worth? Explain.

    _____
    _____
    _____
    _____

4. Ed, an employee of Ace Delivery, was injured in a car accident while making a delivery. The wreck was due to the negligence of Wes, the other driver. If Ace Delivery is covered by workers' compensation, what is the result?

    _____
    _____
    _____
    _____

5. Darla, an employee of First Bank, has brought an action against the bank based upon the alleged sexual harassment of Doug, her co-worker. What must she establish in order to prevail in this action?

    _____
    _____
    _____
    _____

Chapter 43
Antitrust

PURPOSE

Free and fair competition in industry and trade have historically been the backbone of our free enterprise system. However, with the concentrations of economic power created by the combining of forces within the business world, the need for government regulation has become increasingly apparent. With the growth of big business in the last half of the nineteenth century, the federal government came to the aid of state lawmakers in controlling business operations to assure free and fair competition. The Sherman Antitrust Act, enacted in 1890, was the first such legislative action taken by Congress. This act sought to control unfair competition by prohibiting contracts, combinations, and conspiracies that restrain trade as well as monopolies, attempts to monopolize, and conspiracies to monopolize. Other statutes in the field followed, including the Clayton Act, the Robinson-Patman Act, and the Federal Trade Commission Act. These statutes further regulated anticompetitive practices. This chapter discusses these acts and their implications regarding business practices. You will examine the various rights protected by federal legislation and the remedies provided upon infringement of fair competition.

CHAPTER CHECKPOINTS

After reading and studying this chapter, you should be able to:

1. Discuss the Sherman Antitrust Act and its rules governing trade restraints and monopolization.

2. Discuss the Clayton Act and its rules governing (a) tying contracts, (b) exclusive dealing, and (c) mergers.

3. Discuss the Robinson-Patman Act and the various defenses to it.

4. Distinguish between horizontal and vertical restraints and discuss when they are legal and illegal.

5. Discuss the role of the FTC and Justice Department in antitrust enforcement.

CHAPTER OUTLINE

A. Sherman Antitrust Act–Section 1 of the Sherman Act prohibits contracts, combinations, and conspiracies that restrain trade. Section 2 outlaws monopolies and attempts to monopolize. Failure to comply with either section is a crime. The Standards Development Organization Advancement Act of 2004 subjects individual offenders to 10 years in prison and/or fines of up to $1 million. Corporate offenders are subject to fines of up to $100 million per violation. Federal courts have the power to issue injunctions to restrain violations. A person injured by a violation may bring a civil suit for treble damages, which are three times the actual loss sustained.   The United States Department of Justice and the Federal Trade Commission have the duty to institute appropriate enforcement proceedings. Since 1992 the Justice Department also considers conduct by foreign companies that harms U.S. exports.

The case brought by the federal and numerous state governments against Microsoft, Inc. bears particular mention. In this case, Microsoft was accused of illegally maintaining its monopoly over the personal computer operating system market and then attempting to extend it into the market for Internet browsers. The U.S. Department of Justice and a number of states have settled their case with Microsoft, although some states are contesting it. The settlement allows Microsoft to remain as one company but provides that: (1) Microsoft cannot retaliate against a computer maker in any way for dealing with Microsoft's competitors; (2) Microsoft must establish and follow a schedule of fixed prices; (3) other computer makers will be allowed to install non-Microsoft products and desktop shortcuts on their computers; (4) Microsoft will reveal previously confidential programming interfaces that its products rely on to link to Windows; and (5) Microsoft will not retaliate against other companies because their products compete with other Microsoft applications.

1. Restraint of Trade–Section 1 of the Sherman Act provides that "every contract, combination in the form of trust or otherwise, or conspiracy, in restraint of trade or commerce among the several states, or with foreign nations is hereby declared to be illegal."

    a. Standards–The courts have interpreted Section 1 to invalidate only unreasonable restraints of trade. This standard is known as the rule of reason test; it requires that a court balance the anticompetitive effects of an agreement against the procompetitive effects of the restraint. Because this standard places a substantial burden upon the judicial system, the U.S. Supreme Court declared that certain categories of restraints are unreasonable by their very nature and thus illegal *per se*. In such a case, the plaintiff is required to show only that the type of restraint occurred and does not need to prove that it limited competition. During the past third, the courts started using an intermediate test the per se approach is not appropriate but the questioned actions have anticompetitive effects. Under this "quick look" rule of reason analysis, the courts apply a shortened rule of reason standard.

    b. Horizontal and Vertical Restraints–Restraints may be classified as either horizontal or vertical. A horizontal restraint involves collaboration among competitors at the same level in the chain of distribution. An agreement among manufacturers would be horizontal, as would an agreement among retailers. A vertical restraint is one that is made by parties that are not in direct competition at the same level of distribution.   An agreement between a manufacturer and a wholesaler would be vertical. Horizontal market allocations are illegal *per se*, whereas vertical market allocations are subject to the rule of reason.

c. Concerted Action–Section 1 does not prohibit unilateral conduct, only concerted action. Concerted action may be established by express agreement or by circumstantial evidence. Conscious parallelism, or similar patterns of conduct among competitors, is not sufficient in itself to infer a conspiracy in violation of Section 1 without an additional factor.

d. Price Fixing–Price fixing is an agreement with the purpose or effect of inhibiting price competition; it can involve raising, depressing, fixing, pegging, or stabilizing prices. It is the primary and most serious *per se* violation under the Sherman Act. All horizontal price-fixing agreements are illegal *per se*. Retail price maintenance is a vertical form of price fixing in which the wholesaler fixes the prices at which its purchasers must resell the product; it is a *per se* violation of Section 1. The prohibition against price fixing covers any agreement between sellers to establish maximum as well as minimum prices.

e. Market Allocations–In market allocation, competitors agree not to compete with each other in specified markets. These markets may be defined by geographic area, type of customer, or class of product. All horizontal agreements to divide markets are illegal *per se*, because their effect is to give monopoly power in that market to the remaining firm which can control price. Vertical territorial and customer restrictions are no longer illegal *per se* but are judged by the rule of reason. In 1985, the U.S. Department of Justice issued a "market structure screen" which it uses in determining whether vertical territorial restrictions are in compliance with the rule of reason.

f. Boycotts–The refusal of a seller to deal with any particular buyer does not violate the act, because the Sherman Act does not apply to unilateral action. Thus, a manufacturer can refuse to sell to a retailer who persists in selling below the manufacturer's suggested retail price. On the other hand, group boycotts may be prohibited, because they are a concerted refusal to deal. A boycott is an agreement among parties not to deal with a third party. Some group boycotts are illegal *per se*, while others are subject to the rule of reason.

g. Tying Arrangements–A tying arrangement is one in which the sale of a desired product, service, or intangible (the tying product) is conditioned upon the buyer's purchasing of a second product (the tied product) from the seller. An example would be if the manufacturer of photocopying equipment required that all purchasers of its photocopiers also purchase from it all of the paper they will use with the copier. Because these arrangements limit the freedom of choice of buyers and may exclude competitors, the law closely scrutinizes tying arrangements. A tying arrangement exists where a seller exploits its economic power in one market to expand its empire to another market. When the seller has considerable economic power in the tying product and when a substantial amount of interstate commerce in the tied product is affected, the tying arrangement is *per se* illegal. If the seller lacks economic power, the tying arrangement is judged by the rule of reason.

2. Monopolies–According to economic analysis, a monopolist uses its power to limit production and increase prices. A monopolistic market produces fewer goods at a higher price than a competitive market. Section 2 of the Sherman Act prohibits monopolies, attempts to monopolize, and conspiracies to monopolize. Unlike Section 1, it also prohibits unilateral action by one firm.

a. Monopolization–Although Section 2 appears to prohibit all monopolies, the courts have required either the unfair attainment of the monopoly power or the abusive use of that power once attained in addition to the mere possession of market power. Monopoly power is the ability to control price or exclude competitors from the marketplace; the issue of monopoly power involves defining what degree of market dominance constitutes monopoly power. Market share, which is the fractional share of the total relevant product and geographic markets possessed by a firm, is the most common test of monopoly power. The relevant product market includes products that are substitutable for the firm's product on the basis of price, quality, and adaptability for other purposes. The relevant geographic market is the territory in which the firm sells its products or services; it may be local, regional or national depending upon the product. Both monopoly power and unfair conduct must be shown for a firm to violate Section 2. Three different approaches have been used by the courts to determine what constitutes unfair conduct. There is no definitive answer to the basic question of what conduct, beyond the mere possession of monopoly power, violates Section 2.

    b.   Attempts to Monopolize–Section 2 also prohibits attempts to monopolize. The standard test requires proof of a specific intent to monopolize plus a dangerous probability of success, but this standard leaves unanswered such questions as what constitutes a definition of intent and how much power must be achieved.

    c.   Conspiracies to Monopolize–Conspiracies to monopolize, which generally constitute a combination in restraint of trade, are a violation of Section 2 as well as Section 1.

B. Clayton Act–Congress strengthened the Sherman Act by adopting the Clayton Act in 1914. It was expressly designed "to supplement existing laws against unlawful restraints and monopolies." The Act only provides for civil actions which may be brought either by private parties in federal court for treble damages and attorneys' fees or by the Justice Department and the Federal Trade Commission to prevent and restrict violations of the act. The major provisions of the Clayton Act deal with price discrimination, tying contracts, exclusive dealing, and mergers.

    1.   Tying Contracts and Exclusive Dealing–Section 3 of the Clayton Act prohibits tying arrangements and exclusive dealing, selling, or leasing arrangements that prevent purchasers from dealing with the seller's competitors where the effect may be to substantially lessen competition or tend to create a monopoly. It is intended to attack practices before they ripen into violations of Section 1 or 2 of the Sherman Act. Section 3 applies only to practices involving commodities. Exclusive dealing arrangements are agreements by which the seller or lessor of a product conditions the agreement upon the buyer's or lessee's promise not to deal in goods of a competitor. For example, a manufacturer of razors might require that retailers who wish to sell its line not carry a competing brand of razors.

    2.   Mergers–Mergers may be classified as horizontal, vertical, or conglomerate. A horizontal merger involves the acquisition by one company of all or part of the stock or assets of a competing company. A vertical merger is the acquisition by a company of one of its customers or suppliers. It is a forward merger if the acquiring company purchases a customer; it is a backward merger if the acquiring company purchases a supplier. A conglomerate merger is an acquisition that does not involve a competitor, customer, or supplier. Section 7 of the Clayton Act prohibits the merger or acquisition by a corporation of stock or assets of another corporation where the effect may be to substantially lessen competition or tend to create a monopoly. The principal objective of antitrust law governing mergers is to maintain competition. Horizontal mergers are scrutinized most carefully. The courts consider various factors in reviewing the legality of each type of merger.

C. Robinson-Patman Act–The Robinson-Patman Act amended the Clayton Act to prohibit buyers from inducing and sellers from granting price discrimination in interstate commerce of commodities of similar grade and quality. The price discrimination must substantially lessen competition or tend to create a monopoly to be a violation. Under this act, sellers are prevented from granting discounts to buyers, unless the same discounts are offered to all other purchasers on proportionately equal terms. The act imposes liability on the buyer as well as the seller by making it unlawful for a person to knowingly "induce or receive" an illegal discrimination in price. Violations are civil rather than criminal wrongs. Price differentials are permitted when justified by proof of either a cost savings to the seller or a good faith price reduction to meet the lawful price of a competitor.

1. Primary-Line Injury–Injuries accruing to sellers' competitors are called "primary-line" injuries. The Robinson-Patman Act forbids price discrimination only where the effect is to lessen competition or create a monopoly. Thus the plaintiff must show that the defendant, with intent to harm competition, engaged in predatory pricing or present a detailed market analysis that demonstrates how the defendant's price discrimination actually harmed competition.

2. Secondary- and Tertiary-Line Injury–Involves discounts granted to large buyers. To prove the required harm to competition, a plaintiff in a secondary-line injury must either show substantial and sustained intra-market price differentials or offer a detailed market analysis that demonstrates actual harm to competition. Tertiary-line injury occurs when the recipient of a price advantage passes the benefit on to the next level of distribution. Purchases from other secondary-line sellers are thereby injured and may recover damages from the original discriminating seller.

3. Cost Justification–If a seller can show that it costs less to sell a product to a particular buyer, the cost savings may be lawfully passed along. Calculating and proving such savings is difficult.

4. Meeting Competition–A seller may lower its price in a good faith attempt to meet competition. A seller may beat its competitor's price if a seller does not know the competitor's price, cannot reasonably determine it, and acts reasonably in setting its own price.

D. Federal Trade Commission Act–In 1914, Congress enacted the Federal Trade Commission Act, creating the Federal Trade Commission (FTC), which is charged with the duty of preventing unfair methods of competition and unfair or deceptive acts or practices in commerce. The five-member commission is empowered to conduct appropriate investigations and hearings. It may issue cease and desist orders which have the effect of injunctions and which are enforceable in the federal courts against violators. It may also order other relief, such as affirmative disclosure, corrective advertising, and the granting of patent licenses on a reasonable royalty basis. The FTC investigates possible violations of the antitrust laws and also unfair methods of competition.

KEY TERMS

1. Treble damages

2. Rule of reason

3. Illegal *per se*

4. Horizontal restraints of trade

5. Price fixing

6. Retail price maintenance

7. Market allocation

8. Boycott

9. Vertical restraints of trade

10. Conscious parallelism

11. Market share

12. Exclusive dealing arrangement

13. Horizontal merger

14. Vertical merger

15. Forward merger

16. Tying arrangement

17. Monopoly power

18. Backward merger

19. Conglomerate merger

20. Price discrimination

21. Primary-line injury

22. Cease and desist order

TRUE/FALSE

_____ 1. Agreements between parties at the same level in the chain of distribution are horizontal restraints of trade.

_____ 2. Section 1 violations of the Sherman Act require at least two parties.

_____ 3. Justice Department enforcement efforts under the Sherman Act extend to foreign companies that harm U.S. exports.

_____ 4. While the Sherman Act prohibits sellers' agreements to establish minimum prices, sellers are free to agree to establish maximum prices.

_____ 5. Horizontal market allocations are illegal *per se*.

_____ 6. Because of their tendency to exclude competitors from the market, all tying arrangements have been declared illegal *per se*.

_____ 7. Under the Robinson-Patman Act, liability may be imposed upon buyers as well as sellers.

_____ 8. Exclusive dealing arrangements are agreements by which the seller or lessor of a product conditions the agreement upon the buyer's or lessor's promise not to deal in the goods of a competitor.

_____ 9. A good faith price reduction to meet the price of a competitor is a defense to a charge of price discrimination under the Robinson-Patman Act.

_____ 10. A vertical merger occurs when a wholesale manufacturer acquires a retail outlet for its products by way of merger.

_____ 11. The Federal Trade Commission was established to prevent unfair methods of competition in commerce.

_____ 12. The Clayton Act prohibits every contract, combination, or conspiracy in restraint of trade.

_____ 13. A tying arrangement involving a seller who lacks economic power will be judged by the rule of reason test.

_____ 14. A manufacturer who refuses to sell to a retailer who persists in selling below the manufacturer's suggested retail price is a boycott and violates the Sherman Act.

_____ 15. The possession of monopoly power is, by itself, a violation of Section 2 of the Sherman Act.

MULTIPLE CHOICE

_____ 1. Sherman Act corporate offenders are subject to fines up to:
   a. $350,000.
   b. $500,000.
   c. $1,000,000.
   d. $10,000,000.

_____ 2. The rule of reason test is used to determine the legality of:
   a. horizontal price-fixing agreements.
   b. vertical territorial and customer restrictions.
   c. horizontal market allocation agreements.
   d. retail price maintenance agreements.

_____ 3. A company is not in possession of monopoly power if its share of the market is:
   a. 100%.
   b. 85%.
   c. 75%.
   d. 45%.

_____ 4. Labor unions are exempted from the antitrust laws by:
   a. the Sherman Act.
   b. the Clayton Act.
   c. the Robinson-Patman Act.
   d. the FTC Act.

_____ 5. If a seller fixes the price at which its purchasers must resell its product, this would be:
   a. horizontal price fixing.
   b. vertical price fixing.
   c. conscious parallelism.
   d. none of the above.

_____ 6. A person who knowingly induces or receives an illegal discrimination in price has violated:
   a. the Sherman Act.
   b. the Clayton Act.
   c. the Robinson-Patman Act.
   d. none of the above.

_____ 7. A corporation which acquires the stock of another corporation where the effect may be substantially to lessen competition between the two corporations has violated:
   a. the Sherman Act.
   b. the Clayton Act.
   c. the Robinson-Patman Act.
   d. the FTC Act.

_____ 8. A company which engages in unfair methods of competition has violated:
   a. the Sherman Act.
   b. the Clayton Act.
   c. the Robinson-Patman Act.
   d. the FTC Act.

_____ 9. Which one of the following is not a _per se_ violation of the Sherman Act?
   a. Price fixing
   b. Horizontal market allocation
   c. Vertical market allocation
   d. Group boycotts designed to eliminate a competitor

_____ 10. A _____ merger involves the acquisition by a company of all or substantially all or part of the stock or assets of a competing company.
   a. horizontal
   b. vertical
   c. conglomerate
   d. monopolistic

_____ 11. If RAC and Sonny, both manufacturers of color televisions, agree that RAC shall have the exclusive right to sell color televisions in Illinois and Iowa and that Sonny shall have the exclusive right in Minnesota and Wisconsin, they have committed a violation of:
   a. the Clayton Act.
   b. the Sherman Act.
   c. the FTC Act.
   d. none of the above.

_____ 12. Which of the following demonstrates economic power in determining whether a tying arrangement exists?
   a. A dominant position in the tying market
   b. An advantage not shared by competitors in the tying market
   c. A substantial number of customers have accepted the tying arrangement
   d. Any of the above

_____ 13. If IBM purchased a manufacturer of microchips, this would be:
   a. a vertical merger.
   b. a horizontal merger.
   c. a conglomerate merger.
   d. none of the above.

_____ 14. *CPA:* A_____ merger involves the acquisition by a company of one of its suppliers or customers.
   a. horizontal
   b. vertical
   c. conglomerate
   d. monopolistic

_____ 15. *CPA:* A_____ merger involves the acquisition by one company of another that is not a competitor, customer, or supplier.
   a. horizontal
   b. vertical
   c. conglomerate
   d. monopolistic

SHORT ESSAY

1. What is the purpose of the federal antitrust statutes?

    _____

    _____

    _____

    _____

2. According to economic theory, how does a monopolistic market differ from a competitive market?

    _____

    _____

    _____

    _____

3. Discuss the Robinson-Patman Act and defenses to it.

    _____

    _____

    _____

    _____

4. Discuss the Clayton Act.

    _____

    _____

    _____

    _____

5. Disco is a discount chain store that sells goods below the manufacturers' suggested retail prices. X, Y, and Z, three large manufacturers with market power, agree together that they will not sell to Disco unless Disco stops its discount pricing. If Disco refuses and sues X, Y, and Z because they will not sell to Disco, what is the result?

    _____

    _____

    _____

    _____

Chapter 44
Accountants' Legal Liability

PURPOSE

Accountants are subject to potential civil liability arising from the professional services they provide to their clients and third parties. This legal liability is imposed by both the common law at the state level as well as federal securities laws. In addition, accountants may violate criminal laws in connection with their work. In this chapter you study accountants' legal liability under both state and federal law.

CHAPTER CHECKPOINTS

After reading and studying this chapter, you should be able to:

1. Identify situations in which an accountant may have contract liability based upon implicit and explicit contract terms.

2. Identify situations in which an accountant may have tort liability based upon negligence or fraud.

3. Summarize the rights and privileges given to accountants under state law regarding the ownership of working papers and the existence of an accountant-client privilege.

4. Summarize the potential civil and criminal liability of an accountant under the Securities Act of 1933.

5. Summarize the potential civil and criminal liability of an accountant under the Securities Exchange Act of 1934.

CHAPTER OUTLINE

A. Common Law–An accountant's legal responsibility under state law may be based on (1) contract law, (2) tort law, or (3) criminal law. Common law also gives accountants rights and privileges such as the ownership of working papers and, in some states, a limited accountant-client privilege.

   1. Contract Liability–The employment contract between accountant and client is subject to the general principles of contract law. On entering into a binding contract (an engagement), the accountant is bound to perform all of the duties explicitly agreed to under the contract. An accountant also implicitly agrees to perform the contract in a competent and professional manner. An accountant is held to those standards that are generally accepted by the accounting profession, such as Generally Accepted Accounting Standards (GAAS) and Generally Accepted Accounting Principles (GAAP). The accountant may, by agreement, explicitly agree to standards beyond GAAS. An accountant who breaches a contract will incur liability not only to the client but also to third-party beneficiaries who were not parties to the contract but whom the contracting parties intended to benefit under the contract. An accountant who materially breaches a contract will not be entitled to any compensation. An accountant who substantially performs the contractual duties is generally entitled to be compensated the agreed fee less any damages caused by the nonmaterial breach.

   2. Tort Liability–An accountant may incur tort liability to the client or third parties for negligence or fraud. A tort is a private or civil wrong, other than a breach of contract, for which the courts will provide a remedy in the form of an action for damages.

      a. Negligence–An accountant is negligent who does not exercise the degree of care a reasonably competent accountant would exercise under the circumstances. Accountants who exercise reasonable care in performing duties are not liable for honest inaccuracies or errors of judgment. Accountants who act in a reasonably competent and professional manner are not insurers of the accuracy of their reports. Historically, accountants' liability for negligence extended only to the client and to third-party beneficiaries. Privity of contract was required to pursue a cause of action based on negligence according to the landmark case of *Ultramares Corp. v. Touche*. However, in recent years the majority of the states and the Restatement of Torts adopt a foreseen users' test which expands the class of protected individuals to those who the accountant knew would use the work product or those who use the accountant's work for a purpose for which the accountant knew the work would be used. The class does not include potential investors and the general public, although some courts have extended liability to reasonably foreseeable plaintiffs who are neither known nor members of a class of intended recipients.

      b. Fraud–An accountant who commits a fraudulent act is liable to any person who the accountant should have reasonably foreseen would be injured by the misrepresentation and who justifiably relied upon it. The required elements of fraud are: (1) a false representation (2) of fact (3) that is material (4) made with knowledge of its falsity and intention to deceive (5) justifiably relied on, and (6) causes injury to the plaintiff. An accountant who commits fraud is liable for both compensatory and punitive damages.

3. Criminal Liability–An accountant's criminal liability in rendering professional services is based primarily on the federal law of securities regulation and taxation. An accountant who knowingly and willfully certifies false documents, alters or tampers with accounting records, uses false financial reports, gives false testimony under oath, or commits forgery violates state criminal law. Criminal liability exists under the Internal Revenue Code for knowingly preparing false or fraudulent tax returns and for willfully assisting or advising a client to prepare a false return. Violators are subject to a fine not to exceed $250,000 ($500,000 for a corporation) or three years' imprisonment or both.

4. Client Information–Two legal issues arise concerning client information obtained while providing services: (a) who owns the working papers generated by the accountant and (b) whether the client information is privileged.

   a. Working Papers–Accountants are held to be the owners of their working papers and thus need not surrender them to their clients. Nevertheless, accountants may not disclose the contents of these papers unless (1) the client consents or (2) a court orders the disclosure.

   b. Accountant-Client Privilege–The question of a possible accountant-client privilege frequently arises in tax disputes, criminal prosecution, and civil litigation. If information is considered to be privileged, it may not be admitted into evidence over the objection of the person possessing the privilege. Neither common law nor federal law recognizes a general privilege. However, some states have adopted statutes granting some form of privilege, usually to the client, although a few extend the privilege to the accountant. It is generally considered to be professionally unethical for an accountant to disclose confidential communications from the client, unless the disclosure is in accordance with (1) the AICPA or GAAS requirements, (2) a court order, or (3) the client's request.

B. Federal Securities Law–Accountants may be both civilly and criminally liable under provisions of the 1933 and 1934 acts.

1. 1933 Act–Accountants are subject to civil liability under Section 11 of the 1933 act if the financial statements they prepare or certify for inclusion in a registration statement contain any untrue statement or omission of material fact. Liability extends to anyone who acquires the security without knowledge of the untruth or omission. There is no requirement of privity or proof of reliance on the financial statements under Section 11. An accountant may raise the defense of due diligence, which requires that the accountant had, after reasonable investigation, reasonable grounds to believe and did believe that the financial statements were true, complete, and accurate. The standard of reasonableness is that required of a prudent person in the management of his or her own property. Section 11 imposes liability for negligence in the conduct of the audit or the presentation of information in the financial statements. An accountant who willfully violates this section may be held criminally liable for a fine of not more than $10,000 or imprisonment of not more than five years, or both. An accountant, however, is not liable for any portion of the amount recoverable under Section 11 that the accountant proves was caused by something other than his or her improper disclosure.

2. 1934 Act

   a. Civil Liability–Section 18 of the 1934 act imposes civil liability on an accountant who makes or causes to be made any false or misleading statement about any material fact in any application, report, document, or registration filed with the SEC under the 1934 act.

Liability extends to any person who purchased or sold a security in reliance on that false or misleading statement. An accountant is not liable who acted in good faith and had no knowledge the statement was false or misleading. Thus, an accountant is not liable for false or misleading statements that result from good faith negligence.

Accountants may also be civilly liable for violations of Rule 10b-5, which applies to both oral and written misstatements or omissions of material facts and to all securities. Liability extends to purchasers and sellers who rely on the misstatement or omission of material fact in connection with the purchase or sale of a security. Liability is imposed only if the accountant acted with scienter, which includes intentional or knowing conduct, as well as with a reckless disregard of the truth.

b. Criminal Liability–Accountants are subject to criminal liability for any willful violation of either Section 18 or Rule 10b-5. Violators are subject to a fine of not more than $1 million or imprisonment for not more than ten years, or both. An accounting firm may be fined up to $2.5 million.

c. Sarbanes-Oxley Act–This Act amends federal securities law in order to protect investors by improve the accuracy of corporate disclosures. This Act establishes a five member Public Company Accounting Oversight Board to oversee the audit of public companies. The Board's duties include: (i) registering public accounting firms that prepare audit reports for issuers; (ii) overseeing the audit of public companies; (iii) establishing audit report standards and rules; and (iv) inspecting, investigating, and enforcing compliance by registered public accounting firms. In order to make auditors more independent from their clients, the Act forbids accounting firms from performing eight specified non-audit services for audit clients. The lead audit partner who has primary responsibility for the audit and the audit partner who is responsible for reviewing the audit must rotate at least every five years. Auditors must report directly to the company's audit committee and make timely disclosure of certain accounting matters.

d. Audit Requirements–The Private Securities Litigation Reform Act of 1995 authorized SEC to adopt rules to be followed by auditors. Auditors must, under the Reform Act, establish procedures capable of detecting material illegal acts.

KEY TERMS

1. Engagement

2. Third-party beneficiary

3. Negligence

4. Privity

5. Foreseen users

6. Fraud

7. Working papers

8. Accountant-client privilege

9. Due diligence

10. Scienter

TRUE/FALSE

_____ 1. An accountant is required to disclose confidential information from a client if a court orders the disclosure.

_____ 2. An accountant who does not perform an audit on time when time is of the essence is entitled to be compensated for the contractually agreed-upon fee less damages.

_____ 3. Scienter is required for an accountant to violate l0b-5 of the Securities Exchange Act of 1934.

_____ 4. An accountant who does not exercise the degree of care a reasonably competent accountant would exercise under the same circumstances is negligent.

_____ 5. An accountant who commits fraud is liable only to the party with whom the accountant has contracted.

_____ 6. Contributory negligence is a common defense raised by accountants in professional liability cases.

_____ 7. The client is held to be the owner of working papers prepared by an accountant.

_____ 8. Both common law and federal law recognize the existence of an accountant-client privilege.

_____ 9. No criminal liability exists under the Securities Exchange Act of 1934.

_____ 10. By agreeing to render services, an accountant is held to those standards generally accepted by the accounting profession, such as GAAS.

_____ 11. An accountant who breaches a contract will be liable not only to the client but also to third-party beneficiaries.

_____ 12. Due diligence is a defense to an action brought under the Securities Act of 1933.

_____ 13. All communication between an accountant and client is privileged and may not be admitted into evidence in a court proceeding.

_____ 14. Accountants may be both civilly and criminally liable under the provisions of the federal securities laws.

_____ 15. Criminal sanctions may be imposed on accountants under the Internal Revenue Code for knowingly preparing false or fraudulent tax returns.

MULTIPLE CHOICE

_____ 1. Which of the following is a defense under Section 11 of the 1933 act?
   a. Lack of scienter
   b. Due diligence
   c. Lack of privity
   d. All of the above are defenses under Section 11

_____ 2. Historically, an accountant's liability for negligence extended to which of the following?
   a. The client
   b. Third-party beneficiaries
   c. The client and third-party beneficiaries
   d. The client, third-party beneficiaries, and foreseen users

_____ 3. An accountant's legal responsibility under state law may be based upon:
   a. Contract law.
   b. Tort law.
   c. Criminal law.
   d. Any of the above.

_____ 4. In which of the following situations may an accountant disclose the contents of working papers?
   a. When the client consents
   b. When a court orders the disclosure
   c. When the IRS summons them as part of criminal investigation
   d. An accountant may disclose working papers in all of the above situations.

_____ 5. The legal basis for the accountant-client privilege is:
   a. state common law.
   b. state statute.
   c. federal statute.
   d. state common law, as well as both state and federal statute.

_____ 6. Amber, who is a CPA, was hired to audit the books of Fry Co. During the audit, Oscar, an officer of the corporation, notified Amber that he suspected the company's treasurer was engaged in a scheme to embezzle money from the corporation. Amber did not pursue the matter, because she was anxious to complete the job in time for her scheduled summer vacation. If it later becomes known that the treasurer was in fact embezzling corporation money, which of the following is correct?
   a. Amber has no liability if she followed Generally Accepted Auditing Standards.
   b. Amber is guilty of negligence.
   c. If the audit involves financial statements required by the Securities Exchange Act of 1934, Amber has probably violated the Private Securities Litigation Reform Act.
   d. Both (b) and (c) are correct.

_____ 7. Which of the following can give rise to an accountant's criminal liability?
   a. Knowingly preparing a fraudulent tax return
   b. Falsely certifying a document
   c. Willfully violating Section 18 of the 1934 act or Rule 10b-5
   d. All of the above can give rise to criminal liability.

_____ 8. Penalties for the fraudulent preparation of a tax return may be three years in prison and a fine of:
   a. $5,000.
   b. $10,000.
   c. $50,000.
   d. $100,000.

_____ 9. Which of the following is necessary for an accountant to have liability under Rule 10b-5?
   a. Scienter
   b. Mere negligence
   c. Reckless disregard of the truth
   d. Two of the above are correct, (a) or (c).

_____ 10. Who owns an accountant's working papers?
   a. The client
   b. The accountant
   c. The IRS
   d. The SEC

_____ 11. The Restatement of Torts has adopted the rule that accountants are liable for negligence to:
   a. reasonably foreseeable plaintiffs.
   b. clients and third-party beneficiaries.
   c. those the accountant knew would use the work.
   d. two of the above are correct, (b) and (c).

_____ 12. Under the Securities Exchange Act of 1934, an accountant can be held criminally liable for making any false or misleading statement about any material fact in any report filed with the SEC and acting:
   a. willfully.
   b. negligently.
   c. in violation of GAAS.
   d. none of the above.

_____ 13. Under Section 11 of the Securities Act of 1933, an accountant may be civilly liable to:
   a. only those in privity with the accountant.
   b. only those who rely on the financial statements containing the untrue statement or omission.
   c. only those in privity and who rely on the financial statement.
   d. anyone who acquires the security without knowledge of the untrue statement or omission.

_____ 14. **CPA:** In a common law action against an accountant, lack of privity is a viable defense if the plaintiff:
   a. is the client's creditor who sues the accountant for negligence.
   b. can prove the presence of gross negligence that amounts to a reckless disregard for the truth.
   c. is the accountant's client.
   d. bases the action upon fraud.

_____ 15. **CPA:** Which of the following statements concerning an accountant's disclosure of confidential client data is generally correct?
   a. Disclosure may be made to any state agency without subpoena.
   b. Disclosure may be made to any party on consent of the client.
   c. Disclosure may be made to comply with an IRS audit request.
   d. Disclosure may be made to comply with Generally Accepted Accounting Principles.

SHORT ESSAY

1. Kind and Kind, CPAs, has audited the Consumer Credit Corporation (CCC) for the past ten years. The SEC has recently commenced an investigation against CCC for possible violations of the federal securities laws. As part of its investigation, the SEC has subpoenaed all of Kind and Kind's working papers pertaining to the audit of CCC. Does Kind have to produce its working papers? Explain.

_____

_____

_____

_____

2. Arthur and Arthur Company, CPAs, audited the financial statements included in the annual report submitted by Bettren Lane Company to the SEC. The audit failed to detect numerous false and misleading statements in the financial statements. If the SEC initiates criminal proceedings against Arthur and Arthur Company under the 1934 act, what must the SEC prove for Arthur and Arthur to be held criminally liable?

_____

_____

_____

_____

3. Explain the difference in explicit and implicit contract terms which may lead to liability for an accountant.

    _____

    _____

    _____

    _____

4. Wilson and Mathers, CPAs, prepare an audit report for Zandoli Company. Zandoli uses the audit report to obtain a loan from First Bank. If the audit report is not accurate and Zandoli defaults on the loan because of insolvency, what is the result?

    _____

    _____

    _____

    _____

5. Briefly identify the sources of accountants' liability.

    _____

    _____

    _____

    _____

Chapter 45
Consumer Protection

PURPOSE

Historically, consumers were subject to the rule of *caveat emptor* or "let the buyer beware." However, the law has largely abandoned this principle in consumer transactions and today gives greater protection to consumers in the form of federal and state statutes. A consumer transaction is one involving goods, credit, services, or land acquired for personal, household, or family purposes. In this chapter, you study the most important consumer protection statutes and the governmental agencies charged with statutory enforcement.

CHAPTER CHECKPOINTS

After reading and studying this chapter, you should be able to:

1. Discuss the role of the Federal Trade Commission (FTC) in consumer protection and list the remedies used by this agency.

2. Discuss the purpose and authority of the Consumer Product Safety Commission.

3. Explain the principal provisions of the Magnuson-Moss Warranty Act, and distinguish between a full and limited warranty.

4. Summarize the major provisions of the Equal Credit Opportunity Act, the Federal Consumer Credit Protection Act, the Truth-in-Lending Act, the Fair Credit Billing Act, the Credit Card Fraud Act, the Real Estate Settlement Procedures Act, the Fair Credit Reporting Act, and the Fair Debt Collection Practices Act.

5. Distinguish between an open-ended credit account and a closed-ended credit account.

CHAPTER OUTLINE

A. State and Federal Consumer Protection Agencies–Legislatures and administrative bodies at the federal, state, and local levels actively seek to protect consumers through the enactment of laws and regulations. The most common abuses in consumer transactions occur in extension of credit, deceptive trade practices, unsafe products, and unfair pricing.

   1. State and Local Consumer Protection Agencies–These agencies deal with fraudulent and deceptive trade practices and fraudulent sales practices and help consumers resolve complaints about defective goods or poor service. State attorneys general enforce consumer protection laws by seeking injunctions and restitution.

   2. The Federal Trade Commission–In 1914, Congress established the Federal Trade Commission (FTC) and charged it with the duty to prevent unfair methods of competition in commerce and unfair or deceptive trade practices in commerce. It has the power to issue substantive rules, to conduct appropriate investigations and hearings, and to obtain cease and desist orders.

      a. Standards–The FTC has issued three policy statements. The first one dealt with the meaning of unfairness and applies a cost-benefit analysis. The second statement dealt with the meaning of deception and provides that it is a misrepresentation, omission, or practice that is likely to mislead the consumer acting reasonably in the circumstances, to the consumer's detriment. The third statement involved ad substantiation and requires that advertisers have a reasonable basis for their claims at the time their claims are made.

      b. Remedies–The FTC has three additional remedies. Affirmative disclosure is frequently employed by the FTC and requires the offender to provide certain information in its advertisement so that it is not deceptive. Corrective advertising requires disclosure in an advertisement that previous ads were deceptive. Multiple product orders require the deceptive advertiser to cease and desist from deceptive statements on all products it sells.

   3. The Consumer Product Safety Commission–The Consumer Product Safety Act (CPSA) established a federal agency, the Consumer Product Safety Commission (CPSC). The CPSC can set safety standards for consumer products; ban unsafe products; issue administrative "recall" orders to compel repair, replacement, or refunds for products that present hazards; and seek court orders to require recall of "imminently hazardous" products. The CPSC enforces the Federal Hazardous Substances Act, the Flammable Fabrics Act, the Poison Prevention Packaging Act, and the Refrigerator Safety Act. The agency relies on industry to establish voluntary safety standards.

   4. Other Federal Consumer Protection Agencies–Other federal agencies that play a major consumer protection role are the National Highway Traffic Safety Administration (NHTSA), which sets safety standards for motor vehicles to address crash prevention and crashworthiness, and the Food and Drug Administration (FDA), which sets standards for products or requires premarket approval of products to regulate adulterated and misbranded products. The Gramm-Leach-Bliley Act Financial Modernization Act (GLB Act) includes provisions to protect consumers' personal financial information that is possessed by financial institutions.

B. Consumer Purchases–A number of laws protect consumers in their purchases, but state contract law still provides many of the consumers' rights and duties. UCC Article 2 provides the basic rules governing contracts for the sale of goods.   It is the basic building block of laws that protect consumers in sales transactions, but there is also common law and federal and state statutes.

1. Federal Warranty Protection–In 1974 Congress enacted the Magnuson-Moss Warranty Act, which requires that sellers of consumer products give adequate information about warranties. The FTC administers and enforces the act. The act applies to consumer products with written warranties. A consumer product is any item of tangible personal property that is normally used for family, household, or personal use and that is distributed in commerce.

    a. Presale Disclosures–The act contains presale disclosure provisions intended to prevent confusion and deception and to enable purchasers to make educated personal comparisons. A person making a warranty must fully and conspicuously disclose in simple language the terms and conditions of such warranty.

    b. Labeling Requirements–The second major part of the act contains labeling requirements in which written warranties are divided into two categories–limited and full. A full warranty is one under which the warrantor will repair the product and, if unsuccessful, will replace or refund. No limitation may be placed on the duration of any implied warranty by a full warranty. A limited warranty is any warranty not designated as full.

    c. Limitations on Disclaimers–The act provides that a written warranty may not disclaim any implied warranty. A full warranty must not disclaim, modify, or limit any implied warranty, and a limited warranty may not disclaim or modify any implied warranty but may limit its duration to that of the written warranty.

2. State "Lemon Laws"–State legislatures have enacted lemon laws that attempt to provide rights to new car purchasers that are similar to full warranties under the Magnuson-Moss Warranty Act. A lemon is a car that continues to have a defect substantially impairing the use, value, or safety of a car after a reasonable number of attempts by the manufacturer to repair the defect. These laws require the manufacturer to repair the defect. Most of these laws require the manufacturer to replace an unrepairable car or refund the retail price, less an allowance for the use of the car. Some states have broadened their laws to cover used cars and motorcycles as well.

3. Consumer Right of Rescission–Rescission is the right to cancel a contract.   Ordinarily a consumer is legally obligated after signing a contract. However, in many states, statutes allow a consumer a brief period (usually two or three days) in which to rescind an otherwise binding credit obligation if the solicitation occurred in the consumer's home. The FTC also has a trade regulation that applies to door-to-door sales of goods and services for more than $25. That regulation allows a consumer to rescind the contract within three days of signing regardless of whether the sale is for cash or on credit. The Federal Consumer Credit Protection Act (FCCPA) allows consumers three days to withdraw from any credit obligation secured by a mortgage on their homes, unless the credit was used to acquire the dwelling. The Interstate Land Sales Full Disclosure Act requires the developer of unimproved land to file a detailed statement of record with information about subdivisions with the Department of Housing and Urban Development before offering the lots for sale or lease and to provide a property report to each prospective purchaser or lessee. The contract may be revoked at the option of the purchaser within seven days of signing. If the property report is not given to the purchaser before signing the contract, the purchaser has two years to revoke.

C. Consumer Credit Transactions–In the absence of special regulation, consumer credit transactions are governed by laws regulating commercial transactions generally. A consumer credit transaction is any credit transaction involving goods, services, or land acquired for personal, household, or family purposes. Regulation of consumer credit has increased due to the dramatic expansion and the numerous abuses in credit transactions. In response, Congress passed the Federal Consumer Credit Protection Act (FCCPA) in 1968 which requires disclosure of finance charges, credit extension charges, and sets limits on garnishment proceedings. Also in 1968, the National Conference of Commissioners on Uniform State Laws promulgated the Uniform Consumer Credit Code (UCCC) which integrated into one law the regulation of all consumer credit transactions.

1. Access to the Market–The Equal Credit Opportunity Act prohibits all businesses that regularly extend credit from discriminating in extending credit on the basis of sex, marital status, race, color, religion, national origin, or age. The FTC has overall enforcement authority. FTC Regulation B and the Women's Business Ownership Act forbid potential creditors from asking about or using information regarding a credit applicant's marital status or her likelihood of having children.

2. Disclosure Requirements–Title One of the FCCPA is known as the Truth-in-Lending Act. It has superseded state disclosure requirements relating to credit terms for consumer loans and credit sales under $25,000. An important requirement in the act is that sales finance and interest rates must be quoted in terms of an APR (annual percentage rate) and must be calculated on a uniform basis. The Federal Reserve Board issued Regulation Z to carry out its enforcement and interpretation of the act. Congress passed the Fair Credit and Charge Card Disclosure Act of 1988 which adds to the Truth-in-Lending Act a new section requiring all credit and charge card applications and solicitations to include extensive disclosures.

   a. Credit Accounts–The Truth-in-Lending Act requires creditors to tell consumers who open revolving or open-end credit accounts how the finance charge is computed and when it is charged, what other charges may be imposed, and whether the creditor has a security interest. The Federal Reserve Board requires marketing material to clearly display a table that shows the APR and other important information such as the annual fee. An open-end credit account is one that permits the debtor to enter into a series of credit transactions that may be paid off either in installments or in a lump sum, such as most credit cards. With this type of credit, the creditor is required to provide a statement of account for each billing period. Among other things, the Bankruptcy Act of 2005 requires disclosure of low or discounted introductory rates, how long these rates apply, and the rates that will later take effect.

   b. ARMs–The ARM disclosure rule applies to any loan that is (1) a closed-end consumer transaction, (2) secured by the consumer's principal residence, (3) longer than one year in duration, and (4) subject to interest rate variation. Disclosures required must be made when a creditor furnishes an application to a prospective borrower or before the creditor receives payment of a nonrefundable fee, whichever occurs first.

   c. Home Equity Loans–The Home Equity Loan Consumer Protection Act (HELCPA) requires lenders to provide a disclosure statement and consumer pamphlet to a prospective consumer borrower. The act applies to all open-end credit plans to be secured by the consumer's principal dwelling. The disclosure statement must include a statement that (1) a default on the loan may result in the consumer's loss of the dwelling, (2) some conditions must be met, and (3) the creditor may, under certain circumstances terminate the plan and accelerate the outstanding balance, prohibit further extension of credit, reduce the plan's credit limit, or impose fees upon the termination of the account. Regulation Z provides the consumer with the right to rescind such a plan until midnight on the third day following the opening of the plan, until delivery of a notice of the right to rescind, or until delivery of all material disclosures, whichever comes last.

    d. Billing Errors–The 1975 Fair Credit Billing Act sets forth procedures for the consumer to follow in making complaints about specified errors in billing.

    e. Settlement Charges–The Real Estate Settlement Procedures Act (RESPA) provides home purchasers with greater and timelier information on the nature and cost of the settlement process and protects them from unnecessarily high settlement charges. The act, administered by the Secretary of Housing and Urban Development, prohibits kickbacks and referral fees.

3. Contract Terms– Frequently, contract documents are printed forms containing blank spaces to be filled in by the creditor at the time of the extension of credit. Standardization facilitates transfer of the rights of the creditor to a third party. Almost all states impose statutory ceilings on the amount that may be charged for the extension of consumer credit. Most statutes require a creditor to permit the debtor to pay the obligation in full at any time before the date of maturity. The FTC has adopted a rule that limits the rights of a holder in due course of an instrument evidencing a debt that arises out of a consumer credit contract. A similar rule applies to credit card issuers under the Fair Credit Billing Act.

4. Consumer Credit Card Fraud–In 1984 Congress enacted the Credit Card Fraud Act which prohibits possessing unauthorized cards, counterfeiting credit cards, using account numbers alone, and using cards obtained from a third party with his consent. The FCCPA provides protection to the credit card holder from loss by limiting the card holder's liability for unauthorized use of a credit card to $50.

5. Fair Reportage–In 1970 Congress enacted the Fair Credit Reporting Act (FCRA), which applies to consumer reports used for purposes of securing employment, insurance, and credit. The act prohibits inaccurate or specified obsolete information in consumer reports. Agencies must give written advance notice to consumers that an investigative report may be made. The consumer may request information in the agency's files. If the consumer notifies the agency of disagreement with the accuracy and completeness of information in the file, the agency must reinvestigate the latter. If the matter is unresolved, the consumer may submit a brief statement to be incorporated into the report. As of 1997, an employer's right to use credit reports is restricted. The FCRA requires each of the national consumer reporting firms to provide a requesting individual with a free copy of his or her credit report once every 12 months.

6. Creditors' Remedies–The creditor may impose a delinquency charge for late payments. If the consumer defaults, the creditor may declare the entire balance immediately due and payable and may sue on the debt.

    a. Wage Assignments and Garnishment–Some states prohibit wage assignments. Under the FCCPA and the laws of most states, a limitation is imposed on the amount that may be deducted per pay period. The FCCPA prohibits discharge of an employee solely because a creditor uses a wage assignment for any one debt.

    b. Security Interest–In the case of credit sales, the seller may retain a security interest in the goods sold. Where the debt is secured by property as collateral, the creditor, on default of the debtor, may take possession of the property and either retain it in full satisfaction of the debt or sell it. If the proceeds are less than the debt, the creditor can sue for the balance.

c. Debt Collection Practices–In 1977 Congress enacted the Fair Debt Collection Practices Act to eliminate abusive, deceptive, and unfair practices in collecting consumer debts by debt collection agencies. The act is enforced by the FTC, and consumers may recover damages from the collection agency for violations.

KEY TERMS

1. Cease and desist order

2. Affirmative disclosure

3. Corrective advertising

4. Multiple product order

5. Warranty

6. Consumer product

7. Full warranty

8. Limited warranty

9. Consumer credit transaction

10. APR

11. Open-ended credit

12. Closed-ended credit

TRUE/FALSE

_____ 1. The Food and Drug Administration is the oldest federal consumer protection agency.

_____ 2. Under Federal Trade Commission standards, deception may occur through either false representations or material omissions.

_____ 3. Under the Magnuson-Moss Warranty Act, a written warranty may disclaim or modify any implied warranty.

_____ 4. A contract subject to the Interstate Land Sales Full Disclosure Act must clearly provide that the contract may be revoked at the option of the purchaser within two years of signing the contract.

_____ 5. Violators of the Equal Credit Opportunity Act are subject to civil actions to recover actual and punitive damages.

_____ 6. The Federal Trade Commission has as one of its major responsibilities the enforcement of rules to prevent unfair business practices by interstate moving companies.

_____ 7. The Fair Credit Billing Act requires creditors to explain or correct billing errors.

_____ 8. Most states impose statutory ceilings on the amount that may be charged for the extension of consumer credit.

_____ 9. Under the Fair Credit Reporting Act, consumers are entitled to read and copy all information pertaining to them in the consumer reporting agency's files.

_____ 10. The Consumer Product Safety Commission has authority to ban unsafe products.

_____ 11. The Fair Debt Collection Practices Act prohibits harassing, oppressive, or abusive debt collection conduct by debt collectors other than the creditor.

_____ 12. A multiple product order requires the advertiser to cease and desist from deceptive statements on all products it sells.

_____ 13. Deception may occur by a misrepresentation, but not by a material omission.

_____ 14. The FTC ad substantiation policy requires that advertisers have a reasonable basis for their claims at the time their claims are made.

_____ 15. Some state legislatures have enacted lemon laws that attempt to provide rights to used car purchasers.

MULTIPLE CHOICE

_____ 1. Today, most consumer protection takes the form of statutory enactments. Which of the following normally initiates complaints?
   a. The FTC
   b. The injured party
   c. The attorney general of the state in which the injured party resides
   d. Any of the above

_____ 2. An FTC remedy which requires an advertiser to include in its advertisements information that will render the ads nondeceptive is:
   a. an affirmative disclosure.
   b. a correcting advertising.
   c. a multiple product order.
   d. none of the above.

_____ 3. Under the Magnuson-Moss Warranty Act, a seller may disclaim any and all implied warranties if:
   a. the seller gives no written warranty.
   b. the product is for personal use only.
   c. the product costs $10 or less.
   d. none of the above.

_____ 4. Under the FTC's door-to-door sales rule, a consumer may only revoke a door-to-door sales contract if:
   a. the sale is on credit.
   b. any credit obligation incurred pursuant to the contract is secured by a home mortgage.
   c. the sale is for $25 or more.
   d. it is within 5 days.

_____ 5. Which of the following acts requires a creditor, within 30 days of receiving an application for credit, to notify the applicant of action taken and to provide specific reasons for a denial of credit?
   a. Consumer Credit Protection Act
   b. Equal Credit Opportunity Act
   c. Fair Credit Reporting Act
   d. Fair Credit Billing Act

_____ 6. The Equal Credit Opportunity Act prohibits businesses that regularly extend credit from discriminating in extending credit on the basis of:
   a. sex.
   b. marital status.
   c. age.
   d. all of the above.

_____ 7. Under the Consumer Credit Protection Act, sales finance charges and interest rates must be quoted in terms of:
   a. add-ons.
   b. discounts.
   c. annual percentage rates.
   d. none of the above.

_____ 8. Which of the following laws prohibits kickbacks and referral fees with respect to federally related mortgage loans?
   a. Interstate Land Sales Full Disclosure Act
   b. Real Estate Settlement Procedures Act
   c. Fair Credit Billing Act
   d. Consumer Credit Protection Act

_____ 9. Which of the following was the Consumer Product Safety Act enacted to accomplish?
   a. To protect the public against unreasonable risk of injury
   b. To assist consumers in evaluating the comparative safety of consumer products
   c. To develop uniform safety standards
   d. All of the above

_____ 10. The FTC is charged with which of the following major functions?
    a. To prevent unfair methods of competition
    b. To prevent unfair and deceptive trade practices
    c. To prevent mail fraud operations
    d. (a) and (b), but not (c)

_____ 11. Under the _____, a consumer has three days within which to withdraw from a credit obligation secured by a home mortgage unless the credit is made to acquire the dwelling.
    a. Interstate Land Sales Full Disclosure Act
    b. Federal Consumer Credit Protection Act
    c. Equal Credit Opportunity Act
    d. Uniform Consumer Credit Code

_____ 12. Under the _____, creditors must disclose finance charges and credit extension charges.
    a. Interstate Land Sales Full Disclosure Act
    b. Federal Consumer Credit Protection Act
    c. Equal Credit Opportunity Act
    d. Uniform Consumer Credit Code

_____ 13. Which of the following would not be prohibited by the Equal Credit Opportunity Act?
    a. First Bank only issues its VISA cards to married women in their husband's name.
    b. First Bank refuses to extend credit to men over the age of 70.
    c. First Bank refuses to extend credit to people having an income of less than $12,000.
    d. First Bank refuses to extend credit to members of the Unification Church.

_____ 14. Which of the following is/are covered by the Fair Credit Reporting Act?
    a. Reports by credit agencies
    b. A creditor calling the debtor in the middle of the night
    c. A credit check done by a credit agency
    d. Two of the above are correct, (a) and (c).

_____ 15. The FTC has issued an order of affirmative disclosure against the Warner-Lambert Company. What does the order require?
    a. It requires that they provide certain information in their advertisement in order for the ad not to be considered deceptive.
    b. It provides affirmative disclosure of the source of the information used in the original ad.
    c. It requires that the company cease and desist from deception with regard to all products that it markets.
    d. All of the above are required by affirmative disclosure.

SHORT ESSAY

1. What is the purpose of the FTC and the CPSC?

_____

_____

_____

_____

2. What are the characteristics of a "full" warranty under the Magnuson-Moss Warranty Act?

_____

_____

_____

_____

3. What information must a creditor give to a consumer who is opening an open-ended credit account?

_____

_____

_____

_____

4. What information must a creditor give to a consumer who is opening a closed-end credit account?

_____

_____

_____

5. List and briefly describe several creditor remedies.

_____

_____

_____

_____

Chapter 46
Environmental Law

PURPOSE

With the advancement of urbanization, the effect on the environment became a matter of greater concern. Air became dirtier and water more polluted. Individuals and environmental groups brought private actions against polluters, but the common law proved unable to control environmental damage. In response, the federal and state governments enacted a variety of statutes designed to promote environmental concerns and prevent environmental harm. In this chapter, you study both common law cause of action for environmental damage and federal regulation of the environment.

CHAPTER CHECKPOINTS

After reading and studying this chapter, you should be able to:

1. Identify and discuss the various common law theories supporting actions for environmental damage.

2. Distinguish between a public nuisance and a private nuisance and explain the difficulties involved in prevailing in an attempt to recover or abate either.

3. Identify important legislative acts regulating the environment.

4. Discuss the procedure for an environmental impact statement and explain its scope.

5. Explain the purpose and scope of the Comprehensive Environmental Response, Compensation and Liability Act (CERCLA).

CHAPTER OUTLINE

I. Common Law Actions for Environmental Damage–Private tort actions may be used to recover for harm to the environment. Such suits rely on the theories of nuisance, trespass, and strict liability.

   A. Nuisance–Nuisance encompasses two distinct types of wrong: private nuisance and public nuisance. A private nuisance involves an interference with the use and enjoyment of a person's land, while a public nuisance is an act which interferes with a public right.
      1. Private Nuisance–Private nuisance is a substantial and unreasonable interference with the use and enjoyment of another's land. In an action for damages a plaintiff need not prove that the defendant's conduct is unreasonable, only that the interference was unreasonable. However, in an action seeking an injunction, the reasonableness of the defendant's conduct is an issue. Courts balance the equities.
      2. Public Nuisance–A public nuisance is an interference with the health, safety, or comfort of the public. Suits to stop a public nuisance are brought by a public representative, such as the attorney general. Because public representatives often will not, and private parties may not, sue, relatively few public nuisance actions have been brought against polluters.

   B. Trespass to Land–Trespass to land involves action by one party which directly results in an invasion which interferes with the right of exclusive possession of the property of another. Trespass differs from private nuisance in that nuisance does not require an interference with the plaintiff's possession of the land.

   C. Strict Liability for Abnormally Dangerous Activities–To establish strict liability, a plaintiff must show that the defendant is carrying on an unduly dangerous (ultrahazardous) activity in an inappropriate location and that the plaintiff has suffered damage because of this activity.

   D. Problems Common to Private Causes of Action–Problems associated with the bringing of a private cause of action include: (1) high costs; (2) relief for aesthetic injury is generally not available; (3) there may be a question of causation if more than one defendant is polluting; and (4) recovery is often limited to monetary damages and the defendant remains free to continue to pollute.

II. Federal Regulation of the Environment–Because private causes of action proved inadequate, federal, state, and some local governments have enacted statutes designed to protect the environment.

   A. The National Environmental Policy Act–In 1969 Congress enacted the National Environmental Policy Act (NEPA) to establish environmental protection as a goal of federal policy. NEPA has two major substantive sections, one of which created the Council on Environmental Quality (CEQ), and the other established the requirement for an environmental impact statement (EIS) in those cases where legislation or federal action would have a significant environmental effect.
      1. Council on Environmental Quality–CEQ, part of the Executive Office of the President, makes recommendations and prepares annual reports on the condition of the environment.
      2. Environmental Impact Statements (EIS)–NEPA's promotion of environmental protection considerations is effected through the EIS requirement. An EIS is required if a proposed action (1) is Federal, (2) is "major," and (3) may have a significant environmental impact.

    a. Procedure for Preparing an EIS–When proposing legislation or considering a major federal action the federal agency initially makes an "environmental assessment," which is a short analysis of the need for an EIS. If the agency decides no EIS is required, the public must be informed of this decision. If an EIS is required, a determination is made of the "scope" of the EIS. A draft EIS is made available for comments, followed by a final EIS.

    b. Scope of EIS Requirement–The EIS requirement of NEPA applied to a broad range of projects. "Federal action" occurs when an agency proposes to build a facility itself, and also whenever an agency makes a decision which permits action by other parties which will affect the quality of the environment. The EIS requirement also applies to a broad range of effects.

    c. Content of an EIS–The EIS must contain a statement of any adverse environmental effects which cannot be avoided, reasonable alternatives, the relationship between local short-term uses of the environment and the maintenance and enhancement of long-term productivity, as well as any irreversible and irretrievable commitments of resources involved.

    d. Nature of EIS Requirement–NEPA requirements are primarily procedural and impose no requirement that the relevant federal agency take steps to mitigate the adverse effects of a proposed federal action.

B. The Clean Air Act–This act establishes two regulatory schemes. The states retain primary responsibility for regulating existing stationary sources and motor vehicles then in use. The federal government regulates new sources, new vehicles, and hazardous air pollutants.

    1. Existing Stationary Sources and Motor Vehicles Then in Use–The 1970 amendments provided that, with respect to existing stationary sources and motor vehicles then in use, the federal government would set national air quality standards that the states would be primarily responsible for achieving.

        a. National Ambient Air Quality Standards (NAAQS)–The EPA administrator must establish "primary" standards to protect the public health and "secondary" standards to protect the public welfare. Quality standards were established for seven major classes of pollutants.

        b. State Implementation Plans–After the EPA promulgates a new NAAQS, each state must submit to the EPA a state implementation plan (SIP). If it meets certain statutory conditions and if the state adopts the SIP after public hearings, the SIP must be approved by the EPA.

        c. Prevention of Significant Deterioration (PSD) Areas–Congress, in 1977 amendments, established a policy of preventing deterioration of the quality of air which exceeded the NAAQS levels. In PSD areas, only limited increases in air pollution are allowed.

        d. Nonattainment Areas–The 1977 and 1990 amendments also established special rules for areas that did not meet the applicable NAAQS. In these nonattainment areas, total emissions from existing stationary sources and the proposed new or modified source together must be less than the total emissions allowed from existing sources at the time the permit is sought. To obtain a permit in such an area the owner/operator must reduce total emissions from all sources.

    2. New Source Standards–The Clean Air Act authorizes the federal government to establish national emission standards for new stationary sources, hazardous air pollutants, and new vehicles.

        a. New Stationary Sources–The administrator must establish standards of performance for stationary sources that are constructed or modified after the publication of applicable regulations.   The standard governing new sources is more stringent than the standard governing existing sources.

b. New Vehicles–The act requires the administrator to establish emission standards for new motor vehicles and new motor vehicle engines. The 1990 amendments require reformulated fuels to be employed in order to reduce ozone and carbon monoxide pollution.

c. Hazardous Air Pollutants–The act authorizes the administrator to establish national emission standards for hazardous or toxic air pollutants which may result in an increase in mortality or an increase in serious irreversible, or incapacitating reversible, illness. The standard must be set at a level which "provides an ample margin of safety to protect the public health."

d. Acid Rain–The 1990 amendments attempt to halt environmental destruction due to precipitation containing high levels of sulfuric or nitric acid. A schedule of allowances was established to significantly reduce the emissions of sulfur dioxide and nitrous oxides by 2000.

C. The Clean Water Act–This act applies to all navigable waters in the United States and to tributaries of navigable waters, interstate waters and their tributaries, nonnavigable intrastate waters if misuse could affect interstate commerce, and freshwater wetlands. The act attempts to comprehensively restore and maintain the chemical, physical, and biological integrity of the nation's waters. It establishes different schemes for existing sources and new sources. The act also provides different programs for point sources of pollution and nonpoint sources.

1. Point Sources–A point source is "any discernible, confined and discrete conveyance . . . from which pollutants are or may be discharged." The act requires that the EPA administrator establish limitations on pollutants existing point sources may discharge into a body of water.

a. Effluent Limitations–Effluent limitations required application of the best practicable control technology currently available by 1977 and application of the best available technology economically achievable by 1983. Somewhat different standards apply to publicly owned treatment works.

b. National Pollutant Discharge Elimination System–NPDES requires any person responsible for the discharge from a point source of a pollutant into U.S. waters to obtain a discharge permit from EPA, the Army Corps of Engineers, or the relevant state.

c. The 1977 Amendments–Recognizing that the deadlines set in 1972 would not be met, Congress extended and modified the deadlines in the 1977 amendments, which divided pollutants into three categories–toxic, conventional, and nonconventional–and established different deadlines and standards for each.

2. Nonpoint Source Pollution–Because of the difficulty in controlling nonpoint source pollution, Congress amended the Clean Water Act in 1987. These amendments require states to identify state waters that will not meet the act's requirements without management of nonpoint sources of-pollution and to institute "best management practices" to control those sources. The EPA must approve each state's management plan.

3. New Source Performance Standards–The administrator is required to establish federal standards of performance for new sources. A performance standard should "reflect the greatest degree of effluent reduction . . . achievable through application of the best available demonstrated control technology." Permitting no discharge of pollutants is the preferred standard for new sources.

D. Hazardous Substances–Advances in technology allow for the production of numerous new substances, some of which have proven extremely hazardous to health. In response to this, Congress enacted various statutes to deal with different aspects of the harm.

1. Federal Insecticide, Fungicide, and Rodenticide Act–FIFRA requires that a pesticide be registered with the EPA before any person may distribute it. Registration is legal only if the pesticide's composition warrants the proposed claims for it, the pesticide will perform its intended function without "unreasonable adverse effects on the environment," the pesticide will not generally cause unreasonable adverse effects on the environment when used in accordance with widespread and commonly recognized practice, and the pesticide complies with FIFRA labeling requirements

2. The Toxic Substances Control Act–The TSCA requires a manufacturer to notify the EPA before it manufactures a new chemical or makes a significant new use of an existing chemical. The EPA may require testing of any substance, whether existing or new, if (1) the manufacture or distribution of the substance may present an unreasonable risk of injury to health or the environment, (2) there is insufficient data on the effects of the substance, and (3) testing is necessary to develop such data. If a substance "presents or will present an unreasonable risk of injury to health or the environment," the EPA may restrict or prohibit use of the substance.

3. The Resource Conservation and Recovery Act–RCRA provides a comprehensive scheme for treatment of solid waste, particularly hazardous waste. Responsibility is divided such that the states have primary responsibility for nonhazardous waste and the EPA regulates all phases of hazardous waste. The statute requires the EPA to establish a manifest system, providing a form on which the generator (an entity that produces hazardous waste) must specify the quantity, composition, origin, routing, and destination of a hazardous waste. Transporters of hazardous wastes and owner/operators of hazardous waste treatment, storage, and disposal sites must maintain records and comply with the manifest.

4. The Superfund–The Comprehensive Environmental Response, Compensation, and Liability Act (CERCLA) was enacted to provide for the cleanup of abandoned or inactive hazardous waste sites. CERCLA, as amended, requires the federal government to establish a National Contingency Plan (NCP) to set procedures and standards for responding to hazardous substance releases. This Act authorizes the federal government to take removal or remedial actions in response to a release or threatened release of hazardous substances.

    CERCLA establishes a trust fund to pay for hazardous waste removal and other remedial actions. The trust fund is financed in by a surtax on certain businesses, other taxes, and funds recovered from persons responsible for the release of hazardous substances. These parties include owners and operators of hazardous waste disposal facilities from which there has been a release. "Innocent landowners", however, do not have liability under CERCLA for clean-up costs. The Superfund Recycling Act of 1999 also exempts recyclers from liability to third parties although they may be liable in suits brought by government agencies. The Small Business Liability Relief and Brownfields Revitalization Act promotes the purchase, development, and use of brownfields, which are industrially polluted property that are not sufficiently contaminated to be classified as a priority by either the EPA or state environmental agencies.

E. International Protection of the Ozone Layer–In 1987 a treaty entitled the Montreal Protocol on Substances that Deplete the Ozone Layer was signed by the United States and 23 other countries.

Under the Montreal Protocol all signatories are obligated to reduce their production and consumption of all chemicals that deplete the ozone layer. In 1992, 165 nations negotiated a treaty to control greenhouse gases, but this treaty is voluntary. In 1997, the Kyoto Protocol was proposed to set binding greenhouse gas emission targets for developed nations. Japan and the European Union agreed to reductions, but the U.S. has not yet ratified this treaty.

KEY TERMS

1. Private nuisance

2. Public nuisance

3. Trespass to land

4. Strict liability

5. Environmental impact statement

6. Environmental assessment

7. Scoping

8. National ambient air quality standards

9. State implementation plan

10. Prevention of significant deterioration areas

11. Nonattainment areas

12. Bubble concept

13. Acid rain

14. Point source

15. Nonpoint source

16. Effluent limitation

17. BPT

18. BAT

19. BCT

20. Superfund

TRUE/FALSE

_____ 1. Private tort actions may be used to recover for harm to the environment.

_____ 2. Trespass differs from private nuisance in that nuisance does not require an interference with plaintiff's possession of the land.

_____ 3. To be treated as a public nuisance, an activity must interfere with the health, safety, or comfort of the public.

_____ 4. Comparable to other federal environmental statutes, the National Environmental Policy Act focuses on particular environmental damage and specific harmful substances.

_____ 5. The NEPA's EIS requirement applies not only to a broad range of projects but also to a broad range of environmental effects.

_____ 6. Environmental impact statements provide a basis for evaluating the benefits of a proposed project in light of its environmental risks.

_____ 7. NEPA's requirements are primarily procedural and do not require the relevant federal agency to take steps to mitigate the adverse effects of the proposed federal action.

_____ 8. Under the Clean Air Act the states' primary responsibility is to regulate new sources within the state, new vehicles, and hazardous air pollutants.

_____ 9. Once the EPA promulgates a new ambient air quality standard, every state must submit a state implementation plan detailing how they will maintain the new standard.

_____ 10. In prevention of significant deterioration areas, the EPA will allow increases in air pollution equal to the difference between the current level and the established standard.

_____ 11. Under the "bubble concept" an entire plant is viewed as one source, so that a permit process applies only if total emissions from the plant increase.

_____ 12. Air quality emission standards governing existing sources are more stringent than the standard governing new sources.

_____ 13. Under the 1977 amendments to the Clean Water Act, a new standard of best conventional pollution control technology was to be achieved for conventional pollutants.

_____ 14. An effluent limitation is a technology-based standard that limits the amount of pollutant that may be discharged by a nonpoint source into the water.

_____ 15. The FIFRA requires that a pesticide be registered with the EPA before any person in any state may distribute it.

MULTIPLE CHOICE

_____ 1. An invasion of land which interferes with the right of exclusive possession of the property would be a:
   a. private nuisance.
   b. public nuisance.
   c. trespass.
   d. none of the above.

_____ 2. While tort liability is generally based on fault, a person may be held strictly liable if the plaintiff can show that the defendant was engaged in an activity that was:
   a. ultrahazardous.
   b. inappropriate for its locale.
   c. either (a) or (b).
   d. both (a) and (b).

_____ 3. In a private nuisance action, what factor(s) will a court consider before issuing an injunction?
   a. Gravity of harm to the plaintiff
   b. Social value of defendant's activity
   c. Public interest
   d. All of the above

_____ 4. When the EPA proposes a federal action and an EIS is required, the next step in the procedure is:
   a. an environmental assessment.
   b. a comment period.
   c. scoping.
   d. a draft EIS.

_____ 5. NEPA's EIS requirement applies to a broad range of types of effects within the urban environment. To which one of the following would the EIS requirement not apply?
   a. Noise
   b. Overburdened mass transportation systems
   c. Crime
   d. It would apply to all the above as they all affect the urban environment.

_____ 6. Under the Clean Air Act, the EPA may impose civil penalties of up to:
   a. $32,500 per violation.
   b. $32,500 per day of violation.
   c. $50,000 per violation.
   d. $50,000 per day of violation.

_____ 7. In a PSD area, an owner, in order to receive a permit, must demonstrate that the source:
   a. will not add to pollution beyond the permitted increase.
   b. will utilize the best available control technology.
   c. either (a) or (b).
   d. both (a) and (b).

_____ 8. The Clean Air Act places responsibility on the federal government to establish national emission standards for all of the following except:
   a. existing stationary sources.
   b. new stationary sources.
   c. hazardous air pollutants.
   d. new vehicles.

_____ 9. Under the Clean Water Act, the maximum criminal penalties for knowing violations are 3 years imprisonment and:
   a. $32,500 per violation.
   b. $32,500 per day of violation.
   c. $50,000 per violation.
   d. $50,000 per day of violation.

_____ 10. Under the Clean Water Act "any discernible, confined and discrete conveyance . . . from which pollutants are or may be discharged" is known as:
a. a point source.
b. a nonpoint source.
c. a nonattainment area.
d. none of the above.

_____ 11. To which of the following would the Clean Water Act not apply?
a. Navigable waters in the United States
b. Interstate waters and their tributaries
c. Freshwater wetlands
d. The Clean Water Act would apply to all of the above.

_____ 12. *CPA:* Which of the following remedies is available against a real property owner to enforce the provisions of federal acts regulating air and water pollution?

	Citizen Suits against the Environmental Protection Agency to Enforce Compliance with the Laws	State Suits Against Violators	Citizen Suits Against Violators
a.	Yes	Yes	Yes
b.	Yes	Yes	No
c.	No	Yes	Yes
d.	Yes	No	Yes

_____ 13. Which of the following would be the most widely used regulatory approach by the federal government?
a. Establishment of standards and penalties for violations
b. A charge or fee system for pollution rights
c. Reliance on state regulation
d. None of the above is widely used.

_____ 14. Which of the following would be grounds for the EPA to require testing of a substance?
a. The manufacture or distribution of the substance may present an unreasonable risk of injury to health or the environment.
b. There is insufficient data on the effects of the substance on health and the environment and testing is necessary to develop such data.
c. Both (a) and (b).
d. Neither (a) nor (b).

_____ 15. The Resource Conservation and Recovery Act regulates:
   a. Current and future hazardous waste.
   b. Transportation of hazardous waste.
   c. Disposal of hazardous waste.
   d. All of the above.

SHORT ESSAY

1. Identify and discuss the common law actions for environmental damage.

   _____

   _____

   _____

   _____

2. What is the major difference between a private nuisance and a public nuisance?

   _____

   _____

   _____

   _____

3. List and briefly describe the two major substantive sections of the National Environmental Policy Act.

   _____

   _____

   _____

   _____

4. What is the difference between a "point source" and a "nonpoint source"?

   _____

   _____

   _____

   _____

5. What is the "Superfund"?

   _____

   _____

   _____

   _____

Chapter 47
International Business Law

PURPOSE

Today business requires some understanding of international business practices, because the entire global economy has become increasingly interconnected. Laws vary greatly from country to country and there is no single authority in international law. When the laws of two or more nations conflict, or when one party has violated an agreement that the other party wishes to enforce or to recover damages, it is often difficult to establish who will adjudicate the matter, which laws will be applied, what remedies are available, or where the matter should be decided. In this chapter, you study some of the basic international organizations, agreements, and principles that affect international business.

CHAPTER CHECKPOINTS

After reading and studying this chapter, you should be able to:

1. List and discuss the sources and institutions of international law.

2. Discuss the purpose and major provisions of GATT.

3. Compare the doctrines of sovereign immunity and act of state, and distinguish between expropriation and confiscation.

4. Discuss the legal controls imposed on the flow of trade, labor, and capital across national borders.

5. List and briefly describe the forms that a multinational enterprise may choose when conducting its business in a foreign country.

CHAPTER OUTLINE

A. The International Environment–International law includes law that deals with the conduct and relations of nation-states and international organizations as well as some of their relations with persons. As a general rule, international law cannot be enforced, because international courts do not have compulsory jurisdiction to resolve disputes. The courts of a sovereign nation may enforce an international law to the same extent as its domestic law if the nation has adopted the international law as the law of the nation.

1. International Court of Justice–The United Nations has a judicial branch called the International Court of Justice. The ICJ consists of 15 judges, no two of whom may be from the same sovereign state. Only nations and not private parties may be parties to an action before the court. It has jurisdiction only when nations agree to be bound by its decision, and when countries do not like its decision, they may ignore it.

2. Regional Trade Communities–International organizations, conferences, and treaties that focus on business and trade regulation are of greater significance than the ICJ. Regional trade communities such as the European Union (EU) promote common trade policies among member nations. Other important regional trade communities are the Central American Common Market (CACM), the Caribbean Common Market (CARICOM), the Association of South East Asian Nations (ASEAN), the Andean Common Market (ANCOM), the Economic Community of West African States (ECOWAS), and the Gulf Cooperation Council (GCC).

   a. European Union–The European Economic Community (EEC), better known as the Common Market, and later the European Community (EC) were predecessors to the EU and worked to remove trade barriers between member nations and to unify their economic policies. As of 2004, it was comprised of 25 countries.

   b. NAFTA–The North American Free Trade Agreement (NAFTA) took effect in 1994 and established a free trade area among the United States, Canada, and Mexico. Over 15 years, the treaty will gradually eliminate all tariffs between these three countries.

3. International Treaties–A treaty is an agreement between or among independent nations. The U.S. Constitution authorizes the president to enter into treaties with the advice and consent of the Senate "providing two-thirds of the Senators present concur." The Constitution also provides that all valid treaties are the "law of the land," having the legal force of a federal statute. Probably the most important multilateral trade treaty is the General Agreement on Tariffs and Trade (GATT). The GATT, now called the World Trade Organization, has as its basic purpose to facilitate the flow of trade by establishing agreements on potential trade barriers such as import quotas, customs, export regulations, subsidies, and import fees. GATT's most favored nation provision states that all signatories must treat each other as favorably as they treat any other country. Nevertheless, nations may also enter in free trade areas with one or more other nations.

B. Jurisdiction Over Actions of Foreign Governments–This section focuses on the power, and the limits upon the power, of a sovereign nation to exercise jurisdiction over a foreign nation or to take property owned by foreign citizens.

1. Sovereign Immunity–Every nation has absolute and total authority over what goes on within its own territory. This principle of absolute immunity of a foreign sovereign from the courts of the host country is known as sovereign immunity. Congress has enacted the Foreign Sovereign

Immunities Act in order to establish legislatively when immunity would be extended to foreign nations. The act specifically provides that a foreign state shall not be immune from the jurisdiction of courts of the U.S. or of the states if the suit is based upon (1) a commercial activity carried on in the U.S. by the foreign state, (2) an act performed in the U.S. in connection with a commercial activity of the foreign state carried on elsewhere, or (3) a commercial activity of a foreign state carried on outside the U.S. that causes a direct effect in the U.S.

2. Act of State Doctrine–The act of state doctrine provides that the judicial branch of a nation should not question the validity of actions taken by a foreign government within that foreign sovereign's own borders. The U.S. Supreme Court said in 1987 that "Every sovereign State is bound to respect the independence of every other sovereign State, and the courts of one country will not sit in judgment on the acts of the government of another done within its own territory." Exceptions to the act of state doctrine include the following: (a) a sovereign may waive its right to raise the act of state defense and (b) the doctrine may be inapplicable to commercial activities of a foreign sovereign.

3. Taking of Foreign Investment Property–An expropriation or nationalization occurs when a host government seizes foreign-owned property or assets for a public purpose and pays the owner just compensation for what is taken. Confiscation is the term used when no payment (or an inadequate payment) is given in exchange for the seized property, or it is seized for a nonpublic purpose. U.S. firms should obtain insurance from a private insurer or the Overseas Private Investment Corporation (OPIC).

C. Transacting Business Abroad–Business abroad may involve selling goods, information, or services or investing capital or arranging for the movement of labor. This section examines the legal controls imposed on the flow of trade, labor, and capital across national borders.

1. Flow of Trade–A device that is frequently applied by nations to protect domestic businesses is the tariff, which is a duty or tax imposed on goods moving into or out of a country. Tariffs raise the price of imported goods, causing some consumers to purchase less expensive, domestically produced items. Nontariff barriers include unilateral or bilateral import quotas, import bans, overly restrictive safety or manufacturing standards, complicated customs procedures, and subsidies to local industry. Export controls are used to control the flow of goods out of a country. They are usually imposed for policy reasons such as national defense, foreign policy, or protection of scarce national resources.

2. Flow of Labor–Almost all countries require that foreigners obtain valid passports before entering their borders. In addition, they may issue visas to foreign citizens permitting them to enter the country for an identified purpose or specified period of time. The U.S. Immigration and Naturalization Service issues various types of visas depending on the purpose of an individual's visit.

3. Flow of Capital–The International Monetary Fund (IMF) was established to facilitate the expansion and balanced growth of international trade, to assist in the elimination of foreign exchange restrictions, and to shorten the duration and lessen the disequilibrium in the international balance of payments of its members. There are also international and regional banks to facilitate the flow of capital and trade.

4. International Contracts–The legal issues associated with domestic commercial contracts also arise in international contracts. There also are additional issues, such as differences in language,

customs, legal systems and currency. The contract should specify the official language, currency, choice of law designating the governing law, and which nation's court will resolve disputes or whether arbitration will be used. It should also include a force majeure clause apportioning the liabilities and duties of the parties in the event of an unforeseeable occurrence. The UNCITRAL Model Law on Electronic Signatures creates a presumption that electronic signatures, which meet certain reliability criteria, are equivalent to hand-written signatures.

   a. CISG–The United States, as well as over 60 other countries, has ratified the U.N. Convention on Contracts for the International Sale of Goods. The CISG governs all contracts for the international sales of goods between parties located in nations that have ratified the CISG.

   b. Letters of Credit–A letter of credit is a promise by a buyer's bank to pay the seller provided certain conditions are met. The buyer enters into a second contract with a local bank, called an issuer, requesting the bank to pay the price upon presentation of specified documents. The commitment by the buyer's bank is the irrevocable letter of credit. Typically, a correspondent or paying bank located in the seller's country makes payment to the seller.

5. Antitrust Laws–Section 1 of the Sherman Act provides for a broad, extraterritorial reach of U.S. antitrust laws. These laws apply only if unfair methods of competition that have a direct, substantial, and reasonably foreseeable effect on U.S. domestic commerce, U.S. import commerce, or U.S. export commerce.

6. Securities Regulation–Due to increasingly internationalized securities markets, questions regarding applicable laws governing a particular transaction in securities are not uncommon. The Securities Act of 1933 and the Securities Exchange Act of 1934 apply to those securities issued in the United States unless an exemption is available. The antifraud provisions apply, and courts generally find jurisdiction where there is either *conduct* or *effects* in the United States relating to a violation of the federal securities laws.

7. Protection of Intellectual Property–U.S. intellectual property protection laws do not apply in foreign countries. The owner of an intellectual property right obtains protection from the country in question or from certain international treaties.

    The United States belongs to some multinational treaties designed to protect intellectual property. In 2002, the United States became a signatory of the Madrid Protocol, an agreement allowing U.S. trademark owners to file for registration in over 65 member countries by filing a single application in English and paying a single fee. The World Intellectual Property Organization (WIPO), also seeks to promote protection of intellectual property throughout the world. WIPO administers twenty-one international treaties dealing with intellectual property protection and includes more than 175 nations as member states.

8. Foreign Corrupt Practices Act–The Foreign Corrupt Practices Act (FCPA) prohibits all domestic concerns from bribing foreign governmental or political officials. Violations can result in fines for individuals of up to $100,000 and/or imprisonment of up to five years. Companies violating this law can be fined up to $2 million.

9. Employment Discrimination–Title VII, the Americans with Disabilities Act, and the Age Discrimination in Employment Act apply to U.S. citizens employed abroad by U.S. employers or by foreign companies controlled by U.S. employers, unless compliance violates laws of the country in which the workplace is located.

D. Forms of Multinational Enterprises–A multinational enterprise is a business that engages in transactions involving the movement of goods, information, money, people, or services across national borders. Factors to be considered in determining the form of a multinational business enterprise include financing, tax consequences, legal restrictions imposed by the host country, and the degree of control over the business sought by the multinational enterprise.

1. Direct Export Sales–The seller contracts directly with the buyer in the other country. This is the simplest and least involved form of multinational enterprise.

2. Foreign Agents–Agency relationships are often used by companies that want limited involvement in the international market.

3. Distributorships–Unlike an agent, a distributor takes title to merchandise it receives. This commonly used form is susceptible to antitrust violations.

4. Licensing–This involves the sale of an intellectual property right, such as patent, trademark, trade secret, or innovative production technology. The foreign firm pays royalties in exchange for the use of the right. Franchising is a form of licensing in which the owner grants permission to a foreign business to use the intellectual property under carefully specified conditions.

5. Joint Ventures–In a joint venture, two or more independent businesses from different countries agree to coordinate their efforts to achieve a common result. They share profits and liabilities according to a contract. Each company can be assigned responsibility for what it does best.

6. Wholly Owned Subsidiaries–The creation of a foreign wholly owned subsidiary can offer numerous advantages, including the opportunity to retain authority and control over all phases of operation and the ability to safeguard technology.

KEY TERMS

1. International law

2. Treaty

3. Sovereign immunity

4. Act of state doctrine

5. Expropriation

6. Confiscation

7. Tariff

8. Letter of credit

9. Multinational enterprise

10. Licensing

TRUE/FALSE

_____ 1. Only nations may be parties to an action before the International Court of Justice.

_____ 2. The European Community has the power to make rules which are binding on member nations and which preempt its members' domestic laws.

_____ 3. Sovereign nations which adopt international laws will enforce those laws to the same extent as all of its domestic laws.

_____ 4. The tariff is a frequently used device designed to protect domestic businesses.

_____ 5. The North American Free Trade Agreement established free trade among the United States, Mexico, and Brazil.

_____ 6. A simple majority of the senators present may ratify a treaty under the U.S. Constitution.

_____ 7. A letter of credit transaction is an effective means of managing the risks of international trade and involves three or four different parties and three underlying contracts.

_____ 8. Under GATT's most favored nation provision, signatories are not required to treat other signatories equally with regard to privileges, immunities, and favors.

_____ 9. The U.S. Supreme Court holding that a court should not question the validity of actions a foreign government takes in its own country is known as the act of state doctrine.

_____ 10. The simplest and least involved multinational enterprise is a direct export sale.

_____ 11. International courts have authority to resolve a dispute only if the parties to the dispute accept the court's jurisdiction over the matter.

_____ 12. Currently, the International Monetary Fund has more than 150 counties as members.

_____ 13. U.S. laws protecting intellectual property do not apply to transactions in other countries.

_____ 14. The United Nations Convention on Contracts for the International Sales of Goods (CISG) governs all contracts for the international sales of goods between parties located in different nations that have ratified the CISG.

_____ 15. The term "multinational enterprise" refers to any business that engages in transactions involving the movement of goods across national borders.

MULTIPLE CHOICE

_____ 1. The EEC is better known as:
  a. the Warsaw Pact.
  b. the Common Market.
  c. the General Agreement on Tariffs and Trade.
  d. the International Monetary Fund.

_____ 2. What is the purpose of a *force majeure* clause?
  a. It determines what law applies to a contract.
  b. It determines the method of payment for goods sold between a buyer in one country and a seller in another country.
  c. It determines the forum in which a dispute must be decided.
  d. It apportions the liabilities and duties of the parties in case of an unforeseeable occurrence.

_____ 3. Which of the following is NOT a nontariff barrier?
   a. Quotas
   b. Taxes
   c. Bans
   d. Subsidies

_____ 4. One precaution that can be taken by U.S. firms to avoid economic loss caused by seizure of property by a foreign government is to obtain insurance from which federal agency:
   a. OPIC.
   b. ASEAN.
   c. the Commerce Department.
   d. the U.S. State Department.

_____ 5. Examples of noncommercial activities to which the doctrine of _____ would extend include nationalizing a corporation, determining the limitations upon the use of natural resources, and granting licenses to export a natural resource.
   a. act of state
   b. sovereign immunity
   c. confiscation
   d. expropriation

_____ 6. Which of the following is the west African states' counterpart to the European Union?
   a. CARICOM
   b. ANCOM
   c. COMECON
   d. ECOWAS

_____ 7. Which of the following are objectives of NAFTA?
   a. To promote conditions of fair competition in the free trade area
   b. To promote adequate and effective enforcement of intellectual property rights
   c. To increase investment opportunities in the area
   d. All of the above

_____ 8. Almost all countries have their own immigration policies and regulations which require:
   a. that foreigners obtain valid passports before entering their borders.
   b. that their citizens have a passport to leave or reenter the country.
   c. that foreign citizens obtain a visa to enter the country for an identified purpose.
   d. all of the above.

_____ 9. Which of the following could be an exception to the act of state doctrine?
   a. The doctrine may be inapplicable to commercial activities of a foreign sovereign.
   b. A sovereign may waive its right to raise the doctrine as a defense.
   c. Either (a) or (b).
   d. Neither (a) nor (b), exceptions are not allowed.

_____ 10. The CISG specifically excludes which of the following?
   a.   Sales of goods bought for personal, family, or household use
   b.   Sale of ships or aircraft
   c.   Both (a) and (b)
   d.   Neither (a) nor (b)

_____ 11. Which of the following should be used by Americana Computer Corporation, a multinational enterprise, if they want the least involvement in the international market?
   a.   Foreign agents
   b.   Direct export sales
   c.   Joint ventures
   d.   Licensing

_____ 12. An international contract should specify:
   a.   what law will govern any breach or dispute.
   b.   the official language of the contract.
   c.   which nation's court will resolve disputes.
   d.   all of the above.

_____ 13. The choice of which multinational enterprise form of business to select depends upon which of the following?
   a.   Financing considerations
   b.   Tax consequences
   c.   Degree of desired control
   d.   All of the above

_____ 14. The rule that a court should not question the validity of actions taken by a foreign government in its own country is known as the:
   a.   act of state doctrine.
   b.   doctrine of sovereign immunity.
   c.   U.S. conflicts of laws.
   d.   none of the above.

_____ 15. Denmark seized all of the property of Chemco, Inc., an American company located in Denmark, and assumed ownership of the property for a public purpose after payment of just compensation. This is known as:
   a.   confiscation.
   b.   nationalization.
   c.   sovereign immunity.
   d.   none of the above.

SHORT ESSAY

1. The Widget Corporation of America would like to begin marketing its products in the international sector. What forms of multinational business enterprise should it consider?

   _____

   _____

   _____

   _____

2. How do expropriation and confiscation differ? What precautions should a firm which deals in the international sector take in order to protect itself against confiscation?

   _____

   _____

   _____

   _____

3. Assume you are the manager of a company that has just begun the direct export of your product. What precautions can you take to assure that you will in fact be paid for your products when you have never dealt with the buyer before and you are new to the international legal environment?

   _____

   _____

   _____

   _____

4. What items should be specified in a contract involving the sale of goods between a seller in the United States and a buyer in a foreign country?

   _____

   _____

   _____

5. What is the purpose of the Foreign Corrupt Practices Act?

   _____

   _____

   _____

   _____

Part IX
Sample Examination

MULTIPLE CHOICE

_____ 1. Which of the following is prohibited by the Sherman Act?
   a. A manufacturer assigns exclusive territories to each of its distributors.
   b. Two manufacturers enter into an agreement allocating exclusive territories to each manufacturer.
   c. A manufacturer suggests retail prices for its products.
   d. A manufacturer grants a franchise to a distributor and requires that the franchisee meet certain standards.

_____ 2. With regard to price-fixing agreements, which of the following is generally correct?
   a. They are legal when the parties to the agreement agree to lower their prices for consumers.
   b. They are legal if they meet the rule of reason test.
   c. They are _per se_ illegal under the Sherman Act.
   d. They are legal if they benefit consumers.

_____ 3. A seller of a product conditions its sale on the buyer's purchase of a second product or service. This is an example of a:
   a. market allocation.
   b. group boycott.
   c. vertical restraint.
   d. tying arrangement.

_____ 4. Which of the following is a valid defense against a discrimination charge under the Civil Rights Act of 1964?
   a. A _bona fide_ seniority or merit system
   b. A _bona fide_ occupational qualification
   c. A professionally developed ability test
   d. All of the above

_____ 5. *CPA:* Which of the following is least likely to be considered a security under the Securities Act of 1933?
   a. General partnership interests
   b. Limited partnership interests
   c. Stock options
   d. Warrants

_____ 6. Which of the following is NOT required under the *Howey* test for an investment transaction?
   a. An investment in a common venture.
   b. Premised on an expectation of profit.
   c. Derived from one's own effort.
   d. All of the above are required.

_____ 7. Title I of the FCCPA, which is also known as the _____, has superseded state disclosure requirements relating to credit terms for both consumer loans and credit sales under $25,000.
   a. Equal Credit Opportunity Act
   b. Truth-in-Lending Act
   c. Magnuson-Moss Warranty Act
   d. Fair Credit Billing Act

_____ 8. Margaret requests a credit card in her own name at Greene's Department Store. The store manager tells her the store has a policy of only issuing cards to married women in their husband's name. The manager says Margaret can have a card issued in her husband's name if he completes the application. In all likelihood, Greene's Department Store is in violation of:
   a. the Federal Consumer Credit Protection Act.
   b. the Fair Credit Reporting Act.
   c. the Equal Credit Opportunity Act.
   d. no laws, because this is an acceptable practice.

_____ 9. What is a "yellow dog" contract?
   a. It is a contract that allows an employer to terminate an employee at will.
   b. It is a contract that prohibits discrimination against persons of oriental heritage.
   c. It is a contract by which an employer requires employees to promise they will not join a union.
   d. It is a contract that requires the employer to hire only union members.

_____ 10. *CPA:* Under Title VII of the 1964 Civil Rights Act, which of the following forms of discrimination is not prohibited?
   a. Sex
   b. Age
   c. Race
   d. Religion

_____ 11. Sexual harassment is prohibited by which of the following?
   a. The Equal Pay Act
   b. Title VII of the Civil Rights Act of 1964
   c. The Rehabilitation Act of 1973
   d. All of the above

_____ 12. A grant by the federal government of a limited monopoly right of an author to control the copying, publication, or other use of works of authorship fixed in any tangible medium of expression is a:
   a. patent.
   b. copyright.
   c. trade secret.
   d. trademark.

_____ 13. Courts have generally interpreted the statutory definition of the term "security" found in the 1933 Securities Act to include investments in which of the following?
   a. Limited partnership interests
   b. Citrus groves
   c. Both (a) and (b)
   d. Neither (a) nor (b)

_____ 14. Which of the following transactions would not be exempt from the registration requirements found in the 1933 Securities Act?
   a. An offering to local resident investors in the city where a corporation is located and in the state in which the corporation is incorporated with $6 million in securities.
   b. An offering of stock in the Valley National Bank of Southern Minnesota.
   c. A private placement to an insurance company.
   d. An offering of limited partnerships in pecan groves to investors in two states where $6 million in the partnerships are offered.

_____ 15. *CPA:* When performing an audit, a CPA:
   a. must exercise the level of care, skill, and judgment expected of a reasonably prudent CPA under the circumstances.
   b. must strictly adhere to generally accepted accounting principles.
   c. is strictly liable for failing to discover client fraud.
   d. is not liable unless the CPA commits gross negligence or intentionally disregards generally accepted auditing standards.

_____ 16. *CPA:* A CPA will be liable to a tax client for damages resulting from all of the following actions except:
   a. failing to timely file a client's return.
   b. failing to advise a client of certain tax elections.
   c. refusing to sign a client's request for a filing extension.
   d. neglecting to evaluate the option of preparing joint or separate returns that would have resulted in a substantial tax savings for a married client.

_____ 17. The federal statute establishing environmental protection as a major national goal and mandating environmental impact statements in certain situations is the:
a. Resource Conservation and Recovery Act (RCRA).
b. National Environmental Policy Act (NEPA).
c. Clean Air Act.
d. Comprehensive Environmental Response, Compensation, and Liability Act (CERCLA).

_____ 18. Under the _____, a foreign country would be free from a host country's laws.
a. sovereign immunity rule
b. General Agreement on Tariffs and Trade
c. act of state doctrine
d. Convention on the International Sale of Goods

_____ 19. The government of Parador seizes an American-owned factory for a public purpose and pays the owner compensation for the factory based upon what it considers fair.
a. If the American owner is not satisfied with the compensation, it could sue in the International Court of Justice.
b. If the American owner is not satisfied with the compensation, it could sue in an American court under the General Agreement on Tariffs and Trade.
c. This is an example of a confiscation.
d. This is an example of an expropriation.

_____ 20. An FTC ruling requiring an advertiser to include in its advertisements information that will insure that the advertisements are not deceptive is called:
a. affirmative disclosure.
b. corrective advertising.
c. multiple product order.
d. none of the above.

Try The Web

1. What is the definition of a "person" under the Civil Rights Act of 1964?

One solution:
   Go to: http://www.law.cornell.edu/
   Select: Constitutions & Codes–US Code
   Select: Table of Popular Names
   Select: Part 4
   Select: Civil Rights Act of 1964

Chapter 48
CyberLaw

PURPOSE

The purpose of this chapter is to identify and discuss some of the important legal and regulatory issues that have arisen relating to the Internet and business conducted in cyberspace. This chapter examines the response of the legal system to this evolving area of commercial trade and its attempt to adjust existing laws to help regulate this area of commerce, as well as to adopt new laws that target certain matters of concern. This chapter focuses primarily on the following areas of the law that have been affected by e-commerce: defamation, intellectual property, contract and sales law, privacy, securities regulation, and criminal law.

CHAPTER CHECKPOINTS

After reading and studying this chapter, you should be able to:

1. Identify the major types of intellectual property that are involved in e-commerce and explain how parties' rights to this type of property may be adversely affected by conduct on the Internet.

2. Discuss special laws that address contracting on the Internet.

3. Explain how the law attempts to protect the privacy of individuals from private and governmental invasions involving the Internet.

4. Discuss the right to conduct securities transactions via the Internet.

5. Identify and discuss different types of crimes that may be conducted online.

CHAPTER OUTLINE

A. Defamation – Defamation is the wrongful injury to the reputation of another. The elements of defamation are (1) a false and defamatory statement concerning another person, (2) an unprivileged communication of this statement to a third party, (3) in some situations, fault on the part of the defendant in knowing or failing to determine the falsity of the statement, and (4) in some situations, proof that the statement caused special harm to the plaintiff. A defamatory statement set forth in writing or print medium is called libel. Oral defamation is slander. To date, defamation on the Internet has been treated as libel.

The Communications Decency Act of 1996 ("CDA") grants Internet service providers ("ISPs") immunity from defamation when publishing information communicated by third parties. Because the CDA grants immunity only to ISPs, it is possible that an employer that intentionally and unreasonably fails to remove defamatory material posted by employees on the employer's electronic system may be held for such defamatory material.

B. Intellectual Property
   1. Copyrights – The Federal Copyright Act grants copyright owners the exclusive right to use, reproduce, and sell original works, such as written, musical, and dramatic works, sound recordings, and computer programs. It protects original works in any tangible form. Federal laws seeking to help protect copyrights include those set forth below.
      a. The No Electronic Theft Act ("NET Act") makes it clear that infringement includes pirating copyrighted works (1) for commercial advantage or private financial gain or (2) by reproducing or distributing, during any 180-day period, one or more copies of one or more copyrighted works with a total retail value of more than $1,000. This Act extends the statute of limitations for criminal copyright infringement to 5 years and increases criminal penalties for certain copyright violations. Imprisonment for up to five years (ten years for subsequent violations) may be imposed for certain willful infringements.
      b. The Family Entertainment and Copyright Act of 2005 establishes criminal penalties for willful copyright infringement by distribution of certain works, such as a computer program, musical work, or motion picture.
      c. The Anti-counterfeiting Amendments Act of 2004 prohibits knowingly trafficking in various works including counterfeit computer programs and motion pictures, or counterfeit documentation or packaging.
      d. The federal Digital Millennium Copyright Act ("DCMA") forbids: (1) circumventing a technological protection measure that is put in place by a copyright owner to control access to a copyrighted work, e.g., descrambling a scrambled work; (2) creating or making available technologies that are developed to defeat technological protections against unauthorized access; and (3) creating or making available technologies developed to defeat technological protections against unauthorized copying or other copyright infringement. This Act allows a wronged party to obtain injunctions, damages (actual and statutory), attorneys' fees, and destruction of the offending device. Criminal penalties also may be levied.

e. The Digital Theft Deterrence and Copyright Damages Improvement Act of 1999 increases the maximum statutory damages that may be awarded under federal copyright law to $30,000. It increases to $150,000 the additional damages that a court may award for willful conduct.

f. Different types of infringing conduct - The posting or e-mailing of a copyrighted work may constitute copyright infringement. The DCMA, however, immunizes ISPs from liability for third-party infringement of this nature. Web site operators who enable others to commit copyright infringement, however, may be held vicariously liable for others' infringement, e.g., Napster. "Hyperlinking" enables Internet users to move quickly from one web site to another by clicking on highlighted text or graphics. Unauthorized hyperlinking using copyrighted material may be copyright infringement. "Framing" occurs when information from a linked web site is viewed from within a linking web site. This can be misleading because the user may mistakenly believe that the linking site is supplying the information. This conduct may be infringement.

g. Defenses to copyright infringement-The Copyright Act provides that the "fair use" of copyrighted works for purposes of criticism, comment, news reporting, teaching, scholarship, or research is not copyright infringement. In determining whether use of a work is fair use, courts consider: (1) the purpose of the use, including whether it is used for commercial gain; (2) the nature of the work; (3) the amount of the work used and how substantial a portion of the work is used; and (4) the effect of the use on the potential market for or value of the copyrighted work.

2. Trademarks - Federal law primarily governs trademark law. The Federal Trademark Act (Lanham Act) recognizes four types of marks: (1) trademark – mark, word, letter, number, design, picture, or combination that a party uses to identify its goods and to distinguish them from those of others, e.g., "Nike;" (2) service mark – mark used to identify and distinguish one's services from those of others, e.g., "Jenny Craig Weight Loss Clinic;" (3) certification mark - mark used to certify that goods or services satisfy specific requirements for receiving such certification, e.g., "Good Housekeeping Seal of Approval;" and (4) collective mark - mark used to indicate that a producer or provider belongs to a trade union, trade association, or other organization, or that members of a collective group produced the goods or services, e.g., "Union Made." To be protected, a mark must be distinctive enough to clearly identify the origin of goods or services, and it cannot be immoral or deceptive. Trademark infringement occurs when a person without authorization uses an identical or substantially similar mark that is likely to cause confusion, mistake, or deception.

a. Cybersquatting-Cybersquatting is the registering of a domain name that contains another's trademark with the intent to sell the rights to the domain name to the party who owns the mark. Example: Joe registers the domain name "DenverBroncos.com." The Anticybersquatting Consumer Protection Act allows the owner of a mark to civilly sue any person who, with a bad faith intent to profit from that mark, registers or uses a domain name that (1) is identical or confusingly similar to a protected mark, (2) dilutes a protected mark, or (3) is a protected mark.

The Fraudulent Online Identity Sanctions Act of 2004 provides that if a person knowingly and falsely registers and uses a domain name in the course of committing another felony offense, then the maximum imprisonment provided for that felony offense is to be doubled or increased by seven years, whichever is less.

b. Metatags are key words that describe the contents of web sites. These words are embedded in a web site's pages and are used by search engines, such as Yahoo!, to create large indexes that are scanned for matches when users ask a search engine to find a particular type of site. Some courts have enjoined parties from embedding others' metatags in their site.

3. Patents – A patent grants its owner the exclusive right to make, use, and sell an invention for the life of the patent. Utility patents may be obtained for a process, machine, manufactured item, or composition of matter if it is (1) novel, (2) useful, and (3) nonobvious. Utility patents are valid for 20 years. A patent cannot be renewed and, upon its expiration, the invention enters the public domain and anyone can use it. Internet-related programs can be patented.

4. Trade Secrets - A trade secret is commercially valuable information that is kept secret and is not general knowledge, e.g., the recipe for Coca-Cola. Trade secrets are governed by state law, which provides civil remedies for their misappropriation. The federal Economic Espionage Act of 1996 forbids the theft of trade secrets. This Act establishes criminal penalties for violations, but it does not create any federal civil remedies for theft of trade secrets. The unauthorized downloading or uploading of another's trade secret is a violation of this Act.

C. Contracts and Sales - A contract is a legally binding agreement. Contracts are primarily governed by state common law, although the sale of goods is governed by UCC Article 2 in nearly all states. While it is sometimes unclear which law governs Internet business transactions, many firms follow Article 2. It similarly is unclear whether an enforceable contract is created by a "shrinkwrap license" (license agreement is included in software that is covered by plastic) or by a "clickwrap license" (before buying item on the Internet, a buyer must click on a button that displays a license agreement).

1. *UCITA* - In 1999, the National Conference of Commissioners on Uniform State Laws adopted the Uniform Computer Information Transaction Act ("UCITA"), which establishes comprehensive rules for computer information transactions. To date, only two states have enacted UCITA.

2. Electronic Records - The Uniform Electronic Transactions Act ("UETA"), which has been enacted by nearly 40 states, gives full legal effect to electronic contracts and establishes uniform rules for their use provided that the parties to a transaction have agreed to conduct transactions by electronic means. Among other things, UETA provides that electronic signatures and contracts satisfy the writing requirement of the statute of frauds. UETA This Act also validates contracts that are created by machines that function as electronic agents for parties to a transaction, e.g., ATM machines.

   The federal Electronic Signatures in Global and National Commerce ("E-Sign") makes electronic records and signatures valid and enforceable in the United States for many transactions that are conducted in interstate or foreign commerce. Transactions covered by this Act include the sale, lease, exchange, and licensing of personal property and services, as well as the sale, lease, or exchange of real property. E-Sign does not require anyone to agree to accept electronic records or electronic signatures. E-Sign does not preempt the UETA. E-sign also assures that Internet and e-mail agreements are not rendered unenforceable by the statute of frauds.

3. Non-Compete Agreements – An employee's covenant not to compete (agreement not to engage in a given trade, profession, or business) is enforceable if (1) the purpose of the covenant is to protect a property interest of the employer and (2) the covenant is no more extensive than is reasonably necessary to protect that interest. The reasonableness of a covenant depends on its geographic scope, length of time, and hardship it imposes. Non-compete agreements generally are valid in the context of e-commerce employment. Nonetheless, some courts have held that the scope of these covenants are more limited in the context of Internet-related employment than in other types of employment.

D. Privacy and the Internet
   1. Protection of Personal Identifiable Information on the Internet

a. Privacy and Intrusion by Private Parties - The U.S. Constitution does not protect a person's right to privacy from conduct of private parties – tort law protects against such intrusions. The tort of invasion of privacy consists of four distinct torts: (1) appropriation of a person's name or likeness; (2) unreasonable intrusion on another's seclusion; (3) unreasonable public disclosure of private facts about another; and (4) unreasonable publicity that places another in a false light in the public's eye. The Federal Trade Commission has recommended that Congress enact laws to establish four basic privacy protections for consumer-oriented web sites.

b. Protecting Children – The Children's Online Privacy Protection Act ("COPPA") protects the privacy of children who are under the age of 13 and their parents in connection with the Internet. This Act requires certain web sites to (1) post a notice on the web site regarding the information that is being collected from children by the operator, how the operator uses such information, and the operator's disclosure practices for such information and (2) obtain verifiable parental consent for the collection, use, or disclosure of personal information on such children.

2. Freedom from Unwanted Government Intrusion – In general, the U.S. Constitution and individual constitutional guarantees apply to governmental conduct involving the Internet.

3. Employee Privacy Intrusions by Employers – Unless otherwise agreed, an employer may legally examine employees' communications that are made using the employer's e-mail system.

E. Securities Regulation – A security is broadly defined to include stocks, bonds, notes, and investment contracts. The Securities Act of 1933 and the Securities Exchange Act of 1934 are the primary federal laws regulating the offering and sale of securities in interstate commerce.

The 1933 Act forbids the offer or sale of any security by mail or any other means of interstate commerce unless a registration statement for that security is in effect or the issuer secures an exemption from registration. The 1933 Act also forbids fraud in all sales of securities involving interstate commerce or the mails. The 1934 Act deals mainly with the resale of securities. The SEC has adopted regulations for the electronic delivery of information required by federal securities laws. It also has established EDGAR (Electronic Data Gathering, Analysis, and Retrieval), a computer system that automatically processes reports required to be filed with the SEC.

1. Permitted Securities Activities over the Internet - For public offerings registered under the 1933 Act, the SEC allows electronic delivery of a prospectus provided that the issuer satisfies requirements relating to notice, access, and evidence of delivery. Electronic disclosure via a firm's web site does not satisfy the delivery requirements under the 1933 Act unless an investor gives prior consent to receive electronic delivery via that web site or the investor actually accesses the document on the web site. Private offerings of securities, which do not permit general or public solicitations, cannot be made via the Internet unless an effective procedure is used to restrict access solely to investors who are qualified to participate in such offerings.

2. Fraudulent Use of the Internet – Fraudulent conduct used to sell securities online in violation of federal securities law often involves (1) selling worthless securities or (2) manipulation of the price of securities traded in the secondary market, e.g., "pump and dump" fraudulent scheme.

F. Cyber Crime - Computer crimes are often categorized on whether a computer is (1) the target of the crime, e.g., theft or destruction of proprietary information, vandalism, denial of service, web site defacing, and malicious code, or (2) the instrument of the crime, e.g., distribution of child pornography, money laundering, illegal gambling, copyright infringement, and fraud.

The Computer Fraud and Abuse Act makes the following conduct a crime with respect to any computer that is used in interstate commerce: (1) unauthorized access or damage to the computer; (2) access to the computer with the intent to commit fraud; (3) trafficking in confidential passwords; and (4) threatening to damage the computer with the intent to extort money or anything of value. Parties also may be prosecuted under other federal laws, such as copyright, mail fraud, or wire fraud laws, for unlawful conduct committed in cyber space.

The Controlling the Assault of Non-Solicited Pornography and Marketing Act of 2003 ("CAN-SPAM Act of 2003") seeks to help protect parties from spam (unsolicited commercial electronic mail) by forbidding false or misleading transmission information, deceptive subject headings, and sending spam after objection.

KEY TERMS

1. CyberLaw
2. Defamation
3. Libel
4. Slander
5. Communications Decency Act of 1996 (CDA)
6. No Electronic Theft Act (NET Act)
7. Digital Theft Deterrence and Copyright Damages Improvement Act
8. Copyright
9. Digital Millennium Copyright Act (DCMA)
10. Lanham Act
11. Hyperlinking
12. Framing
13. Fair use
14. Trademark
15. Service mark
16. Certification mark
17. Collective mark
18. Cybersquatting
19. Anticybersquatting Consumer Protection Act
20. Metatags
21. Keying
22. Patent
23. Trade secret
24. Shrinkwrap license
25. Clickwrap license
26. Uniform Computer Information Transaction Act (UCITA)
27. Electronic records
28. Uniform Electronic Transactions Act (UETA)
29. Electronic Signatures in Global and National Commerce (E-Sign)
30. Non-Compete agreement
31. Children's Online Privacy Protection Act (COPPA)
32. Security
33. Securities Act of 1933
34. Securities Exchange Act of 1934
35. Pump and dump
36. Electronic Data Gathering, Analysis, and Retrieval (EDGAR)
37. Regulation A
38. Private Offerings under Regulation D
39. Cyber crime
40. Computer Fraud and Abuse Act

TRUE/FALSE

_____ 1. Courts have ruled that employees' non-compete agreements are invalid whenever made in connection with Internet-related employment.

_____ 2. The U.S. Constitution does not apply to e-commerce or the Internet.

_____ 3. Employers may look at employees' e-mail that is communicated via the employers' e-mail system.

_____ 4. Computer crime refers only to special crimes in which a computer is the target of a crime.

_____ 5. Federal securities law may apply to stock transactions conducted via the Internet.

_____ 6. Federal intellectual property law does not apply to the World Wide Web.

_____ 7. "Pump and dump" refers to the unlawful practice of releasing false positive statements on the Internet in order to cause a company's stock price to increase and then selling one's stock in that company before the market learns that these statements are false.

_____ 8. The tort of invasion of privacy is committed when a party wrongly uses another's name, likeness, or image for commercial advantage.

_____ 9. CyberLaw refers only to new legislation and case law dealing with legal issues associated with the Internet and e-commerce.

_____ 10. Unauthorized hyperlinking to others' web sites that involves the use of others' copyrighted material may constitute copyright infringement.

_____ 11. Cybersquatting is lawful if a person who registers a domain name containing a second party's trademark do so before the second party registers a domain name using this mark.

_____ 12. The Uniform Electronic Transactions Act (UETA), which has been enacted by at least 20 states, provides that electronic signatures and contracts do not satisfy the writing requirement of the statute of frauds and, therefore, they are invalid unless set forth in an appropriate signed writing.

_____ 13. A party may be granted a utility patent on an Internet-related process if the process satisfies the general requirements for obtaining a patent.

_____ 14. The unauthorized downloading of another's trade secret is a violation of the Lanham Act.

_____ 15. The Digital Theft Deterrence and Copyright Damages Improvement Act of 1999 increases the maximum statutory damages that may be awarded under federal copyright law to $1 million.

MULTIPLE CHOICE

___ 1. Carl created a web site for a fictitious company called "Get Rich Quick." Carl used his web site and the Internet to make a general public offering of common stock in this firm. In the offering, Carl falsely misrepresented that the company had $50 million in sales and was profitable even though it had never had any sales or profits. Five thousand investors bought stock in Get Rich Quick and subsequently lost their entire investment when Carl absconded with the proceeds. Under these facts:

   a. Carl violated the 1933 Act.
   b. Carl did not commit any wrongs because his statements were made only on the Internet.
   c. Carl committed no wrongs because federal securities laws do not apply to conduct on the Internet.
   d. b and c.

___ 2. Jim stated in a public Internet chat room that May, a former girlfriend, had a sexually transmitted disease. As Jim knew, this statement was false. Under these facts, Jim committed:

   a. The tort of invasion of privacy.
   b. The tort of libel.
   c. The tort of slander.
   d. Jim did not commit any tort because he did not know who would read his false statement.

___ 3. In which case did Grace probably commit a cyber crime?

   a. Grace used her computer and the Internet to make an unauthorized transfer of $50,000 from Acme's bank account into her personal bank account.
   b. Grace used her computer and the Internet to hack into Direct Book's web site to obtain others' credit card numbers. Grace then used these numbers to make unauthorized purchases.
   c. a and b.
   d. Grace did not commit any cyber crimes.

___ 4. Selma developed new computer software and copyrighted it under U.S. copyright law. Data Corporation bought a copy Selma's software and, without Selma's authorization, Data Corporation began to resell this software via its web site on the Internet. Under these facts:

   a. Data Corporation did not commit any wrongs since it purchased the original software.
   b. Data Corporation did not commit any wrongs since software cannot be copyrighted.
   c. Data Corporation did not commit any wrongs since it sold the software only via the Internet.
   d. Data Corporation committed copyright infringement.

_____ 5. Ginger is an employee at Acme Corporation. In which of the following situations, did Acme commit the tort of invasion of privacy?

   a. Acme monitored Ginger's e-mail that she sent and received via Acme's e-mail system. Acme had previously told Ginger that it reserved the right to monitor her e-mail at work.

   b. Acme monitored Ginger's e-mail that she sent and received via Acme's e-mail system. Acme had NOT previously informed Ginger that it reserved the right to monitor her e-mail at work.

   c. Acme monitored Ginger's e-mail that she sent and received via her personal computer at her home. Ginger had not consented to this monitoring.

   d. Acme committed the tort of invasion of privacy in all of the foregoing situations.

_____ 6. Acme Inc. developed a Web site called the PEPSI Drug Site, a site that provided information to teenagers on how to manufacture drug paraphernalia. Under these facts, Acme has violated:

   a. The Digital Millennium Copyright Act.

   b. The Electronic Signatures in Global and National Commerce Act.

   c. The Anticybersquatting Consumer Protection Act.

   d. The Electronic Communications Privacy Act of 1986.

_____ 7. Sam operates an Internet business that specializes in the sale of electronic games to children and teenagers. Sam required all visitors to provide certain personal information, which he intends to use internally and to sell to others. Under the Children's Online Privacy Protection Act:

   a. Sam cannot collect personal information from children 13 or under without parental authorization.

   b. Sam cannot collect personal information from minors under 18 without parental authorization.

   c. Sam can collect personal information from anyone without parental authorization.

   d. a and b.

_____ 8. A person could obtain a patent for which of the following?

   a. A new book on how to use Windows software.

   b. A new process for washing windows: use hot water and white vinegar.

   c. A new software program that teaches a person how to clone himself in 5 minutes.

   d. b and c.

_____ 9. The Copyright Act allows parties to make "fair use" of copyrighted works for what purposes:

   a. News reporting.

   b. Research.

   c. Commercial gain.

   d. a and b.

_____ 10. The federal Economic Espionage Act of 1996 forbids:
   a.   Hyperlinking.
   b.   Framing.
   c.   Keying.
   d.   Theft of trade secrets.

_____ 11. Select the correct answer:
   a.   EDGAR allows companies to electronically file reports with the SEC.
   b.   EDGAR forbids companies from electronically filing reports with the SEC.
   c.   Private offerings under Regulation D can be made to the general public via the Internet.
   d.   a and c.

_____ 12. The federal law that prohibits creating or making available technologies that are developed to defeat technological protections against unauthorized access of copyrighted material is the:
   a.   Digital Millennium Copyright Act (DCMA).
   b.   Uniform Computer Information Transaction Act (UCITA).
   c.   Uniform Electronic Transactions Act (UETA).
   d.   Electronic Signatures in Global and National Commerce (E-Sign).

_____ 13. The federal law that grants Internet service providers immunity from defamation when publishing information communicated by third parties is the:
   a.   Communications Decency Act of 1996 (CDA).
   b.   No Electronic Theft Act (NET Act).
   c.   Anticybersquatting Consumer Protection Act.
   d.   Children's Online Privacy Protection Act (COPPA).

_____ 14. The federal law that prohibits the unauthorized access of another's computer that is used in interstate commerce is the:
   a.   Communications Decency Act of 1996 (CDA).
   b.   No Electronic Theft Act (NET Act).
   c.   Computer Fraud and Abuse Act.
   d.   Children's Online Privacy Protection Act (COPPA).

_____ 15. The federal law that validates digital signatures for purposes of contract formation in connection with interstate and foreign commerce is the:
   a.   Digital Millennium Copyright Act (DCMA).
   b.   Uniform Computer Information Transaction Act (UCITA).
   c.   Uniform Electronic Transactions Act (UETA).
   d.   Electronic Signatures in Global and National Commerce (E-Sign).

SHORT ESSAY

1. Analyze whether ISPs or web site operators may be held liable for wrongs committed by their Internet customers.

    _____

    _____

    _____

    _____

2. Identify and briefly discuss three types of conduct on the Internet that may be copyright infringement.

    _____

    _____

    _____

3. Identify and briefly discuss the four types of marks or symbols that are protected by the Lanham Act.

    _____

    _____

    _____

4. Identify the types of conduct that are made a crime by the Computer Fraud and Abuse Act.

    _____

    _____

    _____

    _____

5. Discuss whether electronic contracts are generally valid.

    _____

    _____

    _____

    _____

Chapter 49
Introduction to Property, Property Insurance, Bailments, and Documents of Title

PURPOSE

In this chapter you study various concepts associated with property, because in America it occupies a unique status because of the protection expressly granted it by the federal Constitution as well as by most state constitutions. Two significant aspects of property law concern the transfer of ownership of property and the protection of property through property insurance. Insurance is a contractual undertaking by the insurer to pay a sum of money or give something of value to the insured or a beneficiary on the happening of a contingency or fortuitous event that is beyond the control of the contracting parties. In this chapter you will study primarily personal property, transfer of title to personal property, and fire and property insurance.

You also will study in this chapter the bailment relationship and documents of title. A bailment is a temporary transfer of personal property without transfer of title, by one person (the bailor) to another person (the bailee) for the accomplishment of a certain purpose, after which the property is to be returned to the bailor or disposed of according to the bailor's directions. Documents of title are frequently used in bailment transactions. A document of title is a warehouse receipt, bill of lading, or other document evidencing a right to receive, hold, and dispose of the document and the goods it covers. To be a document of title, a document must be issued or addressed to a bailee and cover goods in the bailee's possession that are either identified or are fungible portions of an identified mass. Article 7 of the UCC governs documents of title.

CHAPTER CHECKPOINTS

After reading and studying this chapter, you should be able to:

1. Distinguish between tangible and intangible property, real and personal property, as well as fixtures, and give examples of each.

2. Identify and discuss the various methods of transfer of title of personal property.

3. Define an insurable interest and explain why the law requires it.

4. Distinguish between waiver, estoppel, representations, and warranties as they affect forfeiture and avoidance of an insurance policy.

5. Discuss the essential elements of a bailment.

6. List the rights and duties on the part of the bailor and bailee, and those of a warehouser, carrier, and innkeeper.

7. Define a document of title and discuss the requirements of negotiability for a document of title.

8. Identify and discuss the different types of documents of title and the rights acquired by due negotiation of a negotiable document of title.

CHAPTER OUTLINE

I. Introduction to Property and Personal Property–Property is a legally protected interest or group of interests. Certain consequences follow from ownership of it.

   A. Kinds of Property–Property may be classified as (1) tangible or intangible, and (2) real or personal. These classifications are not mutually exclusive.

      1. Tangible and Intangible–Tangible property consists of physical objects such as a chair, a farm, or a household pet. Intangible property is a protected interest in a thing that is not physical, such as a stock certificate, which represents ownership of stock.

      2. Real and Personal–Real property is land and all interests in it (also called realty). Personal property consists of all property that is not real property.

      3. Fixtures–A fixture is an article of personal property so firmly attached to real property that an interest in it arises under real property law. In determining whether personal property becomes a fixture, the intention of the parties with conflicting claims to it as expressed in their agreement will control. If there is no agreement, the following factors are relevant in determining whether a particular item is a fixture: (1) the physical relationship of the item to the land or building; (2) the intention of the person who attached the item to the land or building; (3) the purpose served by the item in relation to the land or building and in relation to the person who brought it there; and (4) the interest of that person in the land or building at the time of the attachment of the item. Although physical attachment is significant, a more important test is whether the item can be removed without material injury to the land or the building. A trade fixture is an affixed item used in connection with the tenant's trade but not intended to become part of the realty. The law of landlord and tenant permits a tenant to remove a trade fixture if the removal can be done without material injury to the structure.

   B. Transfer of Title to Personal Property–The acquisition or transfer of title to real property is generally a formal affair. In contrast, title to personal property may be transferred with relative ease and a minimum of formality. The law concerning personal property has been largely codified in the

Uniform Commercial Code, especially Article 2 of the UCC dealing with sale of goods, Article 3 dealing with negotiable instruments, and Article 8 governing investment securities. However, certain issues involving ownership and transfer of title are not covered by the Code. Transfer of title to personal property may be:

1. By Sale–A sale of tangible personal property (goods) is the transfer of title to specified existing goods for a consideration known as the price. Title passes when the parties intend it to pass; transfer of possession is not required for transfer of title. Sales of intangible personal property also involve the transfer of title. Some of these sales are governed by the UCC and some, such as copyrights and patents, are governed by specialized federal legislation.

2. By Gift–A gift is the transfer of title to property from one person to another without consideration. The lack of consideration is the basic distinction between a gift and a sale. To be effective a gift must be completed by delivery. The donor is the person who makes a gift; the donee is the recipient of a gift. A gratuitous promise to make a gift is not binding.

    a. Delivery–Delivery is essential to a valid gift. The term delivery refers to the manual transfer of the item to the donee. Constructive delivery refers to the delivery of something symbolic of control over an item. An irrevocable gift may be effected by constructive delivery when actual delivery of the gift item itself is not possible.

    b. Intent–The law requires that there must be an intent on the part of the donor to make a present gift of the property. Gifts, other than engagement gifts, cannot be conditional.

    c. Acceptance–The final requirement of a valid gift is acceptance by the donee.

    d. Classification–Gifts may be either *inter vivos* or *causa mortis*. An *inter vivos* gift is one made by a donor during her lifetime. A gift *causa mortis* is one made by a donor in contemplation of her imminent death.

3. By Will or Descent–Title to personal property is frequently acquired by inheritance from a person who dies, either with or without a will.

4. By Accession–Accession means the right of the owner of property to any increase in it, whether caused by natural or artificial means. The owner of a cow acquires title by accession to any calves born to that cow.

5. By Confusion–Confusion is the intermixing of goods belonging to two or more owners such that the property of all of them can no longer be identified except as part of the mass of like goods. Confusion may result from accident, mistake, willful act, or agreement of the parties. If the goods can be apportioned, each owner who proves his proportion of the whole is entitled to receive his share. If, however, the confusion results from the willful and wrongful act of one of the parties, he will lose his entire interest if he cannot prove his share.

6. By Possession–In some instances, a person may acquire title to movable personal property by taking possession of it. Abandoned property is property intentionally disposed of by the owner. Lost property is property that is unintentionally left by the owner. If the property has been intentionally abandoned, a finder is entitled to the property. Under the general rule, the finder of lost property is entitled to it as against everyone except the true owner. If lost property is in the ground, the owner of the land has a superior claim to that of the finder. Mislaid property is property that is intentionally placed by the owner but unintentionally left. If property is mislaid, most courts hold that the owner of the premises, not the finder, has first claim if the true owner is

not discovered. Many states now have statutes that provide a means of vesting title to lost property in the finder when a prescribed search for the owner is fruitless.

II. Property Insurance–Insurance distributes risk among a large number of members (the insureds) through an insurance company (insurer). Insurance is a contractual undertaking by the insurer to pay a sum of money or give something of value to the insured upon the happening of a contingency or fortuitous event that is beyond the control of the contracting parties. The McCarran-Ferguson Act places the regulation of insurance on the states.

   A. Fire and Property Insurance–Fire insurance protects against loss resulting from damage to or destruction of property by fire and related perils, such as damage caused by lightning, explosion, earthquake, water, wind, rain, collision, and riot. Coverage is frequently enlarged through an "endorsement" or "rider" to include other perils. Fire policies are standardized in the United States.
     1. Types of Fire–Policies are generally held to cover damage from "hostile" fires, but not from "friendly" fires. A friendly fire is one that is contained in its intended location, such as a fire in a fireplace, furnace, or stove. A hostile fire includes all fires outside their intended or usual locales.
     2. Co-insurance Clauses–Co-insurance is a means of sharing the risk between insurer and insured, in which a person insures property for less than its full or stated value and agrees to share the risk of loss. The formula for recovery is:

        Recovery = (Face value of policy) / (Fair market value of property × co-insurance %) × loss

     3. Other Insurance Clauses–Recovery under property insurance policies may be limited by other insurance clauses, which require that liability be distributed pro rata among the various insurers.
     4. Types of Policies–Property insurance may be either a valued policy or an open policy. A valued policy provides for payment of the full value of the property, which is specifically agreed upon by the insured and the insurer at the time the policy is issued. An open policy contains no agreement as to the specific value of the property to be insured. The insurer pays the fair market value of the property calculated immediately prior to its loss. Insurance of property under a marine policy is considered to be valued, whereas non-marine property insurance is presumed to be unvalued or open.

   B. Nature of Insurance Contracts–The basic principles of contract law apply to insurance policies, and insurance companies tend to standardize their policies. Some states legally require standardization.
     1. Offer and Acceptance–The applicant is the one who makes the offer, and contract is created when that offer is accepted by the company. A life insurance agent may issue a binding receipt acknowledging payment of the premium and providing for the issuance of a standard policy effective from the date of the medical examination. In fire and casualty insurance, agents use binders making an agreement legally binding until the completion of the formal contract.
     2. Insurable Interest–Insurable interest in property is a relationship which a person has with respect to certain property such that the happening of a possible, specific, damage-causing contingency would result in direct loss or injury to her. The purpose of insurance is to protect against the risk of loss, not to realize gain or profit. The concept of insurable interest has been developed to

eliminate gambling and to lessen the moral hazard. The insurable interest must exist at the time the property loss occurs.

3. Premiums–Premiums are the amount to be paid, often in installments, for an insurance policy. Regulatory authorities are under a duty to require that companies' rates be reasonable, and not unfairly discriminatory. State law regulates the rates that may be charged for fire and various types of casualty insurance.

4. Defenses of the Insurer–The insurer may assert certain defenses in addition to the ordinary defenses to a contract.

    a. Misrepresentation–For a misrepresentation to have legal consequences, it must have been material, relied on by the insurer as an inducement to enter into the contract, and substantially false when made or it must have become so, to the insured's knowledge, before the contract was created. The principal remedy of the insurer is rescission of the contract, and the insurer must return all the premiums that have been paid unless the misrepresentation was fraudulent. An innocent misrepresentation of a material fact is a sufficient ground for avoidance of a policy by the insurer. To be effective, a rescission must be made as soon as possible after discovery of the misrepresentation.

    b. Breach of Warranty–Warranties are conditions that must exist before the contract is effective or before the insurer's promise to pay is enforceable. Failure of the condition to exist relieves the insurer from any obligation to perform its promise. Conditions are either precedent or subsequent. To be a warranty, ;the provision must be expressly included in the insurance contract or clearly incorporated by reference.

    c. Concealment–Concealment is the failure of an applicant for insurance to disclose material facts that the insurer does not know. The nondisclosure must normally be fraudulent as well as material to invalidate the policy.

5. Waiver and Estoppel–Waiver is the intentional relinquishment of a known right. Estoppel means that a person is prevented by his own conduct from asserting a position that is inconsistent with acts of his on which another person justifiably relied.

6. Termination–Performance terminates the insurer's obligation. Normally, the insurer pays the principal sum due and the contract is performed and discharged. Cancellation of an insurance contract by mutual consent is another way of terminating it. To cancel a policy, the insurer must return the unearned portion of the premium.

III. Bailments–A bailment is the temporary transfer of possession, without title, of personal property by one party to another. The bailor is the transferor of the bailed property. The bailee is the recipient of the bailed property. The bailment may be with or without compensation. Bailments are classified as follows: (1) Bailments for the bailor's sole benefit. These include the gratuitous custody of personal property and the gratuitous services that involve custody of personal property, such as repairs or transportation. (2) Bailments for the bailee's sole benefit. These are usually limited to the gratuitous loan of personal property for use by the bailee. (3) Bailments for the mutual benefit of both parties. These include ordinary commercial bailments, such as when goods are delivered to a repairperson or when an automobile is delivered to a parking lot attendant.

A. Essential Elements of a Bailment–The essential elements of a bailment are: (1) delivery of possession by a bailor to a bailee, (2) delivery of personal property, not real property, (3) possession without ownership by the bailee, (4) a determinable period of time, and (5) an absolute duty on the bailee to return the property to the bailor or to dispose of it according to the bailor's directions.

1. Delivery of Possession–Possession by a bailee in a bailment relationship involves (1) the bailee's power to control, and (2) either an intention to control or an awareness on the part of the bailee that the rightful possessor has given up physical control of the personal property. Parking lot cases, depending on the circumstances, may be either a lease arrangement (a right to use the space) or a bailment (where the attendant exercises control over the car).

2. Personal Property–A bailment can only exist with respect to personal property. Intangible property, such as corporate bonds, promissory notes, and life insurance policies that are evidenced by written instruments, may be the subject matter of bailments.

3. Possession for a Determinable Time–The person receiving possession must be under a duty to return the personal property and must not obtain title to it. If the identical property transferred is to be returned, the transaction is a bailment; if other property of equal value or the money value may be returned, there is a transfer of title, and the transaction is a sale.

4. Restoration of Possession to the Bailor–The bailee is legally obligated to restore possession of the property to the bailor when the period of the bailment ends. Normally, the bailee is required to return the identical goods bailed. Fungible goods are equivalent goods where each unit is the equivalent of every other unit. In the case of fungible goods, such as grain, the bailee is obligated simply to return goods of the same quality and quantity. If the bailee, by mistake or intentionally, misdelivers the property to someone other than the bailor and that person has no right to its possession, the bailee is guilty of conversion and is liable to the bailor.

B. Rights and Duties of Bailor and Bailee–The bailee is under a duty to exercise due care for the safety of the property and to return it to the right person. The bailee has the exclusive right to possess the property for the term of the bailment. The bailee may have the right to limit its liability, as well as to receive compensation and reimbursement of expenses.

1. Bailee's Duty to Exercise Due Care–The bailee must exercise due care not to permit injury to or destruction of the property by him or third parties. The degree of care depends on the nature of the bailment relationship and the character of the property. In the case of a commercial bailment, from which both parties derive a mutual benefit, the law requires the bailee to exercise care that a reasonably prudent person would exercise under the same circumstances. Where the bailment is for the benefit of the bailee alone, the law requires more than reasonable care. Where the bailment is for the benefit of the bailor alone, the law requires a lesser degree of care. Standards will vary according to the character of the property. When property is lost, damaged, or destroyed while in the possession of the bailee, the burden rests on the bailee to prove that he exercised the required degree of care.

2. Bailee's Absolute Liability to Return Property–The bailee is free from liability if she has exercised the degree of care required. This general rule has certain important exceptions that impose an absolute duty on the bailee to return the property undamaged to the proper person. The bailee has liability where he has an obligation by express agreement with the bailor or by custom to insure against certain risks but fails to do so. Where the bailee uses the bailed

property in a manner not authorized by the bailor and the property is damaged, the bailee is liable.

3. Bailee's Right to Limit Liability–The law permits certain bailees, including common carriers, public warehousers, and innkeepers, to limit their liability for breach of their duties to the bailor as provided by statute. Other bailees may vary their duties and liabilities by contract with the bailor. The law requires that any such limitation be properly brought to the attention of the bailor before the property is bailed.

4. Bailee's Right to Compensation–A bailee who by express or implied agreement undertakes to perform work on or render services in connection with the bailed goods is entitled to reasonable compensation for those services or work. Most bailees who are entitled to compensation for work and services performed in connection with bailed goods acquire a possessory lien on the goods to secure the payment of such compensation.

5. Bailor's Duties–In a bailment for the sole benefit of the bailee, the bailor warrants that she is unaware of any defects in the bailed property. In all other instances, the bailor has a duty to warn the bailee of all defects she knows of or should have discovered upon reasonable inspection. Implied warranties may be imposed on the lease of goods.

C. Special Types of Bailments–An ordinary bailee is liable for loss or injury to the bailed property only where it resulted from the bailee's failure to exercise ordinary or reasonable care. In general, the liability of an extraordinary bailee is absolute; the extraordinary bailee is liable to the bailor for any loss or injury to the bailed goods regardless of the bailee's care or negligence as to their safety. Innkeepers and common carriers are extraordinary bailees, where all other bailees are ordinary bailees. However, pledgees, warehousers, and safe deposit companies may also have extraordinary duties of care and liability.

1. Pledges–A pledge is a bailment for security in which the owner gives possession of her personal property to another (the secured party) to secure a debt or the performance of some obligation.

2. Warehousing–A warehouser is a bailee who receives goods to be stored in a warehouse for compensation. At common law his duties were the same as those of an ordinary bailee for compensation. Today warehousers are subject to extensive state and federal regulation.

3. Safe Deposit Boxes–Most states hold that a person who rents a safe deposit box enters into a mutual benefit bailment with the bank, which is liable only if negligent.

4. Carriers of Goods–A carrier is anyone who transports goods from one place to another, either gratuitously or for compensation. A common carrier offers its services to the general public. A private or contract carrier limits its services and does not offer them to the general public. The consignor is the person who delivers goods to a carrier for shipment. The consignee is the person to whom the goods are to be delivered by the carrier. The instrument that contains the terms of the contract of transportation is called a bill of lading. A common carrier is under a duty to serve the public to the limits of its capacity and, within those limits, to accept for carriage goods of the kind that it normally transports. A private carrier has no such duty. Both the common and private carriers are under an absolute duty to deliver the goods to the person to whom they are consigned by the shipper. In the absence of special contract terms, a private carrier is liable for the goods it undertakes to carry. On the other hand, a common carrier is under a stricter liability that approaches that of an insurer.

5. Innkeepers–An innkeeper is a hotel or motel operator. At common law, innkeepers were held to the same strict or absolute liability for their guests' belongings as a common carrier. Today, the old common law of strict liability has been substantially modified by case law and statutes.

IV. Documents of Title–A document of title is a warehouse receipt, bill of lading, or other document evidencing a right to receive, hold, and dispose of the document and the goods it covers. To be a document of title, a document must be issued by or addressed to a bailee and cover goods in the bailee's possession that are either identified or are fungible portions of an identified mass. A document of title is a symbol of ownership of the goods it describes. Its ownership is equivalent to the ownership or control of the goods it represents. Article 7 of the UCC governs documents of title.

A. Types of Documents of Title
   1. Warehouse Receipts–A warehouse receipt is a receipt issued by a person engaged in the business of storing goods for hire. A warehouser is liable for damages for loss or injury to the goods caused by failure to exercise such care in regard to them as a reasonably careful person would exercise under the circumstances. The warehouser must deliver the goods to the person entitled to receive them under the terms of the warehouse receipt. The liability of a warehouser may be limited by a provision in the warehouse receipt fixing a specific maximum liability per article. A warehouse does not have to keep the goods indefinitely. Depending upon the contract, the warehouser may notify the person on whose account the goods are held to pay storage and remove the goods. To enforce the payment of the charges and necessary expenses in connection with keeping and handling of goods, a warehouser has a lien on the goods. The goods may be sold at public or private sale after notice. The net proceeds are to be applied to the amount of the charges.
   2. Bills of Lading–A bill of lading is a document issued by a carrier on receipt of goods for transportation. It serves a threefold function: (1) as a receipt for the goods, (2) as evidence of the contract of carriage, and (3) as a document of title. A bill of lading may be negotiable or nonnegotiable. The carrier must deliver the goods to the person entitled to receive them under the terms of the bill of lading. Common carriers are extraordinary bailees and subject to a greater degree of liability than ordinary bailees, such as warehousers. The Code allows a carrier to limit liability by contract. The carrier has a lien on goods in its possession covered by a bill of lading for its charges and expenses necessary for preservation of the goods.

B. Negotiability of Documents of Title–The Code provides that a warehouse receipt, bill of lading, or other document of title is negotiable if, by its terms, the goods are to be delivered to bearer or to the order of a named person or, in overseas trade, it runs to a named person or assigns. Any other document is nonnegotiable and may be transferred by assignment but not negotiation.

C. Due Negotiation–Due negotiation is a term peculiar to Article 7 and requires not only that the purchaser of the negotiable document take it in good faith without notice of any adverse claim or defense and pay value, but also that she must take it in the regular course of business or financing and not in settlement or payment of a money obligation. The effect of due negotiation is that it creates new rights in the holder of the document. Defects and defenses available against the transferor are not available against the new holder. The rights of a holder to whom a document has been duly negotiated are that the holder has: (1) title to the document, (2) title to the goods, (3) all rights accruing under the law of agency or estoppel, and (4) the direct obligation of the issuer to hold or deliver the goods according to the terms of the document.

D. Warranties–The transferor of a document of title for value warrants to the immediate transferee that the document is genuine, that she had no knowledge of any fact that would impair its validity or worth, and that the negotiation or transfer is rightful.

E. Ineffective Documents of Title–In order for a person to obtain title to goods by a negotiation of a document, the goods must have been delivered to the issuer of the document by the owner of the goods or by one to whom the owner has delivered them with actual or apparent authority to ship, store, or sell them. A thief or finder may not deliver them to a warehouser or carrier in return for a negotiable document of title and thus defeat the rights of the owner.

KEY TERMS

1. Property
2. Tangible property
3. Intangible property
4. Real property
5. Personal property
6. Fixture
7. Sale
8. Gift
9. Donor
10. Donee
11. Constructive delivery
12. Bailment for sole benefit of bailee
13. Bailment for sole benefit of bailor
14. Bailor
15. Bailee

16. Confusion
17. Insurance
18. Fire insurance
19. Co-insurance
20. Binder
21. Insurable interest
22. Premiums
23. Misrepresentation
24. Warranty
25. Concealment
26. Waiver
27. Carrier
28. Ordinary bailee
29. Extraordinary bailee
30. Pledge

31. Due negotiation
32. Innkeeper
33. Document of title
34. Consignee
35. Consignor
36. Fungible goods
37. Commercial bailment
38. Bill of lading
39. Private carrier
40. Warehouse receipt
41. Common carrier
42. Estoppel
43. Accession
44. Bailment
45. Warehouser

TRUE/FALSE

_____ 1. All property interests that are not classified as real property or as fixtures are classified as personal property.

_____ 2. The intention of the parties with conflicting claims to the property, as expressed in their agreement, is controlling in determining whether personal property has become a fixture.

_____ 3. A tenant may remove trade fixtures provided he can do so without causing material injury to the real property to which it is affixed.

_____ 4. A fixture is personal property which is so firmly attached to real property that an interest in it arises under real property law.

_____ 5. As in contract law, in order for a gift to be valid it must be supported by consideration.

_____ 6. The owner of a cow acquires title by accession to any calves born to that cow.

_____ 7. If confusion of goods results by accident and there is not enough left to distribute a full share to each owner, each party will lose his entire interest if he cannot prove his share.

_____ 8. A gift must be completed by delivery to be effective.

_____ 9. A gratuitous promise to make a gift is binding and may be enforced in a court of law.

_____ 10. Hereford cattle owned by the Cartright Ranch are accidentally mixed with Hereford cattle owned by the Reagon Ranch. Neither rancher's herd can be specifically identified. If the cattle can be apportioned, each ranch is entitled to its proportional share.

_____ 11. Fire insurance policies are standardized in the United States, but coverage may be enlarged through an "endorsement."

_____ 12. Co-insurance is a means of sharing the risk between multiple insurers of the same property of an insured.

_____ 13. The principal remedy of the insurer upon discovery of a misrepresentation by the insured is rescission of the contract.

_____ 14. To invalidate an insurance policy, a nondisclosure must generally be material and fraudulent.

_____ 15. The insurer, in order to cancel a policy, must tender any unearned portion of the premium to the insured.

_____ 16. Bailed property must be both personal and tangible.

_____ 17. In order to establish a bailment relationship, the person receiving possession of the property must be under a duty to return the property.

_____ 18. The bailee has the exclusive right to possess the bailed goods for the term of the bailment.

_____ 19. Except in the case of fungible goods, the bailee is required to return the identical goods bailed.

_____ 20. A private carrier has no duty to accept goods for carriage except where it has agreed to do so by contract.

_____ 21. The extent of a warehouser's liability may be limited by a provision in the warehouse receipt fixing a specific maximum liability.

_____ 22. When a customer rents a safe deposit box, the bailee bank owes the customer the duty to act with ordinary care.

_____ 23. Innkeepers and common carriers are known as ordinary bailees.

_____ 24. After an indorsement in blank or to bearer, a negotiable document of title may be negotiated by delivery alone.

_____ 25. States may by statute prohibit professional bailees from disclaiming liability for their own negligence.

_____ 26. If Julia hangs her coat on a rack at Nick's Restaurant, the restaurant owner is a bailee of the coat.

_____ 27. Under the Code, bills of lading may be issued only by common carriers, not by contract carriers or freight forwarders.

_____ 28. A private carrier is liable for the loss of or damage to goods it undertakes to deliver as one who insures the safety of the goods.

_____ 29. A warehouser has a lien against the goods stored and in her possession.

_____ 30. Fred, without compensation, loans his textbook to his friend Elmer, so that Elmer may study for a test. This is a bailment for the sole benefit of the bailee.

MULTIPLE CHOICE

_____ 1. A speedboat would be classified as:
a. tangible property.
b. intangible property.
c. personal property.
d. both (a) and (c).

_____ 2. Which of the following would be considered intangible personal property?
   a. A stock certificate
   b. A patent
   c. A promissory note
   d. All of the above

_____ 3. In the absence of a binding agreement between the parties, the court, in determining whether an item is a fixture, will consider the following factors:
   a. the physical relationship of the item to the land.
   b. the intention of the person who attached the item to the land.
   c. the interest of the person who attached the item to the land at the time of attachment.
   d. all of the above.

_____ 4. In determining whether an item is a fixture, the test of "purpose or use" applies only if the item:
   a. is affixed to the realty in some way.
   b. can be removed without material injury to the realty.
   c. either (a) or (b).
   d. both (a) and (b).

_____ 5. The basic distinction between a gift and a sale is that a gift:
   a. requires delivery.
   b. lacks any consideration.
   c. requires intent on the part of the donor.
   d. must be accepted by the donee.

_____ 6. Which of the requirements of an effective gift is presumed?
   a. Delivery to the donee
   b. Intent on donor's part to make a present gift
   c. Acceptance by the donee
   d. None of the above

_____ 7. If an item is determined to be a fixture, it:
   a. can be removed by the seller of the land.
   b. is not a part of the realty.
   c. will be sold with the land.
   d. none of the above.

_____ 8. Under the doctrine of confusion, if James, Kevin, and Loren accidentally commingle identical cases of soda, and there is not enough left to distribute a full share to each:
   a. the first owners proving their proportion of the whole are entitled to receive their share.
   b. the loss will be borne by each in proportion to his share.
   c. no party will recover anything unless he can prove his share.
   d. none of the above.

_____ 9. Which of the following are ways by which title to personal property may be obtained?
   a. Possession
   b. Accession
   c. Confusion
   d. All of the above are means by which title to personal property may be obtained.

_____ 10. Which of the following would be considered intangible personal property?
   a. A pen
   b. A chair
   c. A stock certificate
   d. A book

_____ 11. *CPA:* Which of the following would change if an asset is treated as personal property rather than as real property?

	Requirements for transfer	Creditor's rights
a.	Yes	No
b.	No	Yes
c.	Yes	Yes
d.	No	No

_____ 12. An insurable interest in property must exist at:
   a. the time that the insurance contract is entered into.
   b. the time that the property loss occurs.
   c. either (a) or (b).
   d. both (a) and (b).

_____ 13. A misrepresentation by or on behalf of an insurance applicant will have legal consequences if:
   a. it was relied upon by the insurer as an inducement to enter into a contract.
   b. it was substantially false when made or it became so with the insured's knowledge before the contract was created.
   c. either (a) or (b).
   d. both (a) and (b).

_____ 14. *CPA:* Which of the following factors help determine whether an item of personal property is a fixture?
   (I) degree of the item's attachment to the property
   (II) intent of the person who had the item installed
   a. I only
   b. II only
   c. Both I and II
   d. Neither I nor II

_____ 15. Jenna owns a piece of property on which she has an 80% co-insurance policy for fire and property damage. The property is valued at $100,000 and the policy amount is $60,000. If the property is 50% destroyed by fire, how much can Jenna recover from the insurance company?
   a. $30,000
   b. $37,500
   c. $40,000
   d. $48,000

_____ 16. Carlos parks his car in a parking lot, receives a claim check, locks his car, and takes the keys. This is probably a:
   a. bailment for the benefit of the bailor.
   b. bailment for the benefit of the bailee.
   c. mutual benefit bailment.
   d. lease.

_____ 17. Which of the following is not an essential element of a bailment relationship?
   a. Delivery of lawful possession of specific personal property by the bailor to the bailee
   b. Transfer of title to the property from the bailor to the bailee for a determinable period of time
   c. An obligation of the bailee to return the property to the bailor or to dispose of it according to the bailor's directions
   d. All of the above are essential elements of a bailment relationship.

_____ 18. A mutual benefit bailment terminates on the happening of the conditions listed below except:
   a. when the purpose of the bailment is fully accomplished.
   b. when the time for which the bailment was created expires.
   c. when the bailed goods are destroyed.
   d. all of the above.

_____ 19. A bailee is free from liability for casualty to the bailed goods if he exercised the requisite degree of care unless he:
   a. agrees with the bailor to insure the goods against a certain risk, then failed to do so and the casualty to the goods occurred through such a risk.
   b. used the bailed property in a manner not authorized by the bailment and damage results from that use.
   c. delivers the property to the wrong person by mistake.
   d. all of the above.

_____ 20. In order to be a common carrier, a carrier must meet all of the following conditions except:
   a. the carriage must be a part of its business.
   b. the carrier serves a limited number of customers under individual contracts.
   c. the carriage must be for remuneration.
   d. the carrier must represent to the general public that it is willing to serve the public in the transportation of property.

_____ 21. Which of the following is characteristic of a bill of lading?
  a. It serves as a receipt for the goods.
  b. It serves as evidence of the contract of carriage.
  c. It serves as a document of title.
  d. All of the above.

_____ 22. A document of title is negotiable if it is made payable to any of the following except:
  a. to a named person.
  b. to bearer.
  c. to order.
  d. a document of title is negotiable if made payable to any of the above.

_____ 23. A holder of a negotiable document of title to whom it has been duly negotiated obtains all of the following except:
  a. title to the document.
  b. proof that the document is genuine.
  c. title to the goods.
  d. the holder has all of the above rights.

_____ 24. A person who transfers a document of title for value to other than a collecting bank or other intermediary warrants to the immediate purchaser that:
  a. the document is genuine.
  b. he has no knowledge of any fact that would impair the validity or worth of the document.
  c. his transfer is rightful and fully effective with respect to the document of title and the goods it represents.
  d. all of the above.

_____ 25. A purchaser will obtain title to goods by negotiation to her of a document of title provided the goods have been delivered to the issuer of the document by:
  a. a finder of the goods.
  b. a thief of the goods.
  c. the true owner of the goods.
  d. none of the above.

_____ 26. *CPA:* The procedure to negotiate a document of title depends principally on whether the document is:
  a. an order document or bearer document.
  b. issued by a bailee or a consignee.
  c. a receipt for goods stored or goods already shipped.
  d. a bill of lading or a warehouse receipt.

_____ 27. **CPA:** Under the UCC, a warehouse receipt:
   a. will not be negotiable if it contains a contractual limitation on the warehouser's liability.
   b. may qualify as both a negotiable warehouse receipt and negotiable commercial paper if the instrument is payable either in cash or by the delivery or goods.
   c. may be issued only by a bonded and licensed warehouser.
   d. is negotiable if, by its terms, the goods are to be delivered to bearer or the order of a named person.

_____ 28. Arlene brings her car to the garage to have some work done on it. In the trunk of the car is a set of valuable jewels. Is there a bailment relationship between Arlene and the garage?
   a. There is a bailment relationship with respect to both the car and the jewels.
   b. There is a bailment relationship for the car but not the jewels.
   c. There is a bailment relationship for the jewels but not the car.
   d. There is no bailment relationship of either the car or the jewels.

_____ 29. Amos takes his radio to a repairman who gives a claim check containing a statement limiting the repairman's liability. This will be effective only if:
   a. the repairman-bailee draws Amos's attention to the writing.
   b. the repairman-bailee informs Amos that it contains a limitation of liability.
   c. the repairman-bailee does not coerce Amos into agreeing with the liability limitation.
   d. all of the above are necessary for the repairman-bailee to effectively limit his liability.

_____ 30. A written limitation of liability contained in a claim check will not bind the bailor unless the bailee possesses equal bargaining power and:
   a. draws the bailor's attention to the writing.
   b. informs the bailor of its contents.
   c. either (a) or (b).
   d. both (a) and (b).

SHORT ESSAY

1. Distinguish between real property, personal property, and fixtures and between tangible and intangible property. Discuss the legal significance, if any, of these distinctions.

_____

_____

_____

_____

2. What is a trade fixture? How does it differ from a fixture?

_____

_____

_____

_____

3. Distinguish between "valued" and "open" fire and property insurance policies.

_____

_____

_____

_____

4. Discuss briefly the concept of insurable interest. What purpose does it serve?

_____

_____

_____

_____

5. Of what significance are warranties in insurance contracts? How do they operate?

_____

_____

_____

_____

6. Identify the five essential elements of a bailment.

_____

_____

_____

_____

7. What are the three basic kinds of bailments and what standard is applied to the bailee's duty to exercise due care under each?

   _____

   _____

   _____

   _____

8. Identify four special types of bailments.

   _____

   _____

   _____

   _____

9. Identify and briefly describe the types of documents of title.

   _____

   _____

   _____

   _____

10. Explain negotiability with respect to documents of title.

   _____

   _____

   _____

   _____

Chapter 50
Interests in Real Property

PURPOSE

This chapter discusses the different ways one may hold ownership or claim on real property. Possessory interests in real property are called estates and are classified to indicate quantity, nature, and extent of rights. When the ownership is for an indefinite period of time or for the life of a person, it is known as a freehold estate. This ownership may be with or without condition, depending on the terms by which the property was acquired. Leasehold estates, which include landlord-tenant relationships, are those that exist for a predetermined time. In addition, there are several nonpossessory interests in property, including easements, *profits à prendre*, and licenses. The ownership of interests in property may be held by one individual or concurrently by two or more persons, each of whom is entitled to an undivided interest in the entire property. You will study all of these topics in this chapter.

CHAPTER CHECKPOINTS

After reading and studying this chapter, you should be able to:

1. Define and discuss the various freehold estates.

2. Distinguish between reversion and remainder future interests.

3. Define a leasehold estate and discuss the primary rights and obligations of landlords and tenants.

4. Identify and discuss the various forms of concurrent ownership of real property.

5. Discuss the different forms of nonpossessory interests.

CHAPTER OUTLINE

A. Freehold Estates–A freehold estate is a right of ownership of real property for an indefinite time (fee estate) or for the life of a person (life estate).

1. Fee Estates–Fee estate refers to the right to immediate possession for an indefinite period of time with the right to transfer the interest by deed or will. Fee estates include both fee simple and qualified fee estates.

   a. Fee Simple Estate–Fee simple means that the property is owned absolutely and can be sold or passed on at will. The absolute rights of transferability and of transmitting by inheritance are basic characteristics of a fee simple estate.

   b. Qualified or Base Fee Estate–A qualified fee is an ownership interest subject to its being taken away upon the happening of an event.

2. Life Estates–A life estate is an ownership right in the property for the life of a designated individual, while the remainder is the ownership estate that takes effect when the prior life estate terminates. A grant or devise "to Alex for life" creates in Alex an estate that terminates on his death. Alex is the life tenant. A grant "to Alex for life and then to Mario and his heirs" makes Alex the life tenant and Mario the remainderman. Generally, a life tenant may make reasonable use of the property so long as he does not commit "waste," which is any act or omission that does permanent injury to the realty or unreasonably changes its characteristics or value. No particular words are necessary to create a life estate, as long as the words clearly reflect the grantor's intent. A conveyance by a life tenant passes only the interest of the life tenant. However, a life tenant and the remainderman may join in a conveyance to pass the entire fee to the property.

3. Future Interests–Not all interests in property carry the right to immediate possession, even though the right and title to an interest is absolute. In a grant, "to Adam during his life and then to Bea and her heirs," Bea has a definite, existing interest in the property but she is not entitled to immediate possession. Bea's right is a future interest, as her right to possession will become effective at a future time. Future interests may be classified as either reversions or remainders.

   a. Reversions–A reversion is the grantor's right to property upon termination of another estate. For example, if Charles conveys property to Rhonda "for life" but specifies no disposition after her life estate, Charles holds the reversion. A possibility of reverter is a conditional reversionary interest and exists where property may return to the grantor or his successor in interest because of the happening of an event on which a fee simple was to terminate. Reversions may be transferred by deed or will and pass by intestate succession. A possibility of reverter may pass by will or intestate succession and, in some states, by deed.

   b. Remainders–A remainder is an estate in property that, like a reversion, will take effect in possession, if at all, on the termination of a prior estate created by the same instrument. Unlike a reversion, a remainder is held by a person other than the grantor or his successors. A vested remainder is an unconditional remainder that is a fixed, present interest to be enjoyed in the future. A contingent remainder is a remainder interest conditional upon the happening of an event in addition to the termination of the preceding estate. A provision in a will "to David for life and then to his children but if he has no children then to Julie," creates contingent remainders both as to the children and as to Julie.

B. Leasehold Estates–A leasehold estate is the right to possess real property. A lease is a contract in which the landlord grants to the tenant an exclusive right to use and possession of the land for a definite period of time. A tenant has a leasehold interest in real property. The landlord retains an interest in the property called a reversion. The principal characteristics of a leasehold estate are that it continues for a definite term and that it carries with it the obligation on the part of the tenant to pay rent to the landlord.

The law of leasehold estates has changed considerably in recent decades. Traditionally, the common law viewed a leasehold estate less as a contract than as a conveyance of the use of land. Today, the landlord-tenant relationship is primarily viewed as a contract and subject to contractual doctrines of unconscionability, implied warranties, and constructive conditions.   Numerous ordinances and statutes, such as the Uniform Residential Landlord and Tenant Act enacted by at least twenty states, also now protect tenants' rights further modifying the landlord-tenant relationship.

1. Creation and Duration–Leaseholds are created by contract and must comply with the usual requirements for formation of a contract. Leases for a statutorily specified period of time, usually from one to three years, must be in writing.

    a. Definite Term–A lease for a definite term automatically expires at the end of the term. Such a lease is frequently termed an estate for years, even though it may be for one year or shorter. No notice to terminate is required.

    b. Periodic Tenancy–A periodic tenancy is a lease of indefinite duration that continues for successive periods unless terminated by notice to the other party. A periodic tenancy may be terminated by either party at the expiration of any one period but only on adequate notice to the other party.

    c. Tenancy at Will–A tenancy at will is a lease that is terminable at any time by either party, usually upon notice.

    d. Tenancy at Sufferance–A tenancy at sufferance exists when a tenant fails to vacate the premises when the lease expires.

2. Transfer of Interests–Both the tenant's possessory interest in the leasehold and the landlord's reversionary interest in the property may be freely transferred in the absence of contractual or statutory prohibition. One major exception is the tenancy at will.

    a. Transfers by Landlord–After conveying the leasehold interest, a landlord is left with a reversionary interest in the property plus the right to rent and other benefits acquired under the lease. The landlord may transfer either or both of these interests.

    b. Transfers by Tenant–A tenant may dispose of his interest either by (1) assignment, or (2) sublease. Most standard leases, however, require the consent of the landlord to an assignment or sublease of the premises. A tenant who transfers all interest in the leasehold so that he has no reversionary rights has made an assignment. The agreement to pay rent and certain other contractual covenants (express promises) pass to and obligate the assignee of the lease as long as he remains in possession of the leasehold estate. However, the original tenant is not relieved of the obligation to pay rent if the assignee fails to pay. A sublease differs from an assignment in that it involves the transfer by the tenant to another of less than all the tenant's rights in the lease, such that the tenant retains a reversion in the leasehold. The legal effects of a sublease are different from those of an assignment.

3. Tenant's Obligations–Although the leasehold estate carries with it an implied obligation on the part of the tenant to pay reasonable rent, the lease contract almost always contains an express

promise or covenant by the tenant to pay rent in specified amounts at specified times. Most leases contain a provision to the effect that if the tenant breaches any of the covenants in the lease, the landlord is entitled to declare the lease at an end and may regain possession of the premises. A tenant is under no duty to make any repairs to the leased premises, unless the lease has specific provisions to the contrary. The tenant is obliged to use the premises so that no substantial injury is caused them.

    a. Destruction of the Premises–Where the tenant leases land together with a building and the building is destroyed by fire or some other chance event, the common law does not relieve the tenant of the obligation to pay rent or permit the tenant to terminate the lease. The common law rule has been modified by statute in most states.

    b. Eviction–To evict is to remove from the premises. When the tenant breaches one of the covenants in the lease and the landlord evicts the tenant, the lease is terminated. If the tenant is wrongfully evicted by the landlord, the tenant's obligations under the lease are terminated, and the landlord is liable for breach of the tenant's right of quiet enjoyment.

    c. Abandonment–If the tenant wrongfully abandons the premises before the expiration of the term of the lease and the landlord reenters the premises or relets them to another, a majority of the courts hold that the tenant's obligation to pay rent after reentry terminates.

4. Landlord's Obligations–Under the Fair Housing Act, a landlord cannot discriminate against a tenant regarding race, color, gender, religion, national origin, or familial status. Nevertheless, under the common law, the landlord has few obligations to the tenant. Under the majority rule, at the beginning of the lease, the landlord must only give a tenant the right to possession.

    a. Quiet Enjoyment–The landlord is bound to provide the tenant with quiet and peaceful enjoyment. Quiet enjoyment is the right of a tenant not to have physical possession of the premises interfered with by the landlord. Under the doctrine of constructive eviction, a failure by the landlord in any of the undertakings under the lease that causes a substantial and lasting injury to the tenant's enjoyment of the premises is regarded as being an eviction. If there is constructive eviction, the tenant may abandon the premises and terminate the lease.

    b. Fitness for Use–Under the common law, the landlord has no obligation to maintain the premises in a livable condition or to make them fit for any purpose. However, most courts have abandoned this rule in residential leases by imposing an implied warranty of habitability that the leased premises are fit for ordinary residential purposes. A number of states have statutes requiring landlords to keep the residential premises fit for occupation. Zoning and health regulations and building codes may also apply.

    c. Repair–Under the common law, unless there is a specific provision in the lease or a statutory duty to do so, the landlord has no obligation to repair or restore the premises. The landlord does have a duty to maintain, repair, and keep in safe condition the common areas of the premises under her control. While at common law the landlord is under no duty to repair, restore, or keep the premises in a livable condition, she may assume those duties in the lease.

    d. Landlord's Liability for Injury Caused by Third Parties–Some states hold landlords liable for injuries suffered by their tenants and others as a result of foreseeable criminal conduct of third parties. While landlords are not insurers of the safety of tenants, they have been held liable for failure "to take minimal precautions to protect members of the public from the reasonably foreseeable criminal acts of third persons."

C. Concurrent Ownership–Two or more persons who hold title concurrently are generally referred to as co-tenants. The two major types of concurrent ownership are joint tenancy and tenancy in common.

1. Tenancy in Common–Tenancy in common is co-ownership whereby each tenant holds an undivided interest with no right of survivorship. The interest of tenants in common may be devised by will or pass by intestate succession. Partition is a physical division of the property, changing undivided interests into smaller parcels owned by each person individually.

2. Joint Tenancy–The most significant feature of joint tenancy is the right of survivorship. On the death of one of the joint tenants, title to the entire property passes by operation of law to the survivor or survivors, and neither the heirs of the deceased joint tenant nor his general creditors have a claim to his interest after his death. To sever means to lose the right of survivorship and to make the tenancy a tenancy in common among the remaining joint tenants and the transferee. A joint tenant may sever the joint tenancy by conveying or mortgaging his interest to a third party. To sustain a joint tenancy, the common law requires the presence of the four unities of time, title, interest, and possession. A failure of any one of the first three unities will result in a tenancy in common, because the only unity required of a tenancy in common is unity of possession.

3. Tenancy by the Entireties–Tenancy by the entireties is created only by a conveyance to a husband and wife. It is co-ownership by spouses in which neither may convey his or her interest during life and thus destroy the right of survivorship.

4. Community Property–In Arizona, California, Idaho, Louisiana, Nevada, New Mexico, Puerto Rico, Texas, Washington, and Wisconsin, under the community property system one-half of any property acquired by the efforts of either the husband or the wife belongs to each spouse. The only property that belongs separately to either spouse is that acquired before the marriage or acquired subsequent to it by gift or inheritance.

5. Condominiums–Condominiums are a form of concurrent ownership that have become common-place in the United States. The purchaser of a condominium acquires separate ownership to the unit and becomes a tenant in common with respect to the common facilities. The transfer of a condominium conveys the separate ownership of the unit and the share in the common elements.

6. Cooperatives–A cooperative, usually a corporation, buys or constructs the dwelling units. It then leases the units to shareholders as tenants, who acquire the right to use and occupy their units.

D. Nonpossessory Interests–A nonpossessory interest in land entitles the holder to use the land or to take something from the land, but the interest does not include the right to possess the land.

1. Definition of Easements–An easement is a limited right to make use of the land or a portion of the land of another in a specific manner that is created by the acts of the parties or by operation of law and that has all the attributes of an estate in the land itself. The dominant parcel of land is the one whose owner has rights in other land. The servient parcel of land is the one that is subject to an easement.

2. Types of Easements–Easements fall into two classes: easements appurtenant and easements in gross. Appurtenant easements are by far the more common. Rights and duties created by such easements pertain to the land itself and not to the particular individuals who may have created them. Therefore, the easement stays with the land when it is sold. The second type of easement is an easement in gross, which is personal to the particular individual who received the right. It amounts to an irrevocable personal right to use another's land.

3. Creation of Easements–The most common way to create an easement is by express grant or reservation. Easements by implication arise whenever an owner of adjacent properties establishes an apparent and permanent use in the nature of an easement, and then conveys one of the properties without mention of any easement. The law implies the grant of an easement by necessity to give purchasers of land access to their property across the land of the seller. An easement may arise by prescription if certain conditions are met. To obtain an easement by prescription, a person must use a portion of land owned by another in a way (1) that is adverse to the rightful owner's use, (2) that is open and generally known, and (3) that is continuous and uninterrupted for a period of time that varies from state to state. A claimant of an easement by prescription acquires no easement if given the owner's permission to use the land.

4. Profits à Prendre–A *profit à prendre* is the right to remove the produce from the land of another. Like an easement, a *profit à prendre* may arise by prescription, but if it comes about by an act of the parties, it must be created with all the formalities of a grant of an estate in real property.

5. Licenses–A license is permission to make use of another's land. Generally a license creates no interest in the property. It is usually exercised only at the will of and subject to revocation by the owner at any time.

KEY TERMS

1. Freehold estate

2. Fee estate

3. Fee simple estate

4. Qualified fee estate

5. Life estate

6. Remainder

7. Waste

8. Future interest

9. Reversion

10. Possibility of reverter

11. Vested remainder

12. Contingent remainder

13. Landlord

14. Tenant

15. Leasehold estate

16. Estate for years

17. Periodic tenancy

18. Tenancy at will

19. Tenancy at sufferance

20. Assignment

21. Covenants

22. Sublease

23. Evict

24. Abandonment

25. Quiet enjoyment

26. Constructive eviction

27. Implied warranty of habitability

28. Co-tenants

29. Tenancy in common

30. Partition

31. Joint tenancy

32. Four unities

33. Tenancy by the entireties

34. Community property

35. Condominiums

36. Cooperatives

37. Easement

38. Dominant

39. Servient

40. Appurtenant easement

41. Easement in gross

42. *Profit à prendre*

43. License

TRUE/FALSE

_____ 1. A qualified fee is the largest estate in land.

_____ 2. A fee simple estate is created by any words which indicate an intent to convey absolute ownership.

_____ 3. The holder of a qualified fee interest may transfer that interest, but all transferees will take the property subject to the initial condition imposed by the interest.

_____ 4. A reversion, a life estate, and a remainder are all considered future interests.

_____ 5. A fee simple estate may be sold, but it may not be passed by will.

_____ 6. A lease that does not specify any duration is treated as a tenancy at sufferance.

_____ 7. Unless specifically permitted in the lease, leases are not freely assignable without the landlord's consent.

_____ 8. A tenant is under no duty to make any repairs to the leased premises unless the lease expressly so provides.

_____ 9. Like joint tenants, tenants in common are persons who hold undivided interests in the property, each having the right to possession, but neither claiming any specific portion of the property.

_____ 10. A tenancy by the entireties can only be created in a conveyance to a husband and wife.

_____ 11. The purchaser of a cooperative acquires separate ownership to the unit and becomes a tenant in common in the common facilities.

_____ 12. A creditor of the wife only can attach the wife's interest in real property held by tenancy by the entireties, but not an interest held as a joint tenant with her husband.

_____ 13. The interests of the parties holding land as tenants in common may be devised by will as there is no right of survivorship.

_____ 14. Either party to a joint tenancy may sever the tenancy and thus convert the estate into a tenancy in common.

_____ 15. A license is a nonpossessory interest to use the land of another.

MULTIPLE CHOICE

_____ 1. All of the following conveyances will create an unqualified fee simple estate in the transferee except:
   a. "To B absolutely."
   b. "To B forever."
   c. "To B so long as she does not remarry."
   d. "To B in fee simple."

_____ 2. In his will, a man conveys his house and lot to his widow in "fee simple forever so long as she does not remarry." The widow has:
   a. a fee simple estate.
   b. a fee simple defeasible estate.
   c. a life estate.
   d. an estate for years.

_____ 3. O conveys Greenacre "to A for life, then to B." What interest, if any, does B have in Greenacre?
   a. A reversion
   b. A vested remainder
   c. A contingent remainder
   d. No interest

_____ 4. A leases a factory to B for three years. The written lease provides that rent is to be paid on the first day of each month, and that either party may terminate the lease at any time. The lease can best be described as:
   a. an estate for years.
   b. a periodic tenancy "from year to year."
   c. a periodic tenancy "from month to month."
   d. a tenancy at will.

_____ 5. A freehold estate is a right of ownership of real property for:
   a. an indefinite time.
   b. the life of a person.
   c. either (a) or (b).
   d. neither (a) nor (b).

_____ 6. If a tenant assigns her leasehold interest without the written consent of the landlord as required by the lease, the assignment is:
   a. valid and enforceable.
   b. void and unenforceable by either party.
   c. voidable at the landlord's election.
   d. treated as a sublease.

_____ 7. Which of the following "unities" would be required in joint tenancy?
   a. Time
   b. Title
   c. Interest
   d. All of the above

_____ 8. A conveys "the back forty" to B. The parcel is bordered on three sides by the remainder of A's farm and on the fourth by a river. At present, B has no access to the highway and the deed from A grants none. Which of the following is correct?
   a. B has an express easement across A's land to the highway.
   b. B has an implied easement across A's land to the highway.
   c. B has an easement by necessity across A's land to the highway.
   d. B has no right to cross A's land to the highway.

_____ 9. If A gives B permission to extract oil from his land, he has given B:
   a. an easement in gross.
   b. a license.
   c. a _profit à prendre_.
   d. none of the above.

_____ 10. Co-ownership of land by spouses in which neither may convey his or her interest during life is a:
   a. joint tenancy.
   b. tenancy in common.
   c. tenancy by the entireties.
   d. tenancy at sufferance.

_____ 11. A lease which has specific terms that continue in indefinite succession would be classified as:
   a. tenancy at sufferance.
   b. tenancy at will.
   c. periodic tenancy.
   d. none of the above.

_____ 12. Which of the following is correct with regard to a *profit à prendre?*
   a. Unless it is clearly designated as exclusive, it is subject to similar use by the owner.
   b. It is sometimes difficult to distinguish from a license.
   c. It is the right to remove the produce from another's land.
   d. All of the above are correct.

_____ 13. *CPA:* Which of the following unities (elements) are required to establish a joint tenancy?

	Time	*Title*	*Interest*	*Possession*
a.	Yes	Yes	Yes	Yes
b.	Yes	Yes	No	No
c.	No	No	Yes	Yes
d.	Yes	No	Yes	No

_____ 14. *CPA:* Court, Fell, and Miles own a parcel of land as joint tenants with right of survivorship. Court's interest was sold to Plank. As a result of the sale from Court to Plank:
   a. Fell, Miles, and Plank each own a one-third interest in the land as joint tenants.
   b. Fell and Miles each own a one-third interest in the land as tenants in common.
   c. Plank owns a one-third interest in the land as a tenant in common.
   d. Plank owns a one-third interest in the land as a joint tenant.

_____ 15. Trevor and two of his friends rent an apartment near the campus of Northern University. When winter comes and the outside temperature is below zero, they discover that the furnace does not work. They notify the landlord, but he says that is not his problem. Does the landlord have any responsibility to maintain the furnace?
   a. Yes, because of his obligation of quiet enjoyment.
   b. Yes, because of the implied warranty of habitability.
   c. Yes, because of his obligation of repair.
   d. Two of the above are correct, (b) and (c).

SHORT ESSAY

1. What are the basic characteristics of a fee simple estate? How do these estates differ from a qualified fee simple estate?

_____

_____

_____

_____

2. Distinguish among a reversion, a possibility of reverter, and a remainder.

    _____

    _____

    _____

    _____

3. Distinguish between tenancy in common, joint tenancy, and tenancy by the entireties.

    _____

    _____

    _____

    _____

4. What obligations does a landlord owe to her tenant?

    _____

    _____

    _____

    _____

5. Identify several obligations owed the tenant by the landlord.

    _____

    _____

    _____

Chapter 51
Transfer and Control of Real Property

PURPOSE

The law has always been extremely cautious about the transfer of title to real property. Title to land may be transferred in three principal ways: (1) by deed, (2) by will or by the law of descent on the death of the owner, and (3) by open, continuous, and adverse possession for a statutorily prescribed period of time. In this chapter, you study the transfer of possession of real property by deed and adverse possession, and you study the public and private controls that affect the use of real property.

CHAPTER CHECKPOINTS

After reading and studying this chapter, you should be able to:

1. List the essential elements in the formation of a contract of sale for real property and a valid deed.

2. Distinguish among the following types of deeds: (a) warranty, (b) special warranty, and (c) quitclaim.

3. Explain what is meant by a secured transaction and distinguish between "assumption of a mortgage" and "subject to the mortgage."

4. Explain how title to land is acquired by adverse possession.

5. Describe the public and private controls placed on land including zoning, eminent domain, and restrictive covenants.

CHAPTER OUTLINE

I. Transfer of Real Property–The most common way in which real property is transferred is by contract for sale of the land and delivery of the deed upon payment of the agreed-upon consideration. A far less common method of transfer is by adverse possession.

   A. Contract of Sale–General contract law, as modified by the Fair Housing Act (Title VIII of the Civil Rights Act), governs the sale of real property.

      1. Formation–The buyer and seller must put their agreement in writing in order to meet the requirements of the statute of frauds. Neither party can enforce the agreement unless the other party signs it. The agreement should contain the names and addresses of the parties, a description of the property, time for the conveyance, type of deed, and price and manner of payment.

      2. Marketable Title–The law of conveyance provides that a contract for the sale of land carries with it an implied obligation on the part of the seller to transfer marketable title. Marketable title means that the title is free from (1) encumbrances; (2) defects in the chain of title appearing in the land records; and (3) events depriving the seller of title, such as adverse possession or eminent domain. A title search should be done to check for defects in title.

      3. Implied Warranty of Habitability–The obligation of marketable title has nothing to do with the quality of any improvements to the land. The traditional common law rule is *caveat emptor*–let the buyer beware. The buyer has to inspect the property before the sale is completed. The seller is liable only for any misrepresentations or express warranties. A majority of states have relaxed the harshness of this rule in sales by the builder of residential dwellings. In such a sale, the builder-seller impliedly warrants that a newly constructed house is free of latent defects.

   B. Deeds–A deed is a formal document transferring any type of interest in land.

      1. Types of Deeds–There are three basic types of deeds: warranty, special warranty, and quitclaim.

         a. Warranty Deed–In a warranty deed, the grantor (seller) promises the grantee (buyer) that the grantor has a valid title to the property. In addition, the grantor obliges herself to make the grantee whole if the grantee suffers any damage because the grantor's title was defective. The promises or covenants in a warranty deed include title, against encumbrances, quiet enjoyment, and warranty.

         b. Special Warranty Deed–A special warranty deed warrants only that the title has not been impaired, encumbered, or made defective because of any act or omission of the grantor. It does not warrant title as to acts or omissions of others.

         c. Quitclaim Deed–In a quitclaim deed the grantor transfers whatever interest he has in the property. They are used most frequently when it is desired that persons who appear to have an interest in land release their interest.

      2. Formal Requirements–Any transfer of an interest in land is within the statute of frauds if it is an interest of more than a limited duration. The description in the deed must be sufficiently clear and certain to permit identification of the property conveyed. After describing the property, the deed generally describes the quantity of the estate conveyed to the grantee. Deeds generally end with the signature of the grantor, a seal, and an acknowledgment before a notary public or other official authorized to verify the authenticity of documents.

3. Delivery of Deeds–A deed does not transfer title to land until it is delivered. Delivery means an intent that the deed is to take effect and is evidenced by the acts or statements of the grantor. Manual or physical transfer of the deed is usually the best evidence of intent, but it is not necessary. A deed is frequently turned over to a third party, called an escrow agent. Escrow is the holding by a third party of a document or funds until all conditions in the contract are fulfilled.

4. Recordation–In almost all states, it is not necessary to record a deed in order to pass title from grantor to grantee. However, unless the grantee has the deed recorded, a subsequent good faith purchaser of the property will acquire superior title to the grantee. Recordation consists of delivery of a duly executed and acknowledged deed to the recorder's office in the county where the property is located. In notice states, unrecorded instruments are invalid against any subsequent purchaser without notice. In notice-race states, an unrecorded deed is invalid against any subsequent purchaser without notice who records first. In race states, an unrecorded deed is invalid against any deed recorded before it.

C. Secured Transactions–A secured transaction includes two elements: (1) a debt or obligation to pay money, and (2) an interest of the creditor in specific property that secures performance of the obligation. Transactions involving the use of real estate as security for a debt are subject to real estate law, which consists of statutes and rules developed by the common laws regarding mortgages and trust deeds. In these cases, the real estate itself is used to secure the obligation, which is evidenced by either a mortgage or a deed of trust. A mortgagor is a debtor who uses real estate to secure an obligation. A mortgagee is a creditor of a secured transaction involving real estate.

1. Form of Mortgages–A mortgage is an interest in land created by a written document that provides security for payment of a debt. The instrument creating a mortgage must meet all the requirements for such documents–it must be in writing, contain an adequate description of the property, and be executed and delivered. A deed of trust is nearly identical to a mortgage, except that under a deed of trust, the property is conveyed not to the creditor as security, but to a third person as trustee for the benefit of a creditor.

2. Rights and Duties–The rights and duties of the parties to a mortgage may depend on whether it is viewed as creating a lien or as transferring legal title to the mortgagee. Most states have adopted the lien theory, which states that the mortgagor retains title, and is entitled to possession of the premises to the exclusion of the mortgagee even in the event of default by the mortgagor. Redemption is the right of the debtor to remove the mortgage by payment of the debt.

3. Transfer of the Interests Under the Mortgage–The interests of the original mortgagor and mortgagee can be transferred, and the rights and obligations of the assignees will depend primarily on (1) the agreement of the parties to the assignment, and (2) the legal rules protecting the interest of the one who is party to the mortgage but not to the transfer. A purchaser who assumes the mortgage is personally obligated to pay the mortgagor's debt owing to the mortgagee. The mortgagee can also hold the mortgagor on his promise to pay. A purchaser who purchases the property subject to the mortgage is not personally obligated to pay the debt. In such a case, the transferee's loss is limited to the property. A mortgagee has the right to assign the mortgage to another person without the consent of the mortgagor. However, an assignee of a mortgage is well advised to obtain the assignment in writing duly executed by the mortgagee and

to record it promptly in order to protect his rights against any subsequent persons who acquire an interest in the property without knowledge of the assignment.

4. Foreclosure–Foreclosure is the sale of the mortgaged property upon default to satisfy the debt. The mortgagee will obtain a deficiency judgment for any unsatisfied balance of the debt and may proceed to enforce payment out of other assets of the mortgagor.

D. Adverse Possession–Adverse possession is the acquisition of title to land by open, continuous, and adverse occupancy for a statutorily prescribed period. Any act of dominion by the true owner will stop the period from running, and the period would have to begin from that time.

II. Public and Private Controls–In the exercise of its police power, the state can place controls on the use of privately owned land for the benefit of the community. The state does not pay the owner any compensation for loss or damage sustained by the owner because of legitimate controls. The enforcement of zoning laws is not a taking of property but a regulation of its use. However, the taking of private property for a public purpose or use under eminent domain is not the exercise of police power. The owners of the property so taken are entitled to be paid its fair and reasonable value. Private controls of the use of privately owned property are possible by means of restrictive covenants.

A. Zoning–Zoning is public control over private land use. The validity of zoning is based on the police power of the state. The police power to provide for the public health, safety, morals, and welfare is an inherent power of government.
1. Enabling Acts and Zoning Ordinances–The power to zone is generally delegated to local city and village authorities by statutes known as enabling statutes. A typical enabling statute grants the following powers to municipalities: (1) to regulate and limit the height and bulk of buildings; (2) to establish, regulate, and limit setback lines; (3) to regulate and determine the area of open spaces; (4) to classify, regulate, and restrict the location of businesses; (5) to divide the municipality into districts; and (6) to set standards to which buildings or structures must conform.
2. Variance–A variance is a use differing from that provided in the zoning ordinance in order to avoid undue hardship.
3. Nonconforming Uses–A zoning ordinance may not immediately terminate a lawful use that existed before it was enacted. The use must be permitted to continue as a nonconforming use for at least a reasonable time.
4. Judicial Review of Zoning–The zoning process is traditionally viewed as legislative. However, it is subject to judicial review on grounds (1) that the zoning ordinance is invalid, (2) that the zoning ordinance has been applied unreasonably, and (3) that the zoning ordinance amounts to a confiscation or taking of property.
5. Subdivision Master Plans–Most states have legislation enabling local authorities to require municipality approval of every land subdivision plat. These enabling statutes provide penalties for failure to secure approval where required by local ordinance.

B. Eminent Domain–Eminent domain is the power to take (buy) private property for public use. The power is carefully circumscribed and controlled. The Fifth Amendment to the federal Constitution provides, "Nor shall private property be taken for public use without just compensation." Similar provisions are found in the constitutions of the states.

1. Public Use–Most states interpret public use to mean "public advantage." Under this definition the power of eminent domain may be delegated to railroad and public utility companies. As society becomes more complex, other public purposes are accepted as legitimate grounds for exercise of the power of eminent domain.

2. Just Compensation–The owners of the property taken must receive just compensation as measured by the fair market value of the property as of the time of taking.

C. Private Restrictions on Land Use–Owners of real property may impose restrictive covenants on the use of land. A restrictive covenant is a private restriction on property contained in a conveyance.

1. Requirements for Covenants Running with the Land–If certain conditions are satisfied, then a restrictive covenant will bind not only the original parties to it but also remote parties who subsequently acquire the property. Such a restrictive covenant is said to "run with the land."

2. Restrictive Covenants in Subdivisions–If the entire subdivision has been subjected to a general building plan designed to benefit all the lots, any lot owner in the subdivision has the right to enforce the restriction against a purchaser whose title descends from a common grantor. Many types of restrictive covenants are used in subdivisions. The more common ones limit the use of property to residential purposes, restrict the area of the lot on which a structure can be built, or provide for a special type of architecture. Restrictive covenants are strictly construed against the party asserting their applicability.

3. Termination of Restrictive Covenants–A restrictive covenant may end by the terms of the original agreement. A court will not enforce a restrictive covenant if changed circumstances make enforcement inequitable and oppressive.

4. Validity of Restrictive Covenants–If it appears that the restriction will operate to the general benefit of the owners of all the land intended to be affected, the restriction will be enforced. The usual method of enforcing such agreements is by injunction to restrain violation.

KEY TERMS

1. Marketable title

2. Deed

3. Warranty deed

4. Special warranty deed

5. Quitclaim deed

6. Delivery

7. Escrow

8. Mortgagor

9. Mortgagee

10. Mortgage

11. Deed of trust

12. Redemption

13. Foreclosure

14. Adverse possession

15. Zoning

16. Variance

17. Nonconforming use

18. Eminent domain

19. Restrictive covenant

TRUE/FALSE

_____ 1. The transfer of real estate by deed must be supported by consideration to be valid.

_____ 2. To be enforceable, a contract for the sale of an interest in land must be in writing and signed by the party against whom enforcement is sought.

_____ 3. An agreement for the sale of an interest in land need not contain the price or manner of payment.

_____ 4. In most jurisdictions, consideration must pass between the parties for a deed to be valid.

_____ 5. A deed is not effective to pass title unless and until it is both delivered and recorded.

_____ 6. The provisions of Article 9 of the UCC govern real estate mortgages and deeds of trust.

_____ 7. A mortgagee has the right to assign a mortgage to a third person without a mortgagor's consent.

_____ 8. When the power of eminent domain is exercised, the award of compensation is given to the holders of all vested and contingent interests in the condemned property.

_____ 9. In a notice-race state, an unrecorded deed is invalid against any subsequent purchaser without notice who records first.

_____ 10. A special warranty deed warrants only that the title has not been impaired, encumbered, or made defective because of anything the grantor has done.

_____ 11. The enforcement of zoning laws constitutes a taking for which the owner of the property must be compensated.

_____ 12. The implied warranty of habitability requires the seller to be responsible for latent defects in a newly constructed home.

_____ 13. A court will enforce a restrictive covenant regardless of whether circumstances have changed to make the covenant inequitable and oppressive.

_____ 14. The courts will uphold a restrictive covenant prohibiting the owner of property from selling to someone of a particular race or ethnic background.

_____ 15. Illegal covenants can be removed from an agreement provided it will not affect the intent of the remaining covenants.

MULTIPLE CHOICE

_____ 1. Zoning ordinances are subject to judicial review on the grounds that:
   a.   the ordinance amounts to a confiscation or taking of property.
   b.   the ordinance bears no reasonable relation to public health, safety, morals, or welfare.
   c.   the ordinance has been applied unreasonably.
   d.   any of the above.

_____ 2. Which of the following would render title to be unmarketable?
   a.   Defects in the chain of title appearing in the land records
   b.   Events depriving the seller of title, such as adverse possession
   c.   A mortgage not excepted in the contract for sale
   d.   All of the above

_____ 3. By a _____ deed, the grantor obliges herself to make the grantee whole if the grantee suffers any damage because the grantor's title was defective.
   a.   warranty
   b.   special warranty
   c.   quitclaim
   d.   none of the above

_____ 4. Which of the following are requirements for an effective deed?
   a.   Be written
   b.   Be delivered
   c.   Both (a) and (b)
   d.   Neither (a) nor (b)

_____ 5. Title to land may be acquired in which of the following ways?
   a.   By gift
   b.   By will
   c.   By adverse possession
   d.   Title may be transferred by any of the above ways

_____ 6. Which of the following are elements of a secured transaction?
   a.   A debt or obligation to pay money
   b.   An interest of the creditor in specific property which secures performance of the obligation
   c.   Neither (a) nor (b)
   d.   Both (a) and (b)

_____ 7. The mortgagor retains title to the property in:
   a.   a "lien" theory state.
   b.   a "title" theory state.
   c.   neither (a) nor (b).
   d.   both (a) and (b).

_____ 8. Which of the following would be grounds for judicial review of a zoning ordinance?
    a. The zoning ordinance is invalid.
    b. The ordinance has been unreasonably applied.
    c. The ordinance amounts to a confiscation.
    d. All of the above would be grounds.

_____ 9. In many states, if a person openly and continuously occupies the land of another without permission for a statutorily prescribed period, that person will gain title to the land by:
    a. foreclosure.
    b. redemption.
    c. eminent domain.
    d. adverse possession.

_____ 10. Under which of the following circumstances would a nonconforming use be eliminated?
    a. When the use is discontinued
    b. When a nonconforming structure is destroyed or is substantially damaged
    c. When a nonconforming structure has been permitted to exist for the period of its useful life
    d. All of the above

_____ 11. A restrictive covenant is enforceable only if:
    a. the restriction will operate to the general benefit of the owners of all the land the restriction will affect.
    b. the restriction appears somewhere in the chain of title to which the land of the person seeking to enforce the covenant is subject.
    c. neither (a) nor (b).
    d. both (a) and (b).

_____ 12. Which of the following is/are typically found in the enabling statutes which delegate zoning power to local authorities?
    a. The power to regulate and limit the height and bulk of buildings
    b. The power to set standards to which buildings must conform
    c. The power to restrict the location of trades and industries
    d. All of the above are typically found in enabling statutes.

_____ 13. An attorney does a title search on property that Ron wishes to purchase. The search indicates a title defect, because the abstract shows that Wesley could possibly have an interest in the land even though he is not the seller. What type of deed should Ron ask Wesley to give him in order to clear up the title defect?
    a. A warranty deed
    b. A special warranty deed
    c. A quitclaim deed
    d. A contract for deed

_____ 14. *CPA:* Which of the following is a defect in marketable title to real property?
   a.   Recorded zoning restrictions
   b.   Recorded easements referred to in the contract of sale
   c.   Unrecorded lawsuit for negligence against the seller
   d.   Unrecorded easement

_____ 15. *CPA:* For a deed to be effective between the purchaser and seller of real estate, one of the conditions is that the deed must:
   a.   contain the signatures of the seller and purchaser.
   b.   contain the actual sales price.
   c.   be delivered by the seller with an intent to transfer title.
   d.   be recorded within the permissible statutory time limits..

SHORT ESSAY

1.   What are the two essential documents involved in the sale of real estate? What must or should each document contain?

   _____

   _____

   _____

   _____

2.   What are the three types of deeds? How do they differ in effect?

   _____

   _____

   _____

   _____

3. Discuss what is meant by marketable title.

_____

_____

_____

_____

4. Discuss eminent domain.

_____

_____

_____

_____

5. List and briefly and define three public or private controls over real property.

_____

_____

_____

_____

Chapter 52
Trusts and Wills

PURPOSE

In addition to the transfer of property by sale and gift, another important way in which a person may convey property is through trusts and wills. Trusts may be either inter vivos (taking effect during the transferor's lifetime) or testamentary (taking effect upon the transferor's death). Wills enable individuals to control the transfer of their property at their death. However, if a person dies intestate (without a will), state law prescribes who shall receive the property. In this chapter, you study both trusts and wills, as well as the manner in which property descends when a person dies intestate.

CHAPTER CHECKPOINTS

After reading and studying this chapter, you should be able to:

1. Describe the differences between an express trust and an implied trust.

2. List the essential elements of a trust.

3. Discuss the formal requirements of making a valid will and how a will may be revoked.

4. Discuss the general rules of intestate succession.

5. Discuss the process involved in the administration of an estate.

CHAPTER OUTLINE

I.   Trusts–A trust is the transfer of property to one party for the benefit of another. It may be created by agreement of the parties, by a grant in a will, or by a court decree for any purpose that is not against the law or public policy. The settlor is the creator of the trust. The trustee is the holder of legal title to property for the benefit of another. The beneficiary is the equitable owner of the trust property.

   A. Types of Trusts–All trusts may be divided into two major groups: express and implied. Implied trusts are known as either "constructive" or "resulting" trusts.

      1. Express Trusts–An express trust is established by voluntary action and is represented by a written document or, in some circumstances, an oral statement or by conduct of the settlor. An express trust of real property must be in writing to meet the requirements of the statute of frauds. No particular words are necessary to create a trust, provided the intent of the settlor is unmistakable. A precatory expression is one that expresses a wish. It must be definite and certain in order to impose a trust upon the property.

         a. Testamentary Trust–A testamentary trust is one incorporated into a will. Such a trust becomes operative after the settlor's death.

         b. Inter Vivos Trust–An inter vivos trust is one made and operative during the settlor's lifetime.

         c. Charitable Trusts–A charitable trust is designed to benefit humankind.

         d. Spendthrift Trusts–Trust designed to remove the trust estate from the beneficiary's control.

         e. Totten Trusts–A totten trust is a tentative trust consisting of a joint bank account opened by the settlor. The trust may be revoked by withdrawing the funds or changing the form of the account. The transfer of ownership becomes complete only upon the depositor's death.

      2. Implied Trusts–In some cases, the courts will impose a trust on property to correct wrongdoing, to prevent unjust enrichment, or to undo a morally-wrongful situation.

         a. Constructive Trusts–A constructive trust is one that arises by operation of law to prevent unjust enrichment. A constructive trust is created when there is abuse of a confidential relationship or when actual fraud or duress is an equitable ground for creating the trust.

         b. Resulting Trusts–A resulting trust arises to fulfill the presumed intent of the settler which was inadequately expressed. A resulting trust does not depend on contract or agreement. A resulting trust represents a legal presumption that the apparent holder of legal title does not hold the property personally but as a trustee for another. A resulting trust also may arise when an express trust fails and the trustee then holds the property in trust for the settlor to whom the property is returned.

   B. Creation of Trusts–Each trust has (1) a creator or settlor, (2) a "corpus" or trust property, (3) a trustee, and (4) a beneficiary. No special words are needed to create a trust provided that the intent of the settlor to make a trust is unmistakable. Consideration is not essential to an enforceable trust.

      1. Settlor–Any person legally capable of making a contract may create a trust.

      2. Subject Matter–A trust corpus or res must be property that is definite and specific.

      3. Trustee–Anyone legally capable of holding title to and dealing with property may be a trustee. The lack of a trustee will not destroy the trust. The court will appoint someone to act as trustee if the settlor neglects to appoint one.

    a. Duties of the Trustee–A trustee has three primary duties: (1) to carry out the purposes of the trust, (2) to act with prudence and care in the administration of the trust, and (3) to exercise a high degree of loyalty toward the beneficiary. The trustee is required to act with the same degree of care that a prudent person would use to carry out his personal affairs. The trustee is a fiduciary who has a duty of loyalty.

    b. Powers of the Trustee–The powers of the trustee are determined by: (1) the authority granted him by the settlor in the instrument creating the trust, and (2) the rules of law in the jurisdiction in which the trust is established. State laws determine the investments a trustee may make with trust funds. Most states prescribe a prudent investor rule.

    c. Allocation of Principal and Income–Trusts often settle a life estate in the corpus on one beneficiary and a remainder interest on another beneficiary. In these instances, the trustee must distribute the principal to one party (the remainderman) and the income to another (the life tenant or income beneficiary). The trustee must also allocate receipts and charge expenses between the income beneficiary and the remainderman. The general rule in allocating benefits and burdens is that ordinary or current receipts and expenses are chargeable to the income beneficiary, whereas extraordinary receipts and expense are allocated to the remainderman.

  4. Beneficiary–There are very few restrictions on who (or what) may be a beneficiary. In the absence of restrictive provisions, a beneficiary's interest may be reached by creditors, or the beneficiary may sell or dispose of the interest.

C. Termination of a Trust–Unless a power of revocation is reserved by the settlor, the general rule is that a trust, once validly created, is irrevocable. If so reserved, the trust may be terminated at the discretion of the settlor. Normally, the instrument creating a trust establishes a termination date. If both the equitable and legal title are held by the same beneficiary, the merger doctrine applies and the beneficiary holds the property outright.

II. Decedent's Estates–The assets (estate) of a person who dies leaving a valid will are to be distributed according to the directions contained in the will. A will is also called a testament; the maker of a will is called a testator; and gifts made in the will are called devises or bequests. If a person dies without leaving a will (intestate), her property will pass to her heirs and next of kin as provided by state statute. This is known as intestate succession. If a person dies without a will and leaves no heirs or next of kin, her property escheats (reverts) to the state.

A. Wills–A will is a written instrument executed with the formalities required by statutes, whereby a person makes a disposition of his property to take effect after his death. A will is revocable at any time during life. A will takes effect only on the death of the testator.

  1. Mental Capacity–In order to make a valid will, the testator must have both the "power" and the "capacity" to do so. In addition, testamentary intent must be present.

    a. Testamentary Capacity and Power–The power to make a will is granted by the state to persons who are of a class believed generally able to handle their affairs without regard to personal limitations. In most states, a child under a certain age cannot make a valid will. The capacity to make a will refers to the limits placed on particular persons in the class generally granted the power to make wills because of personal mental deficiencies. A person has sufficient mental capacity to make a will if she is capable of understanding the nature and extent of her property, appreciating the natural objects of her bounty, and formulating a plan of disposition.

    b. Conduct Invalidating a Will–A will that transmits property as a result of duress, undue influence, or fraud is no will at all, because it reflects an intent other than the testator's.

2. Formal Requirements of a Will–To be valid, a will must comply with certain formalities. These are necessary to indicate that the testator understood her actions and to help prevent fraud.

    a. Writing–A basic requirement to a valid will is that it be in writing. The writing may be informal, as long as it meets the basic requirements of the statute. Pencil, ink, and photocopy are all valid methods.

    b. Signature–A will must be signed by the testator. The signature verifies that the will has been executed. Most statutes require the signature to be at the end of the will.

    c. Attestation–With a few isolated exceptions, a written will must be attested or certified by witnesses. Usually two or three witnesses are required. The most common restriction is that a witness must not have any interest under the will.

3. Revocation of a Will–A will is revocable by the testator if certain formalities are followed. Under certain circumstances, a will may be revoked by operation of law.

    a. Destruction or Alteration–Tearing, burning, or otherwise destroying a will is a strong sign that the testator intended to revoke it. Unless it can be shown that the destruction was inadvertent, it is an effective way of revoking a will. In some states the testator may partially revoke a will by erasure or obliteration of a part of a will. Substituted or additional bequests made by insertions between the written or printed lines are not effective without reexecution and reattestation.

    b. Subsequent Will–The execution of a second will does not in itself constitute a revocation of an earlier will. The first will is revoked only to the extent it is inconsistent with the second. The most certain manner of revocation is the execution of a later will containing declaration that all former wills are revoked.

    c. Codicils–A codicil is an addition to or a revision of a will. Codicils must be executed with all the formal requirements of a will.

    d. Operation of Law–A marriage generally revokes a will executed before the marriage. Divorce, however, does not revoke a will for the benefit of the other party. The birth of a child after execution of a will may revoke a will, at least as far as that child is concerned, but this is not true in all states.

    e. Renunciation by the Surviving Spouse–Statutes generally provide a surviving spouse the election of taking under the will or under intestate succession.

4. Special Types of Wills–There are many special types of wills.

    a. Nuncupative Wills–A nuncupative will is an oral declaration made before witnesses without any writing. They are authorized in only a few jurisdictions and are valid to pass limited amounts of personal property.

    b. Holographic Wills–A holographic will is one entirely in the handwriting of the testator. In some jurisdictions it is valid without witnesses. It must strictly comply with statutory requirements for such wills.

c. Soldiers' and Sailors' Wills–Most statutes relax the formal will requirements for soldiers on active duty and sailors while at sea.

d. Living Wills–Almost all states have adopted statutes permitting living wills. A living will is a document that complies with the statutory requirements by which an individual declares that she does not wish to receive extraordinary medical treatment to preserve her life.

B. Intestate Succession–Property not effectively disposed of before death or by will passes in accordance with the law of intestate succession. The rules set forth in statutes for determining to whom the decedent's property shall be distributed assure an orderly transfer of title to property and purport to carry out what would probably be the wishes of the decedent. The rules of descent vary widely from state to state. Except for the statutory rights of the widow, the intestate property passes in equal shares to each child of the decedent living at the time of his death. The share of any child who dies before the decedent is equally divided among that child's children. Per stirpes is a class or group of distributees that take the share their deceased ancestor would have been entitled to. Thus they take by their right of representing such ancestor and not as so many individuals. Per capita is an equal share given to each of a number of persons, all of whom stand in equal degree to the decedent without reference to the right of representation.

C. Administration of Estates–The procedure of managing the distribution of decedents' estates is referred to as probate. The rules and procedures are statutory. The first legal step after death is to determine whether the deceased left a will. If there is a will, most likely the testator named an executor. If there is no will or no one named as executor in the will, the court will on petition appoint an administrator. Soon after the admission of the will to probate, the personal representative, who is a fiduciary, must file an inventory. The executor or administrator will then begin the duties of collecting the assets, paying the debts, and disbursing the remainder according to the will or intestate succession. An executor is the person named in the will and appointed by the court to administer the will. An administrator is a person appointed by the court to administer the estate when there is no will or the person named in the will fails to qualify. In the administration of every estate, there are probate expenses as well as fees to be paid to the executor or administrator, attorneys' fees, and taxes imposed by both the federal and state governments.

KEY TERMS

1. Trust

2. Settlor

3. Trustee

4. Beneficiary

5. Express trust

6. Testamentary trust

7. *Inter vivos* trust

8. Charitable trust

9. Spendthrift trust

10. Totten trust

11. Implied trust

12. Constructive trust

13. Resulting trust

14. Trust corpus

15. Intestate

16. Will

17. Codicil

18. Nuncupative will

19. Holographic will

20. Living will

21. Intestate succession

22. *Per stirpes*

23. *Per capita*

24. Probate

25. Executor

26. Administrator

TRUE/FALSE

_____ 1. Legal title to property may be held by one or more persons while at the same time its use, enjoyment, and benefit belong to one or more others.

_____ 2. An express trust is established by voluntary action.

_____ 3. A court may impose a constructive trust to prevent unjust enrichment of a person who has abused a confidential relationship with another.

_____ 4. A trust established during the lifetime of the settlor is called a testamentary trust.

_____ 5. In a spendthrift trust the beneficiary's interest may be reached by his creditors.

_____ 6. Anyone legally capable of holding title to and dealing with property may be a trustee.

_____ 7. The death of a trustee destroys the trust.

_____ 8. In general, unless the settlor reserves a power of revocation, a trust once validly created is irrevocable.

_____ 9. A valid will requires the testator to have mental capacity and be free from the undue influence of others.

_____ 10. In certain circumstances, a testator may execute an irrevocable will.

_____ 11. A witness to a will must not have any interest under the will.

_____ 12. A codicil must be executed with all of the formal requirements of a will.

_____ 13. Legally adopted children are generally recognized as lawful heirs of their adopting parents.

_____ 14. The rules of descent are uniform throughout the United States.

_____ 15. Marriage generally revokes a will executed before the marriage, but divorce generally does not revoke a provision in the will of one party for the benefit of the other.

MULTIPLE CHOICE

_____ 1. Implied trusts imposed upon property by court order are:
   a. constructive trusts.
   b. resulting trusts.
   c. either (a) or (b).
   d. neither (a) nor (b).

_____ 2. If a director of a corporation is found to have taken advantage of a "corporate opportunity," the court will impose:
   a. an express trust.
   b. a constructive trust.
   c. a resulting trust.
   d. a charitable trust.

_____ 3. In order to have a valid trust, there must be all of the following except:
   a. settlor.
   b. codicil.
   c. trustee.
   d. beneficiary.

_____ 4. A spendthrift clause in a trust instrument will insulate income already received from the trust by the beneficiary from:
   a. the claims of the beneficiary's creditors.
   b. the beneficiary's control.
   c. neither (a) nor (b).
   d. both (a) and (b).

_____ 5. Sally deposits money into a joint bank account in the name of "Sally, in trust for Roger." This is known as:
  a. a charitable trust.
  b. a totten trust.
  c. a resulting trust.
  d. an *inter vivos* trust.

_____ 6. Which of the following is not a duty of a trustee?
  a. To carry out the purposes of the trust
  b. To act with prudence and care in the administration of the trust
  c. To exercise a high degree of loyalty toward the beneficiary
  d. To act as a guarantor for the liabilities of the trust

_____ 7. In order to make a valid will, the testator must have:
  a. the "power" to make a valid will, as defined by state law.
  b. the "capacity" to make a valid will.
  c. either (a) or (b).
  d. both (a) and (b).

_____ 8. To incorporate by reference a memorandum into a will, all of the following conditions must exist except:
  a. it must be in writing.
  b. it must be in existence when the will is executed.
  c. it must be physically attached to the will.
  d. it must be adequately described in the will.

_____ 9. Which of the following will result in the revocation of a will?
  a. The testator is divorced after having executed the will.
  b. The testator executes a codicil.
  c. The testator marries after having executed the will.
  d. The testator tears the will in half thinking that it is a void "I.O.U."

_____ 10. If *A* executes a will leaving Blackacre to *B*, but then sells the land for $20,000 before he dies, on *A*'s death, *B* will receive:
  a. Blackacre.
  b. $20,000.
  c. $20,000 and Blackacre.
  d. nothing.

_____ 11. In which of the following situations will a will be declared invalid?
 a. The testator was incompetent most of the time, but executed the will during a period of lucidity.
 b. The will was executed under fraudulent circumstances.
 c. A will is invalid in both of the above circumstances.
 d. A will is not invalid under either of the above circumstances.

_____ 12. A _____ is an addition to or a revision of a will by a separate instrument.
 a. devise
 b. hologram
 c. codicil
 d. settlor

_____ 13. Which of the following is generally correct regarding the course of descent?
 a. At common law, property could not lineally ascend to one's parents.
 b. At common law, a stepchild was considered an heir.
 c. All states distribute property on a per capita basis.
 d. None of the above is correct.

_____ 14. *CPA:* Which of the following is **not** necessary to create an express trust?
 a. A trust corpus
 b. A successor trustee
 c. A valid trust purpose
 d. A beneficiary

_____ 15. *CPA:* To properly create an *inter vivos* trust funded with cash, the grantor must:
 a. execute a written trust instrument.
 b. transfer the cash to the trustee.
 c. provide for payment of fees to the trustee.
 d. designate an alternate trust beneficiary.

SHORT ESSAY

1. What are the four essential elements of a trust?

_____

_____

_____

_____

2. What is the difference between an express trust and an implied trust?

3. List and define four special types of wills.

4. List ways in which a will may be revoked.

5. Outline briefly the steps involved in the administration of an estate.

Part X
Sample Examination

MULTIPLE CHOICE

_____ 1. *CPA:* Which of the following items is tangible property?
   a. Share of stock
   b. Trademark
   c. Promissory note
   d. Oil painting

_____ 2. Which of the following would not be considered in determining whether property had become a fixture?
   a. The physical relationship of the item to the land
   b. The intent of the owner of the land to which the item is attached
   c. The purpose the item serves with respect to the land
   d. The intent of the person who attached the item to the land

_____ 3. A _____ is a transfer of title to property from one person to another for consideration.
   a. sale
   b. gift
   c. bailment
   d. trust

_____ 4. The individual designated to manage a trust is known as the:
   a. trustee.
   b. beneficiary.
   c. settlor.
   d. executor.

_____ 5. When Arthur dies and his will is probated, Brad receives a life estate in Arthur's house. What happens to the house when Brad dies, if no one else is mentioned in the will as receiving an interest in the house?
   a. It goes to Brad's heirs.
   b. It reverts to Arthur's heirs.
   c. It goes to the state.
   d. It is shared by Brad's heirs and Arthur's heirs.

_____ 6. When Jane dies and her will is probated, Wayne receives a life estate in Jane's house. The will also states that on Wayne's death, the house will go to Clark. Clark's interest in the house is known as a:
   a. possibility of reverter.
   b. vested remainder.
   c. contingent remainder.
   d. periodic tenancy.

_____ 7. Max conveys part of his land to Tina. The part conveyed to Tina is so situated that she would have no access to it except across Max's remaining land. Under these facts, Tina has an easement by:
   a. express grant or reservation.
   b. implied grant or reservation.
   c. necessity.
   d. prescription.

_____ 8. Dale grants to Brian, an adjoining landowner, the right to cross his land and to gather black walnuts from the trees located there. Brian has a(n):
   a. easement by prescription.
   b. _profit à prendre._
   c. license.
   d. either a _profit à prendre_ or a license.

_____ 9. Lorraine rents a car from Ajax Car Rental while on a business trip to Los Angeles. This is an example of a(n):
   a. extraordinary bailment.
   b. constructive bailment.
   c. gratuitous bailment.
   d. bailment for mutual benefit.

_____ 10. If a mortgagor sells the land that is the security for the mortgage, the purchaser is personally liable for the mortgage debt:
   a. if the purchaser expressly assumed the mortgage.
   b. if the purchaser bought the property "subject to" the mortgage.
   c. in both situation (a) and (b).
   d. in no case, because a mortgage is a personal security interest that cannot be transferred.

_____ 11. Neil borrows his neighbor's snowblower to clear his own driveway of snow. This is an example of a:
   a. bailment for mutual benefit.
   b. bailment for the benefit of the bailor.
   c. bailment for the benefit of the bailee.
   d. gift.

_____ 12. Which of the following is correct regarding a trade fixture?
   a. It is considered to be personal property belonging to the tenant.
   b. It belongs to the landlord upon termination of the lease agreement.
   c. It becomes so attached as to be considered part of the real property.
   d. Two of the above are correct, (b) and (c).

_____ 13. Zoning:
   a. is the principal method of private control over land use.
   b. is an exercise of police power.
   c. allows no deviations from the ordinance once it has been adopted.
   d. is considered a legislative process and, as such, is not subject to judicial review.

_____ 14. Sharon rents an apartment from Gibson Realty. The lease is for a six-month period, and no notice is required to terminate at the end of the six months. The rental agreement is for a(n):
   a. estate for years.
   b. tenancy from month to month.
   c. tenancy at will.
   d. tenancy at sufferance.

_____ 15. Vernon rents an apartment for a six-month period with rent due on the first of each month. At the end of six months, Vernon continues in possession of the apartment, but no new lease is drafted and signed by either Vernon or the landlord. The continued occupancy is a:
   a. periodic tenancy.
   b. tenancy from month to month.
   c. tenancy at will.
   d. tenancy at sufferance.

_____ 16. *CPA:* Which of the following statements correctly describes the requirement of insurable interest relating to property insurance? An insurable interest:
   a. must exist when any loss occurs.
   b. must exist when the policy is issued and when any loss occurs.
   c. is created only when the property is owned in fee simple.
   d. is created only when the property is owned by an individual.

_____ 17. Lowell has a building valued at $100,000. He has an 80% co-insurance policy on the property, but only purchased insurance in the face amount of $65,000. If the building is totally destroyed in an earthquake, Lowell will be able to recover what amount of money?
   a. $64,000.
   b. $65,000.
   c. $81,250.
   d. $100,000.

_____ 18. *CPA:* Which of the following is **not** necessary to create an express trust?
   a. A successor trustee
   b. A trust corpus
   c. A beneficiary
   d. A valid trust purpose

_____ 19. *CPA:* If **not** expressly granted, which of the following implied powers would a trustee have:
   (I) power to sell trust property, (II) power to borrow from the trust, or (III) power to pay trust expenses.
   a. I and II
   b. I and III
   c. II and III
   d. I, II, and III

_____ 20. Sarah and her boyfriend go to a restaurant for dinner. While washing her hands in the restroom, Sarah removes her watch and accidentally leaves it there. Later in the evening, a waitress finds it and turns it over to the restaurant owner. The owner puts it in the restaurant safe and then forgets about it until six months later when the cleaning lady finds it there and shows it to the restaurant manager. Assuming that Sarah never returned to the restaurant to look for the watch, who has first claim to it?
   a. The waitress
   b. The restaurant owner
   c. The cleaning lady
   d. None of the above, because Sarah is the true owner and has only mislaid the property.

Try The Web

Review and select (or compile from options) a suitable will and testament.

Solution:

Go to: http://www.lectlaw.com./formb.htm
Select: Will I

Answers to Chapter Tests and Sample Examinations

Chapter 1

True/False:
1. T	6. T	11. T
2. F	7. F	12. T
3. F	8. T	13. F
4. T	9. F	14. F
5. F	10. T	15. T

Multiple Choice:
1. c	6. d	11. c
2. c	7. b	12. a
3. c	8. d	13. c
4. d	9. d	14. d
5. c	10. a	15. c

Short Essay:

1. In civil law systems, the legislatures create the laws and the judges initiate and conduct the litigation through the inquisitorial method of adjudication. In common law systems, the judges have a major role in creating the laws, the parties initiate and conduct the litigation through the adversary system, and the judges act as referees to insure that the parties follow the procedural rules.

2. A right is the capacity of a person, aided by the law, to require another person or persons to perform or refrain from performing a certain act. A duty is the obligation the law imposes upon a person to perform a certain act or to refrain from performing a certain act. Duty and right are correlatives.

3. *Stare decisis* literally means to stand by the decisions. It is a principle that courts should adhere to and rely on rules applied in prior, substantially similar cases. This principle lends stability to the law.

4. They are similar in that they were both drafted by legal scholars who were concerned that legal rules be good rules that have wide applicability nationwide. They are different in that the Restatements of Law are not law in and of themselves, but are statements of what legal scholars believe the common law to be. In contrast, the UCC is statutory law in all fifty states, because the UCC has been adopted by the state legislatures. Restatements reflect the law developed by judicial decisions and by court application and interpretation of statutes in force for years.

5. A civil action in tort could be brought by Alice against George, and also a criminal action could be brought against George by the state. In a civil action, the plaintiff brings the action against the defendant, the burden of proof is preponderance of the evidence, and the action in this case would result in money damages. In a criminal action, the government brings the action against the defendant, the burden of proof is beyond a reasonable doubt, and the action results in a fine and/or imprisonment.

Chapter 2

True/False:

1. T	6. F	11. T
2. F	7. T	12. T
3. T	8. T	13. F
4. F	9. T	14. F
5. T	10. F	15. T

Multiple Choice:

1. d	6. b	11. d
2. d	7. c	12. d
3. d	8. d	13. c
4. c	9. d	14. a
5. a	10. b	15. d

Short Essay:

1. Utilitarians believe that moral actions are those that produce the greatest net pleasure compared to the net pain. They assess good and evil in terms of consequences of actions. Deontologists believe that actions must be judged by their motives and means as well as their results. They address the practical problems of utilitarianism by holding that certain underlying principles are right or wrong irrespective of any pleasure or pain calculations.

2. Kant asserted that conduct should be such that the actor would want that conduct to become a universal, consistent law of conduct. Additionally, one should respect the autonomy and rationality of all human beings and never treat another human being merely as a means to an end.

3. The arguments for corporate social responsibility include: (1) corporations have limited liability and other rights which carry a responsibility to contribute to the betterment of society; (2) the more socially responsible that companies act, the less the government must regulate; and (3) enhanced goodwill created by involvement in social causes means stronger profits in the long run. The arguments against corporate social responsibility include: (1) businesses are established to permit people to engage in profit-making, not social activities; (2) whenever companies stray from their designated role of profit maker, they take unfair advantage of company employees and shareholders; (3) corporations are private institutions that are subject to a lower standard of accountability than public bodies; and (4) corporations may not possess the ability to recognize and manage socially useful activities.

4. Three social ethics theories would be: Social Egalitarian, where society should provide all its members with equal goods and services regardless of their relative contributions; Distributive Justice, which stresses equality of opportunity rather than results; and Libertarian, which stresses market outcomes as the basis for distributing society's rewards.

5. While corporations should be socially responsible, some feel that their greatest social obligation is to return as much money as possible to their stakeholders from their profit-making activities. The argument has been made that when companies such as Big Bucks provide funding for social causes that they are taking unfair advantage of company employees and shareholders. The argument is that these funds rightfully belong to the shareholders or employees, so a decision by the board of directors to support social concerns with the money is unfair. The feeling is that shareholders and employees can decide independently if they wish to make charitable contributions. On the other hand, some feel that corporations carry a responsibility to society to contribute to its overall well-being. The proponents of this view feel that corporate America cannot ignore the multitude of pressing needs that remain, despite the efforts of government and private charities.

Chapter 3

True/False:

1. F	6. T	11. T
2. T	7. T	12. F
3. T	8. F	13. T
4. F	9. T	14. F
5. T	10. F	15. T

Multiple Choice:

1. d	6. b	11. a
2. b	7. a	12. d
3. c	8. d	13. d
4. d	9. b	14. a
5. c	10. c	15. b

Short Essay:

1. Jurisdiction is the power or authority of a court to hear a case. Venue is the geographical location where the case should be heard when there are several courts of the same jurisdiction.

2. The judge assumes that all the evidence introduced by the non-moving party is true. The judge then decides whether this evidence, if true, would be sufficient for the jury to find in favor of the non-moving party. If the evidence of the non-moving party, assumed to be true, is not sufficient for the jury to find in favor of the non-moving party, then there is no point in requiring the moving party to try to disprove that evidence. Thus, the moving party will be entitled to a directed verdict.

3. The major advantages of court adjudication are that it is binding, and it is based upon public norms and precedents; the major disadvantages include that it is expensive, it is time-consuming, it has limited remedies, and judges may lack special expertise. The major advantages of arbitration are that it is binding, the parties control the process, there is privacy, arbitrators have special expertise, and you can get a speedy resolution of your dispute; the major disadvantages include that there are no public norms, no precedents, and no uniformity. The major advantages of mediation are that it preserves relations, the parties control the process, and there is privacy; the major disadvantages include that it is not binding, it lacks finality, and there is no precedent nor uniformity.

4. *In personam* jurisdiction is that jurisdiction based upon claims against a person in contrast to jurisdiction over that person's property, whereas *in rem* jurisdiction is based upon a claim against the property of a person.

5. (a) Pleadings: filing of a complaint, service of a summons, and filing of an answer, reply, and/or counterclaim; (b) Possible demurrer or motion to dismiss for failure to state a claim; (c) Discovery in the form of depositions, interrogatories, requests for admission, and examinations of various sorts; (d) Pretrial conference to clarify issues and set a date for a trial; (e) Trial: consists of jury selection or *voir dire*, opening statements, examination and cross-examination of witnesses, closing statements, jury instructions, and verdict; (f) Motion for a new trial or executing of judgment if no appeal; and (g) Appeal.

Chapter 4

True/False:

1. T	6. T	11. F
2. T	7. F	12. F
3. F	8. T	13. T
4. T	9. T	14. T
5. F	10. F	15. F

Multiple Choice:

1. d	6. c	11. a
2. d	7. a	12. c
3. b	8. c	13. b
4. c	9. b	14. b
5. d	10. d	15. a

Short Essay:

1. Procedural due process requires that governmental decision-making be fair and impartial in those situations where an individual may be deprived of life, liberty, or property, whereas substantive due process requires a determination of whether a particular governmental action is compatible with individual liberties.

2. The rational relationship test is applied to economic regulation. It must be conceivable that the classification used bear a rational relationship to a bona fide governmental interest the classification seeks to further. The strict scrutiny test is more stringent. It is applied to legislation affecting fundamental rights. The classification must be necessary to promote a compelling governmental interest.

3. The court would be concerned with (1) the necessity and importance of the state regulation, (2) the burden it imposes on interstate commerce, and (3) the extent to which it discriminates against interstate commerce in favor of local concerns.

4. A state may not regulate activities if it would produce an undue burden on interstate commerce. The Supreme Court considers whether the regulation is necessary as well as the burden it would impose on interstate commerce. Note that states may not tax goods that continue to remain in the stream of commerce. Taxes may only be imposed after the movement of the goods has ceased.

5. The First Amendment's guarantee of free speech applies to corporations. Accordingly, corporations may not be prohibited from speaking out on political issues. Commercial speech is also protected under the First Amendment but to a lesser degree than private speech. Government regulation of false and misleading advertising is permissible under the First Amendment. Because defamation involves a communication, the protection extended to speech by the First Amendment applies. However, the Supreme Court has ruled that a public official who is defamed may not recover in an action of defamation unless the statement was made with actual malice.

Chapter 5

True/False:

1. F	6. F	11. T
2. F	7. T	12. T
3. T	8. T	13. T
4. T	9. F	14. F
5. F	10. T	15. F

Multiple Choice:

1. d	6. d	11. d
2. d	7. a	12. a
3. d	8. d	13. b
4. c	9. d	14. d
5. c	10. b	15. d

Short Essay:

1. Administrative agencies exercise powers that have been allocated by the Constitution to the three separate branches of government. Agencies exercise legislative power when they make rules, executive power when they enforce the law, and judicial power when they adjudicate disputes.

2. In informal rulemaking, the agency must provide prior notice of a proposed rule–usually by publication in the *Federal Register*, an opportunity for interested parties to participate, and publication of a final draft containing a concise general statement of its basis and purpose at least 30 days before the rule's effective date. In formal rulemaking, the agency must base its rules upon consideration of the record of the trial-like agency hearing and include a statement of "findings and conclusions, and the reasons or basis therefore, on all the material issues of fact, law, or discretion presented on the record." Hybrid rulemaking results from combining the informal procedures of the APA with the additional procedures specified by the enabling statute.

3. In exercising judicial review of agency action, the court may either compel agency action unlawfully withheld or set aside impermissible agency action. In making these determinations, the court must review the whole record and may set aside agency action only if the error is prejudicial. The court decides all relevant questions of law, interprets constitutional and statutory provisions, and determines the meaning or applicability of the terms of an agency action.

4. Control of administrative processes comes from all three major branches of government. Legislative control comes through the passage of enabling statutes and approval of budgets. Executive control includes the president's power to appoint members of the agency, and judicial control can be found in the court's power to review a particular rule or order of an administrative agency. In addition, disclosure statutes, such as the Freedom of Information Act and the Government in the Sunshine Act, make agencies more accountable to the public.

5. The three types of rules promulgated by administrative agencies include: legislative rules, interpretative rules, and procedural rules. Legislative rules are substantive rules issued by an administrative agency under the authority delegated to it by the legislature. Interpretative rules are statements issued by an administrative agency indicating its construction of its governing statute. Procedural rules are rules issued by an administrative agency establishing its organization, methods of operation, and rules of conduct for practice before it.

Chapter 6

True/False:

1. F	6. F	11. F
2. F	7. F	12. F
3. F	8. T	13. T
4. T	9. T	14. T
5. T	10. T	15. F

Multiple Choice:

1. d	6. d	11. d
2. c	7. a	12. c
3. a	8. a	13. b
4. d	9. a	14. c
5. b	10. d	15. c

Short Essay:

1. Both crimes and torts involve breaches of duty. In criminal law, the duty is one owed to society as a whole and punishment can be fines, imprisonment, or even death. Elements necessary in order to obtain a conviction are the *actus reus,* the wrongful act, and the *mens rea,* or criminal intent. Tort law involves a wrong committed against another individual and punishment includes injunctions or fines.

2. The four defenses most relevant to white-collar crimes and crimes against business include: (1) defense of person or property which allows individuals to use reasonable force to protect themselves, others, and their property, and deadly force to protect themselves and others if they are threatened with death or serious bodily harm; (2) duress, which is coercion by threat of serious bodily injury; (3) mistake of fact which occurs if persons honestly and reasonably believe the facts to be such that their conduct would not constitute a crime; and (4) entrapment which arises when a government official induces persons to commit a crime they would not otherwise commit.

3. The Racketeer Influenced and Corrupt Organizations Act (RICO) was enacted to terminate the infiltration of organized crime into legitimate business. The act subjects enterprises that engage in a pattern of racketeering to severe civil and criminal penalties.

4. A search warrant is not required in the following situations: (a) hot pursuit of a fugitive, (b) voluntary consent is given, (c) an emergency, (d) search incident to a lawful arrest, (e) evidence of a crime in plain view of a law enforcement officer, or (f) a delay which would hinder an investigation.

5. The Fourth, Fifth, and Sixth Amendments to the U.S. Constitution provide important protections for those accused of criminal conduct. The Fourth protects all persons against unreasonable searches and seizures, thereby protecting privacy and safeguarding against arbitrary invasions by governmental officials. The Fifth Amendment protects persons against self-discrimination, double jeopardy, and being charged with a capital or infamous crime except by grand jury indictment. The Sixth Amendment ensures that the accused shall receive a speedy and public trial by an impartial jury. All of these protections are extended to state actions by the Fourteenth Amendment.

Chapter 7

True/False:

1. T	6. T	11. T
2. F	7. T	12. T
3. T	8. T	13. T
4. F	9. T	14. T
5. T	10. T	15. T

Multiple Choice:

1. d	6. d	11. c
2. a	7. a	12. b
3. c	8. d	13. b
4. b	9. b	14. a
5. d	10. d	15. a

Short Essay:

1. Trespass is an interference with a person's right to the exclusive possession of his property, while nuisance is an interference with a person's right to use and enjoy his property. Trespass usually occurs when the wrongdoer attempts to exercise possession of the land by actually coming onto the land. Nuisance usually occurs when the wrongdoer makes it difficult or impossible for the property owner to use or enjoy his land by subjecting it to such irritants as dirt, smoke, noise, or unpleasant odors.

2. For purposes of tort law, a wrongdoer intends to commit a particular tort if she acts with the purpose or motive of achieving the tortious result or with the knowledge that such tortious result is substantially certain to occur as a natural consequence of her actions. For example, if *A* throws a rock at *B*, hoping to hit him, she has acted with the purpose of battering him and so she has the requisite intent. If, however, *A* throws a rock into a large crowd at a rock concert, not hoping to hit anyone at all, she can hardly be surprised when someone is in fact hit. Thus, she will have acted with the knowledge that a battery was substantially certain to occur as a natural consequence of her action and would have the requisite intent.

3. Interference with contractual relations is the tort of interfering intentionally and improperly with the performance of a contract by inducing a party not to perform it. The tort of disparagement imposes liability on a person who knowingly or recklessly publishes a false statement that harms another's monetary interests. Fraudulent misrepresentation imposes liability for monetary loss caused by justifiable reliance on an intentional misrepresentation of fact made to induce the relying party to act.

4. (a) Arnold has probably committed assault, battery, and conversion, because he put Benjamin in fear for his life or safety, inflicted offensive bodily harm, and permanently deprived him of his property in the form of the wallet. (b) Arnold has committed the crimes of assault, theft, and robbery. (c) In a tort action, Benjamin sues to recover compensation for the injury he sustained as a result of Arnold's wrongful conduct. For the commission of the crimes, the state may bring appropriate action against Arnold resulting in payment of a fine and/or imprisonment.

5. Both reputation and privacy are important to everyone. Uttering false communications which injure a person's reputation constitutes a tort. This may take either the form of written (libelous) or oral (slanderous) communications. One's privacy may be invaded in several ways. Appropriation occurs with the unauthorized use of a person's identity. Intrusion is an unreasonable and offensive interference with the seclusion of another. Public disclosure of private facts is the offensive publicity of private information, and false light is the offensive and false publicity about another, giving them an untrue image.

Chapter 8

True/False:

1. T	6. T	11. F
2. T	7. T	12. T
3. F	8. T	13. F
4. T	9. T	14. T
5. T	10. F	15. T

Multiple Choice:

1. d	6. a	11. d
2. c	7. d	12. b
3. b	8. c	13. c
4. b	9. c	14. b
5. a	10. a	15. d

Short Essay:

1. The reasonable person standard is ordinarily used to determine a defendant's negligence by comparing what the defendant did to what a reasonable person acting prudently and with due care under the circumstances would have done. Some statutes impose a specific standard of care upon certain classes of defendants for the protection of certain classes of plaintiffs. Thus, the courts may take the requirements of a statute as the applicable standard of care in determining the negligence of a particular defendant if the defendant violated a statute which is intended to protect a particular class of persons of which the plaintiff is a member against the particular hazard and kind of harm which resulted.

2. The concept of *res ipsa loquitur* allows a jury to infer both negligent conduct and causation from the mere occurrence of an event when the event is of a kind that ordinarily would not occur in the absence of negligence. Translated, *res ipsa loquitur* means "the thing speaks for itself," and the concept operates where other possible causes are sufficiently eliminated by the evidence.

3. The doctrine of strict liability or liability without fault is not based upon any particular fault of the defendant. Rather, it is based upon the nature of the activity in which the defendant is engaged. Certain types of activities are socially desirable but pose significant risks of harm regardless of how carefully they are conducted. Thus, where the activities are in themselves abnormally dangerous, or where one keeps animals, or where one sells defective, unreasonably dangerous products, liability may be imposed even though the actor neither intended any harm nor acted in a negligent manner.

4. A few states have abandoned any distinction between these three classifications of persons. For those states which still recognize a difference, however, the courts generally recognize a duty not to intentionally injure trespassers, a duty to warn to licensees of known dangers the licensees are unlikely to discover, and a duty to exercise reasonable care to protect invitees against dangerous conditions about which the possessor knows or should know and which the invitee is unlikely to discover. Most courts hold that upon discovering the presence of trespassers, a lawful occupier of land must use reasonable care in his or her activities and warn trespassers of dangerous conditions that the trespassers are unlikely to discover.

5. Contributory negligence is defined as failure of a plaintiff to exercise reasonable care that legally causes the plaintiff's harm. If negligence of the plaintiff together with negligence of the defendant proximately caused the injury sustained by the plaintiff, he cannot recover any damages from the defendant in those few states where contributory negligence is still recognized. Comparative negligence divides damages between the plaintiff and defendant where the negligence of each has caused the harm. Under the "modified" comparative negligence doctrine followed by many states, however, a plaintiff cannot recover anything if the plaintiff's negligence was 50% or more the cause of the harm.

Parts I & II: Sample Examination

1. b	8. c	15. b
2. b	9. d	16. d
3. a	10. b	17. a
4. c	11. d	18. c
5. c	12. c	19. b
6. d	13. d	20. b
7. b	14. c	

Chapter 9

True/False:

1. T	6. T	11. T
2. T	7. F	12. F
3. F	8. T	13. T
4. F	9. F	14. F
5. T	10. T	15. T

Multiple Choice:

1. a	6. d	11. d
2. b	7. c	12. b
3. a	8. a	13. d
4. d	9. c	14. d
5. a	10. c	15. a

Short Essay:
1. The law of contracts is governed primarily by state common law. An often-cited source of this law is found in the Restatements of the Law of Contracts promulgated by the American Law Institute. In all states except Louisiana, however, Article 2 of the UCC governs sales. A sale is a contract involving the transfer of title to goods from seller to buyer for a price. In all transactions to which Article 2 does not apply, and in all those governed by Article 2 but where general contract law has not been specifically modified by the Code, contract common law continues to apply.

2. The contract to provide accounting services to Clem for $15,000 involves an oral manifestation of willingness by both parties to enter into a contract. Therefore the contract is express, even though not in writing. The contract also involves an exchange of promises. Arthur promised to provide accounting services for one year in exchange for Clem's promise to pay $15,000 to Arthur. Therefore the contract is bilateral. There is no evidence that the contract is void, voidable, or otherwise unenforceable. Therefore it is valid. Finally, since, at its inception, neither party has performed any of its duties, the contract is executory.

3. Under the doctrine of promissory estoppel and the theory of quasi-contract, promises are sometimes enforced even though they do not meet contractual requirements. Under promissory estoppel a noncontractual promise will be enforced where there has been justifiable reliance on the promise and justice requires enforcement. A quasi-contract is not actually a contract at all because it is based neither on an express nor an implied promise but rather is an obligation imposed by law to avoid injustice.

4. A contract has the element of consideration associated with it. The duties associated with a contract have been bargained for, whereas the making of a gift is a gratuitous situation and thus not enforceable.

5. Promissory estoppel is an equitable doctrine under which noncontractual promises will be enforced where there has been justifiable reliance on the promise by the injured party and justice requires enforcement.

Chapter 10

True/False:

1. T	6. T	11. T
2. T	7. T	12. T
3. F	8. F	13. F
4. F	9. F	14. T
5. T	10. T	15. F

Multiple Choice:

1. d	6. c	11. b
2. d	7. b	12. d
3. c	8. d	13. c
4. c	9. c	14. d
5. c	10. b	15. b

Short Essay:

1. An offer need not take any particular form to have legal effect but it must (1) be communicated to the offeree; (2) manifest an intent to enter into a contract; and (3) be sufficiently definite and certain. Those being present, if a communication creates in the mind of a reasonable person in the position of the offeree an expectation that his acceptance will conclude a contract, then the communication is an offer.

2. An offer may lapse either upon the running of the period of time specified in the offer itself, or if no such time is stated, upon the expiration of a reasonable period of time. The offeror may also revoke his offer at any time prior to acceptance unless the offer is held open by an option contract, is a merchant's firm offer under the Code, is statutorily irrevocable, or is for a unilateral contract and the offeree has begun the requested performance. An offeree's power of acceptance may also be terminated by the offeree's communicated rejection. The rejection is effective from the moment that it is received by the offeror. A counteroffer or conditional acceptance both indicate an unwillingness to agree to the terms of an offer and operate as a rejection. They are to be distinguished from mere inquiries about the possibility of obtaining new or different terms for the contract, as these do not terminate the offer. Finally, an offer will be terminated by the death or incompetency of the offeror or offeree, by the destruction of the specific subject matter of a contract, or if performance of a valid offer is later made illegal.

3. Under the common law "mirror image rule," an acceptance must be positive and unequivocal. It may not change any of the terms of the offer, nor add to, subtract from, or otherwise qualify the terms of the offer in any way. Any communication that attempts to do so is not acceptance but rather is a mere counteroffer. In contrast, the Code modifies this rule to account for the realities of modern business practices, the most notable being the extensive use of the standardized business form. The Code focuses on the intent of the parties; if the offeree definitely and seasonably expresses his acceptance of the offer and does not expressly make his acceptance conditional on the buyer's assent to the different or additional terms, then a contract is formed. Here the issue becomes whether the seller's different or additional terms are part of the contract. The Code provides rules to resolve these disputes depending on whether the parties are merchants and on whether the terms are additional or different terms.

4. Both an option contract and a firm offer under the Code have the result of holding an offer to be irrevocable for a period of time. The main distinctions between the two are that an option contract is a common law agreement which requires consideration be valid, whereas a firm offer under the UCC is a Code provision and when in writing from a merchant needs no consideration to be enforceable.

5. (a) The common law follows the "mirror image rule" which states that offers and acceptances must be mirror images of each other. The Code (in §2-207, the battle of the forms section) allows for the acceptance of an offer where the terms of the acceptance vary from those of the offer. (b) The common law required definiteness and certainty in the terms of an offer. The UCC has "gap filler" provisions (in §§ 2-305, 2-308 and 2-309) that allow a contract to exist when certain terms are left open. (c) At common law, an offer which says it will be kept open for a specified period of time can be terminated at any time in the absence of consideration. Under the UCC (§ 2-205), a firm offer in writing by a merchant is binding even without consideration. (d) At common law, an offer must be accepted in the manner specified. Under the UCC, an offer may be accepted in any manner and by any medium reasonable under the circumstances. In general, the Code looks at whether the parties intended to form a contract rather than at technical rules regarding the exact moment of acceptance of an offer.

Chapter 11

True/False:
1. F
2. F
3. F
4. T
5. T

6. T
7. T
8. F
9. T
10. F

11. T
12. T
13. T
14. F
15. F

Multiple Choice:
1. a
2. c
3. b
4. d
5. d

6. d
7. a
8. b
9. a
10. c

11. c
12. c
13. d
14. b
15. b

Short Essay:
1. There are two basic types of duress. The first occurs when a party is compelled to assent to a contract through physical force. This form of duress renders the purported agreement void. The second type of duress involves the use of improper threats to compel a person to enter into a contract. The threat may be explicit or inferred from words or conduct. A subjective test is used to determine whether the threat actually induced assent on the part of the person claiming to be the victim of duress. Duress of this kind renders the resulting contract voidable at the option of the coerced.

2. (a) The elements necessary to establish fraud in the inducement include: false representation, of fact, that is material, made with knowledge of its falsity and the intention to deceive, and that is justifiably relied on. (b) In general, a statement of opinion cannot constitute fraud in the inducement. However, a statement of opinion by an expert is treated as being a statement of fact. (c) Puffing is rather general and is considered to be "sales talk." A statement such as "This is the best car in town" is puffing. A statement such as "*Consumer Reports* rates this the best car of the year" is a statement of the fact that it has in fact been so rated by *Consumer Reports*.

3. Both parties to the contract mistakenly believed that the train schedule would allow the papers to arrive in time. The contract is voidable due to mutual mistake of fact.

4. To be material, a fact must be of substantial importance. When considering materiality as related to misrepresentation, a fact is material if (1) it would be likely to induce a reasonable person to manifest his assent to an agreement or (2) the maker knows that it would be likely to induce the recipient to do so.

5. Undue influence is the unfair persuasion of a person by a party in a dominant position based on a relationship of trust and confidence. It generally occurs where there is a confidential relationship such as a guardian and ward or physician and patient where the dominant party takes unfair advantage of the other.

Chapter 12

True/False:

1. F	6. T	11. T
2. T	7. F	12. F
3. F	8. T	13. T
4. F	9. F	14. T
5. T	10. T	15. F

Multiple Choice:

1. c	6. c	11. b
2. c	7. d	12. c
3. a	8. d	13. c
4. c	9. a	14. c
5. d	10. c	15. b

Short Essay:

1. Mutuality of consideration means that the promises or performance of both parties to a contract must be legally sufficient for the contract to be enforceable by either. To be legally sufficient, a promise or performance must be either a legal benefit to the promisor or a legal detriment to the promisee. In this regard, legal benefit means the obtaining by the promisor of that which he had no legal right to obtain. A legal detriment means the doing of that which the promisee was under no prior legal obligation to do, or the refraining from doing that which he was previously under no legal obligation to refrain from doing.

2. The two essential elements of consideration are (1) legal sufficiency (value) and (2) bargained-for exchange. In short, consideration is a bargained-for exchange of value. The adequacy of consideration, however, is irrelevant and the subject matter that the parties respectively have exchanged need not have approximately the same value. Rather, the law will treat the parties as having considered the subject of the exchange adequate by reason of their having freely agreed to the exchange.

3. This doctrine prohibits a party from denying a promise made in those cases where the promisee takes action, or forbears to act, to his detriment when those actions were reasonably based on the promise made. The doctrine is applied when necessary to avoid injustice.

4. Sam has reasonably and detrimentally relied upon Big Bucks' promise of a job. He can sue to enforce the contract based upon promissory estoppel.

5. There are several situations governed by Article 2 of the UCC in which no consideration is required for enforceability. Modification of a preexisting contract, firm offers by merchants, and a written waiver or renunciation to settle a dispute are all enforceable without consideration.

Chapter 13

True/False:
1. T
2. F
3. F
4. F
5. F
6. F
7. F
8. T
9. T
10. F
11. F
12. T
13. T
14. T
15. T

Multiple Choice:
1. d
2. b
3. d
4. c
5. b
6. d
7. d
8. c
9. d
10. d
11. d
12. a
13. d
14. a
15. a

Short Essay:

1. The Restatement does not define "unconscionable" but, like the UCC, provides that a court may scrutinize contracts to determine whether in their commercial settings, purposes, and effects, the contracts are grossly unfair or unconscionable. Courts may refuse to enforce unconscionable contracts or any part of a contract they find to be unconscionable.

2. The two types of licensing statutes are those which are regulatory in nature and those enacted in order to raise revenue. A regulatory licensing statute is one designed to protect the public against services provided by unqualified individuals. If violated, there can be no recovery for professional services rendered by a person not having the required license. A revenue-raising licensing statute is one designed solely to raise revenue. It does not seek to protect the public from services provided by incompetents. Accordingly, agreements by persons not having the license required by such a statute are enforceable.

3. Unconscionable contracts are grossly unfair or unduly harsh. The doctrine of unconscionability permits the courts to resolve issues of unfairness with regard to either procedural or substantive unfairness. The doctrine with regard to contracts of adhesion is related to the doctrine of unconscionability in that it allows the courts to scrutinize standard form contracts offered on a "take-it-or-leave-it" basis for procedural or substantive unconscionability..

4. With few exceptions, illegal agreements are unenforceable. As a general rule, where the parties to an illegal agreement are in *pari delicto* the courts will not aid either party. However, where one party withdraws prior to performance or is protected by statute, or where one party is not equally at fault or can make a claim of excusable ignorance, the courts may allow certain actions regarding the agreement.

5. A covenant not to compete is an agreement to refrain from entering into a competing trade, profession, or business. Such a covenant will be upheld if the purpose of the restraint is to protect a legitimate property interest of the promisee and the restraint is no more extensive than is reasonably necessary to protect that interest. Covenants not to compete are typically found in contracts to sell a business and in employment contracts.

Chapter 14

True/False:
1. T	6. T	11. T
2. T	7. T	12. F
3. T	8. F	13. F
4. T	9. F	14. T
5. T	10. T	15. T

Multiple Choice:
1. d	6. d	11. b
2. d	7. d	12. c
3. a	8. b	13. d
4. c	9. d	14. c
5. b	10. d	15. d

Short Essay:

1. Generally, all persons are regarded as having capacity to contract unless specifically designated otherwise. Minors, incompetent persons, and intoxicated persons are limited to some extent. Minors' contracts are voidable at the option of the minor. If one has been adjudicated incompetent and a guardian appointed, contracts entered into by the incompetent are void. One not so adjudicated but who is nevertheless unable to understand the nature and consequence of his acts or one who cannot understand the nature and consequence of her actions due to intoxication, entered into voidable contracts.

2. Not all contracts entered into by minors are voidable. Where minors contract for a necessary, they will be held liable for the reasonable value of the item contracted for. Today the courts generally define "necessaries" as those things that the minor needs to maintain himself in his particular station in life.

3. The act of ratification makes the contract binding, and if properly ratified a contract may not thereafter be disaffirmed. Ratification may occur in three ways: (1) through express language, (2) as implied from conduct, and (3) through failure to make a timely disaffirmance.

4. States do not agree whether a minor who misrepresents his age has the power to disaffirm a contract. Under the prevailing view, Tyrone may disaffirm the contract. However, some states would not allow Tyrone to disaffirm if the bank officer in good faith relied upon the misrepresentation.

5. The contract between Don and Lucy is voidable at the option of Don if he is unable to comprehend the subject of the contract, its nature, and its probable consequences. If Don has been adjudicated incompetent by a court, the contract is void and has no legal effect.

Chapter 15

True/False:

1. F	6. T	11. F
2. T	7. F	12. F
3. T	8. T	13. F
4. T	9. F	14. T
5. T	10. T	15. T

Multiple Choice:

1. c	6. a	11. c
2. d	7. c	12. c
3. d	8. d	13. a
4. b	9. b	14. c
5. b	10. c	15. a

Short Essay:

1. The following five kinds of contracts are within most state statutes: (1) promises to answer for the duty of another, (2) promises of an executor or administrator to answer personally for a duty of the decedent whose funds he is administering, (3) agreements upon consideration of marriage, (4) agreements for the transfer of an interest in land and, (5) agreements that cannot be performed within one year.

2. As a general rule, a promise to transfer an interest in land is within the statute of frauds and therefore must comply with its requirements. There are two exceptions to that rule, however. The first involves a promise to make a short-term lease. In most states, this is defined by statute to include leases that are for one year or less in duration. The second involves an oral contract that may be enforced if the party seeking enforcement has so changed his position in reasonable reliance upon the contract that injustice can only be prevented by enforcing the contract.

3. The general statute of frauds requires that an agreement be in writing to be enforceable. The writing has to be signed by the party to be charged or his agent, specify the parties to the contract, and specify with reasonable certainty the subject matter and the essential terms of the unperformed promises. The statute of frauds provision under the UCC is more liberal. The Code requires only a writing that is sufficient to indicate that a contract has been made between the parties, signed by the party against whom enforcement is sought or by his authorized agent, and specify the quantity of goods to be sold. An oral contract for the sale of goods may comply with the requirements of the Code in the following three instances: (1) where the party defending against the contract admits it by pleading, testimony, or otherwise in court; (2) under certain circumstances, where the goods are to be specially manufactured; and (3) where there has been payment or delivery and acceptance.

4. Parties frequently put their agreements in writing, intending the writing to be the final expression of their agreement. Generally, evidence of their prior oral or written negotiations or agreements or their contemporaneous oral agreements that might vary or change the written expression would not be admissible in court on the presumption that the final written expression is the best evidence of the true agreement.

5. Oral contracts modifying previously existing contracts are unenforceable if the resulting contract is within the statute of frauds. The contract between Betty and Interlock is within the statute of frauds–it cannot be performed in one year. Therefore, the oral contract modifying the existing contract is unenforceable.

Chapter 16

True/False:

1. T	6. T	11. T
2. F	7. T	12. T
3. T	8. F	13. F
4. F	9. T	14. T
5. T	10. F	15. F

Multiple Choice:

1. a	6. b	11. c
2. d	7. a	12. b
3. d	8. c	13. a
4. a	9. a	14. c
5. c	10. c	15. a

Short Essay:

1. Parties involved might be the assignor, the assignee, the delegator, the delegatee, the obligor, and the obligee. The assignor would be the party transferring her rights under a contract to some third party known as the assignee. Duties may sometimes be delegated and the delegator would be the person transferring her duty to perform to some third party known as the delegatee. The person who then must perform the obligations imposed by the contract would be the obligor and the person to whom that performance is owed would be the obligee.

2. An assignment of rights is the voluntary transfer to a third party (the assignee) of the rights arising from a contract. A delegation of duties, on the other hand, is a transfer to a third party (the delegatee) of the contractual duty to perform. An effective assignment extinguishes the assignor's right of performance by the obligor. Therefore, only the assignee has a right to the obligor's performance. A delegation of duty, however, does not extinguish the delegator's duty to perform. It only results in an additional party, the delegatee, being obligated as well.

3. Under the majority rule, the first assignee in point of time prevails over the later assignees. This is contrasted with the minority rule that the first assignee to notify the obligor will prevail.

4. Rocky's duty to perform at the university is a nondelegable duty because it is personal in nature; therefore his duty may not be delegated. However, his right to payment of money may be assigned.

5. Where contracts are made which benefit a third party, i.e. not a party to the contract, the third party may be classified as either an intended beneficiary or an incidental beneficiary. The intended beneficiary may be either a donee or creditor beneficiary and in either case the beneficiary may enforce the agreement against the obligor. The incidental beneficiary, however, does not have the right of enforcement.

Chapter 17

True/False:

1. F	6. F	11. T
2. F	7. T	12. T
3. T	8. F	13. F
4. T	9. T	14. F
5. T	10. T	15. T

Multiple Choice:

1. b	6. b	11. b
2. d	7. d	12. c
3. d	8. d	13. d
4. d	9. c	14. c
5. a	10. c	15. d

Short Essay:

1. A condition in a contract is an event whose happening or non-happening affects a duty of performance. Many times express conditions are explicitly set forth in the contractual language and call for a personal satisfaction of one party as approval of the other's performance. The courts, depending upon the circumstances, recognize both a subjective satisfaction based upon a party's honestly held opinion, or an objective satisfaction based upon whether a reasonable person would be satisfied.

2. At common law, a party was discharged from the duty to perform under the contract on grounds of impossibility only if it was objectively impossible for anyone to perform. The courts also generally regarded frustration of purpose as a discharge where the purpose of the contract was frustrated by fortuitous circumstances that deprived the performance of the value attached to it by the parties. The Restatement and Code positions, however, are that literal impossibility is not required, and that commercial impracticability resulting from a supervening event will excuse nonperformance. The supervening event, however, must have been a "basic assumption" of both parties when they entered the contract.

3. The Code requires that performance of a sales contract must conform exactly to the contract or it discharges the other party. Common law requires only a material breach before a party can sue.

4. There are several ways a contract might be discharged by agreement. First, the parties might mutually agree to terminate their respective duties. This is called mutual rescission. Secondly, they might substitute a new contract which would be accepted by both parties. Thirdly, an accord and satisfaction occurs where there is a substituted duty under a contract (the accord) and a discharge of the prior contractual obligation by performance of that new duty (the satisfaction). Lastly, there could be a novation which occurs where there is a substituted contract involving a new third-party promisor or promisee.

5. If Lisa promises to buy Jim's land for $100,000, provided she can obtain financing in the amount of $75,000 at 10 percent or less, Lisa's obtaining the financing is a condition precedent to her duty. If Lisa promises to work for Hillcrest, Inc. for one year unless she is admitted to graduate school at Towers University, her admission to graduate school is a condition subsequent. If she is admitted to graduate school, then her duty to work is terminated. If the contract for the sale of Jim's land to Lisa provides that Jim is to deliver the deed on payment of the purchase price, then Jim has no duty to deliver the deed until Lisa pays the purchase price and Lisa has no duty to pay until Jim delivers the deed. These are concurrent conditions and each party's duty is conditioned on performance by the other.

Chapter 18

True/False:

1. T	6. T	11. T
2. F	7. T	12. F
3. T	8. F	13. T
4. T	9. T	14. T
5. T	10. F	15. T

Multiple Choice:

1. d	6. a	11. c
2. c	7. d	12. b
3. b	8. d	13. c
4. c	9. d	14. d
5. c	10. b	15. d

Short Essay:
1. Should more than one remedy be available to an aggrieved party, his manifestation of a choice of one remedy, such as bringing suit, does not prevent him from seeking another unless the remedies are inconsistent and the other party materially changes her position in reliance on the manifestation.

2. Under the doctrine of mitigation of damages, the party injured by a breach of contract must take such steps as may be reasonably calculated to lessen the damages that he may sustain. Damages are not recoverable for losses that the injured party could have avoided without undue risk, burden, or humiliation.

3. The two major equitable remedies applicable to a breach of contract are the decree of specific performance and the injunction. A decree of specific performance orders a breaching party to render the performance promised under the contract. In contrast, an injunction is an order issued by a court commanding a person to refrain from doing a specific act or engaging in specified conduct. Generally, equitable remedies are available only where damages for a breach would be inadequate. A court will not decree specific performance of a contract for personal services. A court may issue an injunction against serving another employer as a means of enforcing an exclusive personal service contract if the probable result would not be to leave the employee without other reasonable means of making a living.

4. Restitution is the act of returning to the aggrieved party the consideration, or the value thereof if the actual consideration cannot be returned, which was given to the other party. Such an award would be available in several situations: (1) as an alternative remedy for a party injured by breach; (2) for a party in default; (3) for a party who may not enforce a contract because of a limitation; or (4) for a party wishing to rescind a voidable contract.

5. The right to recover compensatory damages for breach of contract is always available to the injured party. Therefore, Jill may recover $2,000 to compensate her for her loss due to American's failure to perform. She may also recover $300 in incidental damages which are damages arising directly out of a breach of contract.

Part III: Sample Examination

1. c	8. d	15. b
2. a	9. a	16. b
3. c	10. d	17. b
4. b	11. d	18. a
5. b	12. d	19. d
6. c	13. b	20. c
7. c	14. a	

Chapter 19

True/False:

1. T	6. T	11. T
2. T	7. F	12. F
3. T	8. F	13. T
4. T	9. F	14. T
5. T	10. F	15. F

Multiple Choice:

1. b	6. a	11. b
2. c	7. c	12. c
3. d	8. d	13. c
4. d	9. b	14. d
5. d	10. a	15. c

Short Essay:

1. Article 2 of the Uniform Commercial Code is expressly applicable to contracts for the sale of goods, as it defines those terms. General contract law, however, continues to govern aspects of the sale of goods not specifically modified by the Code as well as contracts outside the scope of the Code. These include transactions other than sales, such as bailments, leases, and gifts, as well as sales of things other than goods, such as services, real property, and intangibles. Nevertheless, the Code is often applied by analogy to nonsales transactions, thereby expanding the scope of its principles and policies.

2. A "sale" is the transfer of title to goods from a seller to a buyer for a price which may be either money, other goods, real property, or services. "Goods" are defined as personal property which is tangible and movable.

3. Where an agreement is so one-sided as to be oppressive and unfair, a court may refuse to enforce the contract, or refuse to enforce any part of a contract found to be unconscionable. The court may find either procedural unconscionability, which is unfairness of the bargaining process, or substantive unconscionability, which is oppressive or grossly unfair contractual provisions.

4. A firm offer is a signed writing by a merchant to hold open an offer for the sale or purchase of goods for a period of time of up to three months. Under the Code, such offers are binding on the merchant even though no consideration is given and cannot be revoked for the time stated or if no time is stated, for a reasonable period of time.

5. No. An agreement modifying a contract for the sale of goods must be in writing if the resulting contract is within the statute of frauds. Even though the original contract for the sale of the wheat was not required to be in writing, the subsequent modification resulted in a contract that was within the statute of frauds. Therefore, the modified contract is unenforceable.

Chapter 20

True/False:

1. T	6. F	11. T
2. T	7. T	12. T
3. T	8. T	13. T
4. T	9. T	14. F
5. F	10. T	15. T

Multiple Choice:

1. c	6. d	11. a
2. c	7. a	12. b
3. c	8. b	13. c
4. d	9. d	14. c
5. d	10. d	15. c

Short Essay:

1. Tender requires the seller to make available goods that conform to the contract at the buyer's disposition and give the buyer reasonable notification to enable her to take delivery. Once a seller tenders conforming goods to the buyer, the seller is then entitled to have the goods accepted and to be paid the contract price.

2. Unless the parties otherwise agree, the place for delivery of goods is the seller's place of business. Under a shipment contract, however, the seller is obligated to send the goods to the buyer (although he is not required to deliver them to a particular place as in a destination contract). Discharge of his duty of performance under a shipment contract requires the seller to: (1) deliver the goods to a carrier, (2) make a reasonable contract for their shipment, (3) obtain and promptly deliver or tender to the buyer any documents necessary to allow the buyer to obtain possession of the goods from the carrier, and (4) promptly notify the buyer of the shipment.

3. Under the perfect tender rule, the seller's tender of performance must conform exactly to the contract. There are three qualifications to this rule: (1) agreement of the parties may limit the operation of this rule; (2) if the time for performance has not expired, the seller may cure or correct the nonconforming tender; and (3) in installment contracts the buyer may reject a nonconforming installment if it substantially impairs the value of that installment and cannot be cured.

4. A rejection is a manifestation by the buyer of unwillingness to become owner of the goods. To be effective, it must be made within a reasonable time after the goods have been tendered or delivered and the seller must be reasonably notified. A buyer may rightfully reject goods that do not conform to the contract, but any exercise of ownership of the goods by the buyer after rejection is wrongful as against the seller. Finally, a buyer's duty after rejection varies depending on whether or not he is a merchant. A revocation of acceptance is a manifestation of unwillingness to remain the owner of the goods after the buyer has already accepted them. A buyer may revoke acceptance of nonconforming goods only if the nonconformity substantially impairs the value of the goods and the acceptance was (a) based on the reasonable assumption that the seller would cure the nonconformity and did not, or (b) without discovery of the nonconformity and such acceptance was reasonably induced by the difficulty of discovery before acceptance or by assurances of the seller. Upon revocation of acceptance, the buyer is in the same position with respect to the goods and has the same rights and duties with regard to them as if he had rejected them.

5. When the buyer accepts nonconforming goods on the assumption that the nonconformity would be cured by the seller and the seller has failed to do so, a revocation of the acceptance is appropriate. Also, if the nonconformity was an undiscovered, hidden defect, the buyer may revoke a previous acceptance.

Chapter 21

True/False:

1. F	6. F	11. F
2. T	7. F	12. T
3. F	8. T	13. F
4. T	9. F	14. F
5. T	10. F	15. T

Multiple Choice:

1. b	6. b	11. c
2. d	7. d	12. a
3. c	8. c	13. c
4. b	9. b	14. b
5. b	10. c	15. b

Short Essay:

1. At common law, risk of loss was placed upon the party that had title to the goods at the time in question. The Code, however, employs a transactional approach that diminishes the importance of the concept of title. Accordingly, the Code sets forth a detailed set of rules for allocating risk of loss depending on whether there has been a breach of the sales contract. In the absence of a breach, the Code attempts to place the risk of loss upon the party who is more likely to have greater control over the goods or is better able to prevent the loss.

2. Two types of trial sales, where the buyer is permitted to try the goods for a period of time to determine satisfaction, are recognized by the Code. First, in a sale on approval possession, but not title, is transferred to the buyer for a designated or reasonable time. Both title and risk of loss remain with the seller. Second, in a sale or return the goods are sold and delivered to the buyer who also accepts the risk of loss. Return of the goods is at the buyer's risk and expense. In the absence of agreement, if the goods are delivered primarily for the buyer's use, the transaction is a sale of approval but if the goods are delivered primarily for resale by the buyer, it is a sale or return.

3. Where the owner of goods entrusts those goods to a merchant who deals in goods of that kind, the merchant has the power to transfer title to those goods to a buyer in the ordinary course of business. A buyer in the ordinary course of business is one who in good faith and without knowledge that the sale to him is in violation of the ownership rights or security interest of another buys those goods. In such a case the "true" owner has a right of recourse against the merchant bailee for value of the goods but the Code protects the buyer in the ordinary course of business who acquires good title.

4. Where the buyer has accepted nonconforming goods, and thereafter by timely notice to the seller rightfully revokes her acceptance, she may treat the risk of loss, to the extent of any deficiency in insurance coverage, as resting from the beginning on the seller.

5. Goods should be protected against loss whenever possible, but for a policy of insurance to be valid, the insured must have an insurable interest. The common law allowed only one with title or a lien to purchase such protection. The Code, however, extends this right to a buyer who has an interest in goods that have been identified to the contract. This allows both the seller and buyer to protect themselves.

Chapter 22

True/False:

1. T	6. F	11. T
2. F	7. T	12. T
3. T	8. F	13. F
4. T	9. F	14. T
5. F	10. F	15. F

Multiple Choice:

1. b	6. d	11. b
2. d	7. a	12. d
3. d	8. c	13. a
4. b	9. c	14. b
5. d	10. a	15. b

Short Essay:

1. Generally a warranty is considered to be an obligation of the seller to the buyer concerning the title, quality, characteristics, or condition of goods sold. The seller will warrant, unless properly disclaimed, that she has and can transfer title to the goods without any lien that the buyer is not aware of. The seller may also make either an express warranty or an implied warranty. Express warranties may arise by the seller making an affirmation of fact about the goods, or by describing the goods, or through the use of a sample or model of the goods. Implied warranties, such as the warranty of fitness for a particular purpose, arise out of the circumstances of the sale.

2. Under the implied warranty of merchantability, a merchant seller impliedly warrants that the goods that are of the kind in which he deals are merchantable, i.e., that they are reasonably fit for the ordinary purpose for which they are manufactured and sold, and also that they are of fair, average quality. The warranty may be disclaimed, unless barred by the Magnuson-Moss Act, by a conspicuous writing containing language that specifically includes "merchantability." Under the implied warranty of fitness for a particular purpose, any seller, whether a merchant or a nonmerchant, impliedly warrants that the goods are reasonably fit for the particular purpose of the buyer for which the goods are required, provided at the time of contracting the seller has reason to know such particular purpose and knows that the buyer is relying upon the seller's skill and judgment to furnish suitable goods. The disclaimer of an implied warranty to fitness for the particular purpose must be in writing and conspicuous.

3. In order to recover under a theory of strict liability in tort, a seller must show that: (1) the defendant was engaged in the business of selling such a product; (2) the defendant sold the product in a defective condition; (3) the defective condition made the product unreasonably dangerous to the user or consumer or to his property; (4) the defect in the product existed at the time it left the hands of the defendant; (5) the plaintiff sustained physical harm or property damage by use or consumption of the product; and (6) the defective condition was the proximate cause of such injury or damage. Many of the traditional obstacles to recovery are not applicable to a claim of strict liability in tort. Liability cannot generally be modified or disclaimed, and there is no requirement of horizontal or vertical privity. Moreover, contributory negligence is, for the most part, not recognized as a valid defense; comparative negligence, however, has been applied by most courts to limit a plaintiff's recovery to account for his degree of fault. Voluntary assumption of risk and misuse or abuse of a product are valid defenses to an action based on strict liability in tort. Subsequent alternation and waiting to sue beyond the time in the statute of repose are defenses.

4. The kinds of defects that give rise to a defective condition include: (a) manufacturing defects that occur when the product is not properly made and fails to meet its own manufacturing specifications; (b) design defects that occur when a product is produced as specified but is dangerous or hazardous because its design is inadequate; and (c) inadequate warnings or instructions that are considered a defect when as a result of a failure to warn or to provide adequate directions for safe use, the product becomes dangerous.

5. The Magnuson-Moss Warranty Act is a federal law intended to protect purchasers of consumer goods from deception and to ensure the availability of adequate information concerning warranties. Administered by the Federal Trade Commission, it provides that a seller who makes a written warranty cannot disclaim any implied warranty and must provide certain information to the buyer.

Chapter 23

True/False:

1. T	6. T	11. T
2. F	7. T	12. T
3. T	8. T	13. F
4. T	9. F	14. T
5. T	10. T	15. T

Multiple Choice:

1. c	6. b	11. c
2. b	7. d	12. c
3. b	8. a	13. a
4. c	9. b	14. a
5. d	10. d	15. b

Short Essay:

1. If a buyer has rightfully rejected the seller's nonconforming tender of goods, the buyer has several nonexclusive remedies for the seller's breach. First, the buyer may cancel the contract and recover any payments already made. The buyer may establish a security interest in any of the seller's goods that are already in the buyer's possession to the extent of any payment of the price already made. Finally, the buyer may also cover and recover damages or simply seek market price damages for the seller's breach.

2. All of the remedies outlined in Question 1 are available to a buyer if the seller repudiates a contract, and several more are also available. First, the buyer may maintain an action for replevin of goods that have been identified to the contract if the buyer after a reasonable effort is unable to effect cover for such goods, or if the goods have been shipped under reservation of a security interest in the seller and satisfaction of this security interest has been made or tendered. In addition, if the goods are unique or if money damages would not be an adequate remedy, the buyer may seek specific performance.

3. Several remedies are available to the seller after buyer has wrongfully rejected a conforming tender of goods. First, the seller may cancel the contract. The seller may also withhold delivery of additional goods and identify goods to the contract. The seller may resell and recover damages or just recover market price damages. Finally, if appropriate, a seller may bring an action for price. This is most likely to occur if conforming goods have been lost or damaged after the risk of loss has passed to the buyer, or where goods have been identified to the contract and there is no ready market available for their resale at a reasonable price.

4. Cover is a remedy which allows an aggrieved buyer to purchase needed goods to replace those due under the terms of the contract with the original seller. The buyer must act in good faith, and without unreasonable delay. The buyer may then recover from the original seller the difference between the cost of cover and the contract price, plus any incidental and consequential damages, less expenses saved, if any, because of the seller's breach.

5. Provided that the agreed-upon damages are reasonable, the parties to an agreement may provide in their agreement a specific amount or measure of damages recoverable should either party breach the contract.

Part IV: Sample Examination

1. b	8. d	15. a
2. a	9. b	16. c
3. b	10. b	17. c
4. b	11. d	18. a
5. b	12. d	19. c
6. b	13. c	20. b
7. b	14. c	

Chapter 24

True/False:
1. T
2. F
3. T
4. F
5. F

6. F
7. T
8. F
9. F
10. F

11. T
12. F
13. F
14. T
15. T

Multiple Choice:
1. d
2. c
3. c
4. d
5. b

6. c
7. d
8. c
9. a
10. b

11. a
12. d
13. b
14. a
15. d

Short Essay:
1. Negotiability is a concept that makes written instruments a readily accepted form of payment in substitution for money. Negotiability invests negotiable instruments with a high degree of marketability and commercial utility. It allows negotiable instruments to be freely transferable and enforceable.

2. It is nonnegotiable because it is not payable to order or to bearer, and it does not contain an unconditional promise or order to pay.

3. Order paper has an instruction to pay it to a named person or anyone designated by that person. Bearer paper is payable to anyone in possession of it. "Order" and "bearer" are words of negotiability which indicate that the maker or drawer intends that the instrument pass into the hands of someone other than the payee. Revised Article 3 provides that a *check* which meets all of the negotiability requirements, except it does not state whether it is an order instrument or a bearer instrument, is nevertheless negotiable. This applies only to checks.

4. The notation does not destroy the negotiability of the draft. It is a mere bookkeeping notation.

5. One requirement of negotiability is that the instrument must be unconditional. Thus, the instrument may not be dependent upon any other agreement or document to determine its conditions. However, reference to other agreements does not destroy negotiability unless the recital makes the instrument subject to or governed by the terms of the other agreement. To cite another agreement merely as a reference has no effect and does not render the instrument conditional.

Chapter 25

True/False:
1. F
2. F
3. T
4. T
5. F
6. F
7. T
8. F
9. F
10. T
11. F
12. T
13. F
14. T
15. F

Multiple Choice:
1. c
2. b
3. b
4. d
5. c
6. b
7. d
8. c
9. b
10. a
11. d
12. d
13. c
14. d
15. d

Short Essay:
1. Order paper is an instrument that is payable to order and requires both possession and indorsement by the appropriate parties for the transferee to be a holder. Bearer paper is an instrument payable to bearer and is transferred by mere possession. Because bearer paper runs to whoever is in possession of it, a finder or a thief would be a holder even though he did not receive possession by voluntary transfer.

2. A transfer by negotiation is the transfer of a negotiable instrument in such a manner that the transferee becomes a holder. An assignment is the voluntary transfer to some third party of the rights arising from a contract. Whether the transfer is by negotiation or by assignment, the transferee acquires the rights that her transferor had, but a transferee by negotiation can acquire greater rights than the transferor.

3. A restrictive indorsement is an indorsement attempting to limit the rights of the indorsee by: (a) placing a condition in the indorsement, or (b) prohibiting further transfer, or (c) limiting further negotiation to those consistent with the indorsement, or (d) requiring the indorsee to pay or apply all funds in accordance with the indorsement.

4. No, negotiation of a negotiable instrument is separate from the underlying contractual transaction. This rule is followed in order to allow negotiable instruments to move freely in the marketplace. It is this feature of negotiability that gives the holder of an instrument the right to payment and that allows a holder in due course a unique legal position in that the holder in due course has greater rights in the instrument than the transferor from whom he received it.

5. An indorsement "without recourse" is the customary manner of disclaiming an indorser's liability on an instrument. It is a qualified indorsement which disclaims contract liability but does not entirely remove the warranty liability of the indorser.

Chapter 26

True/False:

1. T	6. T	11. T
2. T	7. F	12. F
3. F	8. T	13. F
4. F	9. T	14. F
5. T	10. T	15. T

Multiple Choice:

1. c	6. c	11. d
2. d	7. d	12. d
3. c	8. a	13. c
4. a	9. b	14. c
5. d	10. c	15. b

Short Essay:

1. To be classified as an HDC, one must meet the requirements of the Code or inherit these rights under the shelter rule. The Code requirements are: (1) be a holder, (2) take for value, (3) in good faith, (4) without notice that it is overdue or has been dishonored, or that the instrument contains an unauthorized signature or alteration, or that any person has any defense against or claim to it, and (5) take without reason to question its authenticity.

2. A mere holder is nothing more than an assignee. Thus, a holder takes the rights the transferor had and is subject to the claims and defenses that could be asserted against the transferor. A holder in due course, on the other hand, takes the instrument free from any claims and free from most defenses. Thus, a holder in due course will be entitled to payment in many cases where a mere holder would not be.

3. Under the shelter rule a holder who does not qualify to be a holder in due course may nevertheless acquire all the rights of a holder in due course if some previous holder had been a holder in due course. The rule does not apply to a transferee (1) who has been a party to any fraud or illegality affecting the instrument or (2) who, as a prior holder, had notice of a claim or defense.

4. *B* is not a holder in due course, since he has taken the instrument when overdue, did not pay value, and has notice of *M*'s defense. However, due to the shelter rule *B* acquires *H*'s rights as a holder in due course, and *M* cannot successfully assert her defense against *B* because it is only a personal defense. The shelter rule confers on a transferee all the rights of the transferor.

5. Any alteration that changes the contract of any party to the instrument in any way is a material alteration. In keeping with the preferential position accorded a holder in due course, the holder in due course may enforce any altered instrument according to its original terms. Therefore, because Melissa is a holder in due course, she may enforce the note in the amount of $2,000.

Chapter 27

True/False:
1. T
2. T
3. T
4. F
5. F

6. T
7. F
8. T
9. T
10. T

11. T
12. F
13. T
14. T
15. T

Multiple Choice:
1. d
2. d
3. c
4. d
5. b

6. b
7. b
8. c
9. c
10. a

11. a
12. a
13. c
14. c
15. c

Short Essay:
1. Contractual liability is imposed upon those parties who have signed negotiable instruments, whether in a primary or secondary status. There are parties to negotiable instruments who may never sign them and will therefore not be liable on a contractual basis or theory. Warranty liability is imposed on both parties who do sign and on those who do not sign negotiable instruments. It would apply to (1) those who transfer an instrument, and (2) those who receive payment or acceptance of an instrument.

2. The drawers and indorsers of an instrument are secondarily liable to pay the instrument, unless they disclaim their liability by adding the notation "without recourse." Their liability is subject to the conditions of presentment, dishonor, and notice of dishonor. Because Cathy indorsed the instrument "without recourse," she has disclaimed her secondary liability. Ben may proceed against you and your roommate on the basis of your secondary liability, but your liability is contingent upon the conditions being met. The check has been presented for payment and has been dishonored. In order for Ben to succeed against you or your roommate, each of you must be given proper notice of the dishonor. Any notice by a bank must be given before midnight on the first banking day after it receives notice of dishonor. Any nonbank must give notice before midnight of the third business day after dishonor or receipt of notice of dishonor.

3. Under primary liability, one is absolutely and unconditionally liable to pay a negotiable instrument, while under secondary liability, one is only liable to pay a negotiable instrument subject to the conditions of presentment, dishonor, and notice of dishonor.

4. An instrument may be signed by the individual making or drawing it or by her authorized agent. If an instrument is signed by an authorized agent on behalf of the principal, the agent will not be liable if the instrument is properly executed. Agents may, however, lack the power to sign on behalf of the principal. Where this is the case or where the signature is a forgery, the named person on the instrument will generally not be liable, but the unauthorized signer will be liable.

5. The unnamed principal is not liable on the note, but you would be liable. Parol evidence is admissible to prove the agency relationship and to establish liability of the unnamed principal.

Chapter 28

True/False:

1. F	6. T	11. T
2. T	7. F	12. F
3. T	8. T	13. T
4. F	9. F	14. F
5. F	10. T	15. T

Multiple Choice:

1. c	6. c	11. d
2. d	7. c	12. b
3. b	8. d	13. d
4. a	9. c	14. a
5. c	10. a	15. c

Short Essay:

1. When an item is restrictively indorsed with words such as "pay any bank," it is locked into the bank collection system, and only a bank may acquire the rights of a holder.

2. A stop payment order is a command from a drawer to a drawee bank not to pay a particular instrument. Such an order is binding on the bank for a period of fourteen calendar days if the order is an oral order, but binding for a period of six months if in writing.

3. Arthur must examine his bank statement and report the payment of the forged check to the bank. The bank will in all likelihood bear the loss, unless it can find Carl, who will have liability for the forgery both criminally and based upon several of the civil provisions in the Code. The forged signature is that of Carl even though he signed Brad's name. Carl has also breached both the indorser's warranties and the presenter's warranties and thus has liability based on both the contract of indorsement and the warranty provisions of the Code. The bank has liability to Brad for conversion.

4. David is liable for only $50, because he immediately notified the bank within two days of learning of the loss or theft. If he had not immediately notified the bank, his liability would have been for $500. If he had failed to notify the bank within sixty days, he would bear the entire loss.

5. East Company is the originator which is the sender of the first payment order. East Company is also a sender which is the party who gives an instruction to the receiving bank. First National (FNB) is the receiving bank who receives the sender's instructions. FNB is also the originator's bank and the beneficiary's bank. West is the beneficiary who is to be paid by the beneficiary bank.

Part V: Sample Examination

1. a	8. a	15. c
2. b	9. b	16. a
3. c	10. b	17. a
4. c	11. c	18. c
5. b	12. d	19. c
6. d	13. b	20. a
7. c	14. b	

Chapter 29

True/False:

1. T	6. F	11. T
2. F	7. T	12. T
3. T	8. T	13. T
4. T	9. F	14. F
5. T	10. F	15. T

Multiple Choice:

1. c	6. d	11. b
2. b	7. d	12. b
3. d	8. d	13. d
4. d	9. d	14. c
5. d	10. d	15. c

Short Essay:

1. A principal-agency relationship is a consensual relationship which may be formed by either an oral or written agreement. Consideration is not necessary, nor are any other formal requirements, but the statute of frauds would apply if the agency is going to last longer than one year or, in some states, if the agent will be selling land.

2. An agent may not (a) represent his principal in any transaction in which he has a personal interest; (b) take a position in conflict with the interests of his principal; (c) compete with his principal; (d) act on behalf of a competitor or for persons whose interests conflict with those of the principal; (e) use for his own benefit, and contrary to the interests of his principal, information obtained in the course of the agency; or (f) make a secret profit out of any transaction subject to the agency.

3. Should an agent violate any fiduciary duty, she would be liable to her principal for breach of contract. Additionally, she would be liable in tort for any losses caused by her conduct as well as restitution for profits made or property received. Of course, the relationship may be terminated.

4. From time to time an agent will contribute her own funds or property to the agency. Where the agency is thus coupled with an interest of the agent in the subject matter, the authority of the agent may not be revoked by the principal. Additionally, neither the incapacity nor the bankruptcy of the principal will terminate the authority of the agent. Normally not even the death of the principal will terminate the agency, unless the duty for which the security was given terminates with her death.

5. An agent must act with reasonable care and skill in performing the work for which he is employed. Therefore, *A* would be liable to *P* for breach of the duty of diligence.

Chapter 30

True/False:

1. T	6. F	11. F
2. T	7. T	12. T
3. T	8. T	13. T
4. T	9. F	14. F
5. F	10. F	15. T

Multiple Choice:

1. d	6. b	11. d
2. c	7. d	12. b
3. c	8. b	13. b
4. a	9. c	14. a
5. d	10. c	15. c

Short Essay:

1. Actual authority is based upon words or conduct of the principal manifested to the agent. Apparent authority is based upon words or conduct of the principal that lead a third person to believe that the agent has actual authority, on which belief the third person justifiably relies. Actual authority gives an agent both the power and the right to bind the principal in legal relations with third persons, while apparent authority gives the agent the power but not necessarily the right to bind the principal.

2. An agent has the power to bind the principal when the principal is legally bound by the act of the agent. An agent has the right to bind the principal whenever the agent may do so without violating the duty of obedience by exceeding actual authority. For example, an agent with apparent authority but not actual authority has the power, but not the right, to bind the principal. Thus, the principal is legally bound by the act of the agent, but by exceeding actual authority, the agent has violated the duty of obedience and is liable to the principal for any resulting loss.

3. One of the ways liability to third parties may be imposed upon the principal would be in a situation where the principal was not careful in the hiring process. Called the negligent hiring doctrine, this arises when the principal does not exercise proper care in selecting an agent for the job to be performed. This doctrine has also been used to impose liability on a principal for intentional torts committed by an agent against customers of the principal.

4. A principal may be liable to third parties for the tortious acts of agents under the doctrine of *respondeat superior*. If the act that created the problem was committed during or within the line and scope of the agent's employment, the principal will likely be liable. Under certain circumstances, a principal may also be liable for the conduct of an independent contractor, though not generally if the act was an unauthorized one.

5. To avoid personal liability, an agent must disclose both that he is acting as an agent and the identity of his principal. Therefore, because Rob is acting on behalf of an undisclosed principal, he would be personally liable on the contract with Dan.

Part VI: Sample Examination

1. T	8. F	15. c
2. T	9. F	16. c
3. T	10. F	17. c
4. T	11. d	18. b
5. T	12. d	19. b
6. T	13. b	20. c
7. T	14. b	

Chapter 31

True/False:

1. F	8. F	15. F
2. T	9. T	16. F
3. T	10. F	17. F
4. T	11. F	18. F
5. T	12. F	19. F
6. T	13. T	20. T
7. F	14. T	

Multiple Choice:

1. a	6. d	11. d
2. d	7. c	12. b
3. d	8. a	13. c
4. b	9. a	14. c
5. a	10. d	15. c

Short Essay:
1. The court will look for three components to determine whether a partnership exists. Specifically, the court will determine whether there exists: (a) an association of two or more persons who agree to become partners, (b) a business with an intention to acquire profits and a continuous series of

commercial activities, and (c) co-ownership and a sharing of profits and the right to manage and control the business.

2. A partnership agreement should include the following: (1) names of each partner and partnership name, (2) nature of business, (3) length of time partnership is to last, (4) capital contribution of each partner, (5) how profits and losses are to be shared, (6) who is to have what authority, (7) how the partners are to be paid, (8) special restrictions on partners, if any, (9) withdrawal rights of partners, and (10) distribution upon termination.

3. At common law, a partnership was regarded as a legal aggregate; that is, a group of individuals having no legal existence apart from its members. However, under the RUPA partnerships may be treated as a legal entity–that is as an organization having a legal existence separate from that of its members. The assets of the firm and title to real estate are but two ways the RUPA treats partnerships as a legal entity. Other ways the RUPA recognizes the legal entity theory are the fiduciary duty of partners to the partnership and the partners' roles as agents of the partnership. The UPA on the other hand, ascribes more to the legal aggregate theory. For example, the UPA holds that a partnership cannot be sued or sue in the firm name unless authorized by statute to do so.

4. Partners are provided, by law, with various rights because of their status as partners. They have rights in the partnership itself. Additionally, they have a right to share in distributions, a right to participate in management, a right to choose associates, and a right of enforcement.

5. All partners within a partnership have a fiduciary duty to one another and to the partnership. They must operate in a loyal, fair manner demonstrating good faith in all partnership business. In addition, they have a duty of obedience, to follow the partnership agreement and other business decisions, and the duty of care.

Chapter 32

True/False:

1. T	6. F	11. T
2. T	7. F	12. T
3. T	8. F	13. F
4. T	9. T	14. T
5. T	10. F	15. F

Multiple Choice:

1. c	6. b	11. d
2. c	7. c	12. d
3. b	8. d	13. d
4. b	9. d	
5. b	10. c	

Short Essay:

1. The general rule is that partners are jointly and severally liable for all the debts of the partnership. However, when a new partner is accepted into an existing partnership, she would be liable only to the extent of her capital contribution for antecedent debts. Caution should be used here for the liability of an incoming partner for subsequent debts of the partnership is unlimited. What happens if the partnership refinances its current obligations? This is a new debt.

2. In the absence of an agreement on the sharing of profits, the RUPA provides that profits must be shared equally regardless of the capital contribution of each of the partners. Each partner would receive $12,000.

3. The RUPA provides that a partnership is liable for loss or injury caused by any wrongful act or omission of any partner while acting within the ordinary course of the business of the partnership. If the partnership is liable, then each partner has unlimited personal liability for the obligation. The liability of partners for a tort committed by any partner or by an employee of the firm in the course of partnership business is joint and several. Thus the partnership, as well as the individual partners, is liable to Sue.

4. Partnerships may be dissolved in any of the following ways: (1) by act of the partners, (2) by operation of law, or (3) by court order. Dissolution is defined as the change in the relation of partners caused by any partner's ceasing to be associated with the carrying on of the business.

5. During the winding up process, liabilities of a partnership are paid out of partnership assets in the following order: (1) amounts owing to creditors including advances and loans owed to partners, (2) amounts owing to partners for capital contributions, and (3) amounts owing to partners for profits.

Chapter 33

True/False:

1. T	6. F	11. F
2. F	7. T	12. T
3. T	8. T	13. T
4. T	9. F	14. T
5. T	10. F	15. T

Multiple Choice:

1. d	6. b	11. d
2. a	7. c	12. a
3. d	8. b	13. b
4. c	9. d	14. d
5. d	10. b	15. c

Short Essay:
1. A limited partner may withdraw as provided in the limited partnership certificate or, under the 1985 act, the written partnership agreement.

2. The RULPA provides that a person who has contributed capital to a business mistakenly believing in good faith that he is a limited partner in a limited partnership is not liable as a general partner provided that on learning of the mistake he either (1) withdraws from the business and renounces future profits or (2) files a certificate or an amendment curing the defect. However, this party is liable to a third party who did business with the enterprise before the withdrawal or amendment and who in good faith believed that the this party was a general partner at the time of the transaction.

3. Known as the "safe harbor" provisions of both versions of the RULPA, activities listed may be performed without being deemed to be management activities which endanger liability protection. These provisions are: (1) being a contractor for, or an agent or employee of, the limited partnership or a general partner; (2) consulting with or advising a general partner with respect to the business of the limited partnership; (3) acting as surety for the limited partnership; (4) approving or disapproving an amendment to the partnership agreement; and (5) voting on various fundamental changes in the limited partnership.

4. A limited liability company is another form of unincorporated business association which provides its membership with liability protection, allows all members to participate in management, and generally provides taxation as a partnership.

5. A limited liability partnership is a general partnership that, by making the statutorily-required filing, limits the liability of its partners for some or all of the partnership obligations. Three different approaches have arisen with respect to limiting the partners' liability. Early statutes limited liability only for negligent acts of the partners but retained unlimited liability for all other obligations. Later statutes extended limited liability to any partnership tort or contract obligation. Recent statutes have provided limited liability for all debts and obligations of the partnership.

Chapter 34

True/False:

1. T	6. T	11. T
2. T	7. T	12. T
3. T	8. F	13. T
4. F	9. F	14. F
5. T	10. T	15. F

Multiple Choice:

1. a	6. d	11. d
2. d	7. a	12. a
3. c	8. b	13. d
4. b	9. d	14. c
5. c	10. a	15. b

Short Essay:

1. The principal attributes of a corporation are: (1) it is considered to be a legal entity, (2) it provides the shareholders with limited liability, (3) ownership, represented by shares of stock, is freely transferable, (4) it is designed to have perpetual existence, and (5) its management is centralized. Additionally, it is considered for some purposes a citizen and for other purposes a person.

2. Corporations may be classified as: (1) public or private, (2) profit or nonprofit, (3) domestic or foreign, (4) publicly or closely held, (5) Subchapter S, and/or (6) professional. Any combination of these is generally possible. For example: A corporation may be private, nonprofit, domestic, and closely held.

3. A court will pierce the corporate veil where the shareholders (a) have not conducted the business on a corporate basis, (b) have not provided an adequate financial basis for the business, or (c) have used the corporation to defraud.

4. The doctrine of *respondeat superior* imposes full liability on a corporation for the torts committed by its agents and employees during the course of their employment. Because Albert was acting within the scope of employment, both Albert and Carryall Corporation are liable to Brenda for the injuries she sustained as a result of Albert's negligence.

5. Corporations derive their powers from three primary sources. State statutes contain a great many powers extended to properly formed corporations, including perpetual existence, the right to hold property in the corporate name, and all powers necessary or convenient to effect the corporation's purpose. The corporate charter will grant further powers to the corporation as enumerated in the articles of incorporation. Additionally, the corporation may exercise implied powers necessary or convenient to and consistent with the express powers contained in the corporate articles.

Chapter 35

True/False:

1. F	6. F	11. F
2. T	7. F	12. T
3. F	8. F	13. F
4. T	9. F	14. T
5. T	10. T	15. T

Multiple Choice:

1. c	6. c	11. c
2. d	7. d	12. b
3. a	8. c	13. c
4. c	9. d	14. b
5. d	10. b	15. b

Short Essay:

1. According to the RMBCA, a distribution is "a direct or indirect transfer of money or other property or incurrence of indebtedness by a corporation to or for the benefit of its shareholders with respect to any of its shares." Examples include a purchase, redemption, or acquisition of shares, or a payment of a dividend. Stock dividends or stock splits are not distributions.

2. A debt security or bond is a source of capital creating no ownership interest and involving the corporation's promise to repay funds loaned to it. An equity security is a source of capital creating an ownership interest in the corporation.

3. For cumulative dividends, if the board does not declare regular dividends on the preferred stock, such omitted dividends cumulate, and no dividend may be declared on the common stock until all dividend arrearages on the preferred stock are declared and paid. If noncumulative, regular dividends do not cumulate on failure of the board to declare them. Cumulative to the extent earned shares cumulate unpaid dividends only to the extent funds were legally available to pay such dividends in that fiscal period.

4. The Revised Act imposes personal liability to the corporation upon directors who wrongfully vote for or assent to the declaration of a dividend or other distribution of corporate assets. A shareholder has an obligation to repay an illegally declared dividend under certain circumstances. Good or bad faith, knowledge of the facts, and solvency or insolvency of the corporation are all taken into consideration.

5. If Julie has preemptive rights, a shareholder's right to purchase a pro rata share of new stock offerings, she will be offered one share of the newly issued stock for every two shares she owns. If she accepts the offer and buys the stock, she will have 150 shares out of a total of 1500 outstanding, and her relative interest in the corporation will be unchanged.

Chapter 36

True/False:

1. T	6. T	11. F
2. F	7. F	12. T
3. F	8. T	13. T
4. F	9. T	14. T
5. T	10. F	15. F

Multiple Choice:

1. c	6. c	11. d
2. a	7. c	12. b
3. b	8. b	13. d
4. a	9. d	14. b
5. b	10. c	15. b

Short Essay:

1. A shareholder may only inspect the books and records of the corporation for a proper purpose. Thus, a shareholder may be denied the right if the shareholder attempts to obtain the information for improper purposes, such as use by a competitor or sale to a third party. Also, the shareholder may be denied the right to inspect if the request was in bad faith or not during regular business hours at the corporation's principal office.

2. Shareholder approval is required to make certain fundamental changes in the corporation. These changes include: (a) amending the articles of incorporation, (b) effecting a merger or consolidation, (c) effecting a dissolution, (d) selling or leasing all or substantially all of the assets of the corporation other than in the usual and regular course of business, and (e) effecting a compulsory share exchange.

3. The board of directors has general authority to manage the business and affairs of the corporation. This authority invests the board with the power to: (a) select and remove officers, (b) set management compensation, (c) determine the capital structure, (d) declare dividends, and (e) initiate fundamental changes.

4. Both officers and directors are fiduciaries of the corporation and thus owe the duties of obedience, requiring them to act within their respective authority; diligence, requiring them to exercise ordinary care and prudence in the conduct of their business; and loyalty, requiring them to place the corporation first in any and all business decisions.

5. Directors and officers may be liable for their actions under certain circumstances. The "business judgment rule" acts as a protection against personal liability where it can be shown that the mistake in judgment was an honest mistake made in the belief that the decision would benefit the corporation. When the directors or officers act in good faith, and with due care in arriving at their decisions, they will not be liable when those decisions go wrong.

Chapter 37

True/False:

1. F	6. T	11. F
2. T	7. F	12. F
3. F	8. T	13. T
4. T	9. F	14. F
5. T	10. T	15. F

Multiple Choice:

1. a	6. d	11. d
2. c	7. d	12. c
3. c	8. a	13. c
4. a	9. b	14. b
5. c	10. c	15. d

Short Essay:

1. Fundamental changes include: (a) charter amendments, (b) mergers, (c) consolidations, (d) dissolution, (e) sale or lease of all or substantially all of the corporation's assets not in the usual and regular course of business, and (f) compulsory share exchanges.

2. Under modern statutes, the typical procedure involves: (a) adoption of a resolution by the board setting forth the proposed amendment, (b) approval by a majority vote of the shareholders, and (c) execution and filing of articles of amendment with the secretary of state. The secretary of state then issues a certificate of amendment.

3. This may be accomplished by: (a) purchase or lease of the assets, (b) purchase of a controlling stock interest in the other corporation, (c) merger with the other corporation, or (d) consolidation with the other corporation.

4. Most states grant dissenters' rights to dissenting shareholders of (1) a corporation selling or leasing all or substantially all of its property or assets not in the usual or regular course of business; (2) a corporation whose shares are acquired in a compulsory share exchange; (3) each corporation that is a party to a merger, except in short-form mergers where only the dissenting shareholders of the subsidiary have dissenters' rights; and (4) each corporation that is a party to a consolidation.

5. Dissolution of a corporation may be either voluntary or involuntary. A voluntary dissolution may be brought about by a resolution of the board of directors and thereafter approved by the shareholders. An involuntary dissolution may occur either by administrative or judicial action. These actions may be taken by the attorney general of the state, by shareholders under certain circumstances, or by a creditor if it can show that the corporation has been unable to pay debts as they come due.

Part VII: Sample Examination

1. d	8. c	15. a
2. d	9. b	16. c
3. c	10. a	17. d
4. b	11. d	18. d
5. a	12. c	19. c
6. c	13. a	20. b
7. c	14. d	

Chapter 38

True/False:

1. F	6. T	11. F
2. F	7. F	12. F
3. T	8. T	13. T
4. T	9. T	14. T
5. F	10. T	15. F

Multiple Choice:

1. c	6. c	11. a
2. d	7. b	12. c
3. d	8. b	13. b
4. b	9. c	14. d
5. c	10. a	15. c

Short Essay:

1. A secured transaction can be defined as a consensual security interest wherein the debtor grants a creditor the right to reach specified property of the debtor to pay off the debt in the case where the debtor fails to do so. Two elements of a secured transaction are: (1) a debt or obligation to pay money and (2) an interest of the creditor in specific property of the debtor that secures performance of the obligation.

2. There are two steps that a lender must execute in order to obtain a perfected security interest in the boat as collateral for a loan. The first is to create a security interest and have it "attach" to the collateral, the boat. Attachment occurs upon: (1) the giving of value by the secured party (the lender); (2) the debtor's acquiring rights in the boat; and (3) the secured party's taking possession of the boat or a security agreement is entered into which is in writing and which contains a description of the collateral and is signed by the debtor. The second step is for the secured party to perfect the security interest. In this case, where the collateral is a boat, perfection is most likely to be effected by filing a financing statement, signed by the debtor, in the appropriate offices. However, perfection can also be obtained by possession or by automatic perfection if the lender satisfies the requirements of a PMSI in consumer goods.

3. Collateral is classified according to its nature as being either (1) goods, (2) indispensable paper or, (3) intangibles. Goods are movable, tangible personal property which may be further classified as consumer goods, farm products, inventory, equipment, or fixtures. Indispensable paper is further classified as either: chattel paper, which is a writing that evidences both a debt and a security interest; instruments, which are negotiable; and documents, which represent title. Intangibles are generally accounts receivable and other forms of collateral not otherwise covered.

4. Jeremy is a buyer in the ordinary course of business from a merchant. Under the Code, even though Equity Credit has a perfected security interest in the goods, Jeremy takes the television free of that interest regardless of whether he had knowledge of the security interest of Equity Credit.

5. A surety has the following rights: (1) exoneration, the right to be relieved of his obligation by having the principal debtor perform the obligation; (2) reimbursement, the right to be repaid by the principal debtor; (3) subrogation, the right to assume all the rights the creditor has against the principal debtor; and (4) contribution, the right to payment from each cosurety of his proportionate share of the amount paid to the creditor.

Chapter 39

True/False:
1. F
2. F
3. T
4. T
5. T
6. F
7. T
8. F
9. T
10. F
11. T
12. F
13. T
14. T
15. T

Multiple Choice:
1. b
2. d
3. c
4. c
5. d
6. b
7. d
8. c
9. d
10. d
11. c
12. a
13. a
14. b
15. a

Short Essay:
1. Any person who is eligible to be a debtor under a given bankruptcy proceeding may file a voluntary petition. It is not necessary to be insolvent. Once a petition is filed, an order for relief is automatic. An involuntary petition may be filed (1) by three or more creditors who have unsecured claims that total $12,300 or more, or (2) if the debtor has fewer than twelve creditors, by one or more creditors whose total unsecured claims equal $12,330 or more. Involuntary petition may be filed only under Chapter 7 or Chapter 11 and may not be filed against a farmer or a banking, insurance, or nonprofit corporation.

2. Whether the filing of a petition is voluntary or involuntary, it operates as a stay against all creditors. That is, it restrains all creditors from beginning or continuing to recover claims against the debtor, or creating or enforcing liens against property of the debtor. The stay applies to both secured and unsecured creditors.

3. Chapter 7, Liquidation, applies to most creditors and distributes equitably the debtor's nonexempt assets and thereafter discharges all dischargeable debts. Chapter 11, Reorganization, attempts to preserve the troubled entity and allow a continuation of business. Finally, Chapter 13, Adjustment of Debts of Individuals, permits an individual debtor to file a repayment plan which when all payments under the plan are paid will discharge the petitioner from most other debts.

4. (a) Claim for $50,000 secured by inventory worth $10,000 (gets $10,000 from the inventory or sale); (b) Child support in arrears ($3,000) (c) Fees earned by the attorneys of the bankruptcy estate; (d) Claim for wages of the employee earned within 180 days of filing the petition; (e) Unsecured claim for income tax; (f) Balance of claim ($40,000) that was secured by the inventory.

5. Chapter 13 applies to individuals with regular income who owe liquidated, unsecured debts of less than $307,675 and secured debts of less than $922,975. The adjustment of debt provision is intended to permit an individual to file a repayment plan with the ultimate goal of discharging her from debts. The plan must be (1) in good faith, (2) of a value such that property distributed to creditors will be not less than the amount that would be paid them under Chapter 7, (3) all secured creditors must accept the plan, (4) the debtor must be able to make all payments and comply with the plan, (5) if the debtor's net current monthly income is equal to or greater than the state median income, the plan may not provide for payments over a period longer than five years, but if the debtor's net current monthly income is less than the state median income then the plan generally may not provide for payments over a period longer than three years, and (6) the debtor must pay all domestic support obligations that became payable after the filing.

Part VIII: Sample Examination

1. d	8. b	15. a
2. b	9. b	16. b
3. a	10. d	17. a
4. a	11. d	18. c
5. d	12. b	19. d
6. a	13. d	20. a
7. d	14. c	

Chapter 40

True/False:

1. F	6. T	11. T
2. T	7. T	12. T
3. T	8. F	13. T
4. T	9. T	14. F
5. F	10. T	15. T

Multiple Choice:

1. c	6. d	11. d
2. c	7. a	12. a
3. d	8. c	13. d
4. d	9. c	14. b
5. d	10. d	15. a

Short Essay:
1. The primary purpose of federal securities regulation is to prevent fraudulent practices in the sale of securities and thereby maintain public confidence in the securities markets.

2. A registration statement usually includes: (a) a description of the registrant's properties and business, (b) a description of the significant provisions of the security to be offered for sale and its relationship to the registrant's other capital securities, (c) information about the management of the registrant, and (d) financial statements certified by independent public accountants.

3. A two-tier analysis has been developed by the court to identify securities. Under this analysis, the court will treat as a security any financial instrument designated as a note, stock, bond, or other instrument specifically named in the act such as a debenture, preorganization certificate or subscription, investment contract, voting-trust, etc. If a financial transaction lacks the traditional characteristics of an instrument the court will apply a three-part test. Under this test a financial instrument or transaction constitutes an investment contract if it involves (1) an investment in common venture, (2) having a reasonable expectation of profit and, (3) that profit to be derived from the efforts of others not a party to the instrument or transaction.

4. Rule 10b-5 is the antifraud provision of the 1934 act. This rule makes it unlawful to use the mail or facilities of interstate commerce to: (1) employ any device, scheme, or artifice to defraud; (2) make any untrue statement of a material fact; or (3) omit to state a material fact; or (4) engage in any act that operates as fraud. Scienter and reliance are both required for recovery, as is materiality and a connection with the purchase or sale of a security. This also contains the "insider trading" provision.

5. The Breakers has assets of less than $5 million and the class of stock involved is less than 500 shareholders, so the issue is exempt from registration under Rule 505 as long as the issue does not exceed $5 million over 12 months. General advertising or general solicitation is not permitted. The issue may be purchased by an unlimited number of accredited investors and by no more than 35 other purchasers.

Chapter 41

True/False:

1. T	6. F	11. F
2. F	7. T	12. T
3. F	8. F	13. T
4. F	9. T	14. T
5. T	10. F	15. T

Multiple Choice:

1. b	6. a	11. b
2. c	7. d	12. c
3. c	8. c	13. d
4. d	9. d	14. d

5. c   10. d   15. a

Short Essay:

1. Registration is advisable, because it is a condition of certain remedies for copyright infringement. Some rights can be permanently lost by failure to register soon enough. If an infringement occurs after registration, the following remedies are available: (1) injunction; (2) impoundment and possible destruction of infringing articles; (3) actual damages plus profits made by the infringer that are in addition to those damages or the statutory damages; or (4) criminal penalties. Registration also serves as proof of the time at which the copyrighted item was fixed in tangible form.

2. The four types of trade symbols recognized by the Lanham Act include: (1) a trademark which is a distinctive symbol, word, or design on a good that is used to identify the manufacturer; (2) a service mark which is a distinctive symbol, word, or design that is used to identify the services of a provider; (3) certification mark which is a distinctive symbol, word, or design used with goods or services to certify specific characteristics; and (4) collective mark which is a distinctive symbol used to indicate membership in an organization.

3. The rights of a copyright owner are very broad but are limited in several ways, the most important two of which are: (1) compulsory licenses and (2) fair use. Compulsory licenses permit certain limited uses of copyrighted material upon the payment of specified royalties and compliance with statutory conditions. Fair use allows use of a copyrighted work for purposes such as criticism, comment, news reporting, teaching, or scholarship.

4. In the absence of a contract restriction, an employee is under no duty upon termination of his employment to refrain from competing or working for a competitor of his former employer, but he may not use trade secrets, such as customer lists, or disclose them to third persons. Because Mark has misappropriated a trade secret, Briarton may obtain damages and possibly injunctive relief.

5. Under the Lanham Act, several remedies for infringement are provided. Injunctive relief, an accounting for profits, damages, destruction of infringing articles are all available. Additionally, attorneys' fees in some exceptional cases and costs may be available.

Chapter 42

True/False:

1. T	6. T	11. T
2. T	7. F	12. T
3. F	8. F	13. T
4. T	9. T	14. F
5. F	10. F	15. T

Multiple Choice:

1. b	6. c	11. d

2. c	7. d	12. d
3. d	8. c	13. d
4. c	9. a	14. c
5. d	10. d	15. a

Short Essay:
1. This act prohibits employment discrimination of the basis of race, color, gender, religion, or national origin and is enforced by the EEOC. Discrimination may occur through the use of proscribed criteria which produces disparate treatment, engaging in conduct that perpetuates past discrimination, or adopting neutral rules that have a disparate impact.

2. The remedies are: (a) injunctive relief, (b) affirmative action, and (c) reinstatement and award of back pay.

3. The Equal Pay Act only requires equal pay for equal work. Where jobs are different but comparable, the statute provides no remedy for women who have been systematically undervalued and underpaid. The concept of comparable worth provides that employers should compare the relative values of different jobs in such a way that workers in both jobs would receive the same pay if the jobs were in fact comparable.

4. If Ed can establish that he was in fact injured and that the injury arose out of and in the course of his employment, he can recover workers' compensation. Because a third party, Wes, caused the injury, Ed may also bring a tort action against Wes.

5. Darla would need to prove that the conduct of Doug did in fact constitute sexual harassment within the EEOC guidelines and that First Bank did not take immediate action when it knew or should have known of the harassment. The courts have generally held that sexual harassment that creates a hostile or offensive working environment, even if it does not condition employment benefits upon sexual favors, is a violation. Also, when the employee engaging in sexual harassment is an agent of the employer or is in a supervisory position over the victim, the employer may be liable without knowledge or reason to know of the harassment.

Chapter 43

True/False:

1. T	6. F	11. T
2. T	7. T	12. F
3. T	8. T	13. T
4. F	9. T	14. F
5. T	10. T	15. F

Multiple Choice:

1. d	6. c	11. b
2. b	7. b	12. d

3. d	8. d	13. a
4. b	9. c	14. b
5. b	10. a	15. c

Short Essay:

1. Federal antitrust statutes are designed to prevent unreasonable concentration of economic power which would weaken or destroy free and open competition in the marketplace.

2. Economic theory predicts that the goal of every monopolist is to utilize its power to limit production and increase prices. Thus, a monopolistic market will produce fewer goods at a higher price than a competitive market.

3. The Robinson-Patman Act deals with price discrimination and prohibits sellers from giving different prices to buyers of commodities of similar grade and quality. It also prohibits buyers from inducing sellers to do the above. Defenses to charges of a violation include (1) cost justification, (2) meeting competition, and (3) functional discounts.

4. The Clayton Act was passed in 1914 with the express purpose of supplementing existing laws against unlawful restraints and monopolies. It provides only civil remedies. The act primarily deals with price discrimination, tying arrangements, exclusive dealings, and mergers. Subsequently price discrimination became the subject of an amendment called the Robinson-Patman Act. Tying arrangements are prohibited if they tend to create a monopoly or substantially lessen competition. Exclusive dealing arrangements are likewise prohibited if they would tend to create a monopoly or substantially lessen competition, as are mergers.

5. The court would probably rule for Disco, because X, Y, and Z have jointly refused to deal with Disco. Such agreement not to deal with a third party constitutes a group boycott which may violate Section 1 of the Sherman Act.

Chapter 44

True/False:

1. T	6. F	11. T
2. F	7. F	12. T
3. T	8. F	13. F
4. T	9. F	14. T
5. F	10. T	15. T

Multiple Choice:

1. b	6. d	11. d
2. c	7. d	12. a
3. d	8. d	13. d
4. d	9. d	14. a

5. b   10. b   15. b

Short Essay:
1. Kind and Kind will probably have to produce its working papers. Although many states have statutes that establish an accountant-client privilege, an accountant's work papers are not subject to the same protection afforded the attorney-client work product. The accountant's duty is owed to the general investing public. Work papers cannot be shielded from public scrutiny. The U.S. Supreme Court case of *United States v. Arthur Young & Company* may have relevance to this case also, even though that case involved tax accrual work papers and this one involves securities work papers.

2. The SEC must prove that Arthur willfully and knowingly caused false and misleading statements to be made with respect to material facts in the annual report filed with the SEC.

3. One of the primary ways an accountant may face liability is through breach of contract. An accountant normally enters into a binding contract to perform work through an engagement letter, the contents of which are the express, or explicit, obligations to be performed. Failure to perform these explicit obligations may result in the accountant's liability. Also the accountant implicitly agrees to perform in a competent and professional manner, and implicitly promises to perform to those standards expected of all accountants as expressed in guidelines such as GAAS and GAAP.

4. First Bank can recover from the accountants for negligence if it can establish that it was a foreseen user, which is one the accountants knew would use the work.

5. Accountants' liability may arise from contract, tort, or criminal law. Under contract law, the accountant could be liable based upon explicit or implicit duties to the other contract party. Additionally, liability may extend to third parties as beneficiaries. Tort liability might arise based upon either the negligence or fraud of the accountant. Criminal liability may be imposed based upon several federal or state statutes.

Chapter 45

True/False:
1. T	6. F	11. T
2. T	7. T	12. T
3. F	8. T	13. F
4. F	9. F	14. T
5. T	10. T	15. T

Multiple Choice:
1. d	6. d	11. b
2. a	7. c	12. b

3. a	8. b	13. c
4. c	9. d	14. d
5. b	10. d	15. a

Short Essay:

1. These two consumer protection commissions have a broad range of responsibility. The Federal Trade Commission has two major functions: (1) to prevent "unfair methods of competition in commerce" and (2) to prevent "unfair and deceptive" trade practices. To accomplish these ends the commission has established standards. The Consumer Product Safety Commission was established to (1) protect the public against unreasonable risks of injury associated with consumer products, (2) to assist consumers in evaluating the comparative safety of consumer products, (3) to develop uniform safety standards for consumer products and to minimize conflicting state and local regulations, and (4) to promote research and investigation into the causes and prevention of product-related deaths, illnesses, and injuries.

2. Under a "full" warranty, the warrantor must: (a) agree to repair without charge the product to conform with the warranty; (b) not limit the duration of any implied warranty; (c) give the consumer the option of a refund or replacement if repair is unsuccessful; and (d) not exclude consequential damages unless conspicuously noted.

3. The creditor must disclose: (a) the cost of the credit; (b) when the finance charge is imposed and how it is computed; (c) what other charges may be imposed; and (d) whether a security interest is retained or acquired by the creditor.

4. The creditor must disclose: (a) the total amount financed; (b) the cash price; (c) the number, amount, and due dates of installments; (d) delinquency charges; and (e) a description of the security, if any.

5. Creditors generally may garnish wages, seek an assignment of wages, or retain a security interest in goods sold or other collateral of the buyer.

Chapter 46

True/False:

1. T	6. T	11. T
2. T	7. T	12. F
3. T	8. F	13. T
4. F	9. T	14. F
5. T	10. F	15. T

Multiple Choice:

1. c	6. b	11. d
2. d	7. d	12. c
3. d	8. a	13. a
4. c	9. d	14. c

5. d   10. a   15. d

Short Essay:
1. Three theories of private tort actions include (1) nuisance, (2) trespass, and (3) strict liability. Nuisance encompasses the two distinct types of wrongs: public nuisance which is an act interfering with a public right, and private nuisance, which is interference by another with the use and enjoyment of a person's own land. Trespass to land involves an invasion which interferes with the plaintiff's right of exclusive possession of the property and which is the direct result of an action by the defendant. Strict liability would be available where an individual is engaged in an abnormally dangerous activity which is both ultrahazardous and inappropriate for its locale.

2. A private nuisance occurs when the defendant has substantially and unreasonably interfered with the use and enjoyment of the plaintiff's land. A public nuisance requires some interference with the health, safety, or comfort of the public.

3. The National Environment Policy Act establishes protection of the environment as a goal of federal policy and has two major substantive sections: (1) the creation of the Council of Environmental Quality, which is a Presidential advisory group charged with the tasks of making recommendations to the president on environmental matters and preparing annual reports on the condition of the environment, and (2) the requirement that each federal agency, when proposing legislation or other major federal action, prepare an environmental impact statement.

4. A "point source" is any discernible, confined, and discrete conveyance from which pollutants are or may be discharged. This applies to industry etc., other than publicly owned treatment works. A "nonpoint source" pertains mostly to farming and other land uses which cause pollution, such as a pesticide runoff from farming operations.

5. In 1980 Congress enacted the Comprehensive Environmental Response, Compensation, and Liability Act (CERCLA or the Superfund). It is designed to fill the gap left by RCRA with regard to cleanup of abandoned or inactive hazardous waste sites. The federal government may now take either removal or remedial action in response to either a release or threatened release of hazardous substances, as long as such actions are consistent with the National Contingency Plan. States and private parties may also engage in response actions.

Chapter 47

True/False:
1. T   6. F   11. T
2. T   7. T   12. T
3. T   8. F   13. T
4. T   9. T   14. T

5. F   10. T   15. T

Multiple Choice:
1. b   6. d   11. b
2. d   7. d   12. d
3. b   8. d   13. d
4. a   9. c   14. a
5. b   10. c   15. b

Short Essay:

1. There are many forms of multinational enterprises. They include: (a) direct export sales, (b) the use of foreign agents, (c) the use of foreign distributors, (d) licensing to a foreign firm, (e) joint ventures, and (f) the use of a wholly owned subsidiary. As a company just entering the foreign market, WCA should first look at direct export, the use of a foreign agent, or the use of a foreign distributor. If it considers the use of a foreign agent or the use of a foreign distributor, it should carefully study the agent or the distributor before entering into agreements and should consult legal counsel regarding the laws of the particular country in which it wishes to do business with particular reference to any special provisions regarding the termination of an agent or distributor.

2. Expropriation is a governmental taking of foreign-owned property for a public purpose. When property is expropriated by a foreign government, the government must pay for it. Confiscation is a governmental taking of foreign-owned property without payment or with inadequate payment. To protect itself, a company should take out insurance with a private company or with the Overseas Private Investment Company.

3. The company should have a good working relationship with a bank that deals in the international sector and that has correspondent banks around the world. The company should consider requiring the buyer to furnish a letter of credit, which is a promise by a buyer's bank to pay the seller provided that certain conditions are met. A letter of credit transaction affords the seller protection against the possibility of nonpayment when dealing in the international sector.

4. A contract involving the sale of goods between a seller in the United States and a buyer in a foreign country should consider such items as: (a) the official language of the contract, (b) the law that governs any breach and if the other country is a party to the CISG whether that will govern the transaction, (c) how any disputes will be settled, (d) acceptable currencies and methods of payment, and (e) a *force majeure* clause apportioning liabilities and responsibilities in the event of any unforeseen occurrences.

5. The FCPA prohibits all domestic concerns from bribing foreign governmental or political officials. Domestic concerns, or any officer, director, employee, or agent thereof may not offer or give anything of value for the purpose of (1) influencing any act or decision in an official capacity, (2) inducing an act or omission in violation of a lawful duty, or (3) inducing anyone to use his influence to affect a decision of a foreign government in order to assist the domestic concern in obtaining or retaining business.

Chapter 48

True/False:

1. F	6. F	11. F
2. F	7. T	12. F
3. T	8. T	13. T
4. F	9. F	14. T
5. T	10. T	15. F

Multiple Choice:

1. a	6. c	11. a
2. b	7. a	12. a
3. c	8. c	13. a
4. d	9. d	14. c
5. c	10. d	15. d

Short Essay:

1. The Communications Decency Act of 1996 (CDA) grants Internet service providers (ISPs) immunity from defamation when publishing information communicated by third parties. Because the CDA grants immunity only to ISPs, it is possible that an employer that intentionally and unreasonably fails to remove defamatory material posted by employees on the employer's electronic system may be held for such defamatory material.

2. The posting or e-mailing of a copyrighted work may constitute copyright infringement. Hyperlinking, which enables Internet users to move quickly from one web site to another by clicking on highlighted text or graphics, may be copyright infringement if the party hyperlinking uses someone else's copyrighted material without authorization. Framing occurs when information from a linked web site is viewed from within a linking web site. This may be infringement if it misleads others into mistakenly believing that the linking site is providing the information.

3. The Lanham Act recognizes four types of marks: (1) trademarks, which identify a party's goods and distinguishes them from those of others; (2) service marks, which identify and distinguish one's services from those of others; (3) certification marks, which certify that goods or services satisfy specific requirements for receiving such certification; and (4) collective marks, which indicate that a producer or provider belongs to a trade union, trade association, or other organization, or that members of a collective group produced the goods or services.

4. The Computer Fraud and Abuse Act makes the following conduct a crime with respect to any computer that is used in interstate commerce: (1) unauthorized access or damage to the computer; (2) access to the computer with the intent to commit fraud; (3) trafficking in confidential passwords; and (4) threatening to damage the computer with the intent to extort money or anything of value.

5. The Uniform Electronic Transactions Act (UETA), which has been enacted by more than 20 states, gives full legal effect to electronic contracts and provides that electronic signatures and contracts satisfy the writing requirement of the statute of frauds. The federal Electronic Signatures in Global and National Commerce (E-Sign) makes electronic records and signatures valid and enforceable in the United States for many transactions that are conducted in interstate or foreign commerce including the sale, lease, exchange, and licensing of personal property and services, and the sale, lease, or exchange of real property.

Part IX: Sample Examination

1. b
2. c
3. d
4. d
5. a
6. c
7. b

8. c
9. c
10. b
11. b
12. b
13. c
14. d

15. a
16. c
17. b
18. a
19. d
20. a

Chapter 49

True/False:

1. T
2. T
3. T
4. T
5. F
6. T
7. F
8. T
9. F
10. T

11. T
12. F
13. T
14. T
15. T
16. F
17. T
18. T
19. T
20. T

21. T
22. T
23. F
24. T
25. T
26. F
27. F
28. F
29. T
30. T

Multiple Choice:

1. d	11. c	21. d
2. d	12. b	22. a
3. d	13. d	23. b
4. d	14. c	24. d
5. b	15. b	25. c
6. c	16. d	26. a
7. c	17. b	27. d
8. b	18. d	28. b
9. d	19.	d 29. d
10. c	20. b	30. d

Short Essay:

1. Real property consists of all interests in land. Personal property, in contrast, is every other thing or interest identified as property. A fixture is an item of personal property that has been attached to realty so that an interest in it arises under real property law. These classifications are significant in that real and personal property rights are governed by different principles of law. Tangible property is property that exists in a physical form; all other property is classified as intangible property. Once again, the determination of various property rights can depend on whether property is classified as tangible or intangible.

2. A fixture is an article or piece of personal property that has been attached in some manner to land or a building so that an interest in it arises under real property law. A trade fixture is one which is used in connection with a trade. Whereas a fixture is likely to become part of the realty, and thus may not be removable, a trade fixture may usually be removed by a lessee provided she may remove the item without material injury to the realty.

3. Fire and property insurance policies are designed to distribute risk of loss. There are several ways to determine what the loss has been and to insure against that. A valued policy covers the full value of property as agreed upon by the parties whenever the policy is issued. An open policy covers the fair market value of property which will need to be calculated as of the time immediately prior to the loss.

4. An insurable interest is a relationship that a person has to another person, or to certain property, such that the happening of a possible specific damage-causing contingency would result in direct loss or injury to him. The purpose of the concept is to ensure that insurance is used as protection against the risk of loss resulting from the happening of an event, not the realization of profit from idle wagering.

5. Warranties operate as conditions that must exist before the contract of insurance is effective or before the insured's obligation to pay is enforceable. Failure of a certain condition to exist or to occur relieves the insurer from any obligations to perform its promise.

6. The five essential elements of a bailment are: (1) delivery of possession by a bailor to a bailee, (2) delivery of personal property, (3) possession without ownership by the bailee, (4) a determinable period of time, and (5) an absolute duty on the bailee to return the property to the bailor or dispose of it according to the bailor's directions.

7. The three kinds of bailments are those for the benefit of the bailee, those for the benefit of the bailor, and mutual benefit bailments. In a mutual benefit bailment, the bailee must exercise the degree of care that a reasonably prudent person would exercise under the same circumstances. If the bailment is one for the benefit of the bailee only, a higher degree of care is expected, and if for the bailor's benefit only, a lower degree of care.

8. A pledge is simply a security interest by possession. A second special bailment is storage of goods for compensation by a warehouser. Third is transportation of goods by a carrier. Carriers may be classified as either common carriers or private carriers. Fourth is storage of goods for patrons by an operator of a hotel or motel.

9. A document of title symbolizes ownership of the goods described by the document. One type of document of title is a warehouse receipt, which is a receipt issued by a person engaged in the storing of goods for hire. The warehouser must deliver the goods to the person entitled to receive them under the terms of the warehouse receipt. Another type of document of title is a bill of lading, which is a document issued by a carrier on receipt of goods for transportation. It serves a threefold function: (1) as a receipt for the goods, (2) as evidence of the contract of carriage, and (3) as a document of title.

10. If, by its terms, a document of title calls for the goods to be delivered to bearer or to the order of a named person, the document of title is negotiable and subject to due negotiation in the regular course of business to a holder, who takes in good faith, for value, and without notice of any defense or claim. Such a person who negotiates or transfers a document of title for value, other than a collecting bank or other intermediary, incurs warranty liability unless otherwise agreed.

Chapter 50

True/False:

1. F	6. F	11. F
2. T	7. F	12. F
3. T	8. T	13. T
4. F	9. T	14. T
5. F	10. T	15. T

Multiple Choice:

1. c	6. c	11. c
2. b	7. d	12. d
3. b	8. c	13. a
4. d	9. c	14. c
5. c	10. c	15. b

Short Essay:

1. The two basic characteristics of the fee simple estate are the holder's absolute ownership and the right of transferability by sale or by inheritance. In contrast, a qualified fee is one that it is possible to convey or will to another to enjoy absolutely, subject, however, to the possibility that it will be taken away at a later date if a certain event takes place.

2. A reversion is the general interest that the grantor retains if he conveys away less than his entire estate. It is a present estate to be enjoyed in the future. A possibility of reverter exists when the property conveyed may return to the grantor or his successor in interest because of the happening of an event upon which a fee simple estate was to terminate. A possibility of reverter is just an expectancy and is not a present estate. Finally, a remainder is an estate in property that, like a reversion, will take effect in possession, if at all, upon the termination of a prior estate created by the same instrument. Unlike a reversion, however, a remainder is held by a person other than the grantor or his successors. There are two kinds of remainders: vested and contingent.

3. All three are forms of concurrent ownership, with tenancy in common being the most frequently used. Tenancy in common and joint tenancy both provide an undivided interest in the whole, the right of both tenants to possession, and the right of either to sell his interest during life and thus terminate the original relationship. Tenancy in common does not have a right of survivorship, thus the interests may be devised by will or pass by intestate succession. Joint tenancy has a right of survivorship and thus passes by operation of law to the surviving co-owner. Neither the heirs of the deceased nor his general creditors have a claim to the deceased's interest. A joint tenant may not transfer his interest by executing a will. Tenancy by the entireties is not recognized in all states, but where recognized is created only by a conveyance to a husband and wife. Neither spouse may convey separately his or her interest during life. The right of survivorship remains and creditors cannot attach the interests of either spouse.

4. A landlord must provide quiet enjoyment, which is the right of the tenant to physical possession of the property without interference from the landlord. Also, the tenant would receive an implied warranty of habitability from the landlord. However, unless there is a statute or a specific provision in the lease, the landlord has no duty to repair or restore the premises.

5. The landlord owes a tenant the obligation of quiet enjoyment, fitness for use, and nondiscrimination. This means that the tenant must have physical possession of the premises free from interference. Additionally, the premises must be habitable or fit for ordinary residential purposes. Under the Fair Housing Act, a landlord cannot discriminate against a tenant on the basis of race, color, gender, religion, national origin, or familial status. Unless there is a statute or specific agreement to the contrary, the landlord has no duty to repair or restore the premises.

...se:

~~1.~~ F	6. F	11. F
2. T	7. T	12. T
3. F	8. F	13. F
4. F	9. T	14. F
5. F	10. T	15. T

Multiple Choice:

1. d	6. d	11. d
2. d	7. a	12. d
3. a	8. d	13. c
4. c	9. d	14. d
5. d	10. d	15. c

Short Essay:

1. The two essential documents involved in the sale of real estate are the contract of sale and the deed. The contract of sale must be in writing and signed by the party against whom enforcement is sought to satisfy the statute of frauds. A deed must contain a description of the property that is sufficiently clear and certain to permit identification of the property conveyed. It will also usually describe the quantity of the estate conveyed. It will also contain the appropriate covenants of title, if any. Finally, it must be signed by the grantor, and for purposes of recordation, it must be acknowledged before a notary public.

2. The three types of deeds are the warranty deed, the special warranty deed, and the quitclaim deed. By the warranty deed, the seller promises that he has title to the property and that he will do what is necessary to make the grantee whole if the latter suffers any damage because the grantor's title was defective. In contrast, a special warranty deed is one that warrants only that the title has not been impaired, encumbered, or rendered defective by any act or omission of the grantor. The grantor does not warrant that the title may not be defective by reason of the acts or omissions of others. Finally, a quitclaim deed is used to convey all of one's interest in certain property, whatever it might be. No warranties of title are made.

3. Marketable title refers to the condition of the title with respect to (1) encumbrances (such as mortgages, easements, liens, leases, and restrictive covenants), (2) defects in the chain of title, and (3) events that deprive the seller of title, such as adverse possession or eminent domain. It assures the buyer that title is free from any of the above not listed in the contract. The buyer's remedies for breach include specific performance with a price reduction, rescission and restitution, or damages for loss of bargain.

4. Eminent domain is the power of a government to take private land for public use. Such a use need only provide a public advantage. When the government "takes" land in this manner, the fair market value of the land must be given to the landowner from whom the land is taken.

5. Property may be controlled by both public and private restrictions placed upon the property. For example, the government might zone the property. That is, the government may regulate the land with respect to its permissible use. Additionally, the government has the constitutional power to take private property for public use. Just compensation must be awarded in these cases. Individual sellers may restrict land use through restrictive covenants in the deed.

Chapter 52

True/False:

1. T	6. T	11. T
2. T	7. F	12. T
3. T	8. T	13. T
4. F	9. T	14. F
5. F	10. F	15. T

Multiple Choice:

1. c	6. d	11. b
2. b	7. d	12. c
3. b	8. c	13. a
4. c	9. c	14. b
5. b	10. d	15. b

Short Essay:

1. The four essential elements of a trust are as follows: (1) the trust must have a creator, known as the settlor; (2) there must be a subject matter of the trust, or the trust "corpus" that is definite and certain; (3) there must be a trustee, but the trust will not fail for want of a trustee because the court will appoint one; and (4) there must be a beneficiary of the trust.

2. The primary difference between an express and an implied trust is in the origination of the trust. An express trust is created by voluntary action and may be either oral or written. Examples of an express trust would be: charitable trust, spendthrift trust, and totten trust. An implied trust, however, arises by operation of law where a trust would be imposed to rectify a fraud, to prevent unjust enrichment, or to fulfill a presumed intent of the settlor. Examples are constructive and resulting trusts.

3. Four types of special wills are: Nuncupative, Holographic, Soldiers' and Sailors', and Living Wills. A nuncupative will is an oral declaration made before witnesses. A holographic will is one entirely in the handwriting of the testator. Soldiers on active duty or sailors at sea may make a disposition of personal property in a document less formal than normally required for a will. A living will is not a true will, but is a document by which an individual rejects use of extraordinary medical treatment in order to prolong his life if he becomes incurably ill.

time a will becomes operative, it may be revoked in several ways. Destruction or alteration, ne intent to revoke, revokes a will. Any subsequent, conflicting will or codicil, or a will that declares it revokes prior wills, revokes an earlier will. Marriage or the birth of a child may revoke wills as far as those involved are concerned. And, finally, most states give the surviving spouse the power to renounce a will and elect to take under the statues of descent and distribution, effectively revoking the will.

5. The first step involved in administering an estate is to see if the deceased left a will. If so, the named executor will handle the administration. If there is no will, the court will appoint an administrator. If there is a will, it is submitted to probate by the personal representative, who then must file an inventory of the estate. Assets are then collected, debts paid, and the remainder disbursed according to either the terms of the will, or if there is no will, the laws of intestate succession.

Part X: Sample Examination

1. d	8. b	15. d
2. b	9. d	16. a
3. a	10. a	17. b
4. a	11. c	18. a
5. b	12. a	19. b
6. b	13. b	20. b
7. c	14. a	